D0627719

The Life and Memoirs of

CASANOVA

The Life and Memoirs of
CASANOVA

Translated from the French by
ARTHUR MACHEN

&

Selected and Edited with Connecting Links
by
GEORGE DUNNING GRIBBLE

New Introduction by
ERICA JONG

A Da Capo Paperback

Library of Congress Cataloging in Publication Data

Casanova, Giacomo, 1725–1798.
    The life and memoirs of Casanova.

    (A Da Capo paperback)
    Translation of: Mémoires.
    Reprint. Previously published: New York: Knopf, 1929.
    1. Casanova, Giacomo, 1725–1798. 2. Europe—Biography. I.
Machen, Arthur, 1863–1947. II. Gribble, George Dunning. III. Title.
D285.8.C4A362513   1984   940.2′53   83-27324
ISBN 0-306-80208-2

This Da Capo Press paperback edition of *Life and Memoirs of Casanova*
is an unabridged republication of the edition published in New York
in 1929, here supplemented with a new introduction by Erica Jong.
It is reprinted by arrangement with the Estate of Arthur Machen.

Copyright © 1929 by Alfred A. Knopf
New introduction copyright © 1984 by Erica Jong

Published by Da Capo Press, Inc.
A Subsidiary of Plenum Publishing Corporation
233 Spring Street, New York, N.Y. 10013

All Rights Reserved

Manufactured in the United States of America

INTRODUCTION TO THE DA CAPO EDITION

"I am a free agent"—thus Casanova begins his famous book of memoirs, and indeed freedom is his theme. He is a true eighteenth century spirit—more libertarian than libertine, a born vagabond and adventurer whose life reads like the lustiest of picaresque novels. But it is lusty in the old (Anglo-Saxon and Middle English) sense of the word—meaning pleasure or delight, not lusty in the modern sense—meaning carnal appetite. Is this surprising? Casanova's name has become synonymous with carnal appetite. Yet one looks in vain through these pages for explicit descriptions of sex. Our author *alludes* to his multitudinous sexual romps quite openly, but his language is hardly explicit. We hear of "conflagrations," of "seas of delight," of "ecstasies of enjoyment." The contemporary reader, sated with explicit sexual description, may indeed wonder (with Casanova no less than with Cleland) what all the centuries of fuss have been about. Casanova is open, but he is never explicit. He is a free spirit, but he is never a pornographer. His memoirs do not fall into that deliciously-named category—"books of one hand." He is no "wanker" (as the English say), but an eighteenth-century lover of life, a *viveur* whose *joie de vivre* abounds.

And yet there are the tell-tale signs of the sensualist everywhere in Casanova's work—even if they do not occur in the descriptions of the sexual act itself. He tells us that he loves strong cheeses and the odors of women. He tells of his lust for good food and wine. The visual clarity with which he describes places and people mark him above all as a sensualist. Casanova, like every good writer, is a sponge. He soaks up life. He lives to look, to feel, to taste.

It is this avidity for life that finally accounts for the charm of his memoirs. No less than Tom Jones, Candide, and Fanny Hill, Casanova is an eighteenth-century *naif*. Life delights and amazes him. Life is a groaning board before which he stands amazed, not knowing which delicacy to pluck and place upon his tongue.

How then account for Casanova's reputation as "a Casanova"? Is the love of life so rare a commodity that it has the power to shock the puritan? Apparently.

That tells us more about our culture than it tells us about Casanova. "The look of lust is always gloomy," says Humbert Humbert in *Lolita*. And Sade and Sacher-Masoch would certainly agree. But not Casanova. The look of *his* lust is always jolly. Is it that very jollity which is more shocking to the gloomy life-deniers than the lust itself? I think so. Casanova seems an anomaly in our guilt-bound culture. For two hundred years his critics have projected on him feelings they should have rather exorcised from themselves.

Vive Casanova! He knew how.

— Erica Jong
January, 1984

"IF these Memoirs, only written to console me in the dreadful weariness which is slowly killing me in Bohemia — and which perhaps would kill me anywhere, since, though my body is old, my spirit and desires are as young as ever — if these Memoirs are ever read, I repeat, they will only be read when I am gone, and all censure will be lost on me. Nevertheless, seeing that men are divided into two sections, the one and by far the greater composed of the ignorant and superficial, and the other of the learned and reflective, I beg to state that it is to the latter I would appeal. Their judgment, I believe, will be in favour of my veracity, and, indeed, why should I not be veracious? A man can have no object in deceiving himself, and it is for myself that I chiefly write."

CASANOVA

CONTENTS
VOLUME I

AUTHOR'S PREFACE

THE reader of these Memoirs will discover that I never had any fixed aim before my eyes, and that my system, if it can be called a system, has been to glide away unconcernedly on the stream of life, trusting to the wind wherever it led. How many changes arise from such an independent mode of life! My success and my misfortunes, the bright and the dark days I have gone through, everything has proved to me that in this world, either physical or moral, good comes out of evil just as well as evil comes out of good. My errors will point to thinking men the various roads, and will teach them the great art of treading on the brink of the precipice without falling into it. It is only necessary to have courage, for strength without self-confidence is useless. I have often met with happiness after some imprudent step which ought to have brought ruin upon me, and although passing a vote of censure upon myself I would thank God for his mercy. But, by way of compensation, dire misfortune has befallen me in consequence of actions prompted by the most cautious wisdom. This would humble me; yet conscious that I had acted rightly I would easily derive comfort from that conviction.

In spite of a good foundation of sound morals, the natural offspring of the divine principles which had been early rooted in my heart, I have been throughout my life the victim of my senses; I have found delight in losing the right path, I have constantly lived in the midst of error, with no consolation but the consciousness of my being mistaken. Therefore, dear reader, I trust that, far from attaching to my history the character of impudent boasting, you will find in my Memoirs only the characteristic proper to a general confession, and that my narratory style will be the manner neither of a repenting sinner, nor of a man ashamed to acknowledge his frolics. They are the follies inherent to youth; I make sport of them, and, if you are kind, you will not yourself refuse them a good-natured smile. You will be amused when you see that I have more than once deceived, without the slightest qualm of conscience, both knaves and fools. As to the deceit perpetrated upon women, let it pass, for, when love is in the way, men and women as a general rule dupe each other. But on the score of fools it is a very different matter. I always feel the greatest bliss when I recollect those I have caught in my snares, for fools generally are insolent, and so self-conceited that they challenge wit. We avenge intellect when we dupe a fool, and it is a victory not to be despised, for a fool is covered with steel, and it is often very hard to find his vulnerable part. In fact, to gull a fool seems to me an exploit worthy of a witty man. I have felt in my very blood, ever since I was born, a most unconquerable hatred towards the whole tribe of fools, and it arises from the fact that I feel myself a blockhead whenever I am in their company. I am very far from placing them in the same class with those men whom we call stupid, for the latter are stupid only from deficient education, and I rather like them. I have met with some of them — very honest fellows who, with all their stupidity, had a kind of intelligence and an upright good sense, which cannot be the characteristics of fools. They are like eyes veiled with the cataract, which, if the disease could be removed, would be very beautiful.

Dear reader, examine the spirit of this preface, and you will at once guess at my purpose. I have written a preface because I wish you to know me thoroughly before you begin the reading of my Memoirs. It is only in a coffee-room or at a "table d'hôte" that we like to converse with strangers.

I have written the history of my life, and I have a perfect right to do so; but am I wise in throwing it before a public of which I know nothing but evil? No, I am aware it is sheer folly, but I want to be busy, I want to laugh, and why should I deny myself this gratification?

Expulit elleboro morbum bilemque mero.

An ancient author tells us somewhere, with the tone of a pedagogue, if you have not done anything worthy of being recorded, at least write something worthy of being read. It is a precept as beautiful as a diamond of the first water cut in England, but it cannot be applied to me, because I have not written either a novel, or the life of an illustrious character. Worthy or not, my life is my subject, and my subject is my life. I have lived without dreaming that I should ever take a fancy to write the history of my life, and, for that very reason, my Memoirs may claim from the reader an interest and a sympathy which they would not have obtained had I always entertained the design to write them in my old age, and, still more, to publish them.

I have reached, in 1797, the age of three-score years and twelve; I can now say "Vixi," and I could not find a more agreeable pastime than to relate my own adventures, and to cause pleasant laughter amongst the good company listening to me, from which I have received so many tokens of friendship, and in the midst of which I have ever lived. To enable me to write well, I have only to think that my readers will belong to that polite society:

Quæcunque dixi, si placuerint, dictavit auditor.

Should there be a few intruders whom I cannot prevent from perusing my Memoirs, I must find comfort in the idea that my history was not written for them.

By recollecting the pleasures I have had formerly, I renew them, I enjoy them a second time, while I laugh at the remembrance of troubles now past, which I no longer feel. A member of this great universe, I speak to the air, and I fancy myself rendering an account of my administration, as a steward is wont to do before leaving his situation. For my future I have no concern, and as a true philosopher I never would have any, for I know not what it may be; as a Christian, on the other hand, faith must believe without discussion, and the stronger it is, the more it keeps silent. I know that I have lived because I have felt, and, feeling giving me the knowledge of my existence, I know likewise that I shall exist no more when I shall have ceased to feel.

Should I perchance still feel after my death, I would no longer have any doubt, but I would most certainly give the lie to anyone asserting before me that I was dead.

I have had in turn every temperament: phlegmatic in my infancy; sanguine in my youth; later on, bilious; and now I have a disposition which engenders melancholy, and most likely will never change. I always made my food congenial to my constitution, and my health was always excellent. I learned very early that our health is always impaired by some excess either of food or of abstinence, and I never had any physician except myself. I am bound to add that the excess in too little has ever proved in me more dangerous than the excess in too much; the last may cause indigestion, but the first causes death.

Now, old as I am, and although enjoying good digestive organs,

I must have only one meal every day; but I find a set-off to that privation in my delightful sleep, and in the ease which I experience in writing down my thoughts without having recourse to paradox or sophism, which would be calculated to deceive myself even more than my readers, for I never could make up my mind to palm counterfeit coin upon them if I knew it to be such.

The sanguine temperament rendered me very sensible to the attractions of voluptuousness: I was always cheerful and ever ready to pass from one enjoyment to another, and I was at the same time very skilful in inventing new pleasures. Thence, I suppose, my natural disposition to make fresh acquaintances, and to break with them so readily, although always for a good reason, and never through mere fickleness. The errors caused by temperament are not to be corrected because our temperament is perfectly independent of our strength; it is not the case with our character. Heart and head are the constituent parts of character; temperament has almost nothing to do with it, and, therefore, character is dependent upon education and is susceptible of being corrected and improved.

The chief business of my life has always been to indulge my senses; I never knew anything of greater importance. I felt myself born for the fair sex, I have ever loved it dearly, and I have been loved by it as often and as much as I could. I have likewise always had a great weakness for good living, and I ever felt passionately fond of every object which excited my curiosity.

I have had friends who have acted kindly towards me, and it has been my good fortune to have it in my power to give them substantial proofs of my gratitude. I have had also bitter enemies who have persecuted me, and whom I have not crushed simply because I could not do it. I never would have forgiven them, had I not lost the memory of all the injuries they had heaped upon me. The man who forgets does not forgive, he only loses the remembrance of the harm inflicted upon him; forgiveness is the offspring of a feeling of heroism, of a noble heart, of a generous mind; whilst forgetfulness is only the result of a weak memory, or of an easy carelessness, and still oftener of a natural desire for calm and quietness. Hatred, in the course of time, kills the unhappy wretch who delights in nursing it in his bosom.

Should anyone bring against me an accusation of sensuality, he would be wrong, for all the fierceness of my senses never caused me to neglect any of my duties. For the same excellent reason, the

*accusation of drunkenness ought not to have been brought against
Homer:*

Laudibus arguitur vini vinosus Homerus.

*I have always been fond of highly seasoned, rich dishes, such as
macaroni prepared by a skilful Neapolitan cook, the olla-podrida of
the Spaniards, the glutinous codfish from Newfoundland, game with
a strong flavour, and cheese, the perfect state of which is attained
when the tiny animalcula formed from its very essence begin to show
signs of life. As for women, I have always found the odour of my
beloved ones exceeding pleasant.*

*What depraved tastes! some people will exclaim. Are you not
ashamed to confess such inclinations without blushing! Dear critics,
you make me laugh heartily! Thanks to my coarse tastes, I believe
myself happier than other men, because I am convinced that they
enhance my enjoyment. Happy are those who know how to obtain
pleasures without injury to anyone; insane are those who fancy
that the Almighty can enjoy the sufferings, the pains, the fasts and
abstinences which they offer to Him as a sacrifice, and that His
love is granted only to those who tax themselves so foolishly. God
can only demand from His creatures the practice of virtues the seed
of which He has sown in their soul, and all He has given unto us
has been intended for our happiness: self-love, thirst for praise,
emulation, strength, courage, and a power of which nothing can deprive us — the power of self-destruction, if, after due calculation,
whether false or just, we unfortunately reckon death to be advanta-
geous. This is the strongest proof of our moral freedom so much
attacked by sophists. Yet this power of self-destruction is repugnant
to nature, and has been rightly opposed by every religion.*

*A so-called free-thinker told me at one time that I could not con-
sider myself a philosopher if I placed any faith in revelation. But
when we accept it readily in physics, why should we reject it in
religious matters? The form alone is the point in question. The
spirit speaks to the spirit, and not to the ears. The principles of
everything we are acquainted with must necessarily have been revealed to those from whom we have received them by the great, supreme principle which contains them all. The bee erecting its hive,
the swallow building its nest, the ant constructing its cave, and the
spider warping its web, would never have done anything but for a
previous and everlasting revelation. We must either believe that it is*

so or admit that matter is endowed with thought. But as we dare not pay such a compliment to matter, let us stand by revelation. I pretend to the friendship, to the esteem, to the gratitude of my readers. I claim their gratitude, if my Memoirs can give them instruction and pleasure; I claim their esteem if, rendering me justice, they find more good qualities in me than faults; and I claim their friendship as soon as they deem me worthy of it by the candour and the good faith with which I abandon myself to their judgment, without disguise and exactly as I am in reality. They will find that I have always had such sincere love for truth, that I have often begun by telling stories for the purpose of getting truth to enter the heads of those who could not appreciate its charms. They will not form a wrong opinion of me when they see me emptying the purse of my friends to satisfy my fancies, for those friends entertained idle schemes, and by giving them the hope of success I trusted to disappointment to cure them. I would deceive them to make them wiser, and I did not consider myself guilty, for I applied to my own enjoyment sums of money which would have been lost in the vain pursuit of possessions denied by nature; therefore I was not actuated by any avaricious rapacity. I might think myself guilty if I were rich now, but I have nothing. I have squandered everything; it is my comfort and my justification. The money was intended for extravagant follies, and by applying it to my own frolics I did not turn it into a very different channel.

If I were deceived in my hope to please, I candidly confess I would regret it, but not sufficiently so to repent having written my Memoirs, for, after all, writing them has given me pleasure. Oh, cruel ennui! It must be by mistake that those who have invented the torments of hell have forgotten to ascribe thee the first place among them. Yet I am bound to own that I entertain a great fear of hisses; it is too natural a fear for me to boast of being insensible to them, and I cannot find any solace in the idea that, when these Memoirs are published, I shall be no more. I cannot think without a shudder of contracting any obligations towards death: I hate death; for, happy or miserable, life is the only blessing which man possesses, and those who do not love it are unworthy of it. If we prefer honour to life, it is because life is blighted by infamy; and if, in the alternative, man sometimes throws away his life, philosophy must remain silent.

Oh, death, cruel death! Fatal law which nature necessarily rejects because thy very office is to destroy nature! Cicero says that death frees us from all pains and sorrows, but this great philosopher books all the expense without taking the receipts into account. I do not recollect if, when he wrote his Tusculan Disputations, *his own* Tullia *was dead. Death is a monster which turns away from the great theatre an attentive hearer before the end of the play which deeply interests him, and this is reason enough to hate it.*

All my adventures are not to be found in these Memoirs; I have left out those which might have offended the persons who have played a sorry part therein. In spite of this reserve, my readers will perhaps often think me indiscreet, and I am sorry for it. Should I perchance become wiser before I give up the ghost, I might burn every one of these sheets, but now I have not courage enough to do it.

It may be that certain love scenes will be considered too explicit, but let no one blame me, unless it be for lack of skill, for I ought not to be scolded because, in my old age, I can find no other enjoyment but that which recollections of the past afford to me. After all, virtuous and prudish readers are at liberty to skip over any offensive pictures, and I think it my duty to give them this piece of advice; so much the worse for those who may not read my preface; it is no fault of mine if they do not, for everyone ought to know that a preface is to a book what the play-bill is to a comedy; both must be read.

My Memoirs are not written for young persons, who, in order to avoid false steps and slippery roads, ought to spend their youth in blissful ignorance, but for those who, having thorough experience of life, are no longer exposed to temptation, and who, having but too often gone through the fire, are like salamanders, and can be scorched by it no more. True virtue is but a habit, and I have no hesitation in saying that the really virtuous are those persons who can practise virtue without the slightest trouble; such persons are always full of toleration; and it is to them that my Memoirs are addressed.

I have written in French, and not in Italian, because the French language is more universal than mine, and the purists who may criticise in my style some Italian turns will be quite right, but only in case it should prevent them from understanding me clearly. The Greeks admired Theophrastus in spite of his Eresian style, and the Romans delighted in their Livy in spite of his patavinity. Provided I amuse my readers, it seems to me that I can claim the same indulgence. After all, every Italian reads Algarotti with pleasure, although his works are full of French idioms.

[7]

The motto I have adopted justifies my digressions, and all the commentaries, perhaps too numerous, in which I indulge upon my various exploits: "Nequidquam sapit qui sibi non sapit." *For the same reason I have always felt a great desire to receive praise and applause from polite society:*

Excitat auditor studium, laudataque virtus
Crescit, et immensum gloria calcar habet.

I would willingly have displayed here the proud axiom: "Nemo læditur nisi a se ipso" *had I not feared to offend the immense number of persons who, whenever anything goes wrong with them, are wont to exclaim,* "It is no fault of mine!" *I cannot deprive them of that small particle of comfort, for, were it not for it, they would soon feel hatred for themselves, and self-hatred often leads to the fatal idea of self-destruction.*

As for myself, I always willingly acknowledge my own self as the principal cause of every good or of every evil which may befall me; therefore I have always found myself capable of being my own pupil, and ready to love my teacher.

CHAPTER I

THE YOUTH OF CASANOVA

*G*IACOMO CASANOVA, *self-styled Chevalier de Seingalt, was born in Venice on April 2nd, 1725, the eldest of a family of six. Of his three brothers, two achieved some reputation as painters. Francesco, or François, specialised in military subjects and had a considerable vogue in Paris and Vienna, where his work can still be seen. Giovanni, the younger of the two, became Director of the Academy of Painting at Dresden, where his mother, engaged at the Court Theatre, resided, as well as one of the sisters, who was married there.*

In the opening chapter of his Memoirs, Casanova is at some pains to establish the family pedigree, which he traces back to a certain Don Jacob Casanova, a native of Saragossa, and "secretary to King Alfonso." Don Jacob, who was of illegitimate birth, started his ancestral duties in the approved Casanovian manner by eloping with a young nun the day after she had taken the veil. After seeking refuge in Rome, where their uncle, Don Juan Casanova, filled the post of major-domo at the Vatican, the young couple were successful in obtaining the pardon of Pope Martin III, who very obligingly not only released the lady from her vows, but even bestowed his nuptial blessing on the pair — so at least we are assured by their descendant.

The father of our hero, Gaëtan-Joseph (to keep the French form, as given in the Memoirs), was a native of Parma, which city he abandoned to follow the fortunes of "La Fragoletta," an actress, whose mature charms had captivated the young man. While acting with her in Venice, he transferred his affections to Zanetta Farusi, the daughter of a shoe-maker, whom he married in 1724. Although one of the conditions of the marriage was that Zanetta should not embrace her husband's career, the lure of the footlights proved too much; for soon after the birth of her first son, Giacomo, she followed her husband to London, where apparently she made her début as an actress. Naturally gifted for the stage, Zanetta Casanova, nicknamed "La Buranella," soon eclipsed her husband and became a "leading lady." Goldoni, who met her in Verona, refers to her as a "very handsome, very adroit widow," who, despite her ignorance of music, was able to sing well enough to content her audiences, while her acting never failed to delight them. Her husband having died after seven years of marriage, "La Buranella" seems to have made the best of things and provided a comfortable home in Venice, as well as a good education, for her numerous offspring. Giacomo was still a boy when his mother removed to Dresden, where she accepted a lifelong engagement at the Court Theatre and enjoyed the favours of the Elector of Saxony, an enthusiastic patron of Italian art.

Giacomo, left to the care of his maternal grandmother, old Marzia, who seems to have had a particular affection for him, showed at first very little promise of developing either physically or mentally. In an "Outline of My Life," discovered among his papers at Dux, Casanova affirms that he was "imbecile up to the age of eight and a half." Among other ominous symptoms, which seemed to hint at an early demise, were nasal hæmorrhages, with which he was afflicted. Old Marzia, determined to save the boy's life, and probably as distrustful of medical science as her grandson was to be, submitted Giacomo without hesitation to the treatment of a local sorceress, whose remedies and incantations proved so successful that the hæmorrhages ceased. It is possible that this first contact with magical practices was the origin of Casanova's lifelong interest in cabalistic science, which he was later to turn to such personal profit in his career. Significantly enough, this miraculous cure, which is the starting-point of his conscious life, was also to give him a foretaste of his other and greatest ruling passion: the pursuit of women. In return for his promise of secrecy regarding his "treatment," the boy was promised by the witch that he would receive the visit of a beautiful lady, who would be very kind to him, provided he could keep his mouth shut; and he relates that that same night he was awakened from his sleep by the arrival, by way of the chimney, of "a dazzling woman, with immense hoops, splendidly attired. and wearing on her head a crown set with precious stones, which seemed to me sparkling with fire." Having anointed the boy's head, uttered a long speech, which proved unintelligible to the listener, and given him a kiss, the mysterious visitor withdrew by the same way she had come.

[10]

THE YOUTH OF CASANOVA

At the age of nine, after receiving a little preliminary instruction from the poet Baffo, a friend of his deceased father's, Giacomo was sent to school at Padua. It is in this famous seat of learning that young Casanova, awakening from his mental lethargy, showed signs of such singular precociousness that he was able within a few years to take his degree in utroque jure (that is, in civil and canon law). For this, as for many of his other achievements, we have to take Casanova's word, patient researches having so far failed to discover any record either of his matriculation at the University of Padua or of the conferring of a doctor's degree. It is possible, however, that, like Goldoni (whose Memoirs, it is worth recording, were published during Casanova's lifetime), he was, by special dispensation, admitted to his thesis without having to furnish the usual certificates of matriculation and attendance.

Enhanced with the prestige of academic honours, real or fictitious, we find Casanova at the age of fifteen once more in Venice, preparing to enter the Church, as the quickest road to material welfare and social distinctions. To the delight of his devoted grandmother, he receives the tonsure and the minor orders from the Patriarch of Venice, frequents literary circles, and hobnobs with young patricians. His motto is that of every good Venetian of his day: "La mattina una messetta, l'aposdisnar una bassetta e la notte una donnetta," and he applies it to the letter. After listening to the sermons of Father Concina at San-Moïse or the lectures at San-Samuele (the church of the parish in which he resides with old Marzia, his grandmother), Giacomo dines with his new patron, Senator Malipiero, and the old gentleman's charming young protégée, Térèse Imer, just embarking on her chequered and brilliant career; puts in an appearance at the afternoon receptions of Giulietta Cavamacchi, the courtesan in vogue; takes a turn at the faro-tables established in the various private casinos, before or after the play; and rounds off his busy day with a picnic supper in the bedroom of his two "adorable friends" Nanette and Marton, the young nieces of the pious Madame Orio and the tender confidantes of his thwarted passion for the prudish Angela.

During the Christmas celebrations of that year (1740) Giacomo, thanks to the influence of Senator Malipiero, delivers his first sermon in the Church of the Holy Sacrament, with such success that the sexton finds no less than fifty sequins and several billets-doux in the bag of offerings sent round for the benefit of the preacher. Casanova, elated and triumphant, seriously intends training for the pulpit and confides this intention to the parson of the church in which he had made his début. Unfortunately the parson's sister is the very Angela for whom he is consumed with love and who refuses to listen to him unless he gives up the priesthood and leads her to the altar. Unable at the moment to solve this "case of conscience," Casanova decides to preach a second sermon, which was also destined to be his last. This is his own account of the affair:

The priest, who had at last confessed his admiration for my first sermon, asked me, some time afterwards, to prepare another for St. Joseph's Day, with an invitation to deliver it on the 19th of March, 1741. I composed it, and the abbé spoke of it with enthusiasm, but fate had decided that I should never preach but once in my life. It is a sad tale, unfortunately for me very true, which some persons are cruel enough to consider very amusing.

Young and rather self-conceited, I fancied that it was not necessary for me to spend much time in committing my sermon to memory. Being the author, I had all the ideas contained in my work classified in my mind, and it did not seem to me within the range of possibilities that I could forget what I had written. Perhaps I might not remember the exact words of a sentence, but I was at liberty to replace them by other expressions as good, and as I never happened to be at a loss, or to be struck dumb, when I spoke in society, it was not likely that such an untoward accident would befall me before an audience amongst whom I did not know anyone who could intimidate me and cause me suddenly to lose the faculty of reason or of speech. I therefore took my pleasure as usual, being satisfied with reading my sermon morning and evening, in order to impress it upon my memory, which until then had never betrayed me.

The 19th of March came, and on that eventful day at four o'clock in the afternoon I was to ascend the pulpit; but, believing myself quite secure and thoroughly master of my subject, I had not the moral courage to deny myself the pleasure of dining with Count Mont-Réal, who was then residing with me, and who had invited the patrician Barozzi, engaged to be married to his daughter after the Easter holidays.

I was still enjoying myself with my fine company, when the sexton of the church came in to tell me that they were waiting for me in the vestry. With a full stomach and my head rather heated, I took my leave, ran to the church, and entered the pulpit. I went through the exordium with credit to myself, and I took breathing time; but scarcely had I pronounced the first sentences of the narration, before I forgot what I was saying or what I had to say, and in my endeavours to proceed, I fairly wandered from my subject and I lost myself entirely. I was still more discomforted by a half-repressed murmur of the audience, as my deficiency appeared evident. Several persons left the church, others began to smile, I lost all presence of mind and every hope of getting out of the scrape.

I could· not say whether I feigned a fainting fit, or whether I truly swooned; all I know is that I fell down on the floor of the pulpit, striking my head against the wall, with an inward prayer for annihilation.

Two of the parish clerks carried me to the vestry, and after a few moments, without addressing a word to anyone, I took my cloak and my hat, and went home to lock myself in my room. I immediately dressed myself in a short coat, after the fashion of travelling priests, I packed a few things in a trunk, obtained some money from my grandmother, and took my departure for Padua, where I intended to pass my third examination. I reached Padua at midnight, and went to Doctor Gozzi's house, but I did not feel the slightest temptation to mention to him my unlucky adventure.

I remained in Padua long enough to prepare myself for the doctor's degree, which I intended to take the following year, and after Easter I returned to Venice, where my misfortune was already forgotten; but preaching was out of the question, and when any attempt was made to induce me to renew my efforts, I manfully kept to my determination never to ascend the pulpit again.

Two years later, his grandmother having died, "La Buranella," now definitely established in Dresden, decided to give up her house in Venice, and her son Giacomo was left to shift for himself. His exuberant temperament and wild associates soon got him into trouble with the authorities, who, thinking that a taste of prison fare would act as a salutary cure for his reckless spirit, sent him to meditate on his misdemeanours in the Fort of Saint André.

Casanova's stay in the fortress was enlivened by various incidents, the principal of which was his breaking bounds one night, returning to Venice, waylaying the rascally Razetta, who had been the cause of his captivity, and treating him to a sound thrashing. Owing to a carefully prepared ruse, entailing a sprained ankle, Casanova was able to prove an alibi, though he affirms that all Venice knew and applauded the hero of this vendetta.

At Saint André occurred also another incident, which for the first time brought the heedless youth face to face with an aspect of human tragedy only too common in the voluptuous city of the doges. A young lady of quality came to visit the fort in the company of her parents. Casanova was introduced by the governor, with whom he had become very friendly, and spent a delightful afternoon squiring the charming creature, basking in her smiles, and inordinately flattered by her mother's invitation to call on her in Venice. Once set free, he hurries to pay his respects to the lady, and — But Casanova shall take up the tale:

I found the house without difficulty; the count was not at home. The countess received me very kindly, but her appearance caused me so great a surprise that I did not know what to say to her. I had fancied that I was going to visit an angel, that I would find her in a lovely paradise, and I found myself in a large sitting-room furnished with four rickety chairs and a dirty old table. There was hardly any light in the room because the shutters were nearly closed. It might have been a precaution against the heat, but I judged that it was more probably for the purpose of concealing the windows, the glass of which was all broken. But this visible darkness did not prevent me from remarking that the countess was wrapped up in an old tattered gown, and that her chemise did not shine by its cleanliness. Seeing that I was ill at ease, she left the room, saying that she would send her daughter, who, a few minutes afterwards, came in with an easy and noble appearance, and told me that she had expected me with great impatience, but that I had surprised her at a time at which she was not in the habit of receiving any visits.

I did not know what to answer, for she did not seem to me to be the same person. Her miserable dishabille made her look almost ugly, and I wondered at the impression she had produced upon me at the fortress. She saw my surprise, and partly guessed my thoughts, for she put on a look, not of vexation, but of sorrow which called forth all my pity. If she had been a philosopher she might have rightly despised me as a man whose sympathy was enlisted only by her fine dress, her nobility, or her apparent wealth; but she endeavoured to bring me round by her sincerity. She felt that if she could call a little sentiment into play, it would certainly plead in her favour.

"I see that you are astonished, reverend sir, and I know the reason of your surprise. You expected to see great splendour here, and you find only misery. The government allows my father but a small salary, and there are nine of us. As we must attend church on Sundays and holidays in a style proper to our condition, we are often compelled to go without our dinner, in order to get out of pledge the clothes which urgent need too often obliges us to part with, and which we pledge anew on the following day. If we did not attend mass, the curate would strike our names off the list of those who share the alms of the Confraternity of the Poor, and those alms alone keep us afloat."

What a sad tale! She had guessed rightly. I was touched, but rather with shame than true emotion. I was not rich myself, and, as I was no longer in love, I only heaved a deep sigh, and remained as cold as ice. Nevertheless, her position was painful, and I answered politely, speaking with kindness and assuring her of my sympathy. "Were I wealthy," I said, "I would soon show you that your tale of woe has not fallen on unfeeling ears; but I am poor, and, being at the eve of my departure from Venice, even my friendship would be useless to you." Then, after some desultory talk, I expressed a hope that her beauty would yet win happiness for her. She seemed to consider for a few moments, and said, "That may happen some day, provided that the man who feels the power of my charms understands that they can be bestowed only with my heart, and is willing to render me the justice I deserve; I am only looking for a lawful marriage, without dreaming of rank or fortune; I no longer believe in the first, and I know how to live without the second; for I have been accustomed to poverty, and even to abject need; but you cannot realise that. Come and see my drawings."

"You are very good, mademoiselle."

Alas! I was not thinking of her drawings, and I could no longer feel interested in her Eve, but I followed her.

We came to a chamber in which I saw a table, a chair, a small toilet-glass, and a bed with the straw palliasse turned over, very likely for the purpose of allowing the looker-on to suppose that there were sheets underneath, but I was particularly disgusted by a certain smell, the cause of which was recent; I was thunderstruck, and if I had been still in love, this antidote would have been sufficiently powerful to cure me instanter. I wished for nothing but to make my escape, never to return, and I regretted that I could not throw on the table a handful of ducats, which I should have considered the price of my ransom.

The poor girl showed me her drawings; they were fine, and I praised them, without alluding particularly to Eve, and without venturing a joke upon Adam. I asked her, for the sake of saying something, why she did not try to render her talent remunerative by learning pastel drawing.

"I wish I could," she answered, "but the box of chalks alone costs two sequins."

"Will you forgive me if I am bold enough to offer you six?"

"Alas! I accept them gratefully, and to be indebted to you for such a service makes me truly happy."

Unable to keep back her tears, she turned her head round to conceal them from me, and I took that opportunity of laying the money on the table, and out of politeness, wishing to spare her every unnecessary humiliation, I saluted her lips with a kiss which she was at liberty to consider a loving one, as I wanted her to ascribe my reserve to the respect I felt for her. I then left her with a promise to call another day to see her father. I never kept my promise. The reader will see how I met her again after ten years.

How many thoughts crowded upon my mind as I left that house! What a lesson! I compared reality with the imagination, and I had to give the preference to the last, as reality is always dependent on it. I then began to foresee a truth which has been clearly proved to me in my after life — namely, that love is only a feeling of curiosity more or less intense, grafted upon the inclination placed in us by nature that the species may be preserved. And truly, woman is like a book, which, good or bad, must at first please us by the frontispiece. If this is not interesting, we do not feel any wish to read the book, and our wish is in direct proportion to the interest we feel. The frontispiece of woman runs from top to bottom like that of a book, and her feet, which are most important to every man who shares my taste, offer the same interest as the edition of the work.   If it is true that most amateurs bestow little or no attention upon the feet of a woman, it is likewise a fact that most readers care little or nothing whether a book is of the first edition or the tenth.   At all events, women are quite right to take the greatest care of their face, of their dress, of their general appearance; for it is only by that part of the frontispiece that they can call forth a wish to read them in those men who have not been endowed by nature with the privilege of blindness.   And just in the same manner that men who have read a great many books are certain to feel at last a desire for perusing new works even if they are bad, a man who has known many women, and all handsome women, feels at last a curiosity for ugly specimens when he meets with entirely new ones.   It is all very well for his eye to discover the paint which conceals the reality, but his passion has become a vice, and suggests some argument in favour of the lying frontispiece. It is possible, at least he thinks so, that the work may prove better than the title-page, and the reality more acceptable than the paint which hides it.   He then tries to peruse the book, but the leaves have not been opened; he meets with some resistance, the living book must be read according to established rules, and the bookworm falls a victim to coquetry, the monster which persecutes all those who make a business of love.

As for thee, intelligent man who hast read the few preceding lines, let me tell thee that, if they do not assist in opening thy eyes, thou art lost; I mean that thou art certain of being a victim to the fair sex to the very last moment of thy life.   If my candour does not displease thee, accept my congratulations.

Meanwhile Casanova's mother, anxious to get her enfant terrible safely into the arms of the Church, had prevailed on a good acquaintance of hers, Bernado de Bernardis, whom "La Buranella" had helped to obtain the bishopric of Martorano in Calabria, to take her son into his service.   It was the least the good bishop could do and he graciously consented.   Giacomo was informed of the arrangement, which met with his hearty approval, for not only was Venice becoming uncomfortably hot for him — the boy was wildly ambitious. The prospect of such high patronage to start him on his ecclesiastical career, as well as that of seeing the world, outweighed all other considerations.   So, after a night of tender farewells with Nanette and

Marton, during which they mingled their tears and their ecstasies, Giacomo Casanova in July 1743 embarked from the Piazzetta for a voyage of adventures which was to last for half a century and, after taking him through all the countries of Europe, finally bring him to anchor in a remote castle in Bohemia.

As the bishop of Martorano, to whom Casanova was presented in Venice by his guardian the abbé Grimani, was unable to take the young man with him, it was arranged that the latter should travel as far as Ancona in the retinue of the Venetian ambassador, who was proceeding to that city, and from there find his way to Rome, where he was to join the bishop.

The story of Casanova's journey to Calabria is one of the liveliest chapters of the Memoirs. We give it in full:

I embarked from St. Mark's landing. M. Grimani had given me ten sequins, which he thought would keep me during my stay in the lazzaretto of Ancona for the necessary quarantine, after which it was not to be supposed that I could want any money. I shared Grimani's certainty on the subject, and with my natural thoughtlessness I cared nothing about it. Yet I must say that, unknown to everybody, I had in my purse forty bright sequins, which powerfully contributed to increase my cheerfulness, and I left Venice full of joy and without one regret.

The retinue of the ambassador, which was styled "grand," appeared to me very small. It was composed of a Milanese steward, named Carcinelli, of a priest who fulfilled the duties of secretary because he could not write, of an old woman acting as housekeeper, of a man cook with his ugly wife, and eight or ten servants.

We reached Chiozza about noon. Immediately after landing, I politely asked the steward where I should put up, and his answer was:

"Wherever you please, provided you let this man know where it is, so that he can give you notice when the *peotta* is ready to sail. My duty," he added, "is to leave you at the lazzaretto of Ancona free of expense from the moment we leave this place. Until then enjoy yourself as well as you can."

The man to whom I was to give my address was the captain of the *peotta*. I asked him to recommend me a lodging.

"You can come to my house," he said, "if you have no objection to share a large bed with the cook, whose wife remains on board."

Unable to devise any better plan, I accepted the offer, and a sailor, carrying my trunk, accompanied me to the dwelling of the honest captain. My trunk had to be placed under the bed, which filled up the room. I was amused at this, for I was not in a position to be over-fastidious, and, after partaking of some dinner at the inn, I went about the town. Chiozza is a peninsula, a seaport belonging to Venice, with a population of ten thousand inhabitants, seamen, fishermen, merchants, lawyers, and government clerks.

I entered a coffee-room, and I had scarcely taken a seat when a young doctor-at-law, with whom I had studied in Padua, came up to me and introduced me to a druggist whose shop was near by, saying that his house was the rendezvous of all the literary men of the place. A few minutes afterwards, a tall Jacobin friar, blind of one eye, called Corsini, whom I had known in Venice, came in and paid me many compliments. He told me that I had arrived just in time to go to a picnic got up by the Macaronic academicians for the next day, after a sitting of the academy in which every member was to recite something of his composition. He invited me to join them, and to gratify the meeting with the delivery of one of my productions. I accepted the invitation, and, after the reading of ten stanzas which I had written for the occasion, I was unanimously elected a member. My success at the picnic was still greater, for I disposed of such a quantity of macaroni, that I was found worthy of the title of prince of the academy.

The young doctor, himself one of the academicians, introduced me to his family. His parents, who were in easy circumstances, received me very kindly. One of his sisters was very amiable, but the other, a professed nun, appeared to me a prodigy of beauty. I might have enjoyed myself in a very agreeable way in the midst of that charming family during my stay in Chiozza, but I suppose that it was my destiny to meet in that place with nothing but sorrows. The young doctor forewarned me that the monk Corsini was a very worthless fellow, despised by everybody, and advised me to avoid him. I thanked him for the information, but my thoughtlessness prevented me from profiting by it. Of a very easy disposition, and too giddy to fear any snares, I was foolish enough to believe that the monk would, on the contrary, be the very man to throw plenty of amusement in my way.

[19]

On the third day the worthless dog took me to a house of ill-fame, where I might have gone without his introduction, and, in order to show my mettle, I obliged a low creature whose ugliness ought to have been a sufficient antidote against my fleshly desire. On leaving the place, he brought me for supper to an inn, where we met four scoundrels of his own stamp. After supper one of them began a bank of faro, and I was invited to join in the game. I gave way to that feeling of false pride which so often causes the ruin of young men, and after losing four sequins I expressed a wish to retire, but my honest friend, the Jacobin, contrived to make me risk four more sequins in partnership with him. He held the bank, and it was broken. I did not wish to play any more, but Corsini, feigning to pity me and to feel great sorrow at being the cause of my loss, induced me to try myself a bank of twenty-five sequins; my bank was likewise broken. The hope of winning back my money made me keep up the game, and I lost everything I had. Deeply grieved, I went away and laid myself down near the cook, who woke up and said I was a libertine.

"You are right," was all I could answer.

I was worn out with fatigue and sorrow, and I slept soundly. My vile tormentor, the monk, woke me at noon, and informed me with a triumphant joy that a very rich young man had been invited by his friends to supper, that he would be sure to play and to lose, and that it would be a good opportunity for me to retrieve my losses.

"I have lost all my money. Lend me twenty sequins."

"When I lend money I am sure to lose; you may call it superstition, but I have tried it too often. Try to find money somewhere else, and come. Farewell."

I felt ashamed to confess my position to my friend, and sending for a money-lender I emptied my trunk before him. We made an inventory of my clothes, and the honest broker gave me thirty sequins, with the understanding that if I did not redeem them within three days, all my things would become his property. I am bound to call him an honest man, for he advised me to keep three shirts, a few pairs of stockings, and a few handkerchiefs; I was disposed to let him take everything, having a presentiment that I would win back all I had lost; a very common error. A few years later I took my revenge by writing a diatribe against presentiments. I am of opinion that the only foreboding in which man can have any sort of faith is the one which forebodes evil, because it comes from the mind, while a presentiment of happiness has its origin in the heart, and the heart is a fool worthy of reckoning foolishly upon fickle fortune.

I did not lose any time in joining the honest company, which was alarmed at the thought of not seeing me. Supper went off without any allusion to gambling, but my admirable qualities were highly praised, and it was decided that a brilliant fortune awaited me in Rome. After supper there was no talk of play, but giving way to my evil genius I loudly asked for my revenge. I was told that if I would take the bank everyone would punt. I took the bank, lost every sequin I had, and retired, begging the monk to pay what I owed to the landlord, which he promised to do.

I was in despair, and to crown my misery I found out as I was going home that I had met the day before with another living specimen of the Greek woman, less beautiful but as perfidious. I went to bed stunned by my grief, and I believe that I must have fainted into a heavy sleep, which lasted eleven hours; my awaking was that of a miserable being, hating the light of heaven, of which he felt himself unworthy, and I closed my eyes again, trying to sleep for a little while longer. I dreaded to rouse myself up entirely, knowing that I would then have to take some decision; but I never once thought of returning to Venice, which would have been the very best thing to do, and I would have destroyed myself rather than confide my sad position to the young doctor. I was weary of my existence, and I entertained vaguely some hope of starving where I was, without leaving my bed. It is certain that I should not have got up if M. Alban, the master of the *peotta*, had not roused me by calling upon me and informing me that the boat was ready to sail.

The man who is delivered from great perplexity, no matter by what means, feels himself relieved. It seemed to me that Captain Alban had come to point out the only thing I could possibly do; I dressed myself in haste, and tying all my worldly possessions in a handkerchief I went on board. Soon afterwards we left the shore, and in the morning we cast anchor in Orsara, a seaport of Istria. We all landed to visit the city, which would more properly be called a village. It belongs to the Pope, the Republic of Venice having abandoned it to the Holy See.

A young monk of the order of the Recollets, who called himself Friar Stephano of Belun, and had obtained a free passage from the devout Captain Alban, joined me as we landed and inquired whether I felt sick.

"Reverend father, I am unhappy."

"You will forget all your sorrow, if you will come and dine with me at the house of one of our devout friends."

I had not broken my fast for thirty-six hours, and having suffered much from sea-sickness during the night, my stomach was quite empty. My erotic inconvenience made me very uncomfortable, my mind felt deeply the consciousness of my degradation, and I did not possess a groat! I was in such a miserable state that I had no strength to accept or to refuse anything. I was thoroughly torpid, and I followed the monk mechanically.

He presented me to a lady, saying that he was accompanying me to Rome, where I intended to become a Franciscan. This untruth disgusted me, and under any other circumstances I would not have let it pass without protest, but in my actual position it struck me as rather comical. The good lady gave us a good dinner of fish cooked in oil, which in Orsara is delicious, and we drank some exquisite refosco. During our meal, a priest happened to drop in, and, after a short conversation, he told me that I ought not to pass the night on board the tartan, and pressed me to accept a bed in his house and a good dinner for the next day in case the wind should not allow us to sail; I accepted without hesitation. I offered my most sincere thanks to the good old lady, and the priest took me all over the town. In the evening, he brought me to his house, where we partook of an excellent supper prepared by his housekeeper, who sat down to the table with us, and with whom I was much pleased. The refosco, still better than that which I had drunk at dinner, scattered all my misery to the wind, and I conversed gaily with the priest. He offered to read to me a poem of his own composition, but, feeling that my eyes would not keep open, I begged he would excuse me and postpone the reading until the following day.

I went to bed, and in the morning, after ten hours of the most profound sleep, the housekeeper, who had been watching for my awakening, brought me some coffee. I thought her a charming woman, but, alas! I was not in a fit state to prove to her the high estimation in which I held her beauty.

THE YOUTH OF CASANOVA

Entertaining feelings of gratitude for my kind host, and disposed to listen attentively to his poem, I dismissed all sadness, and I paid his poetry such compliments that he was delighted, and, finding me much more talented than he had judged me to be at first, he insisted upon treating me to the reading of his idylls, and I had to swallow them, bearing the infliction cheerfully. The day passed off very agreeably; the housekeeper surrounded me with the kindest attentions — a proof that she was smitten with me; and, giving way to the pleasing idea, I felt that, by a very natural system of reciprocity, she had made my conquest. The good priest thought that the day had passed like lightning, thanks to all the beauties I had discovered in his poetry, which, to speak the truth, was below mediocrity, but time seemed to me to drag along very slowly, because the friendly glances of the housekeeper made me long for bedtime, in spite of the miserable condition in which I felt myself morally and physically. But such was my nature; I abandoned myself to joy and happiness, when, had I been more reasonable, I ought to have sunk under my load of grief and sadness.

But the golden time came at last. I found the pretty housekeeper full of compliance, but only up to a certain point, and as she offered some resistance when I showed myself disposed to pay a full homage to her charms, I quietly gave up the undertaking, very well pleased for both of us that it had not been carried any further, and I sought my couch in peace. But I had not seen the end of the adventure, for the next morning, when she brought my coffee, her pretty, enticing manners allured me to bestow a few loving caresses upon her, and if she did not abandon herself entirely, it was only, as she said, because she was afraid of some surprise. The day passed off very pleasantly with the good priest, and at night, the housekeeper no longer fearing detection, and I having on my side taken every precaution necessary in the state in which I was, we passed two most delicious hours. I left Orsara the next morning.

Friar Stephano amused me all day with his talk, which plainly showed me his ignorance combined with knavery under the veil of simplicity. He made me look at the alms he had received in Orsara — bread, wine, cheese, sausages, preserves, and chocolate; every nook and cranny of his holy garment was full of provisions.

"Have you received money likewise?" I inquired.

[23]

"God forbid! In the first place, our glorious order does not permit me to touch money, and, in the second place, were I to be foolish enough to receive any when I am begging, people would think themselves quit of me with one or two sous, whilst they give me ten times as much in eatables. Believe me, Saint Francis was a very judicious man."

I bethought myself that what this monk called wealth would be poverty to me. He offered to share with me, and seemed very proud at my consenting to honour him so far.

The tartan touched at the harbour of Pola, called Veruda, and we landed. After a walk up hill of nearly a quarter of an hour, we entered the city, and I devoted a couple of hours to visiting the Roman antiquities, which are numerous. Yet I saw no other trace of grand buildings except the ruins of the arena. We returned to Veruda, and went again to sea. On the following day we sighted Ancona, but the wind being against us we were compelled to tack about, and we did not reach the port till the second day. The harbour of Ancona, although considered one of the great works of Trajan, would be very unsafe if it were not for a causeway, which has cost a great deal of money, and which makes it somewhat better. I observed a fact worthy of notice — namely, that, in the Adriatic, the northern coast has many harbours, while the opposite coast can only boast of one or two. It is evident that the sea is retiring by degrees towards the east, and that in three or four more centuries Venice must be joined to the land.

We landed at the old lazzaretto, where we received the pleasant information that we would go through a quarantine of twenty-eight days, because Venice had admitted, after a quarantine of three months, the crew of two ships from Messina, where the plague had recently been raging. I requested a room for myself and for Brother Stephano, who thanked me very heartily. I hired from a Jew a bed, a table, and a few chairs, promising to pay for the hire at the expiration of our quarantine. The monk would have nothing but straw. If he had guessed that without him I might have starved, he would most likely not have felt so much vanity at sharing my room. A sailor, expecting to find in me a generous customer, came to inquire where my trunk was, and, hearing from me that I did not know, he, as well as Captain Alban, went to a great deal of trouble to find it, and I could hardly keep down my merriment when the captain called, begging to be excused for having left it behind, and assuring me that he would take care to forward it to me in less than three weeks.

The friar, who had to remain with me four weeks, expected to live at my expense, while, on the contrary, he had been sent by Providence to keep me. He had provisions enough for one week, but it was necessary to think of the future.

After supper, I drew a most affecting picture of my position, showing that I should be in need of everything until my arrival at Rome, where I was going, I said, to fill the post of secretary of memorials, and my astonishment may be imagined when I saw the blockhead delighted at the recital of my misfortunes.

"I undertake to take care of you until we reach Rome; only tell me whether you can write."

"What a question! Are you joking?"

"Why should I? Look at me; I cannot write anything but my name. True, I can write it with either hand; and what else do I want to know?"

"You astonish me greatly, for I thought you were a priest."

"I am a monk; I say the mass, and, as a matter of course, I must know how to read. Saint Francis, whose unworthy son I am, could not read, and that is the reason why he never said a mass. But as you can write, you will to-morrow pen a letter in my name to the persons whose names I will give you, and I warrant you we shall have enough sent here to live like fighting cocks all through our quarantine."

The next day he made me write eight letters, because, in the oral tradition of his order, it is said that, when a monk has knocked at seven doors and has met with a refusal at every one of them, he must apply to the eighth with perfect confidence, because there he is certain of receiving alms. As he had already performed the pilgrimage to Rome, he knew every person in Ancona devoted to the cult of Saint Francis, and was acquainted with the superiors of all the rich convents. I had to write to every person he named, and to set down all the lies he dictated to me. He likewise made me sign the letters for him, saying that, if he signed himself, his correspondents would see that the letters had not been written by him, which would injure him, for, he added, in this age of corruption, people will esteem only learned men. He compelled me to fill the letters with Latin passages and quotations, even those addressed to ladies, and I remonstrated in vain, for, when I raised any objection, he threatened to leave me without anything to eat. I made up my mind to do exactly as he wished. He desired me to write to the superior of the Jesuits that he would not apply to the Capuchins, because they were no better than atheists, and that that was the reason of the great dislike of Saint Francis for them. It was in vain that I reminded him of the fact that in the time of Saint Francis there were neither Capuchins nor Recollets. His answer was that I had proved myself an ignoramus. I firmly believed that he would be thought a madman, and that we should not receive anything, but I was mistaken, for such a quantity of provisions came pouring in that I was amazed. Wine was sent from three or four different quarters, more than enough for us during all our stay, and yet I drank nothing but water, so great was my wish to recover my health. As for eatables, enough was sent in every day for six persons; we gave all our surplus to our keeper, who had a large family. But the monk felt no gratitude for the kind souls who bestowed their charity upon him; all his thanks were reserved for Saint Francis.

He undertook to have my linen washed by the keeper; I would not have dared to give it myself, and he said that he had nothing to fear, as everybody was well aware that the monks of his order never wear any kind of linen.

I kept my bed nearly all day, and thus avoided showing myself to visitors. The persons who did not come wrote letters full of incongruities cleverly worded, which I took good care not to point out to him. It was with great difficulty that I tried to persuade him that those letters did not require any answer.

A fortnight of repose and severe diet brought me round towards complete recovery, and I began to walk in the yard of the lazzaretto from morning till night; but the arrival of a Turk from Thessalonia with his family compelled me to suspend my walks, the ground-floor having been given to him. The only pleasure left me was to spend my time on the balcony overlooking the yard. I soon saw a Greek slave, a girl of dazzling beauty, for whom I felt the deepest interest. She was in the habit of spending the whole day sitting near the door with a book or some embroidery in her hand. If she happened to raise her eyes and to meet mine, she modestly bent her head down, and sometimes she rose and went in slowly, as if she meant to say, "I did not know somebody was looking at me." Her figure was tall and slender, her features proclaimed her to be very young; she had a very fair complexion, with beautiful black hair and eyes. She wore the Greek costume, which gave her person a certain air of very exciting voluptuousness.

I was perfectly idle, and with the temperament which nature and habit had given me, was it likely that I could feast my eyes constantly upon such a charming object without falling desperately in love? I had heard her conversing in Lingua Franca with her master, a fine old man, who, like her, felt very weary of the quarantine, and used to come out but seldom, smoking his pipe, and remaining in the yard only a short time. I felt a great temptation to address a few words to the beautiful girl, but I was afraid she might run away and never come out again; however, unable to control myself any longer, I determined to write to her; I had no difficulty in conveying the letter, as I had only to let it fall from my balcony. But she might have refused to pick it up, and this is the plan I adopted in order not to risk any unpleasant result.

Availing myself of a moment during which she was alone in the yard, I dropped from my balcony a small piece of paper folded like a letter, but I had taken care not to write anything on it, and held the true letter in my hand. As soon as I saw her stooping down to pick up the first, I quickly let the second drop at her feet, and she put both into her pocket. A few minutes afterwards she left the yard. My letter was somewhat to this effect:

"Beautiful angel from the East, I worship you. I will remain all night on this balcony in the hope that you will come to me for a quarter of an hour, and listen to my voice through the hole under my feet. We can speak softly, and in order to hear me you can climb up to the top of the bale of goods which lies beneath the same hole."

I begged from my keeper not to lock me in as he did every night, and he consented on condition that he would watch me, for if I had jumped down in the yard his life might have been the penalty, and he promised not to disturb me on the balcony.

At midnight, as I was beginning to give her up, she came forward. I then laid myself flat on the floor of the balcony, and I placed my head against the hole, about six inches square. I saw

[27]

her jump on the bale, and her head reached within a foot from the balcony. She was compelled to steady herself with one hand against the wall for fear of falling, and in that position we talked of love, of ardent desires, of obstacles, of impossibilities, and of cunning artifices. I told her the reason for which I dared not jump down in the yard, and she observed that, even without that reason, it would bring ruin upon us, as it would be impossible to come up again, and that, besides, God alone knew what her master would do if he were to find us together. Then, promising to visit me in this way every night, she passed her hand through the hole. Alas! I could not leave off kissing it, for I thought that I had never in my life touched so soft, so delicate a hand. But what bliss when she begged for mine! I quickly thrust my arm through the hole, so that she could fasten her lips to the bend of the elbow. How many sweet liberties my hand ventured to take! But we were at last compelled by prudence to separate, and when I returned to my room I saw with great pleasure that the keeper was fast asleep.

Although I was delighted at having obtained every favour I could possibly wish for in the uncomfortable position we had been in, I racked my brain to contrive the means of securing more complete enjoyment for the following night, but I found during the afternoon that the feminine cunning of my beautiful Greek was more fertile than mine.

Being alone in the yard with her master, she said a few words to him in Turkish, to which he seemed to give his approval, and soon after a servant, assisted by the keeper, brought under the balcony a large basket of goods. She overlooked the arrangement, and in order to secure the basket better, she made the servant place a bale of cotton across two others. Guessing at her purpose, I fairly leaped for joy, for she had found the way of raising herself two feet higher; but I thought that she would then find herself in the most inconvenient position, and that, forced to bend double, she would not be able to resist the fatigue. The hole was not wide enough for her head to pass through, otherwise she might have stood erect and been comfortable. It was necessary at all events to guard against that difficulty; the only way was to tear out one of the planks of the floor of the balcony, but it was not an easy undertaking. Yet I decided upon attempting it, regardless of consequences; and I went to my room to provide myself with a large pair of pincers. Luckily the keeper was absent, and availing myself of the opportunity, I succeeded in dragging out carefully the four large nails which fastened the plank. Finding that I could lift it at my will, I replaced the pincers, and waited for the night with amorous impatience.

The darling girl came exactly at midnight. Noticing the difficulty she experienced in climbing up, and in getting a footing upon the third bale of cotton, I lifted the plank, and, extending my arm as far as I could, I offered her a steady point of support. She stood straight, and found herself agreeably surprised, for she could pass her head and her arms through the hole. We wasted no time in empty compliments; we only congratulated each other upon having both worked for the same purpose.

If, the night before, I had found myself master of her person more than she was of mine, this time the position was entirely reversed. Her hand roamed freely over every part of my body, but I had to stop half-way down hers. She cursed the man who had packed the bale for not having made it half a foot bigger, so as to get nearer to me. Very likely even that would not have satisfied us, but she would have felt happier.

Our pleasures were barren, yet we kept up our enjoyment until the first streak of light. I put back the plank carefully, and I lay down in my bed in great need of recruiting my strength.

My dear mistress had informed me that the Turkish Bairam began that very morning, and would last three days, during which it would be impossible for her to see me.

The night after Bairam, she did not fail to make her appearance, and, saying that she could not be happy without me, she told me that, as she was a Christian woman, I could buy her, if I waited for her after leaving the lazzaretto. I was compelled to tell her that I did not possess the means of doing so, and my confession made her sigh. On the following night she informed me that her master would sell her for two thousand piastres, that she would give me the amount, that she was yet a virgin, and that I would be pleased with my bargain. She added that she would give me a casket full of diamonds, one of which was alone worth two thousand piastres, and that the sale of the others would place us beyond the reach of poverty for the remainder of our life. She assured me that her master would not notice the loss of the casket, and that if he did, he would never think of accusing her.

I was in love with this girl; and her proposal made me uncomfortable; but when I woke in the morning I did not hesitate any longer. She brought the casket in the evening, but I told her that I never could make up my mind to be accessory to a robbery; she was very unhappy, and said that my love was not as deep as her own, but that she could not help admiring me for being so good a Christian.

This was the last night; probably we should never meet again. The flame of passion consumed us. She proposed that I should lift her up to the balcony through the open space. Where is the lover who would have objected to so attractive a proposal? I rose, and, without being a Milo, placed my hands under her arms, I drew her up towards me, and my desires are on the point of being fulfilled. Suddenly I feel two hands upon my shoulders, and the voice of the keeper exclaims, "What are you about?" I let my precious burden drop; she regains her chamber, and I, giving vent to my rage, throw myself flat on the floor of the balcony, and remain there without a movement, in spite of the shaking of the keeper, whom I was sorely tempted to strangle. At last I rose from the floor and went to bed without uttering one word, and not even caring to replace the plank.

In the morning the governor informed us that we were free. As I left the lazzaretto, with a breaking heart, I caught a glimpse of the Greek slave drowned in tears.

I agreed to meet Friar Stephano at the exchange, and I took the Jew from whom I had hired the furniture, to the convent of the Minims, where I received from Father Lazari ten sequins and the address of the bishop, who, after performing quarantine on the frontiers of Tuscany, had proceeded to Rome, where he would expect me to meet him.

I paid the Jew, and made a poor dinner at an inn. As I was leaving it to join the monk, I was so unlucky as to meet Captain Alban, who reproached me bitterly for having led him to believe that my trunk had been left behind. I contrived to appease his anger by telling him all my misfortunes, and I signed a paper in which I declared that I had no claim whatever upon him. I then purchased a pair of shoes and an overcoat, and met Stephano, whom I informed of my decision to make a pilgrimage to Our

Lady of Loretto. I said I would wait there for him, and that we would afterwards travel together as far as Rome. He answered that he did not wish to go through Loretto, and that I would repent of my contempt for the grace of Saint Francis. I did not alter my mind, and I left for Loretto the next day in the enjoyment of perfect health.

I reached the Holy City, tired almost to death, for it was the first time in my life that I had walked fifteen miles, drinking nothing but water, although the weather was very warm, because the dry wine used in that part of the country parched me too much. I must observe that, in spite of my poverty, I did not look like a beggar.

As I was entering the city, I saw coming towards me an elderly priest of very respectable appearance, and, as he was evidently taking notice of me, as soon as he drew near, I saluted him, and inquired where I could find a comfortable inn. "I cannot doubt," he said, "that a person like you, travelling on foot, must come here from devout motives; come with me." He turned back, I followed him, and he took me to a fine-looking house. After whispering a few words to a man who appeared to be a steward, he left me, saying, very affably, "You shall be well attended to."

My first impression was that I had been mistaken for some other person, but I said nothing.

I was led to a suite of three rooms; the chamber was decorated with damask hangings, the bedstead had a canopy, and the table was supplied with all materials necessary for writing. A servant brought me a light dressing-gown, and another came in with linen and a large tub full of water, which he placed before me; my shoes and stockings were taken off, and my feet washed. A very decent-looking woman, followed by a servant girl, came in a few minutes after, and curtsying very low, she proceeded to make my bed. At that moment the Angelus bell was heard; everyone knelt down, and I followed their example. After the prayer, a small table was neatly laid out, I was asked what sort of wine I wished to drink, and I was provided with newspapers and two silver candlesticks. An hour afterwards I had a delicious fish supper, and, before I retired to bed, a servant came to inquire whether I would take chocolate in the morning before or after mass.

As soon as I was in bed, the servant brought me a night-lamp with a dial, and I remained alone. Except in France I have never had such a good bed as I had that night. It would have cured the most chronic insomnia, but I was not labouring under such a disease, and I slept for ten hours.

This sort of treatment easily led me to believe that I was not in any kind of hostelry; but where was I? How was I to suppose that I was in a hospital?

When I had taken my chocolate, a hairdresser — quite a fashionable, dapper fellow — made his appearance, dying to give vent to his chattering propensities. Guessing that I did not wish to be shaved, he offered to clip my soft down with the scissors, saying that I would look younger.

"Why do you suppose that I want to conceal my age?"

"It is very natural, because, if your lordship did not wish to do so, your lordship would have shaved long ago. Countess Marcolini is here; does your lordship know her? I must go to her at noon to dress her hair."

I did not feel interested in the Countess Marcolini, and, seeing it, the gossip changed the subject.

"Is this your lordship's first visit to this house? It is the finest hospital throughout the papal states."

"I quite agree with you, and I shall compliment His Holiness on the establishment."

"Oh! His Holiness knows all about it, he resided here before he became Pope. If Monsignor Caraffa had not been well acquainted with you, he would not have introduced you here."

Such is the use of barbers throughout Europe; but you must not put any questions to them, for, if you do, they are sure to treat you to an impudent mixture of truth and falsehood, and instead of you pumping them, they will worm everything out of you.

Thinking that it was my duty to present my respectful compliments to Monsignor Caraffa, I desired to be taken to his apartment. He gave me a pleasant welcome, showed me his library, and entrusted me to the care of one of his abbés, a man of parts, who acted as my cicerone everywhere. Twenty years afterwards, this same abbé was of great service to me in Rome, and, if still alive, he is a canon of St. John Lateran.

On the following day I took the communion in the Santa-Casa. The third day was entirely employed in examining the exterior of this truly wonderful sanctuary, and early the next day I resumed my journey, having spent nothing except three paoli for the barber. Half-way to Macerata, I overtook Brother Stephano walking on at a very slow rate. He was delighted to see me again, and told me that he had left Ancona two hours after me, but that he never walked more than three miles a day, being quite satisfied to take two months for a journey which, even on foot, can easily be accomplished in a week. "I want," he said, "to reach Rome without fatigue and in good health. I am in no hurry, and if you feel disposed to travel with me and in the same quiet way, Saint Francis will not find it difficult to keep us both during the journey."

This lazy fellow was a man about thirty, red-haired, very strong and healthy; a true peasant who had turned himself into a monk only for the sake of living in idle comfort. I answered that, as I was in a hurry to reach Rome, I could not be his travelling companion.

"I undertake to walk six miles, instead of three, to-day," he said, "if you will carry my cloak, which I find very heavy."

The proposal struck me as a rather funny one; I put on his cloak, and he took my greatcoat, but, after the exchange, we cut such a comical figure that every peasant we met laughed at us. His cloak would truly have proved a load for a mule. There were twelve pockets quite full, without taking into account a pocket behind, which he called *il batticulo*, and which contained alone twice as much as all the others. Bread, wine, fresh and salt meat, fowls, eggs, cheese, ham, sausages — everything was to be found in those pockets, which contained provisions enough for a fortnight.

I told him how well I had been treated in Loretto, and he assured me that I might have asked Monsignor Caraffa to give me letters for all the hospitals on my road to Rome, and that everywhere I would have met with the same reception. "The hospitals," he added, "are all under the curse of Saint Francis, because the mendicant friars are not admitted in them; but we do not mind their gates being shut against us, because they are too far apart from each other. We prefer the homes of the persons attached to our order; these we find everywhere."

"Why do you not ask hospitality in the convents of your order?"

"I am not so foolish. In the first place, I should not be admitted, because, being a fugitive, I have not the written obedience which must be shown at every convent, and I should even run the risk of being thrown into prison; your monks are a cursed bad lot. In the second place, I should not be half so comfortable in the convents as I am with our devout benefactors."

"Why and how are you a fugitive?"

He answered my question by the narrative of his imprisonment and flight, the whole story being a tissue of absurdities and lies. The fugitive Recollet friar was a fool, with something of the wit of harlequin, and he thought that every man listening to him was a greater fool than himself. Yet with all his folly he was not deficient in a certain species of cunning. His religious principles were singular. As he did not wish to be taken for a bigoted man he was scandalous, and for the sake of making people laugh he would often make use of the most disgusting expressions. He had no taste whatever for women, and no inclination towards the pleasures of the flesh; but this was only owing to a deficiency in his natural temperament, and yet he claimed for himself the virtue of continence. On that score, everything appeared to him food for merriment, and when he had drunk rather too much, he would ask questions of such an indecent character that they would bring blushes to everybody's countenance. Yet the brute would only laugh.

As we were getting within one hundred yards from the house of the devout friend whom he intended to honour with his visit, he took back his heavy cloak. On entering the house he gave his blessing to everybody, and everyone in the family came to kiss his hand. The mistress of the house requested him to say mass for them, and the compliant monk asked to be taken to the vestry, but when I whispered in his ear:

"Have you forgotten that we have already broken our fast to-day?" he answered, dryly:

"Mind your own business."

I dared not make any further remark, but during the mass I was indeed surprised, for I saw that he did not understand what he was doing. I could not help being amused at his awkwardness, but I had not yet seen the best part of the comedy. As soon as he had somehow or other finished his mass he went to the confessional, and after hearing in confession every member of the family he took it into his head to refuse absolution to the daughter of his hostess, a girl of twelve or thirteen, pretty and quite charming. He gave his refusal publicly, scolding her and threatening her with the torments of hell. The poor girl, over-whelmed with shame, left the church crying bitterly, and I, feel-ing real sympathy for her, could not help saying aloud to Stephano that he was a madman. I ran after the girl to offer her my consolations, but she had disappeared, and could not be induced to join us at dinner. This piece of extravagance on the part of the monk exasperated me to such an extent that I felt a very strong inclination to thrash him. In the presence of all the family I told him that he was an impostor, and the infamous destroyer of the poor child's honour; I challenged him to ex-plain his reasons for refusing to give her absolution, but he closed my lips by answering very coolly that he could not betray the secrets of the confessional. I could eat nothing, and was fully determined to leave the scoundrel. As we left the house I was compelled to accept one paolo as the price of the mock mass he had said. I had to fulfil the sorry duty of his treasurer.

The moment we were on the road, I told him that I was going to part company, because I was afraid of being sent as a felon to the galleys if I continued my journey with him. We exchanged high words; I called him an ignorant scoundrel, he styled me beggar. I struck him a violent slap on the face, which he re-turned with a blow from his stick, but I quickly snatched it from him, and, leaving him, I hastened towards Macerata. A carrier who was going to Tolentino took me with him for two paoli, and for six more I might have reached Foligno in a waggon, but un-fortunately a wish for economy made me refuse the offer. I felt well, and I thought I could easily walk as far as Valcimare, but I arrived there only after five hours of hard walking, and thor-oughly beaten with fatigue. I was strong and healthy, but a walk of five hours was more than I could bear, because in my infancy I had never gone a league on foot. Young people cannot practise too much the art of walking.

The next day, refreshed by a good night's rest, and ready to resume my journey, I wanted to pay the innkeeper, but, alas! a new misfortune was in store for me! Let the reader imagine my sad position! I recollected that I had forgotten my purse, containing seven sequins, on the table of the inn at Tolentino.

What a thunderbolt! I was in despair, but I gave up the idea
of going back, as it was very doubtful whether I would find my
money. Yet it contained all I possessed, save a few copper coins
I had in my pocket. I paid my small bill, and, deeply grieved at
my loss, continued my journey towards Seraval. I was within
three miles of that place, when, in jumping over a ditch, I
sprained my ankle, and was compelled to sit down on one side of
the road, and to wait until someone should come to my assistance.

In the course of an hour a peasant happened to pass with his
donkey, and he agreed to carry me to Seraval for one paolo.
As I wanted to spend as little as possible, the peasant took me
to an ill-looking fellow who, for two paoli, paid in advance, consented to give me a lodging. I asked him to send for a surgeon,
but I did not obtain one until the following morning. I had a
wretched supper, after which I lay down in a filthy bed. I was
in hope that sleep would bring me some relief, but my evil genius
was preparing for me a night of torments.

Three men, armed with guns and looking like banditti, came
in shortly after I had gone to bed, speaking a kind of slang
which I could not make out, swearing, raging, and paying no
attention to me. They drank and sang until midnight, after
which they threw themselves down on bundles of straw brought
for them, and my host, who was drunk, came, greatly to my dis-
may, to lie down near me. Disgusted at the idea of having such
a fellow for my bed-companion, I refused to let him come, but
he answered, with fearful blasphemies, that all the devils in hell
could not prevent him from taking possession of his own bed. I
was forced to make room for him, and exclaimed, "Heavens,
where am I?" He told me that I was in the house of the most
honest constable in all the papal states.

Could I possibly have supposed that the peasant would have
brought me amongst those accursed enemies of humankind!

I got out of bed, and crawling along as well as I could, I found
a chair on which I passed the night. At daybreak, my tormentor, called up by his honest comrades, joined them in drinking
and shouting, and the three strangers, taking their guns, departed. Left alone by the departure of the vile rabble, I passed
another unpleasant hour, calling in vain for someone. At last a
young boy came in, I gave him some money and he went for a

surgeon. The doctor examined my foot, and assured me that three or four days would set me to rights. He advised me to be removed to an inn, and I most willingly followed his counsel. As soon as I was brought to the inn, I went to bed, and was well cared for, but my position was such that I dreaded the moment of my recovery. I feared that I should be compelled to sell my coat to pay the innkeeper, and the very thought made me feel ashamed. I began to consider that if I had controlled my sympathy for the young girl so ill-treated by Stephano, I should not have fallen into this sad predicament, and I felt conscious that my sympathy had been a mistake. If I had put up with the faults of the friar, if this and if that, and every other if was conjured up to torment my restless and wretched brain. Yet I must confess that the thoughts which have their origin in misfortune are not without some advantage to a young man, for they give him the habit of thinking, and the man who does not think never does anything right.

The morning of the fourth day came, and I was able to walk, as the surgeon had predicted; I made up my mind, although reluctantly, to beg the worthy man to sell my greatcoat for me — a most unpleasant necessity, for rain had begun to fall. I owed fifteen paoli to the innkeeper and four to the surgeon. Just as I was going to proffer my painful request, Brother Stephano made his appearance in my room, and burst into loud laughter inquiring whether I had forgotten the blow from his stick!

I was struck with amazement! I begged the surgeon to leave me with the monk, and he immediately complied.

I must ask my readers whether it is possible, in the face of such extraordinary circumstances, not to feel superstitious! What is truly miraculous in this case is the precise minute at which the event took place, for the friar entered the room as the word was hanging on my lips. What surprised me most was the force of Providence, of fortune, of chance, whatever name is given to it, of that very necessary combination which compelled me to find no hope but in that fatal monk, who had begun to be my protective genius in Chiozza at the moment my distress had likewise commenced. And yet, a singular guardian angel, this Stephano! I felt that the mysterious force which threw me in his hands was a punishment rather than a favour.

Nevertheless he was welcome, because I had no doubt of his

relieving me from my difficulties, and whatever might be the power that sent him to me, I felt that I could not do better than to submit to its influence; the destiny of that monk was to escort me to Rome.

"*Chi va piano va sano*," said the friar as soon as we were alone. He had taken five days to traverse the road over which I had travelled in one day, but he was in good health, and he had met with no misfortune. He told me that, as he was passing, he had heard that an abbé, secretary to the Venetian ambassador at Rome, was lying ill at the inn, after having been robbed in Valcimara. "I came to see you," he added, "and as I find you recovered from your illness, we can start again together; I agree to walk six miles every day to please you. Come, let us forget the past, and let us be at once on our way."

"I cannot go; I have lost my purse, and I owe twenty paoli."

"I will go and find the amount in the name of Saint Francis."

He returned within an hour, but he was accompanied by the infamous constable, who told me that, if I had let him know who I was, he would have been happy to keep me in his house. "I will give you," he continued, "forty paoli, if you will promise me the protection of your ambassador; but if you do not succeed in obtaining it for me in Rome, you will undertake to repay me. Therefore you must give me an acknowledgment of the debt."

"I have no objection." Every arrangement was speedily completed; I received the money, paid my debts, and left Seraval with Stephano.

About one o'clock in the afternoon, we saw a wretched-looking house at a short distance from the road, and the friar said: "It is a good distance from here to Collefiorito, we had better put up there for the night." It was in vain that I objected, remonstrating that we were certain of having very poor accommodation; I had to submit to his will. We found a decrepit old man lying on a pallet, two ugly women of thirty or forty, three children entirely naked, a cow, and a cursed dog which barked continually. It was a picture of squalid misery; but the niggardly monk, instead of giving alms to the poor people, asked them to entertain us to supper in the name of Saint Francis.

"You must boil the hen," said the dying man to the females, "and bring out of the cellar the bottle of wine which I have kept now for twenty years." As he uttered those few words, he was seized with such a fit of coughing that I thought he would die. The friar went near him, and promised him that, by the grace of Saint Francis, he would get young and well. Moved by the sight of so much misery, I wanted to continue my journey as far as Collefiorito, and to wait there for Stephano, but the women would not let me go, and I remained. After boiling for four hours the hen set the strongest teeth at defiance, and the bottle which I uncorked proved to be nothing but sour vinegar. Losing patience, I got hold of the monk's *batticulo*, and took out of it enough for a plentiful supper, and I saw the two women opening their eyes very wide at the sight of our provisions.

We all ate with good appetite, and after our supper the women made for us two large beds of fresh straw, and we lay down in the dark, as the last bit of candle to be found in the miserable dwelling was burnt out. We had not been lying on the straw five minutes, when Stephano called out to me that one of the women had just placed herself near him, and at the same instant the other one takes me in her arms and kisses me. I push her away, and the monk defends himself against the other; but mine, nothing daunted, insists upon laying herself near me; I get up, the dog springs up at my neck, and fear compels me to remain quiet on my straw bed; the monk screams, swears, struggles, the dog barks furiously, the old man coughs; all is noise and confusion. At last Stephano, protected by his heavy garments, shakes off the too loving shrew, and, braving the dog, manages to find his stick. Then he lays about to right and left, striking in every direction; one of the women exclaims, "Oh, God!" the friar answers, "She has her quietus." Calm reigns again in the house, the dog, most likely dead, is silent; the old man, who perhaps has received his death-blow, coughs no more; the children sleep, and the women, afraid of the singular caresses of the monk, sheer off into a corner: the remainder of the night passed off quietly.

At daybreak I rose; Stephano was likewise soon up. I looked all round, and my surprise was great when I found that the women had gone out, and seeing that the old man gave no sign of life, and had a bruise on his forehead, I showed it to Stephano, remarking that very likely he had killed him.

"It is possible," he answered, "but I have not done it intentionally."

Then taking up his *batticulo* and finding it empty he flew into a violent passion; but I was much pleased, for I had been afraid that the women had gone out to get assistance and to have us arrested, and the robbery of our provisions reassured me, as I felt certain that the poor wretches had gone out of the way so as to secure impunity for their theft. But I laid great stress upon the danger we should run by remaining any longer, and I succeeded in frightening the friar out of the house. We soon met a waggoner going to Folligno; I persuaded Stephano to take the opportunity of putting a good distance between us and the scene of our last adventures; and, as we were eating our breakfast at Folligno, we saw another waggon, quite empty, got a lift in it for a trifle, and thus rode to Pisignano, where a devout person gave us a charitable welcome, and I slept soundly through the night without the dread of being arrested.

Early the next day we reached Spoleti, where Brother Stephano had two benefactors, and, careful not to give either of them a cause of jealousy, he favoured both; we dined with the first, who entertained us like princes, and we had supper and lodging in the house of the second, a wealthy wine merchant, and the father of a large and delightful family. He gave us a delicious supper, and everything would have gone on pleasantly had not the friar, already excited by his good dinner, made himself quite drunk. In that state, thinking to please his new host, he began to abuse the other, greatly to my annoyance; he said the wine he had given us to drink was adulterated, and that the man was a thief. I gave him the lie to his face, and called him a scoundrel. The host and his wife pacified me, saying that they were well acquainted with their neighbour, and knew what to think of him; but the monk threw his napkin at my face, and the host took him very quietly by the arm and put him to bed in a room in which he locked him up. I slept in another room.

In the morning I rose early, and was considering whether it would not be better to go alone, when the friar, who had slept himself sober, made his appearance and told me that we ought for the future to live together like good friends, and not to give way to angry feelings; I followed my destiny once more. We resumed our journey, and at Soma, the innkeeper, a woman of rare beauty, gave us a good dinner, and some excellent Cyprus wine which the Venetian couriers exchanged with her against delicious truffles found in the vicinity of Soma, which sold for a good price in Venice. I did not leave the handsome innkeeper without losing a part of my heart.

It would be difficult to draw a picture of the indignation which overpowered me when, as we were about two miles from Terni, the infamous friar showed me a small bag full of truffles which the scoundrel had stolen from the amiable woman by way of thanks for her generous hospitality. The truffles were worth two sequins at least. In my indignation I snatched the bag from him, saying that I would certainly return it to its lawful owner. But, as he had not committed the robbery to give himself the pleasure of making restitution, he threw himself upon me, and we came to a regular fight. But victory did not remain long in abeyance; I forced his stick out of his hands, knocked him into a ditch, and went off. On reaching Terni, I wrote a letter of apology to our beautiful hostess of Soma, and sent back the truffles.

From Terni I went on foot to Otricoli, where I only stayed long enough to examine the fine old bridge, and from there I paid four paoli to a waggoner who carried me to Castel-Nuovo, from which place I walked to Rome. I reached the celebrated city on the 1st of September, at nine in the morning.

I must not forget to mention here a rather peculiar circumstance, which, however ridiculous it may be in reality, will please many of my readers. An hour after I had left Castel-Nuovo, the atmosphere being calm and the sky clear, I perceived on my right, and within ten paces of me, a pyramidal flame about two feet long and four or five feet above the ground. This apparition surprised me, because it seemed to accompany me. Anxious to examine it, I endeavoured to get nearer to it, but the more I advanced towards it the further it went from me. It would stop when I stood still, and when the road along which I was travelling happened to be lined with trees, I no longer saw it, but it was sure to reappear as soon as I had reached a portion of the road without trees. I several times retraced my steps purposely, but, every time I did so, the flame disappeared, and would not show itself again until I proceeded towards Rome. This extraordinary beacon left me when daylight chased darkness from the sky.

What a splendid field for ignorant superstition, if there had been any witnesses to that phenomenon, and if I had chanced to make a great name in Rome! History is full of such trifles, and the world is full of people who attach great importance to them in spite of the so-called light of science. I must candidly confess that, although somewhat versed in physics, the sight of that small meteor gave me singular ideas. But I was prudent enough not to mention the circumstance to anyone.

When I reached the ancient capital of the world, I possessed only seven paoli, and consequently I did not loiter about. I paid no attention to the splendid entrance through the gate of the *poplar*, which is by mistake pompously called of *the people*, or to the beautiful square of the same name, or to the portals of the magnificent churches, or to all the stately buildings which generally strike the traveller as he enters the city. I went straight towards Monte-Magnanopoli, where, according to the address given to me, I was to find the bishop. There I was informed that he had left Rome ten days before, leaving instructions to send me to Naples free of expense. A coach was to start for Naples the next day; not caring to see Rome, I went to bed until the time for the departure of the coach. I travelled with three low fellows to whom I did not address one word through the whole of the journey. I entered Naples on the 6th day of September.

I went immediately to the address which had been given to me in Rome; the bishop was not there. I called at the Convent of the Minims, and I found that he had left Naples to proceed to Martorano. I inquired whether he had left any instructions for me, but all in vain, no one could give me any information. And there I was, alone in a large city, without a friend, with eight carlini in my pocket, and not knowing what to do! But never mind; fate calls me to Martorano, and to Martorano I must go. The distance, after all, is only two hundred miles.

I found several drivers starting for Cosenza, but when they heard that I had no luggage, they refused to take me, unless I paid in advance. They were quite right, but their prudence placed me under the necessity of going on foot. Yet I felt I must reach Martorano, and I made up my mind to walk the distance, begging food and lodging like the very reverend Brother Stephano.

First of all I made a light meal for one-fourth of my money,

and, having been informed that I had to follow the Salerno road,
I went towards Portici, where I arrived in an hour and a half.
I already felt rather fatigued; my legs, if not my head, took me
to an inn, where I ordered a room and some supper. I was
served in good style, my appetite was excellent, and I passed a
quiet night in a comfortable bed. In the morning, I told the
innkeeper that I would return for my dinner, and I went out to
visit the royal palace. As I passed through the gate, I was met
by a man of prepossessing appearance, dressed in the Eastern
fashion, who offered to show me all over the palace, saying that
I would thus save my money. I was in a position to accept any
offer; I thanked him for his kindness.

Happening during the conversation to state that I was a Venetian, he told me that he was my subject, since he came from
Zante. I acknowledged his polite compliment with a reverence.

"I have," he said, "some very excellent muscatel wine grown
in the East, which I could sell you cheap."

"I might buy some, but I warn you I am a good judge."

"So much the better. Which do you prefer?"

"The Cerigo wine."

"You are right. I have some rare Cerigo muscatel, and we can
taste it if you have no objection to dine with me."

"None whatever."

"I can likewise give you the wines of Samos and Cephalonia.
I have also a quantity of minerals, plenty of vitriol, cinnabar,
antimony, and one hundred quintals of mercury."

"Are all these goods here?"

"No, they are in Naples. Here I have only the muscatel wine
and the mercury."

It is quite naturally and without any intention to deceive, that
a young man accustomed to poverty, and ashamed of it when
he speaks to a rich stranger, boasts of his means — of his fortune.
As I was talking with my new acquaintance, I recollected an
amalgam of mercury with lead and bismuth, by which the mercury increases one-fourth in weight. I said nothing, but I bethought myself that if the mystery should be unknown to the
Greek I might profit by it. I felt that some cunning was necessary, and that he would not care for my secret if I proposed to
sell it to him without preparing the way. The best plan was to
astonish my man with the miracle of the augmentation of the

mercury, treat it as a jest, and see what his intentions would be. Cheating is a crime, but honest cunning may be considered as a species of prudence. True, it is a quality which is near akin to roguery; but that cannot be helped, and the man who, in time of need, does not know how to exercise his cunning nobly is a fool. The Greeks call this sort of wisdom *Cerdaleophron* from the word *cerdo*, fox, and it might be translated by *foxdom* if there were such a word in English.

After we had visited the palace we returned to the inn, and the Greek took me to his room, in which he ordered the table to be laid for two. In the next room I saw several large vessels of muscatel wine and four flagons of mercury, each containing about ten pounds. My plans were laid, and I asked him to let me have one of the flagons of mercury at the current price, and took it to my room. The Greek went out to attend to his business, reminding me that he expected me to dinner. I went out likewise, and bought two pounds and a half of lead and an equal quantity of bismuth; the druggist had no more. I came back to the inn, asked for some large empty bottles, and made the amalgam.

We dined very pleasantly, and the Greek was delighted because I pronounced his Cerigo excellent. In the course of conversation he inquired laughingly why I had bought one of his flagons of mercury.

"You can find out if you come to my room," I said.

After dinner we repaired to my room, and he found his mercury divided in two vessels. I asked for a piece of chamois leather, strained the liquid through it, filled his own flagon, and the Greek stood astounded at the sight of the fine mercury, about one-fourth of a flagon, which remained over, with an equal quantity of a powder unknown to him; it was the bismuth. My merry laugh kept company with his astonishment, and calling one of the servants of the inn I sent him to the druggist to sell the mercury that was left. He returned in a few minutes and handed me fifteen carlini.

The Greek, whose surprise was complete, asked me to give him back his own flagon, which was there quite full, and worth sixty carlini. I handed it to him with a smile, thanking him for the opportunity he had afforded me of earning fifteen carlini, and took care to add that I should leave for Salerno early the next morning.

"Then we must have supper together this evening," he said. During the afternoon we took a walk towards Mount Vesuvius. Our conversation went from one subject to another, but no allusion was made to the mercury, though I could see that the Greek had something on his mind. At supper he told me, jestingly, that I ought to stop in Portici the next day to make forty-five carlini out of the three other flagons of mercury. I answered gravely that I did not want the money, and that I had augmented the first flagon only for the sake of procuring him an agreeable surprise.

"But," said he, "you must be very wealthy."

"No, I am not, because I am in search of the secret of the augmentation of gold, and it is a very expensive study for us."

"How many are there in your company?"

"Only my uncle and myself."

"What do you want to augment gold for? The augmentation of mercury ought to be enough for you. Pray, tell me whether the mercury augmented by you to-day is again susceptible of a similar increase."

"No, if it were so, it would be an immense source of wealth for us."

"I am much pleased with your sincerity."

Supper over I paid my bill, and asked the landlord to get me a carriage and pair of horses to take me to Salerno early the next morning. I thanked the Greek for his delicious muscatel wine, and, requesting his address in Naples, I assured him that he would see me within a fortnight, as I was determined to secure a cask of his Cerigo.

We embraced each other, and I retired to bed well pleased with my day's work, and in no way astonished at the Greek's not offering to purchase my secret, for I was certain that he would not sleep for anxiety, and that I should see him early in the morning. At all events, I had enough money to reach the Tour-du-Grec, and there Providence would take care of me. Yet it seemed to me very difficult to travel as far as Martorano, begging like a mendicant friar, because my outward appearance did not excite pity; people would feel interested in me only from a conviction that I needed nothing — a very unfortunate conviction, when the object of it is truly poor.

As I had foreseen, the Greek was in my room at daybreak. I

received him in a friendly way, saying that we could take coffee together.

"Willingly; but tell me, reverend abbé, whether you would feel disposed to sell me your secret."

"Why not? When we meet in Naples —"

"But why not now?"

"I am expected in Salerno; besides, I would only sell the secret for a large sum of money, and I am not acquainted with you."

"That does not matter, as I am sufficiently known here to pay you in cash. How much would you want?"

"Two thousand ounces."

"I agree to pay you that sum provided that I succeed in making the augmentation myself with such matter as you name to me, which I will purchase."

"It is impossible, because the necessary ingredients cannot be got here; but they are common enough in Naples."

"If it is any sort of metal, we can get it at the Tour-du-Grec. We could go there together. Can you tell me what is the expense of the augmentation?"

"One and a half per cent.; but are you likewise known at the Tour-du-Grec, for I should not like to lose my time?"

"Your doubts grieve me."

Saying which he took a pen, wrote a few words, and handed to me this order:

"At sight, pay to bearer the sum of fifty gold ounces, on account of Panagiotti."

He told me that the banker resided within two hundred yards of the inn, and he pressed me to go there myself. I did not stand upon ceremony, but went to the banker, who paid me the amount. I returned to my room, in which he was waiting for me, and placed the gold on the table, saying that we could now proceed together to the Tour-du-Grec, where we would complete our arrangements after the signature of a deed of agreement. The Greek had his own carriage and horses; he gave orders for them to be got ready, and we left the inn; but he had nobly insisted upon my taking possession of the fifty ounces.

When we arrived at the Tour-du-Grec, he signed a document by which he promised to pay me two thousand ounces as soon as I should have discovered to him the process of augmenting mercury by one-fourth without injuring its quality, the amalgam to be equal to the mercury which I had sold in his presence at Portici.

He then gave me a bill of exchange payable at sight in eight days on M. Genaro de Carlo. I told him that the ingredients were lead and bismuth; the first combining with mercury, and the second giving to the whole the perfect fluidity necessary to strain it through the chamois leather. The Greek went out to try the amalgam — I do not know where, and I dined alone, but towards evening he came back, looking very disconsolate, as I had expected.

"I have made the amalgam," he said, "but the mercury is not perfect."

"It is equal to that which I have sold in Portici, and that is the very letter of your engagement."

"But my engagement says likewise *without injury to the quality*. You must agree that the quality is injured, because it is no longer susceptible of further augmentation."

"You knew that to be the case; the point is its equality with the mercury I sold in Portici. But we shall have to go to law, and you will lose. I am sorry the secret should become public. Congratulate yourself, sir, for, if you should gain the lawsuit, you will have obtained my secret for nothing. I would never have believed you capable of deceiving me in such a manner."

"Reverend sir, I can assure you that I would not willingly deceive anyone."

"Do you know the secret, or do you not? Do you suppose I would have given it to you without the agreement we entered into? Well, there will be some fun over this affair in Naples, and the lawyers will make money out of it. But I am much grieved at this turn of affairs, and I am very sorry that I allowed myself to be so easily deceived by your fine talk. In the meantime, here are your fifty ounces."

As I was taking the money out of my pocket, frightened to death lest he should accept it, he left the room, saying that he would not have it. He soon returned; we had supper in the same room, but at separate tables; war had been openly declared, but I felt certain that a treaty of peace would soon be signed. We did not exchange one word during the evening, but in the morning he came to me as I was getting ready to go. I again offered to return the money I received, but he told me to keep it, and proposed to give me fifty ounces more if I would give him back his bill of exchange for two thousand. We began to argue the matter quietly, and after two hours of discussion I gave in. I received fifty ounces more, we dined together like old friends, and embraced each other cordially. As I was bidding him adieu, he gave me an order on his house at Naples for a barrel of muscatel wine, and he presented me with a splendid box containing twelve razors with silver handles, manufactured in the Tour-du-Grec. We parted the best friends in the world and well pleased with each other.

I remained two days in Salerno to provide myself with linen and other necessaries. Possessing about one hundred sequins, and enjoying good health, I was very proud of my success, in which I could not see any cause of reproach to myself, for the cunning I had brought into play to ensure the sale of my secret could not be found fault with except by the most intolerant of moralists, and such men have no authority to speak on matters of business. At all events, free, rich, and certain of presenting myself before the bishop with a respectable appearance, and not like a beggar, I soon recovered my natural spirits, and congratulated myself upon having bought sufficient experience to ensure me against falling a second time an easy prey to a Father Corsini, to thieving gamblers, to mercenary women, and particularly to the impudent scoundrels who barefacedly praise so well those they intend to dupe — a species of knaves very common in the world, even amongst people who form what is called good society.

I left Salerno with two priests who were going to Cosenza on business, and we traversed the distance of one hundred and forty-two miles in twenty-two hours. The day after my arrival in the capital of Calabria, I took a small carriage and drove to Martorano. During the journey, fixing my eyes upon the famous *mare Ausonium,* I felt delighted at finding myself in the middle of Magna Grecia, rendered so celebrated for twenty-four centuries by its connection with Pythagoras. I looked with astonishment upon a country renowned for its fertility, and in which, in spite of nature's prodigality, my eyes met everywhere the aspect of terrible misery, the complete absence of that pleasant superfluity which helps man to enjoy life, and the degradation of

[48]

the inhabitants sparsely scattered on a soil where they ought to be so numerous; I felt ashamed to acknowledge them as originating from the same stock as myself. Such is, however, the Terra di Lavoro where labour seems to be execrated, where everything is cheap, where the miserable inhabitants consider that they have made a good bargain when they have found anyone disposed to take care of the fruit which the ground supplies almost spontaneously in too great abundance, and for which there is no market. I felt compelled to admit the justice of the Romans who had called them *Brutes* instead of *Brutians*. The good priests with whom I had been travelling laughed at my dread of the tarantula and of the charsydra, for the disease brought on by the bite of those insects appeared to me more fearful even than a certain disease with which I was already too well acquainted. They assured me that all the stories relating to those creatures were fables; they laughed at the lines which Virgil has devoted to them in the *Georgics* as well as at all those I quoted to justify my fears.

I found Bishop Bernard de Bernardis occupying a hard chair near an old table on which he was writing. I fell on my knees, as it is customary to do before a prelate, but, instead of giving me his blessing, he raised me up from the floor, and, folding me in his arms, embraced me tenderly. He expressed his deep sorrow when I told him that in Naples I had not been able to find any instructions to enable me to join him, but his face lighted up again when I added that I was indebted to no one for money, and that I was in good health. He bade me take a seat, and with a heavy sigh he began to talk of his poverty, and ordered a servant to lay the cloth for three persons. Besides this servant, his lordship's suite consisted of a most devout-looking housekeeper, and of a priest whom I judged to be very ignorant from the few words he uttered during our meal. The house inhabited by his lordship was large, but badly built and poorly kept. The furniture was so miserable that, in order to make up a bed for me in the room adjoining his chamber, the poor bishop had to give up one of his two mattresses! His dinner, not to say any more about it, frightened me, for he was very strict in keeping the rules of his order, and this being a fast day, he did not eat any meat, and the oil was very bad. Nevertheless, monsignor was an intelligent man, and, what is still better, an honest man. He told me, much to my surprise, that his bishopric, although not one of little importance, brought him in only five hundred ducati-di-regno yearly, and that, unfortunately, he had contracted debts to the amount of six hundred. He added, with a sigh, that his only happiness was to feel himself out of the clutches of the monks, who had persecuted him, and made his life a perfect purgatory for fifteen years. All these confidences caused me sorrow and mortification, because they proved to me, not only that I was not in the promised land where a mitre could be picked up, but also that I would be a heavy charge for him. I felt that he was grieved himself at the sorry present his patronage seemed likely to prove.

I inquired whether he had a good library, whether there were any literary men, or any good society in which one could spend a few agreeable hours. He smiled and answered that throughout his diocese there was not one man who could boast of writing decently, and still less of any taste or knowledge in literature; that there was not a single bookseller, nor any person caring even for the newspapers. But he promised me that we would follow our literary tastes together, as soon as he received the books he had ordered from Naples. That was all very well, but was this the place for a young man of eighteen to live in, without a good library, without good society, without emulation and literary intercourse? The good bishop, seeing me full of sad thoughts, and almost astounded at the prospect of the miserable life I should have to lead with him, tried to give me courage by promising to do everything in his power to secure my happiness.

The next day, the bishop having to officiate in his pontifical robes, I had an opportunity of seeing all the clergy, and all the faithful of the diocese, men and women, of whom the cathedral was full; the sight made me resolve at once to leave Martorano. I thought I was gazing upon a troop of brutes for whom my external appearance was a cause of scandal. How ugly were the women! What a look of stupidity and coarseness in the men! When I returned to the bishop's house I told the prelate that I did not feel in me the vocation to die within a few months a martyr in this miserable city.

"Give me your blessing," I added, "and let me go; or, rather, come with me. I promise you that we shall make a fortune somewhere else."

The proposal made him laugh repeatedly during the day. Had he agreed to it he would not have died two years afterwards in the prime of manhood. The worthy man, feeling how natural was my repugnance, begged me to forgive him for having summoned me to him, and, considering it his duty to send me back to Venice, having no money himself and not being aware that I had any, he told me that he would give me an introduction to a worthy citizen of Naples who would lend me sixty ducati-di-regno to enable me to reach my native city. I accepted his offer with gratitude, and going to my room I took out of my trunk the case of fine razors which the Greek had given me, and I begged his acceptance of it as a souvenir of me. I had great difficulty in forcing it upon him, for it was worth the sixty ducats, and to conquer his resistance I had to threaten to remain with him if he refused my present. He gave me a very flattering letter of recommendation for the Archbishop of Cosenza, in which he requested him to forward me as far as Naples without any expense to myself. It was thus that I left Martorano sixty hours after my arrival, pitying the bishop whom I was leaving behind, and who wept as he was pouring heartfelt blessings upon me.

The Archbishop of Cosenza, a man of wealth and of intelligence, offered me a room in his palace. During the dinner I made, with an overflowing heart, the eulogy of the Bishop of Martorano; but I railed mercilessly at his diocese and at the whole of Calabria in so cutting a manner that I greatly amused the archbishop and all his guests, amongst whom were two ladies, his relatives, who did the honours of the dinner-table. The youngest, however, objected to the satirical style in which I had depicted her country, and declared war against me; but I contrived to obtain peace again by telling her that Calabria would be a delightful country if one-fourth only of its inhabitants were like her. Perhaps it was with the idea of proving to me that I had been wrong in my opinion that the archbishop gave on the following day a splendid supper.

Cosenza is a city in which a gentleman can find plenty of amusement; the nobility are wealthy, the women are pretty, and men generally well-informed, because they have been educated in Naples or in Rome.

I left Cosenza on the third day with a letter from the archbishop for the far-famed Genovesi.

I had five travelling companions, whom I judged, from their appearance, to be either pirates or banditti, and I took very good care not to let them see or guess that I had a well-filled purse. I likewise thought it prudent to go to bed without undressing during the whole journey — an excellent measure of prudence for a young man travelling in that part of the country.

I reached Naples on the 16th of September, 1743, and I lost no time in presenting the letter of the Bishop of Martorano. It was addressed to a M. Gennaro Polo at St.-Anne's. This excellent man, whose duty was only to give me the sum of sixty ducats, insisted, after perusing the bishop's letter, upon receiving me in his house, because he wished me to make the acquaintance of his son, who was a poet like myself. The bishop had represented my poetry as sublime. After the usual ceremonies, I accepted his kind invitation, my trunk was sent for, and I was a guest in the house of M. Gennaro Polo.

Naples, always a city of good luck for Casanova, as he himself declares, proved no exception on this occasion. At Dr. Gennaro's he made the acquaintance of various literati, to whom he was introduced by his enthusiastic host as a rising poet, as well as of a Don Antonio Casanova, who claimed him as a kinsman and treated him with lavish hospitality, delighted to find that his Venetian cousin had no intention of disputing Don Antonio's claim of representing the "illustrious" Casanovas of Saragossa. After a few days of feasting, Casanova, armed with letters of introduction to various people of note, including the Spanish Cardinal Acquaviva, set out for Rome.

His carriage is not yet outside Naples, and the tears of parting from his affectionate friends are still in the process of drying, when the vision of two smiling faces opposite him suggests new means of improving the shining hour. Needless to say, he is not slow to avail himself of the occasion, and, as the husband of one of the enchantresses proves to be a genial and loquacious Neapolitan lawyer, the journey to Rome is anything but dull, especially as, owing to scanty accommodation at the inns, the quartet shared a bedroom.

A born tactician in matters amorous, Casanova loses no time in tergiversation between two possible objectives. He already realises that dispersion of effort ends in defeat, and that, although it is possible to kill two birds with one stone, it is no use aiming at both at the same time. All things being equal as regards youth and physical attractions, a young Latin will prefer the married woman to the spinster. In this case it was the lawyer's wife, Donna Lucrezia, on whom he concentrated his attacks, but with sufficient discretion not to alienate the sympathies of her husband or her sister. On reaching Rome the company part on the best of terms and in high spirits, Casanova going so far as to predict (in this case with some plausibility) that the lawyer would become the father of a son. Meanwhile it was arranged' that during the lawyer's stay in Rome, the party would forgather as often as possible.

For the second time Casanova is in Rome, but in what different conditions from the first visit! Here is the picture he gives of himself:

I was in Rome with a good wardrobe, pretty well supplied with money and jewellery, not wanting in experience, and with excellent letters of introduction. I was free, my own master, and just reaching the age in which a man can have faith in his own fortune, provided he is not deficient in courage, and is blessed with a face likely to attract the sympathy of those he mixes with. I was not handsome, but I had something better than beauty — a striking expression which almost compelled a kind interest in my favour, and I felt myself ready for anything. I knew that Rome is the one city in which a man can begin from the lowest rung, and reach the very top of the social ladder. This knowledge increased my courage, and I must confess that a most inveterate feeling of self-esteem which, on account of my inexperience, I could not distrust, enhanced wonderfully my confidence in myself.

The man who intends to make his fortune in this ancient capital of the world must be a chameleon susceptible of reflecting all the colours of the atmosphere that surrounds him — a Proteus apt to assume every form, every shape. He must be supple, flexible, insinuating, close, inscrutable, often base, sometimes sincere, sometimes perfidious, always concealing a part of his knowledge, indulging but in one tone of voice, patient, a perfect master of his own countenance, as cold as ice when any other man would be all fire; and if unfortunately he is not religious at heart — a very common occurrence for a soul possessing the above requisites — he must have religion in his mind, that is to say, on his face, on his lips, in his manners; he must suffer quietly, if he be an honest man, the necessity of knowing himself

[53]

an arrant hypocrite. The man whose soul would loathe such a life should leave Rome and seek his fortune elsewhere. I do not know whether I am praising or excusing myself, but of all those qualities I possessed but one — namely, flexibility; for the rest, I was only an interesting, heedless young fellow, a pretty good blood horse, but not broken, or, rather, badly broken; and that is much worse.

The letters of introduction to Cardinal Acquaviva and Father Georgi, a learned monk, much in favour with the Pope, proved more than efficacious, and before long, Casanova was fairly launched in Roman society. The only requirement for social success which he lacked being a knowledge of the French language, which both his sponsors declared to be essential, the young man lost no time in making up this deficiency. The teacher recommended to him by the cardinal's secretary, and whose services he at once engaged, lived opposite his eminence's palace, where Casanova had been given a lodging. As luck would have it, this teacher had a daughter Barbara, who had started an intrigue with one of her father's pupils. The young people were violently in love and, as the girl's father objected to their marrying, had decided to run away together. Though at first Casanova wisely refused to have anything to do with the matter, which the lovers had confided to him, he suddenly, and, as he declares, quite innocently, became involved in a serious scandal. The father, having got wind of the proposed elopement, notified the sbirri (the police), who arrested the lover as he was about to carry off the girl. The latter, disguised as a man, sought refuge in Casanova's apartment in the cardinal's palace, threw herself on his mercy, and so wrought on his feelings that he consented to let her remain. There she was safe, for not even the bargello (head of the police) would dare to violate the premises of a prince of the Church. Although the cardinal, on hearing the details of the story, behaved with generosity and gallantry, refusing to give up the girl, whom he placed in a convent until a marriage with her lover became possible, he found it advisable to dispense with the services of so compromising a secretary. The fact that the latter had been paying assiduous and, if we are to believe the Memoirs, not unsuccessful court to the beautiful and gifted Lucrezia Monti, who enjoyed his eminence's special favour, was probably an added motive for Casanova's dismissal.

To see the ladder by which he was to climb to fortune and his lady's chamber so roughly withdrawn, just as he had triumphantly placed his foot on the first rung, was a bitter blow for poor Giacomo, who on this occasion, as on many others, indulged in some salutary reflections on the folly of his conduct, promising himself to profit by the lesson. The cardinal, who throughout seems to have behaved with magnanimity, wishing to offer some compensation, promised the lad letters of recommendation for any destination he had in mind. He was not a little surprised when he heard that Constantinople was the place selected. Casanova, who had replied on the impulse of the moment, decided, on thinking the matter over, that he must be either mad or inspired by some mysterious genius to have made such a choice.

Besides the cardinal's letter, which was addressed to Osman Bonneval, Pacha of Caramania, a renegade Frenchman who had embraced the religion of Islam, Casanova was handed a purse of one hundred ounces of gold (value: seven hundred sequins, about three hundred and fifty pounds in English money) as a parting gift. With this viaticum, to which he added his own reserve funds of three hundred sequins and a letter from the Venetian ambassador for a wealthy Turk, Casanova, now nineteen years of age, set out for Ancona, en route for the Turkish capital. "I left Rome," he recounts, "in a coach with a lady going to Our Lady of Loretto, to fulfil a vow made during a severe illness of her daughter, who accompanied her. The young lady was ugly; my journey was rather a tedious one."

After a short stay in Ancona, where he made the acquaintance of a mysterious youth, called Bellino, exercising the profession of castrato, or "male soprano," who on closer inspection turned out to be a girl — a discovery which, needless to say, was not without a reward for the discoverer — Casanova crosses the lines of the Austrian and Spanish armies, then in winter quarters in the Romagna, in a manner worthy of Baron Münchhausen (the account of this adventure also bears the mark of the illustrious baron), and eventually reaches Venice.

Whether it was his brief contact with military life, or a reluctance to admit that his ecclesiastical career had proved a failure, or both, Casanova on reaching his native city feels suddenly impelled to exchange his clerical dress for a military uniform. An impulse in Casanova is tantamount to a considered decision and brooks of no delay — not longer than it takes for the tailor to supply him with the necessary garments, which, for being somewhat irregular, are none the less resplendent. Those were the happy days, it must be remembered, when a plume, a sword, and a swagger would easily hold lieu of a gazetted commission — at least for travelling purposes. He relates:

The day before my departure from Venice I did not go out; I devoted the whole of the day to friendship. Madame Orio and her lovely nieces shed many tears, and I joined them in that delightful employment. During the last night that I spent with both of them, the sisters repeated over and over, in the midst of the raptures of love, that they never would see me again. They guessed rightly; but if they had happened to see me again they would have guessed wrongly. Observe how wonderful prophets are. I went on board, on the 5th of May, with a good supply of clothing, jewels, and ready cash. Our ship carried twenty-four guns and two hundred Sclavonian soldiers. We sailed from Malamacca to the shores of Istria during the night, and we came to anchor in the harbour of Orsera to take ballast. I landed with several others to take a stroll through the wretched place where I had spent three days nine months before, a recollection which caused me a pleasant sensation when I compared my present position to what it was at that time. What a difference in everything — health, social condition, and money! I felt quite certain that in the splendid uniform I was now wearing nobody would recognise the miserable-looking abbé who, but for Friar Stephano, would have become — God knows what!

CHAPTER II

THE SOLDIER OF FORTUNE

*A*FTER *encountering a severe storm, during which Casanova, suspected of being a sorcerer by a fanatical priest, nearly shared the fate of Jonah, the ship arrived at Corfu, where Casanova passed a month, waiting for the arrival of the* bailo, *who was to take him to Constantinople in his suite. We now turn again to the Memoirs:*

During the month that I spent in Corfu, waiting for the arrival of M. Vénier, I did not devote any time to the study, either moral or physical, of the country, for, excepting the days on which I was on duty, I passed my life at the coffee-house, intent upon the game, and sinking, as a matter of course, under the adverse fortune which I braved with obstinacy. I never won, and I had not the moral strength to stop till all my means were gone. The only comfort I had, and a sorry one truly, was to hear the banker himself call me — perhaps sarcastically — a fine player, every time I lost a large stake. My misery was at its height, when new life was infused in me by the booming of the guns fired in honour of the arrival of the *bailo*. He was on board the *Europa*, a frigate of seventy-two guns, and he had taken only eight days to sail from Venice to Corfu. The moment he cast anchor, the *bailo* hoisted his flag of captain-general of the Venetian navy, and the *proveditore* hauled down his own colours. The Republic of Venice has not on the sea any authority greater than that of *Bailo* to the Porte. The Chevalier Vénier had with him a distinguished and brilliant suite; Count Annibal Gambera, Count Charles Zenobio, both Venetian noblemen of the first class, and the Marquis d'Anchotti of Bressan, accompanied him to Constantinople for their own amusement. The *bailo* remained a week in Corfu, and all the naval authorities entertained him and his suite in turn, so that there was a constant succession of balls and suppers. When I presented myself to his excellency, he informed me that he had already spoken to the *proveditore*, who had granted me a furlough of six months to enable me to accompany him to Constantinople as his adjutant; and as soon as the official document for my furlough had been delivered to me, I sent my small stock of worldly goods on board the *Europa*, and we weighed anchor early the next day.

We sailed with a favourable wind which remained steady and brought us in six days to Cerigo, where we stopped to take in some water. Feeling some curiosity to visit the ancient Cythera, I went on shore with the sailors on duty, but it would have been better for me if I had remained on board, for in Cerigo I made a bad acquaintance. I was accompanied by the captain of marines.

The moment we set foot on shore, two men, very poorly dressed and of unprepossessing appearance, came to us and begged for assistance. I asked them who they were, and one, quicker than the other, answered: —

"We are sentenced to live, and perhaps to die, in this island by the despotism of the Council of Ten. There are forty others as unfortunate as ourselves, and we are all born subjects of the Republic.

"The crime of which we have been accused, which is not considered a crime anywhere, is that we were in the habit of living with our mistresses, without being jealous of our friends, when, finding our ladies handsome, they obtained their favours with our ready consent. As we were not rich, we felt no remorse in availing ourselves of the generosity of our friends in such cases, but it was said that we were carrying on an illicit trade, and we have been sent to this place, where we receive every day ten sous in *moneta lunga*. We are called *mangia-marroni*, and are worse off than galley-slaves, for we are dying of ennui, and we are often starving without knowing how to stay our hunger. My name is Don Antonio Pocchini, I am of a noble Paduan family, and my mother belongs to the illustrious family of Campo San-Piero."

We gave them some money, and went about the island, returning to the ship after we had visited the fortress. I shall have to speak of that Pocchini in a few years.

The wind continued in our favour, and we reached the Dardanelles in eight or ten days; the Turkish barges met us there to carry us to Constantinople. The sight offered by that city at the distance of a league is truly wonderful; and I believe that a more magnificent panorama cannot be found in any part of the world. It was that splendid view which was the cause of the fall of the Roman, and of the rise of the Greek Empire. Constantine the Great, arriving at Byzantium by sea, was so much struck with the wonderful beauty of its position, that he exclaimed, "Here is the proper seat of the empire of the whole world!" and, in order to secure the fulfilment of his prediction, he left Rome for Byzantium. If he had known the prophecy of Horace, or rather if he had believed in it, he would not have been guilty of such folly. The poet had said that the downfall of the Roman Empire would begin only when one of the successors of Augustus bethought him of removing the capital of the empire to where it had originated. The Troad is not far distant from Thrace.

We arrived at the Venetian Embassy in Pera towards the middle of July, and, for a wonder, there was no talk of the plague in Constantinople just then. We were all provided with very comfortable lodgings, but the intensity of the heat induced the *bailo* to seek for a little coolness in a country mansion which had been hired by the Bailo Dona. It was situated at Bouyou-dere. The very first order laid upon me was never to go out un-known to the *bailo*, and without being escorted by a janissary, and this order I obeyed to the letter. In those days the Russians had not tamed the insolence of the Turkish people. I am told that foreigners can now go about as much as they please in per-fect security.

The day after our arrival, I took a janissary to accompany me to Osman Pacha, of Caramania, the name assumed by Count de Bonneval ever since he had adopted the turban. I sent in my letter, and was immediately shown into an apartment on the ground-floor, furnished in the French fashion, where I saw a stout elderly gentleman, dressed like a Frenchman, who, as I entered the room, rose, came to meet me with a smiling coun-tenance, and asked me how he could serve the protégé of a cardinal of the Roman Catholic Church, which he could no longer call his mother. I gave him all the particulars of the circumstances which, in a moment of despair, had induced me to ask the cardinal for letters of introduction for Constantinople, and I added that, the letters once in my possession, my supersti-tious feelings had made me believe that I was bound to deliver them in person.

"Then, without this letter," he said, "you never would have come to Constantinople, and you have no need of me?"

"True, but I consider myself fortunate in having thus made the acquaintance of a man who has attracted the attention of the whole of Europe, and who still commands that attention."

His excellency made some remark respecting the happiness of young men who, like me, without care, without any fixed pur-pose, abandon themselves to fortune with that confidence which knows no fear, and telling me that the cardinal's letter made it desirable that he should do something for me, he promised to introduce me to three or four of his Turkish friends who deserved to be known. He invited me to dine with him every Thursday, and undertook to send me a janissary who would protect me from the insults of the rabble, and show me everything worth seeing.

The cardinal's letter representing me as a literary man, the pacha observed that I ought to see his library. I followed him through the garden, and we entered a room furnished with grated cupboards; curtains could be seen behind the wire-work; the books were most likely behind the curtains.

Taking a key out of his pocket, he opened one of the cupboards, and, instead of folios, I saw long rows of bottles of the finest wines. We both laughed heartily.

"Here are," said the pacha, "my library and my harem. I am old, women would only shorten my life, but good wine will prolong it, or, at least, make it more agreeable."

"I imagine your excellency has obtained a dispensation from the mufti?"

"You are mistaken, for the Pope of the Turks is very far from enjoying as great a power as the Christian Pope. He cannot in any case permit what is forbidden by the *Koran;* but everyone is at liberty to work out his own damnation if he likes. The Turkish devotees pity the libertines, but they do not persecute them; there is no inquisition in Turkey. Those who do not follow the precepts of religion, say the Turks, will suffer enough in the life to come; there is no need to make them suffer in this life. The only dispensation I have asked and obtained, has been respecting circumcision, although it can hardly be called so, because, at my age, it might have proved dangerous. That ceremony is generally performed, but it is not compulsory."

During the two hours that we spent together, the pacha inquired after several of his friends in Venice, and particularly after Marc Antonio Dieto. I told him that his friends were still faithful to their affection for him, and did not find fault with his apostasy. He answered that he was a Mahometan as he had been a Christian, and that he was not better acquainted with the *Koran* than he had been with the Gospel. "I am certain," he added, "that I shall die calmer and much happier than Prince Eugène. I have had to say that God is God, and that Mahomet is the prophet. I have said it, and the Turks care very little whether I believe it or not. I wear the turban as the soldier wears the uniform. I was nothing but a military man; I could not have turned my hand to any other profession, and I made up my mind to become lieutenant-general of the Grand Turk only when I found myself entirely at a loss how to earn my living. When I left Venice, the pitcher had gone too often to the well, it was broken at last, and if the Jews had offered me the command of an army of fifty thousand men, I would have gone and besieged Jerusalem!"

Bonneval was handsome, but too stout. He had received a sabre-cut in the lower part of the abdomen, which compelled him to wear constantly a bandage supported by a silver plate. He had been exiled to Asia, but only for a short time, for, as he told me, the cabals are not so tenacious in Turkey as they are in Europe, and particularly at the court of Vienna. As I was taking leave of him, he was kind enough to say that, since his arrival in Turkey, he had never passed two hours as pleasantly as those he had just spent with me, and that he would compliment the *bailo* about me.

The Bailo Dona, who had known him intimately in Venice, desired me to be the bearer of all his friendly compliments for him, and M. Vénier expressed his deep regret at not being able to make his acquaintance.

The second day after my first visit to him being a Thursday, the pacha did not forget to send a janissary according to his promise. It was about eleven in the morning when the janissary called for me, I followed him, and this time I found Bonneval dressed in the Turkish style. His guests soon arrived, and we sat down to dinner, eight of us, all well disposed to be cheerful and happy. The dinner was entirely French, in cooking and service; his steward and his cook were both worthy French renegades.

He had taken care to introduce me to all his guests and at the same time to let me know who they were, but he did not give me an opportunity of speaking before dinner was nearly over. The conversation was entirely kept up in Italian, and I remarked that the Turks did not utter a single word in their own language, even to say the most ordinary thing. Each guest had near him a bottle which might have contained either white wine or hydromel; all I know is that I drank, as well as M. de Bonneval, next to whom I was seated, some excellent white Burgundy.

The guests got me on the subject of Venice, and particularly of Rome, and the conversation very naturally fell upon religion, but not upon dogmatic questions; the discipline of religion and liturgical questions were alone discussed.

One of the guests, who was addressed as *effendi*, because he had been secretary for foreign affairs, said that the ambassador from Venice to Rome was a friend of his, and he spoke of him in the highest manner. I told him that I shared his admiration for that ambassador, who had given me a letter of introduction for

[61]

a Turkish nobleman, whom he had represented as an intimate friend. He inquired for the name of the person to whom the letter was addressed, but I could not recollect it, and took the letter out of my pocket-book. The *effendi* was delighted when he found that the letter was for himself. He begged leave to read it at once, and after he had perused it, he kissed the signature and came to embrace me. This scene pleased M. de Bonneval and all his friends. The *effendi*, whose name was Ismail, entreated the pacha to come to dine with him, and to bring me; Bonneval accepted, and fixed a day.

Notwithstanding all the politeness of the *effendi*, I was particularly interested during our charming dinner in a fine elderly man of about sixty, whose countenance breathed at the same time the greatest sagacity and the most perfect kindness. Two years afterwards I found again the same features on the handsome face of M. de Bragadin, a Venetian senator of whom I shall have to speak at length when we come to that period of my life. That elderly gentleman had listened to me with the greatest attention, but without uttering one word. In society, a man whose face and general appearance excite your interest, stimulates strongly your curiosity if he remains silent. When we left the dining-room I inquired from M. de Bonneval who he was; he answered that he was wealthy, a philosopher, a man of acknowledged merit, of great purity of morals, and strongly attached to his religion. He advised me to cultivate his acquaintance if he made any advances to me.

I was pleased with his advice, and when, after a walk under the shady trees of the garden, we returned to a drawing-room furnished in the Turkish fashion, I purposely took my seat near Yusuf Ali. Such was the name of the Turk for whom I felt so much sympathy. He offered me his pipe in a very graceful manner; I refused it politely, and took one brought to me by one of M. de Bonneval's servants. Whenever I have been amongst smokers I have smoked or left the room; otherwise I would have fancied that I was swallowing the smoke of the others, and that idea, which is true and unpleasant, disgusted me. I have never been able to understand how in Germany the ladies, otherwise so polite and delicate, could inhale the suffocating fumes of a crowd of smokers.

Yusuf, pleased to have me near him, at once led the conversation to subjects similar to those which had been discussed at table, and particularly to the reasons which had induced me to give up the peaceful profession of the Church and to choose a military life; and in order to gratify his curiosity without losing his good opinion, I gave him, but with proper caution, some of the particulars of my life, for I wanted him to be satisfied that, if I had at first entered the career of the holy priesthood, it had not been through any vocation of mine. He seemed pleased with my recital, spoke of natural vocations as a Stoic philosopher, and I saw that he was a fatalist; but as I was careful not to attack his system openly, he did not dislike my objections, most likely because he thought himself strong enough to overthrow them.

I must have inspired the honest Mussulman with very great esteem, for he thought me worthy of becoming his disciple; it was not likely that he could entertain the idea of becoming himself the disciple of a young man of nineteen, lost, as he thought, in a false religion.

After spending an hour in examining me, in listening to my principles, he said that he believed me fit to know the real truth, because he saw that I was seeking for it, and that I was not certain of having obtained it so far. He invited me to come and spend a whole day with him, naming the days when I would be certain to find him at home, but he advised me to consult the Pacha Osman before accepting his invitation. I told him that the pacha had already mentioned him to me and had spoken very highly of his character; he seemed much pleased. I fixed a day for my visit, and left him.

I informed M. de Bonneval of all that had occurred; he was delighted, and promised that his janissary would be every day at the Venetian palace, ready to execute my orders.

I received the congratulation of the *bailo* upon the excellent acquaintances I had already made, and M. Vénier advised me not to neglect such friends in a country where weariness of life was more deadly to foreigners than the plague.

On the day appointed I went early to Yusuf's palace, but he was out. His gardener, who had received his instructions, showed me every attention, and entertained me very agreeably for two hours in doing the honours of his master's splendid garden, where I found the most beautiful flowers. This gardener was a Neapolitan, and had belonged to Yusuf for thirty years.

His manners made me suspect that he was well born and well educated, but he told me frankly that he had never been taught even to read, that he was a sailor when he was taken in slavery, and that he was so happy in the service of Yusuf that liberty would be a punishment to him. Of course I did not venture to address him any questions about his master, for his reserve might have put my curiosity to the blush.

Yusuf had gone out on horseback; he returned, and, after the usual compliments, we dined alone in a summer-house, from which we had a fine view of the sea, and in which the heat was cooled by a delightful breeze, which blows regularly at the same hour every day from the north-west, and is called the *mistral*. We had a good dinner; there was no prepared dish except the *cauroman*, a peculiar delicacy of the Turks. I drank water and hydromel, and I told Yusuf that I preferred the last to wine, of which I never took much at that time. "Your hydromel," I said, "is very good, and the Mussulmans who offend against the law by drinking wine do not deserve any indulgence; I believe they drink wine only because it is forbidden." "Many of the true believers," he answered, "think that they can take it as a medicine. The Grand Turk's physician has brought it into vogue as a medicine, and it has been the cause of his fortune, for he has captivated the favour of his master, who is in reality constantly ill, because he is always in a state of intoxication." I told Yusuf that in my country drunkards were scarce, and that drunkenness was a vice to be found only amongst the lowest people; he was much astonished. "I cannot understand," he said, "why wine is allowed by all religions, when its use deprives man of his reason." "All religions," I answered, "forbid excess in drinking wine, and the crime is only in the abuse." I proved him the truth of what I had said by telling him that opium produced the same results as wine, but more powerfully, and consequently Mahomet ought to have forbidden the use of it. He observed that he had never taken either wine or opium in the course of his life.

After dinner, pipes were brought in and we filled them ourselves. I was smoking with pleasure, but, at the same time, was expectorating. Yusuf, who smoked like a Turk, that is to say, without spitting, said: —

"The tobacco you are now smoking is of a very fine quality, and you ought to swallow its balsam, which is mixed with the saliva."

[64]

"I suppose you are right; smoking cannot be truly enjoyed without the best tobacco."

"That is true to a certain extent, but the enjoyment found in smoking good tobacco is not the principal pleasure, because it only pleases our senses; true enjoyment is that which works upon the soul, and is completely independent of the senses."

"I cannot realise pleasures enjoyed by the soul without the instrumentality of the senses."

"Listen to me. When you fill your pipe do you feel any pleasure?"

"Yes."

"Whence does that pleasure arise, if it is not from your soul? Let us go further. Do you not feel pleased when you give up your pipe after having smoked all the tobacco in it — when you see that nothing is left but some ashes?"

"It is true."

"Well, there are two pleasures in which your senses have certainly nothing to do, but I want you to guess the third, and the most essential."

"The most essential? It is the perfume."

"No; that is a pleasure of the organ of smelling — a sensual pleasure."

"Then I do not know."

"Listen. The principal pleasure derived from tobacco smoking is the sight of the smoke itself. You must never see it go out of the bowl of your pipe, but only from the corner of your mouth, at regular intervals which must not be too frequent. It is so truly the greatest pleasure connected with the pipe, that you cannot find anywhere a blind man who smokes. Try yourself the experiment of smoking a pipe in your room, at night, and without a light; you will soon lay the pipe down."

"It is all perfectly true; yet you must forgive me if I give the preference to several pleasures, in which my senses are interested, over those which afford enjoyment only to my soul."

"Forty years ago I was of the same opinion, and in forty years, if you succeed in acquiring wisdom, you will think like me. Pleasures which give activity to our senses, my dear son, disturb the repose of our soul — a proof that they do not deserve the name of real enjoyments."

"But if I feel them to be real enjoyments, it is enough to prove that they are truly so."

"Granted; but if you would take the trouble of analysing them after you have tasted them, you would not find them unalloyed."

"It may be so, but why should I take a trouble which would only lessen my enjoyment?"

"A time will come when you will feel pleasure in that very trouble."

"It strikes me, dear father, that you prefer mature age to youth."

"You may boldly say old age."

"You surprise me. Must I believe that your early life has been unhappy?"

"Far from it. I was always fortunate in good health, and the master of my own passions; but all I saw in my equals was for me a good school in which I have acquired the knowledge of man, and learned the real road to happiness. The happiest of men is not the most voluptuous, but the one who knows how to choose the highest standard of voluptuousness, which can be found, I say again, not in the pleasures which excite our senses, but in those which give greater repose to the soul."

"That is the voluptuousness which you consider unalloyed."

"Yes, and such is the sight of a vast prairie all covered with grass. The green colour, so strongly recommended by our divine prophet, strikes my eyes, and at the same moment I feel that my soul is wrapped up in a calm so delightful that I fancy myself nearer the Creator. I enjoy the same peace, the same repose, when I am seated on the banks of a river, when I look upon the water so quiet, yet always moving, which flows constantly, yet never disappears from my sight, never loses any of its clearness in spite of its constant motion. It strikes me as the image of my own existence, and of the calm which I require for my life in order to reach, like the water I am gazing upon, the goal which I do not see, and which can only be found at the other end of the journey."

Thus did the Turk reason, and we passed four hours in this sort of conversation. He had buried two wives, and he had two sons and one daughter. The eldest son, having received his patrimony, had established himself in the city of Salonica, where he was a wealthy merchant; the other was in the seraglio, in the service of the Grand Turk, and his fortune was in the hands of a trustee. His daughter, Zelmi, then fifteen years of age, was to inherit all his remaining property. He had given her all the accomplishments which could minister to the happiness of the man whom Heaven had destined for her husband. We shall hear more of that daughter anon. The mother of the three children was dead, and, five years previous to the time of my visit, Yusuf had taken another wife, a native of Scio, young and very beautiful, but he told me himself that he was now too old, and could not hope to have any child by her. Yet he was only sixty years of age. Before I left, he made me promise to spend at least one day every week with him.

At supper, I told the *baili* how pleasantly the day had passed.

"We envy you," they said, "the prospect you have before you of spending agreeably three or four months in this country, while, in our quality of ministers, we must pine away with melancholy."

A few days afterwards, M. de Bonneval took me with him to dine at Ismail's house, where I saw Asiatic luxury on a grand scale, but there were a great many guests, and the conversation was held almost entirely in the Turkish language — a circumstance which annoyed me and M. de Bonneval also. Ismail saw it, and he invited me to breakfast whenever I felt disposed, assuring me that he would have much pleasure in receiving me. I accepted the invitation, and I went ten or twelve days afterwards. For the present I must return to Yusuf, who, during my second visit, displayed a character which inspired me with the greatest esteem and the warmest affection.

We had dined alone as before, and, conversation happening to turn upon the fine arts, I gave my opinion upon one of the precepts in the *Koran*, by which the Mahometans are deprived of the innocent enjoyment of paintings and statues. He told me that Mahomet, a very sagacious legislator, had been right in removing all images from the sight of the followers of Islam.

"Recollect, my son, that the nations to which the prophet brought the knowledge of the true God were all idolaters. Men are weak; if the disciples of the prophet had continued to see the same objects, they might have fallen back into their former errors."

"No one ever worshipped an image as an image; the deity of which the image is a representation is what is worshipped."

"I may grant that, but God cannot be matter, and it is right

[67]

to remove from the thoughts of the vulgar the idea of a material divinity. You are the only men, you Christians, who believe that you see God."

"It is true, we are sure of it, but observe that faith alone gives us that certainty."

"I know it; but you are idolaters, for you see nothing but a material representation, and yet you have a complete certainty that you see God, unless you should tell me that faith disaffirms it."

"God forbid I should tell you such a thing! Faith, on the contrary, affirms our certainty."

"We thank God that we have no need of such self-delusion, and there is not one philosopher in the world who could prove to me that you require it."

"That would not be the province of philosophy, dear father, but of theology — a very superior science."

"You are now speaking the language of our theologians, who differ from yours only in this; they use their science to make clearer the truths we ought to know, whilst your theologians try to render those truths more obscure."

"Recollect, dear father, that they are mysteries."

"The existence of God is a sufficiently important mystery to prevent men from daring to add anything to it. God can only be simple; any kind of combination would destroy His essence; such is the God announced by our prophet, who must be the same for all men and in all times. Agree with me that we can add nothing to the simplicity of God. We say that God is *one;* that is the image of simplicity. You say that He is *one* and *three* at the same time, and such a definition strikes us as contradictory, absurd, and impious."

"It is a mystery."

"Do you mean God or the definition? I am speaking only of the definition, which ought not to be a mystery or absurd. Common sense, my son, must consider as absurd an assertion which is substantially nonsensical. Prove to me that *three* is not a compound, that it cannot be a compound, and I will become a Christian at once."

"My religion tells me to believe without arguing, and I shudder, my dear Yusuf, when I think that, through some specious reasoning, I might be led to renounce the creed of my fathers.

I must first be convinced that they lived in error. Tell me whether, respecting my father's memory, I ought to have such a good opinion of myself as to sit in judgment over him, with the intention of giving my sentence against him?"

My lively remonstrance moved Yusuf deeply, but after a few instants of silence he said to me: —

"With such feelings, my son, you are sure to find grace in the eyes of God, and you are, therefore, one of the elect. If you are in error, God alone can convince you of it, for no just man on earth can refute the sentiment you have just given expression to."

We spoke of many other things in a friendly manner, and in the evening we parted with the often repeated assurance of the warmest affection and of the most perfect devotion.

But my mind was full of our conversation, and as I went on pondering over the matter, I thought that Yusuf might be right in his opinion as to the essence of God, for it seemed evident that the Creator of all beings ought to be perfectly simple; but I thought at the same time how impossible it would be for me, because the Christian religion had made a mistake, to accept the Turkish creed, which might perhaps have a just conception of God, but which caused me to smile when I recollected that the man who had given birth to it had been an arrant impostor. I had not the slightest idea, however, that Yusuf wished to make a convert of me.

The third time I dined with him religion was again the subject of conversation.

"Do you believe, dear father, that the religion of Mahomet is the only one in which salvation can be secured?"

"No, my dear son, I am not certain of it, and no man can have such a certainty; but I am sure that the Christian religion is not the true one, because it cannot be universal."

"Why not?"

"Because there is neither bread nor wine to be found in three-fourths of the world. Observe that the precepts of the *Koran* can be followed everywhere."

I did not know how to answer, and I would not equivocate.

"If God cannot be matter," I said, "then He must be a spirit?"

"We know what He is not, but we do not know what He is:

man cannot affirm that God is a spirit, because he can only realise the idea in an abstract manner. God is immaterial; that is the extent of our knowledge, and it can never be greater."

I was reminded of Plato, who had said exactly the same, and most certainly Yusuf had never read Plato.

He added that the existence of God could be useful only to those who did not entertain a doubt of that existence, and that, as a natural consequence, Atheists must be the most miserable of men. God has made in man His own image in order that, amongst all the animals created by Him, there should be one that can understand and confess the existence of the Creator. Without man, God would have no witness of His own glory, and man must therefore understand that his first and highest duty is to glorify God by practising justice and trusting to His providence.

"Observe, my son, that God never abandons the man who, in the midst of his misfortunes, falls down in prayer before Him, and that He often allows the wretch who has no faith in prayer to die miserably."

"Yet we meet with Atheists who are fortunate and happy."

"True; but, in spite of their tranquillity, I pity them because they have no hope beyond this life, and are on a level with animals. Besides, if they are philosophers, they must linger in dark ignorance, and, if they never think, they have no consolation, no resource, when adversity reaches them. God has made man in such a manner that he cannot be happy unless he entertains no doubt of the existence of his Divine Creator; in all stations of life man is naturally prone to believe in that existence, otherwise man would never have admitted one God, Creator of all beings and of all things."

"I should like to know why Atheism has only existed in the systems of the learned, and never as a national creed."

"Because the poor feel their wants much more than the rich. There are amongst us a great many impious men who deride the true believers because they have faith in the pilgrimage to Mecca. Wretches that they are! they ought to respect the ancient customs which, exciting the devotion of fervent souls, feed religious principles, and impart courage under all misfortunes. Without such consolation, people would give way to all the excess of despair."

Much pleased with the attention I gave to all he said, Yusuf would thus yield to the inclination he felt to instruct me, and, on my side, feeling myself drawn towards him by the charm which amiable goodness exerts upon all hearts, I would often go and spend the day with him, even without any previous invitation, and Yusuf's friendship soon became one of my most precious treasures.

Five or six weeks after the commencement of our intimacy, Yusuf asked me one day whether I was married. I answered that I was not; the conversation turned upon several moral questions, and at last fell upon chastity, which, in his opinion, could be accounted a virtue only if considered from one point of view — namely, that of total abstinence; but he added that it could not be acceptable to God, because it transgressed against the very first precept He had given to man.

"I would like to know, for instance," he said, "what name can be given to the chastity of your knights of Malta. They take a vow of chastity, but it does not mean that they will renounce women altogether, they renounce marriage only. Their chastity, and therefore chastity in general, is violated only by marriage, yet I observe that marriage is one of your sacraments. Therefore, those knights of Malta promise not to give way to lustful incontinence in the only case in which God might forgive it, but they reserve the licence of being lustful unlawfully as often as they please, and whenever an opportunity may offer itself; and that immoral, illicit licence is granted to them to such an extent that they are allowed to acknowledge legally a child which can be born to them only through a double crime! The most revolting part of it all is that these children of crime, who are of course perfectly innocent themselves, are called natural children, as if children born in wedlock came into the world in an unnatural manner! In one word, my dear son, the vow of chastity is so much opposed to divine precepts and to human nature that it can be agreeable neither to God nor to society, nor to those who pledge themselves to keep it, and, being in such opposition to every divine and human law, it must be a crime."

He inquired for the second time whether I was married; I replied in the negative, and added that I had no idea of ever getting married.

"What!" he exclaimed; "I must then believe that you are

not a perfect man, or that you intend to work out your own damnation; unless you should tell me that you are a Christian only outwardly."

"I am a man in the very strongest sense of the word, and I am a true Christian. I must even confess that I adore women, and that I have not the slightest idea of depriving myself of the most delightful of all pleasures."

"According to your religion, damnation awaits you."

"I feel certain of the contrary, because, when we confess our sins, our priests are compelled to give us absolution."

"I know it, but you must agree with me that it is absurd to suppose that God will forgive a crime which you would, perhaps, not commit if you did not think that, after confession, a priest, a man like you, will give you absolution. God forgives only the repenting sinner."

"No doubt of it, and confession supposes repentance; without it, absolution has no effect."

After many such conversations, in which he seemed to consider me as endowed with reason and talent, even when I was not of his opinion, Yusuf Ali surprised me greatly one day by the following proposition: —

"I have two sons and a daughter. I no longer think of my sons, because they have received their share of my fortune. As far as my daughter is concerned she will, after my death, inherit all my possessions, and I am, besides, in a position while I am alive to promote the fortune of the man who may marry her. Five years ago I took a young wife, but she has not given me any progeny, and I know to a certainty that no offspring will bless our union. My daughter, whose name is Zelmi, is now fifteen; she is handsome, her eyes are black and lovely like her mother's, her hair is of the colour of the raven's wing, her complexion is animated alabaster; she is tall, well made, and of a sweet disposition; I have given her an education which would make her worthy of our master the Sultan. She speaks Greek and Italian fluently, she sings delightfully, and accompanies herself on the harp; she can draw and embroider, and is always contented and cheerful. No living man can boast of having seen her features, and she loves me so dearly that my will is hers. My daughter is a treasure, and I offer her to you if you will consent to go for one year to Adrianople to reside with a relative of mine, who will teach you our religion, our language, and our manners. You will return at the end of one year, and as soon as you have become a Mussulman my daughter shall be your wife. You will find a house ready furnished, slaves of your own, and an income which will enable you to live in comfort. I have no more to say at present. I do not wish you to answer me either to-day, or to-morrow, or on any fixed day. You will give me your decision whenever you feel yourself called upon by your genius to give it, and you need not give me any answer unless you accept my offer, for, should you refuse it, it is not necessary that the subject should be again mentioned. I do not ask you to give full consideration to my proposal, for now that I have thrown the seed in your soul it must fructify. Without hurry, without delay, without anxiety, you can but obey the decrees of God and follow the immutable decision of fate. Such as I know you, I believe that you only require the possession of Zelmi to be completely happy, and that you will become one of the pillars of the Ottoman Empire."

Saying those words, Yusuf pressed me affectionately in his arms, and left me by myself to avoid any answer I might be inclined to make. I went away in such wonder at all I had just heard, that I found myself at the Venetian Embassy without knowing how I had reached it. The *baili* thought me very pensive, and asked whether anything was the matter with me, but I did not feel disposed to gratify their curiosity. I found that Yusuf had indeed spoken truly: his proposal was of such importance that it was my duty, not only not to mention it to anyone, but even to abstain from thinking it over, until my mind had recovered its calm sufficiently to give me the assurance that no external consideration would weigh in the balance and influence my decision. I had to silence all my passions; prejudices, principles already formed, love, and even self-interest were to remain in a state of complete inaction.

When I awoke the next morning I began to think the matter over, and I soon discovered that, if I wanted to come to a decision, I ought not to ponder over it, as the more I considered, the less likely I should be to decide. This was truly a case for the *sequere Deum* of the Stoics.

I did not visit Yusuf for four days, and when I called on him on the fifth day, we talked cheerfully without once mentioning his proposal, although it was very evident that we were both thinking of it. We remained thus for a fortnight, without ever alluding to the matter which engrossed all our thoughts, but our silence was not caused by dissimulation, or by any feeling contrary to our mutual esteem and friendship; and one day Yusuf suggested that very likely I had communicated his proposal to some wise friend, in order to obtain good advice. I immediately assured him it was not so, and that in a matter of so delicate a nature I thought I ought not to ask anybody's advice.

"I have abandoned myself to God, dear Yusuf, and, full of confidence in Him, I feel certain that I shall decide for the best, whether I make up my mind to become your son, or believe that I ought to remain what I am now. In the meantime, my mind ponders over it day and night, whenever I am quiet and feel myself composed and collected. When I come to a decision, I will impart it to you alone, and from that moment you shall have over me the authority of a father."

At these words the worthy Yusuf, his eyes wet with tears, placed his left hand over my head, and the first two fingers of the right hand on my forehead, saying: —

"Continue to act in that way, my dear son, and be certain that you can never act wrongly."

"But," I said to him, "one thing might happen, Zelmi might not accept me."

"Have no anxiety about that. My daughter loves you; she, as well as my wife and her nurse, sees you every time that we dine together, and she listens to you with pleasure."

"Does she know that you are thinking of giving her to me as my wife?"

"She knows that I ardently wish you to become a true believer, so as to enable me to link her destiny to yours."

"I am glad that your habits do not permit you to let me see her, because she might dazzle me with her beauty, and then passion would soon have too much weight in the scale; I could no longer flatter myself that my decision had been taken in all the unbiassed purity of my soul."

Yusuf was highly delighted at hearing me speak in that manner, and I spoke in perfect good faith. The mere idea of seeing Zelmi caused me to shudder. I felt that, if I had fallen in love with her, I would have become a Mussulman in order to possess her, and that I might soon have repented such a step, for the religion of Mahomet presented to my eyes and to my mind nothing but a disagreeable picture, as well for this life as for a future one. As for wealth, I did not think it deserved the immense sacrifice demanded from me. I could find equal wealth in Europe, without stamping my forehead with the shameful brand of apostasy. I cared deeply for the esteem of the persons of distinction who knew me, and did not want to render myself unworthy of it. Besides, I felt an immense desire to obtain fame amongst civilised and polite nations, either in the fine arts or in literature, or in any other honourable profession, and I could not reconcile myself to the idea of abandoning to my equals the triumph which I might win if I lived amongst them. It seemed to me, and I am still of the same opinion, that the decision of wearing the turban befits only a Christian despairing of himself and at the end of his wits, and fortunately I was not in that predicament. My greatest objection was to spend a year in Adrianople to learn a language for which I did not feel any liking, and which I should therefore have learned but imperfectly. How could I, at my age, renounce the prerogative, so pleasant to my vanity, of being reputed a fine talker? And I had secured that reputation wherever I was known. Then I would often think that Zelmi, the eighth wonder of creation in the eyes of her father, might not appear such in my eyes, and it would have been enough to make me miserable, for Yusuf was likely to live twenty years longer, and I felt that gratitude, as well as respect, would never have permitted me to give that excellent man any cause for unhappiness by ceasing to show myself a devoted and faithful husband to his daughter. Such were my thoughts, and, as Yusuf could not guess them, it was useless to make a confidant of him.

A few days afterwards, I dined with the Pacha Osman and met my Effendi Ismail. He was very friendly to me, and I reciprocated his attentions, though I paid no attention to the reproaches he addressed to me for not having come to breakfast with him for such a long time. I could not refuse to dine at his house with Bonneval, and he treated me to a very pleasing sight; Neapolitan slaves, men and women, performed a pantomime and some Calabrian dances. M. de Bonneval happened to mention the dance called *forlana*, and, Ismail expressing a great wish to know it, I told him that I could give him that pleasure if I had a Venetian woman to dance it with and a fiddler who knew the tune. I took a violin, and played the *forlana*, but, even if the partner had been found, I could not play and dance at the same time.

Ismail whispered a few words to one of his eunuchs, who went out of the room and returned soon with some message that he delivered to him. The *effendi* told me that he had found the partner I wanted, and I answered that the musician could be had easily, if he would send a note to the Venetian Embassy, which was done at once. The Bailo Dona sent one of his men who played the violin well enough for dancing purposes. As soon as the musician was ready, a door was thrown open, and a fine-looking woman came in, her face covered with a black velvet mask, such as we call *moretta* in Venice. The appearance of that beautiful masked woman surprised and delighted every one of the guests, for it was impossible to imagine a more interesting object, not only on account of the beauty of that part of the face which the mask left exposed, but also for the elegance of her shape, the perfection of her figure, and the exquisite taste displayed in her costume. The nymph took her place, I did the same, and we danced the *forlana* six times without stopping.

I was in perspiration and out of breath, for the *forlana* is the most violent of our national dances; but my beautiful partner stood near me without betraying the slightest fatigue, and seemed to challenge me to a new performance. At the round of the dance, which is the most difficult step, she seemed to have wings. I was astounded, for I had never seen anyone, even in Venice, dance the *forlana* so splendidly. After a few minutes' rest, rather ashamed of my feeling tired, I went up to her, and said, "*Ancora sei, e poi basta, se non volete vedermi a morire.*" She would have answered me if she had been able, but she wore one of those cruel masks which forbid speech. But a pressure of her hand which nobody could see made me guess all I wanted to know. The moment we finished dancing, the eunuch opened the door, and my lovely partner disappeared.

Ismail could not thank me enough, but it was I who owed him my thanks, for it was the only real pleasure which I enjoyed in Constantinople. I asked him whether the lady was from Venice, but he only answered by a significant smile.

"The worthy Ismail," said M. de Bonneval to me, as we were leaving the house late in the evening, "has been to-day the dupe of his vanity, and I have no doubt that he is sorry already for what he has done. To bring out his beautiful slave to dance with you! According to the prejudices of this country it is injurious to his dignity, for you are sure to have kindled an amorous flame in the poor girl's breast. I would advise you to be careful and to keep on your guard, because she will try to get up some intrigue with you; but be prudent, for intrigues are always dangerous in Turkey."

I promised to be prudent, but I did not keep my promise; for, three or four days afterwards, an old slave woman met me in the street, and offered to sell for one piastre a tobacco-bag embroidered in gold; and as she put it in my hand she contrived to make me feel that there was a letter in the bag.

I observed that she tried to avoid the eyes of the janissary who was walking behind me; I gave her one piastre, she left me, and I proceeded towards Yusuf's house. He was not at home, and I went to his garden to read the letter with perfect freedom. It was sealed and without any address, and the slave might have made a mistake; but my curiosity was excited to the highest pitch; I broke the seal, and found the following note written in good enough Italian: —

"Should you wish to see the person with whom you danced the *forlana*, take a walk towards evening in the garden beyond the fountain, and contrive to become acquainted with the old servant of the gardener by asking her for some lemonade. You may perchance manage to see your partner in the *forlana* without running any risk, even if you should happen to meet Ismail; she is a native of Venice. Be careful not to mention this invitation to any human being."

"I am not such a fool, my lovely countrywoman," I exclaimed, as if she had been present, and put the letter in my pocket. But at that very moment, a fine-looking elderly woman came out of a thicket, pronounced my name, and inquired what I wanted and how I had seen her. I answered that I had been speaking to the wind, not supposing that anyone could hear me, and without any more preparation, she abruptly told me that she was very glad of the opportunity of speaking with me, that she was from Rome, that she had brought up Zelmi, and had taught her to sing and to play the harp. She then praised highly the beauty and the excellent qualities of her pupil, saying that, if I saw her, I would certainly fall in love with her, and expressing how much she regretted that the law should not allow it.

"She sees us at this very moment," she added, "from behind that green window-blind, and we love you ever since Yusuf has informed us that you may, perhaps, become Zelmi's husband."

"May I mention our conversation to Yusuf?" I inquired.

"No."

Her answering me in the negative made me understand that, if I had pressed her a little, she would have allowed me to see her lovely pupil, and perhaps it was with that intention that she had contrived to speak to me, but I felt great reluctance to do anything to displease my worthy host. I had another reason of even greater importance; I was afraid of entering an intricate maze in which the sight of a turban hovering over me made me shudder.

Yusuf came home, and, far from being angry when he saw me with the woman, he remarked that I must have found much pleasure in conversing with a native of Rome, and he congratulated me upon the delight I must have felt in dancing with one of the beauties from the harem of the voluptuous Ismail.

"Then it must be a pleasure seldom enjoyed, if it is so much talked of?"

"Very seldom indeed, for there is amongst us an invincible prejudice against exposing our lovely women to the eyes of other men; but everyone may do as he pleases in his own house: Ismail is a very worthy and a very intelligent man."

"Is the lady with whom I danced known?"

"I believe not. She wore a mask, and everybody knows that Ismail possesses half a dozen slaves of surpassing beauty."

I spent a pleasant day with Yusuf, and when I left him, I ordered his janissary to take me to Ismail's. As I was known by his servants, they allowed me to go in, and I proceeded to the spot described in the letter. The eunuch came to me, informed me that his master was out, but that he would be delighted to hear of my having taken a walk in the garden. I told him that I would like a glass of lemonade, and he took me to the summer-house, where I recognised the old woman who had sold me the tobacco-pouch. The eunuch told her to give me a glass of some liquid which I found delicious, and would not allow me to give her any money. We then walked towards the fountain, but he told me abruptly that we were to go back, as he saw three ladies to whom he pointed, adding that, for the sake of decency, it was necessary to avoid them. I thanked him for his attentions, left my compliments for Ismail, and went away not dissatisfied with my first attempt, and with the hope of being more fortunate another time.

The next morning I received a letter from Ismail inviting me to go fishing with him on the following day, and stating that he intended to enjoy the sport by moonlight. I immediately gave way to my suppositions, and I went so far as to fancy that Ismail might be capable of arranging an interview between me and the lovely Venetian. I did not mind his being present. I begged permission of Chevalier Vénier to stop out of the palace for one night, but he granted it with the greatest difficulty, because he was afraid of some love affair and of the results it might have. I took care to calm his anxiety as much as I could, but without acquainting him with all the circumstances of the case, for I thought I was wise in being discreet.

I was exact to the appointed time, and Ismail received me with the utmost cordiality, but I was surprised when I found myself alone with him in the boat. We had two rowers and a man to steer; we took some fish, fried in oil, and ate it in the summer-house. The moon shone brightly, and the night was delightful.

"Let us leave this place quietly," said Ismail, "I have just heard a slight noise which heralds something that will amuse us."

He dismissed his attendants, and took my hand, saying: —

"Let us go to a small room, the key of which I luckily have with me, but let us be careful not to make any noise. That room has a window overlooking the fountain where I think that two or three of my beauties have just gone to bathe. We will see them and enjoy a very pleasing sight, for they do not imagine that anyone is looking at them. They know that the place is forbidden to everybody except me."

We entered the room, we went to the window, and, the moon shining right over the basin of the fountain, we saw three nymphs who, now swimming, now standing or sitting on the marble steps, offered themselves to our eyes in every possible position, and in all the attitudes of graceful voluptuousness. Dear reader, I must not paint in too vivid colours the details of that beautiful picture, but if nature has endowed you with an ardent imagination and with equally ardent senses, you will easily imagine the fearful havoc which that unique, wonderful, and enchanting sight must have made upon my poor body.

A few days after that delightful fishing and bathing party by moonlight, I called upon Yusuf early in the morning; as it was raining, I could not go to the garden, and I went into the dining-room, in which I had never seen anyone. The moment I entered the room, a charming female form rose, covering her features with a thick veil which fell to the feet. A slave was sitting near the window, doing some tambour-work, but she did not move. I apologised, and turned to leave the room, but the lady stopped me, observing, with a sweet voice, that Yusuf had commanded her to entertain me before going out. She invited me to be seated, pointing to a rich cushion placed upon two larger ones, and I obeyed, while, crossing her legs, she sat down upon another cushion opposite to me. I thought I was looking upon Zelmi, and fancied that Yusuf had made up his mind to show me that he was not less courageous than Ismail. Yet I was surprised, for, by such a proceeding, he strongly contradicted his maxims, and ran the risk of impairing the unbiassed purity of my consent by throwing love in the balance. But I had no fear of that, because, to become enamoured, I should have required to see her face.

"I suppose," said the veiled beauty, "that you do not know who I am?"

"I could not guess, if I tried."

"I have been for the last five years the wife of your friend, and I am a native of Scio. I was thirteen years of age when I became his wife."

I was greatly astonished to find that my Mussulman philosopher had gone so far as to allow me to converse with his wife, but I felt more at ease after I had received that information, and fancied that I might carry the adventure further, but it would be necessary to see the lady's face, for a finely-dressed body, the head of which is not seen, excites but feeble desires. The fire lighted by amorous desires is like a fire of straw; the moment it burns up it is near its end. I had before me a magnificent appearance, but I could not see the soul of the image, for a thick gauze concealed it from my hungry gaze. I could see arms as white as alabaster, and hands like those of Alcina, *dove ne nodo apparisce ne vena accede,* and my active imagination fancied that all the rest was in harmony with those beautiful specimens, for the graceful folds of the muslin, leaving the outline all its perfection, hid from me only the living satin of the surface; there was no doubt that everything was lovely, but I wanted to see, in the expression of her eyes, that all that my imagination created had life and was endowed with feeling. The Oriental costume is a beautiful varnish placed upon a porcelain vase to protect from the touch the colours of the flowers and of the design, without lessening the pleasure of the eyes. Yusuf's wife was not dressed like a sultana; she wore the costume of Scio, with a short skirt which concealed neither the perfection of the leg nor the round form of the thigh, nor the voluptuous plump fall of the hips, nor the slender, well-made waist encompassed in a splendid band embroidered in silver and covered with arabesques.

Enraptured, unable to control myself, I thrust my arm forward by a movement almost independent of my will, and my hand, too audacious, was on the point of lifting the hateful veil, but she prevented me by raising herself quickly on tiptoe, upbraiding me at the same time for my perfidious boldness, with a voice as commanding as her attitude.

"Dost thou deserve," she said, "Yusuf's friendship, when thou abusest the sacred laws of hospitality by insulting his wife?"

"Madam, you must kindly forgive me, for I never had any intention to insult you. In my country the lowest of men may fix his eyes upon the face of a queen."

"Yes, but he cannot tear off her veil, if she chooses to wear it. Yusuf shall avenge me."

The threat, and the tone in which it was pronounced, frightened me. I threw myself at her feet, and succeeded in calming her anger.

"Art thou excited?" she said.

"How could I be otherwise," I answered, "when thou art scorching me with an ardent fire?"

I had become more prudent, and I seized her hand without thinking any more of her face.

"Here is my husband," she said, and Yusuf came into the

[81]

room. We rose, Yusuf embraced me, I complimented him, the slave left the room. Yusuf thanked his wife for having entertained me, and offered her his arm to take her to her own apartment. She took it, but when she reached the door she raised her veil, and kissing her husband she allowed me to see her lovely face as if it had been done unwittingly. I followed her with my eyes as long as I could, and Yusuf, coming back to me, said with a laugh that his wife had offered to dine with us.

"I thought," I said to him, "that I had Zelmi before me."

"That would have been too much against our established rules. What I have done is not much, but I do not know an honest man who would be bold enough to bring his daughter into the presence of a stranger."

"I think your wife must be handsome; is she more beautiful than Zelmi?"

"My daughter's beauty is cheerful, sweet, and gentle; that of Sophia is proud and haughty. She will be happy after my death. The man who will marry her will find her a virgin."

I gave an account of my adventure to M. de Bonneval, somewhat exaggerating the danger I had run in trying to raise the veil of the handsome daughter of Scio.

"She was laughing at you," said the count, "and you ran no danger. She felt very sorry, believe me, to have to deal with a novice like you. You have been playing the comedy in the French fashion, when you ought to have gone straight to the point. What on earth did you want to see her nose for? She knew very well that she would have gained nothing by allowing you to see her. If I were young I would perhaps manage to give her a revenge, and to punish my friend Yusuf. You have given that lovely woman a poor opinion of Italian valour. The most reserved of Turkish women has no modesty except on her face, and, with her veil over it, she knows to a certainty that she will not blush at anything."

A few days after, I happened to be in the shop of an Armenian merchant, looking at some beautiful goods, when Yusuf entered the shop and praised my taste; but, although I had admired a great many things, I did not buy, because I thought they were too dear. I said so to Yusuf, but he remarked that they were, on the contrary, very cheap, and he purchased them all. We parted company at the door, and the next morning I received all the beautiful things he had bought; it was a delicate attention of my friend, and to prevent my refusal of such a splendid present, he had enclosed a note stating that, on my arrival in Corfu, he would let me know to whom the goods were to be delivered. He had thus sent me gold and silver filigrees from Damascus, portfolios, scarves, belts, handkerchiefs, and pipes, the whole worth four or five hundred piastres. When I called to thank him, I compelled him to confess that it was a present offered by his friendship.

The day before my departure from Constantinople, the excellent man burst into tears as I bade him adieu, and my grief was as great as his own. He told me that, by not accepting the offer of his daughter's hand, I had so strongly captivated his esteem that his feelings for me could not have been warmer if I had become his son. When I went on board ship with the Bailo Jean Dona, I found another case given to me by him, containing two quintals of the best Mocha coffee, one hundred pounds of tobacco leaves, two large flagons filled, one with Zabandi tobacco, the other with camussa, and a magnificent pipe tube of jessamine wood, covered with gold filigrane, which I sold in Corfu for one hundred sequins. I had not it in my power to give my generous Turk any mark of my gratitude until I reached Corfu, but there I did not fail to do so. I sold all his beautiful presents, which made me the possessor of a small fortune.

Ismail gave me a letter for the Chevalier de Lezze, but I could not forward it to him because I unfortunately lost it; he presented me with a barrel of hydromel, which I turned likewise into money. M. de Bonneval gave me a letter for Cardinal Acquaviva, which I sent to Rome with an account of my journey, but his eminence did not think fit to acknowledge the receipt of either. Bonneval made me a present of twelve bottles of malmsey from Ragusa, and of twelve bottles of genuine scopolo — a great rarity, with which I made a present in Corfu which proved very useful to me.

The only foreign minister I saw much in Constantinople was the Lord Marshal of Scotland, the celebrated Keith, who represented the King of Prussia, and who, six years later, was of great service to me in Paris.

We sailed from Constantinople in the beginning of September in the same man-of-war which had brought us, and we reached

Corfu in fourteen days. The Bailo Dona did not land. He had with him eight splendid Turkish horses; I saw two of them still alive in Gorizia in the year 1773.

As soon as I had landed with my luggage, and had engaged a rather mean lodging, I presented myself to M. André Dolfin, the *proveditore-generale,* who promised me again that I should soon be promoted to a lieutenancy. After my visit to him, I called upon M. Camporese, my captain, and was well received by him. My third visit was to the commander of galleasses M. D ** R **, to whom M. Antonio Dolfin, with whom I had travelled from Venice to Corfu, had kindly recommended me. After a short conversation, he asked me if I would remain with him with the title of adjutant. I did not hesitate one instant, but accepted, saying how deeply honoured I felt by his offer, and assuring him that he would always find me ready to carry out his orders. He immediately had me taken to my room, and, the next day, I found myself established in his house. I obtained from my captain a French soldier to serve me, and I was well pleased when I found that the man was a hairdresser by trade, and a great talker by nature, for he could take care of my beautiful head of hair, and I wanted to practise French conversation. He was a good-for-nothing fellow, a drunkard and a debauchee, a peasant from Picardy, and he could hardly read or write, but I did not mind all that; all I wanted from him was to serve me, and to talk to me, and his French was pretty good. He was an amusing rogue, knowing by heart a quantity of erotic songs and of smutty stories which he could tell in the most laughable manner.

When I had sold my stock of goods from Constantinople (except the wines), I found myself the owner of nearly five hundred sequins. I redeemed all the articles which I had pledged in the hands of Jews, and turned into money everything of which I had no need. I was determined not to play any longer as a dupe, but to secure in gambling all the advantages which a prudent young man could obtain without sullying his honour.

*After leaving Constantinople, Casanova made a protracted stay at Corfu, serving as adjutant to the commander of the Venetian galleasses, whom he designates by the initials D ** R **. This officer was the cicisbeo of the reigning beauty of the colony, a certain Madame F **, whose husband commanded one of the ships. Need-*

less to say, Casanova lost no time in emulating his superior and, after some skilful manœuvring, managed to get himself transferred to her husband's service. With the prestige of his Turkish adventures, the recital of which, he assures us, delighted his audiences, he now feels himself a man of the world, poses as an arbiter of fashion, unmasks and beats an impostor masquerading as a French prince, is ordered under arrest, escapes to a small Greek island, where he falls foul of the local priest and terrorises the inhabitants, is finally taken back to Corfu, obtains his pardon, and is on the point of winning the lady of his desire, when, as usual, he upsets his own apple-cart by an act of folly. Again he vows to profit by the lesson.

During the last two months of my stay in Corfu, I learned the most bitter and important lessons. In after years I often derived useful hints from the experience I acquired at that time.

Before my adventure with the worthless Melulla, I enjoyed good health, I was rich, lucky at play, liked by everybody, beloved by the most lovely woman of Corfu. When I spoke, everybody would listen and admire my wit; my words were taken for oracles, and everyone coincided with me in everything. After my fatal meeting with the courtesan I rapidly lost my health, my money, my credit; cheerfulness, consideration, wit, everything, even the faculty of eloquence vanished with fortune. I would talk, but people knew that I was unfortunate, and I no longer interested or convinced my hearers. The influence I had over Madame F ** faded away little by little, and, almost without her knowing it, the lovely woman became completely indifferent to me.

I left Corfu without money, although I had sold or pledged everything I had of any value. Twice I had reached Corfu rich and happy, twice I left it poor and miserable. But this time I had contracted debts which I have never paid, not through want of will but through carelessness.

Rich and in good health, everyone received me with open arms; poor and looking sick, no one showed me any consideration. With a full purse and the tone of a conqueror, I was thought witty, amusing; with an empty purse and a modest air, all I said appeared dull and insipid. If I had become rich again, how soon I would have been again accounted the eighth wonder of the world! Oh, men! oh, fortune! Everyone avoided me as if the ill luck which crushed me down was infection.

We left Corfu towards the end of September, with five galleys, two galleasses, and several smaller vessels, under the command of M. Renier. We sailed along the shores of the Adriatic, towards the north of the gulf, where there are a great many harbours, and we put in at one of them every night. I saw Madame F ** every evening; she always came with her husband to take supper on board our galleass. We had a fortunate voyage, and cast anchor in the harbour of Venice on the 14th of October, 1745, and after having performed quarantine on board our ships, we landed on the 25th of November. Two months afterwards, the galleasses were set aside altogether. The use of these vessels could be traced very far back in ancient times; their maintenance was very expensive, and they were useless. A galleass had the frame of a frigate with the rowing apparatus of the galley, and when there was no wind, five hundred slaves had to row.

Before simple good sense managed to prevail and to enforce the suppression of these useless carcasses, there were long discussions in the senate, and those who opposed the measure took their principal ground of opposition in the necessity of respecting and conserving all the institutions of olden times. That is the disease of persons who can never identify themselves with the successive improvements born of reason and experience; worthy persons who ought to be sent to China, or to the dominions of the Grand Lama, where they would certainly be more at home than in Europe.

That ground of opposition to all improvements, however absurd it may be, is a very powerful one in a republic, which must tremble at the mere idea of novelty either in important or in trifling things. Superstition has likewise a great part to play in these conservative views.

There is one thing that the Republic of Venice will never alter: I mean the galleys, because the Venetians truly require such vessels to ply, in all weathers and in spite of the frequent calms, in a narrow sea, and because they would not know what to do with the men sentenced to hard labour.

I have observed a singular thing in Corfu, where there are often as many as three thousand galley-slaves; it is that the men who row on the galleys, in consequence of a sentence passed upon them for some crime, are held in a kind of opprobrium, whilst those who are there voluntarily are, to some extent, respected.

I have always thought it ought to be the reverse, because misfortune, whatever it may be, ought to inspire some sort of respect; but the vile fellow who condemns himself voluntarily and as a trade to the position of a slave seems to me contemptible in the highest degree. The convicts of the Republic, however, enjoy many privileges, and are, in every way, better treated than the soldiers. It very often occurs that soldiers desert and give themselves up to a *sopracomito* to become galley-slaves. In those cases, the captain who loses a soldier has nothing to do but to submit patiently, for he would claim the man in vain. The reason of it is that the Republic has always believed galley-slaves more necessary than soldiers. The Venetians may perhaps now (I am writing these lines in the year 1797) begin to realise their mistake.

A galley-slave, for instance, has the privilege of stealing with impunity. It is considered that stealing is the least crime they can be guilty of, and that they ought to be forgiven for it.

"Keep on your guard," says the master of the galley-slave; "and if you catch him in the act of stealing, thrash him, but be careful not to cripple him; otherwise you must pay me the one hundred ducats the man has cost me."

A court of justice could not have a galley-slave taken from a galley without paying the master the amount he has disbursed for the man.

As soon as I had landed in Venice, I called upon Madame Orio, but I found the house empty. A neighbor told me that she had married the Procurator Rosa, and had removed to his house. I went immediately to M. Rosa and was well received. Madame Orio informed me that Nanette had become Countess R **, and was living in Guastalla with her husband.

Twenty-four years afterwards, I met her eldest son, then a distinguished officer in the service of the Infante of Parma.

As for Marton, the grace of Heaven had touched her, and she had become a nun in the convent at Muran. Two years afterwards, I received from her a letter full of unction in which she adjured me, in the name of Our Saviour and of the Holy Virgin, never to present myself before her eyes. She added that she was bound by Christian charity to forgive me for the crime I had committed in seducing her, and she felt certain of the reward of the elect, and she assured me that she would ever pray earnestly for my conversion.

[87]

I never saw her again, but she saw me in 1754, as I will mention when we reach that year.

I found Madame Manzoni still the same. She had predicted that I would not remain in the military profession, and when I told her that I had made up my mind to give it up, because I could not be reconciled to the injustice I had experienced, she burst out laughing. She inquired about the profession I intended to follow after giving up the army, and I answered that I wished to become an advocate. She laughed again, saying that it was too late. Yet I was only twenty years old.

When I called upon M. Grimani I had a friendly welcome from him, but, having inquired after my brother François, he told me that he had had him confined in Fort Saint André, the same to which I had been sent before the arrival of the Bishop of Martorano.

"He works for the major there," he said; "he copies Simonetti's battle-pieces, and the major pays him for them; in that manner he earns his living, and is becoming a good painter."

"But he is not a prisoner?"

"Well, very much like it, for he cannot leave the fort. The major, whose name is Spiridion, is a friend of Razetta, who could not refuse him the pleasure of taking care of your brother."

I felt it a dreadful curse that the fatal Razetta should be the tormentor of all my family, but I concealed my anger.

"Is my sister," I inquired, "still with him?"

"No, she has gone to your mother in Dresden."

This was good news.

I took a cordial leave of the Abbé Grimani, and I proceeded to Fort Saint André. I found my brother hard at work, neither pleased nor displeased with his position, and enjoying good health. After embracing him affectionately, I inquired what crime he had committed to be thus a prisoner.

"Ask the major," he said, "for I have not the faintest idea."

The major came in just then, so I gave him the military salute, and asked by what authority he kept my brother under arrest.

"I am not accountable to you for my actions."

"That remains to be seen."

I then told my brother to take his hat, and to come and dine with me. The major laughed, and said that he had no objection provided the sentinel allowed him to pass.

I saw that I should only waste my time in discussion, and I left the fort fully bent on obtaining justice.

The next day I went to the war office, where I had the pleasure of meeting my dear Major Pelodoro, who was then commander of the Fortress of Chiozza. I informed him of the complaint I wanted to prefer before the secretary of war respecting my brother's arrest, and of the resolution I had taken to leave the army. He promised me that, as soon as the consent of the secretary for war could be obtained, he would find a purchaser for my commission at the same price I had paid for it.

I had not long to wait. The war secretary came to the office and everything was settled in half an hour. He promised his consent to the sale of my commission as soon as he ascertained the abilities of the purchaser, and, Major Spiridion happening to make his appearance in the office while I was still there, the secretary ordered him, rather angrily, to set my brother at liberty immediately, and cautioned him not to be guilty again of such reprehensible and arbitrary acts.

I went at once for my brother, and we lived together in furnished lodgings.

A few days afterwards, having received my discharge and one hundred sequins, I threw off my uniform, and found myself once more my own master.

I had to earn my living in one way or another, and I decided for the profession of gamester. But Dame Fortune was not of the same opinion, for she refused to smile upon me from the very first step I took in the career, and in less than a week I did not possess a groat. What was to become of me? One must live, and I turned fiddler. Doctor Gozzi had taught me well enough to enable me to scrape on the violin in the orchestra of a theatre, and having mentioned my wishes to M. Grimani he procured me an engagement at his own theatre of Saint Samuel, where I earned a crown a day, and supported myself while I awaited better things.

Fully aware of my real position, I never showed myself in the fashionable circles which I used to frequent before my fortune had sunk so low. I knew that I was considered as a worthless fellow, but I did not care. People despised me, as a matter of course; but I found comfort in the consciousness that I was worthy of contempt. I felt humiliated by the position to which

I was reduced after having played so brilliant a part in society; but as I kept the secret to myself I was not degraded, even if I felt some shame. I had not exchanged my last word with Dame Fortune, and was still in hope of reckoning with her some day, because I was young, and youth is dear to Fortune.

CHAPTER III

THE YOUNG COUNTESS

C ASANOVA, twenty years of age, having finished with the Church and the army, is now fairly started on his career as a soldier of fortune. If we are to believe the Memoirs — the "if" is a constantly recurring factor in the case of these records — it was with a chastened spirit that our hero made his reappearance on the scene of his first exploits. His own words are as follows:

With an education which ought to have ensured me an honourable standing in the world, with some intelligence, wit, good literary and scientific knowledge, and endowed with those accidental physical qualities which are such a good passport into society, I found myself, at the age of twenty, the mean follower of a sublime art, in which, if great talent is rightly admired, mediocrity is as rightly despised. I was compelled by poverty to become a member of a musical band, in which I could expect neither esteem nor consideration, and I was well aware that I should be the laughing-stock of the persons who had known me as a doctor in divinity, as an ecclesiastic, and as an officer in the army, and had welcomed me in the highest society.

I knew all that, for I was not blind to my position; but contempt, the only thing to which I could not have remained indifferent, never showed itself anywhere under a form tangible enough for me to have no doubt of my being despised, and I set it at defiance, because I was satisfied that contempt is due only to cowardly, mean actions, and I was conscious that I had never been guilty of any. As to public esteem, which I had ever been anxious to secure, my ambition was slumbering, and satisfied with being my own master I enjoyed my independence without puzzling my head about the future. I felt that in my first profession, as I was not blessed with the vocation necessary to it, I should have succeeded only by dint of hypocrisy, and I should have been despicable in my own estimation, even if I had seen the purple mantle on my shoulders, for the greatest dignities cannot silence a man's own conscience. If, on the other hand, I had continued to seek fortune in a military career, which is surrounded by a halo of glory, but is otherwise the worst of professions for the constant self-abnegation, for the complete surrender of one's will which passive obedience demands, I should have required a patience to which I could not lay any claim, as every kind of injustice was revolting to me, and as I could not bear to feel myself dependent. Besides, I was of opinion that a man's profession, whatever it might be, ought to supply him with enough money to satisfy all his wants; and the very poor pay of an officer would never have been sufficient to cover my expenses, because my education had given me greater wants than those of officers in general. By scraping my violin I earned enough to keep myself without requiring anybody's assistance, and I have always thought that the man who can support himself is happy. I grant that my profession was not a brilliant one, but I did not mind it, and, calling prejudices all the feelings which rose in my breast against myself, I was not long in sharing all the habits of my degraded comrades. When the play was over, I went with them to the drinking-booth, which we often left intoxicated to spend the night in houses of ill-fame. When we happened to find those places already tenanted by other men, we forced them by violence to quit the premises, and defrauded the miserable victims of prostitution of the mean salary the law allows them, after compelling them to yield to our brutality. Our scandalous proceedings often exposed us to the greatest danger.

We would very often spend the whole night rambling about the city, inventing and carrying into execution the most impertinent practical jokes. One of our favourite pleasures was to unmoor the patricians' gondolas, and to let them float at random along the canals, enjoying by anticipation all the curses that the gondoliers would not fail to indulge in. We would rouse up hurriedly, in the middle of the night, an honest midwife, telling her to hasten to Madame So-and-so, who, not being even pregnant, was sure to tell her she was a fool when she called at the house. We did the same with physicians, whom we often sent half dressed to some nobleman who was enjoying excellent health. The priests fared no better; we would send them to carry the last sacraments to married men who were peacefully slumbering near their wives, and not thinking of extreme unction.

We were in the habit of cutting the wires of the bells in every house, and if we chanced to find a gate opened we would go up the stairs in the dark, and frighten the sleeping inmates by telling them very loudly that the house door was not closed, after which we would go down, making as much noise as we could, and leave the house with the gate wide open.

During a very dark night we formed a plot to overturn the large marble table of St. Angelo's Square, on which it was said that in the days of the League of Cambray the commissaries of the Republic were in the habit of paying the bounty to the recruits who engaged to fight under the standard of St. Mark — a circumstance which secured for the table a sort of public veneration.

Whenever we could contrive to get into a church tower we thought it great fun to frighten all the parish by ringing the alarm bell, as if some fire had broken out; but that was not all, we always cut the bell ropes, so that in the morning the bell-ringers had no means of summoning the faithful to early mass. Sometimes we would cross the canal, each of us in a different gondola, and take to our heels without paying as soon as we landed on the opposite side, in order to make the gondoliers run after us.

The city was alive with complaints, and we laughed at the useless search made by the police to find out those who disturbed the peace of the inhabitants. We took good care to be careful, for if we had been discovered we stood a very fair chance of being sent to practise rowing at the expense of the Council of Ten.

We were seven, and sometimes eight, because, being much attached to my brother François, I gave him a share now and then in our nocturnal orgies. But at last fear put a stop to our criminal jokes, which in those days I used to call only the frolics of young men. This is the amusing adventure which closed our exploits.

In every one of the seventy-two parishes of the city of Venice, there is a large public-house called *magazzino*. It remains open all night, and wine is retailed there at a cheaper price than in all the other drinking houses. People can likewise eat in the *magazzino*, but they must obtain what they want from the pork butcher near by, who has the exclusive sale of eatables, and likewise keeps his shop open throughout the night. The pork butcher is usually a very poor cook; but as he is cheap, poor people are willingly satisfied with him, and these resorts are considered very useful to the lower class. The nobility, the merchants, even workmen in good circumstances, are never seen in the *magazzini*, for cleanliness is not exactly worshipped in such places. Yet there are a few private rooms which contain a table surrounded with benches, in which a respectable family or a few friends can enjoy themselves in a decent way.

It was during the Carnival of 1745, after midnight; we were, all the eight of us, rambling about together with our masks on, in quest of some new sort of mischief to amuse us, and we went into the *magazzino* of the parish of the Holy Cross to get something to drink. We found the public room empty, but in one of the private chambers we discovered three men quietly conversing with a young and pretty woman, and enjoying their wine.

Our chief, a noble Venetian belonging to the Balbi family, said to us, "It would be a good joke to carry off those three blockheads, and to keep the pretty woman in our possession." He immediately explained his plan, and under cover of our masks we entered their room, Balbi at the head of us. Our sudden appearance rather surprised the good people, but you may fancy their astonishment when they heard Balbi say to them: "Under penalty of death, and by order of the Council of Ten, I command you to follow us immediately, without making the slightest noise; as to you, my good woman, you need not be frightened, you will be escorted to your house." When he had finished his speech, two of us got hold of the woman to take her where our chief had arranged beforehand, and the others seized the three poor fellows, who were trembling all over, and had not the slightest idea of opposing any resistance.

The waiter of the *magazzino* came to be paid, and our chief gave him what was due, enjoining silence under penalty of death. We took our three prisoners to a large boat. Balbi went to the stern, ordered the boatman to stand at the bow, and told him that he need not inquire where we were going, that he would steer himself whichever way he thought fit. Not one of us knew where Balbi wanted to take the three poor devils.

He sails all along the canal, gets out of it, takes several turnings, and in a quarter of an hour, we reach Saint George, where Balbi lands our prisoners, who are delighted to find themselves at liberty. After this, the boatman is ordered to take us to Saint Geneviève, where we land, after paying for the boat.

We proceed at once to Palombo Square, where my brother and another of our band were waiting for us with our lovely prisoner, who was crying.

"Do not weep, my beauty," says Balbi to her, "we will not hurt you. We intend only to take some refreshment at the Rialto, and then we will take you home in safety."

"Where is my husband?"

"Never fear; you shall see him again to-morrow."

Comforted by that promise, and as gentle as a lamb, she follows us to the Two Swords. We order a good fire in a private room, and, everything we wanted to eat and drink having been brought in, we send the waiter away, and remain alone. We take off our masks, and the sight of eight young, healthy faces seems to please the beauty we had so unceremoniously carried off. We soon manage to reconcile her to her fate by the gallantry of our proceedings; encouraged by a good supper and by the stimulus of wine, prepared by our compliments and by a few kisses, she realises what is in store for her, and does not seem to have any unconquerable objection. My brother François alone exempted himself from paying the tribute, saying that he was ill, the only excuse which could render his refusal valid, for we had established as a law that every member of our society was bound to do whatever was done by the others.

After that fine exploit, we put on our masks, and, the bill being paid, escorted the happy victim to Saint Job, where she lived, and did not leave her till we had seen her safe in her house, and the street door closed.

My readers may imagine whether we felt inclined to laugh when the charming creature bade us good-night, thanking us all with perfect good faith!

Two days afterwards, our nocturnal orgy began to be talked of. The young woman's husband was a weaver by trade, and so were his two friends. They joined together to address a complaint to the Council of Ten. The complaint was candidly written and contained nothing but the truth, but the criminal portion of the truth was veiled by a circumstance which must have brought a smile on the grave countenances of the judges, and highly amused the public at large: the complaint setting forth that the eight masked men had not rendered themselves guilty of any act disagreeable to the wife. It went on to say that the two men who had carried her off had taken her to such a place, where they had, an hour later, been met by the other six, and that they had all repaired to the Two Swords, where they had spent an hour in drinking. The said lady having been handsomely entertained by the eight masked men, had been escorted to her house, where she had been politely requested to excuse the joke perpetrated upon her husband. The three plaintiffs had not been able to leave the island of Saint George until daybreak, and the husband, on reaching his house, had found his wife quietly asleep in her bed. She had informed him of all that had happened; she complained of nothing but of the great fright she had experienced on account of her husband, and on that count she entreated justice and the punishment of the guilty parties.

That complaint was comic throughout, for the three rogues showed themselves very brave in writing, stating that they would certainly not have given way so easily if the dreaded authority of the council had not been put forth by the leader of the band. The document produced three different results; in the first place, it amused the town; in the second, all the idlers of Venice went to Saint Job to hear the account of the adventure from the lips of the heroine herself, and she got many presents from her numerous visitors; in the third place, the Council of Ten offered a reward of five hundred ducats to any person giving such information as would lead to the arrest of the perpetrators of the practical joke, even if the informer belonged to the band, provided he was not the leader.

The offer of that reward would have made us tremble if our leader, precisely the one who alone had no interest in turning informer, had not been a patrician. The rank of Balbi quieted my anxiety at once, because I knew that, even supposing one of us were vile enough to betray our secret for the sake of the reward, the tribunal would have done nothing to implicate a patrician.

[95]

There was no cowardly traitor amongst us, although we were all poor; but fear had its effect, and our nocturnal pranks were not renewed.

Three or four months afterwards the Chevalier Nicolas Iron, then one of the Inquisitors, astonished me greatly by telling me the whole story, giving the names of all the actors. He did not tell me whether any one of the band had betrayed the secret, and I did not care to know; but I could clearly see the characteristic spirit of the aristocracy, for which the *solo mihi* is the supreme law.

Towards the middle of April of the year 1746 M. Girolamo Cornaro, the eldest son of the family Cornaro de la Reine, married a daughter of the house of Soranzo de St. Pol, and I had the honour of being present at the wedding . . . as a fiddler. I played the violin in one of the numerous bands engaged for the balls which were given for three consecutive days in the Soranzo Palace.

On the third day, towards the end of the dancing, an hour before daybreak, feeling tired, I left the orchestra abruptly; and as I was going down the stairs I observed a senator, wearing his red robes, on the point of getting into a gondola. In taking his handkerchief out of his pocket he let a letter drop on the ground. I picked it up, and coming up to him just as he was going down the steps I handed it to him. He received it with many thanks, and inquired where I lived. I told him, and he insisted upon my coming with him in the gondola, saying that he would leave me at my house. I accepted gratefully, and sat down near him. A few minutes afterwards he asked me to rub his left arm, which, he said, was so benumbed that he could not feel it. I rubbed it with all my strength, but he told me in a sort of indistinct whisper that the numbness was spreading all along the left side, and that he was dying.

I was greatly frightened; I opened the curtain, took the lantern, and found him almost insensible, and the mouth drawn on one side. I understood that he was seized with an apoplectic stroke, and called out to the gondoliers to land me at once, in order to procure a surgeon to bleed the patient.

I jumped out of the gondola, and found myself on the very spot where three years before I had taught Razetta such a forcible lesson; I inquired for a surgeon at the first coffee-house, and ran to the house that was pointed out to me. I knocked as hard as I could; the door was at last opened, and I made the surgeon follow me in his dressing-gown as far as the gondola, which was waiting; he bled the senator while I was tearing my shirt to make the compress and the bandage.

The operation being performed, I ordered the gondoliers to row as fast as possible, and we soon reached St. Marina; the servants were roused up, and taking the sick man out of the gondola we carried him to his bed almost dead.

Taking everything upon myself, I ordered a servant to hurry out for a physician, who came in a short time, and ordered the patient to be bled again, thus approving the first bleeding prescribed by me. Thinking I had a right to watch the sick man, I settled myself near his bed to give him every care he required.

An hour later, two noblemen, friends of the senator, came in, one a few minutes after the other. They were in despair; they had inquired about the accident from the gondoliers, and having been told that I knew more than they did, they loaded me with questions, which I answered. They did not know who I was, and did not like to ask me; whilst I thought it better to preserve a modest silence.

The patient did not move; his breathing alone showed that he was still alive; fomentations were constantly applied, and the priest who had been sent for, and was of very little use under such circumstances, seemed to be there only to see him die. All visitors were sent away by my advice, and the two noblemen and myself were the only persons in the sick man's room. At noon we partook silently of some dinner, which was served in the sick room.

In the evening one of the two friends told me that if I had any business to attend to I could go, because they would both pass the night on a mattress near the patient.

"And I, sir," I said, "will remain near his bed in this armchair, for if I went away the patient would die, and he will live as long as I am near him."

This sententious answer struck them with astonishment, as I expected it would, and they looked at each other in great surprise.

We had supper, and in the little conversation we had I gathered the information that the senator, their friend, was M.

de Bragadin, the only brother of the procurator of that name.
He was celebrated in Venice not only for his eloquence and his
great talents as a statesman, but also for the gallantries of his
youth. He had been very extravagant with women, and more
than one of them had committed many follies for him. He had
gambled and lost a great deal, and his brother was his most bitter enemy, because he was infatuated with the idea that he had
tried to poison him. He had accused him of that crime before
the Council of Ten, which, after an investigation of eight months,
had brought in a verdict of not guilty: but that just sentence,
although given unanimously by that high tribunal, had not had
the effect of destroying his brother's prejudices against him.

M. de Bragadin, who was perfectly innocent of such a crime
and oppressed by an unjust brother who deprived him of half of
his income, spent his days like an amiable philosopher, surrounded by his friends, amongst whom were the two noblemen
who were then watching him; one belonged to the Dandolo
family, the other was a Barbaro, and both were excellent men.
M. de Bragadin was handsome, learned, cheerful, and most
kindly disposed; he was then about fifty years old.

The physician who attended him was named Terro; he
thought, by some peculiar train of reasoning, that he could cure
him by applying a mercurial ointment to the chest, to which no
one raised any objection. The rapid effect of the remedy delighted the two friends, but it frightened me, for in less than
twenty-four hours the patient was labouring under great excitement of the brain. The physician said that he had expected that
effect, but that on the following day the remedy would act less
on the brain, and diffuse its beneficial action through the whole
of the system, which required to be invigorated by a proper
equilibrium in the circulation of the fluids.

At midnight the patient was in a state of high fever, and in
a fearful state of irritation. I examined him closely, and found
him hardly able to breathe. I roused up his two friends, and declared that in my opinion the patient would soon die unless the
fatal ointment was at once removed. And without waiting for
their answer, I bared his chest, took off the plaster, washed the
skin carefully with lukewarm water, and in less than three minutes he breathed freely and fell into a quiet sleep. Delighted
with such a fortunate result, we lay down again.

[98]

The physician came very early in the morning, and was much pleased to see his patient so much better, but when M. Dandolo informed him of what had been done, he was angry, said it was enough to kill his patient, and asked who had been so audacious as to destroy the effect of his prescription. M. de Bragadin, speaking for the first time, said to him:

"Doctor, the person who has delivered me from your mercury, which was killing me, is a more skilful physician than you"; and, saying these words, he pointed to me.

It would be hard to say who was the more astonished: the doctor, when he saw an unknown young man, whom he must have taken for an impostor, declared more learned than himself; or I, when I saw myself transformed into a physician, at a moment's notice. I kept silent, looking very modest, but hardly able to control my mirth, whilst the doctor was staring at me with a mixture of astonishment and of spite, evidently thinking me some bold quack who had tried to supplant him. At last, turning towards M. de Bragadin, he told him coldly that he would leave him in my hands; he was taken at his word, he went away, and behold! I had become the physician of one of the most illustrious members of the Venetian Senate! I must confess that I was very glad of it, and I told my patient that a proper diet was all he needed and that nature, assisted by the approaching fine season, would do the rest.

The dismissed physician related the affair through the town, and, as M. de Bragadin was rapidly improving, one of his relations, who came to see him, told him that everybody was astonished at his having chosen for his physician a fiddler from the theatre; but the senator put a stop to his remarks by answering that a fiddler could know more than all the doctors in Venice, and that he owed his life to me.

The worthy nobleman considered me as his oracle, and his two friends listened to me with the deepest attention. Their infatuation encouraging me, I spoke like a learned physician, I dogmatised, I quoted authors whom I had never read.

M. de Bragadin, who had the weakness to believe in the occult sciences, told me one day that, for a young man of my age, he thought my learning too extensive, and that he was certain I was the possessor of some supernatural endowment. He entreated me to tell him the truth.

[99]

What extraordinary things will sometimes occur from mere chance, or from the force of circumstances! Unwilling to hurt his vanity by telling him that he was mistaken, I took the wild resolution of informing him, in the presence of his two friends, that I possessed a certain numeral calculus which gave answers (also in numbers), to any questions I liked to put.

M. de Bragadin said that it was Solomon's key, vulgarly called cabalistic science, and he asked me from whom I had learnt it.

"From an old hermit," I answered, "who lives on the Carpegna Mountain, and whose acquaintance I made quite by chance when I was a prisoner in the Spanish army."

"The hermit," remarked the senator, "has, without informing you of it, linked an invisible spirit to the calculus he has taught you, for simple numbers cannot have the power of reason. You possess a real treasure, and you may derive great advantages from it."

"I do not know," I said, "in what way I could make my science useful, because the answers given by the numerical figures are often so obscure that I have felt discouraged, and I very seldom tried to make any use of my calculus. Yet, it is very true that, if I had not formed my pyramid, I never should have had the happiness of knowing your excellency."

"How so?"

"On the second day, during the festivities at the Soranzo Palace, I inquired of my oracle whether I would meet at the ball anyone whom I should not care to see. The answer I obtained was this: 'Leave the ball-room precisely at four o'clock.' I obeyed implicitly, and met your excellency."

The three friends were astounded. M. Dandolo asked me whether I would answer a question he would ask, the interpretation of which would belong only to him, as he was the only person acquainted with the subject of the question.

I declared myself quite willing, for it was necessary to brazen it out, after having ventured as far as I had done. He wrote the question, and gave it to me; I read it, I could not understand either the subject or the meaning of the words, but it did not matter, I had to give an answer. If the question was so obscure that I could not make out the sense of it, it was natural that I should not understand the answer. I therefore answered, in ordinary figures, four lines of which he alone could be the interpreter, not caring much, at least in appearance, how they would be understood. M. Dandolo read them twice over, seemed astonished, said that it was all very plain to him; it was divine, it was unique, it was a gift from Heaven, the numbers being only the vehicle, but the answer emanating evidently from an immortal spirit.

M. Dandolo was so well pleased that his two friends very naturally wanted also to make an experiment. They asked questions on all sorts of subjects, and my answers, perfectly unintelligible to myself, were all held as divine by them. I congratulated them on their success, and congratulated myself in their presence upon being the possessor of a thing to which I had until then attached no importance whatever, but which I promised to cultivate carefully, knowing that I could thus be of some service to their excellencies.

They all asked me how long I would require to teach them the rules of my sublime calculus. "Not very long," I answered, "and I will teach you as you wish, although the hermit assured me that I would die suddenly within three days if I communicated my science to anyone, but I have no faith whatever in that prediction." M. de Bragadin, who believed in it more than I did, told me in a serious tone that I was bound to have faith in it, and from that day they never asked me again to teach them. They very likely thought, that, if they could attach me to them, it would answer the purpose as well as if they possessed the science themselves. Thus I became the hierophant of those three worthy and talented men, who, in spite of their literary accomplishments, were not wise, since they were infatuated with occult and fabulous sciences, and believed in the existence of phenomena impossible in the moral as well as in the physical order of things. They believed that through me they possessed the philosopher's stone, the universal panacea, the intercourse with all the elementary, heavenly, and infernal spirits; they had no doubt whatever that, thanks to my sublime science, they could find out the secrets of every government in Europe.

After they had assured themselves of the reality of my cabalistic science by questions respecting the past, they decided to turn it to some use by consulting it upon the present and upon the future. I had no difficulty in showing myself a good guesser, because I always gave answers with a double meaning, one of the meanings being carefully arranged by me, so as not to be understood until after the event; in that manner, my cabalistic science, like the oracle of Delphi, could never be found in fault. I saw how easy it must have been for the ancient heathen priests to impose upon ignorant, and therefore credulous mankind. I saw how easy it will always be for impostors to find dupes, and I realised, even better than the Roman orator, why two augurs could never look at each other without laughing; it was because they had both an equal interest in giving importance to the deceit they perpetrated, and from which they derived such immense profits. But what I could not, and probably never shall, understand, was the reason for which the Fathers, who were not so simple or so ignorant as our Evangelists, did not feel able to deny the divinity of oracles, and, in order to get out of the difficulty, ascribed them to the devil. They never would have entertained such a strange idea if they had been acquainted with cabalistic science. My three worthy friends were like the Holy Fathers; they had intelligence and wit, but they were superstitious, and no philosophers. But, although believing fully in my oracles, they were too kind-hearted to think them the work of the devil, and it suited their natural goodness better to believe my answers inspired by some heavenly spirit.

They were not only good Christians and faithful to the Church, but even real devotees and full of scruples. They were not married, and, after having renounced all commerce with women, they had become the enemies of the female sex; perhaps a strong proof of the weakness of their minds. They imagined that chastity was the condition *sine qua non* exacted by the spirits from those who wished to have intimate communication or intercourse with them: they fancied that spirits excluded women, and *vice versa*.

With all these oddities, the three friends were truly intelligent and even witty, and, at the beginning of my acquaintance with them, I could not reconcile these antagonistic points. But a prejudiced mind cannot reason well, and the faculty of reasoning is the most important of all. I often laughed when I heard them talk on religious matters; they would ridicule those whose intellectual faculties were so limited that they could not understand the mysteries of religion. The incarnation of the Word, they would say, was a trifle for God, and therefore easy to understand,

and the resurrection was so comprehensible that it did not appear to them wonderful, because, as God cannot die, Jesus Christ was naturally certain to rise again. As for the Eucharist, transubstantiation, the real presence, it was all no mystery to them, but palpable evidence, and yet they were not Jesuits. They were in the habit of going to confession every week, without feeling the slightest trouble about their confessors, whose ignorance they kindly regretted. They thought themselves bound to confess only what was a sin in their own opinion, and in that, at least, they reasoned with good sense.

With those three extraordinary characters, worthy of esteem and respect for their moral qualities, their honesty, their reputation, and their age, as well as for their noble birth, I spent my days in a very pleasant manner; although, in their thirst for knowledge, they often kept me hard at work for ten hours running, all four of us being locked up together in a room, and unapproachable to everybody, even to friends or relatives.

I completed the conquest of their friendship by relating to them the whole of my life, only with some proper reserve, so as not to lead them into any capital sins. I confess candidly that I deceived them, as the Papa Deldimopulo used to deceive the Greeks who applied to him for the oracles of the Virgin. I certainly did not act towards them with a true sense of honesty, but if the reader to whom I confess myself is acquainted with the world and with the spirit of society, I entreat him to think before judging me, and perhaps I may meet with some indulgence at his hands.

I might be told that if I had wished to follow the rules of pure morality I ought either to have declined intimate intercourse with them or to have undeceived them. I cannot deny these premises, but I will answer that I was only twenty years of age, I was intelligent, talented, and had just been a poor fiddler. I should have lost my time in trying to cure them of their weaknesses; I should not have succeeded, for they would have laughed in my face, deplored my ignorance, and the result of it all would have been my dismissal. Besides, I had no mission, no right, to constitute myself an apostle, and if I had heroically resolved on leaving them as soon as I knew them to be foolish visionaries, I should have shown myself a misanthrope, the enemy of those worthy men for whom I could procure innocent pleasures, and my own enemy at the same time; because, as a young man, I liked to live well, to enjoy all the pleasures natural to youth and to a good constitution. By acting in that manner I should have failed in common politeness, I should perhaps have caused or allowed M. de Bragadin's death, and I should have exposed those three honest men to becoming the victims of the first bold cheat who, ministering to their monomania, might have won their favour, and would have ruined them by inducing them to undertake the chemical operations of the Great Work. There is also another consideration, dear reader, and as I love you I will tell you what it is. An invincible self-love would have prevented me from declaring myself unworthy of their friendship either by my ignorance or by my pride; and I should have been guilty of great rudeness if I had ceased to visit them.

I took, at least it seems to me so, the best, the most natural, and the noblest decision, if we consider the disposition of their mind when I decided upon the plan of conduct which ensured me the necessaries of life: and of those necessaries who could be a better judge than your very humble servant?

Through the friendship of those three men, I was certain of obtaining consideration and influence in my own country. Besides, I found it very flattering to my vanity to become the subject of the speculative chattering of empty fools who, having nothing else to do, are always trying to find out the cause of every moral phenomenon they meet with, which their narrow intellect cannot understand.

People racked their brains in Venice to find out how my intimacy with three men of that high character could possibly exist; they were wrapped up in heavenly aspirations, I was a world's devotee; they were very strict in their morals, I was thirsty of all pleasures!

At the beginning of summer, M. de Bragadin was once more able to take his seat in the senate, and, the day before he went out for the first time, he spoke to me thus: —

"Whoever you may be, I am indebted to you for my life. Your first protectors wanted to make you a priest, a doctor, an advocate, a soldier, and ended by making a fiddler of you; those persons did not know you. God had evidently instructed your guardian angel to bring you to me. I know you and appreciate you. If you will be my son, you have only to acknowledge me for your father, and, for the future, until my death, I will treat you as my own child. Your apartment is ready, you may send your clothes; you shall have a servant, a gondola at your orders, my own table, and ten sequins a month. It is the sum I used to receive from my father when I was your age. You need not think of the future; think only of enjoying yourself, and take me as your adviser in everything that may happen to you, in everything you may wish to undertake, and you may be certain of always finding me your friend."

I threw myself at his feet to assure him of my gratitude, and embraced him calling him my father. He folded me in his arms, called me his dear son; I promised to love and to obey him; his two friends, who lived in the same palace, embraced me affectionately, and we swore eternal fraternity.

Such is the history of my metamorphosis, and of the lucky stroke which, taking me from the vile profession of a fiddler, raised me to the rank of a grandee.

The metamorphosis was, indeed, complete. Unfortunately it had been so swift that it partook of the miraculous and only served to encourage the young man in the belief, dear to all who worship the blind goddess, that a genius,[1] whose lead he had only to follow, had singled him out and would assure his triumph, regardless of what he might do to further or spoil his chances. Fifty years later, in the monotonous seclusion of Dux, he realised the folly of the system of life he had adopted:

Fortune, which had taken pleasure in giving me a specimen of its despotic caprice, and had ensured my happiness through means which sages would disavow, had not the power to make me adopt a system of moderation and prudence which alone could establish my future welfare on a firm basis.

[1] *Throughout the Memoirs this belief in his "genius" is given as explanation for actions or decisions which may surprise the reader. Though doubtless often a useful pretext, a means of concealing more embarrassing reasons, Casanova, like all his kind, believed in his "star." We may believe him when he says: "I had always a strong tincture of superstition, which has exercised considerable influence on my career. Like Socrates, I, too, had a dæmon to whom I referred my doubtful counsels, doing his will, and obeying blindly when I felt a voice within me telling me to forbear. A hundred times have I thus followed my genius, and occasionally I have felt inclined to complain that it did not impel me to act against my reason more frequently. Whenever I did so I found that impulse was right and reason wrong, and for all that I have still continued reasoning."*

My ardent nature, my irresistible love of pleasure, my unconquerable independence, would not allow me to submit to the reserve which my new position in life demanded from me. I began to lead a life of complete freedom, caring for nothing but what ministered to my tastes, and I thought that, as long as I respected the laws, I could trample all prejudices under my feet. I fancied that I could live free and independent in a country ruled entirely by an aristocratic government, but this was not the case, and would not have been so even if fortune had raised me to a seat in that same government, for the Republic of Venice, considering that its primary duty is to preserve its own integrity, finds itself the slave of its own policy, and is bound to sacrifice everything to self-preservation, before which the laws themselves cease to be inviolable.

But let us abandon the discussion of a principle now too trite, for humankind, at least in Europe, is satisfied that unlimited liberty is nowhere consistent with a properly regulated state of society. I have touched lightly on the matter, only to give to my readers some idea of my conduct in my own country, where I began to tread a path which was to lead me to a state prison as inscrutable as it was unconstitutional.

With enough money, endowed by nature with a pleasing and commanding physical appearance, a confirmed gambler, a true spendthrift, a great talker, very far from modest, intrepid, always running after pretty women, supplanting my rivals, and acknowledging no good company but that which ministered to my enjoyment, I was certain to be disliked; but, ever ready to expose myself to any danger, and to take the responsibility of all my actions, I thought I had a right to do anything I pleased, for I always broke down abruptly every obstacle I found in my way.

Such conduct could not but be disagreeable to the three worthy men whose oracle I had become, but they did not like to complain. The excellent M. de Bragadin would only tell me that I was giving him a repetition of the foolish life he had himself led at my age, but that I must prepare to pay the penalty of my follies, and to feel the punishment when I should reach his time of life. Without wanting in the respect I owed him, I would turn his terrible forebodings into jest, and continue my course of extravagance.

It was about that time that my brother Jean came to Venice

with Guarienti, a converted Jew, a great judge of paintings, who was travelling at the expense of His Majesty the King of Poland, and Elector of Saxony. It was the converted Jew who had purchased for His Majesty the gallery of the Duke of Modena for one hundred thousand sequins. Guarienti and my brother left Venice for Rome, where Jean remained in the studio of the celebrated painter Raphael Mengs, whom we shall meet again hereafter.

Now, as a faithful historian, I must give my readers the story of a certain adventure in which were involved the honour and happiness of one of the most charming women in Italy, who would have been unhappy if I had not been a thoughtless fellow.

In the early part of October, 1746, the theatres being opened, I was walking about with my mask on when I perceived a woman, whose head was well enveloped in the hood of her mantle, getting out of the Ferrara barge which had just arrived. Seeing her alone, and observing her uncertain walk, I felt myself drawn towards her as if an unseen hand had guided me.

I come up to her, and offer my services if I can be of any use to her. She answers timidly that she only wants to make some inquiries.

"We are not here in the right place for conversation," I say to her; "but if you would be kind enough to come with me to a café, you would be able to speak and to explain your wishes."

She hesitates, I insist, and she gives way. The tavern was close at hand; we go in, and are alone in a private room. I take off my mask, and out of politeness she must put down the hood of her mantle. A large muslin head-dress conceals half of her face, but her eyes, her nose, and her pretty mouth are enough to let me see on her features beauty, nobleness, sorrow, and that candour which gives youth such an undefinable charm. I need not say that, with such a good letter of introduction, the unknown at once captivated my warmest interest. After wiping away a few tears which are flowing, in spite of all her efforts, she tells me that she belongs to a noble family, that she has run away from her father's house, alone, trusting in God, to meet a Venetian nobleman who had seduced her and then deceived her, thus sealing her everlasting misery.

"You have then some hope of recalling him to the path of duty? I suppose he has promised you marriage?"

"He has engaged his faith to me in writing. The only favour

I claim from your kindness is to take me to his house, to leave me there, and to keep my secret."

"You may trust, madam, to the feelings of a man of honour. I am worthy of your trust. Have entire confidence in me, for I already take a deep interest in all your concerns. Tell me his name."

"Alas! sir, I give way to fate."

With these words, she takes out of her bosom a paper which she gives me; I recognise the handwriting of Zanetto Steffani. It was a promise of marriage by which he engaged his word of honour to marry within a week, in Venice, the young countess A ** S **. When I have read the paper, I return it to her, saying that I knew the writer quite well, that he was connected with the chancellor's office, known as a great libertine, and deeply in debt, but that he would be rich after his mother's death.

"For God's sake take me to his house."

"I will do anything you wish; but have entire confidence in me, and be good enough to hear me. I advise you not to go to his house. He has already done you great injury, and, even supposing that you should happen to find him at home, he might be capable of receiving you badly; if he should not be at home, it is most likely that his mother would not exactly welcome you, if you should tell her who you are and what is your errand. Trust to me, and be quite certain that God has sent me on your way to assist you. I promise you that to-morrow at the latest you shall know whether Steffani is in Venice, what he intends to do with you, and what we may compel him to do. Until then my advice is not to let him know your arrival in Venice."

"Good God! where shall I go to-night?"

"To a respectable house, of course."

"I will go to yours, if you are married."

"I am a bachelor."

I knew an honest widow who resided in a lane, and who had two furnished rooms. I persuade the young countess to follow me, and we take a gondola. As we are gliding along, she tells me that, one month before, Steffani had stopped in her neighbourhood for necessary repairs to his travelling carriage, and that, on the same day, he had made her acquaintance at a house where she had gone with her mother for the purpose of offering their congratulations to a newly-married lady.

"I was unfortunate enough," she continued, "to inspire him with love, and he postponed his departure. He remained one month in C **, never going out but in the evening, and spending every night under my windows conversing with me. He swore a thousand times that he adored me, that his intentions were honourable. I entreated him to present himself to my parents to ask me in marriage, but he always excused himself by alleging some reasons, good or bad, assuring me that he could not be happy unless I showed him entire confidence. He would beg of me to make up my mind to run away with him, unknown to everybody, promising that my honour should not suffer from such a step, because, three days after my departure, everybody should receive notice of my being his wife, and he assured me that he would bring me back on a visit to my native place shortly after our marriage. Alas, sir! what shall I say now? Love blinded me; I fell into the abyss; I believed him; I agreed to everything. He gave me the paper which you have read, and the following night I allowed him to come into my room through the window under which he was in the habit of conversing with me. I consented to be guilty of a crime which I believed would be atoned for within three days, and he left me, promising that the next night he would be again under my window, ready to receive me in his arms. Could I possibly entertain any doubt after the fearful crime I had committed for him? I prepared a small parcel, and waited for his coming, but in vain. Oh! what a cruel long night it was! In the morning I heard that the monster had gone away with his servant one hour after sealing my shame. You may imagine my despair! I adopted the only plan that despair could suggest, and that, of course, was not the right one. One hour before midnight I left my father's roof, alone, thus completing my dishonour, but resolved on death, if the man who has cruelly robbed me of my most precious treasure, and whom a natural instinct told me I could find here, does not restore me the honour which he alone can give me back. I walked all night and nearly the whole day, without taking any food, until I got into the barge, which brought me here in twenty-four hours. I travelled in the boat with five men and two women, but no one saw my face or heard my voice, I kept constantly sitting down in a corner, holding my head down, half asleep, and with this prayer-book in my hands. I was left alone, no one spoke to me, and I thanked God for it. When I landed on the wharf, you did not give me time to think how I could find out the dwelling of my perfidious seducer, but you may imagine the impression produced upon me by the sudden apparition of a masked man who, abruptly, and as if placed there purposely by Providence, offered me his services; it seemed to me that you had guessed my distress, and, far from experiencing any repugnance, I felt that I was acting rightly in trusting myself in your hands, in spite of all prudence, which, perhaps, ought to have made me turn a deaf ear to your words, and refuse the invitation to enter alone with you the house to which you took me.

"You know all now, sir; but I entreat you not to judge me too severely; I have been virtuous all through my life; one month ago I had never committed a fault which could call a blush upon my face, and the bitter tears which I shed every day will, I hope, wash out my crime in the eyes of God. I have been carefully brought up, but love and the want of experience have thrown me into the abyss. I am in your hands, and I feel certain that I shall have no cause to repent it."

I needed all she had just told me to confirm me in the interest which I had felt in her from the first moment. I told her unsparingly that Steffani had seduced and abandoned her of malice aforethought, and that she ought to think of him only to be revenged of his perfidy. My words made her shudder, and she buried her beautiful face in her hands.

We reached the widow's house; I established her in a pretty, comfortable room, and ordered some supper for her, desiring the good landlady to show her every attention and to let her want for nothing. I then took an affectionate leave of her, promising to see her early in the morning.

On leaving this interesting but hapless girl, I proceeded to the house of Steffani. I heard from one of his mother's gondoliers that he had returned to Venice three days before, but that, twenty-four hours after his return, he had gone away again without any servant, and nobody knew his whereabouts, not even his mother. The same evening, happening to be seated next to an abbé from Bologna at the theatre, I asked him several questions respecting the family of my unfortunate *protégée;* the abbé being intimately acquainted with them, I gathered from him all the information I required, and, amongst other things, I heard that the young countess had a brother, then an officer in the papal service.

Very early the next morning I called upon her. She was still asleep. The widow told me that she had made a pretty good supper, but without speaking a single word, and that she had locked herself up in her room immediately afterwards. As soon as she had opened her door, I entered her room, and, cutting short her apologies for having kept me waiting, I informed her of all I had heard.

Her features bore the stamp of deep sorrow, but she looked calmer, and her complexion was no longer pale. She thought it unlikely that Steffani would have left for any other place but for C **. Admitting the possibility that she might be right, I immediately offered to go to C ** myself, and to return without loss of time to fetch her, in case Steffani should be there. Without giving her time to answer I told her all the particulars I had learned concerning her honourable family, which caused her real satisfaction.

"I have no objection," she said, "to your going to C **, and I thank you for the generosity of your offer, but I beg you will postpone your journey. I still hope that Steffani will return, and then I can take a decision."

"I think you are quite right," I said. "Will you allow me to have some breakfast with you?"

"Do you suppose I could refuse you?"

"I should be very sorry to disturb you in any way. How did you use to amuse yourself at home?"

"I am very fond of books and music; my harpsichord was my delight."

I left her after breakfast, and in the evening I came back with a basket full of good books and music, and I sent her an excellent harpsichord. My kindness confused her, but I surprised her much more when I took out of my pocket three pairs of slippers. She blushed, and thanked me with great feeling. She had walked a long distance, her shoes were evidently worn out, her feet sore, and she appreciated the delicacy of my present. As I had no improper design with regard to her, I enjoyed her gratitude, and felt pleased at the idea she evidently entertained of my kind attentions. I had no other purpose in view but to restore calm to her mind, and to obliterate the bad opinion which the unworthy Steffani had given her of men in general. I never thought of inspiring her with love for me, and I had not the slightest idea that I could fall in love with her. She was unhappy, and her unhappiness — a sacred thing in my eyes — called all the more for my most honourable sympathy, because, without knowing me, she had given me her entire confidence. Situated as she was, I could not suppose her heart susceptible of harbouring a new affection, and I would have despised myself if I had tried to seduce her by any means in my power.

I remained with her only a quarter of an hour, being unwilling that my presence should trouble her at such a moment, as she seemed to be at a loss how to thank me and to express all her gratitude.

I was thus engaged in a rather delicate adventure, the end of which I could not possibly foresee, but my warmth for my *protégée* did not cool down, and having no difficulty in procuring the means to keep her I had no wish to see the last scene of the romance. That singular meeting, which gave me the useful opportunity of finding myself endowed with generous dispositions, stronger even than my love for pleasure, flattered my self-love more than I could express. I was then trying a great experiment, and conscious that I wanted sadly to study myself, I gave up all my energies to acquire the great science of the γνῶθι σεαυτόν.

On the third day, in the midst of expressions of gratitude which I could not succeed in stopping, she told me that she could not conceive why I showed her so much sympathy, because I ought to have formed but a poor opinion of her in consequence of the readiness with which she had followed me into the café. She smiled when I answered that I could not understand how I had succeeded in giving her so great a confidence in my virtue, when I appeared before her with a mask on my face, in a costume which did not indicate a very virtuous character.

"It was easy for me, madam," I continued, "to guess that you were a beauty in distress, when I observed your youth, the nobleness of your countenance, and, more than all, your candour. The stamp of truth was so well affixed to the first words you uttered that I could not have the shadow of a doubt left in me as to your being the unhappy victim of the most natural of all feelings, and as to your having abandoned your home through a sentiment of honour. Your fault was that of a warm heart seduced by love, over which reason could have no sway, and your flight — the action of a soul crying for reparation or for revenge — fully justifies you. Your cowardly seducer must pay with his life the penalty due to his crime, and he ought never to receive, by marrying you, an unjust reward, for he is not worthy of possessing you after degrading himself by the vilest conduct."

"Everything you say is true. My brother, I hope, will avenge me."

"You are greatly mistaken if you imagine that Steffani will fight your brother; Steffani is a coward who will never expose himself to an honourable death."

As I was speaking, she put her hand in her pocket and drew forth, after a few moments' consideration, a stiletto six inches long, which she placed on the table.

"What is this?" I exclaimed.

"It is a weapon upon which I reckoned until now to use against myself in case I should not succeed in obtaining reparation for the crime I have committed. But you have opened my eyes. Take away, I entreat you, this stiletto, which henceforth is useless to me. I trust in your friendship, and I have an inward certainty that I shall be indebted to you for my honour as well as for my life."

I was struck with the words she had just uttered, and I felt that those words, as well as her looks, had found their way to my heart, besides enlisting my generous sympathy. I took the stiletto, and left her with so much agitation that I had to acknowledge the weakness of my heroism, which I was very near turning into ridicule; yet I had the wonderful strength to perform, at least by halves, the character of a Cato until the seventh day.

I must explain how a certain suspicion of the young lady arose in my mind. That doubt was heavy on my heart, for, if it had proved true, I should have been a dupe, and the idea was humiliating. She had told me that she was a musician; I had immediately sent her a harpsichord, and, yet, although the instrument had been at her disposal for three days, she had not opened it once, for the widow had told me so. It seemed to me that the best way to thank me for my attentive kindness would have been to give me a specimen of her musical talent. Had she deceived me? If so, she would lose my esteem. But, unwilling to form a hasty judgment, I kept on my guard, with a firm determination to make good use of the first opportunity that might present itself to clear up my doubts.

I called upon her the next day after dinner, which was not my usual time, having resolved on creating the opportunity myself. I caught her seated before a toilet-glass, while the widow dressed the most beautiful auburn hair I had ever seen. I tendered my apologies for my sudden appearance at an unusual hour; she excused herself for not having completed her toilet, and the widow went on with her work. It was the first time I had seen the whole of her face, her neck, and half of her arms, which the graces themselves had moulded. I remained in silent contemplation. I praised, quite by chance, the perfume of the pomatum, and the widow took the opportunity of telling her that she had spent in combs, powder, and pomatum the three livres she had received from her. I recollected then that she had told me the first day that she had left C ** with ten paoli. I blushed for very shame, for I ought to have thought of that.

As soon as the widow had dressed her hair, she left the room to prepare some coffee for us. I took up a ring which had been laid by her on the toilet-table, and I saw that it contained a portrait exactly like her; I was amused at the singular fancy she had had of having her likeness taken in a man's costume, with black hair. "You are mistaken," she said, "it is a portrait of my brother. He is two years older than I, and is an officer in the papal army."

I begged her permission to put the ring on her finger; she consented, and when I tried, out of mere gallantry, to kiss her hand, she drew it back, blushing. I feared she might be offended, and I assured her of my respect.

"Ah, sir!" she answered, "in the situation in which I am placed, I must think of defending myself against my own self much more than against you."

The compliment struck me as so fine, and so complimentary to me, that I thought it better not to take it up, but she could easily read in my eyes that she would never find me ungrateful for whatever feelings she might entertain in my favour. Yet I felt my love taking such proportions that I did not know how to keep it a mystery any longer.

[114]

Soon after that, as she was again thanking me for the books I had given her, saying that I had guessed her taste exactly, because she did not like novels, she added, "I owe you an apology for not having sung to you yet, knowing that you are fond of music." These words made me breathe freely; without waiting for any answer, she sat down before the instrument and played several pieces with a facility, with a precision, with an expression of which no words could convey any idea. I was in ecstacy. I entreated her to sing; after some little ceremony, she took one of the music books I had given her, and she sang at sight in a manner which fairly ravished me. I begged that she would allow me to kiss her hand, and she did not say yes, but when I took it and pressed my lips on it, she did not oppose any resistance; I had the courage to smother my ardent desires, and the kiss I imprinted on her lovely hand was a mixture of tenderness, respect, and admiration.

I took leave of her, smitten, full of love, and almost determined on declaring my passion. Reserve becomes silliness when we know that our affection is returned by the woman we love, but as yet I was not quite sure.

The disappearance of Steffani was the talk of Venice but I did not inform the charming countess of that circumstance. It was generally supposed that his mother had refused to pay his debts, and that he had run away to avoid his creditors. It was very possible. But, whether he returned or not, I could not make up my mind to lose the precious treasure I had in my hands. Yet I did not see in what manner, in what quality, I could enjoy that treasure, and I found myself in a regular maze. Sometimes I had an idea of consulting my kind father, but I would soon abandon it with fear, for I had made a trial of his empiric treatment in the Rinaldi affair, and still more in the case of l'Abbadie. His remedies frightened me to that extent that I would rather remain ill than be cured by their means.

One morning I was foolish enough to inquire from the widow whether the lady had asked her who I was. What an egregious blunder! I saw it when the good woman, instead of answering me, said:

"Does she not know who you are?"

"Answer me, and do not ask questions," I said, in order to hide my confusion.

The worthy woman was right; through my stupidity she would now feel curious; the tittle-tattle of the neighbourhood would of course take up the affair and discuss it; and all through my thoughtlessness! It was an unpardonable blunder. One ought never to be more careful than in addressing questions to half-educated persons. During the fortnight that she had passed under my protection, the countess had shown me no curiosity whatever to know anything about me, but it did not prove that she was not curious on the subject. If I had been wise, I should have told her the very first day who I was, but I made up for my mistake that evening better than anybody else could have done it, and, after having told her all about myself, I entreated her forgiveness for not having done so sooner. Thanking me for my confidence, she confessed how curious she had been to know me better, and she assured me that she would never have been imprudent enough to ask any questions about me from her landlady. Women have a more delicate, a surer tact than men, and her last words were a home-thrust for me.

Our conversation having turned to the extraordinary absence of Steffani, she said that her father must necessarily believe her to be hiding with him somewhere. "He must have found out," she added, "that I was in the habit of conversing with him every night from my window, and he must have heard of my having embarked for Venice on board the Ferrara barge. I feel certain that my father is now in Venice, making secretly every effort to discover me. When he visits this city he always puts up at Boncousin; will you ascertain whether he is there?"

She never pronounced Steffani's name without disgust and hatred, and she said she would bury herself in a convent, far away from her native place, where no one could be acquainted with her shameful history.

I intended to make some inquiries the next day, but it was not necessary for me to do so, for in the evening, at supper-time, M. Barbaro said to us:

"A nobleman, a subject of the Pope, has been recommended to me, and wishes me to assist him with my influence in a rather delicate and intricate matter. One of our citizens has, it appears, carried off his daughter, and has been hiding somewhere with her for the last fortnight, but nobody knows where. The affair ought to be brought before the Council of Ten, but the mother of the ravisher claims to be a relative of mine, and I do not intend to interfere."

I pretended to take no interest in M. Barbaro's words, and early the next morning I went to the young countess to tell her the interesting news. She was still asleep; but, being in a hurry, I sent the widow to say that I wanted to see her only for two minutes in order to communicate something of great importance. She received me, covering herself up to the chin with the bed-clothes.

As soon as I had informed her of all I knew, she entreated me to enlist M. Barbaro as a mediator between herself and her father, assuring me that she would rather die than become the wife of the monster who had dishonoured her. I undertook to do it, and she gave me the promise of marriage used by the deceiver to seduce her, so that it could be shown to her father.

In order to obtain M. Barbaro's mediation in favour of the young countess, it would have been necessary to tell him that she was under my protection, and I felt it would injure my *protégée*. I took no determination at first, and most likely one of the reasons for my hesitation was that I saw myself on the point of losing her, which was particularly repugnant to my feelings.

After dinner Count A ** S ** was announced as wishing to see M. Barbaro. He came in with his son, the living portrait of his sister. M. Barbaro took them to his study to talk the matter over, and within an hour they had taken leave. As soon as they had gone, the excellent M. Barbaro asked me, as I had expected, to consult my heavenly spirit, and to ascertain whether he would be right in interfering in favour of Count A ** S **. He wrote the question himself, and I gave the following answer with the utmost coolness:

"You ought to interfere, but only to advise the father to forgive his daughter and to give up all idea of compelling her to marry her ravisher, for Steffani has been sentenced to death by the will of God."

The answer seemed wonderful to the three friends, and I was myself surprised at my boldness, but I had a foreboding that Steffani was to meet his death at the hands of somebody; love might have given birth to that presentiment. M. de Bragadin, who believed my oracle infallible, observed that it had never given such a clear answer, and that Steffani was certainly dead. He said to M. de Barbaro:

"You had better invite the count and his son to dinner here to-morrow. You must act slowly and prudently; it would be necessary to know where the daughter is before you endeavour to make the father forgive her."

M. Barbaro very nearly made me drop my serious countenance by telling me that if I would try my oracle I could let them know at once where the girl was. I answered that I would certainly ask my spirit on the morrow, thus gaining time in order to ascertain beforehand the disposition of the father and of his son. But I could not help laughing, for I had placed myself under the necessity of sending Steffani to the next world, if the reputation of my oracle was to be maintained.

I spent the evening with the young countess, who entertained no doubt either of her father's indulgence or of the entire confidence she could repose in me.

What delight the charming girl experienced when she heard that I would dine the next day with her father and brother, and that I would tell her every word that would be said about her! But what happiness it was for me to see her convinced that she was right in loving me, and that, without me, she would certainly have been lost in a town where the policy of the government tolerates debauchery as a solitary species of individual freedom! We congratulated each other upon our fortuitous meeting and upon the conformity in our tastes, which we thought truly wonderful. We were greatly pleased that her easy acceptance of my invitation, or my promptness in persuading her to follow and to trust me, could not be ascribed to the mutual attraction of our features, for I was masked, and her hood was then as good as a mask. We entertained no doubt that everything had been arranged by Heaven to get us acquainted, and to fire us both, even unknown to ourselves, with love for each other.

"Confess," I said to her, in a moment of enthusiasm, and as I was covering her hand with kisses, "confess that if you found me to be in love with you you would fear me."

"Alas! my only fear is to lose you."

That confession, the truth of which was made evident by her voice and by her looks, proved the electric spark which ignited the latent fire. Folding her rapidly in my arms, pressing my

[118]

mouth on her lips, reading in her beautiful eyes neither a proud indignation nor the cold compliance which might have been the result of a fear of losing me, I gave way entirely to the sweet inclination of love, and swimming already in a sea of delights I felt my enjoyment increased a hundredfold when I saw, on the countenance of the beloved creature who shared it, the expression of happiness, of love, of modesty, and of sensibility, which enhances the charm of the greatest triumph.

She had scarcely recovered her composure when she cast her eyes down and sighed deeply. Thinking that I knew the cause of it, I threw myself on my knees before her, and speaking to her words of the warmest affection I begged, I entreated her, to forgive me.

"What offence have I to forgive you for, dear friend? You have not rightly interpreted my thoughts. Your love caused me to think of my happiness, and in that moment a cruel recollection drew that sigh from me. Pray rise from your knees."

Midnight had struck already; I told her that her good fame made it necessary for me to go away; I put my mask on and left the house. I was so surprised, so amazed at having obtained a felicity of which I did not think myself worthy, that my departure must have appeared rather abrupt to her. I could not sleep; I passed one of those disturbed nights during which the imagination of an amorous young man is unceasingly running after the shadows of reality. I had tasted, but not savoured, that happy reality, and all my being was longing for her who alone could make my enjoyment complete. In that nocturnal drama love and imagination were the two principal actors; hope, in the background, performed only a dumb part. People may say what they please on that subject, but hope is in fact nothing but a deceitful flatterer accepted by reason only because it is often in need of palliatives. Happy are those men who, to enjoy life to the fullest extent, require neither hope nor foresight.

In the morning, recollecting the sentence of death which I had passed on Steffani, I felt somewhat embarrassed about it. I wished I could have recalled it, as well for the honour of my oracle, which was seriously implicated by it, as for the sake of Steffani himself, whom I did not hate half so much since I was indebted to him for the treasure in my possession.

The count and his son came to dinner. The father was simple,

artless, and unceremonious. It was easy to read on his countenance the grief he felt at the unpleasant adventure of his
daughter, and his anxiety to settle the affair honourably, but
no anger could be traced on his features or in his manners. The
son, as handsome as the god of love, had wit and great nobility
of manner. His easy, unaffected carriage pleased me, and wishing to win his friendship I showed him every attention.

After the dessert, M. Barbaro contrived to persuade the count
that we were four persons with but one head and one heart, and
the worthy nobleman spoke to us without any reserve. He
praised his daughter very highly; he assured us that Steffani
had never entered his house, and therefore he could not conceive
by what spell, speaking to his daughter only at night and from
the street under the window, he had succeeded in seducing her
to such an extent as to make her leave her home alone, on foot,
two days after he had left himself in his post-chaise.

"Then," observed M. Barbaro, "it is impossible to be certain
that he actually seduced her, or to prove that she went off with
him."

"Very true, sir; but although it cannot be proved, there is
no doubt of it, and now that no one knows where Steffani is,
he can be nowhere but with her. I only want him to marry
her."

"It strikes me that it would be better not to insist upon a
compulsory marriage which would seal your daughter's misery,
for Steffani is, in every respect, one of the most worthless young
men we have amongst our government clerks."

"Were I in your place," said M. de Bragadin, "I would let
my daughter's repentance disarm my anger, and I would forgive
her."

"Where is she? I am ready to fold her in my arms; but how
can I believe in her repentance when it is evident that she is
still with him."

"Is it quite certain that in leaving C ** she proceeded to this
city?"

"I have it from the master of the barge himself, and she
landed within twenty yards of the Roman gate. An individual
wearing a mask was waiting for her, joined her at once, and they
both disappeared without leaving any trace of their whereabouts."

[120]

"Very likely it was Steffani waiting there for her."

"No, for he is short, and the man with the mask was tall. Besides, I have heard that Steffani had left Venice two days before the arrival of my daughter. The man must have been some friend of Steffani and he has taken her to him."

"But, my dear count, all this is mere supposition."

"There are four persons who have seen the man with the mask, and pretend to know him; only they do not agree. Here is a list of four names, and I will accuse these four persons before the Council of Ten, if Steffani should deny having my daughter in his possession."

The list, which he handed to M. Barbaro, gave not only the names of the four accused persons, but likewise those of their accusers. The last name, which M. Barbaro read, was mine. When I heard it, I shrugged my shoulders in a manner which caused the three friends to laugh heartily.

M. de Bragadin, seeing the surprise of the count at such un-called-for mirth, said to him:

"This is Casanova my son, and I give you my word of honour that, if your daughter is in his hands, she is perfectly safe, although he may not look exactly the sort of man to whom young girls should be trusted."

The surprise, the amazement, and the perplexity of the count and his son were an amusing picture. The loving father begged me to excuse him, with tears in his eyes, telling me to place myself in his position. My only answer was to embrace him most affectionately.

The man who had recognised me was a noted pimp whom I had thrashed some time before for having deceived me. If I had not been there just in time to take care of the young countess, she would not have escaped him, and he would have ruined her for ever by taking her to some house of ill-fame.

The result of the meeting was that the count agreed to postpone his application to the Council of Ten until Steffani's place of refuge should be discovered.

"I have not seen Steffani for six months, sir," I said to the count, "but I promise you to kill him in a duel as soon as he returns."

"You shall not do it," answered the young count, very coolly, "unless he kills me first."

"Gentlemen," exclaimed M. de Bragadin, "I can assure you that you will neither of you fight a duel with him, for Steffani is dead."

"Dead!" said the count.

"We must not," observed the prudent Barbaro, "take that word in its literal sense, but the wretched man is dead to all honour and self-respect."

After that truly dramatic scene, during which I could guess that the *dénouement* of the play was near at hand, I went to my charming countess, taking care to change my gondola three times — a necessary precaution to baffle spies.

I gave my anxious mistress an exact account of all the conversation. She was very impatient for my coming, and wept tears of joy when I repeated her father's words of forgiveness; but when I told her that nobody knew of Steffani having entered her chamber, she fell on her knees and thanked God. I then repeated her brother's words, imitating his coolness: "You shall not kill him, unless he kills me first." She kissed me tenderly, calling me her guardian angel, her saviour, and weeping in my arms. I promised to bring her brother on the following day, or the day after that at the latest. We had our supper, but we did not talk of Steffani, or of revenge, and after that pleasant meal we devoted two hours to the worship of the god of love.

I left her at midnight, promising to return early in the morning — my reason for not remaining all night with her was that the landlady might, if necessary, swear without scruple that I had never spent a night with the young girl. It proved a very lucky inspiration of mine, for, when I arrived home, I found the three friends waiting impatiently for me in order to impart to me wonderful news which M. de Bragadin had heard at the sitting of the senate.

"Steffani," said M. de Bragadin to me, "is dead, as our angel Paralis revealed it to us; he is dead to the world, for he has become a Capuchin friar. The senate, as a matter of course, has been informed of it. We alone are aware that it is a punishment which God has visited upon him. Let us worship the Author of all things, and the heavenly hierarchy which renders us worthy of knowing what remains a mystery to all men. Now we must achieve our undertaking, and console the poor father. We must inquire from Paralis where the girl is; she cannot now be with

Steffani; of course, God has not condemned her to become a Capuchin nun."

"I need not consult my angel, dearest father, for it is by his express orders that I have been compelled until now to make a mystery of the refuge found by the young countess."

I related the whole story, except what they had no business to know, for, in the opinion of the worthy men, who had paid heavy tribute to Love, all intrigues were fearful crimes. M. Dandolo and M. Barbaro expressed their surprise when they heard that the young girl had been under my protection for a fortnight, but M. de Bragadin said that he was not astonished, that it was according to cabalistic science, and that he knew it.

"We must only," he added, "keep up the mystery of his daughter's place of refuge for the count, until we know for a certainty that he will forgive her, and that he will take her with him to C **, or to any other place where he may wish to live hereafter."

"He cannot refuse to forgive her," I said, "when he finds that the amiable girl would never have left C ** if her seducer had not given her this promise of marriage in his own handwriting. She walked as far as the barge, and she landed at the very moment I was passing the Roman gate. An inspiration from above told me to accost her and to invite her to follow me. She obeyed, as if she was fulfilling the decree of Heaven, I took her to a refuge impossible to discover, and placed her under the care of a God-fearing woman."

My three friends listened to me so attentively that they looked like three statues. I advised them to invite the count to dinner for the day after next, because I needed some time to consult Paralis *de modo tenendi*. I then told M. Barbaro to let the count know in what sense he was to understand Steffani's death. He undertook to do it, and we retired to rest.

I slept only four or five hours, and, dressing myself quickly, hurried to my beloved mistress. I told the widow not to serve the coffee until we called for it, because we wanted to remain quiet and undisturbed for some hours, having several important letters to write.

I found the lovely countess in bed, but awake, and her eyes beaming with happiness and contentment. For a fortnight I had only seen her sad, melancholy, and thoughtful; her pleased countenance, which I naturally ascribed to my influence, filled me with joy. We commenced as all happy lovers always do, and we were both unsparing of the mutual proofs of our love, tenderness, and gratitude.

After our delightful amorous sport, I told her the news, but love had so completely taken possession of her pure and sensitive soul, that what had been important was now only an accessory. But the news of her seducer having turned a Capuchin friar filled her with amazement, and, passing very sensible remarks on the extraordinary event, she pitied Steffani. When we can feel pity, we love no longer, but a feeling of pity succeeding love is the characteristic only of a great and generous mind. She was much pleased with me for having informed my three friends of her being under my protection, and she left to my care all the necessary arrangements for obtaining a reconciliation with her father.

Now and then we recollected that the time of our separation was near at hand, our grief was bitter, but we contrived to forget it in the ecstacy of our amorous enjoyment.

"Ah! why can we not belong for ever to each other?" the charming girl would exclaim. "It is not my acquaintance with Steffani, it is your loss which will seal my eternal misery."

But it was necessary to bring our delightful interview to a close, for the hours were flying with fearful rapidity. I left her happy, her eyes wet with tears of intense felicity.

At the dinner-table M. Barbaro told me that he had paid a visit to his relative, Steffani's mother, and that she had not appeared sorry at the decision taken by her son, although he was her only child.

"He had the choice," she said, "between killing himself and turning friar, and he took the wiser course."

The woman spoke like a good Christian, and she professed to be one; but she spoke like an unfeeling mother, and she was truly one, for she was wealthy, and if she had not been cruelly avaricious her son would not have been reduced to the fearful alternative of committing suicide or of becoming a Capuchin friar.

The last and most serious motive which caused the despair of Steffani, who is still alive, remained a mystery for everybody. My Memoirs will raise the veil when no one will care anything about it.

The count and his son were, of course, greatly surprised, and the event made them still more desirous of discovering the young lady. In order to obtain a clue to her place of refuge, the count had resolved on summoning before the Council of Ten all the parties, accused and accusing, whose names he had on his list, with the exception of myself. His determination made it necessary for us to inform him that his daughter was in my hands, and M. de Bragadin undertook to let him know the truth.

We were all invited to supper by the count, and we went to his hostelry, with the exception of M. de Bragadin, who had declined the invitation. I was thus prevented from seeing my divinity that evening; but early the next morning I made up for lost time, and as it had been decided that her father would on that very day be informed of her being under my care, we remained together until noon. We had no hope of contriving another meeting, for I had promised to bring her brother in the afternoon.

The count and his son dined with us, and after dinner M. de Bragadin said:

"I have joyful news for you, count; your beloved daughter has been found!"

What an agreeable surprise for the father and son! M. de Bragadin handed them the promise of marriage written by Steffani, and said:

"This, gentlemen, evidently brought your lovely young lady to the verge of madness when she found that he had gone from C ** without her. She left your house alone on foot, and as she landed in Venice, Providence threw her in the way of this young man, who induced her to follow him, and has placed her under the care of an honest woman, whom she has not left since, whom she will leave only to fall in your arms as soon as she is certain of your forgiveness for the folly she has committed."

"Oh! let her have no doubt of my forgiving her," exclaimed the father, in the ecstacy of joy, and turning to me, "Dear sir, I beg of you not to delay the fortunate moment on which the whole happiness of my life depends."

I embraced him warmly, saying that his daughter would be restored to him on the following day, and that I would let his son see her that very afternoon, so as to give him an opportunity of preparing her by degrees for that happy reconciliation. M.

Barbaro desired to accompany us, and the young man, approving all my arrangements, embraced me, swearing everlasting friendship and gratitude.

We went out all three together, and a gondola carried us in a few minutes to the place where I was guarding a treasure more precious than the golden apples of the Hesperides. But, alas! I was on the point of losing that treasure, the remembrance of which causes me, even now, a delicious trembling.

I preceded my two companions in order to prepare my lovely young friend for the visit, and when I told her that, according to my arrangements, her father would not see her till on the following day:

"Ah!" she exclaimed with the accent of true happiness, "then we can spend a few more hours together! Go, dearest, go and bring my brother."

I returned with my companions; but how can I paint that truly dramatic situation? Oh! how inferior art must ever be to nature! The fraternal love, the delight beaming upon those two beautiful faces, with a slight shade of confusion on that of the sister, the pure joy shining in the midst of their tender caresses, the most eloquent exclamations followed by a still more eloquent silence, their loving looks which seem like flashes of lightning in the midst of the dew of tears, a thought of politeness which brings blushes on her countenance, when she recollects that she has forgotten her duty towards a nobleman whom she sees for the first time, and finally there was my part, not a speaking one, but yet the most important of all; the whole formed a living picture to which the most skilful painter could not have rendered full justice.

We sat down at last, the young countess between her brother and M. Barbaro, on the sofa; I, opposite to her, on a low footstool.

"To whom, dear sister, are we indebted for the happiness of having found you again?"

"To my guardian angel," she answered, giving me her hand, "to this generous man who was waiting for me, as if Heaven had sent him with the special mission of watching over your sister; it is he who has saved me, who has prevented me from falling into the gulf which yawned under my feet, who has rescued me from the shame threatening me, of which I had then no conception; it is to him I am indebted for all, to him who, as you see, kisses my hand now for the first time."

And she pressed her handkerchief to her beautiful eyes to dry her tears, but ours were flowing at the same time.

Such is true virtue, which never loses its nobleness, even when modesty compels it to utter some innocent falsehood. But the charming girl had no idea of being guilty of an untruth. It was a pure, virtuous soul which was then speaking through her lips, and she allowed it to speak. Her virtue seemed to whisper to her that, in spite of her errors, it had never deserted her. A young girl who gives way to a real feeling of love cannot be guilty of a crime, or be exposed to remorse.

Towards the end of our friendly visit, she said that she longed to throw herself at her father's feet, but that she wished to see him only in the evening, so as not to give any opportunity to the gossips of the place; and it was agreed that the meeting, which was to be the last scene of the drama, should take place the next day towards the evening.

We returned to the count's hostelry for supper, and the excellent man, fully persuaded that he was indebted to me for his honour as well as for his daughter's, looked at me with admiration, and spoke to me with gratitude. Yet he was not sorry to have ascertained himself, and before I had said so, that I had been the first man who had spoken to her after landing. Before parting in the evening, M. Barbaro invited them to dinner for the next day.

I went to my charming mistress very early the following morning, and, although there was some danger in protracting our interview, we did not give it a thought, or, if we did, it only caused us to make good use of the short time that we could still devote to love. I asked her to give me a lock of her hair, which she did at once; I meant to have it made into a chain like the one woven with the hair of Madame F **, which I still wore round my neck.

Towards dusk, the count and his son, M. Dandolo, M. Barbaro, and myself, proceeded together to the abode of the young countess. The moment she saw her father, she threw herself on her knees before him, but the count, bursting into tears, took her in his arms, covered her with kisses, and breathed over her words of forgiveness, of love and blessing. What a scene for a man of sensibility! An hour later we escorted the family to the inn, and, after wishing them a pleasant journey, I went back with my two friends to M. de Bragadin, to whom I gave a faithful account of what had taken place.

We thought that they had left Venice, but the next morning they called at the palace in a *peotta* with six rowers. The count said that they could not leave the city without seeing us once more; without thanking us again, and me particularly, for all we had done for them. M. de Bragadin, who had not seen the young countess before, was struck by her extraordinary likeness to her brother.

They partook of some refreshments, and embarked in their *peotta*, which was to carry them, in twenty-four hours, to Ponte di Lago Oscuro, on the River Po, near the frontiers of the papal states. It was only with my eyes that I could express to the lovely girl all the feelings which filled my heart, but she understood the language, and I had no difficulty in interpreting the meaning of her looks.

Never did an introduction occur in better season than that of the count to M. Barbaro. It saved the honour of a respectable family; and it saved me from the unpleasant consequences of an interrogatory in the presence of the Council of Ten, during which I should have been convicted of having taken the young girl with me, and compelled to say what I had done with her.

A few days afterwards we all proceeded to Padua to remain in that city until the end of autumn. I was grieved not to find Doctor Gozzi in Padua; he had been appointed to a benefice in the country, and he was living there with Bettina; she had not been able to remain with the scoundrel who had married her only for the sake of her small dowry, and had treated her very ill.

I did not like the quiet life of Padua, and to avoid dying from ennui I fell in love with a celebrated Venetian courtesan. Her name was Ancilla; some time after, the well-known dancer, Campioni, married her and took her to London, where she caused the death of a very worthy Englishman. I shall have to mention her again in four years; now I have only to speak of a certain circumstance which brought my love adventure with her to a close after three or four weeks.

Count Medini, a young, thoughtless fellow like myself, and with inclinations of much the same cast, had introduced me to

Ancilla. The count was a confirmed gambler and a thorough enemy of fortune. There was a good deal of gambling going on at Ancilla's, whose favourite lover he was, and the fellow had presented me to his mistress only to give her the opportunity of making a dupe of me at the card-table.

And, to tell the truth, I was a dupe at first; not thinking of any foul play, I accepted ill luck without complaining; but one day I caught them cheating. I took a pistol out of my pocket, and, aiming at Medini's breast, I threatened to kill him on the spot unless he refunded at once all the gold they had won from me. Ancilla fainted away, and the count, after refunding the money, challenged me to follow him out and measure swords. I placed my pistols on the table, and we went out. Reaching a convenient spot, we fought by the bright light of the moon, and I was fortunate enough to give him a gash across the shoulder. He could not move his arm, and he had to cry for mercy.

After that meeting, I went to bed and slept quietly, but in the morning I related the whole affair to my father, and he advised me to leave Padua immediately, which I did.

Count Medini remained my enemy through all his life; I shall have occasion to speak of him again when I reach Naples.

The remainder of the year 1746 passed off quietly, without any events of importance. Fortune was now favourable to me and now adverse.

Towards the end of January, 1747, I received a letter from the young Countess A ** S **, who had married the Marquis of **. She entreated me not to appear to know her, if by chance I visited the town in which she resided, for she had the happiness of having linked her destiny to that of a man who had won her heart after he had obtained her hand.

I had already heard from her brother that, after their return to C **, her mother had taken her to the city from which her letter was written, and there, in the house of a relative with whom she was residing, she had made the acquaintance of the man who had taken upon himself the charge of her future welfare and happiness. I saw her one year afterwards, and if it had not been for her letter, I should certainly have solicited an introduction to her husband. Yet, peace of mind has greater charms even than love; but, when love is in the way, we do not think so.

For a fortnight I was the lover of a young Venetian girl, very handsome, whom her father, a certain Ramon, exposed to public admiration as a dancer at the theatre. I might have remained longer her captive, if marriage had not forcibly broken my chains. Her protectress, Madame Cecilia Valmarano, found her a very proper husband in the person of a French dancer, called Binet, who had assumed the name of Binetti, and thus his young wife had not to become a Frenchwoman; she soon won great fame in more ways than one. She was strangely privileged; time with its heavy hand seemed to have no power over her. She always appeared young, even in the eyes of the best judges of faded, bygone female beauty. Men, as a general rule, do not ask for anything more, and they are right in not racking their brain for the sake of being convinced that they are the dupes of external appearance. The last lover that the wonderful Binetti killed by excess of amorous enjoyment was a certain Mosciuski, a Pole, whom fate brought to Venice seven or eight years ago; she had then reached her sixty-third year!

CHAPTER IV

CHRISTINE

*I*T HAS *been rightly said that, whatever the value of Casanova's Memoirs may be from the point of view of true biography, there can be no question of their novelistic qualities. Over and over again we note the careful contrasting of effects, especially in the early chapters, which contain the story of his youth, while the flow of the narrative continues with apparently artless freedom. It was not for nothing that throughout his life Casanova continued to be an ardent student of Horace, whom he was for ever quoting. The ars celare artem of the master was practised by the disciple. So, after the raffinezza of the episode of the young countess, with its secretive boudoir atmosphere, we are given the bucolic idyll of "Christine." This contrasting of effects had already been essayed almost imperceptibly in an earlier chapter when the Lucie of Paséan episode, with its rustic atmosphere à la Greuze is thrown into relief against the voluptuous and sophisticated vignettes à la Tiepolo or Boucher which depict his gallantries with Teresa Imer, Giulietta, or Marton-*

*Nanette in Venice. As an example of this "manner," as well as for
its own sake, we give the Christine episode in full:*

At the end of January, finding myself under the necessity of
procuring two hundred sequins, Madame Manzoni contrived to
obtain for me from another woman the loan of a diamond ring
worth five hundred. I made up my mind to go to Treviso,
fifteen miles distant from Venice, to pawn the ring at the Mont-
de-pieté, which there lends money upon valuables at the rate of
five per cent. That useful establishment does not exist in Venice,
where the Jews have always managed to keep the monopoly in
their hands.

I got up early one morning, and walked to the end of the
canale regio, intending to engage a gondola to take me as far as
Mestra, where I could take post horses, reach Treviso in less than
two hours, pledge my diamond ring, and return to Venice the
same evening.

As I passed along St. Job's Quay, I saw in a two-oared gondola
a country girl beautifully dressed. I stopped to look at her; the
gondoliers, supposing that I wanted an opportunity of reaching
Mestra at a cheap rate, rowed back to the shore.

Observing the lovely face of the young girl, I do not hesitate,
but jump into the gondola, and pay double fare, on condition
that no more passengers are taken. An elderly priest was seated
near the young girl, he rises to let me take his place, but I
politely insist upon his keeping it.

"Those gondoliers," said the elderly priest, addressing me in
order to begin the conversation, "are very fortunate. They
took us up at the Rialto for thirty soldi, on condition that they
would be allowed to embark other passengers, and here is one
already; they will certainly find more."

"When I am in a gondola, reverend sir, there is no room left
for any more passengers."

So saying I give forty more soldi to the gondoliers, who, highly
pleased with my generosity, thank me and call me excellency.
The good priest, accepting that title as truly belonging to me,
entreats my pardon for not having addressed me as such.

"I am not a Venetian nobleman, reverend sir, and I have no
right to the title of *Eccellenza.*"

"Ah!" says the young lady, "I am very glad of it."

"Why so, signora?"

"Because when I find myself near a nobleman I am afraid. But I suppose that you are an *illustrissimo*."

"Not even that, signora; I am only an advocate's clerk."

"So much the better, for I like to be in the company of persons who do not think themselves above me. My father was a farmer, brother of my uncle here, rector of P **, where I was born and bred. As I am an only daughter I inherited my father's property after his death, and I shall likewise be heiress to my mother, who has been ill a long time and cannot live much longer, which causes me a great deal of sorrow; but it is the doctor who says it. Now, to return to my subject, I do not suppose that there is much difference between an advocate's clerk and the daughter of a rich farmer. I only say so for the sake of saying something, for I know very well that, in travelling, one must accept all sorts of companions: is it not so, uncle?"

"Yes, my dear Christine, and as a proof you see that this gentleman has accepted our company without knowing who or what we are."

"But do you think I would have come if I had not been attracted by the beauty of your lovely niece?"

At these words the good people burst out laughing. As I did not think that there was anything very comic in what I had said, I judged that my travelling companions were rather simple, and I was not sorry to find them so.

"Why do you laugh so heartily, beautiful *damigella?* Is it to show me your fine teeth? I confess that I have never seen such a splendid set in Venice."

"Oh! it is not that, sir, although everyone in Venice has paid me the same compliment. I can assure you that in P ** all the girls have teeth as fine as mine. Is it not a fact, uncle?"

"Yes, my dear niece."

"I was laughing, sir, at a thing which I will never tell you."

"Oh! tell me, I entreat you."

"Oh! certainly not, never."

"I will tell you myself," says the curate.

"You will not," she exclaims, knitting her beautiful eyebrows. "If you do I will go away."

"I defy you to do it, my dear. Do you know what she said, sir, when she saw you on the wharf? 'Here is a very handsome young man who is looking at me, and would not be sorry to be

[132]

with us.' And when she saw that the gondoliers were putting back for you to embark, she was delighted."

While the uncle was speaking to me, the indignant niece was slapping him on the shoulder.

"Why are you angry, lovely Christine, at my hearing that you liked my appearance, when I am so glad to let you know how truly charming I think you?"

"You are glad for a moment. Oh! I know the Venetians thoroughly now. They have all told me that they were charmed with me, and not one of those I would have liked ever made a declaration to me."

"What sort of declaration did you want?"

"There's only one sort for me, sir; the declaration leading to a good marriage in church, in the sight of all men. Yet we remained a fortnight in Venice; did we not, uncle?"

"This girl," said the uncle, "is a good match, for she possesses three thousand crowns. She has always said that she would marry only a Venetian, and I have accompanied her to Venice to give her an opportunity of being known. A worthy woman gave us hospitality for a fortnight, and has presented my niece in several houses where she made the acquaintance of marriageable young men; but those who pleased her would not hear of marriage, and those who would have been glad to marry her did not take her fancy."

"But do you imagine, reverend sir, that marriages can be made like omelets? A fortnight in Venice, that is nothing; you ought to live there at least six months. Now, for instance, I think your niece sweetly pretty, and I should consider myself fortunate if the wife whom God intends for me were like her; but, even if she offered me now a dowry of fifty thousand crowns on condition that our wedding takes place immediately, I would refuse her. A prudent young man wants to know the character of a girl before he marries her, for it is neither money nor beauty which can ensure happiness in married life."

"What do you mean by character?" asked Christine; "is it a beautiful handwriting?"

"No, my dear. I mean the qualities of the mind and the heart. I shall most likely get married some time, and I have been looking for a wife for the last three years, but I am still looking in vain. I have known several young girls almost as lovely as you are, and all with a good marriage portion, but after an acquaintance of two or three months I found out that they could not make me happy."

"In what were they deficient?"

"Well, I will tell you, because you are not acquainted with them, and there can be no indiscretion on my part. One whom I certainly would have married, for I loved her dearly, was extremely vain. She would have ruined me in fashionable clothes and by her love for luxuries. Fancy! she was in the habit of paying one sequin every month to the hairdresser, and as much at least for pomatum and perfumes."

"She was a giddy, foolish girl. Now, I spend only ten soldi in one year on wax, which I mix with goat's grease, and there I have an excellent pomatum."

"Another, whom I would have married two years ago, laboured under a disease which would have made me unhappy; as soon as I knew of it, I ceased my visits."

"What disease was it?"

"A disease which would have prevented her from being a mother, and, if I get married, I wish to have children."

"All that is in God's hands; but I know that my health is excellent. Is it not, uncle?"

"Another was too devout, and that does not suit me. She was so over-scrupulous that she was in the habit of going to her confessor twice a week, and every time her confession lasted at least one hour. I want my wife to be a good Christian, but not bigoted."

"She must have been a great sinner, or else she was very foolish. I confess only once a month, and get through everything in two minutes. Is it not true, uncle? and if you were to ask me any questions, uncle, I should not know what more to say."

"One young lady thought herself more learned than I, although she would, every minute, utter some absurdity. Another was always low-spirited, and my wife must be cheerful."

"Hark to that, uncle! You and my mother are always chiding me for my cheerfulness."

"Another, whom I did not court long, was always afraid of being alone with me, and if I gave her a kiss she would run and tell her mother."

"How silly she must have been! I have never yet listened to a lover, for we have only rude peasants in P **, but I know very well that there are some things which I would not tell my mother."

"One had a rank breath; another painted her face, and, indeed, almost every young girl is guilty of that fault. I am afraid marriage is out of the question for me, because I want, for instance, my wife to have black eyes, and in our days almost every woman colours them by art; but I cannot be deceived, for I am a good judge."

"Are mine black?"

"Ah! Ah!"

"You are laughing?"

"I laugh because your eyes certainly appear to be black, but they are not so in reality. Never mind, you are very charming in spite of that."

"Now, that is amusing. You pretend to be a good judge, yet you say that my eyes are dyed black. My eyes, sir, whether beautiful or ugly, are now the same as God made them. Is is not so, uncle?"

"I never had any doubt of it, my dear niece."

"And you do not believe me, sir?"

"No, they are too beautiful for me to believe them natural."

"Oh, dear me! I cannot bear it."

"Excuse me, my lovely *damigella*, I am afraid I have been too sincere."

After that quarrel we remained silent. The good curate smiled now and then, but his niece found it very hard to keep down her sorrow.

At intervals I stole a look at her face, and could see that she was very near crying; I felt sorry, for she was a charming girl. In her hair, dressed in the fashion of wealthy countrywomen, she had more than one hundred sequins' worth of gold pins and arrows which fastened the plaits of her long locks as dark as ebony. Heavy gold ear-rings, and a long chain, which was wound twenty times round her snowy neck, made a fine contrast to her complexion, on which the lilies and the roses were admirably blended. It was the first time that I had seen a country beauty in such splendid apparel. Six years before, Lucie at Paséan had captivated me, but in a different manner.

Christine did not utter a single word, she was in despair, for her eyes were truly of the greatest beauty, and I was cruel enough to attack them. She evidently hated me, and her anger alone kept back her tears. Yet I would not undeceive her, for I wanted her to bring matters to a climax.

When the gondola had entered the long canal of Marghera, I asked the clergyman whether he had a carriage to go to Treviso, through which place he had to pass to reach P **.

"I intended to walk," said the worthy man, "for my parish is poor and I am the same, but I will try to obtain a place for Christine in some carriage travelling that way."

"You would confer a real kindness on me if you would both accept a seat in my chaise; it holds four persons, and there is plenty of room."

"It is a good fortune which we were far from expecting."

"Not at all, uncle; I will not go with this gentleman."

"Why not, my dear niece?"

"Because I will not."

"Such is the way," I remarked, without looking at her, "that sincerity is generally rewarded."

"Sincerity, sir! nothing of the sort," she exclaimed, angrily, "it is sheer wickedness. There can be no true black eyes now for you in the world, but, as you like them, I am very glad of it."

"You are mistaken, lovely Christine, for I have the means of ascertaining the truth."

"What means?"

"Only to wash the eyes with a little lukewarm rose-water; or if the lady cries, the artificial colour is certain to be washed off."

At those words, the scene changed as if by the wand of a conjuror. The face of the charming girl, which had expressed nothing but indignation, spite, and disdain, took an air of contentment and of placidity delightful to witness. She smiled at her uncle, who was much pleased with the change in her countenance, for the offer of the carriage had gone to his heart.

"Now you had better cry a little, my dear niece, and *il signore* will render full justice to your eyes."

Christine cried in reality, but it was immoderate laughter that made her tears flow.

That species of natural originality pleased me greatly; and as we were going up the steps at the landing-place, I offered her my full apologies; she accepted the carriage. I ordered breakfast, and told a *vetturino* to get a very handsome chaise ready while we had our meal, but the curate said that he must first of all go and say his mass.

"Very well, reverend sir, we will hear it, and you must say it for my intention."

I put a silver ducat in his hand.

"It is what I am in the habit of giving," I observed.

My generosity surprised him so much that he wanted to kiss my hand. We proceeded towards the church, and I offered my arm to the niece, who, not knowing whether she ought to accept it or not, said to me:

"Do you suppose that I cannot walk alone?"

"I have no such idea, but if I do not give you my arm, people will think me wanting in politeness."

"Well, I will take it. But now that I have your arm, what will people think?"

"Perhaps that we love each other and that we make a very nice couple."

"And if anyone should inform your mistress that we are in love with each other, or even that you have given your arm to a young girl?"

"I have no mistress, and I shall have none in future, because I could not find a girl as pretty as you in all Venice."

"I am very sorry for you, for we cannot go again to Venice; and even if we could, how could we remain there six months? You said that six months were necessary to know a girl well."

"I would willingly defray all your expenses."

"Indeed? Then say so to my uncle, and he will think it over, for I could not go alone."

"In six months you would know me likewise."

"Oh! I know you very well already."

"Could you accept a man like me?"

"Why not?"

"And will you love me?"

"Yes, very much, when you are my husband."

I looked at the young girl with astonishment; she seemed to me a princess in the disguise of a peasant girl. Her dress, made of *gros de Tours* and all embroidered in gold, was very handsome, and cost certainly twice as much as the finest dress of a Venetian lady. Her bracelets, matching the neck-chain, completed her rich toilet. She had the figure of a nymph, and the new fashion of wearing a mantle not having yet reached her village, I could see the most magnificent bosom, although her dress was fastened up to the neck. The end of the richly-embroidered skirt did not go lower than the ankles, which allowed me to admire the neatest little foot and the lower part of an exquisitely moulded leg. Her firm and easy walk, the natural freedom of all her movements, a charming look which seemed to say, "I am very glad that you think me pretty," everything, in short, caused the ardent fire of amorous desires to circulate through my veins. I could not conceive how such a lovely girl could have spent a fortnight in Venice without finding a man to marry or to deceive her. I was particularly delighted with her simple, artless way of talking, which in the city might have been taken for silliness.

Absorbed in my thoughts, and having resolved in my own mind on rendering brilliant homage to her charms, I waited impatiently for the end of the mass.

After breakfast I had great difficulty in convincing the curate that my seat in the carriage was the last one, but I found it easier to persuade him on our arrival in Treviso to remain for dinner and for supper at a small, unfrequented inn, as I took all the expense upon myself. He accepted very willingly when I added that immediately after supper a carriage would be in readiness to convey him to P **, where he would arrive in an hour after a pleasant journey by moonlight. He had nothing to hurry him on, except his wish to say mass in his own church the next morning.

I ordered a fire and a good dinner, and the idea struck me that the curate himself might pledge the ring for me, and thus give me the opportunity of a short interview with his niece. I proposed it to him, saying that I could not very well go myself, as I did not wish to be known; he undertook the commission at once, expressing his pleasure at doing something to oblige me.

He left us, and I remained alone with Christine. I spent an hour with her without trying to give her even a kiss, although I was dying to do so, but I prepared her heart to burn with the same desires which were already burning in me by those

[138]

words which so easily inflame the imagination of a young girl.

The curate came back and returned me the ring, saying that it could not be pledged until the day after the morrow, in consequence of the Festival of the Holy Virgin. He had spoken to the cashier, who had stated that if I liked the bank would lend double the sum I had asked.

"My dear sir," I said, "you would greatly oblige me if you would come back here from P ** to pledge the ring yourself. Now that it has been offered once by you, it might look very strange if it were brought by another person. Of course I will pay all your expenses."

"I promise you to come back."

I hoped he would bring his niece with him.

I was seated opposite to Christine during the dinner, and discovered fresh charms in her every minute, but, fearing I might lose her confidence if I tried to obtain some slight favour, I made up my mind not to go to work too quickly, and to contrive that the curate should take her again to Venice. I thought that there only I could manage to bring love into play and to give it the food it requires.

"Reverend sir," I said, "let me advise you to take your niece again to Venice. I undertake to defray all expenses, and to find an honest woman with whom your Christine will be as safe as with her own mother. I want to know her well in order to make her my wife, and if she comes to Venice our marriage is certain."

"Sir, I will bring my niece myself to Venice as soon as you inform me that you have found a worthy woman with whom I can leave her in safety."

While we were talking I kept looking at Christine, and I could see her smile with contentment.

"My dear Christine," I said, "within a week I shall have arranged the affair. In the meantime, I will write to you; I hope that you have no objection to correspond with me."

"My uncle will write for me, for I have never been taught writing."

"What, my dear child! you wish to become the wife of a Venetian, and you cannot write?"

"Is it then necessary to know how to write in order to become a wife? I can read well."

"That is not enough, and although a girl can be a wife and a mother without knowing how to trace one letter, it is generally admitted that a young girl ought to be able to write. I wonder you never learned."

"There is no wonder in that, for not one girl in our village can do it. Ask my uncle."

"It is perfectly true, but there is not one who thinks of getting married in Venice, and as you wish for a Venetian husband, you must learn."

"Certainly," I said, "and before you come to Venice, for everybody would laugh at you, if you could not write. I see that it makes you sad, my dear, but it cannot be helped."

"I am sad, because I cannot learn writing in a week."

"I undertake," said her uncle, "to teach you in a fortnight, if you will only practise diligently. You will then know enough to be able to improve by your own exertions."

"It is a great undertaking, but I accept it; I promise you to work night and day, and to begin to-morrow."

After dinner, I advised the priest not to leave that evening, to rest during the night, and I observed that, by going away before daybreak, he would reach P ** in good time, and feel all the better for it. I made the same proposal to him in the evening, and when he saw that his niece was sleepy, he was easily persuaded to remain. I called for the innkeeper, ordered a carriage for the clergyman, and desired that a fire might be lit for me in the next room, where I would sleep, but the good priest said that it was unnecessary, because there were two large beds in our room, that one would be for me and the other for him and his niece.

"We need not undress," he added, "as we mean to leave very early, but you can take off your clothes, sir, because you are not going with us, and you will like to remain in bed to-morrow morning."

"Oh!" remarked Christine, "I must undress myself, otherwise I could not sleep, but I only want a few minutes to get ready in the morning."

I said nothing, but I was amazed. Christine then, lovely and charming enough to wreck the chastity of a Xenocrates, would sleep naked with her uncle! True, he was old, devout, and without any of the ideas which might render such a position dangerous, yet the priest was a man, he had evidently felt like all men, and he ought to have known the danger he was exposing himself to. My carnal-mindedness could not realise such a state of innocence. But it was truly innocent, so much so that he did it openly, and did not suppose that anyone could see anything wrong in it. I saw it all plainly, but I was not accustomed to such things, and felt lost in wonderment. As I advanced in age and in experience, I have seen the same custom established in many countries amongst honest people whose good morals were in no way debased by it, but it was amongst good people, and I do not pretend to belong to that worthy class.

We had had no meat for dinner, and my delicate palate was not over-satisfied. I went down to the kitchen myself, and I told the landlady that I wanted the best that could be procured in Treviso for supper, particularly in wines.

"If you do not mind the expense, sir, trust to me, and I undertake to please you. I will give you some Gatta wine."

"All right; but let us have supper early."

When I returned to our room, I found Christine caressing the cheeks of her old uncle, who was laughing; the good man was seventy-five years old.

"Do you know what is the matter?" he said to me; "my niece is caressing me because she wants me to leave her here until my return. She tells me that you were like brother and sister during the hour you have spent alone together this morning, and I believe it, but she does not consider that she would be a great trouble to you."

"Not at all, quite the reverse; she will afford me great pleasure, for I think her very charming. As to our mutual behaviour, I believe you can trust us both to do our duty."

"I have no doubt of it. Well, I will leave her under your care until the day after to-morrow. I will come back early in the morning so as to attend to your business."

This extraordinary and unexpected arrangement caused the blood to rush to my head with such violence that my nose bled profusely for a quarter of an hour. It did not frighten me, because I was used to such accidents, but the good priest was in a great fright, thinking that it was a serious hæmorrhage.

When I had allayed his anxiety, he left us on some business of his own, saying that he would return at nightfall. I remained alone with the charming, artless Christine, and lost no time in thanking her for the confidence she placed in me.

"I can assure you," she said, "that I wish you to have a thorough knowledge of me; you will see that I have none of the faults which have displeased you so much in the young ladies you have known in Venice, and I promise to learn writing immediately."

"You are charming and true; but you must be discreet in P **, and confide to no one that we have entered into an agreement with each other. You must act according to your uncle's instructions, for it is to him that I intend to write to make all arrangements."

"You may rely upon my discretion; I will not say anything even to my mother, until you give me permission to do so."

I passed the afternoon, in denying myself even the slightest liberties with my lovely companion, but falling every minute deeper in love with her. I told her a few love stories which I veiled sufficiently not to shock her modesty; she felt interested, and I could see that, although she did not always understand, she pretended to do so, in order not to appear ignorant.

When her uncle returned, I had arranged everything in my mind to make her my wife, and I resolved on placing her, during her stay in Venice, in the house of the same honest widow with whom I had found a lodging for my beautiful Countess A ** S **.

We had a delicious supper. I had to teach Christine how to eat oysters and truffles, which she then saw for the first time. Gatta wine is like champagne, it causes merriment without intoxicating, but it cannot be kept for more than one year. We went to bed before midnight, and it was broad daylight when I awoke. The curate had left the room so quietly that I had not heard him.

I looked towards the other bed, Christine was asleep. I wished her good morning, she opened her eyes, and leaning on her elbow, she smiled sweetly.

"My uncle has gone; I did not hear him."

"Dearest Christine, you are as lovely as one of God's angels; I have a great longing to give you a kiss."

"If you long for a kiss, my dear friend, come and give me one."

I jump out of my bed, decency makes her hide her face, it was cold, and I was in love; I find myself in her arms by one of those spontaneous movements which sentiment alone can cause, and we belong to each other without having thought of it, she happy and rather confused, I delighted, yet unable to realise the truth of a victory won without any contest.

Christine was the first to break the silence:

"What have we done?" she said, softly and lovingly.

"We have become husband and wife."

"What will my uncle say to-morrow?"

"He need not know anything about it until he gives us the nuptial benediction in his own church."

"And when will he do so?"

"As soon as we have completed all the arrangements necessary for a public marriage."

"How long will that be?"

"About a month."

"We cannot be married during Lent."

"I will obtain permission."

"You are not deceiving me?"

"No, for I adore you."

"Then, you no longer want to know me better?"

"No, I know you thoroughly now, and I feel certain that you will make me happy."

"And will you make me happy, too?"

"I hope so."

"Let us get up and go to church. Who could have believed that, to get a husband, it was necessary not to go to Venice, but to come back from that city!"

We got up, and, after partaking of some breakfast, we went to hear mass. The morning passed off quickly, but towards dinner-time I thought that Christine looked different to what she did the day before, and I asked her the reason of that change.

"It must be," she said, "the same reason which causes you to be thoughtful."

"An air of thoughtfulness, my dear, is proper to love when it finds itself in consultation with honour. This affair has become serious, and love is now compelled to think and consider. We want to be married in the church, and we cannot do it before Lent, now that we are in the last days of carnival; yet we cannot wait until Easter, it would be too long. We must therefore obtain a dispensation in order to be married. Have I not reason to be thoughtful?"

Her only answer was to come and kiss me tenderly. I had spoken the truth, yet I had not told her all my reasons for being so pensive. I found myself drawn into an engagement which was not disagreeable to me, but I wished it had not been so very pressing. I could not conceal from myself that repentance was beginning to creep into my amorous and well-disposed mind, and I was grieved at it. I felt certain, however, that the charming girl would never have any cause to reproach me for her misery.

We had the whole evening before us, and as she had told me that she had never gone to a theatre, I resolved on affording her that pleasure. I sent for a Jew from whom I procured everything necessary to disguise her, and we went to the theatre. A man in love enjoys no pleasure but that which he gives to the woman he loves. After the performance was over, I took her to the Casino, and her astonishment made me laugh when she saw for the first time a faro bank. I had not money enough to play myself, but I had more than enough to amuse her and to let her play a reasonable game. I gave her ten sequins, and explained what she had to do. She did not even know the cards, yet in less than an hour she had won one hundred sequins. I made her leave off playing, and we returned to the inn. When we were in our room, I told her to see how much money she had, and when I assured her that all that gold belonged to her, she thought it was a dream.

"Oh! what will my uncle say?" she exclaimed.

We had a light supper, and spent a delightful night, taking good care to part by daybreak, so as not to be caught in the same bed by the worthy ecclesiastic. He arrived early and found us sleeping soundly in our respective beds. He woke me, and I gave him the ring, which he went to pledge immediately. When he returned two hours later, he saw us dressed and talking quietly near the fire. As soon as he came in, Christine rushed to embrace him, and she showed him all the gold she had in her possession. What a pleasant surprise for the good old priest! He did not know how to express his wonder! He thanked God for what he called a miracle, and he concluded by saying that we were made to ensure each other's happiness.

The time to part had come; I promised to pay them a visit in the first days of Lent, but on condition that on my arrival in P ** I would not find anyone informed of my name or of my concerns. The curate gave me the certificate of birth of his niece and the account of her possessions. As soon as they had gone I took my departure for Venice, full of love for the charming girl, and determined on keeping my engagement with her. I knew how easy it would be for me to convince my three friends that my marriage had been irrevocably written in the great book of fate.

My return caused the greatest joy to the three excellent men, because, not being accustomed to see me three days absent, M. Dandolo and M. Barbaro were afraid of some accident having befallen me; but M. de Bragadin's faith was stronger, and he allayed their fears, saying to them that, with Paralis watching over me, I could not be in any danger.

The very next day I resolved on ensuring Christine's happiness without making her my wife. I had thought of marrying her when I loved her better than myself, but after obtaining possession the balance was so much on my side that my self-love proved stronger than my love for Christine. I could not make up my mind to renounce the advantages, the hopes which I thought were attached to my happy independence. Yet I was the slave of sentiment. To abandon the artless, innocent girl seemed to me an awful crime of which I could not be guilty, and the mere idea of it made me shudder. I was aware that she was, perhaps, bearing in her womb a living token of our mutual love, and I shivered at the bare possibility that her confidence in me might be repaid by shame and everlasting misery.

I bethought myself of finding her a husband in every way better than myself; a husband so good that she would not only forgive me for the insult I should thus be guilty of towards her, but also thank me at the end, and like me all the better for my deceit.

To find such a husband could not be very difficult, for Christine was not only blessed with wonderful beauty, and with a well-established reputation for virtue, but she was also the possessor of a fortune amounting to four thousand Venetian ducats.

Shut up in a room with the three worshippers of my oracle,

I consulted Paralis upon the affair which I had so much at heart. The answer was:

"Serenus must attend to it."

Serenus was the cabalistic name of M. de Bragadin, and the excellent man immediately expressed himself ready to execute all the orders of Paralis. It was my duty to inform him of those orders.

"You must," I said to him, "obtain from the Holy Father a dispensation for a worthy and virtuous girl, so as to give her the privilege of marrying during Lent in the church of her village; she is a young country girl. Here is her certificate of birth. The husband is not yet known; but it does not matter, Paralis undertakes to find one."

"Trust to me," said my father, "I will write at once to our ambassador in Rome, and I will contrive to have my letter sent by special express. You need not be anxious, leave it all to me, I will make it a business of state, and I must obey Paralis all the more readily that I foresee that the intended husband is one of us four. Indeed, we must prepare to obey."

I had some trouble in keeping my laughter down, for it was in my power to metamorphose Christine into a grand Venetian lady, the wife of a senator; but that was not my intention. I again consulted the oracle in order to ascertain who would be the husband of the young girl, and the answer was that M. Dandolo was entrusted with the care of finding one, young, handsome, virtuous, and able to serve the Republic, either at home or abroad. M. Dandolo was to consult me before concluding any arrangements. I gave him courage for his task by informing him that the girl had a dowry of four thousand ducats, but I added that his choice was to be made within a fortnight. M. de Bragadin, delighted at not being entrusted with the commission, laughed heartily.

Those arrangements made me feel at peace with myself. I was certain that the husband I wanted would be found, and I only thought of finishing the carnival gaily, and of contriving to find my purse ready for a case of emergency.

Fortune soon rendered me possessor of a thousand sequins. I paid my debts, and the licence for the marriage having arrived from Rome ten days after M. de Bragadin had applied for it, I gave him one hundred ducats, that being the sum it had cost.

The dispensation gave Christine the right of being married in any church in Christendom, she would only have to obtain the seal of the episcopal court of the diocese in which the marriage was to take place, and no publication of banns was required. We wanted, therefore, but one thing — a trifling one — namely, the husband. M. Dandolo had already proposed three or four to me, but I had refused them for excellent reasons. At last he offered one who suited me exactly.

I had to take the diamond ring out of pledge, and not wishing to do it myself, I wrote to the priest making an appointment in Treviso. I was not, of course, surprised when I found he was accompanied by his lovely niece, who, thinking that I had come to complete all arrangements for our marriage, embraced me without ceremony, and I did the same. If the uncle had not been present, I am afraid that those kisses would have caused all my heroism to vanish. I gave the curate the dispensation, and the handsome features of Christine, shone with joy. She certainly could not imagine that I had been working so actively for others, and, as I was not yet certain of anything, I did not undeceive her then. I promised to be in P ** within eight or ten days, when we would complete all necessary arrangements. After dinner, I gave the curate the ticket for the ring and the money to take it out of pledge, and we retired to rest. This time, very fortunately, there was but one bed in the room, and I had to take another chamber for myself.

The next morning, I went into Christine's room, and found her in bed. Her uncle had gone out for my diamond ring, and alone with that lovely girl, I found that I had, when necessary, complete control over my passions. Thinking that she was not to be my wife, and that she would belong to another, I considered it my duty to silence my desires. I kissed her, but nothing more.

I spent one hour with her, fighting like Saint Anthony against the carnal desires of my nature. I could see the charming girl full of love and of wonder at my reserve, and I admired her virtue in the natural modesty which prevented her from making the first advances. She got out of bed and dressed herself without showing any disappointment. She would, of course, have felt mortified if she had had the slightest idea that I despised her, or that I did not value her charms.

Her uncle returned, gave me the ring, and we had dinner, after which he treated me to a wonderful exhibition. Christine had learned how to write, and, to give me a proof of her talent, she wrote very fluently and very prettily in my presence.

We parted, after my promising to come back again within ten days, and I returned to Venice.

On the second Sunday in Lent, M. Dandolo told me with an air of triumph that the fortunate husband had been found, and that there was no doubt of my approval of the new candidate. He was named Charles **, whom I knew by sight — a very handsome young man, of irreproachable conduct, and about twenty-two years of age. He was clerk to M. Ragionato and godson of Count Algarotti, a sister of whom had married M. Dandolo's brother.

"Charles **," said M. Dandolo to me, "has lost his father and his mother, and I feel satisfied that his god-father will guarantee the dowry brought by his wife. I have spoken to him, and I believe him disposed to marry an honest girl whose dowry would enable him to purchase M. Ragionato's office."

"It seems to promise very well, but I cannot decide until I have seen him."

"I have invited him to dine with us to-morrow."

The young man came, and I found him worthy of all M. Dandolo's praise. We became friends at once; he had some taste for poetry, I read some of my productions to him, and having paid him a visit the following day, he showed me several pieces of his own composition which were well written. He introduced me to his aunt, in whose house he lived with his sister, and I was much pleased with their friendly welcome. Being alone with him in his room, I asked him what he thought of love.

"I do not care for love," he answered; "but I should like to get married in order to have a house of my own."

When I returned to the palace, I told M. Dandolo that he might open the affair with Count Algarotti, and the count mentioned it to Charles, who said that he could not give any answer, either one way or the other, until he should have seen the young girl, talked with her, and inquired about her reputation. As for Count Algarotti, he was ready to be answerable for his godson, that is to guarantee four thousand ducats to the wife, provided

her dowry was worth that amount. Those were only the pre-
liminaries; the rest belonged to my province.

Dandolo having informed Charles that the matter was entirely
in my hands, he called on me and inquired when I would be kind
enough to introduce him to the young person. I named the day,
adding that it was necessary to devote a whole day to the visit,
as she resided at a distance of twenty miles from Venice, that
we would dine with her and return the same evening. He promised to be ready for me by daybreak. I immediately sent an
express to the curate to inform him of the day on which I would
call with a friend of mine whom I wished to introduce to his
niece.

On the appointed day, Charles was punctual; I took care to
let him know along the road that I had made the acquaintance
of the young girl and of her uncle as travelling companions from
Venice to Mestra about one month before, and that I would have
offered myself as a husband, if I had been in a position to
guarantee the dowry of four thousand ducats. I did not think it
necessary to go any further in my confidences.

We arrived at the good priest's house two hours before mid-
day, and soon after our arrival, Christine came in with an air of
great ease, expressing all her pleasure at seeing me. She only
bowed to Charles, inquiring from me whether he was likewise a
clerk.

Charles answered that he was clerk to Ragionato.

She pretended to understand, in order not to appear ignorant.

"I want you to look at my writing," she said to me, "and
afterwards we will go and see my mother."

Delighted at the praise bestowed upon her writing by Charles,
when he heard that she had learned only one month, she invited
us to follow her. Charles asked her why she had waited until
the age of nineteen to study writing.

"Well, sir, what does it matter to you? Besides, I must tell
you that I am seventeen, and not nineteen years of age."

Charles entreated her to excuse him, smiling at the quickness
of her answer.

She was dressed like a simple country girl, yet very neatly, and
she wore her handsome gold chains round her neck and on her
arms. I told her to take my arm and that of Charles, which she
did, casting towards me a look of loving obedience. We went

to her mother's house; the good woman was compelled to keep her bed owing to sciatica. As we entered the room, a respect-able-looking man who was seated near the patient, rose at the sight of Charles, and embraced him affectionately. I heard that he was the family physician, and the circumstance pleased me much.

After we had paid our compliments to the good woman, the doctor inquired after Charles's aunt and sister; and alluding to the sister, who was suffering from a secret disease, Charles desired to say a few words to him in private; they left the room to-gether. Being alone with the mother and Christine, I praised Charles, his excellent conduct, his high character, his business abilities, and extolled the happiness of the woman who would be his wife. They both confirmed my praises by saying that every-thing I said of him could be read on his features. I had no time to lose, so I told Christine to be on her guard during dinner, as Charles might possibly be the husband whom God had intended for her.

"For me?"

"Yes, for you. Charles is one of a thousand; you would be much happier with him than you could be with me; the doctor knows him, and you could ascertain from him everything which I cannot find time to tell you now about my friend."

The reader can imagine all I suffered in making this declara-tion, and my surprise when I saw the young girl calm and perfectly composed! Her composure dried the tears already gather-ing in my eyes. After a short silence, she asked me whether I was certain that such a handsome young man would have her. That question gave me an insight into Christine's heart and feelings, and quieted all my sorrow, for I saw that I had not known her well. I answered that, beautiful as she was, there was no doubt of her being loved by everybody.

"It will be at dinner, my dear Christine, that my friend will examine and study you; do not fail to show all the charms and qualities with which God has endowed you; but do not let him suspect our intimacy."

"It is all very strange. Is my uncle informed of this wonder-ful change?"

"No."

"If your friend should feel pleased with me, when would he marry me?"

[150]

"Within ten days. I will take care of everything, and you will see me again in the course of the week."

Charles came back with the doctor, and Christine, leaving her mother's bedside, took a chair opposite to us. She answered very sensibly all the questions addressed to her by Charles, often exciting his mirth by her artlessness, but not showing any silliness.

Oh! charming simplicity! offspring of wit and of ignorance! thy charm is delightful, and thou alone hast the privilege of saying anything without ever giving offence! But how unpleasant thou art when thou art not natural! and thou art the masterpiece of art when thou art imitated with perfection!

We dined rather late, and I took care not to speak to Christine, not even to look at her, so as not to engross her attention, which she devoted entirely to Charles, and I was delighted to see with what ease and interest she kept up the conversation. After dinner, and as we were taking leave, I heard the following words uttered by Charles, which went to my very heart:

"You are made, lovely Christine, to minister to the happiness of a prince."

And Christine? This was her answer:

"I should esteem myself fortunate, sir, if you should judge me worthy of ministering to yours."

These words excited Charles so much that he embraced me!

Christine was simple, but her artlessness did not come from her mind, only from her heart. The simplicity of mind is nothing but silliness, that of the heart is only ignorance and innocence; it is a quality which subsists even when the cause has ceased to be. This young girl, almost a child of nature, was simple in her manners, but graceful in a thousand trifling ways which cannot be described; she was sincere, because she did not know that to conceal some of our impressions is one of the precepts of propriety, and as her intentions were pure, she was a stranger to that false shame and mock modesty which cause pretended innocence to blush at a word or at a movement said or made very often without any wicked purpose.

During our journey back to Venice, Charles spoke of nothing but of his happiness; he had decidedly fallen in love.

"I will call to-morrow morning upon Count Algarotti," he said to me, "and you may write to the priest to come with all

the necessary documents to make the contract of marriage which
I long to sign."

His delight and his surprise were intense when I told him that
my wedding present to Christine was a dispensation from the
Pope for her to be married in Lent.

"Then," he exclaimed, "we must go full speed ahead!"

In the conference which was held the next day between my
young substitute, his god-father, and M. Dandolo, it was decided
that the parson should be invited to come with his niece. I
undertook to carry the message, and leaving Venice two hours
before morning I reached P ** early. The priest said he would
be ready to start immediately after mass. I then called on
Christine, and I treated her to a fatherly and sentimental
sermon, every word of which was intended to point out to her
the true road to happiness in the new condition which she was on
the point of adopting. I told her how she ought to behave towards her husband, towards his aunt and his sister, in order to
captivate their esteem and their love. The last part of my discourse was pathetic and rather disparaging to myself, for, as I
enforced upon her the necessity of being faithful to her husband,
I was necessarily led to entreat her pardon for having seduced
her.

"When you promised to marry me, after we had both been
weak enough to give way to our love, did you intend to deceive
me?"

"Certainly not."

"Then you have not deceived me. On the contrary, I owe
you some gratitude for having thought that, if our union should
prove unhappy, it was better to find another husband for me,
and I thank God that you have succeeded so well. Tell me,
now, what I can answer to your friend in case he should ask me,
during the first night, why I am so different to what a virgin
ought to be."

"It is not likely that Charles, who is full of reserve and propriety, would ask you such a thing, but if he should, tell him
positively that you never had a lover, and that you do not suppose yourself to be different to any other girl."

"Will he believe me?"

"He would deserve your contempt, and entail punishment
on himself if he did not. But dismiss all anxiety; that will not

[152]

occur. A sensible man, my dear Christine, when he has been rightly brought up, never ventures upon such a question, because he is not only certain to displease, but also sure that he will never know the truth, for if the truth is likely to injure a woman in the opinion of her husband, she would be very foolish, indeed, to confess it."

"I understand your meaning perfectly, my dear friend; let us, then, embrace each other for the last time."

"No, for we are alone and I am very weak; I adore thee as much as ever."

"Do not cry, dear friend, for, truly speaking, I have no wish for it."

That simple and candid answer changed my disposition suddenly, and, instead of crying, I began to laugh. Christine dressed herself splendidly, and after breakfast we left P **. We reached Venice in four hours; I lodged them at a good inn, and going to the palace, I told M. Dandolo that our people had arrived, that it would be his province to bring them and Charles together on the following day, and to attend to the matter altogether, because the honour of the future husband and wife, the respect due to their parents and to propriety, forbade any further interference on my part.

He understood my reasons, and acted accordingly. He brought Charles to me, I presented both of them to the curate and his niece, and then left them to complete their business.

I heard afterwards from M. Dandolo that they all called upon Count Algarotti, and at the office of a notary, where the contract of marriage was signed, and that, after fixing a day for the wedding, Charles had escorted his intended back to P **.

On his return, Charles paid me a visit; he told me that Christine had won by her beauty and pleasing manners the affection of his aunt, of his sister, and of his god-father, and that they had taken upon themselves all the expense of the wedding.

"We intend to be married," he added, "on such a day at P **, and I trust that you will crown your work of kindness by being present at the ceremony."

I tried to excuse myself, but he insisted with such a feeling of gratitude, and with so much earnestness, that I was compelled to accept. I listened with real pleasure to the account he gave me of the impression produced upon all his family and upon

Count Algarotti by the beauty, the artlessness, the rich toilet, and especially by the simple talk of the lovely country girl.

"I am deeply in love with her," Charles said to me, "and I feel that it is to you that I shall be indebted for the happiness I am sure to enjoy with my charming wife. She will soon get rid of her country way of talking in Venice, because here envy and slander will but too easily show her the absurdity of it."

His enthusiasm and happiness delighted me, and I congratulated myself upon my own work; yet I felt inwardly some jealousy, and I could not help envying a lot which I might have kept for myself.

M. Dandolo and M. Barbaro having been also invited by Charles, I went with them to P **. We found the dinner-table laid out in the rector's house by the servants of Count Algarotti, who was acting as Charles's father, and having taken upon himself all the expense of the wedding, had sent his cook and his major-domo to P **.

When I saw Christine, the tears filled my eyes, and I had to leave the room. She was dressed as a country girl, but looked as lovely as a nymph. Her husband, her uncle, and Count Algarotti had vainly tried to make her adopt the Venetian costume, but she had very wisely refused.

"As soon as I am your wife," she said to Charles, "I will dress as you please; but here I will not appear before my young companions in any other costume than the one in which they have always seen me; I shall thus avoid being laughed at, and accused of pride, by the girls among whom I have been brought up."

There was in these words something so noble, so just, and so generous, that Charles thought his sweetheart a supernatural being. He told me that he had inquired, from the woman with whom Christine had spent a fortnight, about the offers of marriage she had refused at that time, and that he had been much surprised, for two of those offers were excellent ones.

"Christine," he added, "was evidently destined by Heaven for my happiness, and to you I am indebted for the precious possession of that treasure."

His gratitude pleased me, and I must render myself the justice of saying that I entertained no thought of abusing it. I felt happy in the happiness I had thus given.

We repaired to the church towards eleven o'clock, and were very much astonished at the difficulty we experienced in getting in. A large number of the nobility of Treviso, curious to ascertain whether it was true that the marriage ceremony of a country girl would be publicly performed during Lent when, by waiting only one month, a dispensation would have been useless, had come to P **. Everyone wondered at the permission having been obtained from the Pope, everyone imagined that there was some extraordinary reason for it, and was in despair because it was impossible to guess that reason. In spite of all feelings of envy, every face beamed with pleasure and satisfaction when the young couple made their appearance, and no one could deny that they deserved that extraordinary distinction, that exception to all established rules.

A certain Countess of Tos **, from Treviso, Christine's godmother, went up to her after the ceremony, and embraced her most tenderly, complaining that the happy event had not been communicated to her in Treviso. Christine, in her artless way, answered with as much modesty as sweetness, that the countess ought to forgive her if she had failed in her duty towards her, on account of the marriage having been decided on so hastily. She presented her husband, and begged Count Algarotti to atone for her error towards her god-mother by inviting her to join the wedding repast, an invitation which the countess accepted with great pleasure. That behaviour, which is usually the result of a good education and a long experience of society, was in the lovely peasant girl due only to a candid and well-balanced mind, which shone all the more because it was all nature and not art.

As they returned from the church, Charles and Christine knelt down before the young wife's mother, who gave them her blessing with tears of joy.

Dinner was served, and, of course, Christine and her happy spouse took the seats of honour. Mine was the last, and I was very glad of it; but although everything was delicious, I ate very little, and scarcely opened my lips.

Christine was constantly busy, saying pretty things to every one of her guests, and looking at her husband to make sure that he was pleased with her.

Once or twice she addressed his aunt and sister in such a gracious manner that they could not help leaving their places and kissing her tenderly, congratulating Charles upon his good fortune. I was seated not very far from Count Algarotti, and I heard him say several times to Christine's god-mother that he had never felt so delighted in his life.

When four o'clock struck, Charles whispered a few words to his lovely wife, she bowed to her god-mother, and everybody rose from the table. After the usual compliments — and in this case they bore the stamp of sincerity — the bride distributed among all the girls of the village, who were in the adjoining room, packets full of sugar-plums which had been prepared beforehand, and she took leave of them, kissing them all without any pride. Count Algarotti invited all the guests to sleep at a house he had in Treviso, and to partake there of the dinner usually given the day after the wedding. The uncle alone excused himself, and the mother could not come, owing to her disease, which prevented her from moving; the good woman died three months after Christine's marriage.

Christine therefore left her village to follow her husband, and for the remainder of their lives they lived together in mutual happiness.

Count Algarotti, Christine's god-mother, and my two noble friends went away together; the bride and bridegroom had, of course, a carriage to themselves, and I kept the aunt and the sister of Charles company in another. I could not help envying the happy man somewhat, although in my inmost heart I felt pleased with his happiness.

The sister was not without merit. She was a young widow of twenty-five, and still deserved the homage of men; but I gave the preference to the aunt, who told me that her new niece was a treasure, a jewel which was worthy of everybody's admiration, but that she would not let her go into society until she could speak the Venetian dialect well.

"Her cheerful spirits," she added, "her artless simplicity, her natural wit, are like her beauty, they must be dressed in the Venetian fashion. We are highly pleased with my nephew's choice, and he has incurred everlasting obligations towards you. I hope that for the future you will consider our house as your own."

The invitation was polite, perhaps it was sincere, yet I did not avail myself of it, and they were glad of it. At the end of one year Christine presented her husband with a living token of their mutual love, and that circumstance increased their conjugal felicity.

We all found comfortable quarters in the count's house in Treviso, where, after partaking of some refreshments, the guests retired to rest.

The next morning I was with Count Algarotti and my two friends when Charles came in, handsome, bright, and radiant. While he was answering with much wit some jokes of the count, I kept looking at him with some anxiety, but he came up to me and embraced me warmly. I confess that a kiss never made me happier.

People wonder at the devout scoundrels who call upon their saint when they think themselves in need of heavenly assistance, or who thank him when they imagine that they have obtained some favour from him; but people are wrong, for it is a good and right feeling, which preaches against Atheism.

At the invitation of Charles, his aunt and his sister had gone to pay a morning visit to the young wife, and they returned with her. Happiness never shone on a more lovely face.

M. Algarotti, going towards her, inquired from her affectionately whether she had had a good night; her only answer was to rush to her husband's arms. It was the most artless, and at the same time the most eloquent, answer she could possibly give. Then, turning her beautiful eyes towards me, and offering me her hand, she said:

"M. Casanova, I am happy, and I love to be indebted to you for my happiness."

The tears which were flowing from my eyes, as I kissed her hand, told her better than words how truly happy I was myself.

The dinner passed off delightfully; we then left for Mestra and Venice. We escorted the married couple to their house, and returned home to amuse M. de Bragadin with the relation of our expedition. This worthy and particularly learned man said a thousand things about the marriage, some of great profundity and others of great absurdity.

I laughed inwardly; I was the only one who had the key to the mystery, and could realise the secret of the comedy.

On Low Sunday Charles paid us a visit with his lovely wife, who seemed totally different to what Christine used to be. Her hair dressed with powder did not please me as well as the raven black of her beautiful locks, and her fashionable town attire did not, in my eyes, suit her as well as her rich country dress. But the countenances of husband and wife bore the stamp of happiness. Charles reproached me in a friendly manner because I had not called once upon them, and, in order to atone for my apparent negligence, I went to see them the next day with M. Dandolo. Charles told me that his wife was idolised by his aunt and his sister, who had become her bosom-friend; that she was kind, affectionate, unassuming, and of a disposition which enforced affection. I was not less pleased with this favourable state of things than with the facility with which Christine was learning the Venetian dialect.

When M. Dandolo and I called at their house, Charles was not at home; Christine was alone with his two relatives. The most friendly welcome was proffered to us, and in the course of conversation the aunt praised the progress made by Christine in her writing very highly, and asked her to let me see her copy-book. I followed her to the next room, where she told me that she was very happy; that every day she discovered new virtues in her husband. He had told her, without the slightest appearance of suspicion or displeasure, that he knew that we had spent two days together in Treviso, and that he had laughed at the well-meaning fool who had given him that piece of information in the hope of raising a cloud in the heaven of their felicity.

Charles was truly endowed with all the virtues, with all the noble qualities of an honest and distinguished man. Twenty-six years afterwards I happened to require the assistance of his purse, and found him my true friend. I never was a frequent visitor at his house, and he appreciated my delicacy. He died a few months before my last departure from Venice, leaving his widow in easy circumstances, and three well-educated sons, all with good positions, who may, for what I know, be still living with their mother.

CHAPTER V

HENRIETTE

*H*AD Casanova confined himself to finding husbands and dowries for the partners of his erotic exploits — a form of philanthropy which, he assures us, he often indulged in with notable success — he might have continued in his career unmolested by the paternal government of his native city, which was notably tolerant in such matters and could also close an indulgent eye to other peccadillos, such as card-sharping, or, to use the politer term of those days, "correcting fortune." But it was fated that Casanova could never "leave good enough alone." It was not long before he fell foul of the magistrato alla infamia for indulging in a practical joke which involved the desecrating of a corpse and which cost the reason of the unfortunate victim on whom this beffa was perpetrated. This affair was complicated by a second one — the corporal punishment inflicted by the incensed Casanova on a young wanton whose favours he had duly contracted for with the mother and who declined to fulfil her obligations.

Listening for once to the advice of his generous benefactor, Senator Bragadin, Giacomo decamped, very regretfully, for, as he says: "I had some pleasant intrigues on hand and I was very lucky at cards." For two years he is away, visiting Verona, Milan, Cremona, Mantua — where he is introduced to "La Fragoletta," and contemplates with pity and repulsion the ruin of the charms which had tempted his father to run away from home and to which he owes the fact that he himself was born in Venice. To vary the usual round of gambling and woman-hunting, he turns magician, sparing no pains for preparing the elaborate incantations which are to raise a treasure hidden in the cellar of a wealthy farmer of Cesena, apparently with the sole object of indulging in his love of mystification and impressing the credulous country people; for, except for philandering with the farmer's pretty daughter and selling the magic sheath, manufactured out of an old boot, which was to fit the sword of St. Peter, he seems to have derived little profit out of the adventure.

Doubtless Casanova's own explanation for this aimless undertaking would have been that "his genius" had brought him to Cesena, for it was there he met the mysterious young Frenchwoman

*whom he declares he loved more than any other woman in his life.
The protestations of a Casanova regarding the intensity of his emotions are necessarily not convincing arguments in themselves, but
if he ever was truly in love — and the "if" is justified in the
case of all voluptuaries of his stamp — it was with Henriette, whose
name, whenever he mentions it in his Memoirs, stirs a chord of such
tenderness in the old cynic, that even the sceptical reader cannot
question the sincerity of his feelings. The meeting occurred at the
inn at Cesena, just as he was preparing to start for Naples, under
circumstances worthy of the* opera buffo, *dear to his countrymen:*

The next morning I was awoke by a terrible noise in the
passage, almost at the door of my room.

Getting out of my bed, I open my door to ascertain the cause
of the uproar. I see a troop of *sbirri* at the door of a chamber,
and in that chamber, sitting up in bed, a fine-looking man who
was making himself hoarse by screaming in Latin against that
rabble, the plague of Italy, and against the innkeeper who had
been rascally enough to open the door.

I inquire of the innkeeper what it all means.

"This gentleman," answers the scoundrel, "who, it appears,
can only speak Latin, is in bed with a girl, and the *sbirri* of the
bishop have been sent to know whether she is truly his wife; all
perfectly regular. If she is his wife, he has only to convince
them by showing a certificate of marriage, but if she is not, of
course he must go to prison with her. Yet it need not happen,
for I undertake to arrange everything in a friendly manner for a
few sequins. I have only to exchange a few words with the chief
of the *sbirri*, and they will all go away. If you can speak Latin,
you had better go in, and make him listen to reason."

"Who has broken open the door of his room?"

"Nobody; I have opened it myself with the key, as is my
duty."

"Yes, the duty of a highway robber, but not of an honest innkeeper."

Such infamous dealing roused my indignation, and I made up
my mind to interfere. I enter the room, although I had still
my night-cap on, and inform the gentleman of the cause of the
disturbance. He answers with a laugh that, in the first place, it
was impossible to say whether the person who was in bed with
him was a woman, for that person had only been seen in the

[160]

costume of a military officer, and that, in the second place, he did not think that any human being had a right to compel him to say whether his bed-fellow was his wife or his mistress, even supposing that his companion was truly a woman.

"At all events," he added, "I am determined not to give one crown to arrange the affair, and to remain in bed until my door is shut. The moment I am dressed, I will treat you to an amusing *dénouement* of the comedy. I will drive away all those scoundrels at the point of my sword."

I then see in a corner a broad sword, and a Hungarian costume looking like a military uniform. I ask whether he is an officer.

"I have written my name and profession," he answers, "in the hotel book."

Astonished at the absurdity of the innkeeper, I ask him whether it is so; he confesses it, but adds that the clergy have the right to prevent scandal.

"The insult you have offered to that officer, Mr. Landlord, will cost you very dear."

His only answer is to laugh in my face. Highly enraged at seeing such a scoundrel laugh at me, I take up the officer's quarrel warmly, and ask him to entrust his passport to me for a few minutes.

"I have two," he says; "therefore I can let you have one." And taking the document out of his pocket-book, he hands it to me. The passport was signed by Cardinal Albani; the officer was a captain in a Hungarian regiment belonging to the empress and queen. He was from Rome, on his way to Parma with dispatches from Cardinal Albani Alexander to M. Dutillot, prime minister of the Infante of Parma.

At the same moment, a man burst into the room, speaking very loudly, and asked me to tell the officer that the affair must be settled at once, because he wanted to leave Cesena immediately.

"Who are you?" I asked the man.

He answered that he was the *vetturino* whom the captain had engaged. I saw that it was a regular put-up thing, and begged the captain to let me attend to the business, assuring him that I would settle it to his honour and advantage.

"Do exactly as you please," he said.

Then turning towards the *vetturino*, I ordered him to bring up the captain's luggage, saying that he would be paid at once. When he had done so, I handed him eight sequins out of my own purse, and made him give me a receipt in the name of the captain, who could only speak German, Hungarian, and Latin. The *vetturino* went away, and the *sbirri* followed him in the greatest consternation, except two who remained.

"Captain," I said to the Hungarian, "keep your bed until I return. I am going now to the bishop to give him an account of these proceedings, and make him understand that he owes you some reparation. Besides, General Spada is here, and . . ."

"I know him," interrupted the captain, "and if I had been aware of his being in Cesena, I would have shot the landlord when he opened my door to these scoundrels."

I hurried over my toilet, and without waiting for my hair to be dressed I proceeded to the bishop's palace, and making a great deal of noise I almost compelled the servants to take me to his room. A lackey who was at the door informed me that his lordship was still in bed.

"Never mind, I cannot wait."

I pushed him aside and entered the room. I related the whole affair to the bishop, exaggerating the uproar, making much of the injustice of such proceedings, and railing at a vexatious police daring to molest travellers and to insult the sacred rights of individuals and nations.

The bishop without answering me referred me to his chancellor, to whom I repeated all I had said to the bishop, but with words calculated to irritate rather than to soften, and certainly not likely to obtain the release of the captain. I even went so far as to threaten, and I said that if I were in the place of the officer I would demand a public reparation. The priest laughed at my threats; it was just what I wanted, and after asking me whether I had taken leave of my senses, the chancellor told me to apply to the captain of the *sbirri*.

"I shall go to somebody else," I said, "reverend sir, besides the captain of the *sbirri*."

Delighted at having made matters worse, I left him and proceeded straight to the house of General Spada; but being told that he could not be seen before eight o'clock, I returned to the inn.

The state of excitement in which I was, the ardour with which I had made the affair mine, might have led anyone to suppose that my indignation had been roused only by disgust at seeing an odious persecution perpetrated upon a stranger by an unrestrained, immoral, and vexatious police; but why should I deceive the kind reader, to whom I have promised to tell the truth? I must therefore say that my indignation was real, but my ardour was excited by another feeling of a more personal nature. I fancied that the woman concealed under the bedclothes was a beauty; I longed to see her face, which shame, most likely, had prevented her from showing. She had heard me speak, and the good opinion that I had of myself did not leave the shadow of a doubt in my mind that she would prefer me to her captain.

The door of the room being still open, I went in and related to the captain all I had done, assuring him that in the course of the day he would be at liberty to continue his journey at the bishop's expense, for the general would not fail to obtain complete satisfaction for him. He thanked me warmly, gave back the eight ducats I had paid for him, and said that he would not leave the city till the next day.

"From what country," I asked him, "is your travelling companion?"

"From France, and he only speaks his native language."

"Then you speak French?"

"Not one word."

"That is amusing! Then you converse in pantomime?"

"Exactly."

"I pity you, for it is a difficult language."

"Yes, to express the various shades of thought, but in the material part of our intercourse we understand each other quite well."

"May I invite myself to breakfast with you?"

"Ask my friend whether he has any objection."

"Amiable companion of the captain," I said in French, "will you kindly accept me as a third guest at the breakfast-table?"

At these words I saw coming out of the bed-clothes a lovely head, with dishevelled hair, and a blooming, laughing face which, although it was crowned with a man's cap, left no doubt that the captain's friend belonged to that sex without which man would be the most miserable animal on earth.

Delighted with the graceful creature, I told her that I had been happy enough to feel interested in her even before I had seen her, and that now that I had the pleasure of seeing her, I could but renew with greater zeal all my efforts to serve her.

She answered me with the grace and the animation which are the exclusive privilege of her native country, and retorted my argument in the most witty manner; I was already under the charm. My request was granted; I went out to order breakfast, and to give them an opportunity of making themselves comfortable in bed, for they were determined not to get up until the door of their room was closed again.

The waiter came, and I went in with him; I found my lovely Frenchwoman wearing a blue coat, with her hair badly arranged like a man's, but very charming even in that strange costume. I longed to see her up. She ate her breakfast without once interrupting the officer, who was speaking to me, but to whom I was not listening, or listening with very little attention, for I was in a sort of ecstatic trance.

Immediately after breakfast, I called on the general, and related the affair to him, enlarging upon it in such a manner as to pique his martial pride. I told him that, unless he settled the matter himself, the Hungarian captain was determined to send an express to the cardinal immediately. But my eloquence was unnecessary, for the general liked to see priests attend to the business of Heaven, but he could not bear them to meddle in temporal affairs.

"I shall," he said, "immediately put a stop to this ridiculous comedy, and treat it in a very serious manner."

"Go at once to the inn," he said to his aide-de-camp, "invite that officer and his companion to dine with me to-day, and repair afterwards to the bishop's palace. Give him notice that the officer who has been so grossly insulted by his *sbirri* shall not leave the city before he has received a complete apology, and whatever sum of money he may claim as damages. Tell him that the notice comes from me, and that all the expenses incurred here by the officer shall be paid by him."

What pleasure it was for me to listen to these words! In my vanity, I fancied I had almost prompted them to the general. I accompanied the aide-de-camp, and introduced him to the captain, who received him with the joy of a soldier meeting a comrade. The adjutant gave him the general's invitation for him and his companion, and asked him to write down what satisfaction he wanted, as well as the amount of damages he claimed. At the sight of the general's adjutant, the *sbirri* had quickly vanished. I handed to the captain pen, paper, and ink, and he wrote his claim in pretty good Latin for a native of Hungary. The excellent fellow absolutely refused to ask for more than thirty sequins, in spite of all I said to make him claim one hundred. He was likewise a great deal too easy as to the satisfaction he demanded, for all he asked was to see the landlord and the *sbirri* beg his pardon on their knees in the presence of the general's adjutant. He threatened the bishop to send an express to Rome to Cardinal Alexander unless his demands were complied with within two hours, and to remain in Cesena at the rate of ten sequins a day at the bishop's expense.

The officer left us, and a moment afterwards the landlord came in respectfully, to inform the captain that he was free, but the captain having begged me to tell the scoundrel that he owed him a sound thrashing, he lost no time in gaining the door.

I left my friends alone to get dressed, and to attend to my own toilet, as I dined with them at the general's. An hour afterwards I found them ready in their military costumes. The uniform of the Frenchwoman was of course a fancy one, but very elegant. The moment I saw her, I gave up all idea of Naples, and decided upon accompanying the two friends to Parma. The beauty of the lovely Frenchwoman had already captivated me. The captain was certainly on the threshold of sixty, and, as a matter of course, I thought such a union very badly assorted. I imagined that the affair which I was already concocting in my brain could be arranged amicably.

The adjutant came back with a priest sent by the bishop, who told the captain that he should have the satisfaction as well as the damages he had claimed, but that he must be content with fifteen sequins.

"Thirty or nothing," dryly answered the Hungarian. They were at last given to him, and thus the matter ended. The victory was due to my exertions, and I had won the friendship of the captain and of his lovely companion.

In order to guess, even at first sight, that the friend of the worthy captain was not a man, it was enough to look at the hips. She was too well made as a woman ever to pass for a man, and the women who disguise themselves in a male attire, and boast of being like men, are very wrong, for by such a boast they confess themselves deficient in one of the greatest perfections appertaining to woman.

A little before dinner-time we repaired to General Spada's mansion, and the general presented the two officers to all the ladies. Not one of them was deceived in the young officer, but, being already acquainted with the adventure, they were all delighted to dine with the hero of the comedy, and treated the handsome officer exactly as if he had truly been a man, but I am bound to confess that the male guests offered the Frenchwoman homages more worthy of her sex.

Madame Querini alone did not seem pleased, because the lovely stranger monopolised the general attention, and it was a blow to her vanity to see herself neglected. She never spoke to her, except to show off her French, which she could speak well. The poor captain scarcely opened his lips, for no one cared to speak Latin, and the general had not much to say in German.

An elderly priest, who was one of the guests, tried to justify the conduct of the bishop by assuring us that the innkeeper and the sbirri had acted only under the orders of the Holy Office.

"That is the reason," he said, "for which no bolts are allowed in the rooms of the hotels, so that strangers may not shut themselves up in their chambers. The Holy Inquisition does not allow a man to sleep with any woman but his wife."

Twenty years later I found all the doors in Spain with a bolt outside, so that travellers were, as if they had been in prison, exposed to the outrageous molestation of nocturnal visits from the police. That disease is so chronic in Spain that it threatens to overthrow the monarchy some day, and I should not be astonished if one fine morning the Grand Inquisitor was to have the king shaved, and to take his place.

The conversation was animated, and the young female officer was entertaining everybody, even Madame Querini, although she hardly took the trouble of concealing her spleen.

"It seems strange," she remarked, "that you and the captain should live together without ever speaking to each other."

"Why, madam? We understand one another perfectly, for

speech is of very little consequence in the kind of business we do together."

That answer, given with graceful liveliness, made everybody laugh, except Madame Querini-Juliette, who, foolishly assuming the air of a prude, thought that its meaning was too clearly expressed.

"I do not know any kind of business," she said, "that can be transacted without the assistance of the voice or the pen."

"Excuse me, madam, there are some: playing at cards, for instance, is a business of that sort."

"Are you always playing?"

"We do nothing else. We play the game of the Pharaoh (faro), and I hold the bank."

Everybody, understanding the shrewdness of this evasive answer, laughed again, and Juliette herself could not help joining in the general merriment.

"But tell me," said Count Spada, "does the bank receive much?"

"As for the deposits, they are of so little importance that they are hardly worth mentioning."

No one ventured upon translating that sentence for the benefit of the worthy captain. The conversation continued in the same amusing style, and all the guests were delighted with the graceful wit of the charming officer.

Late in the evening I took leave of the general, and wished him a pleasant journey.

"Adieu," he said, "I wish you a pleasant journey to Naples, and I hope you will enjoy yourself there."

"Well, general, I am not going to Naples immediately; I have changed my mind and intend to proceed to Parma, where I wish to see the Infante. I also wish to constitute myself the interpreter of these two officers who know nothing of Italian."

"Ah, young man! opportunity makes the thief, does it not? Well, if I were in your place, I would do the same."

I also bade farewell to Madame Querini, who asked me to write to her from Bologna. I gave her a promise to do so, but without meaning to fulfil it.

I had felt interested in the young Frenchwoman when she was hiding under the bed-clothes; she had taken my fancy the moment she had shown her features, and still more when I had seen

her dressed. She completed her conquest at the dinner-table by
the display of a wit which I greatly admired. It is rare in Italy,
and seems to belong generally to the daughters of France. I did
not think it would be very difficult to win her love, and I resolved on trying. Putting my self-esteem on one side, I fancied
I would suit her much better than the old Hungarian, a very
pleasant man for his age, but who, after all, carried his sixty
years on his face, while my twenty-three were blooming on my
countenance. It seemed to me that the captain himself would
not raise any great objection, for he seemed one of those men
who, treating love as a matter of pure fancy, accept all circumstances easily, and give way good-naturedly to all the freaks of
fortune. By becoming the travelling companion of this ill-
matched couple, I should probably succeed in my aims. I never
dreamed of experiencing a refusal at their hands, my company
would certainly be agreeable to them, as they could not exchange
a single word by themselves.

With this idea I asked the captain, as we reached our inn,
whether he intended to proceed to Parma by the public coach or
otherwise.

"As I have no carriage of my own," he answered, "we shall
have to take the coach."

"I have a very comfortable carriage, and I offer you the two
back seats if you have no objection to my society."

"That is a piece of good fortune. Be kind enough to propose
it to Henriette."

"Will you, madam, grant me the favour of accompanying you
to Parma?"

"I should be delighted, for we could have some conversation;
but take care, sir, your task will not be an easy one; you will
often find yourself obliged to translate for both of us."

"I shall do so with great pleasure; I am only sorry that the
journey is not longer. We can arrange everything at supper-
time; allow me to leave you now as I have some business to
settle."

My business was in reference to a carriage, for the one I had
boasted of existed only in my imagination. I went to the most
fashionable coffee-house, and, as good luck would have it, heard
that there was a travelling carriage for sale, which no one would
buy because it was too expensive. Two hundred sequins were

asked for it, although it had but two seats and a bracket-stool for a third person. It was just what I wanted. I called at the place where it could be seen; I found a very fine English carriage which could not have cost less than two hundred guineas. Its noble proprietor was then at supper, so I sent him my name, requesting him not to dispose of his carriage until the next morning, and I went back to the hotel well pleased with my discovery. At supper I arranged with the captain that we would not leave Cesena till after dinner on the following day, and the conversation was almost entirely a dialogue between Henriette and myself; it was my first talk with a Frenchwoman. I thought this young creature more and more charming, yet I could not suppose her to be anything else but an adventuress, and I was astonished at discovering in her those noble and delicate feelings which denote a good education. However, as such an idea would not have suited the views I had about her, I rejected it whenever it presented itself to my mind. Whenever I tried to make her talk about the captain she would change the subject of conversation, or evade my insinuations with a tact and a shrewdness which astonished and delighted me at the same time, for everything she said bore the impress of grace and wit. Yet she did not elude this question:

"At least tell me, madam, whether the captain is your husband or your father."

"Neither one nor the other," she answered, with a smile.

That was enough for me, and in reality what more did I want to know?

The worthy captain had fallen asleep; when he awoke I wished them both good night, and retired to my room with a heart full of love and a mind full of projects. I saw that everything had taken a good turn, and I felt certain of success, for I was young, I enjoyed excellent health, I had money and plenty of daring. I liked the affair all the better because it must come to a conclusion in a few days.

Early the next morning I called upon Count Dandini, the owner of the carriage, and as I passed a jeweller's shop I bought a pair of gold bracelets in Venetian filigree, each five yards long and of rare fineness. I intended them as a present for Javotte.

The moment Count Dandini saw me he recognised me. He had seen me in Padua at the house of his father, who was professor of civil law at the time I was a student there. I bought his carriage on condition that he would send it to me in good repair at one o'clock in the afternoon.

Having completed the purchase, I went to my friend Franzia and my present of the bracelets made Javotte perfectly happy. There was not one girl in Cesena who could boast of possessing a finer pair, and with that present my conscience felt at ease, for it paid the expense I had occasioned during my stay of ten or twelve days at her father's house four times over. But this was not the most important present I offered the family. I made the father take an oath to wait for me, and never to trust in any pretended magician for the necessary operation to obtain the treasure, even if I did not return or give any news of myself for ten years.

"Because," said I to him, "in consequence of the agreement in which I have entered with the spirits watching the treasure, at the first attempt made by any other person, the casket containing the treasure will sink to twice its present depth, that is to say as deep as thirty-five fathoms, and then I shall have myself ten times more difficulty in raising it up to the surface. I cannot state precisely the time of my return, for it depends upon certain combinations which are not under my control; but recollect that the treasure cannot be obtained by anyone but I."

I accompanied my advice with threats of utter ruin to his family if he should ever break his oath. And in this manner I atoned for all I had done, for, far from deceiving the worthy man, I became his benefactor by guarding against the deceit of some cheat who would have cared for his money more than for his daughter. I never saw him again, and most likely he is dead; but knowing the deep impression I left on his mind I am certain that his descendants are even now waiting for me, for the name of Farusi must have remained immortal in that family.

Javotte accompanied me as far as the gate of the city, where I kissed her affectionately, which made me feel that the thunder and lightning had had but a momentary effect upon me; yet I kept control over my senses, and I congratulate myself on doing so to this day. I told her, before bidding her adieu, that, her virginity being no longer necessary for my magic operations, I advised her to get married as soon as possible, if I did not return within three months. She shed a few tears, but promised to follow my advice.

I trust that my readers will approve of the noble manner in which I concluded my magic business; I hardly dare to boast of it, but I think I deserve some praise for my behaviour. Perhaps I might have ruined poor Franzia with a light heart, had I not possessed a well-filled purse. I do not wish to inquire whether any young man, having intelligence, loving pleasure, and placed in the same position, would not have done the same, but I beg my readers to address that question to themselves.

As for Capitani, to whom I sold the sheath of St. Peter's knife for rather more than it was worth, I confess that I have not yet repented on his account; for Capitani thought he had duped me in accepting it as security for the amount he gave me, and the count, his father, valued it until his death as more precious than the finest diamond in the world. Dying with such a firm belief, he died rich, and I shall die a poor man. Let the reader judge which of the two made the best bargain. But I must return now to my future travelling companions.

As soon as I had reached the inn, I prepared everything for our departure, for which I was now longing. Henriette could not open her lips without my discovering some fresh perfection, for her wit delighted me even more than her beauty. It struck me that the old captain was pleased with all the attention I showed her, and it seemed evident to me that she would not be sorry to exchange her elderly lover for me. I had all the better right to think so, inasmuch as I was perfection from a physical point of view, and I appeared to be wealthy, although I had no servant. I told Henriette that, for the sake of having none, I spent twice as much as a servant would have cost me, that, by my being my own servant, I was certain of being served according to my taste, and I had the satisfaction of having no spy at my heels and no privileged thief to fear. She agreed with everything I said, and it increased my love.

The honest Hungarian insisted upon giving me in advance the amount to be paid for the post-horses at the different stages as far as Parma. We left Cesena after dinner, but not without a contest of politeness respecting the seats. The captain wanted me to occupy the back seat near Henriette, but the reader will understand how much better the seat opposite to her suited me; therefore I insisted upon taking the bracket-seat, and had the double advantage of showing my politeness, and of having constantly

and without difficulty before my eyes the lovely woman whom
I adored.

My happiness would have been too great if there had been no
drawback to it. But where can we find roses without thorns?
When the charming Frenchwoman uttered some of those witty
sayings which proceed so naturally from the lips of her countrywomen, I could not help pitying the sorry face of the poor Hungarian, and, wishing to make him share my mirth, I would
undertake to translate in Latin Henriette's sallies; but far from
making him merry, I often saw his face bear a look of astonishment, as if what I had said seemed to him rather flat. I had to
acknowledge to myself that I could not speak Latin as well as
she spoke French, and this was indeed the case. The last thing
which we learn in all languages is wit, and wit never shines so
well as in jests. I was thirty years of age before I began to laugh
in reading Terence, Plautus, and Martial.

Something being the matter with the carriage, we stopped
at Forli to have it repaired. After a very cheerful supper, I
retired to my room to go to bed, thinking of nothing else but of
the charming woman by whom I was so completely captivated.
Along the road, Henriette had struck me as so strange that I
would not sleep in the second bed in their room. I was afraid
lest she should leave her old comrade to come to my bed and
sleep with me, and I did not know how far the worthy captain
would have put up with such a joke. I wished, of course,
to possess that lovely creature, but I wanted everything to
be settled amicably, for I felt some respect for the brave
officer.

Henriette had nothing but the military costume in which she
stood, not any woman's linen, not even one chemise. For a
change she took the captain's shirt. Such a state of things was
so new to me that the situation seemed to me a complete enigma.

In Bologna, excited by an excellent supper and by the amorous
passion which was every hour burning more fiercely in me, I
asked her by what singular adventure she had become the friend
of the honest fellow who looked her father rather than her lover.

"If you wish to know," she answered, with a smile, "ask him
to relate the whole story himself, only you must request him not
to omit any of the particulars."

Of course I applied at once to the captain, and, having first ascertained by signs that the charming Frenchwoman had no objection, the good man spoke to me thus:

"A friend of mine, an officer in the army, having occasion to go to Rome, I solicited a furlough of six months, and accompanied him. I seized with great delight the opportunity of visiting a city the name of which has a powerful influence on the imagination, owing to the memories of the past attached to it. I did not entertain any doubt that the Latin language was spoken there in good society, at least as generally as in Hungary. But I was indeed greatly mistaken, for nobody can speak it, not even the priests, who only pretend to write it, and it is true that some of them do so with great purity. I was therefore rather uncomfortable during my stay in Rome, and with the exception of my eyes my senses remained perfectly inactive. I had spent a very tedious month in that city, the ancient queen of the world, when Cardinal Albani gave my friend dispatches for Naples. Before leaving Rome, he introduced me to his eminence, and his recommendation had so much influence that the cardinal promised to send me very soon with dispatches for the Duke of Parma, Piacenza, and Guastella, assuring me that all my travelling expenses would be defrayed. As I wished to see the harbour called in former times *Centum cellæ* and now *Civita-Vecchia*, I gave up the remainder of my time in that visit, and I proceeded there with a cicerone who spoke Latin.

"I was loitering about the harbour when I saw, coming out of a tartan, an elderly officer and this young woman dressed as she is now. Her beauty struck me; but I should not have thought any more about it, if the officer had not put up at my inn, and in an apartment over which I had a complete view whenever I opened my window. In the evening I saw the couple taking supper at the same table, but I remarked that the elderly officer never addressed a word to the young one. When the supper was over, the disguised girl left the room, and her companion did not lift his eyes from a letter which he was reading, as it seemed to me, with the deepest attention. Soon afterwards the officer closed the windows, the light was put out, and I suppose my neighbours went to bed. The next morning, being up early as is my habit, I saw the officer go out, and the girl remained alone in the room.

"I sent my cicerone, who was also my servant, to tell the

girl in the garb of an officer that I would give her ten sequins for an hour's conversation. He fulfilled my instructions, and on his return he informed me that her answer, given in French, had been to the effect that she would leave for Rome immediately after breakfast, and that, once in that city, I should easily find some opportunity of speaking to her.

"'I can find out from the *vetturino*,' said my cicerone, 'where they put up in Rome, and I promise you to inquire of him.'

"She left Civita-Vecchia with the elderly officer, and I returned home on the following day.

"Two days afterwards the cardinal gave me the dispatches, which were addressed to M. Dutillot, the French minister, with a passport and the money necessary for the journey. He told me, with great kindness, that I need not hurry on the road.

"I had almost forgotten the handsome adventuress, when, two days before my departure, my cicerone gave me the information that he had found out where she lived, and that she was with the same officer. I told him to try to see her, and to let her know that my departure was fixed for the day after the morrow. She sent me word by him that, if I would inform her of the hour of my departure, she would meet me outside of the gate, and get into the coach with me to accompany me on my way. I thought the arrangement very ingenious; and during the day I sent the cicerone to tell her the hour at which I intended to leave, and where I would wait for her outside of the Porto del Popolo. She came at the appointed time, and we have remained together ever since. As soon as she was seated near me, she made me understand by signs that she wanted to dine with me. You may imagine what difficulty we had in understanding one another, but we guessed somehow the meaning expressed by our pantomime, and I accepted the adventure with delight.

"We dined gaily together, speaking without understanding; but after the dessert we comprehended each other very well. I fancied that I had seen the end of it, and you may imagine how surprised I was when, upon my offering her the ten sequins, she refused most positively to take any money, making me understand that she would rather go with me to Parma, because she had some business in that city, and did not want to return to Rome.

"The proposal was, after all, rather agreeable to me; I consented to her wishes. I only regretted my inability to make her understand that, if she was followed by anyone from Rome, and if that person wanted to take her back, I was not in a position to defend her against violence. I was also sorry that, with our mutual ignorance of the language spoken by each of us, we had no opportunity of conversation, for I should have been greatly pleased to hear her adventures, which, I think, must be interesting. You can, of course, guess that I have no idea of who she can be. I only know she calls herself Henriette, that she must be a Frenchwoman, that she is as gentle as a turtle-dove, that she has evidently received a good education, and that she enjoys good health. She is witty and courageous, as we have both seen, I in Rome and you in Cesena at General Spada's table. If she would tell you her history, and allow you to translate it for me in Latin, she would indeed please me much, for I am sincerely her friend, and I can assure you that it will grieve me to part from her in Parma. Please to tell her that I intend to give her the thirty sequins I received from the Bishop of Cesena, and that if I were rich I would give her more substantial proofs of my tender affection. Now, sir, I shall feel obliged to you if you will explain it all to her in French."

I asked her whether she would feel offended if I gave her an exact translation; she assured me that, on the contrary, she wished me to speak openly, and I told her literally what the captain had related to me.

With a noble frankness which a slight shade of shame rendered more interesting, Henriette confirmed the truth of her friend's narrative, but she begged me to tell him that she could not grant his wish respecting the adventures of her life.

"Be good enough to inform him," she added, "that the same principle which forbids me to utter a falsehood, does not allow me to tell the truth. As for the thirty sequins which he intends to give me, I will not accept even one of them, and he would deeply grieve me by pressing them upon me. The moment we reach Parma I wish him to allow me to lodge wherever I may please, to make no inquiries whatever about me, and, in case he should happen to meet me, to crown his great kindness to me by not appearing to have ever known me."

As she uttered the last words of this short speech, which she had delivered very seriously and with a mixture of modesty and resolution, she kissed her elderly friend in a manner which indicated esteem and gratitude rather than love. The captain, who did not know why she was kissing him, was deeply grieved when I translated what Henriette had said. He begged me to tell her that, if he was to obey her with an easy conscience, he must know whether she would have everything she required in Parma.

"You can assure him," she answered, "that he need not entertain any anxiety about me."

This conversation had made us all very sad; we remained for a long time thoughtful and silent, until, feeling the situation to be painful, I rose, wishing them good night, and I saw that Henriette's face wore a look of great excitement.

As soon as I found myself alone in my room, deeply moved by conflicting feelings of love, surprise, and uncertainty, I began to give vent to my feelings in a kind of soliloquy, as I always do when I am strongly excited by anything; thinking is not, in those cases, enough for me; I must speak aloud, and I throw so much action, so much animation into these monologues that I forget I am alone. What I knew now of Henriette had upset me altogether.

"Who can she be?" I said, speaking to the walls; "this girl who seems to have the most elevated feelings under the veil of the most cynical libertinism. She says that in Parma she wishes to remain perfectly unknown, her own mistress, and I cannot, of course, flatter myself that she will not place me under the same restrictions as the captain to whom she has already abandoned herself. Good-bye to my expectations, to my money, and my illusions! But who is she — what is she? She must have either a lover or a husband in Parma, or she must belong to a respectable family; or, perhaps, thanks to a boundless love for debauchery and to her confidence in her own charms, she intends to set fortune, misery, and degradation at defiance, and to try to enslave some wealthy nobleman! But that would be the plan of a madwoman or of a person reduced to utter despair, and it does not seem to be the case with Henriette. Yet she possesses nothing. True; but she refused, as if she had been provided with all she needed, the kind assistance of a man who has the right to offer it, and from whom in sooth she can accept without blushing, since she has not been ashamed to grant him favours with which love had nothing to do. Does she think that it is less shameful for a woman to abandon herself to the desires of a man unknown and unloved than to receive a present from an esteemed friend, and particularly at the eve of finding herself in the street, entirely destitute, in the middle of a foreign city, amongst people whose language she cannot even speak? Perhaps she thinks that such conduct will justify the *faux pas* of which she has been guilty with the captain, and give him to understand that she had abandoned herself to him only for the sake of escaping from the officer with whom she was in Rome. But she ought to be quite certain that the captain does not entertain any other idea; he shows himself so reasonable that it is impossible to suppose that he ever admitted the possibility of having inspired her with a violent passion, because she had seen him once through a window in Civita-Vecchia. She might possibly be right, and feel herself justified in her conduct towards the captain, but it is not the same with me, for with her intelligence she must be aware that I would not have travelled with them if she had been indifferent to me, and she must know that there is but one way in which she can obtain my pardon. She may be endowed with many virtues, but she has not the only one which could prevent me from wishing the reward which every man expects to receive at the hands of the woman he loves. If she wants to assume prudish manners towards me and to make a dupe of me, I am bound in honour to show her how much she is mistaken."

After this monologue, which had made me still more angry, I made up my mind to have an explanation in the morning before our departure.

"I shall ask her," said I to myself, "to grant me the same favours which she has so easily granted to her old captain, and if I meet with a refusal the best revenge will be to show her a cold and profound contempt until our arrival in Parma."

I felt sure that she could not refuse me some marks of real or of pretended affection, unless she wished to make a show of a modesty which certainly did not belong to her, and, knowing that her modesty would only be all pretence, I was determined not to be a mere toy in her hands.

As for the captain, I felt certain, from what he had told me, that he would not be angry with me if I risked a declaration, for as a sensible man he could only assume a neutral position.

Satisfied with my wise reasoning, and with my mind full

made up, I fell asleep. My thoughts were too completely absorbed by Henriette for her not to haunt my dreams; but the dream which I had throughout the night was so much like reality that, on awaking, I looked for her in my bed, and my imagination was so deeply struck with the delights of that night that, if the door had not been fastened with a bolt, I should have believed that she had left me during my sleep to resume her place near the worthy Hungarian.

When I was awake I found that the happy dream of the night had turned my love for the lovely creature into a perfect amorous frenzy, and it could not be otherwise. Let the reader imagine a poor devil going to bed broken down with fatigue and starvation; he succumbs to sleep, that most imperative of all human wants, but in his dream he finds himself before a table covered with every delicacy; what will then happen? Why, a very natural result. His appetite, much more lively than on the previous day, does not give him a minute's rest — he must satisfy it or die of sheer hunger.

I dressed myself, resolved on making sure of the possession of the woman who had inflamed all my senses, even before resuming our journey.

"If I do not succeed," I said to myself, "I will not go one step further."

But, in order not to offend against propriety, and not to deserve the reproaches of an honest man, I felt that it was my duty to have an explanation with the captain in the first place.

I fancy that I hear one of those sensible, calm, passionless readers, who have had the advantage of what is called a youth without storms, or one of those whom old age has forced to become virtuous, exclaim:

"Can anyone attach so much importance to such nonsense?"

Age has calmed my passions down by rendering them powerless, but my heart has not grown old, and my memory has kept all the freshness of youth; and far from considering that sort of thing a mere trifle, my only sorrow, dear reader, arises from the fact that I have not the power to practise, to the day of my death, that which has been the principal affair of my life!

When I was ready I repaired to the chamber occupied by my two travelling companions, and after paying them the usual morning compliments I told the officer that I was deeply in love with Henriette, and I asked him whether he would object to my trying to obtain her as my mistress.

"The reason for which she begs you," I added, "to leave her in Parma, and not to take any further notice of her, must be that she hopes to meet some lover of hers there. Let me have half an hour's conversation with her, and I flatter myself I can persuade her to sacrifice that lover for me. If she refuses me, I remain here; you will go with her to Parma, where you will leave my carriage at the post, only sending me a receipt, so that I can claim it whenever I please."

"As soon as breakfast is over," said the excellent man, "I shall go and visit the institute, and leave you alone with Henriette. I hope you may succeed, for I should be delighted to see her under your protection when I part with her. Should she persist in her first resolution, I could easily find a *vetturino* here, and you could keep your carriage. I thank you for your proposal, and it will grieve me to leave you."

Highly pleased at having accomplished half of my task, and at seeing myself near the *dénouement*, I asked the lovely Frenchwoman whether she would like to see the sights of Bologna.

"I should like it very much," she said, "if I had some other clothes; but with such a costume as this I do not care to show myself about the city."

"Then you do not want to go out?"

"No."

"Can I keep you company?"

"That would be delightful."

The captain went out immediately after breakfast. The moment he had gone I told Henriette that her friend had left us alone purposely, so as to give me the opportunity of a private interview with her.

"Tell me now whether you intended the order which you gave him yesterday to forget you, never to inquire after you, and even not to know you if he happened to meet you, from the time of our arrival in Parma, for me as well as for him."

"It is not an order that I gave him; I have no right to do so, and I could not so far forget myself; it is only a prayer I addressed to him, a service which circumstances have compelled me to claim at his hands, and as he has no right to refuse me, I never entertained any doubt of his granting my demand. As

[179]

far as you are concerned, it is certain that I should have addressed the same prayer to you if I had thought that you had any views about me. You have given me some marks of your friendship, but you must understand that if, under the circumstances, I am likely to be injured by the kind attentions of the captain, yours would injure me much more. If you have any friendship for me, you would have felt all that."

"As you know that I entertain great friendship for you, you cannot possibly suppose that I would leave you alone, without money, without resources, in the middle of a city where you cannot even make yourself understood. Do you think that a man who feels for you the most tender affection can abandon you when he has been fortunate enough to make your acquaintance, when he is aware of the sad position in which you are placed? If you think such a thing possible, you must have a very false idea of friendship, and should such a man grant your request, he would only prove that he is not your friend."

"I am certain that the captain is my friend; yet you have heard him, he will obey me, and forget me."

"I do not know what sort of affection that honest man feels for you, or how far he can rely upon the control he may have over himself, but I know that if he can grant you what you have asked from him, his friendship must be of a nature very different to mine, for I am bound to tell you that it is not only impossible for me to afford you willingly the strange gratification of abandoning you in your position, but even that, if I go to Parma, you could not possibly carry out your wishes, because I love you so passionately that you must promise to be mine, or I must remain here. In that case you must go to Parma alone with the captain, for I feel that, if I accompanied you any further, I should soon be the most wretched of men. I could not bear to see you with another lover, with a husband, not even in the midst of your family; in fact, I would fain see you and live with you for ever. Let me tell you, lovely Henriette, that if it is possible for a Frenchman to forget, an Italian cannot do it, at least if I judge from my own feelings. I have made up my mind, you must be good enough to decide now, and tell me whether I am to accompany you or to remain here. Answer yes or no; if I remain here it is all over. I shall leave for Naples to-morrow, and I know I shall be cured in time of the mad passion I feel for you; but if you tell me that I can accompany you to Parma, you must promise me that your heart will for ever belong to me alone. I must be the only one to possess you, but I am ready to accept as a condition, if you like, that you shall not crown my happiness until you have judged me worthy of it by my attentions and by my loving care. Now, be kind enough to decide before the return of the too happy captain. He knows all, for I have told him what I feel."

"And what did he answer?"

"That he would be happy to see you under my protection. But what is the meaning of that smile playing on your lips?"

"Pray, allow me to laugh, for I have never in my life realised the idea of a furious declaration of love. Do you understand what it is to say to a woman in a declaration which ought to be passionate, but at the same time tender and gentle, the following terrible words: 'Madam, make your choice, either one or the other, and decide instanter!' Ha! ha! ha!"

"Yes, I understand perfectly; it is neither gentle, nor gallant, nor pathetic, but it is passionate. Remember that this is a serious matter, and that I have never yet found myself so much pressed by time. Can you, on your side, realise the painful position of a man who, being deeply in love, finds himself compelled to take a decision which may perhaps decide issues of life and death? Be good enough to remark that, in spite of the passion raging in me, I do not fail in the respect I owe you; that the resolution I intend to take, if you should persist in your original decision, is not a threat, but an effort worthy of a hero, which ought to call for your esteem. I beg of you to consider that we cannot afford to lose time. The word "choose" must not sound harshly in your ears, since it leaves my fate as well as yours entirely in your hands. To feel certain of my love, do you want to see me kneeling before you like a simpleton, crying and entreating you to take pity on me? No, madam, that would certainly displease you, and it would not help me. I am conscious of being worthy of your love, I therefore ask for that feeling and not for pity. Leave me, if I displease you, but let me go away; for if you are humane enough to wish that I should forget you, allow me to go far away from you so as to make my sorrow less immense. Should I follow you to Parma, I would not answer for myself, for I might give way to my despair. Consider everything well,

I beseech you; you would indeed be guilty of great cruelty, were you to answer now: 'Come to Parma, although I must beg of you not to see me in that city.' Confess that you cannot, in all fairness, give me such an answer; am I not right?"

"Certainly, if you truly love me."

"Good God! if I love you? Oh, yes! believe me, my love is immense, sincere! Now, decide my fate."

"What! always the same song?"

"Yes."

"But are you aware that you look very angry?"

"No, for it is not so; I am only in a state of uncontrollable excitement, in one of the decisive hours of my life, a prey to the most fearful anxiety. I ought to curse my whimsical destiny and the *sbirri* of Cesena (may God curse them, too!), for, without them, I should never have known you."

"Are you, then, so very sorry to have made my acquaintance?"

"Have I not some reason to be so?"

"No, for I have not given you my decision yet."

"Now I breathe more freely, for I am sure you will tell me to accompany you to Parma."

"Yes, come to Parma."

The reader can easily guess that there was a change as sudden as a transformation in a pantomime, and that the short but magic sentence, "Come to Parma," proved a very fortunate catastrophe, thanks to which I rapidly changed, passing from the tragic to the gentle mood, from the serious to the tender tone. Sooth to say, I fell at her feet, and lovingly pressing her knees I kissed them repeatedly with raptures of gratitude. No more *furore*, no more bitter words; they do not suit the sweetest of all human feelings! Loving, docile, grateful, I swear never to beg for any favour, not even to kiss her hand, until I have shown myself worthy of her precious love! The heavenly creature, delighted to see me pass so rapidly from despair to the most lively tenderness, tells me, with a voice the tone of which breathes of love, to get up from my knees.

"I am sure that you love me," says she, "and be quite certain that I shall leave nothing undone to secure the constancy of your feelings."

Even if she had said that she loved me as much as I adored

her, she would not have been more eloquent, for her words
expressed all that can be felt. My lips were pressed to her
beautiful hands as the captain entered the room. He complimented us with perfect good faith, and I told him, my face
beaming with happiness, that I was going to order the carriage. I left them together, and in a short time we were on our
road, cheerful, pleased, and merry.

Before reaching Reggio the honest captain told me that in his
opinion it would be better for him to proceed to Parma alone,
as, if we arrived in that city all together, it might cause some
remarks, and people would talk about us much less if we were
without him. We both thought him quite right, and we immediately made up our minds to pass the night in Reggio, while the
captain would take a post-chaise and go alone to Parma. According to that arrangement his trunk was transferred to the
vehicle which he hired in Reggio, he bade us farewell and went
away, after having promised to dine with us on the following day
in Parma.

The decision taken by the worthy Hungarian was, doubtless,
as agreeable to my lovely friend as to me, for our delicacy would
have condemned us to a great reserve in his presence. And truly,
under the new circumstances, how were we to arrange for our
lodgings in Reggio? Henriette could not, of course, share the
bed of the captain any more, and she could not have slept with
me as long as he was with us, without being guilty of great im-
modesty. We should all three have laughed at that compulsory
reserve which we would have felt to be ridiculous, but we should,
for all that, have submitted to it. Love is the little impudent
god, the enemy of bashfulness, although he may very often enjoy
darkness and mystery, but if he gives way to it he feels disgraced; he loses three-fourths of his dignity and the greatest
portion of his charms.

Evidently there could be no happiness for Henriette or for me
unless we parted with the person and even with the remembrance
of the excellent captain.

We supped alone; I was intoxicated with a felicity which
seemed too immense, and yet I felt melancholy, but Henriette,
who looked sad likewise, had no reproach to address to me. Our
sadness was in reality nothing but shyness; we loved each other,
but we had had no time to become acquainted. We exchanged

only a few words, there was nothing witty, nothing interesting in our conversation, which struck us both as insipid, and we found more pleasure in the thoughts which filled our minds. We knew that we were going to pass the night together, but we could not have spoken of it openly. What a night! what a delightful creature was that Henriette whom I have loved so deeply, who has made me so supremely happy!

It was only three or four days later that I ventured on asking her what she would have done, without a groat in her possession, having not one acquaintance in Parma, if I had been afraid to declare my love, and if I had gone to Naples. She answered that she would doubtless have found herself in very great difficulties, but that she had all along felt certain of my love, and that she had foreseen what had happened. She added that being impatient to know what I thought of her, she had asked me to translate to the captain what she had expressed respecting her resolution, knowing that he could neither oppose that resolution nor continue to live with her, and that, as she had taken care not to include me in the prayer which she had addressed to him through me, she had thought it impossible that I should fail to ask whether I could be of some service to her, waiting to take a decision until she could have ascertained the nature of my feelings towards her. She concluded by telling me that if she had fallen it was the fault of her husband and of her father-in-law, both of whom she characterised as monsters rather than men.

When we reached Parma, I gave the police the name of Farusi, the same that I had assumed in Cesena; it was the family name of my mother; while Henriette wrote down, "Anne d'Arci, from France." While we were answering the questions of the officer, a young Frenchman, smart and intelligent-looking, offered me his services, and advised me not to put up at the posting-inn, but to take lodgings at d'Andremont's hotel, where I should find good apartments, French cooking, and the best French wines.

Seeing that Henriette was pleased with the proposal, I told the young man to take us there, and we were soon very comfortably lodged. I engaged the Frenchman by the day, and carefully settled all my arrangements with d'Andremont. After that I attended to the housing of my carriage.

Coming in again for a few minutes, I told Henriette that I

would return in time for dinner, and, ordering the servant to remain in the ante-room, I went out alone.

Parma was then groaning under a new government; I had every reason to suppose that there were spies everywhere and under every form; I therefore did not want to have at my heels a valet who might have injured rather than served me. Though I was in my father's native city, I had no acquaintances there, but I knew that I should soon find my way.

When I found myself in the streets, I scarcely could believe that I was in Italy, for everything had a tramontane appearance. I heard nothing but French and Spanish, and those who did not speak one of those languages seemed to be whispering to one another. I was going about at random, looking for a hosier, yet unwilling to inquire where I could find one; at last I saw what I wanted.

I entered the shop, and addressing myself to a stout, good-looking woman, seated behind the counter, I said:

"Madam, I wish to make some purchases."

"Sir, shall I send for someone speaking French?"

"You need not do so, I am an Italian."

"God be praised! Italians are scarce in these days."

"Why scarce?"

"Do you not know that Don Philip has arrived, and that his wife, Madame de France, is on the road?"

"I congratulate you, for it must make trade very good. I suppose that money is plentiful, and that there is abundance of all commodities."

"That is true, but everything is high in price, and we cannot get reconciled to these new fashions. They are a bad mixture of French freedom and Spanish haughtiness which addles our brains. But, sir, what sort of linen do you require?"

"In the first place, I must tell you that I never try to drive a hard bargain, therefore be careful. If you charge me too much, I shall not come again. I want some fine linen for twenty-four chemises, some dimity for stays and petticoats, some muslin, some cambric for pocket-handkerchiefs, and many other articles which I should be very glad to find in your shop, for I am a stranger here, and God knows in what hands I am going to trust myself!"

"You will be in honest ones, if you will give me your confidence."

"I am sure that you deserve it, and I abandon my interests to you. I want likewise to find some needlewomen willing to work in the lady's room, because she requires everything to be made very rapidly."

"And dresses?"

"Yes, dresses, caps, mantles — in fact, everything, for she is naked."

"With money she will soon have all she wants. Is she young?"

"She is four years younger than I; she is my wife."

"Ah! may God bless you! Any children?"

"Not yet, my good lady; but they will come, for we do all that is necessary to have them."

"I have no doubt of it. How pleased I am! Well, sir, I shall send for the very phœnix of all dressmakers. In the meantime, choose what you require; it will amuse you."

I took the best of everything and paid, and the dressmaker making her appearance at that moment, I gave my address, requesting that various sorts of stuff might be sent at once. I told the dressmaker and her daughter, who had come with her, to follow me and to carry the linen. On my way to the hotel I bought several pairs of silk stockings, and took with me a boot-maker who lived close by. Oh, what a delightful moment! Henriette, who had not the slightest idea of what I had gone out for, looked at everything with great pleasure, yet without any of those demonstrations which announce a selfish or interested disposition; she showed her gratitude only by the delicate praise which she bestowed upon my taste and upon the quality of the articles I had purchased. She was not more cheerful on account of my presents, but the tender affection with which she looked at me was the best proof of her grateful feelings.

The valet I had hired had entered the room with the shoemaker; Henriette told him quietly to withdraw, and not to come unless he was called. The dressmaker set to work, the shoemaker took her measure, and I told him to bring some slippers. He returned in a short time, and the valet came in again with him without having been called. The shoemaker, who spoke French, was talking the usual nonsense of dealers, when she interrupted him to ask the valet, who was standing familiarly in the room, what he wanted.

"Nothing, madam, I am only waiting for your orders."

"Have I not told you that you would be called when your services were required?"

"I should like to know who is my master, you or the gentleman?"

"Neither," I replied, laughing. "Here are your day's wages. Be off at once."

The shoemaker, seeing that Henriette spoke only French, begged to recommend a teacher of languages.

"What country does he belong to?" she inquired.

"To Flanders, madam," answered Crispin; "he is a very learned man, about fifty years old; he is said to be a good man. He charges three libbre for each lesson of one hour, and six for two hours, but he requires to be paid each time."

"My dear," said Henriette to me, "do you wish me to engage that master?"

"Yes, dearest, it will amuse you."

The shoemaker promised to send the Flemish professor the next morning.

The dressmakers were hard at work, the mother cutting and the daughter sewing, but, as progress could not be too rapid, I told the mother that she would oblige us if she could procure another seamstress who spoke French.

"You shall have one this very day, sir," she answered; and she offered me the services of her own son as a servant, saying that if I took him I should be certain to have neither a thief nor a spy about me, and that he spoke French pretty well. Henriette thought we could not do better than take the young man; of course that was enough to make me consent at once, for the slightest wish of the woman we love is our supreme law. The mother went for him, and she brought back at the same time the half-French dressmaker. It all amused my goddess, who looked very happy.

The young man was about eighteen, pleasant, gentle, and modest. I inquired his name, and he answered that it was Caudagna.

The reader may very likely recollect that my father's native place had been Parma, and that one of his sisters had married a Caudagna. "It would be a curious coincidence," I thought, "if that dressmaker should be my aunt, and my valet my cousin!" but I did not say it aloud.

Henriette asked me if I had any objection to the first dress-maker dining at our table.

"I entreat you, my darling," I answered, "never, for the future, to ask my consent in such trifling matters. Be quite certain, my beloved, that I shall always approve everything you may do."

She smiled and thanked me. I took out my purse, and said to her: "Take these fifty sequins, dearest, to pay for all your small expenses, and to buy the many trifles which I should be sure to forget."

She took the money, assuring me that she was vastly obliged to me.

A short time before dinner the worthy captain made his appearance. Henriette ran to meet him and kissed him, calling him her dear father, and I followed her example by calling him my friend. My beloved little wife invited him to dine with us every day. The excellent fellow, seeing all the women working busily for Henriette, was highly pleased at having procured such a good position for his young adventuress, and I crowned his happiness by telling him that I was indebted to him for my felicity.

Our dinner was delicious, and it proved a cheerful meal. I found out that Henriette was dainty, and my old friend a lover of good wines. I was both, and felt that I was a match for them. We tasted several excellent wines which d'Andremont had recommended, and altogether we had a very good dinner.

The young valet pleased me in consequence of the respectful manner in which he served everyone, his mother as well as his masters. His sister and the other seamstress had dined apart.

We were enjoying our dessert when the hosier was announced, accompanied by another woman and a milliner who could speak French. The other woman had brought patterns of all sorts of dresses. I let Henriette order caps, head-dresses, etc., as she pleased, but I would interfere in the dress department although I complied with the excellent taste of my charming friend. I made her choose four dresses, I was indeed grateful for her ready acceptance of them, for my own happiness was increased in proportion to the pleasure I gave her and the influence I was obtaining over her heart.

Thus did we spend the first day, and we could certainly not have accomplished more.

In the evening, as we were alone at supper, I fancied that her lovely face looked sad; I told her so.

"My darling," she answered, with a voice which went to my heart, "you are spending a great deal of money on me, and if you do so in the hope of my loving you more dearly I must tell you it is money lost, for I do not love you now more than I did yesterday, but I do love you with my whole heart. All you may do that is not strictly necessary pleases me only because I see more and more how worthy you are of me, but it is not needed to make me feel all the deep love which you deserve."

"I believe you, dearest, and my happiness is indeed great if you feel that your love for me cannot be increased. But learn also, delight of my heart, that I have done it all only to try to love you even more than I do, if possible. I wish to see you beautiful and brilliant in the attire of your sex, and if there is one drop of bitterness in the fragrant cup of my felicity, it is a regret at not being able to surround you with the halo which you deserve. Can I be otherwise than delighted, my love, if you are pleased?"

"You cannot for one moment doubt my being pleased, and as you have called me your wife you are right in one way; but if you are not very rich I leave it to you to judge how deeply I ought to reproach myself."

"Ah, my beloved angel! let me, I beg of you, believe myself wealthy, and be quite certain that you cannot possibly be the cause of my ruin. You were born only for my happiness. All I wish is that you may never leave me; tell me whether I can entertain such a hope."

"I wish it myself, dearest; but who can be sure of the future? Are you free? Are you dependent on anyone?"

"I am free in the broadest meaning of that word; I am dependent on no one but you, and I love to be so."

"I congratulate you, and I am very glad of it, for no one can tear you from my arms; but, alas! you know that I cannot say the same as you. I am certain that some persons are, even now, seeking for me, and they will not find it very difficult to secure me if they ever discover where I am. Alas! I feel how miserable I should be if they ever succeeded in dragging me away from you!"

"You make me tremble. Are you afraid of such a dreadful misfortune here?"

"No, unless I should happen to be seen by someone knowing me."

"Are any such persons likely to be here at present?"

"I think not."

"Then do not let our love take alarm; I trust your fears will never be verified. Only, my darling one, you must be as cheerful as you were in Cesena."

"I shall be more truly so now, dear friend. In Cesena I was miserable, while now I am happy. Do not be afraid of my being sad, for I am of a naturally cheerful disposition."

"I suppose that in Cesena you were afraid of being caught by the officer whom you had left in Rome?"

"Not at all; that officer was my father-in-law, and I am quite certain that he never tried to ascertain where I had gone; he was only too glad to get rid of me. I felt unhappy because I could not bear to be a charge on a man whom I could not love, and with whom I could not even exchange one thought. Recollect also that I could not find consolation in the idea that I was ministering to his happiness, for I had only inspired him with a passing fancy which he had himself valued at ten sequins. I could not help feeling that his fancy, once gratified, was not likely at his time of life to become a more lasting sentiment, and I could therefore only be a burden to him, for he was not wealthy. Besides, there was a miserable consideration which increased my secret sorrow. I thought myself bound in duty to caress him, and on his side, as he thought that he ought to pay me in the same money, I was afraid of his ruining his health for me, and that idea made me very unhappy. Having no love for each other, we allowed a foolish feeling of regard to make both of us uncomfortable. We lavished, for the sake of a well-meant but false decorum, that which belongs to love alone. Another thing troubled me greatly; I was afraid lest people might suppose that I was a source of profit to him. That idea made me feel the deepest shame; yet, whenever I thought of it, I could not help admitting that such a supposition, however false, was not wanting in probability. It is owing to that feeling that you found me so reserved towards you, for I was afraid that you might harbour that fearful idea if I allowed you to read in my looks the favourable impression which you had made on my heart."

"Then it was not owing to a feeling of self-love?"

"No, I confess it; for you could but judge me as I deserved. I had been guilty of the folly now known to you because my father-in-law intended to bury me in a convent, and that did not suit my taste. But, dearest friend, you must forgive me if I cannot confide even to you the history of my life."

"I respect your secret, darling; you need not fear any intrusion from me on that subject. All we have to do is to love one another, and not to allow any dread of the future to mar our actual felicity."

The next day, after a night of intense enjoyment, I found myself more deeply in love than before, and the next three months were spent by us in an intoxication of delight.

At nine o'clock the next morning the teacher of Italian was announced. I saw a man of respectable appearance, polite, modest, speaking little but well, reserved in his answers, and with the manners of olden times. We conversed, and I could not help laughing when he said, with an air of perfect good faith, that a Christian could only admit the system of Copernicus as a clever hypothesis. I answered that it was the system of God Himself because it was that of nature, and that it was not in Holy Scripture that the laws of science could be learned.

The teacher smiled in a manner which betrayed the Tartufe, and if I had consulted only my own feelings I should have dismissed the poor man, but I thought that he might amuse Henriette and teach her Italian; after all it was what I wanted from him. My dear wife told him that she would give him six libbre for a lesson of two hours: the libbra of Parma being worth only about three pence, his lessons were not very expensive. She took her first lesson immediately and gave him two sequins, asking him to purchase her some good novels.

Whilst my dear Henriette was taking her lesson, I had some conversation with the dressmaker, in order to ascertain whether she was a relative of mine.

"What does your husband do?" I asked her.

"He is steward to the Marquis of Sissa."

"Is your father still alive?"

"No, sir, he is dead."

"What was his family name?"

"Scotti."

"Are your husband's parents still alive?"

"His father is dead, but his mother is still alive, and resides with her uncle, Canon Casanova."

That was enough; the good woman was my Welsh cousin, and her children were my Welsh nephews. My niece Jeanneton was not pretty, but she appeared to be a good girl. I continued my conversation with the mother, but I changed the topic.

"Are the Parmesans satisfied with being the subjects of a Spanish prince?"

"Satisfied? Well, in that case, we should be easily pleased, for we are now in a regular maze; everything is upset, we do not know where we are. Oh! happy times of the house of Farnese, whither have you departed? The day before yesterday I went to the theatre, and Harlequin made everybody roar with laughter. Well, now, fancy Don Philipo, our new duke, did all he could to remain serious, and when he could not manage it, he would hide his face in his hat, so that people should not see that he was laughing, for it is said that laughter ought never to disturb the grave and stiff countenance of an Infante of Spain, and he would be dishonoured in Madrid if he did not conceal his mirth. What do you think of that? Can such manners suit us? Here we laugh willingly and heartily! Oh! the good Duke Antonio (God rest his soul!) was certainly as great a prince as Duke Philipo, but he did not hide himself from his subjects when he was pleased, and he would sometimes laugh so heartily that he could be heard in the streets. Now we are all in the most fearful confusion, and for the last three months no one in Parma knows what's o'clock."

"Have all the clocks been destroyed?"

"No; but ever since God created the world, the sun has always gone down at half-past five, and at six the bells have always been tolled for the Angelus; all respectable people knew that at that time the candle had to be lit. Now, it is very strange, the sun has gone mad, for he sets every day at a different hour. Our peasants do not know when they are to come to market. All that is called a regulation, but do you know why? Because now everybody knows that dinner is to be eaten at twelve o'clock. A fine regulation, indeed! Under the Farnese we used to eat when we were hungry, and that was much better."

That way of reasoning was certainly singular, but I did not

think it sounded foolish in the mouth of a woman of humble rank. It seems to me that a government ought never to destroy ancient customs abruptly, and that innocent errors ought to be corrected only by degrees.

Henriette had no watch; I felt delighted at the idea of offering her such a present, and I went out to purchase one, but after I had bought a very fine watch, I thought of ear-rings, of a fan, and of many other pretty nicknacks: of course I bought them all at once. She received all those gifts offered by love with a tender delicacy which overjoyed me. She was still with the teacher when I came back.

"I should have been able," he said to me, "to teach your lady heraldry, geography, history, and the use of the globes, but she knows that already. She has received an excellent education."

The teacher's name was Valentin de la Haye; he told me that he was an engineer and professor of mathematics. I shall have to speak of him very often in these Memoirs, and my readers will make his acquaintance by his deeds better than by any portrait I could give of him, so I will merely say that he was a true Tartufe, a worthy pupil of Escobar.

We had a pleasant dinner with our Hungarian friend; Henriette was still wearing the uniform, and I longed to see her dressed as a woman. She expected a dress to be ready for the next day, and she was already supplied with petticoats and chemises.

Henriette was full of wit and a mistress of repartee. The milliner, who was a native of Lyons, came in one morning, and said in French:

"*Madame et monsieur, j'ai l'honneur de vous souhaiter le bonjour.*"

"Why," said my friend, "do you not say *Monsieur et madame?*"

"I have always heard that in society the precedence is given to the ladies."

"But from whom do we wish to receive that honour?"

"From gentlemen, of course."

"And do you not see that women would render themselves ridiculous if they did not grant to men the same that they expect from them. If we wish them never to fail in politeness towards us, we must show them the example."

"Madam," answered the shrewd milliner, "you have taught

[193]

me an excellent lesson, and I will profit by it. *Monsieur et madame, je suis votre servante.*"

This feminine controversy greatly amused me.

Those who do not believe that a woman can make a man happy through the twenty-four hours of the day have never possessed a woman like Henriette. The happiness which filled me, if I can express it in that manner, was much greater when I conversed with her even than when I held her in my arms. She had read much, she had great tact, and her taste was naturally excellent; her judgment was sane, and, without being learned, she could argue like a mathematician, easily and without pretension; and in everything she had that natural grace which is so charming. She never tried to be witty when she said something of importance, but accompanied her words with a smile which imparted to them an appearance of trifling, and brought them within the understanding of all. In that way she would give intelligence even to those who had none, and she won every heart. Beauty without wit offers love nothing but the material enjoyment of its physical charms, whilst witty ugliness captivates by the charms of the mind, and at last fulfils all the desires of the man it has captivated.

Then what was my position during all the time that I possessed my beautiful and witty Henriette? That of a man so supremely happy that I could scarcely realise my felicity!

Let anyone ask a beautiful woman without wit whether she would be willing to exchange a small portion of her beauty for a sufficient dose of wit. If she speaks the truth, she will say, "No, I am satisfied to be as I am." But why is she satisfied? Because she is not aware of her own deficiency. Let an ugly but witty woman be asked if she would change her wit against beauty, and she will not hesitate in saying no. Why? Because, knowing the value of her wit, she is well aware that it is sufficient by itself to make her a queen in any society.

But a learned woman, a blue-stocking, is not the creature to minister to a man's happiness. Positive knowledge is not a woman's province; it is antipathetic to the gentleness of her nature, to the amenity, to the sweet timidity which are the greatest charms of the fair sex; besides, women never carry their learning beyond certain limits, and the tittle-tattle of blue-stockings can dazzle no one but fools. There has never been one great dis-

covery due to a woman. The fair sex is deficient in that vigorous
power which the body lends to the mind, but women are evidently superior to men in simple reasoning, in delicacy of feelings,
and in that species of merit which appertains to the heart rather
than to the mind.

Hurl some idle sophism at a woman of intelligence; she will
not unravel it, but she will not be deceived by it, and, though
she may not say so, she will let you guess that she does not
accept it. A man, on the contrary, if he cannot unravel the
sophism, takes it in a literal sense, and in that respect the
learned woman is exactly the same as man. What a burden a
Madame Dacier must be to a man! May God save every honest man from such!

When the new dress was brought, Henriette told me that she
did not want me to witness the process of her metamorphosis,
and she desired me to go out for a walk until she had resumed
her original form. I obeyed cheerfully, for the slightest wish of
the woman we love is a law, and our very obedience increases our
happiness.

As I had nothing particular to do, I went to a French bookseller in whose shop I made the acquaintance of a witty hunchback; and I must say that a hunchback without wit is a *rara
avis;* I have found it so in all countries. Of course it is not wit
which gives the hump, for, thank God, all witty men are not
humpbacked, but we may well say that, as a general rule, the
hump gives wit, for the very small number of hunchbacks who
have little or no wit only confirms the rule. The one I was
alluding to just now was called Dubois-Chateleraux. He was a
skilful engraver, and director of the Mint of Parma for the
Infante, although that prince could not boast of such an institution.

I spent an hour with the witty hunchback, who showed me
several of his engravings, and I returned to the hotel, where I
found the Hungarian waiting to see Henriette. He did not know
that she would that morning receive us in the attire of her sex.
The door was thrown open, and a beautiful, charming woman
met us with a curtsy full of grace, which no longer reminded us
of the stiffness or of the too great freedom which belong to the
military costume. Her sudden appearance certainly astonished
us, and we did not know what to say or what to do. She invited

us to be seated, looked at the captain in a friendly manner, and
pressed my hand with the warmest affection, but without giving
way any more to that outward familiarity which a young officer
can assume, but which does not suit a well-educated lady. Her
noble and modest bearing soon compelled me to put myself in
unison with her, and I did so without difficulty, for she was not
acting a part, and the way in which she had resumed her natural
character made it easy for me to follow her on that ground.

I was gazing at her with admiration, and urged by a feeling
which I did not take time to analyse, I took her hand to kiss it
with respect; but, without giving me an opportunity of raising
it to my lips, she offered me her lovely mouth; never did a kiss
taste so delicious.

"Am I not then always the same?" said she to me, with deep
feeling.

"No, heavenly creature, and it is so true that you are no
longer the same in my eyes that I could not now use any familiarity towards you. You are no longer the witty, free young
officer who told Madame Querini about the game of Pharoah,
and about the deposits made to your bank by the captain in so
niggardly a manner that they were hardly worth mentioning."

"It is very true that, wearing the costume of my sex, I should
never dare to utter such words. Yet, dearest friend, it does not
prevent my being your Henriette — that Henriette who has in
her life been guilty of three escapades, the last of which would
have utterly ruined me if it had not been for you, but which I
call a delightful error, since it has been the cause of my knowing
you."

Those words moved me so deeply that I was on the point of
throwing myself at her feet, to entreat her to forgive me for not
having shown her more respect; but Henriette, who saw the
state in which I was, and who wanted to put an end to the
pathetic scene, began to shake our poor captain, who sat as
motionless as a statue, and as if he had been petrified. He felt
ashamed at having treated such a woman as an adventuress, for
he knew that what he now saw was not an illusion. He kept
looking at her with great confusion, and bowing most respectfully, as if he wanted to atone for his past conduct towards her.
As for Henriette, she seemed to say to him, but without the
shadow of a reproach:

"I am glad that you think me worth more than ten sequins."

We sat down to dinner, and from that moment she did the honours of the table with the perfect ease of a person who is accustomed to fulfil that difficult duty. She treated me like a beloved husband, and the captain like a respected friend. The poor Hungarian begged me to tell her that if he had seen her, as she was now, in Civita-Vecchia, when she came out of the tartan, he should never have dreamed of dispatching his cicerone to her room.

"Oh! tell him that I do not doubt it. But is it not strange that a poor little female dress should command more respect than the garb of an officer?"

"Pray do not abuse the officer's costume, for it is to it that I am indebted for my happiness."

"Yes," she said, with a loving smile, "as I owe mine to the *sbirri* of Cesena."

We remained for a long time at the table, and our delightful conversation turned upon no other topic than our mutual felicity; if it had not been for the uneasiness of the poor captain, which at last struck us, we should never have put a stop either to the dinner or to our charming prattle.

The happiness I was enjoying was too complete to last long; I was fated to lose it, but I must not anticipate events. Madame de France, wife of the Infante Don Philip, having arrived in Parma, the opera-house was opened, and I engaged a private box, telling Henriette that I intended to take her to the theatre every night. She had several times confessed that she had a great passion for music, and I had no doubt that she would be pleased with my proposal. She had never yet seen an Italian opera, and I felt certain that she wished to ascertain whether the Italian music deserved its universal fame. But I was indeed surprised when she exclaimed:

"What, dearest! You wish to go every evening to the opera?"

"I think, my love, that, if we did not go, we should give some excuse for scandal-mongers to gossip. Yet, should you not like it, you know that there is no need for us to go; do not think of me, for I prefer our pleasant chat in this room to the heavenly concert of the seraphs."

"I am passionately fond of music, darling, but I cannot help trembling at the idea of going out."

"If you tremble, I must shudder; but we ought to go to the opera or leave Parma; let us go to London or to any other place. Give your orders, I am ready to do anything you like."

"Well, take a private box as little exposed as possible."

"How kind you are!"

The box I had engaged was in the second tier, but the theatre being small it was difficult for a pretty woman to escape observation.

I told her so.

"I do not think there is any danger," she answered; "for I have not seen the name of any person of my acquaintance in the list of foreigners which you gave me to read."

Thus did Henriette go to the opera; I had taken care that our box should not be lighted up. It was an opera-buffet, the music of Burellano was excellent, and the singers were very good.

Henriette made no use of her opera-glass except to look on the stage, and nobody paid any attention to us. As she had been greatly pleased with the finale of the second act, I promised to get it for her, and I asked Dubois to procure it for me. Thinking that she could play the harpsichord, I offered to get one, but she told me that she had never touched that instrument.

On the night of the fourth or fifth performance M. Dubois came to our box, and as I did not wish to introduce him to my friend, I only asked what I could do for him. He then handed me the music I had begged him to purchase for me, and I paid him what it had cost, offering him my best thanks. As we were just opposite the ducal box, I asked him, for the sake of saying something, whether he had engraved the portraits of their highnesses. He answered that he had already engraved two medals, and I gave him an order for both, in gold. He promised to let me have them, and left the box. Henriette had not even looked at him, and that was according to all established rules, as I had not introduced him; but the next morning he was announced as we were at dinner. M. de la Haye, who was dining with us, complimented us upon having made the acquaintance of Dubois, and introduced him to his pupil the moment he came into the room. It was then right for Henriette to welcome him, which she did most gracefully.

After she had thanked him for the *partizione*, she begged he would get her some other music, and the artist accepted her request as a favour granted to him.

"Sir," said Dubois to me, "I have taken the liberty of bringing the medals you wished to have; here they are."

On one were the portraits of the Infante and his wife, on the other was engraved only the head of Don Philip. They were both beautifully engraved, and we expressed our just admiration. "The workmanship is beyond all price," said Henriette, "but the gold can be bartered for other gold." "Madam," answered the modest artist, "the medals weigh sixteen sequins." She gave him the amount immediately, and invited him to call again at dinner-time. Coffee was just brought in at that moment, and she asked him to take it with us. Before sweetening his cup, she inquired whether he liked his coffee very sweet.

"Your taste, madam," answered the hunchback, gallantly, "is sure to be mine."

"Then you have guessed that I always drink coffee without sugar; I am glad we have that taste in common."

And she gracefully offered him the cup of coffee without sugar; she then helped de la Haye and me, not forgetting to put plenty of sugar in our cups, and she poured out one for herself exactly like the one she had handed to Dubois. It was much ado for me not to laugh, for my mischievous Frenchwoman, who liked her coffee in the Parisian fashion, that is to say very sweet, was sipping the bitter beverage with an air of delight which compelled the director of the Mint to smile under the infliction. But the cunning hunchback was even with her; accepting the penalty of his foolish compliment, and praising the good quality of the coffee, he boldly declared that it was the only way to taste the delicious aroma of the precious berry.

When Dubois and de la Haye had left us, we both laughed at the trick.

"But," said I to Henriette, "you will be the first victim of your mischief, for whenever he dines with us, you must keep up the joke, in order not to betray yourself."

"Oh! I can easily contrive to drink my coffee well sweetened, and to make him drain the bitter cup."

At the end of one month, Henriette could speak Italian fluently, and it was owing more to the constant practice she had every day with my cousin Jeanneton, who acted as her maid, than to the lessons of Professor de la Haye. The lessons only taught her the rules, and practice is necessary to acquire a language. I have experienced it myself; I learned more French during the too short period that I spent so happily with my charming Henriette than in all the lessons I had taken from Dalacqua.

We had attended the opera twenty times without making any acquaintance, and our life was indeed supremely happy. I never went out without Henriette and always in a carriage; we never received anyone, and nobody knew us. Dubois was the only person, since the departure of the good Hungarian, who sometimes dined with us; I do not reckon de la Haye, who was a daily guest at our table. Dubois felt great curiosity about us; but he was cunning and did not show his curiosity; we were reserved without affectation, and his inquisitiveness was at fault. One day he mentioned to us that the court of the Infante of Parma was very brilliant since the arrival of Madame de France, and that there were many foreigners of both sexes in the city. Then, turning towards Henriette, he said to her:

"Most of the foreign ladies whom we have here are unknown to us."

"Very likely; many of them would not show themselves if they were known."

"Very likely, madam, as you say; but I can assure you that, even if their beauty and the richness of their toilet made them conspicuous, our sovereigns wish for freedom. I still hope, madam, that we shall have the happiness of seeing you at the court of the duke."

"I do not think so, for, in my opinion, it is superlatively ridiculous for a lady to go to the court without being presented, particularly if she has a right to be so."

The last words, on which Henriette had laid a little more stress than upon the first part of her answer, struck our little hunchback dumb, and my friend, improving her opportunity, changed the subject of conversation.

When he had gone we enjoyed the check she had thus given to the inquisitiveness of our guest, but I told Henriette that, in good conscience, she ought to forgive all those whom she rendered curious, because . . . she cut my words short by covering me with loving kisses.

Thus supremely happy, and finding in one another constant satisfaction, we would laugh at those morose philosophers who deny that complete happiness can be found on earth.

"What do they mean, darling — those crazy fools — by saying that happiness is not lasting, and how do they understand that word? If they mean everlasting, immortal, unintermitting, of course they are right; but the life of man not being such, happiness, as a natural consequence, cannot be such either. Otherwise, every happiness is lasting for the very reason that it does exist, and to be lasting it requires only to exist. But if by complete felicity they understand a series of varied and never-interrupted pleasures, they are wrong, because, by allowing after each pleasure the calm which ought to follow the enjoyment of it, we have time to realise happiness in its reality; in other words, those necessary periods of repose are a source of true enjoyment, because, thanks to them, we enjoy the delight of recollection, which increases twofold the reality of happiness. Man can be happy only when in his own mind he realises his happiness, and calm is necessary to give full play to his mind; therefore without calm man would truly never be completely happy, and pleasure, in order to be felt, must cease to be active. Then what do they mean by that word "lasting"?

"Every day we reach a moment when we long for sleep; and, although it be the very likeness of non-existence, can anyone deny that sleep is a pleasure? No; at least it seems to me that it cannot be denied with consistency, for, the moment it comes to us, we give it the preference over all other pleasures, and we are grateful to it only after it has left us.

"Those who say that no one can be happy throughout life speak likewise frivolously. Philosophy teaches the secret of securing that happiness, provided one is free from bodily sufferings. A felicity which would thus last throughout life could be compared to a nosegay formed of a thousand flowers so beautifully, so skilfully blended together, that it would look like one single flower. Why should it be impossible for us to spend here the whole of our life as we have spent the last month, always in good health, always loving one another, without ever feeling any other want or any weariness? Then, to crown that happiness, which would certainly be immense, all that would be wanted would be to die together, in an advanced age, speaking to the last moment of our pleasant recollections. Surely that felicity would have been lasting. Death would not interrupt it, for death would end it. We could not, even then, suppose ourselves unhappy unless we dreaded unhappiness after death, and such an idea strikes me as absurd, for it is a contradiction of the idea of an almighty and fatherly tenderness."

It was thus that my beloved Henriette would often make me spend delightful hours, talking philosophic sentiment; her logic was better than that of Cicero in his *Tusculan Disputations*, but she admitted that such lasting felicity could exist only between two beings who lived together, and loved each other with constant affection, healthy in mind and in body, enlightened, sufficiently rich, similar in tastes, in disposition, and in temperament. Happy are those lovers who, when their senses require rest, can fall back upon the intellectual enjoyments afforded by the mind! Sweet sleep then comes, and lasts until the body has recovered its general harmony. On awaking, the senses are again active and always ready to resume their action.

The conditions of existence are exactly the same for man as for the universe, I might almost say that between them there is perfect identity, for if we take the universe away, mankind no longer exists, and if we take mankind away, there is no longer an universe; who could realise the idea of the existence of inorganic matter? Now, without that idea, *nibil est*, since the idea is the essence of everything, and since man alone has ideas. Besides, if we abstract the species, we can no longer imagine the existence of matter, and *vice versa*.

I derived from Henriette as great happiness as that charming woman derived from me. We loved one another with all the strength of our faculties, and we were everything to each other. She would often repeat those pretty lines of the good La Fontaine:

> *Soyez-vous l'un à l'autre un monde toujours beau,*
> *Toujours divers, toujours nouveau;*
> *Tenez-vous lieu de tout; comptez pour rien le reste.*

And we did not fail to put the advice into practice, for never did a minute of ennui or of weariness, never did the slightest trouble, disturb our bliss.

The day after the close of the opera, Dubois, who was dining with us, said that on the following day he was entertaining the two first artists, *primo cantatore* and *prima cantatrice*, and added that, if we liked to come, we would hear some of their best pieces, which they were to sing in a lofty hall of his country-house particularly adapted to the display of the human voice. Henriette thanked him warmly, but she said that, her health being very delicate, she could not engage herself beforehand, and she spoke of other things.

When we were alone, I asked her why she had refused the pleasure offered by Dubois.

"I should accept his invitation," she answered, "and with delight, if I were not afraid of meeting at his house some person who might know me, and would destroy the happiness I am now enjoying with you."

"If you have any fresh motive for dreading such an occurrence, you are quite right; but if it is only a vague, groundless fear, my love, why should you deprive yourself of a real and innocent pleasure? If you knew how pleased I am when I see you enjoy yourself, and particularly when I witness your ecstacy in listening to fine music!"

"Well, darling, I do not want to show myself less brave than you. We will go immediately after dinner. The artists will not sing before. Besides, as he does not expect us, he is not likely to have invited any person curious to speak to me. We will go without giving him notice of our coming, without being expected, and as if we wanted to pay him a friendly visit. He told us that he would be at his country-house, and Caudagna knows where it is."

Her reasons were a mixture of prudence and of love, two feelings which are seldom blended together. My answer was to kiss her with as much admiration as tenderness, and the next day at four o'clock in the afternoon we paid our visit to M. Dubois. We were much surprised, for we found him alone with a very pretty girl, whom he presented to us as his niece.

"I am delighted to see you," he said; "but as I did not expect to see you I altered my arrangements, and instead of the dinner I had intended to give I have invited my friends to supper; I hope you will not refuse me the honour of your company. The two virtuosi will soon be here."

We were compelled to accept his invitation.

"Will there be many guests?" I inquired.

"You will find yourselves in the midst of people worthy of you," he answered, triumphantly. "I am only sorry that I have not invited any ladies."

This polite remark, which was intended for Henriette, made her drop him a curtsy, which she accompanied with a smile. I was pleased to read contentment on her countenance; but alas! she was concealing the painful anxiety which she felt acutely. Her noble mind refused to show any uneasiness, and I could not guess her inmost thoughts because I had no idea that she had anything to fear.

I should have thought and acted differently if I had known all her history. Instead of remaining in Parma I should have gone with her to London, and I know now that she would have been delighted to go there.

The two artists arrived soon afterwards; they were the *primo cantatore* Laschi, and the *prima donna* Baglioni, then a very pretty woman. The other guests soon followed; all of them were Frenchmen and Spaniards of a certain age. No introductions took place, and I read the tact of the witty hunchback in the omission; but as all the guests were men used to the manners of the court, that neglect of etiquette did not prevent them from paying every honour to my lovely friend, who received their compliments with that ease and good breeding which are known only in France, and even there only in the highest society, with the exception, however, of a few French provinces in which the nobility, wrongly called good society, show rather too openly the naughtiness which is characteristic of that class.

The concert began by a magnificent symphony, after which Laschi and Baglioni sang a duet with great talent and much taste. They were followed by a pupil of the celebrated Vandini, who played a concerto on the violoncello, and was warmly applauded.

The applause had not yet ceased when Henriette, leaving her seat, went up to the young artist, and told him, with modest confidence, as she took the violoncello from him, that she could bring out the beautiful tone of the instrument still better. I was struck with amazement. She took the young man's seat, placed the violoncello between her knees, and begged the leader of the orchestra to begin the concerto again. The deepest silence prevailed; I was trembling all over, and almost fainting. Fortunately every look was fixed upon Henriette, and nobody thought of me. Nor was she looking towards me, she would not have then ventured even one glance, for she would have lost courage, if she had raised her beautiful eyes to my face. However, not seeing her disposing herself to play, I was beginning to imagine that she had only been indulging in a jest, when she suddenly made the strings resound; my heart was beating with such force that I thought I should drop down dead.

But let the reader imagine my situation when, the concerto being over, well-merited applause burst from every part of the room! The rapid change from extreme fear to excessive pleasure brought on an excitement which was like a violent fever. The applause did not seem to have any effect upon Henriette, who, without raising her eyes from the notes which she saw for the first time, played six pieces with the greatest perfection. As she rose from her seat, she did not thank the guests for their applause, but, addressing the young artist with affability, she told him, with a sweet smile, that she had never played on a finer instrument. Then, curtsying to the audience, she said:

"I entreat your forgiveness for a movement of vanity which has made me encroach on your patience for half an hour."

The nobility and grace of this remark completely upset me, and I ran out to weep like a child, in the garden where no one could see me.

"Who is she, this Henriette?" I said to myself, my heart beating, and my eyes swimming with tears of emotion; "what is this treasure I have in my possession?"

My happiness was so immense that I felt myself unworthy of it.

Lost in these thoughts which enhanced the pleasure of my tears, I should have stayed for a long time in the garden if Dubois had not come out to look for me. He felt anxious about me, owing to my sudden disappearance, and I quieted him by saying that a slight giddiness had compelled me to come out to breathe the fresh air.

Before re-entering the room, I had time to dry my tears, but my eyelids were still red. Henriette, however, was the only one to take notice of it, and she said to me:

"I know, my darling, why you went into the garden."

She knew me so well that she could easily guess the impression made on my heart by the evening's occurrence.

Dubois had invited the most amiable noblemen of the court, and his supper was dainty and well arranged. I was seated opposite Henriette, who was, as a matter of course, monopolising the general attention, but she would have met with the same success if she had been surrounded by a circle of ladies, whom she would certainly have thrown into the shade by her beauty, her wit, and the distinction of her manners. She was the charm of that supper by the animation she imparted to the conversation. M. Dubois said nothing, but he was proud to have such a lovely guest in his house. She contrived to say a few gracious words to everyone, and was shrewd enough never to utter something witty without making me take a share in it. On my side, I openly showed my submissiveness, my deference, and my respect for that divinity, but it was all in vain; she wanted everybody to know that I was her lord and master. She might have been taken for my wife, but my behaviour to her rendered such a supposition improbable.

The conversation having fallen on the respective merits of the French and Spanish nations, Dubois was foolish enough to ask Henriette to which she gave preference.

It would have been difficult to ask a more indiscreet question, considering that the company was composed almost entirely of Frenchmen and Spaniards in about equal proportion. Yet my Henriette turned the difficulty so cleverly that the Frenchmen would have liked to be Spaniards, and *vice versa*. Dubois, nothing daunted, begged her to say what she thought of the Italians; that question made me tremble. A certain M. de la Combe, who was seated near me, shook his head in token of disapprobation, but Henriette did not try to elude the question.

"What can I say about the Italians?" she answered; "I know only one. If I am to judge them all from that one my judgment must certainly be most favourable to them, but one single example is not sufficient to establish the rule."

It was impossible to give a better answer, but as my readers may well imagine, I did not appear to have heard it, and being anxious to prevent any more indiscreet questions from Dubois, I turned the conversation into a different channel.

The subject of music was discussed, and a Spaniard asked Henriette whether she could play any other instrument besides the violoncello.

"No," she answered, "I never felt any inclination for any other. I learned the violoncello at the convent to please my mother, who can play it pretty well, and without an order from my father, sanctioned by the bishop, the abbess would never have given me permission to practise it."

"What objection could the abbess make?"

"That devout spouse of Our Lord pretended that I could not play that instrument without assuming an indecent position."

At this the Spanish guests bit their lips, but the Frenchmen laughed heartily, and did not spare their epigrams against the over-particular abbess.

After a short silence, Henriette rose, and we all followed her example; it was the signal for breaking up the party, and we soon took our leave.

I longed to find myself alone with the idol of my soul. I asked her a hundred questions without waiting for the answers.

"Ah! you were right, my own Henriette, when you refused to go to that concert, for you knew that you would raise many enemies against me. I am certain that all those men hate me, but what do I care? You are my universe! Cruel darling, you almost killed me with your violoncello, because, having no idea of your being a musician, I thought you had gone mad, and when I heard you I was compelled to leave the room in order to weep undisturbed. My tears relieved my fearful oppression. Oh! I entreat you to tell me what other talents you possess; tell me candidly, for you might kill me if you brought them out unexpectedly, as you have done this evening."

"I have no other accomplishments, my best beloved; I have emptied my bag all at once; now you know your Henriette entirely. Had you not chanced to tell me about a month ago that you had no taste for music, I would have told you that I could play the violoncello remarkably well; but if I had mentioned such a thing, I know you well enough to be certain that you would have bought an instrument immediately; and I could not, dearest, find pleasure in anything that would weary you."

The very next morning she had an excellent violoncello, and, far from wearying me, each time she played she caused me a new and greater pleasure. I believe that it would be impossible even to a man disliking music not to become passionately fond of it, if that art were practised to perfection by the woman he adores.

The *vox humana* of the violoncello, the king of instruments, went to my heart every time that my beloved Henriette performed upon it. She knew I loved to hear her play, and every day she afforded me that pleasure. Her talent delighted me so much that I proposed to her to give some concerts, but she was prudent enough to refuse my proposal. But in spite of all her prudence we had no power to hinder the decrees of fate.

The fatal hunchback came the day after his fine supper to thank us and to receive our well-merited praises of his concert, his supper, and the distinction of his guests.

"I foresee, madam," he said to Henriette, "all the difficulty I shall have in defending myself against the prayers of all my friends, who will beg of me to introduce them to you."

"You need not have much trouble on that score: you know that I never receive anyone."

Dubois did not again venture upon speaking of introducing any friend.

On the same day I received a letter from young Capitani, in which he informed me that, being the owner of St. Peter's knife and sheath, he had called upon Franzia with two learned magicians who had promised to raise the treasure out of the earth, and that to his great surprise Franzia had refused to receive him. He entreated me to write to the worthy fellow, and to go to him myself if I wanted to have my share of the treasure. I need not say that I did not comply with his wishes, but I can vouch for the real pleasure I felt in finding that I had succeeded in saving that honest and simple farmer from the impostors who would have ruined him.

One month was gone since the great supper given by Dubois; we had passed it in all the enjoyment which can be derived both from the senses and the mind, and never had one single instant of weariness caused either of us to be guilty of that sad symptom of misery which is called a yawn. The only pleasure we took out of doors was a drive outside of the city when the weather was fine. As we never walked in the streets, and never frequented any public place, no one had sought to make our acquaintance, or at least no one had found an opportunity of doing so, in spite of all the curiosity excited by Henriette amongst the persons whom we had chanced to meet, particularly at the house of

Dubois. Henriette had become more courageous, and I more confident, when we found that she had not been recognised by anyone either at that supper or at the theatre. She only dreaded persons belonging to the high nobility.

One day as we were driving outside the Gate of Colorno, we met the duke and the duchess, who were returning to Parma. Immediately after their carriage another vehicle drove along, in which was Dubois with a nobleman unknown to us. Our carriage had only gone a few yards from theirs when one of our horses broke down. The companion of Dubois immediately ordered his coachman to stop in order to send to our assistance. Whilst the horse was raised again, he came politely to our carriage, and paid some civil compliment to Henriette. M. Dubois, always a shrewd courtier and anxious to show off at the expense of others, lost no time in introducing him as M. Dutillot, the French ambassador. My sweetheart gave the conventional bow. The horse being all right again, we proceeded on our road after thanking the gentlemen for their courtesy. Such an everyday occurrence could not be expected to have any serious consequence, but alas! the most important events are often the result of very trifling circumstances!

The next day, Dubois breakfasted with us. He told us frankly that M. Dutillot had been delighted at the fortunate chance which had afforded him an opportunity of making our acquaintance, and that he had entreated him to ask our permission to call on us.

"On madam or on me?" I asked at once.

"On both."

"Very well, but one at a time. Madam, as you know, has her own room and I have mine."

"Yes, but they are so near each other!"

"Granted; yet I must tell you that, as far as I am concerned, I should have much pleasure in waiting upon his excellency if he should ever wish to communicate with me, and you will oblige me by letting him know it. As for madam, she is here, speak to her, my dear M. Dubois, for I am only her very humble servant."

Henriette assumed an air of cheerful politeness, and said to him:

"Sir, I beg you will offer my thanks to M. Dutillot, and inquire from him whether he knows me."

"I am certain, madam," said the hunchback, "that he does not."

"You see he does not know me, and yet he wishes to call on me. You must agree with me that if I accepted his visits I should give him a singular opinion of my character. Be good enough to tell him that, although known to no one and knowing no one, I am not an adventuress, and therefore I must decline the honour of his visits."

Dubois felt that he had taken a false step, and remained silent. We never asked him how the ambassador had received our refusal.

Three weeks after the last occurrence, the ducal court residing then at Colorno, a great entertainment was given in the gardens, which were to be illuminated all night: everybody had permission to walk about the gardens. Dubois, the fatal hunchback appointed by destiny, spoke so much of that festival, that we took a fancy to see it: always the same old story of Adam's apple. Dubois accompanied us. We went to Colorno the day before the entertainment, and put up at an inn.

In the evening we walked through the gardens, in which we happened to meet the ducal family and suite. According to the etiquette of the French Court, Madame de France was the first to curtsy to Henriette, without stopping. My eyes fell upon a gentleman walking by the side of Don Louis, who was looking at my friend very attentively. A few minutes after, as we were retracing our steps, we came across the same gentleman, who, after bowing respectfully to us, took Dubois aside. They conversed together for a quarter of an hour, following us all the time, and we were passing out of the gardens, when the gentleman, coming forward, and politely apologising to me, asked Henriette whether he had the honour to be known to her.

"I do not recollect having ever had the honour of seeing you before."

"That is enough, madam, and I entreat you to forgive me."

Dubois informed us that the gentleman was the intimate friend of the Infante Don Louis, and that, believing he knew madam, he had begged to be introduced. Dubois had answered that her name was d'Arci, and that, if he was known to the lady, he required no introduction. M. d'Antoine said that the name of d'Arci was unknown to him, and that he was afraid of making a mistake. "In that state of doubt," added Dubois, "and wishing to clear it, he introduced himself; but now he must see that he was mistaken."

After supper, Henriette appeared anxious; I asked her whether she had only pretended not to know M. d'Antoine.

"No, dearest, I can assure you. I know his name, which belongs to an illustrious family of Provence, but I have never seen him before."

"Perhaps he may know you?"

"He might have seen me, but I am certain that he never spoke to me, or I would have recollected him."

"That meeting causes me great anxiety, and it seems to have troubled you."

"I confess it has disturbed my mind."

"Let us leave Parma at once and proceed to Genoa. We will go to Venice as soon as my affairs there are settled."

"Yes, my dear friend, we shall then feel more comfortable. But I do not think we need be in any hurry."

We returned to Parma, and two days afterwards my servant handed me a letter, saying that the footman who had brought it was waiting in the ante-room.

"This letter," I said to Henriette, "troubles me."

She took it, and after she had read it she gave it back to me, saying: "I think M. d'Antoine is a man of honour, and I hope that we have nothing to fear."

The letter ran as follows:

"Either at your hotel or at my residence, or at any place you may wish to appoint, I entreat you, sir, to give me an opportunity of conversing with you on a subject which must be of the greatest importance to you.

"I have the honour to be, etc.

"D'Antoine."

It was addressed to M. Farusi.

"I think I must see him," I said, "but where?"

"Neither here nor at his residence, but in the ducal gardens. Your answer must name only the place and the hour of the meeting."

I wrote to M. d'Antoine that I would see him at half-past eleven in the ducal gardens, only requesting him to appoint another hour in case mine was not convenient to him.

I dressed myself at once in order to be in good time, and meanwhile we both endeavoured, Henriette and I, to keep a cheerful countenance, but we could not silence our sad forebodings. I was exact to my appointment and found M. d'Antoine waiting for me. As soon as we were together, he said to me:

"I have been compelled, sir, to beg from you the favour of an interview, because I could not imagine any surer way to get this letter to Madame d'Arci's hands. I entreat you to deliver it to her, and to excuse me if I give it you sealed. Should I be mistaken, my letter will not even require an answer, but should I be right, Madame d'Arci alone can judge whether she ought to communicate it to you. That is my reason for giving it to you sealed. If you are truly her friend, the contents of that letter must be as interesting to you as to her. May I hope, sir, that you will be good enough to deliver it to her?"

"Sir, on my honour I will do it."

We bowed respectfully to each other, and parted company. I hurried back to the hotel.

As soon as I had reached our apartment, my heart bursting with anxiety, I repeated to Henriette every word spoken by M. d'Antoine, and delivered his letter, which contained four pages of writing. She read it attentively with visible emotion, and then she said:

"Dearest friend, do not be offended, but the honour of two families does not allow of my imparting to you the contents of this letter. I am compelled to receive M. d'Antoine, who represents himself as being one of my relatives."

"Ah!" I exclaimed, "this is the beginning of the end! What a dreadful thought! I am near the end of a felicity which was too great to last! Wretch that I have been! Why did I tarry so long in Parma? What fatal blindness! Of all the cities in the whole world, except France, Parma was the only one I had to fear, and it is here that I have brought you, when I could have taken you anywhere else, for you had no will but mine! I am all the more guilty that you never concealed your fears from me. Why did I introduce that fatal Dubois here? Ought I not to have guessed that his curiosity would sooner or later prove injurious to us? And yet I cannot condemn that curiosity, for it is, alas! a natural feeling. I can only accuse all the perfections which Heaven has bestowed upon you! — perfections which have caused my happiness, and which will plunge me in an abyss of despair, for, alas! I foresee a future of fearful misery."

"I entreat you, dearest, to foresee nothing, and to calm yourself. Let us avail ourselves of all our reason in order to prove ourselves superior to circumstances, whatever they may be. I cannot answer this letter, but you must write to M. d'Antoine to call here to-morrow and to send up his name."

"Alas! you compel me to perform a painful task."

"You are my best, my only friend; I demand nothing, I impose no task upon you, but can you refuse me?"

"No, never, no matter what you ask. Dispose of me, I am yours in life and in death."

"I knew what you would answer. You must be with me when M. d'Antoine calls, but after a few minutes given to etiquette, will you find some pretext to go to your room, and leave us alone? M. d'Antoine knows all my history; he knows in what I have done wrong, in what I have been right; as a man of honour, as my relative, he must shelter me from all affront. He shall not do anything against my will, and if he attempts to deviate from the conditions I will dictate to him, I will refuse to go to France, I will follow you anywhere, and devote to you the remainder of my life. Yet, my darling, recollect that some fatal circumstances may compel us to consider our separation as the wisest course to adopt, that we must husband all our courage to adopt it, if necessary, and to endeavour not to be too unhappy. Have confidence in me, and be quite certain that I shall take care to reserve for myself the small portion of happiness which I can be allowed to enjoy without the man who alone has won all my devoted love. You will have, I trust, and I expect it from your generous soul, the same care of your future, and I feel certain that you must succeed. In the meantime, let us drive away all the sad forebodings which might darken the hours we have yet before us."

"Ah! why did we not go away immediately after we had met that accursed favourite of the Infante?"

"We might have made matters much worse; for in that case M. d'Antoine might have made up his mind to give my family a proof of his zeal by instituting a search to discover our place of residence, and I should then have been exposed to violent proceedings which you would not have endured; it would have been fatal to both of us."

I did everything she asked me; from that moment our love became sad, and sadness is a disease which gives the death-blow to affection. We would often remain a whole hour opposite one another without exchanging a single word, and our sighs would be heard whatever we did to hush them.

The next day, when M. d'Antoine called, I followed exactly the instructions she had given me, and for six mortal hours I remained alone, pretending to write.

The door of my room was open, and a large looking-glass allowed us to see each other. They spent those six hours in writing, occasionally stopping to talk of I do not know what, but their conversation was evidently a decisive one. The reader can easily realise how much I suffered during that long torture, for I could expect nothing but the total wreck of my happiness.

As soon as the terrible M. d'Antoine had taken leave of her, Henriette came to me, and observing that her eyes were red I heaved a deep sigh, but she tried to smile.

"Shall we go away to-morrow, dearest?"

"Oh! yes, I am ready. Where do you wish me to take you?"

"Anywhere you like, but we must be here in a fortnight."

"Here! Oh, fatal illusion!"

"Alas! it is so. I have promised to be here to receive the answer to a letter I have just written. We have no violent proceedings to fear, but I cannot bear to remain in Parma."

"Ah! I curse the hour which brought us to this city. Would you like to go to Milan?"

"Yes."

"As we are unfortunately compelled to come back, we may as well take with us Caudagna and his sister."

"As you please."

"Let me arrange everything. I will order a carriage for them, and they will take charge of your violoncello. Do you not think that you ought to let M. d'Antoine know where we are going?"

"No; it seems to me, on the contrary, that I need not account to him for any of my proceedings. So much the worse for him if he should, even for one moment, doubt my word."

The next morning, we left Parma, taking only what we wanted for an absence of a fortnight. We arrived in Milan without accident, but both very sad, and we spent the following fifteen days in constant *tête-à-tête*, without speaking to anyone, except to the landlord of the hotel and to a dressmaker. I presented my beloved Henriette with a magnificent pelisse made of lynx fur — a present which she prized highly.

Out of delicacy, she had never inquired about my means, and I felt grateful to her for that reserve; I was very careful to conceal from her the fact that my purse was getting very light: when we came back to Parma I had only three or four hundred sequins.

The day after our return M. d'Antoine invited himself to dine with us, and after we had drunk coffee, I left him alone with Henriette. Their interview was as long as the first, and our separation was decided. She informed me of it, immediately after the departure of M. d'Antoine, and for a long time we remained folded in each other's arms, silent, and blending our bitter tears.

"When shall I have to part from you, my beloved, alas! too much beloved, one?"

"Be calm, dearest; only when we reach Geneva, whither you are going to accompany me. Will you try to find me a respectable maid by to-morrow? She will accompany me from Geneva to the place where I am bound to go."

"Oh! then, we shall spend a few days more together! I know no one but Dubois whom I could trust to procure a good *femme-de-chambre;* only I do not want him to learn from her what you might not wish him to know."

"That will not be the case, for I will take another maid as soon as I am in France."

Three days afterwards, Dubois, who had gladly undertaken the commission, presented to Henriette a woman already somewhat advanced in years, pretty well dressed and respectable-looking, who, being poor, was glad of an opportunity of going back to France, her native country. Her husband, an old military officer, had died a few months before, leaving her totally unprovided for. Henriette engaged her, and told her to keep herself ready to start whenever M. Dubois should give her notice. The day before the one fixed for our departure, M. d'Antoine dined with us, and, before taking leave of us, he gave Henriette a sealed letter for Geneva.

[215]

We left Parma late in the evening, and stopped only two hours in Turin, in order to engage a man-servant whose services we required as far as Geneva. The next day we ascended Mont Cenis in sedan-chairs, and we descended to the Novalaise in mountain-sledges. On the fifth day we reached Geneva, and we put up at the Hôtel des Balances. The next morning, Henriette gave me a letter for the banker Tronchin, who, when he had read it, told me that he would call himself at the hotel, and bring me one thousand louis d'or.

I came back and we sat down to dinner. We had not finished our meal when the banker was announced. He had brought the thousand louis d'or, and told Henriette that he would give her two men whom he could recommend in every way.

She answered that she would leave Geneva as soon as she had the carriage which he was to provide for her, according to the letter I had delivered to him. He promised that everything would be ready for the following day, and he left us. It was indeed a terrible moment! Grief almost benumbed us both. We remained motionless, speechless, wrapped up in the most profound despair.

I broke that sad silence to tell her that the carriage which M. Tronchin would provide could not possibly be as comfortable and as safe as mine, and I entreated her to take it, assuring her that by accepting it she would give me a last proof of her affection.

"I will take in exchange, my dearest love, the carriage sent by the banker."

"I accept the change, darling," she answered; "it will be a great consolation to possess something which has belonged to you."

As she said these words, she slipped in my pocket five rolls containing each one hundred louis d'or — a slight consolation for my heart, which was almost broken by our cruel separation! During the last twenty-four hours we could boast of no other eloquence but that which finds expression in tears, in sobs, and in those hackneyed but energetic exclamations, which two happy lovers are sure to address to reason, when in its sternness it compels them to part from one another in the very height of their felicity. Henriette did not endeavour to lure me with any hope for the future, in order to allay my sorrow! Far from that, she said to me:

"Once we are parted by fate, my best and only friend, never inquire after me, and, should chance throw you in my way, do not appear to know me."

She gave me a letter for M. d'Antoine, without asking me whether I intended to go back to Parma; but, even if such had not been my intention, I should have determined at once upon returning to that city. She likewise entreated me not to leave Geneva until I had received a letter which she promised to write to me from the first stage on her journey. She started at daybreak, having with her a maid, a footman on the box of the carriage, and being preceded by a courier on horseback. I followed her with my eyes as long as I could see her carriage, and I was still standing on the same spot long after my eyes had lost sight of it; all my thoughts were wrapped up in the beloved object I had lost for ever; the world was a blank!

I went back to my room, ordered the waiter not to disturb me until the return of the horses which had drawn Henriette's carriage, and I lay down on my bed in the hope that sleep would for a time silence a grief which tears could not drown.

The postillion who had driven Henriette did not return till the next day; he had gone as far as Chatillon. He brought me a letter in which I found one single word: Adieu! He told me that they had reached Chatillon without accident, and that the lady had immediately continued her journey towards Lyons. As I could not leave Geneva until the following day, I spent alone in my room some of the most melancholy hours of my life. I saw on one of the panes of glass of a window these words which she had traced with the point of a diamond I had given her: "You will forget Henriette." That prophecy was not likely to afford me any consolation. But had she attached its full meaning to the word "forget"? No; she could only mean that time would at last heal the deep wounds of my heart, and she ought not to have made it deeper by leaving behind her those words which sounded like a reproach. No, I have not forgotten her; for even now, when my head is covered with white hair, the recollection of her is still a source of happiness for my heart! When I think that in my old age I derive happiness only from my recollections of the past, I find that my long life must have counted more bright than dark days, and, offering my thanks to God, the Giver of all, I congratulate myself, and confess that life is a great blessing.

The next day I set off again for Italy with a servant recommended by M. Tronchin, and although the season was not favourable I took the road over Mont St. Bernard, which I crossed in three days, with seven mules carrying me, my servant, my luggage, and the carriage sent by the banker to the beloved woman now for ever lost to me. One of the advantages of a great sorrow is that nothing else seems painful. It is a sort of despair which is not without some sweetness. During that journey I never felt either hunger or thirst, or the cold which is so intense in that part of the Alps that the whole of nature seems to turn to ice, or the fatigue inseparable from such a difficult and dangerous journey.

I arrived in Parma in pretty good health, and took up my quarters at a small inn, in the hope that in such a place I should not meet any acquaintance of mine. But I was much disappointed, for I found in that inn M. de la Haye, who had a room next to mine. Surprised at seeing me, he paid me a long compliment, trying to make me speak, but I eluded his curiosity by telling him that I was tired, and that we would see each other again.

On the following day I called upon M. d'Antoine, and delivered the letter which Henriette had written to him. He opened it in my presence, and finding another to my address enclosed in his, he handed it to me without reading it, although it was not sealed. Thinking, however, that it might have been Henriette's intention that he should read it because it was open, he asked my permission to do so, which I granted with pleasure as soon as I had myself perused it. He handed it back to me after he had read it, telling me feelingly that I could in everything rely upon him and upon his influence and credit.

Here is Henriette's letter:

"It is I, dearest and best friend, who have been compelled to abandon you; but do not let your grief be increased by any thought of my sorrow. Let us be wise enough to suppose that we have had a happy dream, and not to complain of destiny; for never did so beautiful a dream last so long! Let us be proud of the consciousness that for three months we gave one another the most perfect felicity; few human beings can boast of so much! Let us swear never to forget one another, and to often remember the happy hours of our love, in order to renew them in our souls,

[218]

which, although divided, will enjoy them as acutely as if our hearts were beating one against the other. Do not make any inquiries about me, and if chance should let you know who I am, forget it for ever. I feel certain that you will be glad to hear that I have arranged my affairs so well that I shall, for the remainder of my life, be as happy as I can possibly be without you, dear friend, by my side. I do not know who you are, but I am certain that no one in the world knows you better than I do. I shall not have another lover as long as I live, but I do not wish you to imitate me. On the contrary, I hope that you will love again, and I trust that a good fairy will bring along your path another Henriette. Farewell . . . farewell."

* * * * *

I met that adorable woman, fifteen years later; the reader will see where and how, when we come to that period of my life.

* * * * *

I went back to my room: careless of the future, broken down by the deepest of sorrows, I locked myself in, and went to bed. I felt so low in spirits that I was stunned. Life was not a burden, but only because I did not give a thought to life. In fact I was in a state of complete apathy, moral and physical. Six years later I found myself in a similar predicament; but that time love was not the cause of my sorrow; it was the horrible and too famous prison of The Leads, in Venice.

I was not much better either in 1768, when I was lodged in the prison of Buen Retiro, in Madrid; but I must not anticipate events.

Ten years later, on August 20th, 1760, Casanova, passing through Geneva, stopped at the Hôtel des Balances and found there, on the window-pane of the room he had shared with Henriette, her inscription still intact. The sight so overwhelms him that he breaks down. "In a moment," he says, "my thoughts flew back to the time in which Henriette had written these words, thirteen years [1] ago, and my hair stood on end. We had been lodged in this room when she separated from me to return to France. I was overwhelmed, and fell on a chair, where I abandoned myself to deep thought. Noble Henriette, dear Henriette, whom I had loved so well! where was she

---

[1] *In matters of dates and calculations of time the Memoirs are often misleading. The meeting with Henriette took place in 1749.*

now? I had never heard of her; I had never asked anyone about her. Comparing my present and past estates, I was obliged to confess that I was less worthy of possessing her now than then. I could still love, but I was no longer so delicate in my thoughts. I had not those feelings which justify the faults committed by the senses, nor that probity which serves as a contrast to the follies and frailties of man; but, what was worst of all, I was not so strong. Nevertheless, it seemed that the remembrance of Henriette restored me to my pristine vigour. . . . I experienced a great void; and I felt so enthusiastic that if I had known where Henriette was, I should have gone to seek her out, despite her prohibition."

Twice they were destined to meet again, but, oh, fatality! on neither occasion was he to be aware of the fact! After this second encounter, in Aix-in-Provence, when through her intervention he was nursed back to life during a severe illness, a correspondence took place between the former lovers, which lasted for many years. He states that about forty of these letters, in which she relates the story of her life, were in his possession, and that if he outlived her, they would be added to the Memoirs. No trace has been found among Casanova's papers at Dux of this alleged correspondence, despite the active researches of Casanovists for the last half-century. It has even been held by some that Henriette, as well as certain other "leading ladies" of the Memoirs — "M. M.," "C. C.," Esther, for example — are creatures of the author's fertile imagination. Although there is reason to suspect that some of his enchantresses were indeed bred "or in the heart or in the head," or, if not entirely fictitious, transported from other cytherean preserves and annexed to his own, there are, in the case of Henriette, apart from what we may call the "internal evidence" as manifested in the note and colour of the narration, certain indications given by Casanova which suggest that his heroine was a substantial mortal.

Such, for instance, are the topographical indications regarding the château near Aix-in-Provence where he and Marcoline were so hospitably received in 1763 when their carriage broke down. The lady of the house, whom he refers to as the "countess" or the "châtelaine," and who avoided meeting him face to face, may in fact have been, as he avers, his long-lost Henriette.

A château or manor belonging to the Luynes family, which exists in this region, seems to correspond to the indications given by Casanova. The owner at the time of Casanova's visit was Joseph-Con-

stance de Margalet, a knight of Malta, two of whose three sisters bore the name of Henriette. Unfortunately the certified ages of both these ladies hardly correspond with the age which Casanova's Henriette must have had at that time. But "Henriette" may well have been a nom de guerre. The oldest of the three Margalet sisters, whose name was not Henriette, and who was married in 1757, might, on the other hand, as regards dates, qualify for the rôle of Casanova's grande passion.

CHAPTER VI

PARIS

*A*FTER *nursing his broken heart in Parma for a while, during which time he cultivated the acquaintance of a devout hypocrite, called de la Haye, Casanova received news from Venice that it would be safe for him to return, as his "little affair" was now happily forgotten. So to Venice he returns in company of his friend de la Haye, who by this time had gained such an ascendancy over his mind — enfeebled, as he says, by sorrow, fasting, and sickness — that his devoted friends, the three old senators Bragadin, Dandolo, and Barbaro, have difficulty in recognising the prodigal in the devout and studious young man, who pays off all his debts, goes to church every day, and associates only with pious and God-fearing men.*

But with the return of good health and the carnival season the devil ceases to be a monk — especially when he discovers that de la Haye is another Tartufe — and Casanova resumes, though with more moderation, his old mode of life. For a moment there is even some talk of his marrying damigella *Marchetti, but he quickly thinks better of such rashness, especially after a run of good luck at the tables, capped by winning a handsome prize of money in a lottery, and it needs very little persuasion on the part of young Baletti (son of Silvia Baletti, the famous actress), whom he had met on his travels and who, like his mother, was a member of the troupe of Italian Comedians in Paris, to set out for that city, which for some time had been the goal of his desires.*

So, on June 1st, 1750, he bids farewell to his good friends, promising to return in two years' time, and, well supplied with funds, sets out for France in the company of Baletti. Let us join them.

Baletti, being in a hurry to reach Paris, where great preparations were being made for the birth of a Duke of Burgundy —
for the duchess was near the time of her delivery — easily persuaded me to shorten my stay in Turin. We therefore left that
city, and in five days we arrived at Lyons, where I stayed about
a week.

Lyons is a very fine city in which at that time there were
scarcely three or four noble houses opened to strangers; but,
in compensation, there were more than a hundred hospitable ones
belonging to merchants, manufacturers, and commission agents,
amongst whom was to be found an excellent society remarkable
for easy manners, politeness, frankness, and good style, without
the absurd pride to be met with amongst the nobility in the
provinces, with very few honourable exceptions. It is true that
the standard of good manners is below that of Paris, but one
soon gets accustomed to it. The wealth of Lyons arises from
good taste and low prices, and Fashion is the goddess to whom
that city owes its prosperity. Fashion alters every year, and the
stuff, to which the fashion of the day gives a value equal, say to
thirty, is the next year reduced to fifteen or twenty, and then it
is sent to foreign countries where it is brought up as a novelty.

The manufacturers of Lyons give high salaries to designers of
talent; in that lies the secret of their success. Low prices come
from Competition — a fruitful source of wealth, and a daughter
of Liberty. Therefore, a government wishing to establish on a
firm basis the prosperity of trade must give commerce full
liberty; only being careful to prevent the frauds which private
interests, often wrongly understood, might invent at the expense
of public and general interests. In fact, the government must
hold the scales, and allow the citizens to load them as they
please.

In Lyons I met the most famous courtesan of Venice. It was
generally admitted that her equal had never been seen. Her
name was Ancilla. Every man who saw her coveted her, and
she was so kindly disposed that she could not refuse her favours
to anyone; for if all men loved her one after the other, she returned the compliment by loving them all at once, and with her
pecuniary advantages were only a very secondary consideration.

Venice has always been blessed with courtesans more celebrated by their beauty than their wit. Those who were most

famous in my younger days were Ancilla and another called Spina, both the daughters of gondoliers, and both killed very young by the excesses of a profession which, in their eyes, was a noble one. At the age of twenty-two, Ancilla turned a dancer and Spina became a singer. Campioni, a celebrated Venetian dancer, imparted to the lovely Ancilla all the graces and talents of which her physical perfections were susceptible, and married her. Spina had for her master a *castrato* who succeeded in making of her only a very ordinary singer, and in the absence of talent she was compelled, in order to get a living, to make the most of the beauty she had received from nature.

I shall have occasion to speak again of Ancilla before her death. She was then in Lyons with her husband; they had just returned from England, where they had been greatly applauded at the Haymarket Theatre. She had stopped in Lyons only for her pleasure, and, the moment she showed herself, she had at her feet the most brilliant young men of the town, who were the slaves of her slightest caprice. Every day parties of pleasure, every evening magnificent suppers, and every night a great faro bank. The banker at the gaming-table was a certain Don Joseph Marratti, the same man whom I had known in the Spanish army under the name of Don Pepe il Cadetto, and a few years afterwards assumed the name of Afflisio, and came to such a bad end. That faro bank won in a few days three hundred thousand francs. In a capital that would not have been considered a large sum, but in a commercial and industrial city like Lyons, it raised the alarm amongst the merchants, and the Ultramontanes thought of taking their leave.

It was in Lyons that a respectable individual, whose acquaintance I made at the house of M. de Rochebaron, obtained for me the favour of being initiated in the sublime trifles of Freemasonry. I arrived in Paris a simple apprentice; a few months after my arrival I became companion and master; the last is certainly the highest degree in Freemasonry, for all the other degrees which I took afterwards are only pleasing inventions, which, although symbolical, add nothing to the dignity of master.

No one in this world can obtain a knowledge of everything, but every man who feels himself endowed with faculties, and can realise the extent of his moral strength, should endeavour to obtain the greatest possible amount of knowledge. A well-born young man who wishes to travel and know not only the world, but also what is called good society, who does not want to find himself, under certain circumstances, inferior to his equals, and excluded from participating in all their pleasures, must get himself initiated in what is called Freemasonry, even if it is only to know superficially what Freemasonry is. It is a charitable institution, which, at certain times and in certain places, may have been a pretext for criminal underplots got up for the overthrow of public order; but is there anything under heaven that has not been abused? Have we not seen the Jesuits, under the cloak of our holy religion, thrust into the parricidal hand of blind enthusiasts the dagger with which kings were to be assassinated? All men of importance, I mean those whose social existence is marked by intelligence and merit, by learning or by wealth, can be (and many of them are) Freemasons: is it possible to suppose that such meetings, in which the initiated, making it a law never to speak, *intra muros*, either of politics, or of religions, or of governments, converse only concerning emblems which are either moral or trifling; is it possible to suppose, I repeat, that those meetings, in which the governments may have their own creatures, can offer dangers sufficiently serious to warrant the proscriptions of kings or the excommunications of popes?

In reality such proceedings miss the end for which they are undertaken, and the Pope, in spite of his infallibility, will not prevent his persecutions from giving Freemasonry an importance which it would perhaps have never obtained if it had been left alone. Mystery is the essence of man's nature, and whatever presents itself to mankind under a mysterious appearance will always excite curiosity and be sought, even when men are satisfied that the veil covers nothing but a cypher.

Upon the whole, I would advise all well-born young men, who intend to travel, to become Freemasons; but I would likewise advise them to be careful in selecting a lodge, because, although bad company cannot have any influence while inside of the lodge, the candidate must guard against bad acquaintances.

Those who become Freemasons only for the sake of finding out the secret of the order, run a very great risk of growing old under the trowel without ever realising their purpose. Yet there is a secret, but it is so inviolable that it has never been confided or whispered to anyone. Those who stop at the outward crust of things imagine that the secret consists in words, in signs, or that the main point of it is to be found only in reaching the highest degree. This is a mistaken view: the man who guesses the secret of Freemasonry, and to know it you *must* guess it, reaches that point only through long attendance in the lodges, through deep thinking, comparison, and deduction. He would not trust that secret to his best friend in Freemasonry, because he is aware that if his friend has not found it out, he could not make any use of it after it had been whispered in his ear. No, he keeps his peace, and the secret remains a secret.

Everything done in a lodge must be secret; but those who have unscrupulously revealed what is done in the lodge, have been unable to reveal that which is essential; they had no knowledge of it, and had they known it, they certainly would not have unveiled the mystery of the ceremonies.

The impression felt in our days by the non-initiated is of the same nature as that felt in former times by those who were not initiated in the mysteries enacted at Eleusis in honour of Ceres. But the mysteries of Eleusis interested the whole of Greece, and whoever had attained some eminence in the society of those days had an ardent wish to take a part in those mysterious ceremonies, while Freemasonry, in the midst of many men of the highest merit, reckons a crowd of scoundrels whom no society ought to acknowledge, because they are the refuse of mankind as far as morality is concerned.

We left Lyons in the public diligence, and were five days on our road to Paris. Baletti had given notice of his departure to his family; they therefore knew when to expect him. We were eight in the coach and our seats were very uncomfortable, for it was a large oval in shape, so that no one had a corner. If that vehicle had been built in a country where equality was a principle hallowed by the laws, it would not have been a bad illustration. I thought it was absurd; but I was in a foreign country, and I said nothing. Besides, being an Italian, would it have been right for me not to admire everything which was French, and particularly in France? Example, an oval diligence: I respected the fashion, but I found it detestable, and the singular motion of that vehicle had the same effect upon me as the rolling of a ship in a heavy sea. Yet it was well hung, but the worst jolting would have disturbed me less.

As the diligence undulates in the rapidity of its pace, it has been called a gondola, but I was a judge of gondolas, and I thought that there was no family likeness between the coach and the Venetian boats which, with two hearty rowers, glide along so swiftly and smoothly.

The effect of the movement was that I had to throw up whatever was on my stomach. My travelling companions thought me bad company, but they did not say so: I was in France and among Frenchmen, who know what politeness is. They only remarked that very likely I had eaten too much at my supper, and a Parisian abbé, in order to excuse me, observed that my stomach was weak. A discussion arose.

"Gentlemen," I said, in my vexation, and rather angrily, "you are all wrong, for my stomach is excellent, and I have not had any supper."

Thereupon an elderly man told me, with a voice full of sweetness, that I ought not to say that the gentlemen were wrong, though I might say that they were not right, thus imitating Cicero, who, instead of declaring to the Romans that Catilina and the other conspirators were dead, only said that they had lived.

"Is it not the same thing?"

"I beg your pardon, sir; one way of speaking is polite, the other is not." And after treating me to a long dissertation on politeness, he concluded by saying, with a smile, "I suppose you are an Italian?"

"Yes, I am; but would you oblige me by telling me how you have found it out?"

"Oh! I guessed it from the attention with which you have listened to my long prattle."

Everybody laughed, and I, much pleased with his eccentricity, began to coax him. He was the tutor of a young boy of twelve or thirteen years who was seated near him. I made him give me during the journey lessons in French politeness, and when we parted he took me apart in a friendly manner, saying that he wished to make me a small present.

"What is it?"

"You must abandon, and, if I may say so, forget, the particle *non*, which you use frequently at random. *Non* is not a French word; instead of that unpleasant monosyllable, say, *Pardon*.

Non is equal to giving the lie: never say it, or prepare yourself to give and to receive sword-stabs every moment."

"I thank you, monsieur; your present is very precious, and I promise you never to say *non* again."

During the first fortnight of my stay in Paris, it seemed to me that I had become the most faulty man alive, for I never ceased begging pardon. I even thought, one evening at the theatre, that I should have a quarrel for having begged somebody's pardon in the wrong place. A young fop, coming to the pit, trod on my foot, and I hastened to say:

"Your pardon, sir."

"Sir, pardon me yourself."

"No, yourself."

"Yourself!"

"Well, sir, let us pardon and embrace one another!"

The embrace put a stop to the discussion.

One day during the journey, having fallen asleep from fatigue in the inconvenient gondola, someone pushed my arm.

"Ah, sir! look at that mansion!" said my neighbour.

"I see it; what of it?"

"Ah! I pray you, do you not find it . . ."

"I find nothing particular; and you?"

"Nothing wonderful, if it were not situated at a distance of forty leagues from Paris. But here! Ah! would my *badauds* of Parisians believe that such a beautiful mansion can be found forty leagues distant from the metropolis? How ignorant a man is when he has never travelled!"

"You are quite right."

That man was a Parisian and a *badaud* to the backbone, like a Gaul in the days of Cæsar.

But if the Parisians are lounging about from morning till night, enjoying everything around them, a foreigner like myself ought to have been a greater *badaud* than they! The difference between us was that, being accustomed to see things such as they are, I was astonished at seeing them often covered with a mask which changed their nature, while their surprise often arose from their suspecting what the mask concealed.

What delighted me, on my arrival in Paris, was the magnificent road made by Louis XV., the cleanliness of the hotels, the excellent fare they give, the quickness of the service, the excellent beds, the modest appearance of the attendant, who generally is the most accomplished girl of the house, and whose decency, modest manners, and neatness inspire the most shameless libertine with respect. Where is the Italian who is pleased with the effrontery and the insolence of the hotel-waiters in Italy? In my days, people did not know in France what it was to over-charge; it was truly the home of foreigners. True, they had the unpleasantness of often witnessing acts of odious despotism, *lettres de cachet*, etc.; it was the despotism of a king. Since that time the French have the despotism of the people. Is it less obnoxious?

We dined at Fontainebleau, a name derived from *Fontaine-belle-eau;* and when we were only two leagues from Paris we saw a berlin advancing towards us. As it came near the diligence, my friend called out to the postillions to stop: in the berlin was his mother, who offered me the welcome given to an expected friend. His mother was the celebrated actress Silvia, and when I had been introduced to her she said to me:

"I hope, sir, that my son's friend will accept a share of our family supper this evening."

I accepted gratefully, sat down again in the gondola, Baletti got into the berlin with his mother, and we continued our journey.

On reaching Paris, I found a servant of Silvia's waiting for me with a coach: he accompanied me to my lodging to leave my luggage, and we repaired to Baletti's house, which was only fifty yards distant from my dwelling.

Baletti presented me to his father, who was known under the name of Mario. Silvia and Mario were the stage names assumed by M. and Madame Baletti, and at that time it was the custom in France to call the Italian actors by the names they had on the stage. *Bon jour, Monsieur Arlequin; bon jour, Monsieur Pantalon:* such was the manner in which the French used to address the actors who personified those characters on the stage.

To celebrate the arrival of her son, Silvia gave a splendid supper to which she had invited all her relatives, and it was a good opportunity for me to make their acquaintance. Baletti's father, who had just recovered from a long illness, was not with us, but we had his father's sister, who was older than Mario. She was known, under her theatrical name of Flaminia, in the literary world by several translations, but I had a great wish to make her acquaintance less on that account than in consequence of the story, known throughout Italy, of the stay that three literary men of great fame had made in Paris. Those three *literati* were the Marquis Maffei, the Abbé Conti, and Pierre Jacques Martelli, who became enemies, according to public rumour, owing to the belief entertained by each of them that he possessed the favours of the actress; and, being men of learning, they fought with the pen. Martelli composed a satire against Maffei, in which he designated him by the anagram of Femia.

I had been announced to Flaminia as a candidate for literary fame, and she thought she honoured me by addressing me at all; but she was wrong, for she displeased me greatly by her face, her manners, her style, even by the sound of her voice. Without saying it positively, she made me understand that, being herself an illustrious member of the republic of letters, she was well aware that she was speaking to an insect. She seemed as if she wanted to dictate to everybody around her, and she very likely thought that she had the right to do so at the age of sixty, particularly towards a young novice only twenty-five years old, who had not yet contributed anything to the literary treasury. In order to please her, I spoke to her of the Abbé Conti, and I had occasion to quote two lines of that profound writer. Madam corrected me with a patronising air for my pronunciation of the word "scevra," which means *divided*, saying that it ought to be pronounced "sceura," and she added that I ought to be very glad to have learned as much on the first day of my arrival in Paris; telling me that it would be an important day in my life.

"Madam, I came here to learn and not to unlearn. You will kindly allow me to tell you that the pronunciation of that word is 'scevra' with a *v*, and not 'sceura' with a *u*, because it is a contraction of 'sceverra.'"

"It remains to be seen which of us is wrong."

"You, madam, according to Ariosto, who makes 'scevra' rhyme with 'persevra,' and the rhyme would be false with 'sceura,' which is not an Italian word."

She would have kept up the discussion, but her husband, a man eighty years of age, told her that she was wrong. She held her tongue, but from that time she told everybody that I was an impostor.

Her husband, Louis Riccoboni, better known as Lelio, was the
same who had brought the Italian company to Paris in 1716,
and placed it at the service of the regent: he was a man of great
merit. He had been very handsome, and justly enjoyed the esteem of the public, in consequence not only of his talent but also
of the purity of his life.

During supper my principal occupation was to study Silvia,
who then enjoyed the greatest reputation, and I judged her to be
even above it. She was then about fifty years old, her figure
was elegant, her air noble, her manners graceful and easy; she
was affable, witty, kind to everybody, simple and unpretending.
Her face was an enigma, for it inspired everyone with the warmest sympathy, and yet if you examined it attentively there was
not one beautiful feature; she could not be called handsome, but
no one could have thought her ugly. Yet she was not one of
those women who are neither handsome nor ugly, for she possessed a certain something which struck one at first sight and
captivated the interest. Then what was she?

Beautiful, certainly, but owing to charms unknown to all
those who, not being attracted towards her by an irresistible
feeling which compelled them to love her, had not the courage to
study her, or the constancy to obtain a thorough knowledge of
her.

Silvia was the adoration of France, and her talent was the real
support of all the comedies which the greatest authors wrote for
her, especially of the plays of Marivaux, for without her his
comedies would never have gone to posterity. Never was an
actress found who could replace her, and to find one it would be
necessary that she should unite in herself all the perfections
which Silvia possessed for the difficult profession of the stage:
action, voice, intelligence, wit, countenance, manners, and a deep
knowledge of the human heart. In Silvia every quality was from
nature, and the art which gave the last touch of perfection to her
qualities was never seen.

To the qualities which I have just mentioned, Silvia added
another which surrounded her with a brilliant halo, and the absence of which would not have prevented her from being the
shining star of the stage: she led a virtuous life. She had been
anxious to have friends, but she had dismissed all lovers, refusing
to avail herself of a privilege which she could easily have enjoyed,

but which would have rendered her contemptible in her own estimation. This irreproachable conduct obtained for her a reputation of respectability which, at her age, would have been held as ridiculous and even insulting by any other woman belonging to the same profession; and many ladies of the highest rank honoured her with their friendship more even than with their patronage. Never did the capricious audience of a Parisian pit dare to hiss Silvia, not even in her performance of characters which the public disliked; and it was the general opinion that she was in every way above her profession.

Silvia did not think that her good conduct was a merit, for she knew that she was virtuous only because her self-love compelled her to be so, and she never exhibited any pride or assumed any superiority towards her theatrical sisters, although, satisfied to shine by their talent or their beauty, they cared little about rendering themselves conspicuous by their virtue. Silvia loved them all, and they all loved her; she always was the first to praise, openly and with good faith, the talent of her rivals; but she lost nothing by it, because, being their superior in talent and enjoying a spotless reputation, her rivals could not rise above her.

Nature deprived that charming woman of ten years of life; she became consumptive at the age of sixty, ten years after I had made her acquaintance. The climate of Paris often proves fatal to our Italian actresses. Two years before her death I saw her perform the character of Marianne in the comedy of Marivaux, and in spite of her age and declining health the illusion was complete. She died in my presence, holding her daughter in her arms, and she was giving her the advice of a tender mother five minutes before she breathed her last. She was honourably buried in the church of St. Sauveur, without the slightest opposition from the venerable priest, who, far from sharing the anti-christian intolerance of the clergy in general, said that her profession as an actress had not hindered her from being a good Christian, and that the earth was the common mother of all human beings, as Jesus Christ had been the Saviour of all mankind.

You will forgive me, dear reader, if I have made you attend the funeral of Silvia ten years before her death; believe me I have no intention of performing a miracle; you may console yourself with the idea that I shall spare you that unpleasant task when poor Silvia dies.

Her only daughter, the object of her adoration, was seated next to her at the supper-table. She was then only nine years old, and being entirely taken up by her mother I paid no attention to her; my interest in her was to come.

After the supper, which was protracted to a late hour, I repaired to the house of Madame Quinson, my landlady, where I found myself very comfortable. When I woke in the morning, the said Madame Quinson came to my room to tell me that a servant was outside and wished to offer me his services. I asked her to send him in, and I saw a man of very small stature; that did not please me, and I told him so.

"My small stature, your honour, will be a guarantee that I shall never borrow your clothes to go to some amorous rendezvous."

"Your name?"

"Any name you please."

"What do you mean? I want the name by which you are known."

"I have none. Every master I serve calls me according to his fancy, and I have served more than fifty in my life. You may call me what you like."

"But you must have a family name."

"I never had any family. I had a name, I believe, in my young days, but I have forgotten it since I have been in service. My name has changed with every new master."

"Well! I shall call you Esprit."

"You do me a great honour."

"Here, go and get me change for a louis."

"I have it, sir."

"I see you are rich."

"At your service, sir."

"Where can I inquire about you?"

"At the agency for servants. Madame Quinson, besides, can answer your inquiries. Everybody in Paris knows me."

"That is enough. I shall give you thirty sous a day; you must find your own clothes: you will sleep where you like, and you must be here at seven o'clock every morning."

Baletti called on me and entreated me to take my meals every day at his house. After his visit I told Esprit to take me to the Palais-Royal, and I left him at the gates. I felt the greatest curiosity about that renowned garden, and at first I examined everything. I see a rather fine garden, walks lined with big trees, fountains, high houses all round the garden, a great many men and women walking about, benches here and there forming shops for the sale of newspapers, perfumes, tooth-picks, and other trifles. I see a quantity of chairs for hire at the rate of one sou, men reading the newspaper under the shade of the trees, girls and men breakfasting either alone or in company, waiters who were rapidly going up and down a narrow staircase hidden under the foliage.

I sit down at a small table: a waiter comes immediately to inquire my wishes. I ask for some chocolate made with water; he brings me some, but very bad, although served in a splendid silver-gilt cup. I tell him to give me some coffee, if it is good.

"Excellent, I made it myself yesterday."

"Yesterday! I do not want it."

"The milk is very good."

"Milk! I never drink any. Make me a cup of fresh coffee without milk."

"Without milk! Well, sir, we never make coffee but in the afternoon. Would you like a good bavaroise, or a decanter of orgeat?"

"Yes, give me the orgeat."

I find that beverage delicious, and make up my mind to have it daily for my breakfast. I inquire from the waiter whether there is any news; he answers that the dauphine has been delivered of a prince. An abbé, seated at a table close by, says to him:

"You are mad; she has given birth to a princess."

A third man comes forward and exclaims:

"I have just returned from Versailles, and the dauphine has not been delivered either of a prince or of a princess."

Then, turning towards me, he says that I look like a foreigner, and when I say that I am an Italian he begins to speak to me of the court, of the city, of the theatres, and at last he offers to accompany me everywhere. I thank him and take my leave. The abbé rises at the same time, walks with me, and tells me the names of all the women we meet in the garden.

A young man comes up to him, they embrace one another, and the abbé presents him to me as a learned Italian scholar. I address him in Italian, and he answers very wittily, but his way of speaking makes me smile, and I tell him why. He expressed himself exactly in the style of Boccacio. My remark pleases him, but I soon prove to him that it is not the right way to speak, however perfect may have been the language of that ancient writer. In less than a quarter of an hour we are excellent friends, for we find that our tastes are the same.

My new friend was a poet as I was; he was an admirer of Italian literature, while I admired the French.

We exchange addresses, and promise to see one another very often.

I see a crowd in one corner of the garden, everybody standing still and looking up. I inquire from my friend whether there is anything wonderful going on.

"These persons are watching the meridian; everyone holds his watch in his hand in order to regulate it exactly at noon."

"Is there not a meridian everywhere?"

"Yes; but the meridian of the Palais-Royal is the most exact."

I laugh heartily.

"Why do you laugh?"

"Because it is impossible for all meridians not to be the same. That is true *badauderie*."

My friend looks at me for a moment, then he laughs likewise, and supplies me with ample food to ridicule the worthy Parisians. We leave the Palais-Royal through the main gate, and I observe another crowd of people before a shop, on the sign-board of which I read, "At the Sign of the Civet Cat."

"What is the matter here?"

"Now, indeed, you are going to laugh. All these honest persons are waiting their turn to get their snuff-boxes filled."

"Is there no other dealer in snuff?"

"It is sold everywhere, but for the last three weeks nobody will use any snuff but that sold at the 'Civet Cat.'"

"Is it better than anywhere else?"

"Perhaps it is not as good; but since it has been brought into fashion by the Duchesse de Chartres, nobody will have any other."

"But how did she manage to render it so fashionable?"

"Simply by stopping her carriage two or three times before the shop to have her snuff-box filled, and by saying aloud to the young girl who handed back the box that her snuff was the very best in Paris. The *badauds*, who never fail to congregate near the carriage of princes, no matter if they have seen them a hundred times, or if they know them to be as ugly as monkeys, repeated the words of the duchess everywhere, and that was enough to send here all the snuff-takers of the capital in a hurry. This woman will make a fortune, for she sells at least one hundred crowns' worth of snuff every day."

"Very likely the duchess has no idea of the good she has done."

"Quite the reverse, for it was a cunning artifice on her part. The duchess, feeling interested in the newly-married young woman, and wishing to serve her in a delicate manner, thought of that expedient, which has met with complete success. You cannot imagine how kind the Parisians are. You are now in the only country in the world where wit can make a fortune by selling either a genuine or a false article: in the first case, it receives the welcome of intelligent and talented people, and in the second, fools are always ready to reward it, for silliness is truly a characteristic of the people here, and, however wonderful it may appear, silliness is the daughter of wit. Therefore it is not a paradox to say that the French would be wiser if they were less witty.

"The gods worshipped here — although no altars are raised for them — are Novelty and Fashion. Let a man run, and everybody will run after him. The crowd will not stop, unless the man is proved to be mad; but to prove it is indeed a difficult task, because we have a crowd of men who, mad from their birth, are still considered wise.

"The snuff of the 'Civet Cat' is but one example of the facility with which the crowd can be attracted to one particular spot. The king was one day hunting, and found himself at the Neuilly Bridge; being thirsty, he wanted a glass of ratafia. He stopped at the door of a drinking-booth, and by the most lucky chance the poor keeper of the place happened to have a bottle of that liquor. The king, after he had drunk a small glass, fancied a second one, and said that he had never tasted such delicious ratafia in his life. That was enough to give the ratafia of the good man of Neuilly the reputation of being the best in Europe: the king had said so. The consequence was that the most brilliant society frequented the tavern of the delighted publican, who is now a very wealthy man, and has built on the very spot a splendid house on which can be read the following rather comic motto: '*Ex liquidid solidum,*' which certainly came out of the head of one of the forty immortals. Which gods must the worthy tavern-keeper worship? Silliness, frivolity, and mirth."

"It seems to me," I replied, "that such approval, such ratification of the opinions expressed by the king, the princes of the blood, etc., is rather a proof of the affection felt for them by the nation, for the French carry that affection to such an extent that they believe them infallible."

"It is certain that everything here causes foreigners to believe that the French people adore the king; but all thinking men here know well enough that there is more show than reality in that adoration, and the court has no confidence in it. When the king comes to Paris, everybody calls out '*Vive le Roi!*' because some idle fellow begins, or because some policeman has given the signal from the midst of the crowd; but it is really a cry which has no importance, a cry given out of cheerfulness, sometimes out of fear, and which the king himself does not accept as gospel. He does not feel comfortable in Paris, and he prefers being in Versailles, surrounded by twenty-five thousand men who protect him against the fury of that same people of Paris, who, if ever they became wiser, might very well one day call out, 'Death to the king!' instead of 'Long life to the king!' Louis XIV. was well aware of it, and several councillors of the upper chamber lost their lives for having advised the assembling of the States-General in order to find some remedy for the misfortunes of the country. France never had any love for any kings, with the exception of St. Louis, of Louis XII., and of the great and good Henry IV.; and even in the last case the love of the nation was not sufficient to defend the king against the dagger of the Jesuits, an accursed race, the enemy of nations as well as of kings. The present king, who is weak and entirely led by his ministers, said candidly at the time he was just recovering from illness, 'I am surprised at the rejoicings of the people in consequence of my health being restored, for I cannot imagine why they should love me so dearly.' Many kings might repeat the same words, at least if love is to be measured according to the amount of good actually done. That candid remark of Louis XV. has been highly praised, but some philosopher of the Court ought to have informed him that he was so much loved because he had been surnamed *le bien aimé.*"

"Surname or nickname; but are there any philosophers at the Court of France?"

"No; for philosophers and courtiers are as widely different as light and darkness; but there are some men of intelligence who champ the bit from motives of ambition and interest."

As we were thus conversing, M. Patu (such was the name of my new acquaintance) escorted me as far as the door of Silvia's house; he congratulated me upon being one of her friends, and we parted company.

I found the amiable actress in good company. She introduced me to all her guests, and gave me some particulars respecting every one of them. The name of Crébillon struck my ear.

"What, sir!" I said to him, "am I fortunate enough to see you? For eight years you have charmed me, for eight years I have longed to know you. Listen, I beg of you."

I then recited the finest passage of his *Zénobie et Rhadamiste,* which I had translated into blank verse. Silvia was delighted to see the pleasure enjoyed by Crébillon in hearing, at the age of eighty, his own lines in a language which he knew thoroughly and loved as much as his own. He himself recited the same passage in French, and politely pointed out the parts in which he thought that I had improved on the original. I thanked him, but I was not deceived by his compliment.

We sat down to supper, and, being asked what I had already seen in Paris, I related everything I had done, omitting only my conversation with Patu. After I had spoken for a long time, Crébillon, who had evidently observed better than anyone else the road I had chosen in order to learn the good as well as the bad qualities of his countrymen, said to me:

"For the first day, sir, I think that what you have done gives great hopes of you, and without any doubt you will make rapid progress. You tell your story well, and you speak French in such a way as to be perfectly understood; yet all you say is only Italian dressed in French. That is a novelty which causes you to be listened to with interest, and which captivates the attention of your audience; I must even add that your Franco-Italian language is just the thing to enlist in your favour the sympathy of those who listen to you, because it is singular, new, and because you are in a country where everybody worships those two divinities — novelty and singularity. Nevertheless, you must begin to-morrow and apply yourself in good earnest, in order to acquire a thorough knowledge of our language, for the same persons who warmly applaud you now, will, in two or three months, laugh at you."

"I believe it sir, and that is what I fear; therefore the principal object of my visit here is to devote myself entirely to the study of the French language. But, sir, how shall I find a teacher? I am a very unpleasant pupil, always asking questions, curious, troublesome, insatiable; and even supposing that I could meet with the teacher I require, I am afraid I am not rich enough to pay him."

"For fifty years, sir, I have been looking out for a pupil such as you have just described yourself, and I would willingly pay you myself if you would come to my house and receive my lessons. I reside in the Marais, Rue de Douze Portes. I have the best Italian poets; I will make you translate them into French, and you need not be afraid of my finding you insatiable."

I accepted with joy; I did not know how to express my gratitude, but both his offer and the few words of my answer bore the stamp of truth and frankness.

Crébillon was a giant; he was six feet high, and three inches taller than I. He had a good appetite, could tell a good story without laughing, was celebrated for his witty repartees and his sociable manners; but he spent his life at home, seldom going out, and seeing hardly anyone because he always had a pipe in his mouth and was surrounded by at least twenty cats, with which he would amuse himself all day. He had an old housekeeper, a cook, and a man-servant. His housekeeper had the management of everything; she never allowed him to be in need of anything, and she gave no account of his money, which she kept altogether, because he never asked her to render any accounts. The expression of Crébillon's face was that of the lion's or of the cat's, which is the same thing. He was one of the royal censors, and he told me that it was an amusement for him. His housekeeper was in the habit of reading him the works brought for his examination, and she would stop reading when she came to a passage which, in her opinion, deserved his censure; but sometimes they were of a different opinion, and then their discussions were truly amusing. I once heard the housekeeper send away an author with these words:

"Come again next week; *we* have had no time to examine your manuscript."

During a whole year I paid M. Crébillon three visits every week, and from him I learned all I know of the French language; but I found it impossible to get rid of my Italian idioms. I remark that turn easily enough when I meet with it in other people, but it flows naturally from my pen without my being aware of it. I am satisfied that, whatever I may do, I shall never be able to recognise it any more than I can find out in what consists the bad Latin style so constantly alleged against Livy.

I composed a stanza of eight verses on some subject which I do not recollect, and I gave it to Crébillon, asking him to correct it. He read it attentively, and said to me:

"These eight verses are good and regular; the thought is fine and truly poetical, the style is perfect; and yet the stanza is bad."

"How so?"

"I do not know. I cannot tell you what is wanting. Imagine that you see a man handsome, well made, amiable, witty — in fact, perfect, according to your most severe judgment. A woman comes in, sees him, looks at him, and goes away telling you that the man does not please her. 'But what fault do you find in him, madam?' 'None, only he does not please me.' You look again at the man, you examine him a second time, and you find that, in order to give him a heavenly voice, he has been deprived of that which constitutes a man, and you are compelled to acknowledge that a spontaneous feeling has stood the woman in good stead."

It was by that comparison that Crébillon explained to me a thing almost inexplicable, for taste and feeling alone can account for a thing which is subject to no rule whatever.

We spoke a great deal of Louis XIV., whom Crébillon had

known well for fifteen years, and he related several very curious anecdotes which were generally unknown. Amongst other things he assured me that the Siamese ambassadors were cheats paid by Madame de Maintenon. He told us likewise that he had never finished his tragedy of *Cromwell*, because the king had told him one day not to wear out his pen on a scoundrel.

Crébillon mentioned likewise his tragedy of *Catilina*, and he told me that, in his opinion, it was the most deficient of his works, but that he never would have consented, even to make it a good tragedy, to represent Cæsar as a young man, because he would in that case have made the public laugh, as they would do if Medea were to appear previous to her acquaintance with Jason.

He praised the talent of Voltaire very highly, but he accused him of having stolen from him, Crébillon, the scene of the senate. He, however, rendered him full justice, saying that he was a true historian, and able to write history as well as tragedies, but that he unfortunately adulterated history by mixing with it such a number of light anecdotes and tales for the sake of rendering it more attractive. According to Crébillon, the Man with the Iron Mask was nothing but an idle tale, and he had been assured of it by Louis XIV. himself.

On the day of my first meeting with Crébillon at Silvia's, *Cénie*, a play by Madame de Graffigny, was performed at the Italian Theatre, and I went away early in order to get a good seat in the pit.

The ladies all covered with diamonds, who were taking possession of the private boxes, engrossed all my interest and all my attention. I wore a very fine suit, but my open ruffles and the buttons all along my coat showed at once that I was a foreigner, for the fashion was not the same in Paris. I was gaping in the air and listlessly looking round, when a gentleman, splendidly dressed, and three times stouter than I, came up and inquired whether I was a foreigner. I answered affirmatively, and he politely asked me how I liked Paris; I praised Paris very warmly. But at that moment a very stout lady, brilliant with diamonds, entered the box near us. Her enormous size astonished me, and, like a fool, I said to the gentleman:

"Who is that fat sow?"

"She is the wife of this fat pig."

"Ah! I beg your pardon a thousand times!"

But my stout gentleman cared nothing for my apologies, and very far from being angry he almost choked with laughter. This was the happy result of the practical and natural philosophy which Frenchmen cultivate so well, and which ensures the happiness of their existence under an appearance of frivolity!

I was confused, I was in despair, but the stout gentleman continued to laugh heartily. At last he left the pit, and a minute afterwards I saw him enter the box and speak to his wife. I was keeping an eye on them without daring to look at them openly, and suddenly the lady, following the example of her husband, burst into a loud laugh. Their mirth making me more uncomfortable, I was leaving the pit, when the husband called out to me, "Sir! Sir!"

I could not go away without being guilty of impoliteness, and I went up to their box. Then, with a serious countenance and with great affability, he begged my pardon for having laughed so much, and very graciously invited me to come to his house and sup with them that same evening. I thanked him politely, saying that I had a previous engagement. But he renewed his entreaties, and his wife pressing me in the most engaging manner I told them, in order to prove that I was not trying to elude their invitation, that I was expected to sup at Silvia's house.

"In that case I am certain," said the gentleman, "of obtaining your release if you do not object. Allow me to go myself to Silvia."

It would have been uncourteous on my part to resist any longer. He left the box and returned almost immediately with my friend Baletti, who told me that his mother was delighted to see me making such excellent acquaintances, and that she would expect to see me at dinner the next day. He whispered to me that my new acquaintance was M. de Beauchamp, Receiver-General of Taxes.

As soon as the performance was over, I offered my hand to madame, and we drove to their mansion in a magnificent carriage. There I found the abundance or rather the profusion which in Paris is exhibited by the men of finance; numerous society, high play, good cheer, and open cheerfulness. The supper was not over till one o'clock in the morning. Madame's private carriage drove me to my lodgings. That house offered me a kind welcome during the whole of my stay in Paris, and I must add that my new friends proved very useful to me. Some persons assert that foreigners find the first fortnight in Paris very dull, because a little time is necessary to get introduced; but I was fortunate enough to find myself established on as good a footing as I could desire within twenty-four hours, and the consequence was that I felt delighted with Paris, and certain that my stay would prove an agreeable one.

The next morning Patu called and make me a present of his prose panegyric on the Maréchal de Saxe. We went out together and took a walk in the Tuileries, where he introduced me to Madame du Boccage, who made a good jest in speaking of the Maréchal de Saxe.

"It is singular," she said, "that we cannot have a *De profundis* for a man who makes us sing the *Te Deum* so often."

As we left the Tuileries, Patu took me to the house of a celebrated actress of the opera, Mademoiselle Le Fel, the favourite of all Paris, and member of the Royal Academy of Music. She had three young and charming children, who were fluttering around her like butterflies.

"I adore them," she said to me.

"They deserve adoration for their beauty," I answered, "although they have all a different cast of countenance."

"No wonder! The eldest is the son of the Duke d'Anneci, the second of Count d'Egmont, and the youngest is the offspring of Maison-Rouge, who has just married the Romainville."

"Ah! pray excuse me: I thought you were the mother of the three."

"You were not mistaken; I am their mother."

As she said these words she looked at Patu, and both burst into hearty laughter which did not make me blush, but which showed me my blunder.

I was a novice in Paris, and I had not been accustomed to see women encroach upon the privilege which men alone generally enjoy. Yet Mademoiselle Le Fel was not a bold-faced woman; she was even rather lady-like, but she was what is called above prejudices. If I had known the manners of the time better, I should have been aware that such things were everyday occurrences, and that the noblemen who thus sprinkled their progeny everywhere were in the habit of leaving their children in the hands of their mothers, who were well paid. The more fruit-ful, therefore, these ladies were, the greater was their income.

My want of experience often led me into serious blunders, and Mademoiselle Le Fel would, I have no doubt, have laughed at anyone telling her that I had some wit, after the stupid mistake of which I had been guilty.

Another day, being at the house of Lani, ballet-master of the opera, I saw five or six young girls of thirteen or fourteen years of age accompanied by their mothers, and all exhibiting that air of modesty which is the characteristic of a good education. I addressed a few gallant words to them, and they answered me with downcast eyes. One of them having complained of the headache, I offered her my smelling-bottle, and one of her companions said to her:

"Very likely you did not sleep well last night."

"Oh! it is not that," answered the modest-looking Agnes, "I think I am in the family-way."

On receiving this unexpected reply from a girl I had taken for a maiden, I said to her:

"I should never have supposed that you were married, madam."

She looked at me with evident surprise for a moment, then she turned towards her friend, and both began to laugh immoderately. Ashamed, but for them more than myself, I left the house with a firm resolution never again to take virtue for granted in a class of women amongst whom it is so scarce. To look for, even to suppose, modesty, amongst the nymphs of the green room, is, indeed, to be very foolish; they pride themselves upon having none, and laugh at those who are simple enough to suppose them better than they are.

Thanks to my friend Patu, I made the acquaintance of all the women who enjoyed some reputation in Paris. He was fond of the fair sex, but unfortunately for him he had not a constitution like mine, and his love of pleasure killed him very early. If he had lived, he would have gone down to posterity in the wake of Voltaire, but he paid the debt of nature at the age of thirty.

I learned from him the secret which several young French *literati* employ in order to make certain of the perfection of their prose, when they want to write anything requiring as perfect a style as they can obtain, such as panegyrics, funeral orations, eulogies, dedications, etc. It was by surprise that I wrested that secret from Patu.

Being at his house one morning, I observed on his table several sheets of paper covered with dodecasyllabic blank verse.

I read a dozen of them, and I told him that, although the verses were very fine, the reading caused me more pain than pleasure.

"They express the same ideas as the panegyric of the Maréchal de Saxe, but I confess that your prose pleases me a great deal more."

"My prose would not have pleased you so much, if it had not been at first composed in blank verse."

"Then you take very great trouble for nothing."

"No trouble at all, for I have not the slightest difficulty in writing that sort of poetry. I write it as easily as prose."

"Do you think that your prose is better when you compose it from your own poetry?"

"No doubt of it; it is much better, and I also secure the advantage that my prose is not full of half verses which flow from the pen of the writer without his being aware of it."

"Is that a fault?"

"A great one and not to be forgiven. Prose intermixed with occasional verses is worse than prosaic poetry."

"Is it true that the verses which, like parasites, steal into a funeral oration, must be sadly out of place?"

"Certainly. Take the example of Tacitus, who begins his history of Rome by these words: *Urbem Romam a principio reges habuere.* They form a very poor Latin hexameter, which the great historian certainly never made on purpose, and which he never remarked when he revised his work, for there is no doubt that, if he had observed it, he would have altered that sentence. Are not such verses considered a blemish in Italian prose?"

"Decidedly. But I must say that a great many poor writers have purposely inserted such verses into their prose, believing that they would make it more euphonious. Hence the *tawdriness* which is justly alleged against much Italian literature. But I suppose you are the only writer who takes so much pains."

"The only one? Certainly not. All the authors who can compose blank verses very easily, as I can, employ them when they intend to make a fair copy of their prose. Ask Crébillon, the Abbé de Voisenon, Laharpe, anyone you like, and they will all tell you the same thing. Voltaire was the first to have recourse to that art in the small pieces in which his prose is truly charming. For instance, the epistle to Madame du Chatelet, which is magnificent. Read it, and if you find a single hemistich in it I will confess myself in the wrong."

I felt some curiosity about the matter, and I asked Crébillon about it. He told me that Patu was right, but he added that he had never practised that art himself.

Patu wished very much to take me to the opera in order to witness the effect produced upon me by the performance, which must truly astonish an Italian. *Les Fêtes Vénitiennes* was the title of the opera which was in vogue just then — a title full of interest for me. We went for our forty sous to the pit, in which, although the audience was standing, the company was excellent, for the opera was the favourite amusement of the Parisians.

After a symphony, very fine in its way and executed by an excellent orchestra, the curtain rises, and I see a beautiful scene representing the small St. Mark's Square in Venice, taken from the Island of St. George; but I am shocked to see the ducal palace on my left, and the tall steeple on my right, that is to say the very reverse of reality. I laugh at this ridiculous mistake, and Patu, to whom I say why I am laughing, cannot help joining me. The music, very fine although in the ancient style, at first amused me on account of its novelty, but it soon wearied me. The melopæia fatigued me by its constant and tedious monotony, and by the shrieks given out of season. That melopæia of the French replaces — at least they think so — the Greek melopæia and our recitative, which they dislike, but which they would admire if they understood Italian.

The action of the opera was limited to a day in the carnival, when the Venetians are in the habit of promenading masked in St. Mark's Square. The stage was animated by gallants, procuresses, and women amusing themselves with all sorts of intrigues; the costumes were whimsical and erroneous, but the whole was amusing. I laughed very heartily, and it was truly a curious sight for a Venetian, when I saw the Doge followed by twelve councillors appear on the stage, all dressed in the most ludicrous style, and dancing a *pas d'ensemble*. Suddenly the whole of the pit burst into loud applause at the appearance of a tall, well-made dancer, wearing a mask and an enormous black wig, the hair of which went half-way down his back, and dressed in a robe open in front and reaching to his heels. Patu said, almost reverently, "It is the inimitable Duprès." I had heard of him before, and became attentive. I saw that fine figure coming forward with measured steps, and when the dancer had arrived in front of the stage, he raised slowly his rounded arms, stretched them gracefully backward and forward, moved his feet with precision and lightness, took a few small steps, made some battements and pirouettes, and disappeared like a butterfly. The whole had not lasted half a minute. The applause burst from every part of the house; I was astonished, and asked my friend the cause of all those bravos.

"We applaud the grace of Duprès and the divine harmony of his movements. He is now sixty years of age, and those who saw him forty years ago say that he is always the same."

"What! Has he never danced in a different style?"

"He could not have danced in a better one, for his style is perfect, and what can you want above perfection?"

"Nothing, unless it be a relative perfection."

"But here it is absolute. Duprès always does the same thing, and every day we fancy we see it for the first time. Such is the power of the good and beautiful, of the true and sublime, which speak to the soul. His dance is true harmony, the real dance, of which you have no idea in Italy."

At the end of the second act, Duprès appeared again, still with a mask, and danced to a different tune, but in my opinion doing exactly the same as before. He advanced to the very footlights, and stopped one instant in a graceful attitude. Patu wanted to force my admiration, and I gave way. Suddenly everyone around me exclaimed:

"Look! look! he is developing himself!"

And in reality he was like an elastic body which, in developing itself, would get larger; I made Patu very happy by telling him that Duprès was truly very graceful in all his movements. Immediately after him we had a female dancer, who jumped about like a fury, cutting to right and left, but heavily; yet she was applauded *con furore*.

"This is," said Patu, "the famous Camargo. I congratulate you, my friend, upon having arrived in Paris in time to see her, for she has accomplished her twelfth lustre."

I confessed that she was a wonderful dancer.

"She is the first artist," continued my friend, "who has dared to spring and jump on a French stage; none ventured upon doing it before her, and, what is more extraordinary, she does not wear any drawers."

"I beg your pardon, but I saw —"

"What? Nothing but her skin, which, to speak the truth, is not made of lilies and roses."

"The Camargo," I said, with an air of repentance, "does not please me; I like Duprès much better."

An elderly admirer of Camargo, seated on my left, told me that in her youth she could perform the *saut de basque* and even the *gargouillade*, and that nobody had ever seen her thighs, although she always danced without drawers.

"But if you never saw her thighs, how do you know that she does not wear silk tights?"

"Oh! that is one of those things which can easily be ascertained. I see you are a foreigner, sir."

"You are right."

But I was delighted at the French opera, with the rapidity of the scenic changes which are done like lightning, at the signal of a whistle — a thing entirely unknown in Italy. I likewise admired the start given to the orchestra by the baton of the leader, but he disgusted me with the movements of his sceptre right and left, as if he thought that he could give life to all the instruments by the mere motion of his arm. I admired also the silence of the audience, a thing truly wonderful to an Italian, for it is with great reason that people complain of the noise made in Italy while the artists are singing, and ridicule the silence which prevails through the house as soon as the dancers make their appearance on the stage. One would imagine that all the intelligence of the Italians is in their eyes. At the same time I must observe that there is not one country in the world in which extravagance and whimsicalness cannot be found, because the foreigner can make comparisons with what he has seen elsewhere, whilst the natives are not conscious of their errors. Altogether the opera pleased me, but the French comedy captivated me. There the French are truly in their element; they perform splendidly, in a masterly manner, and other nations cannot refuse them the palm which good taste and justice must award to their superiority. I was in the habit of going there every day, and, although sometimes the audience was not composed of two hundred persons, the actors were perfect. I have seen *Le Misanthrope, L'Avare, Tartufe, Le Loueur, Le Glorieux*, and many other comedies; and, no matter how often I saw them, I always fancied it was the first time. I arrived in Paris to admire Sarrazin, La Dangeville, La Dumesnil, La Gaussin, La Clarion, Préville, and several actresses who, having retired from the stage, were living upon their pension and delighting their circle of friends. I made, amongst others, the acquaintance of the celebrated Le Vasseur. I visited them all with pleasure, and they related to me several very curious anecdotes. They were generally most kindly disposed, in every way.

One evening, being in the box of Le Vasseur, the performance was composed of a tragedy in which a very handsome actress had the part of a dumb priestess.

"How pretty she is!" I said.

"Yes, charming," answered Le Vasseur. "She is the daughter of the actor who plays the confidant. She is very pleasant in company, and is an actress of good promise."

"I should be very happy to make her acquaintance."

"Oh! well, that is not difficult. Her father and mother are very worthy people, and they will be delighted if you ask them to invite you to supper. They will not disturb you; they will go to bed early, and will let you talk with their daughter as long as you please. You are in France, sir; here we know the value of life, and try to make the best of it. We love pleasure, and esteem ourselves fortunate when we can find the opportunity of enjoying life."

"That is truly charming, madam; but how could I be so bold as to invite myself to supper with worthy persons whom I do not know, and who have not the slightest knowledge of me?"

"Oh, dear me! What are you saying? We know everybody. You see how I treat you myself. After the performance, I shall be happy to introduce you, and the acquaintance will be made at once."

"I certainly must ask you to do me that honour, but another time."

"Whenever you like."

CHAPTER VII

HOMME DU MONDE AND CABALIST

MADAME LA DAUPHINE was delivered of a princess, who received the title of Madame de France.

In the month of August the Royal Academy had an exhibition at the Louvre, and as there was not a single battle-piece I conceived the idea of summoning my brother to Paris. He was then in Venice, and he had great talent in that particular style. Passorelli, the only painter of battles known in France, was dead, and I thought that François might succeed and make a fortune. I therefore wrote to M. Grimani and to my brother; I persuaded them both, but François did not come to Paris till the beginning of the following year.

Louis XV., who was passionately fond of hunting, was in the habit of spending six weeks every year at the Château of Fontainebleau. He always returned to Versailles towards the middle of November. That trip cost him, or rather cost France, five millions of francs. He always took with him all that could contribute to the amusement of the foreign ambassadors and of his numerous court. He was followed by the French and the Italian comedians, and by the actors and actresses of the opera.

During those six weeks Fontainebleau was more brilliant than Versailles; nevertheless, the artists attached to the theatres were so numerous that the Opera, the French and Italian Comedies, remained open in Paris.

Baletti's father, who had recovered his health, was to go to Fontainebleau with Silvia and all his family. They invited me to accompany them, and to accept a lodging in a house hired by them.

It was a splendid opportunity; they were my friends, and I accepted, for I could not have met with a better occasion to see the court and all the foreign ministers. I presented myself to M. de Morosini, now Procurator at St. Mark's, and then ambassador from the Republic to the French court.

The first night of the opera he gave me permission to accompany him; the music was by Lulli. I had a seat in the pit precisely under the private box of Madame de Pompadour, whom I did not know. During the first scene the celebrated Le Maur gave a scream so shrill and so unexpected that I thought she had gone mad. I burst into a genuine laugh, not supposing that anyone could possibly find fault with it. But a knight of the Order of the Holy Ghost, who was near the Marquise de Pompadour, dryly asked me what country I came from. I answered, in the same tone:

"From Venice."

"I have been there, and have laughed heartily at the recitative in your operas."

"I believe you, sir, and I feel certain that no one ever thought of objecting to your laughing."

My answer, rather a sharp one, made Madame de Pompadour laugh, and she asked me whether I truly came from down there.

"What do you mean by down there?"

"I mean Venice."

"Venice, madam, is not down there, but up there."

That answer was found more singular than the first, and everybody in the box held a consultation in order to ascertain whether Venice was down or up. Most likely they thought I was right, for I was left alone. Nevertheless, I listened to the opera without laughing; but as I had a very bad cold I blew my nose often. The same gentleman, addressing himself again to me, remarked that very likely the windows of my room did not close well. That gentleman, who was unknown to me, was the Maréchal de Richelieu. I told him he was mistaken, for my windows were well *calfoutrées*. Everyone in the box burst into a loud laugh, and I felt mortified, for I knew my mistake; I ought to have said *calfeutrées*. But these *eus* and *ous* cause dire misery to all foreigners.

Half an hour afterwards, M. de Richelieu asked me which of the two actresses pleased me most by her beauty.

"That one, sir."

"But she has ugly legs."

"They are not seen, sir; besides, whenever I examine the beauty of a woman, *la première chose que j'écarte, ce sont les jambes.*"

That word said quite by chance, and the double meaning of which I did not understand, made at once an important personage of me, and everybody in the box of Madame de Pompadour was curious to know me. The marshal learned who I was from M. de Morosini, who told me that the duke would be happy to receive me. My *jeu de mots* became celebrated, and the marshal honoured me with a very gracious welcome. Among the foreign ministers, the one to whom I attached myself most was Lord Keith, Marshal of Scotland and ambassador of the King of Prussia. I shall have occasion to speak of him.

The day after my arrival in Fontainebleau I went alone to the court, and I saw Louis XV., the handsome king, go to the chapel with the royal family and all the ladies of the court, who surprised me by their ugliness as much as the ladies of the court of Turin had astonished me by their beauty. Yet in the midst of so many ugly ones I found out a regular beauty. I inquired who she was.

"She is," answered one of my neighbours, "Madame de Brionne, more remarkable by her virtue even than by her beauty. Not only is there no scandalous story told about her, but she has never given any opportunity to scandal-mongers of inventing any adventure of which she was the heroine."

"Perhaps her adventures are not known."

"Ah, monsieur! at the court everything is known."

I went about alone, sauntering through the apartments, when suddenly I met a dozen ugly ladies who seemed to be running rather than walking; they were standing so badly upon their legs that they appeared as if they would fall forward on their faces. Some gentleman happened to be near me, curiosity impelled me to inquire where they were coming from, and where they were going in such haste.

"They are coming from the apartment of the queen, who is going to dine, and the reason why they walk so badly is that their shoes have heels six inches high, which compel them to walk on their toes and with bent knees in order to avoid falling on their faces."

"But why do they not wear lower heels?"

"It is the fashion!"

"What a stupid fashion!"

I took a gallery at random, and saw the king passing along, leaning with one arm on the shoulder of M. d'Argenson. "Oh, base servility!" I thought to myself. "How can a man make up his mind thus to bear the yoke, and how can a man believe himself so much above all others as to take such unwarrantable liberties!"

Louis XV. had the most magnificent head it was possible to see, and he carried it with as much grace as majesty. Never did even the most skilful painter succeed in rendering justice to the expression of that beautiful head, when the king turned it on one side to look with kindness at anyone. His beauty and grace compelled love at once. As I saw him, I thought I had found the ideal majesty which I had been so surprised not to find in the King of Sardinia, and I could not entertain a doubt of Madame de Pompadour having been in love with the king when she sued for his royal attention. I was greatly mistaken, perhaps, but such a thought was natural in looking at the countenance of Louis XV.

I reached a splendid room in which I saw several courtiers walking about, and a table large enough for twelve persons, but laid out only for one.

"For whom is this table?"

"For the queen. Her majesty is now coming in."

It was the Queen of France, without rouge, and very simply dressed; her head was covered with a large cap; she looked old and devout. When she was near the table, she graciously thanked two nuns who were placing a plate with fresh butter on it. She sat down, and immediately the courtiers formed a semicircle within five yards of the table; I remained near them, imitating their respectful silence.

Her majesty began to eat without looking at anyone, keeping her eyes on her plate. One of the dishes being to her taste, she desired to be helped to it a second time, and she then cast her eyes round the circle of courtiers, probably in order to see if among them there was anyone to whom she owed an account of her daintiness. She found that person, I suppose, for she said:

"Monsieur de Lowendal!"

At that name, a fine-looking man came forward with a respectful inclination, and said:

"Your majesty?"

"I believe this is a fricassee of chickens."

"I am of the same opinion, madam."

After this answer, given in the most serious tone, the queen

[252]

continued eating, and the marshal retreated backward to his
original place. The queen finished her dinner without uttering a
single word, and retired to her apartments the same way as she
had come. I thought that if such was the way the Queen of
France took all her meals, I would not sue for the honour of being her guest.

I was delighted to have seen the famous captain who had conquered Bergen-op-Zoom, but I regretted that such a man should
be compelled to give an answer about a fricassee of chickens in
the serious tone of a judge pronouncing a sentence of death.

I made good use of this anecdote at the excellent dinner Silvia
gave to the *élite* of polite and agreeable society.

A few days afterwards, as I was forming a line with a crowd
of courtiers to enjoy the ever new pleasure of seeing the king go
to mass, a pleasure to which must be added the advantage of
looking at the naked and entirely exposed arms and bosoms of
Mesdames de France, his daughters, I suddenly perceived the
Cavamacchia, whom I had left in Cesena under the name of
Madame Querini. If I was astonished to see her, she was as
much so in meeting me in such a place. The Marquis of Saint
Simon, *premier gentilhomme* of the Prince de Condé, escorted her.

"Madame Querini in Fontainebleau?"

"You here? It reminds me of Queen Elizabeth saying: '*Pau-
per ubique jacet.*'"

"An excellent comparison, madam."

"I am only joking, my dear friend; I am here to see the king,
who does not know me; but to-morrow the ambassador will
present me to his majesty."

She placed herself in the line within a yard or two from me,
beside the door by which the king was to come. His majesty
entered the gallery with M. de Richelieu, and looked at the so-
called Madame Querini. But she very likely did not take his
fancy, for, continuing to walk on, he addressed to the marshal
these remarkable words, which Juliette must have overheard:

"We have handsomer women here."

In the afternoon I called upon the Venetian ambassador. I
found him in numerous company, with Madame Querini sitting
on his right. She addressed me in the most flattering and
friendly manner; it was extraordinary conduct on the part of a
giddy woman who had no cause to like me, for she was aware

that I knew her thoroughly, and that I had mastered her vanity; but as I understood her manœuvring I made up my mind not to disoblige her, and even to render her all the good offices I could; it was a noble revenge.

As she was speaking of M. Querini, the ambassador congratulated her upon her marriage with him, saying that he was glad M. Querini had rendered justice to her merit, and adding:

"I was not aware of your marriage."

"Yet it took place more than two years since," said Juliette.

"I know it for a fact," I said, in my turn; "for, two years ago, the lady was introduced as Madame Querini and with the title of excellency by General Spada to all the nobility in Cesena, where I was at that time."

"I have no doubt of it," answered the ambassador, fixing his eyes upon me, "for Querini has himself written to me on the subject."

A few minutes afterwards, as I was preparing to take my leave, the ambassador, under pretence of some letters the contents of which he wished to communicate to me, invited me to come into his private room, and he asked me what people generally thought of the marriage in Venice.

"Nobody knows it, and it is even rumoured that the heir of the house of Querini is on the point of marrying a daughter of the Grimani family; but I shall certainly send the news to Venice."

"What news?"

"That Juliette is truly Madame Querini, since your excellency will present her as such to Louis XV."

"Who told you so?"

"She did."

"Perhaps she has altered her mind."

I repeated to the ambassador the words which the king had said to M. de Richelieu after looking at Juliette.

"Then I can guess," remarked the ambassador, "why Juliette does not wish to be presented to the king."

I was informed some time afterwards that M. de Saint Quentin, the king's confidential minister, had called after mass on the handsome Venetian, and had told her that the King of France had most certainly very bad taste, because he had not thought her beauty superior to that of several ladies of his court. Juliette left Fontainebleau the next morning.

In the first part of my Memoirs I have spoken of Juliette's beauty; she had a wonderful charm in her countenance, but she had already used her advantages too long, and her beauty was beginning to fade when she arrived in Fontainebleau.

I met her again in Paris at the ambassador's, and she told me with a laugh that she had only been in jest when she called herself Madame Querini, and that I should oblige her if for the future I would call her by her real name of Countess Preati. She invited me to visit her at the Hôtel de Luxembourg, where she was staying. I often called on her, for her intrigues amused me, but I was wise enough not to meddle with them.

She remained in Paris four months, and contrived to infatuate M. Zanchi, secretary of the Venetian Embassy, an amiable and learned man. He was so deeply in love that he had made up his mind to marry her; but through a caprice which she, perhaps, regretted afterwards, she ill-treated him, and the fool died of grief. Count de Kaunitz, ambassador of Maria Theresa, had some inclination for her, as well as the Count of Zinzendorf. The person who arranged these transient and short-lived intrigues was a certain Guasco, an abbé not over-favoured with the gifts of Plutus. He was particularly ugly, and had to purchase small favours with great services.

But the man whom she really wished to marry was Count Saint Simon. He would have married her if she had not given him false addresses to make inquiries respecting her birth. The Preati family of Verona denied all knowledge of her, as a matter of course, and M. de Saint Simon, who, in spite of all his love, had not entirely lost his senses, had the courage to abandon her. Altogether, Paris did not prove an *el dorado* for my handsome countrywoman, for she was obliged to pledge her diamonds, and to leave them behind her. After her return to Venice she married the son of the Uccelli, who sixteen years before had taken her out of her poverty. She died ten years ago.

I was still taking my French lessons with my good old Crébillon; yet my style, which was full of Italianisms, often expressed the very reverse of what I meant to say. But generally my *quid pro quos* only resulted in curious jokes which made my fortune; and the best of it is that my gibberish did me no harm on the score of wit: on the contrary, it procured me fine acquaintances.

Several ladies of the best society begged me to teach them Italian, saying that it would afford them the opportunity of teaching me French; in such an exchange I always won more than they did.

Madame Prédot, who was one of my pupils, received me one morning; she was still in bed, and told me that she did not feel disposed to have a lesson, because she had taken medicine the night previous. Foolishly translating an Italian idiom, I asked her, with an air of deep interest, whether she had well *déchargé?*

"Sir, what a question! You are unbearable."

I repeated my question; she broke out angrily again.

"Never utter that dreadful word."

"You are wrong in getting angry; it is the proper word."

"A very dirty word, sir, but enough about it. Will you have some breakfast?"

"No, I thank you. I have taken a *café* and two Savoyards."

"Dear me! What a ferocious breakfast! Pray, explain yourself."

"I say that I have drunk a *café* and eaten two Savoyards soaked in it, and that is what I do every morning."

"You are stupid, my good friend. A *café* is the establishment in which coffee is sold, and you ought to say that you have drunk *une tasse de café.*"

"Good indeed! Do you drink the cup? In Italy we say a *caffe*, and we are not foolish enough to suppose that it means the coffee-house."

"He will have the best of it! And the two Savoyards, how did you swallow them?"

"Soaked in my coffee, for they were not larger than these on your table."

"And you call these Savoyards? Say biscuits."

"In Italy, we call them Savoyards because they were first invented in Savoy; and it is not my fault if you imagined that I had swallowed two of the porters to be found at the corner of the streets — big fellows whom you call in Paris, Savoyards, although very often they have never been in Savoy."

Her husband came in at that moment, and she lost no time in relating the whole of our conversation. He laughed heartily, but he said I was right. Her niece arrived a few minutes after; she was a young girl about fourteen years of age, reserved, modest, and very intelligent. I had given her five or six lessons in Italian, and as she was very fond of that language and studied diligently she was beginning to speak.

Wishing to pay me her compliments in Italian, she said to me: "*Signore, sono incantata di vi vedere in buona salute.*"

"I thank you, mademoiselle; but to translate *I am enchanted*, you must say *ho piacere*, and for *to see you*, you must say *di vedervi.*"

"I thought, sir, that the *vi* was to be placed before."

"No, mademoiselle, we always put it *behind.*"

Monsieur and Madame Prédot were dying with laughter; the young lady was confused, and I in despair at having uttered such a gross absurdity; but it could not be helped. I took a book sulkily, in the hope of putting a stop to their mirth, but it was of no use: it lasted a week. That uncouth blunder soon got known throughout Paris, and gave me a sort of reputation which I lost little by little, but only when I understood the double meanings of words better. Crébillon was much amused with my blunder, and he told me that I ought to have said *after* instead of *behind.* Ah! why have not all languages the same genius! But if the French laughed at my mistakes in speaking their language, I took my revenge amply by turning some of their idioms into ridicule.

"Sir," I once said to a gentleman, "how is your wife?"

"You do her great honour, sir."

"Pray tell me, sir, what her honour has to do with her health?"

I meet in the Bois de Boulogne a young man riding a horse which he cannot master, and at last he is thrown. I stop the horse, run to the assistance of the young man, and help him up.

"Did you hurt yourself, sir?"

"Oh! many thanks, sir, *au contraire.*"

"Why *au contraire*! The deuce! It has done you good? Then begin again, sir."

And a thousand similar expressions entirely the reverse of good sense. But it is the genius of the language.

I was one day paying my first visit to the wife of President de N **, when her nephew, a brilliant butterfly, came in, and she introduced me to him, mentioning my name and my country.

"Indeed, sir, you are Italian?" said the young man. "Upon my word, you present yourself so gracefully that I would have betted you were French."

"Sir, when I saw you, I was near making the same mistake; I would have betted you were Italian."

Another time, I was dining at Lady Lambert's in numerous and brilliant company. Someone remarked on my finger a cornelian ring on which was engraved very beautifully the head of Louis XV. My ring went round the table, and everybody thought that the likeness was striking.

A young marquise, who had the reputation of being a great wit, said to me in the most serious tone:

"It is truly an antique?"

"The stone, madam, undoubtedly."

Everyone laughed except the thoughtless young beauty, who did not take any notice of it. Towards the end of the dinner, someone spoke of the rhinoceros, which was then shown for twenty-four sous at the St. Germain's Fair.

"Let us go and see it!" was the cry.

We got into the carriages, and reached the fair. We took several turns before we could find the place. I was the only gentleman; I was taking care of two ladies in the midst of the crowd, and the witty marquise was walking in front of us. At the end of the alley where we had been told that we would find the animal, there was a man placed to receive the money of the visitors. It is true that the man, dressed in the African fashion, was very dark and enormously stout, yet he had a human and very masculine form, and the beautiful marquise had no business to make a mistake. Nevertheless, the thoughtless young creature went up straight to him and said:

"Are you the rhinoceros, sir?"

"Go in, madam, go in."

We were dying with laughing; and the marquise, when she had seen the animal, thought herself bound to apologise to the master; assuring him that she had never seen a rhinoceros in her life, and therefore he could not feel offended if she had made a mistake.

One evening I was in the *foyer* of the Italian Comedy, where between the acts the highest noblemen were in the habit of coming, in order to converse and joke with the actresses who used to sit there waiting for their turn to appear on the stage, and I was seated near Camille, Coraline's sister, whom I amused by making love to her. A young councillor, who objected to my occupying

Camille's attention, being a very conceited fellow, attacked me upon some remark I made respecting an Italian play, and took the liberty of showing his bad temper by criticising my native country. I was answering him in an indirect way, looking all the time at Camille, who was laughing. Everybody had congregated around us and was attentive to the discussion, which, being carried on as an assault of wit, had nothing to make it unpleasant. But it seemed to take a serious turn when the young fop, turning the conversation on the police of the city, said that for some time it had been dangerous to walk alone at night through the streets of Paris.

"During the last month," he added, "the Place de Grève has seen the hanging of seven men, among whom there were five Italians. An extraordinary circumstance."

"Nothing extraordinary in that," I answered; "honest men generally contrive to be hung far away from their native country; and as a proof of it, sixty Frenchmen have been hung in the course of last year between Naples, Rome, and Venice. Five times twelve are sixty; so you see that it is only a fair exchange."

The laughter was all on my side, and the fine councillor went away rather crestfallen. One of the gentlemen present at the discussion, finding my answer to his taste, came up to Camille, and asked her in a whisper who I was. We got acquainted at once.

It was M. de Marigni, whom I was delighted to know for the sake of my brother, whose arrival in Paris I was expecting every day. M. de Marigni was superintendent of the royal buildings, and the Academy of Painting was under his jurisdiction. I mentioned my brother to him, and he graciously promised to protect him. Another young nobleman, who conversed with me, invited me to visit him. It was the Duke de Matalona.

I told him that I had seen him, then only a child, eight years before in Naples, and that I was under great obligations to his uncle, Don Lelio. The young duke was delighted, and we became intimate friends.

My brother arrived in Paris in the spring of 1751, and he lodged with me at Madame Quinson's. He began at once to work with success for private individuals; but his main idea being to compose a picture to be submitted to the judgment of the Academy, I introduced him to M. de Marigni, who received him with great distinction, and encouraged him by assuring him of his protection. He immediately set to work with great diligence.

M. de Morosini had been recalled, and M. de Mocenigo had succeeded him as ambassador of the Republic. M. de Bragadin had recommended me to him, and he tendered a friendly welcome both to me and to my brother, in whose favour he felt interested as a Venetian, and as a young artist seeking to build up a position by his talent.

M. de Mocenigo was of a very pleasant nature; he liked gambling although he was always unlucky at cards; he loved women, and he was not more fortunate with them, because he did not know how to manage them. Two years after his arrival in Paris he fell in love with Madame de Colande, and, finding it impossible to win her affections, he killed himself.

Madame la Dauphine was delivered of a prince, the Duke of Burgundy, and the rejoicings indulged in at the birth of that child seem to me incredible now, when I see what the same nation is doing against the king. The people want to be free; it is a noble ambition, for mankind are not made to be the slaves of one man; but with a nation populous, great, witty, and giddy, what will be the end of that revolution? Time alone can tell us.

The Duke de Matalona procured me the acquaintance of the two princes, Don Marc Antoine and Don Jean Baptiste Borghese, from Rome, who were enjoying themselves in Paris, yet living without display. I had occasion to remark that when those Roman princes were presented at the court of France they were only styled "marquis." It was the same with the Russian princes, to whom the title of prince was refused when they wanted to be presented; they were called "*knees*," but they did not mind it, because that word meant *prince*. The court of France has always been foolishly particular on the question of titles, and is even now sparing of the title of *monsieur*, although it is common enough everywhere: every man who was not titled was called *Sieur*. I have remarked that the king never addressed his bishops otherwise than as abbés, although they were generally very proud of their titles. The king likewise affected to know a nobleman only when his name was inscribed amongst those who served him.

Yet the haughtiness of Louis XV. had been inoculated into him by education; it was not in his nature. When an ambassador presented someone to him, the person thus presented withdrew with the certainty of having been seen by the king, but that was all. Nevertheless, Louis XV. was very polite, particularly with ladies, even with his mistresses, when in public. Whoever failed in respect towards them in the slightest manner was sure of disgrace, and no king ever possessed to a greater extent the grand royal virtue which is called dissimulation. He kept a secret faithfully, and he was delighted when he knew that no one but himself possessed it.

The Chevalier d'Eon is a proof of this, for the king alone knew and had always known that the chevalier was a woman, and all the long discussions which the false chevalier had with the office for foreign affairs was a comedy which the king allowed to go on, only because it amused him.

Louis XV. was great in all things, and he would have had no faults if flattery had not forced them upon him. But how could he possibly have supposed himself faulty in anything when everyone around him repeated constantly that he was the best of kings? A king, in the opinion of which he was imbued respecting his own person, was a being of a nature by far too superior to ordinary men for him not to have the right to consider himself akin to a god. Sad destiny of kings! Vile flatterers are constantly doing everything necessary to reduce them below the condition of man.

The Princess of Ardore was delivered about that time of a young prince. Her husband, the Neapolitan ambassador, entreated Louis XV. to be god-father to the child; the king consented and presented his godson with a regiment; but the mother, who did not like the military career for her son, refused it. The Marshal de Richelieu told me that he had never known the king laugh so heartily as when he heard of that singular refusal.

At the Duchess de Fulvie's I made the acquaintance of Mdlle. Gaussin, who was called Lolotte. She was the mistress of Lord Albemarle, the English ambassador, a witty and very generous nobleman. One evening he complained of his mistress praising the beauty of the stars which were shining brightly over her head, saying that she ought to know he could not give them to

her. If Lord Albemarle had been ambassador to the court of
France at the time of the rupture between France and England,
he would have arranged all difficulties amicably, and the unfortunate war by which France lost Canada would not have
taken place. There is no doubt that the harmony between two
nations depends very often upon their respective ambassadors,
when there is any danger of a rupture. As to the noble lord's
mistress, there was but one opinion respecting her. She was fit
in every way to become his wife, and the highest families of
France did not think that she needed the title of Lady Albemarle
to be received with distinction; no lady considered it debasing
to sit near her, although she was well known as the mistress of
the English lord. She had passed from her mother's arms to
those of Lord Albemarle at the age of thirteen, and her conduct
was always of the highest respectability. She bore children
whom the ambassador acknowledged legally, and she died Countess d'Erouville. I shall have to mention her again in my Memoirs.

I had likewise occasion to become acquainted at the Venetian
Embassy with a lady from Venice, the widow of an English
baronet named Wynne. She was then coming from London with
her children, where she had been compelled to go in order to ensure them the inheritance of their late father, which they would
have lost if they had not declared themselves members of the
Church of England. She was on her way back to Venice, much
pleased with her journey. She was accompanied by her eldest
daughter — a young girl of twelve years, who, notwithstanding
her youth, carried on her beautiful face all the signs of perfection.

She is now living in Venice, the widow of Count de Rosenberg,
who died in Venice ambassador of the Empress-Queen Maria
Theresa. She is surrounded by the brilliant halo of her excellent
conduct and of all her social virtues. No one can accuse her of
any fault, except that of being poor, but she feels it only because
it does not allow her to be as charitable as she might wish.

I went to St. Lawrence's Fair with my friend Patu, who, taking it into his head to sup with a Flemish actress known by the
name of Morphi, invited me to go with him. I felt no inclination for the girl, but what can we refuse to a friend? I did as he
wished. After we had supped with the actress, Patu fancied a

night devoted to a more agreeable occupation, and as I did not want to leave him I asked for a sofa on which I could sleep quietly during the night.

Morphi had a sister, a slovenly girl of thirteen, who told me that if I would give her a crown she would abandon her bed to me. I agreed to her proposal, and she took me to a small closet where I found a straw palliasse on four pieces of wood.

"Do you call this a bed, my child?"

"I have no other, sir."

"Then I do not want it, and you shall not have the crown."

"Did you intend undressing yourself?"

"Of course."

"What an idea! There are no sheets."

"Do you sleep with your clothes on?"

"Oh, no!"

"Well, then, go to bed as usual, and you shall have the crown."

"Why?"

"I want to see you undressed."

"But you won't do anything to me?"

"Not the slightest thing."

She undressed, laid herself on her miserable straw bed, and covered herself with an old curtain. In that state, the impression made by her dirty tatters disappeared, and I only saw a perfect beauty.

The young Hélène faithfully handed to her sister the six francs I had given her, and she told her the way in which she had earned them. Before I left the house she told me that, as she was in want of money, she felt disposed to make some abatement on the price of twenty-five louis. I answered with a laugh that I would see her about it the next day. I related the whole affair to Patu, who accused me of exaggeration; and wishing to prove to him that I was a real connoisseur of female beauty I insisted upon his seeing Hélène as I had seen her. He agreed with me that the chisel of Praxiteles had never carved anything more perfect. As white as a lily, Hélène possessed all the beauties which nature and the art of the painter can possibly combine. The loveliness of her features was so heavenly that it carried to the soul an indefinable sentiment of ecstacy, a delightful calm. She was fair, but her beautiful blue eyes equalled the finest black eyes in brilliance.

I went to see her the next evening, and, not agreeing about the price, I made a bargain with her sister to give her twelve francs every time I paid her a visit, and it was agreed that we would occupy her room until I should make up my mind to pay six hundred francs. It was regular usury, but the Morphi came from a Greek race, and was above prejudices. I had no idea of giving such a large sum, because I felt no wish to obtain what it would have procured me; what I obtained was all I cared for.

The elder sister thought I was duped, for in two months I had paid three hundred francs without having done anything, and she attributed my reserve to avarice. Avarice, indeed! I took a fancy to possess a painting of that beautiful body, and a German artist painted it for me splendidly for six louis. The position in which he painted it was delightful. She was lying on her stomach, her arms and her bosom leaning on a pillow, and holding her head sideways as if she were partly on the back. The clever and tasteful artist had painted her nether parts with so much skill and truth that no one could have wished for anything more beautiful; I was delighted with that portrait; it was a speaking likeness, and I wrote under it, "*O-Morphi*," not a Homeric word, but a Greek one after all, and meaning *beautiful*.

But who can anticipate the wonderful and secret decrees of destiny! My friend Patu wished to have a copy of that portrait; one cannot refuse such a slight service to a friend, and I gave an order for it to the same painter. But the artist, having been summoned to Versailles, showed that delightful painting with several others, and M. de Saint Quentin found it so beautiful that he lost no time in showing it to the king. His Most Christian Majesty, a great connoisseur in that line, wished to ascertain with his own eyes if the artist had made a faithful copy; and in case the original should prove as beautiful as the copy, the son of St. Louis knew very well what to do with it.

M. de Saint Quentin, the king's trusty friend, had the charge of that important affair; it was his province. He inquired from the painter whether the original could be brought to Versailles, and the artist, not supposing there would be any difficulty, promised to attend to it.

He therefore called on me to communicate the proposal; I thought it was delightful, and I immediately told the sister, who jumped for joy. She set to work cleaning, washing, and clothing the young beauty, and two or three days after they went to Versailles with the painter to see what could be done. M. de Saint Quentin's valet, having received his instructions from his master, took the two females to a pavilion in the park, and the painter went to the hotel to await the result of his negotiation. Half an hour afterwards the king entered the pavilion alone, asked the young O-Morphi if she was a Greek woman, took the portrait out of his pocket, and after a careful examination exclaimed:

"I have never seen a better likeness."

His majesty then sat down, took the young girl on his knees, bestowed a few caresses on her, and gave her a kiss.

O-Morphi was looking attentively at her master, and smiled.

"What are you laughing at?" said the king.

"I laugh because you and a crown of six francs are as like as two peas."

That *naïveté* made the king laugh heartily, and he asked her whether she would like to remain in Versailles.

"That depends upon my sister," answered the child.

But the sister hastened to tell the king that she could not aspire to a greater honour. The king locked them up again in the pavilion and went away, but in less than a quarter of an hour Saint Quentin came to fetch them, placed the young girl in an apartment under the care of a female attendant, and with the sister he went to meet at the hotel the German artist, to whom he gave fifty louis for the portrait, and nothing to Morphi. He only took her address, promising her that she would soon hear from him; the next day she received one thousand louis. The worthy German gave me twenty-five louis for my portrait, with a promise to make a careful copy of the one I had given to Patu, and he offered to paint for me gratuitously the likeness of every girl of whom I might wish to keep a portrait.

I enjoyed heartily the pleasure of the good Fleming, when she found herself in possession of the thousand gold pieces which she had received. Seeing herself rich, and considering me as the author of her fortune, she did not know how to show me her gratitude.

The young and lovely O-Morphi — for the king always called her by that name — pleased the sovereign by her simplicity and her pretty ways more even than by her rare beauty — the most perfect, the most regular, I recollect to have ever seen. He placed her in one of the apartments of his Parc-aux-cerfs — the voluptuous monarch's harem, in which no one could get admittance except the ladies presented at the court. At the end of one year she gave birth to a son, who went, like so many others, God knows where! for as long as Queen Mary lived no one ever knew what became of the natural children of Louis XV.

O-Morphi fell into disgrace at the end of three years, but the king, as he sent her away, ordered her to receive a sum of four hundred thousand francs which she brought as a dowry to an officer from Brittany. In 1783, happening to be in Fontainebleau, I made the acquaintance of a charming young man of twenty-five, the offspring of that marriage and the living portrait of his mother, of the history of whom he had not the slightest knowledge, and I thought it my duty not to enlighten him. I wrote my name on his tablets, and I begged him to present my compliments to his mother.

A wicked trick of Madame de Valentinois, sister-in-law of the Prince of Monaco, was the cause of O-Morphi's disgrace. That lady, who was well known in Paris, told her one day that, if she wished to make the king very merry, she had only to ask him how he treated his old wife. Too simple to guess the snare thus laid out for her, O-Morphi actually asked that impertinent question; but Louis XV. gave her a look of fury, and exclaimed:

"Miserable wretch! who taught you to address me that question?"

The poor O-Morphi, almost dead with fright, threw herself on her knees, and confessed the truth.

The king left her and never would see her again. The Countess de Valentinois was exiled for two years from the court. Louis XV., who knew how wrongly he was behaving towards his wife as a husband, would not deserve any reproach at her hands as a king, and woe to anyone who forgot the respect due to the queen!

The French are undoubtedly the most witty people in Europe, and perhaps in the whole world, but Paris is, all the same, the city for impostors and quacks to make a fortune. When their knavery is found out people turn it into a joke and laugh, but in the midst of the merriment another mountebank makes his appearance, who does something more wonderful than those who preceded him, and he makes his fortune whilst the scoffing of the people is in abeyance. It is the unquestionable effects of the power which fashion has over that amiable, clever, and lively nation. If anything is astonishing, no matter how extravagant it may be, the crowd is sure to welcome it greedily, for anyone would be afraid of being taken for a fool if he should exclaim, "It is impossible!" Physicians, are, perhaps, the only men in France who know that an infinite gulf yawns between the will and the deed, whilst in Italy it is an axiom known to everybody; but I do not mean to say that the Italians are superior to the French.

A certain painter met with great success for some time by announcing a thing which was an impossibility — namely, by pretending that he could take a portrait of a person without seeing the individual, and only from the description given. But he wanted the description to be thoroughly accurate. The result of it was that the portrait did greater honour to the person who gave the description than to the painter himself, but at the same time the informer found himself under the obligation of finding the likeness very good; otherwise the artist alleged the most legitimate excuse, and said that if the likeness was not perfect the fault was to be ascribed to the person who had given an imperfect description.

One evening I was taking supper at Silvia's when one of the guests spoke of that wonderful new artist, without laughing, and with every appearance of believing the whole affair.

"That painter," added he, "has already painted more than one hundred portraits, and they are all perfect likenesses."

Everybody was of the same opinion; it was splendid. I was the only one who, laughing heartily, took the liberty of saying it was absurd and impossible. The gentleman who had brought the wonderful news, feeling angry, proposed a wager of one hundred louis. I laughed all the more because his offer could not be accepted unless I exposed myself to being made a dupe.

"But the portraits are all admirable likenesses."

"I do not believe it, or if they are then there must be cheating somewhere."

But the gentleman, being bent upon convincing Silvia and me — for she had taken my part — proposed to make us dine with the artist; and we accepted.

The next day we called upon the painter, where we saw a quantity of portraits, all of which the artist claimed to be speaking likenesses; as we did not know the persons whom they represented we could not deny his claim.

"Sir," said Silvia to the artist, "could you paint the likeness of my daughter without seeing her?"

"Yes, madam, if you are certain of giving me an exact description of the expression of her features."

We exchanged a glance, and no more was said about it. The painter told us that supper was his favourite meal, and that he would be delighted if we would often give him the pleasure of our company. Like all quacks, he possessed an immense quantity of letters and testimonials from Bordeaux, Toulouse, Lyons, Rouen, etc., which paid the highest compliments to the perfection of his portraits, or gave descriptions for new pictures ordered from him. His portraits, by the way, had to be paid for in advance.

Two or three days afterwards I met his pretty niece, who obligingly upbraided me for not having yet availed myself of her uncle's invitation to supper; the niece was a dainty morsel worthy of a king, and, her reproaches being very flattering to my vanity, I promised I would come the next day. In less than a week it turned out a serious engagement. I fell in love with the interesting niece, who, being full of wit and well disposed to enjoy herself, had no love for me, and granted me no favour. I hoped, and, feeling that I was caught, I felt it was the only thing I could do.

One day that I was alone in my room, drinking my coffee and thinking of her, the door was suddenly opened without anyone being announced, and a young man came in. I did not recollect him, but, without giving me time to ask any questions, he said to me:

"Sir, I have had the honour of meeting you at the supper-table of M. Samson, the painter."

"Ah! yes; I beg you to excuse me, sir, I did not at first recollect you."

"It is natural, for your eyes are always on Mdlle. Samson."

"Very likely, but you must admit that she is a charming creature."

"I have no difficulty whatever in agreeing with you; to my misery, I know it but too well."

"You are in love with her?"

"Alas, yes! and I say, again, to my misery."

"To your misery? But why, do not you gain her love?"

"That is the very thing I have been striving for since last year, and I was beginning to have some hope when your arrival has reduced me to despair."

"I have reduced you to despair?"

"Yes, sir."

"I am very sorry, but I cannot help it."

"You could easily help it; and, if you would allow me, I could suggest to you the way in which you could greatly oblige me."

"Speak candidly."

"You might never put your foot in the house again."

"That is a rather singular proposal, but I agree that it is truly the only thing I can do if I have a real wish to oblige you. Do you think, however, that in that case you would succeed in gaining her affection?"

"Then it will be my business to succeed. Do not go there again, and I will take care of the rest."

"I might render you that very great service; but you must confess that you must have a singular opinion of me to suppose that I am a man to do such a thing."

"Yes, sir, I admit that it may appear singular; but I take you for a man of great sense and sound intellect, and after considering the subject deeply I have thought that you would put yourself in my place; that you would not wish to make me miserable, or to expose your own life for a young girl who can have inspired you with but a passing fancy, whilst my only wish is to secure the happiness or the misery of my life, whichever it may prove, by uniting her existence with mine."

"But suppose that I should intend, like you, to ask her in marriage?"

"Then we should both be worthy of pity, and one of us would have ceased to exist before the other obtained her, for as long as I shall live Mdlle. Samson shall not be the wife of another."

This young man, well-made, pale, grave, as cold as a piece of marble, madly in love, who, in his reason mixed with utter despair, came to speak to me in such a manner with the most surprising calm, made me pause and consider. Undoubtedly I was not afraid, but although in love with Mdlle. Samson I did not feel my passion sufficiently strong to cut the throat of a man for the sake of her beautiful eyes, or to lose my own life to defend my budding affection. Without answering the young man, I began to pace up and down my room, and for a quarter of an hour I weighed the following question which I put to myself: Which decision will appear more manly in the eyes of my rival and will win my own esteem to the deeper degree — namely, to accept coolly his offer to cut one another's throats, or to allay his anxiety by withdrawing from the field with dignity?

Pride whispered, Fight; Reason said, Compel thy rival to acknowledge thee a wiser man than he is.

"What would you think of me, sir," I said to him, with an air of decision, "if I consented to give up my visits to Mdlle. Samson?"

"I would think that you had pity on a miserable man, and I say that in that case you will ever find me ready to shed the last drop of my blood to prove my deep gratitude."

"Who are you?"

"My name is Garnier, I am the only son of M. Garnier, wine merchant in the Rue de Seine."

"Well, M. Garnier, I will never again call on Mdlle. Samson. Let us be friends."

"Until death. Farewell, sir."

"Adieu, be happy!"

Patu came in five minutes after Garnier had left me: I related the adventure to him, and he thought I was a hero.

"I would have acted as you have done," he observed, "but I would not have acted like Garnier."

It was about that time that the Count de Melfort, colonel of the Orleans regiment, entreated me through Camille, Coraline's sister, to answer two questions by means of my cabalism. I gave two answers very vague, yet meaning a great deal; I put them under a sealed envelope and gave them to Camille, who asked me the next day to accompany her to a place which she said she could not name to me. I followed her; she took me to the Palais-Royal, and then, through a narrow staircase, up to the apartments of the Duchesse de Chartres. I waited about a quarter of an hour, at the end of which time the duchess came in and loaded Camille with caresses for having brought me. Then addressing herself to me, she told me, with dignity yet very graciously, the difficulty she experienced in understanding the answers I had sent and which she was holding in her hand. At first I expressed some perplexity at the questions having emanated from her royal highness, and I told her afterwards that I understood cabalism, but that I could not interpret the meaning of the answers obtained through it, and that her highness must ask new questions likely to render the answers easier to be understood. She wrote down all she could not make out and all she wanted to know.

"Madam, you must be kind enough to divide the questions, for the cabalistic oracle never answers two questions at the same time."

"Well, then, prepare the questions yourself."

"Your highness will excuse me, but every word must be written with your own hand. Recollect, madam, that you will address yourself to a superior intelligence knowing all your secrets."

She began to write, and asked seven or eight questions. She read them over carefully, and said, with a face beaming with noble confidence:

"Sir, I wish to be certain that no one shall ever know what I have just written."

"Your highness may rely on my honour."

I read attentively, and I saw that her wish for secrecy was reasonable, and that if I put the questions in my pocket I should run the risk of losing them and of implicating myself.

"I only require three hours to complete my task," I said to the duchess, "and I wish your highness to feel no anxiety. If you have any other engagement you can leave me here alone, provided I am not disturbed by anybody. When it is completed, I will put it all in a sealed envelope; I only want your highness to tell me to whom I must deliver the parcel."

"Either to me or to Madame de Polignac, if you know her."

"Yes, madam, I have the honour to know her."

The duchess handed me a small tinder-box to enable me to light a wax-candle, and she went away with Camille. I remained alone locked up in the room, and at the end of three hours, just as I had completed my task, Madame de Polignac came for the parcel and I left the palace.

The Duchesse de Chartres, daughter of the Prince of Conti,

was twenty-six years of age. She was endowed with that particular sort of wit which renders a woman adorable. She was lively, above the prejudices of rank, cheerful, full of jest, a lover of pleasure, which she preferred to a long life. "Short and sweet," were the words she had constantly on her lips. She was pretty but she stood badly, and used to laugh at Marcel, the teacher of graceful deportment, who wanted to correct her awkward bearing. She kept her head bent forward and her feet turned inside when dancing; yet she was a charming dancer. Unfortunately her face was covered with pimples, which injured her beauty very greatly. Her physicians thought that they were caused by a disease of the liver, but they came from impurity of the blood, which at last killed her, and from which she suffered throughout her life.

The questions she had asked from my oracle related to affairs connected with her heart, and she wished likewise to know how she could get rid of the blotches which disfigured her. My answers were rather obscure in such matters as I was not specially acquainted with, but they were very clear concerning her disease, and my oracle became precious and necessary to her highness.

The next day, after dinner Camille wrote me a note, as I expected, requesting me to give up all other engagements in order to present myself at five o'clock at the Palais-Royal, in the same room in which the duchess had already received me the day before. I was punctual. An elderly *valet de chambre*, who was waiting for me, immediately went to give notice of my arrival, and five minutes after the charming princess made her appearance. After addressing me in a very complimentary manner, she drew all my answers from her pocket, and inquired whether I had any pressing engagements.

"Your highness may be certain that I shall never have any more important business than to attend to your wishes."

"Very well; I do not intend to go out, and we can work."

She then showed me all the questions which she had already prepared on different subjects, and particularly those relating to the cure of her pimples. One circumstance had contributed to render my oracle precious to her, because nobody could possibly know it, and I had guessed it. Had I not done so, I dare say it would have been all the same. I had laboured myself under the same disease, and I was enough of a physician to be aware that to attempt the cure of a cutaneous disease by active remedies might kill the patient.

I had already answered that she could not get rid of the pimples on her face in less than a week, but that a year of diet would be necessary to effect a radical cure.

We spent three hours in ascertaining what she was to do, and, believing implicitly in the power and in the science of the oracle, she undertook to follow faithfully everything it ordered. Within one week all the ugly pimples had entirely disappeared.

I took care to purge her slightly; I prescribed every day what she was to eat, and forbade the use of all cosmetics; I only advised her to wash herself morning and evening with plantain water. The modest oracle told the princess to make use of the same water for her ablutions of every part of her body where she desired to obtain the same result, and she obeyed the prescription religiously.

I went to the opera on purpose on the day when the duchess showed herself there with a smooth and rosy skin. After the opera, she took a walk in the great alley of the Palais-Royal, followed by the ladies of her suite, and flattered by everybody. She saw me, and honoured me with a smile. I was truly happy. Camille, Madame de Polignac, and M. de Melfort were the only persons who knew that I was the oracle of the duchess, and I enjoyed my success. But the next day a few pimples reappeared on her beautiful complexion, and I received an order to repair at once to the Palais-Royal.

The valet, who did not know me, showed me into a delightful boudoir near a closet in which there was a bath. The duchess came in; she looked sad, for she had several small pimples on the forehead and the chin. She held in her hand a question for the oracle, and as it was only a short one I thought I would give her the pleasure of finding the answer by herself. The numbers translated by the princess reproached her with having transgressed the regimen prescribed; she confessed to having drunk some liqueurs and eaten some ham; but she was astounded at having found that answer herself, and she could not understand how such an answer could result from an agglomeration of numbers. At that moment, one of her women came in to whisper a few words to her; she told her to wait outside, and turning towards me, she said:

[273]

"Have you any objection to seeing one of your friends who is as delicate as discreet?"

With these words, she hastily concealed in her pocket all the papers which did not relate to her disease; then she called out.

A man entered the room, whom I took for a stable-boy: it was M. de Melfort.

"See," said the princess to him, "M. Casanova has taught me the cabalistic science."

And she showed him the answer she had obtained herself. The count could not believe it.

"Well," said the duchess to me, "we must convince him. What shall I ask?" .

"Anything your highness chooses."

She considered for one instant, and, drawing from her pocket a small ivory box, she wrote, "Tell me why this pomatum has no longer any effect."

She formed the pyramid, the columns, and the key, as I had taught her, and as she was ready to get the answer, I told her how to make the additions and subtractions which seem to come from the numbers, but which in reality are only arbitrary; then I told her to interpret the numbers in letters, and I left the room under some pretext. I came back when I thought that she had completed her translation, and I found her wrapped in amazement.

"Ah, sir!" she exclaimed, "what an answer!"

"Perhaps it is not a right one; but that will sometimes happen, madam."

"Not the right one, sir? It is divine! Here it is: That pomatum has no effect upon the skin of a woman who has been a mother."

"I do not see anything extraordinary in that answer, madam."

"Very likely, sir, but it is because you do not know that the pomatum in question was given to me five years ago by the Abbé de Brosses; it cured me at that time, but it was ten months before the birth of the Duke de Montpensier. I would give anything in the world to be thoroughly acquainted with that sublime cabalistic science."

"What!" said the count, "is it the pomatum the history of which I know?"

"Precisely."

"It is astonishing."

"I wish to ask one more question concerning a woman the name of whom I would rather not give."

"Say the woman whom I have in my thoughts."

She then asked this question: "What disease is that woman suffering from?" She made the calculation, and the answer which I made her bring forth was this: "She wants to deceive her husband." This time the duchess fairly screamed with astonishment.

It was getting very late, and I was preparing to take leave, when M. de Melfort, who was speaking to her highness, told me that we might go together. When we were out, he told me that the cabalistic answer concerning the pomatum was truly wonderful. This was the history of it:

"The duchess, pretty as you see her now, had her face so fearfully covered with pimples that the duke, thoroughly disgusted, had not the courage to come near her to enjoy his rights as a husband, and the poor princess was pining with useless longing to become a mother. The Abbé de Brosses cured her with that pomatum, and her beautiful face having entirely recovered its original bloom she made her appearance at the Théatre Français, in the queen's box. The Duke de Chartres, not knowing that his wife had gone to the theatre, where she went but very seldom, was in the king's box. He did not recognize the duchess, but thinking her very handsome he inquired who she was, and when he was told he would not believe it; he left the royal box, went to his wife, complimented her, and announced his visit for the very same night. The result of that visit was, nine months afterwards, the birth of the Duke de Montpensier, who is now five years old and enjoys excellent health. During the whole of her pregnancy the duchess kept her face smooth and blooming, but immediately after her delivery the pimples reappeared, and the pomatum remained without any effect."

As he concluded his explanation, the count offered me a tortoise-shell box with a very good likeness of her royal highness and said:

"The duchess begs your acceptance of this portrait, and, in case you would like to have it set, she wishes you to make use of this for that purpose."

It was a purse of one hundred louis. I accepted both, and

entreated the count to offer the expressions of my profound gratitude to her highness. I never had the portrait mounted, for I was then in want of money for some other purpose.

After that, the duchess did me the honour of sending for me several times; but her cure remained altogether out of the question; she could not make up her mind to follow a regular diet. She would sometimes keep me at work for five or six hours, now in one corner, now in another, going in and out herself all the time, and having either dinner or supper brought to me by the old valet, who never uttered a word.

Her questions to the oracle alluded only to secret affairs which she was curious to know, and she often found truths with which I was not myself acquainted, through the answers. She wished me to teach her the cabalistic science, but she never pressed her wish upon me. She, however, commissioned M. de Melfort to tell me that, if I would teach her, she would get me an appointment with an income of twenty-five thousand francs. Alas! it was impossible! I was madly in love with her, but I would not for the world have allowed her to guess my feelings. My pride was the corrective of my love. I was afraid of her haughtiness humiliating me, and perhaps I was wrong. All I know is that I even now repent of having listened to a foolish pride. It is true that I enjoyed certain privileges which she might have refused me if she had known my love.

One day she wished my oracle to tell her whether it was possible to cure a cancer which Madame de la Popelinière had in the breast; I took it in my head to answer that the lady alluded to had no cancer, and was enjoying excellent health.

"How is that?" said the duchess; "everyone in Paris believes her to be suffering from a cancer, and she has consultation upon consultation. Yet I have faith in the oracle."

Soon afterwards, seeing the Duke de Richelieu at the court, she told him she was certain that Madame de la Popelinière was not ill. The marshal, who knew the secret, told her that she was mistaken; but she proposed a wager of a hundred thousand francs. I trembled when the duchess related the conversation to me.

"Has he accepted your wager?" I inquired, anxiously.

"No; he seemed surprised; you are aware that he ought to know the truth."

Three or four days after that conversation, the duchess told me triumphantly that M. de Richelieu had confessed to her that the cancer was only a ruse to excite the pity of her husband, with whom Madame de la Popelinière wanted to live again on good terms; she added that the marshal had expressed his willingness to pay one thousand louis to know how she had discovered the truth.

"If you wish to earn that sum," said the duchess to me, "I will tell him all about it."

But I was afraid of a snare; I knew the temper of the marshal, and the story of the hole in the wall, through which he introduced himself into that lady's apartment, was the talk of all Paris. M. de la Popelinière himself had made the adventure more public by refusing to live with his wife, to whom he paid an income of twelve thousand francs.

The Duchesse de Chartres had written some charming poetry on that amusing affair; but out of her own coterie no one knew it except the king, who was very fond of the princess, although she was in the habit of scoffing at him. One day, for instance, she asked him whether it was true that the King of Prussia was expected in Paris. Louis XV. having answered that it was an idle rumour:

"I am very sorry," she said, "for I am longing to see a king."

My brother had completed several pictures, and having decided on presenting one to M. de Marigny, we repaired one morning to the apartment of that nobleman, who lived in the Louvre, where all the artists were in the habit of paying their court to him. We were shown into a hall adjoining his private apartment, and having arrived early we waited for M. de Marigny. My brother's picture was exposed there; it was a battle-piece in the style of Bourguignon.

The first person who passed through the room stopped before the picture, examined it attentively, and moved on, evidently thinking that it was a poor painting; a moment afterwards two more persons came in, looked at the picture, smiled, and said:

"That's the work of a beginner."

I glanced at my brother, who was seated near me; he was in a fever. In less than a quarter of an hour the room was full of people, and the unfortunate picture was the butt of everybody's laughter. My poor brother felt almost dying, and thanked his stars that no one knew him personally.

The state of his mind was such that I heartily pitied him; I rose with the intention of going to some other room, and to console him I told him that M. de Marigny would soon come, and that his approbation of the picture would avenge him for the insults of the crowd. Fortunately, this was not my brother's opinion; we left the room hurriedly, took a coach, went home, and sent our servant to fetch back the painting. As soon as it had been brought back my brother made a battle of it in real earnest, for he cut it up with a sword into twenty pieces. He made up his mind to settle his affairs in Paris immediately, and to go somewhere else to study an art which he loved to idolatry; we resolved on going to Dresden together.

Two or three days before leaving the delightful city of Paris I dined alone at the house of the gate-keeper of the Tuileries; his name was Condé. After dinner his wife, a rather pretty woman, presented me the bill, on which every item was reckoned at double its value. I pointed it out to her, but she answered very curtly that she could not abate one sou. I paid, and as the bill was receipted with the words "*femme Condé*," I took the pen and to the word "*Condé*" I added "*labre*," and I went away leaving the bill on the table.

I was taking a walk in the Tuileries, not thinking any more of my female extortioner, when a small man, with his hat cocked on one side of his head and a large nosegay in his buttonhole, and sporting a long sword, swaggered up to me and informed me, without any further explanation, that he had a fancy to cut my throat.

"But, my small specimen of humanity," I said, "you would require to jump on a chair to reach my throat. I will cut your ears."

"*Sacrebleu,* monsieur!"

"No vulgar passion, my dear sir; follow me; you shall soon be satisfied."

I walked rapidly towards the Porte de l'Etoile, where, seeing that the place was deserted, I abruptly asked the fellow what he wanted, and why he had attacked me.

"I am the Chevalier de Talvis," he answered. "You have insulted an honest woman who is under my protection; unsheath!"

With these words he drew his long sword; I unsheathed mine;

after a minute or two I lunged rapidly, and wounded him in the breast. He jumped backward, exclaiming that I had wounded him treacherously.

"You lie, you rascally mannikin! acknowledge it, or I thrust my sword through your miserable body."

"You will not do it, for I am wounded; but I insist upon having my revenge, and we will leave the decision of this to competent judges."

"Miserable wrangler, wretched fighter, if you are not satisfied, I will cut off your ears!"

I left him there, satisfied that I had acted according to the laws of the duello, for he had drawn his sword before me, and if he had not been skilful enough to cover himself in good time, it was not, of course, my business to teach him. Towards the middle of August I left Paris with my brother. I had made a stay of two years in that city, the best in the world. I had enjoyed myself greatly, and had met with no unpleasantness except that I had been now and then short of money. We went through Metz, Mayence, and Frankfort, and arrived in Dresden at the end of the same month. My mother offered us the most affectionate welcome, and was delighted to see us again. My brother remained four years in that pleasant city, constantly engaged in the study of his art, and copying all the fine paintings of battles by the great masters in the celebrated Electoral Gallery.

He went back to Paris only when he felt certain that he could set criticism at defiance; I shall say hereafter how it was that we both reached that city about the same time. But before that period, dear reader, you will see what good and adverse fortune did for or against me.

My life in Dresden until the end of the carnival in 1753 does not offer any extraordinary adventure. To please the actors, and especially my mother, I wrote a kind of melodrama, in which I brought out two harlequins. It was a parody of the *Frères Ennemis*, by Racine. The king was highly amused at the comic fancies which filled my play, and he made me a beautiful present. The king was grand and generous, and these qualities found a ready echo in the breast of the famous Count de Brühl. I left Dresden soon after that, bidding adieu to my mother, to my brother François, and to my sister, then the wife of Pierre Auguste, chief player of the harpsichord at the court, who died two years ago, leaving his widow and family in comfortable circumstances.

My stay in Dresden was marked by an amorous souvenir of which I got rid, as in previous similar circumstances, by a diet of six weeks. I have often remarked that the greatest part of my life was spent in trying to make myself ill, and when I had succeeded, in trying to recover my health. I have met with equal success in both things; and now that I enjoy excellent health in that line, I am very sorry to be physically unable to make myself ill again; but age, that cruel and unavoidable disease, compels me to be in good health in spite of myself. The illness I allude to, which the Italians call *mal français*, although we might claim the honour of its first importation, does not shorten life, but it leaves indelible marks on the face. Those scars, less honourable perhaps than those which are won in the service of Mars, being obtained through pleasure, ought not to leave any regrets behind.

In Dresden I had frequent opportunities of seeing the king, who was very fond of the Count de Brühl, his minister, because that favourite possessed the double secret of showing himself more extravagant even than his master, and of indulging all his whims. Never was a monarch a greater enemy to economy; he laughed heartily when he was plundered, and he spent a great deal in order to have occasion to laugh often. As he had not sufficient wit to amuse himself with the follies of other kings and with the absurdities of humankind, he kept four buffoons, who are called fools in Germany, although these degraded beings are generally more witty than their masters. The province of those jesters is to make their owner laugh by all sorts of jokes which are usually nothing but disgusting tricks, or low, impertinent jests.

Yet these professional buffoons sometimes captivate the mind of their master to such an extent that they obtain from him very important favours in behalf of the persons they protect, and the consequence is that they are often courted by the highest families. Where is the man who will not debase himself if he be in want? Does not Agamemnon say, in Homer, that in such a case man must necessarily be guilty of meanness? And Agamemnon and Homer lived long before our time! It evidently proves that men are at all times moved by the same motive — namely, self-interest.

It is wrong to say that the Count de Brühl was the ruin of Saxony, for he was only the faithful minister of his royal master's inclinations. His children are poor, and justify their father's conduct.

The court at Dresden was at that time the most brilliant in Europe; the fine arts flourished, but there was no gallantry, for King Augustus had no inclination for the fair sex, and the Saxons were not of a nature to be thus inclined unless the example was set by their sovereign.

At my arrival in Prague, where I did not intend to stop, I delivered a letter I had for Locatelli, manager of the opera, and went to pay a visit to Madame Morelli, an old acquaintance, for whom I had great affection, and for two or three days she supplied all the wants of my heart.

As I was on the point of leaving Prague, I met in the street my friend Fabris, who had become a colonel, and he insisted upon my dining with him. After embracing him, I represented to him, but in vain, that I had made all my arrangements to go away immediately.

"You will go this evening," he said, "with a friend of mine, and you will catch the coach."

I had to give way, and I was delighted to have done so, for the remainder of the day passed in the most agreeable manner. Fabris was longing for war, and his wishes were gratified two years afterwards; he covered himself with glory.

I must say one word about Locatelli, who was an original character well worthy to be known. He took his meals every day at a table laid out for thirty persons, and the guests were his actors, actresses, dancers of both sexes, and a few friends. He did the honours of his well-supplied board nobly, and his real passion was good living. I shall have occasion to mention him again at the time of my journey to St. Petersburg, where I met him, and where he died only lately at the age of ninety.

CHAPTER VIII

The Prodigal's Return: Venice Once More

*B*EFORE *returning to Venice, Casanova, by way of completing the "grand tour," paid a visit to Vienna.*

"In Vienna," he notes, "everything is beautiful; money was then very plentiful, and luxury very great; but the severity of the empress (Maria Theresa) made the worship of Venus difficult, particularly for strangers. A legion of vile spies, who were decorated with the fine title of Commissaries of Chastity, were the merciless tormentors of all the girls." Of the seven cardinal sins the sovereign was indulgent for all except the seventh, lewdness — the very one which Casanova, had he had the ordering of such things, would have eliminated altogether from the divine register.

Following the system he had adopted and to which he remained faithful throughout his life, he made a point of meeting as many people of note, especially in the intellectual world, as would receive him. His countryman the poet Metastasio, in high favour with the empress, was one of the first to receive his visit. Casanova is always an excellent interviewer (he would in that capacity make the fortune of any newspaper to-day), and the short impression of Metastasio is as good as anything he has done in that line:

I arrived for the first time in the capital of Austria, at the age of eight-and-twenty, well provided with clothes, but rather short of money — a circumstance which made it necessary for me to curtail my expenses until the arrival of the proceeds of a letter of exchange which I had drawn upon M. de Bragadin. The only letter of recommendation I had was from the poet Migliavacca, of Dresden, addressed to the illustrious Abbé Metastasio, whom I wished ardently to know. I delivered the letter the day after my arrival, and in one hour of conversation I found him more learned than I should have supposed from his works. Besides, Metastasio was so modest that at first I did not think that modesty natural, but it was not long before I discovered that it was genuine, for when he recited something of his own composition, he was the first to call the attention of his hearers to the important parts or to the fine passages with as much simplicity as he would remark the weak ones. I spoke to him of his tutor

Gravina, and as we were on that subject he recited to me five or six stanzas which he had written on his death, and which had not been printed. Moved by the remembrance of his friend, and by the sad beauty of his own poetry, his eyes were filled with tears, and when he had done reciting the stanzas he said, in a tone of touching simplicity, *"Ditemi il vero, si puo dir meglio?"*

I answered that he alone had the right to believe it impossible. I then asked him whether he had to work a great deal to compose his beautiful poetry; he showed me four or five pages which he had covered with erasures and words crossed and scratched out only because he had wished to bring fourteen lines to perfection, and he assured me that he had never been able to compose more than that number in one day. He confirmed my knowledge of a truth which I had found out before — namely, that the very lines which most readers believe to have flowed easily from the poet's pen are generally those which he has had the greatest difficulty in composing.

"Which of your operas," I inquired, "do you like best?"

"Attilio Regolo; ma questo non vuol già dire che sia il megliore."

"All your works have been translated in Paris into French prose, but the publisher was ruined, for it is not possible to read them, and it proves the elevation and the power of your poetry."

"Several years ago, another foolish publisher ruined himself by a translation into French prose of the splendid poetry of Ariosto. I laugh at those who maintain that poetry can be translated into prose."

"I am of your opinion."

"And you are right."

He told me that he had never written an arietta without composing the music of it himself, but that as a general rule he never showed his music to anyone.

"The French," he added, "entertain the very strange belief that it is possible to adapt poetry to music already composed."

And he made on that subject this very philosophical remark:

"You might just as well say to a sculptor, 'Here is a piece of marble, make a Venus, and let her expression be shown before the features are chiselled.'"

In Vienna he runs across his old acquaintance de la Haye, very conveniently, as he is able to borrow a little money which he urgently needs, having fallen in with some gambling acquaintances, among

[283]

*them the notorious Count Afflisio. To obtain an entrée in the ele-
gant* demi-monde *of Vienna he is "created a baron"; that is, he is
told he must for decency's sake consent to bear at least this title, as
he "cannot be less than baron." In the company of one of his boon
companions and some "lovely fräuleins" he sets out for Pressbourg,
where he meets the Chevalier de Talvis, with whom he had fought a
duel in Paris. The chevalier asks for his revenge, which Casanova
obligingly promises him. Meanwhile they join forces, attend a ball
at the Prince-Bishop's, where de Talvis wins a huge sum from the
prelate, a portion of which goes into Casanova's pocket by way of
a loan; after which the noble chevalier leaves the city as fast as he
can gallop.*

*In Vienna, when Casanova returns there, the adventure with the
Prince-Bishop is already common gossip. "I was not spared by
public rumour," he remarks in an offhand way, "but I took no
notice of it, for I did not think it necessary to defend myself." He
did, however, find it convenient to follow the chevalier's example,
though less precipitously.*

*On Ascension Day he arrives in Venice, after an absence of three
years:*

I found myself again in my native country with that feeling of
delight which is experienced by all true-hearted men, when they
see again the place in which they have received the first lasting
impressions. I had acquired some experience; I knew the laws
of honour and politeness; in one word, I felt myself superior to
most of my equals, and I longed to resume my old habits and
pursuits; but I intended to adopt a more regular and more reserved line of conduct.

I saw with great pleasure, as I entered my study, the perfect
statu quo which had been preserved there. My papers, covered
with a thick layer of dust, testified well enough that no strange
hand had ever meddled with them.

*Having accompanied his protector, Senator Bragadin, to Padua
for a few days, he meets with an adventure which, he says, was
destined to alter the whole course of his life:*

Having, therefore, left Padua at the very instant marked by
fatality, I met at Oriago a cabriolet, drawn at full speed by two
post-horses, containing a very pretty woman and a man wearing
a German uniform. Within a few yards from me the vehicle
was suddenly upset on the side of the river, and the woman,

[284]

falling over the officer, was in great danger of rolling into the Brenta. I jumped out of my chaise without even stopping my postillion, and rushing to the assistance of the lady I remedied with a chaste hand the disorder caused to her toilet by her fall.

Her companion, who had picked himself up without any injury, hastened towards us, and there was the lovely creature sitting on the ground thoroughly amazed, and less confused from her fall than from the indiscretion of her petticoats. In the warmth of her thanks, which lasted until her postillion and mine had righted the cabriolet, she often called me her saviour, her guardian angel.

The vehicle being all right, the lady continued her journey towards Padua, and I resumed mine towards Venice, which I reached just in time to dress for the opera.

The next day I masked myself early to accompany the *Bucentoro*, which, favoured by fine weather, was to be taken to the Lido for the great and ridiculous ceremony. The whole affair is under the responsibility of the admiral of the arsenal, who answers for the weather remaining fine, under penalty of his head, for the slightest contrary wind might capsize the ship and drown the Doge, with all the most serene noblemen, the ambassadors, and the Pope's nuncio, who is the sponsor of that burlesque wedding which the Venetians respect even to superstition. To crown the misfortune of such an accident it would make the whole of Europe laugh, and people would not fail to say that the Doge of Venice had gone at last to consummate his marriage.

I had removed my mask, and was drinking some coffee under the *procuraties* of St. Mark's Square, when a fine-looking female mask struck me gallantly on the shoulder with her fan. As I did not know who she was I did not take much notice of it, and after I had finished my coffee I put on my mask, and walked towards the Spiaggia del Sepulcro, where M. de Bragadin's gondola was waiting for me. As I was getting near the Ponte della Paglia I saw the same masked woman attentively looking at some wonderful monster shown for a few pence. I went up to her, and asked her why she had struck me with her fan.

"To punish you for not knowing me again after having saved my life."

I guessed that she was the person I had rescued the day before on the banks of the Brenta, and after paying her some compliments I inquired whether she intended to follow the *Bucentoro*.

"I should like it," she said, "if I had a safe gondola."

I offered her mine, which was one of the largest, and, after consulting a masked person who accompanied her, she accepted. Before stepping in I invited them to take off their masks, but they told me that they wished to remain unknown. I then begged them to tell me if they belonged to the suite of some ambassador, because in that case I should be compelled, much to my regret, to withdraw my invitation; but they assured me that they were both Venetians. The gondola belonging to a patrician, I might have committed myself with the State Inquisitors — a thing which I wished particularly to avoid.

We were following the *Bucentoro*, and seated near the lady I allowed myself a few slight liberties, but she foiled my intentions by changing her seat. After the ceremony we returned to Venice, and the officer who accompanied the lady told me that I would oblige them by dining in their company at the Savage. I accepted, for I felt somewhat curious about the woman. What I had seen of her at the time of her fall warranted my curiosity. The officer left me alone with her, and went before us to order dinner.

The officer in question turned out to be an adventurer, who tried to inveigle Casanova into backing his bills and taking a share in a cattle transaction. Having failed in his attempt, he introduces him to his young sister, who so dazzles Casanova by her beauty that in half an hour he becomes "the slave of the most perfect woman that the wildest dreams could imagine."

Seeing the impression made by his sister, the rascally brother decided to play this card for all it was worth, in the hope of getting the needed financial assistance. Under such auspicies began Casanova's idyll with C** C**, which, like the Henriette episode, exhales an aroma of true and ardent passion, though of a tenderer, more lyric quality. It is the scherzo amoroso *preceding the ap-passionata of the M** M** episode:*

I took a box at the St. Samuel Opera, and I was waiting for them at the appointed place long before the time. They came at last, and the sight of my young friend delighted me. She was elegantly masked, and her brother wore his uniform. In order not to expose the lovely girl to being recognised on account of her brother, I made them get into my gondola. He insisted upon

[286]

being landed near the house of his mistress, who was ill, he said, and he added that he would soon join us in our box. I was astonished that C ** C ** did not show any surprise or repugnance at remaining alone with me in the gondola; but I did not think the conduct of her brother extraordinary, for it was evident that it was all arranged beforehand in his mind.

I told C ** C ** that we would remain in the gondola until the opening of the theatre, and that as the heat was intense she would do well to take off her mask, which she did at once. The law I had laid upon myself to respect her, the noble confidence which was beaming on her countenance and in her looks, her innocent joy — everything increased the ardour of my love.

Now knowing what to say to her, for I could speak to her of nothing but love — and it was a delicate subject — I kept looking at her charming face, not daring to let my eyes rest upon two budding globes shaped by the Graces, for fear of giving the alarm to her modesty.

"Speak to me," she said at last; "you only look at me without uttering a single word. You have sacrificed yourself for me, because my brother would have taken you with him to his ladylove, who, to judge from what he says, must be as beautiful as an angel."

"I have seen that lady."

"I suppose she is very witty."

"She may be so; but I have no opportunity of knowing, for I have never visited her, and I do not intend ever to call upon her. Do not therefore imagine, beautiful C ** C **, that I have made the slightest sacrifice for your sake."

"I was afraid you had, because as you did not speak I thought you were sad."

"If I do not speak to you it is because I am too deeply moved by your angelic confidence in me."

"I am very glad it is so; but how could I not trust you? I feel much more free, much more confident with you than with my brother himself. My mother says it is impossible to be mistaken, and that you are certainly an honest man. Besides, you are not married; that is the first thing I asked my brother. Do you recollect telling me that you envied the fate of the man who would have me for his wife? Well, at that very moment I was thinking that your wife would be the happiest woman in Venice."

These words, uttered with the most candid artlessness, and with that tone of sincerity which comes from the heart, had upon me an effect which it would be difficult to describe; I suffered because I could not imprint the most loving kiss upon the sweet lips which had just pronounced them, but at the same time it caused me the most delicious felicity to see that such an angel loved me.

"With such conformity of feelings," I said, "we would, lovely C **, be perfectly happy, if we could be united for ever. But I am old enough to be your father."

"You my father? You are joking! Do you know that I am fourteen?"

"Do you know that I am twenty-eight?"

"Well, where can you see a man of your age having a daughter of mine? If my father were like you, he would certainly never frighten me; I could not keep anything from him."

The hour to go to the theatre had come; we landed, and the performance engrossed all her attention. Her brother joined us only when it was nearly over; it had certainly been a part of his calculation. I took them to an inn for supper, and the pleasure I experienced in seeing the charming girl eat with a good appetite made me forget that I had had no dinner. I hardly spoke during the supper, for love made me sick, and I was in a state of excitement which could not last long. In order to excuse my silence, I feigned to be suffering from the toothache.

After supper, P ** C ** told his sister that I was in love with her, and that I should certainly feel better if she would allow me to kiss her. The only answer of the innocent girl was to offer me her laughing lips, which seemed to call for kisses. I was burning; but my respect for that innocent and naive young creature was such that I only kissed her cheek, and even that in a manner very cold in appearance.

"What a kiss!" exclaimed P ** C **. "Come, come, a good lover's kiss!"

I did not move; the impudent fellow annoyed me; but his sister, turning her head aside sadly, said:

"Do not press him; I am not so happy as to please him."

That remark gave the alarm to my love; I could no longer master my feelings.

"What!" I exclaimed warmly, "what! beautiful C **, you do

not condescend to ascribe my reserve to the feeling which you have inspired me with? You suppose that you do not please me? If a kiss is all that is needed to prove the contrary to you, oh! receive it now with all the sentiment that is burning in my heart!"

Then folding her in my arms, and pressing her lovingly against my breast, I imprinted on her mouth the long and ardent kiss which I had so much wished to give her; but the nature of that kiss made the timid dove feel that she had fallen into the vulture's claws. She escaped from my arms, amazed at having discovered my love in such a manner. Her brother expressed his approval, while she replaced her mask over her face, in order to conceal her confusion. I asked her whether she had any longer any doubts as to my love.

"You have convinced me," she answered, "but, because you have undeceived me, you must not punish me."

I thought that this was a very delicate answer, dictated by true sentiment; but her brother was not pleased with it, and said it was foolish. We put on our masks, left the inn, and after I had escorted them to their house, I went home deeply in love, happy in my inmost soul, yet very sad.

The next morning P ** C ** called on me with an air of triumph; he told me that his sister had confessed to her mother that we loved one another, and that if she was ever to be married she would be unhappy with any other husband.

"I adore your sister," I said to him; "but do you think that your father will be willing to give her to me?"

"I think not; but he is old. In the meantime, love one another. My mother has given her permission to go to the opera this evening with us."

"Very well, my dear friend, we must go."

"I find myself under the necessity of claiming a slight service at your hands."

"Dispose of me."

"There is some excellent Cyprus wine to be sold very cheap, and I can obtain a cask of it against my bill at six months. I am certain of selling it again immediately with a good profit; but the merchant requires a guarantee, and he is disposed to accept yours, if you will give it. Will you be kind enough to endorse my note of hand?"

"With pleasure."

I signed my name without hesitation, for where is the man in love who in such a case would have refused that service to a person who to revenge himself might have made him miserable! We made an appointment for the evening, and parted highly pleased with each other.

After I had dressed myself, I went out and bought a dozen pairs of gloves, as many pairs of silk stockings, and a pair of garters embroidered in gold and with gold clasps, promising myself much pleasure in offering that first present to my young friend.

I need not say that I was exact in reaching the appointed place, but they were there already, waiting for me. Had I not suspected the intentions of P ** C **, their coming so early would have been very flattering to my vanity. The moment I had joined them, P ** C ** told me that, having other engagements to fulfil, he would leave his sister with me, and meet us at the theatre in the evening. When he had gone, I told C ** C ** that we would sail in a gondola until the opening of the theatre.

"No," she answered, "let us rather go to the Zuecca Garden."

"With all my heart."

I hired a gondola and we went to St. Blaze, where I knew a very pretty garden which, for one sequin, was placed at my disposal for the remainder of the day, with the express condition that no one else would be allowed admittance. We had not had any dinner, and after I had ordered a good meal we went up to a room where we took off our disguises and masks, after which we went to the garden.

My lovely C ** C ** had nothing on but a bodice made of light silk and a skirt of the same description, but she was charming in that simple costume! My amorous looks went through those light veils, and in my imagination I saw her entirely naked! I sighed with burning desires, with a mixture of discreet reserve and voluptuous love.

The moment we had reached the long avenue, my young companion, as lively as a fawn, finding herself at liberty on the green sward, and enjoying that happy freedom for the first time in her life, began to run about and to give way to the spirit of cheerfulness which was natural to her. When she was compelled to stop for want of breath, she burst out laughing at seeing me gazing at her in a sort of ecstatic silence. She then challenged me to run a race; the game was very agreeable to me. I accepted, but I proposed to make it interesting by a wager.

"Whoever loses the race," I said, "shall have to do whatever the winner asks."

"Agreed!"

We marked the winning-post, and made a fair start. I was certain to win, but I lost on purpose, so as to see what she would ask me to do. At first she ran with all her might while I reserved my strength, and she was the first to reach the goal. As she was trying to recover her breath, she thought of sentencing me to a good penance: she hid herself behind a tree and told me, a minute afterwards, that I had to find her ring. She had concealed it about her, and that was putting me in possession of all her person. I thought it was a delightful forfeit, for I could easily see that she had chosen it with intentional mischief; but I felt that I ought not to take too much advantage of her, because her artless confidence required to be encouraged. The ring was at last found, but I felt such emotion as I drew it out that my hand was trembling.

"What are you trembling for?" she asked.

"Only for joy at having found the ring; you had concealed it so well! But you owe me a revenge, and this time you shall not beat me."

"We shall see."

We began a new race, and seeing that she was not running very fast, I thought I could easily distance her whenever I liked. I was mistaken. She had husbanded her strength, and when we had run about two-thirds of the race she suddenly sprang forward at full speed, left me behind, and I saw that I had lost. I then thought of a trick, the effect of which never fails; I feigned a heavy fall, and I uttered a shriek of pain. The poor child stopped at once, ran back to me in great fright, and, pitying me, she assisted me to raise myself from the ground. The moment I was on my feet again, I laughed heartily and, taking a spring forward, I had reached the goal long before her.

The charming runner, thoroughly amazed, said to me:

"Then you did not hurt yourself?"

"No, for I fell purposely."

"Purposely? Oh, to deceive me! I would never have believed you capable of that. It is not fair to win by fraud; therefore I have not lost the race."

"Oh! yes, you have, for I reached the goal before you. Trick for trick; confess that you tried to deceive me at the start."

"But that is fair, and your trick is a very different thing."

"Yet it has given me the victory, and

Vincasi per fortuna o per ingano,
Il vincer sempre fu laudabil cosa."

"I have often heard those words from my brother, but never from my father. Well, never mind, I have lost. Give your judgment now, I will obey."

"Wait a little. Let me see. Ah! my sentence is that you shall exchange your garters for mine."

"Exchange our garters! But you have seen mine, they are ugly and worth nothing."

"Never mind. Twice every day I shall think of the person I love, and as nearly as possible at the same hours you will have to think of me."

"It is a very pretty idea, and I like it. Now I forgive you for having deceived me. Here are my ugly garters. Ah! my dear deceiver, how beautiful yours are! What a handsome present! How they will please my mother! They must be a present which you have just received, for they are quite new."

"No, they have not been given to me. I bought them for you, and I have been racking my brain to find how I could make you accept them. Love suggested to me the idea of making them the prize of the race. You may now imagine my sorrow when I saw that you would win. Vexation inspired me with a deceitful stratagem, which arose from a feeling you had caused yourself, and which turned entirely to your honour, for you must admit that you would have shown a very hard heart if you had not come to my assistance."

"And I feel certain that you would not have had recourse to that stratagem if you could have guessed how deeply it would pain me."

"Do you, then, feel much interest in me?"

"I would do anything in the world to convince you of it. I like my pretty garters exceedingly; I will never have another pair, and I promise you that my brother shall not steal them from me."

"Can you suppose him capable of such an action?"

"Oh! certainly, especially if the fastenings are in gold."

"Yes, they are in gold; but let him believe that they are in gilt brass."

"Will you teach me how to fasten my beautiful garters?"

"Of course I will."

We went upstairs, and after our dinner, which we both enjoyed with a good appetite, she became more lively and I more excited by love, but at the same time more to be pitied in consequence of the restraint to which I had condemned myself. Very anxious to try her garters, she begged me to help her, and that request was made in good faith, without mischievous coquetry. An innocent young girl, who, in spite of her fifteen years, has not loved yet, who has not frequented the society of other girls, does not know the violence of amorous desires or what is likely to excite them. She has no idea of the danger of a *tête-à-tête*. When a natural instinct makes her love for the first time, she believes the object of her love worthy of her confidence, and she thinks that to be loved herself she must show the most boundless trust.

Seeing that her stockings were too short to fasten the garter above the knee, she told me that she would in the future use longer ones, and I immediately offered her those that I had purchased. Full of gratitude she sat on my knees, and in the effusion of her satisfaction she bestowed upon me all the kisses that she would have given to her father if he had made her such a present. I returned her kisses, forcibly keeping down the violence of my feelings. I only told her that one of her kisses was worth a kingdom. My charming C ** C ** took off her shoes and stockings, and put on one of the pairs I had given her, which went half-way up her thigh. The more innocent I found her to be, the less I could make up my mind to possess myself of that ravishing prey.

We returned to the garden, and after walking about until the evening we went to the opera, taking care to keep on our masks, because, the theatre being small, we might easily have been recognised, and my lovely friend was certain that her father would not allow her to come out again, if he found out that she had gone to the opera.

*Carried away by his infatuation, Casanova approaches the mother of his sweetheart, announcing his intention of marrying her daughter as soon as he has secured a position enabling him to keep a wife — a proviso which he is always careful to add whenever he is assailed by ideas of matrimony. But the infamous brother, set on his object of exploiting his sister's charms, gets the better of Casanova's good intentions and plays the go-between to such good effect that C ** C ** succumbs after another meeting in the Zuecca Garden, both lovers protesting to Heaven that they are only taking an advance on their future and legitimate happiness as man and wife.*

*None the less Casanova is still bent on carrying out his vows, and as soon as C ** C **'s father arrives in Venice, where his son has been imprisoned, Senator Bragadin, in the name of his adopted son, asks for the girl's hand. But Casanova's matrimonial projects were doomed to failure. Not only did the father decline the honours of the proposed alliance, having doubtless learnt something of Giacomo's past record, but, to make assurance doubly sure, he places the girl in a convent at Murano, where she loses no time in finding a postillon d'amour, in the shape of an illiterate lay sister, to carry messages to her lover. The latter passes from "a state of despair to that of extreme felicity" and determines to follow the ancestral example and elope with the fair recluse, whom he continues to call his "wife."*

To carry out this laudable intention it was essential, above all things, to have ample funds, and Casanova's finances were at low ebb once more, owing, he suggests, to an over-concentration on his love affairs. To what extent he had been neglecting his worldly interests was revealed to him when he learned that one of his three protectors, Senator Dandolo, was contemplating marriage with a young widow, the perfidious de la Haye having arranged the affair. Fortunately Paralis, Casanova's oracle, whose advice in the matter having been solicited, gave a negative answer; for, as Casanova frankly pointed out to de la Haye, as long as he lived with his three friends they should have no wife but him.

From that day, de la Haye became my secret enemy, and to him I was in a great measure indebted, two years later, for my imprisonment under The Leads of Venice; not owing to his slanders, for I do not believe he was capable of that, Jesuit though he was — and even amongst such people there is sometimes some honourable feeling — but through the mystical insinuations which he made in the presence of bigoted persons. I must give fair notice to my readers that, if they are fond of such people, they must not read these Memoirs, for they belong to a tribe which I have good reason to attack unmercifully.

The fine marriage was never again alluded to. M. Dandolo continued to visit his beautiful widow every day, and I took care to elicit from Paralis a strong interdiction ever to put my foot in her house.

The financial problem becoming acute, the offer of Don Antonio Croce, "a confirmed gambler, and a downright clever hand in securing the favours of Dame Fortune," to take a share in his gambling enterprise was gratefully, if reluctantly, accepted. The enterprise, which was carried out at Padua, proved successful — too successful, in fact, as Croce was obliged to leave in a hurry, after sharing his booty with his partner, who also withdrew rather hastily to Venice.

The story of Casanova's double love intrigue with C ** C ** and M ** M **, one of the most famous and curious episodes of the Memoirs, shall be told in his own words:

After my return to Venice I resumed my usual habits; but with a nature like mine how could I possibly remain satisfied without positive love? My only pleasure was to receive a letter from my dear recluse every Wednesday, who advised me to wait patiently rather than to attempt carrying her off. Laura [1] assured me that she had become more lovely than ever, and I longed to see her. An opportunity of gratifying my wishes soon offered itself, and I did not allow it to escape. There was to be a taking of the veil — a ceremony which always attracts a large number of persons. On those occasions the nuns always received a great many visitors, and I thought that the boarders were likely to be in the parlour on such an occasion. I ran no risk of being remarked any more than any other person, for I would mingle with the crowd. I therefore went without saying anything about it to Laura, and without acquainting my dear little wife of my intentions. I thought I would fall, so great was my emotion, when I saw her within four yards of me, and looking at me as if she had been in an ecstatic state. I thought her taller and more womanly, and she certainly seemed to me more beautiful than before. I saw no one but her; she never took her eyes off me,

[1] *The messenger between Casanova and C ** C ** in the convent.*

[295]

and I was the last to leave that place, which on that day struck me as being the temple of happiness.

Three days afterwards I received a letter from her. She painted with such vivid colours the happiness she had felt in seeing me, that I made up my mind to give her that pleasure as often as I could. I answered at once that I would attend mass every Sunday at the church of her convent. It cost me nothing; I could not see her, but I knew that she saw me herself, and her happiness made me perfectly happy. I had nothing to fear, for it was almost impossible that anyone could recognise me in the church, which was attended only by the people of Muran.

After hearing two or three masses, I used to take a gondola, the gondolier of which could not feel any curiosity about me. Yet I kept on my guard, for I knew that the father of C ** C ** wanted her to forget me, and I had no doubt he would have taken her away, God knew where! if he had had the slightest suspicion of my being acquainted with the place where he had confined her. Thus was I reasoning in my fear to lose all opportunity of corresponding with my dear C ** C **, but I did not yet know the disposition and the shrewdness of the sainted daughters of the Lord. I did not suppose that there was anything remarkable in my person, at least for the inmates of a convent; but I was yet a novice respecting the curiosity of women, and particularly of unoccupied hearts; I had soon occasion to be convinced.

I had executed my Sunday manœuvring only for a month or five weeks, when my dear C ** C ** wrote to me jestingly that I had become a living enigma for all the convent, boarders and nuns, not even excepting the old ones. They all expected me anxiously; they warned each other of my arrival, and watched me taking the holy water. They remarked that I never cast a glance towards the grating, behind which were all the inmates of the convent; that I never looked at any of the women coming in or going out of the church. The old nuns said that I was certainly labouring under some deep sorrow, of which I had no hope to be cured except through the protection of the Holy Virgin, and the young ones asserted that I was either melancholy or misanthropic.

My dear wife, who knew better than the others, and had no occasion to lose herself in suppositions, was much amused, and she entertained me by sending me a faithful report of it all. I wrote to her that, if she had any fear of my being recognised, I would cease my Sunday visits to the church. She answered that I could not impose upon her a more cruel privation, and she entreated me to continue my visits. I thought it would be prudent, however, to abstain from calling at Laura's house, for fear of the chattering nuns contriving to know it, and discovering in that manner a great deal more than I wished them to find out. But that existence was literally consuming me by slow degrees, and could not last long. Besides, I was made to have a mistress, and to live happily with her. Not knowing what to do with myself, I would gamble, and I almost invariably won; but, in spite of that, weariness had got hold of me and I was getting thinner every day.

With the five thousand sequins which my partner Croce had won for me in Padua I had followed M. de Bragadin's advice. I had hired a casino where I held a faro bank in partnership with a matador, who secured me against the frauds of certain noblemen — tyrants, with whom a private citizen is always sure to be in the wrong in my dear country.

On All Saints' Day, in the year 1753, just as, after hearing mass, I was going to step into a gondola to return to Venice, I saw a woman, somewhat in Laura's style, who, passing near me, looked at me and dropped a letter. I picked it up, and the woman, seeing me in possession of the epistle, quietly went on. The letter had no address, and the seal represented a running knot. I stepped hurriedly into the gondola, and as soon as we were in the offing I broke the seal. I read the following words:

"A nun, who for the last two months and a half has seen you every Sunday in the church of her convent, wishes to become acquainted with you. A pamphlet which you have lost, and which chance has thrown into her hands, makes her believe that you speak French; but, if you like it better, you can answer in Italian, because what she wants above all is a clear and precise answer. She does not invite you to call for her at the parlour of the convent, because, before you place yourself under the necessity of speaking to her, she wishes you to see her, and for that purpose she will name a lady whom you can accompany to the parlour. That lady shall not know you and need not therefore introduce you, in case you should not wish to be known.

[297]

"Should you not approve of that way to become acquainted, the nun will appoint a certain casino in Muran, in which you will find her alone, in the evening, any night you may choose. You will then be at liberty either to sup with her, or to retire after an interview of a quarter of an hour, if you have any other engagements.

"Would you rather offer her a supper in Venice? Name the night, the hour, the place of appointment, and you will see her come out of a gondola. Only be careful to be there alone, masked, and with a lantern.

"I feel certain that you will answer me, and that you will guess how impatiently I am waiting for your letter. I entreat you, therefore, to give it to-morrow to the same woman through whom you will receive mine; you will find her one hour before noon in the church of St. Cancian, near the first altar on the right.

"Recollect that, if I did not suppose you endowed with a noble soul and a high mind, I could never have resolved on taking a step which might give you an unfavourable opinion of my character."

The tone of that letter, which I have copied word by word, surprised me even more than the offer it contained. I had business to attend to, but I gave up all engagements to lock myself in my room in order to answer it. Such an application betokened an extravagant mind, but there was in it a certain dignity, a singularity, which attracted me. I had an idea that the writer might be the same nun who taught French to C ** C **. She had represented her friend in her letters as handsome, rich, gallant, and generous. My dear wife, perhaps, had been guilty of some indiscretion. A thousand fancies whirled through my brain, but I would entertain only those which were favourable to a scheme highly pleasing to me. Besides, my young friend had informed me that the nun who had given her French lessons was not the only one in the convent who spoke that language. I had no reason to suppose that, if C ** C ** had made a confidante of her friend, she would have made a mystery of it to me. But, for all that, the nun who had written to me might be the beautiful friend of my dear little wife, and she might also turn out to be a different person; I felt somewhat puzzled. Here is, however, the letter which I thought I could write without implicating myself:

"I answer in French, madam, in the hope that my letter will have the clearness and the precision of which you give me the example in yours.

"The subject is highly interesting and of the highest importance, considering all the circumstances. As I must answer without knowing the person to whom I am writing, you must feel, madam, that, unless I should possess a large dose of vanity, I must fear some mystification, and my honour requires that I should keep on my guard.

"If it is true that the person who has penned that letter is a respectable woman, who renders me justice in supposing me endowed with feelings as noble as her own, she will find, I trust, that I could not answer in any other way than I am doing now.

"If you have judged me worthy, madam, of the honour which you do me by offering me your acquaintance, although your good opinion can have been formed only from my personal appearance, I feel it my duty to obey you, even if the result be to undeceive you by proving that I had unwittingly led you into a mistaken appreciation of my person.

"Of the three proposals which you so kindly made in your letter, I dare not accept any but the first, with the restriction suggested by your penetrating mind. I will accompany to the parlour of your convent a lady who shall not know who I am, and, consequently, shall have no occasion to introduce me.

"Do not judge too severely, madam, the specious reasons which compel me not to give you my name, and receive my word of honour that I shall learn yours only to render you homage. If you choose to speak to me, I will answer with the most profound respect. Permit me to hope that you will come to the parlour alone. I may mention that I am a Venetian, and perfectly free. The only reason which prevents me from choosing one of the two other arrangements proposed by you, either of which would have suited me better because they greatly honour me, is, allow me to repeat it, a fear of being the victim of a mystification; but these modes of meeting will not be lost when you know me and when I have seen you. I entreat you to have faith in my honour, and to measure my patience by your own. To-morrow, at the same place and at the same hour, I shall be anxiously expecting your answer."

I went to the place appointed, and having met the female

Mercury I gave her my letter with a sequin, and I told her that I would come the next day for the answer. We were both punctual. As soon as she saw me, she handed me back the sequin which I had given her the day before, and a letter, requesting me to read it and to let her know whether she was to wait for an answer. Here is the exact copy of the letter:

"I believe, sir, that I have not been mistaken in anything. Like you, I detest untruth when it can lead to important consequences, but I think it a mere trifle when it can do no injury to anyone. Of my three proposals you have chosen the one which does the greatest honour to your intelligence, and, respecting the reasons which induce you to keep your incognito, I have written the enclosed to the Countess of S **, which I request you to read. Be kind enough to seal it before delivering it to her. You may call upon her whenever convenient to yourself. She will name her own hour, and you will accompany her here in her gondola. The countess will not ask you any questions, and you need not give her any explanation. There will be no presentation; but as you will be made acquainted with my name, you can afterwards call on me here, masked, whenever you please, and by using the name of the countess. In that way we shall become acquainted without the necessity of disturbing you, or of your losing at night some hours which may be precious to you. I have instructed my servant to wait for your answer in case you should be known to the countess and object to her. If you approve of the choice I have made of her, tell the messenger that there is no answer."

As I was an entire stranger to the countess, I told the woman that I had no answer to give, and she left me.

Here are the contents of the note addressed by the nun to the countess, and which I had to deliver to her:

"I beg of you, my dear friend, to pay me a visit when you are at leisure, and to let the masked gentleman — bearer of this note — know the hour, so that he can accompany you. He will be punctual. Farewell. You will much oblige your friend."

That letter seemed to me informed by a sublime spirit of intrigue; there was in it an appearance of dignity which captivated me, although I felt conscious that I was playing the character of a man on whom a favour seemed to be bestowed.

In her last letter, my nun, pretending not to be anxious to

know who I was, approved of my choice, and feigned indifference for nocturnal meetings; but she seemed certain that after seeing her I would visit her. I knew very well what to think of it all, for the intrigue was sure to have an amorous issue. Nevertheless, her assurance, or rather confidence, increased my curiosity, and I felt that she had every reason to hope, if she were young and handsome. I might very well have delayed the affair for a few days, and have learned from C ** C ** who that nun could be; but, besides the baseness of such a proceeding, I was afraid of spoiling the game and repenting it afterwards. I was told to call on the countess at my convenience, but it was because the dignity of my nun would not allow her to show herself too impatient; and she certainly thought that I would myself hasten the adventure. She seemed to me too deeply learned in gallantry to admit the possibility of her being an inexperienced novice, and I was afraid of wasting my time, but I had made up my mind to laugh at my own expense if I happened to meet a superannuated female. It is very certain that if I had not been actuated by curiosity I should not have gone one step further, but I wanted to see the countenance of a nun who had offered to come to Venice to sup with me. Besides, I was much surprised at the liberty enjoyed by those sainted virgins, and at the facility with which they could escape out of their walls.

At three o'clock I presented myself before the countess and delivered the note, and she expressed a wish to see me the next day at the same hour. We dropped a beautiful reverence to one another, and parted. She was a superior woman, already going down the hill, but still very handsome.

The next morning, being Sunday, I need not say that I took care to attend mass at the convent, elegantly dressed, and already unfaithful — at least in idea — to my dear C ** C **, for I was thinking of being seen by the nun, young or old, rather than of showing myself to my charming wife.

In the afternoon I masked myself again, and at the appointed time I repaired to the house of the countess, who was waiting for me. We went in a two-oared gondola, and reached the convent without having spoken of anything but the weather. When we arrived at the gate, the countess asked for M ** M **. I was surprised by that name, for the woman to whom it belonged was celebrated. We were shown into a small parlour, and a few

minutes afterwards a nun came in, went straight to the grating,
touched a spring, and made four squares of the grating revolve,
which left an opening sufficiently large to enable the two friends
to embrace: the ingenious window was afterwards carefully
closed. The opening was at least eighteen inches wide, and a
man of my size could easily have got through it. The countess
sat opposite the nun, and I took my seat a little on one side so
as to be able to observe quietly and at my ease one of the most
beautiful women that it was possible to see. I had no doubt
whatever of her being the person mentioned by my dear C**
C** as teaching her French. Admiration kept me in a sort of
ecstacy, and I never heard one word of their conversation; the
beautiful nun, far from speaking to me, did not even condescend
to honour me with one look. She was about twenty-two or
twenty-three years of age, and the shape of her face was most
beautiful. Her figure was much above the ordinary height, her
complexion rather pale, her appearance noble, full of energy, but
at the same time reserved and modest; her eyes, large and full,
were of a lovely blue; her countenance was soft and cheerful;
her fine lips seemed to breathe the most heavenly voluptuousness,
and her teeth were two rows of the most brilliant enamel. Her
head-dress did not allow me to see her hair, but if she had any
I knew by the colour of her eyebrows that it was of a beautiful
light brown. Her hand and her arm, which I could see as far as
the elbow, were magnificent; the chisel of Praxiteles never
carved anything more gracefully rounded and plump. In spite
of all I could see, of all I guessed, I was not sorry to have refused
the two rendezvous which had been offered to me by the beauty,
for I was sure of possessing her in a few days, and it was a pleasure for me to lay my desires at her feet. I longed to find myself
alone with her near that grating, and I would have considered it
an insult to her if, the very next day, I had not come to tell her
how fully I rendered to her charms the justice they deserved.
She was faithful to her determination not to look at me once,
but after all I was pleased with her reserve. All at once the two
friends lowered their voices, and out of delicacy I withdrew
further. Their private conversation lasted about a quarter of an
hour, during which I pretended to be intently looking at a painting; then they kissed one another again by the same process
as at the beginning of the interview; the nun closed the opening,

turned her back on us, and disappeared without casting one glance in my direction.

As we were on our way back to Venice, the countess, tired perhaps of our silence, said to me, with a smile:

"M ** M ** is beautiful and very witty."

"I have seen her beauty, and I believe in her wit."

"She did not address one word to you."

"I had refused to be introduced to her, and she punished me by pretending not to know that I was present."

The countess made no answer, and we reached her house without exchanging another word. At her door a very ceremonious curtsy, with these words, "Adieu, sir!" warned me that I was not to go any further. I had no wish to do so, and went away dreaming and wondering at the singularity of the adventure, the end of which I longed to see.

My beautiful nun had not spoken to me, and I was glad of it, for I was so astonished, so completely under the spell of her beauty, that I might have given her a very poor opinion of my intelligence by the rambling answers which I should very likely have given to her questions. I knew her to be certain that she had not to fear the humiliation of a refusal from me, but I admired her courage in running the risk of it in her position. I could hardly understand her boldness, and I could not conceive how she contrived to enjoy so much liberty. A casino at Muran! the possibility of going to Venice to sup with a young man! it was all very surprising, and I decided in my own mind that she had an acknowledged lover whose pleasure it was to make her happy by satisfying her caprices. It is true that such a thought was rather unpleasant to my pride, but there was too much piquancy in the adventure, the heroine of it was too attractive, for me to be stopped by any considerations. I saw very well that I was taking the high road to become unfaithful to my dear C ** C **, or rather that I was already so in thought and will, but I must confess that, in spite of all my love for that charming child, I felt no qualms of conscience. It seemed to me that an infidelity of that sort, if she ever heard of it, would not displease her, for that short excursion on strange ground would only keep me alive and in good condition for her, because it would save me from the weariness which was surely killing me.

I had been presented to the celebrated Countess Coronini by

a nun, a relative of M. Dandolo. That countess, who had been very handsome and was very witty, having made up her mind to renounce all the political intrigues which had been the study of her whole life, had sought a retreat in the Convent of St. Justine, in the hope of finding in that refuge the calm which she wanted, and which her disgust of society had rendered necessary to her. As she had enjoyed a very great reputation, she was still visited at the convent by all the foreign ambassadors and by the first noblemen of Venice; inside of the walls of her convent the countess was acquainted with everything that happened in the city. She always received me very kindly, and, treating me as a young man, she took pleasure in giving me, every time I called on her, very agreeable lessons in morals. Being quite certain to find out from her, with a little manœuvring, something concerning M ** M **, I decided on paying her a visit the day after I had seen the beautiful nun.

The countess gave me her usual welcome, and, after the thousand nothings which it is the custom to utter in society before anything worth saying is spoken, I led the conversation up to the convents of Venice. We spoke of the wit and influence of a nun called Celsi, who, although ugly, had an immense credit everywhere and in everything. We mentioned afterwards the young and lovely Sister Michali, who had taken the veil to prove to her mother that she was superior to her in intelligence and wit. After speaking of several other nuns who had the reputation of being addicted to gallantry, I named M ** M **, remarking that most likely she deserved that reputation likewise, but that she was an enigma. The countess answered with a smile that she was not an enigma for everybody, although she was necessarily so for most people.

"What is incomprehensible," she said, "is the caprice that she took suddenly to become a nun, being handsome, rich, free, well-educated, full of wit, and, to my knowledge, a free-thinker. She took the veil without any reason, physical or moral; it was a mere caprice."

"Do you believe her to be happy, madam?"

"Yes, unless she has repented her decision, or if she does not repent it some day. But if ever she does, I think she will be wise enough never to say so to anyone."

Satisfied by the mysterious air of the countess that M ** M ** had a lover, I made up my mind not to trouble myself about it, and having put on my mask I went to Muran in the afternoon. When I reached the gate of the convent I rang the bell, and with an anxious heart I asked for M ** M ** in the name of Madame de S **. The small parlour being closed, the attendant pointed out to me the one in which I had to go. I went in, took off my mask, and sat down waiting for my divinity.

My heart was beating furiously; I was waiting with great impatience; yet that expectation was not without charm, for I dreaded the beginning of the interview. An hour passed pretty rapidly, but I began then to find the time rather long, and thinking that, perhaps, the attendant had not rightly understood me, I rang the bell, and I inquired whether notice of my visit had been given to Sister M ** M **. A voice answered affirmatively. I took my seat again, and a few minutes afterwards an old, toothless nun came in and informed me that Sister M ** M ** was engaged for the whole day. Without giving me time to utter a single word, the woman left the parlour.

This was one of those terrible moments to which the man who worships at the shrine of the god of love is exposed! They are indeed cruel moments; they bring fearful sorrow, they may cause death.

Feeling myself disgraced, my first sensation was utter contempt for myself, an inward despair which was akin to rage; the second was disdainful indignation against the nun, upon whom I passed the severe judgment which I thought she deserved, and which was the only way I had to soothe my grief. Such behaviour proclaimed her to be the most impudent of women, and entirely wanting in good sense; for the two letters she had written to me were quite enough to ruin her character if I had wished to revenge myself, and she evidently could not expect anything else from me. She must have been mad to set at defiance my revengeful feelings, and I should certainly have thought that she was insane if I had not heard her converse with the countess.

Time, they say, brings good counsel; it certainly brings calm, and cool reflection gives lucidity to the mind. At last I persuaded myself that what had occurred was after all in no way extraordinary, and that I would certainly have considered it at first a very common occurrence if I had not been dazzled by the wonderful beauty of the nun, and blinded by my own vanity.

As a very natural result I felt that I was at liberty to laugh at my mishap, and that nobody could possibly guess whether my mirth was genuine or only counterfeit. Sophism is so officious!

But, in spite of all my fine arguments, I still cherished the thought of revenge; no debasing element, however, was to form part of it, and being determined not to leave the person who had been guilty of such a bad practical joke the slightest cause of triumph, I had the courage not to show any vexation. She had sent word to me that she was engaged; nothing more natural; the part I had to play was to appear indifferent. "Most likely she will not be engaged another time," I said to myself, "but I defy her to catch me in the snare again. I mean to show her that I only laugh at her uncivil behaviour." Of course I intended to send back her letters, but not without the acompaniment of a billet-doux, the gallantry of which was not likely to please her.

The worse part of the affair for me was to be compelled to go to church; because, supposing her not to be aware of my going there for C ** C **, she might imagine that the only object of my visits was to give her the opportunity of apologising for her conduct and of appointing a new meeting. I wanted her to entertain no doubt of my utter contempt for her person, and I felt certain that she had proposed the other meetings in Venice and at the casino of Muran only to deceive me more easily.

I went to bed with a great thirst for revenge, I fell asleep thinking of it, and I awoke with the resolution of quenching it. I began to write, but, as I wished particularly that my letter should not show the pique of the disappointed lover, I left it on my table with the intention of reading it again the next day. It proved a useful precaution, for when I read it over, twenty-four hours afterwards, I found it unworthy of me, and tore it to pieces. It contained some sentences which savoured too much of my weakness, my love, and my spite, and which, far from humiliating her, would only have given her occasion to laugh at me.

On the Wednesday after I had written to C ** C ** that very serious reasons compelled me to give up my visits to the church of her convent, I wrote another letter to the nun, but on Thursday it had the same fate as the first, because upon a second perusal I found the same deficiencies. It seemed to me that I had lost the faculty of writing. Ten days afterwards I found out that I was too deeply in love to have the power of expressing myself in any other way than through the feelings of my heart.

Sincerum est nisi vas, quodcunque infundis acescit.

The face of M ** M ** had made too deep an impression on me; nothing could possibly obliterate it except the all-powerful influence of time.

In my ridiculous position I was sorely tempted to complain to Countess S **; but I am happy to say I was prudent enough not to cross the threshold of her door. At last I bethought myself that the giddy nun was certainly labouring under constant dread, knowing that I had in my possession her two letters, with which I could ruin her reputation and cause the greatest injury to the convent, and I sent them back to her with the following note, after I had kept them for ten days:

"I can assure you, madam, that it was owing only to forgetfulness that I did not return your two letters which you will find enclosed. I have never thought of belying my own nature by taking a cowardly revenge upon you, and I forgive you most willingly the two giddy acts of which you have been guilty, whether they were committed thoughtlessly or because you wanted to enjoy a joke at my expense. Nevertheless, you will allow me to advise you not to treat any other man in the same way, for you might meet with one endowed with less delicacy. I know your name, I know who you are, but you need not be anxious; it is exactly as if I did not know it. You may, perhaps, care but little for my discretion, but if it should be so I should greatly pity you.

"You may be aware that I shall not show myself again at your church; but let me assure you that it is not a sacrifice on my part, and that I can attend mass anywhere else. Yet I must tell you why I shall abstain from frequenting the church of your convent. It is very natural for me to suppose that to the two thoughtless acts of which you have been guilty, you have added another not less serious — namely, that of having boasted of your exploits with the other nuns, and I do not want to be the butt of your jokes in cell or parlour. Do not think me too ridiculous if, in spite of being five or six years older than you, I have not thrown off all feelings of self-respect, or trodden under my feet all reserve and propriety; in one word, if I have kept some prejudices, there are a few which in my opinion ought never to be forgotten. Do not disdain, madam, the lesson which I take the liberty to teach you, as I receive in the kindest spirit the one which you have given me, most likely only for the sake of fun, but by which I promise you to profit as long as I live."

I thought that, considering all circumstances, my letter was a very genial one; I made up my parcel, put on my mask, and looked out for a porter who could have no knowledge of me; I gave him half a sequin, and I promised him as much more when he could assure me that he had faithfully delivered my letter at the convent of Muran. I gave him all the necessary instructions, and cautioned him to go away the very moment he had delivered the letter at the gate of the convent, even if he were told to wait. I must say here that my messenger was a man from Forli, and that the Forlanese were then the most trustworthy men in Venice; for one of them to be guilty of a breach of trust was an unheard-of thing. Such were formerly the Savoyards in Paris; but everything is getting worse in this world.

I was beginning to forget the adventure, probably because I thought, rightly or wrongly, that I had put an insurmountable barrier between the nun and myself, when, ten days after I had sent my letter, as I was coming out of the opera, I met my messenger, lantern in hand. I called him, and without taking off my mask I asked him whether he knew me. He looked at me, eyed me from head to foot, and finally answered that he did not.

"Did you faithfully carry the message to Muran?"

"Ah, sir! God be praised! I am very happy to see you again, for I have an important communication to make to you. I took your letter, delivered it according to your instructions, and I went away as soon as it was in the hands of the attendant, although she requested me to wait. When I returned from Muran I did not see you, but that did not matter. On the following day, one of my companions, who happened to be at the gate of the convent when I delivered your letter, came early in the morning to tell me to go to Muran, because the attendant wanted particularly to speak to me. I went there, and after waiting for a few minutes I was shown into the parlour, where I was kept for more than an hour by a nun as beautiful as the light of day, who asked me a thousand questions for the purpose of ascertaining, if not who you are, at least where I should be likely to find you. You know that I could not give her any satisfactory information. She then left the parlour, ordering me to wait, and at the end of two hours she came back with a letter which she entrusted to my hands, telling me that, if I succeeded in finding you out and in bringing her an answer, she would give me two sequins. In the meantime I was to call at the convent every day, show her the letter, and receive forty sous every time. Until now I have earned twenty crowns, but I am afraid the lady will get tired of it, and you can make me earn two sequins by answering a line."

"Where is the letter?"

"In my room under lock and key, for I am always afraid of losing it."

"Then how can I answer?"

"If you will wait for me here, you shall have the letter in less than a quarter of an hour."

"I will not wait, because I do not care about the letter. But tell me how you could flatter the nun with the hope of finding me out? You are a rogue, for it is not likely that she would have trusted you with the letter if you had not promised her to find me."

"I am not a rogue, for I have done faithfully what you told me; but it is true that I gave her a description of your coat, your buckles, and your figure, and I can assure you that for the last ten days I have examined all the masks who are about your size, but in vain. Now I recognise your buckles, but I do not think you have the same coat. Alas, sir! it will not cost you much to write only one line. Be kind enough to wait for me in the coffee-house close by."

I could not resist my curiosity any longer, and I made up my mind not to wait for him but to accompany him as far as his house. I had only to write, "I have received the letter," and my curiosity was gratified and the Forlanese earned his two sequins. I could afterwards change my buckles and my mask, and thus set all inquiries at defiance.

I therefore followed him to his door; he went in and brought me the letter. I took him to an inn, where I asked for a room with a good fire, and I told my man to wait. I broke the seal of the parcel — a rather large one — and the first papers that I saw were the two letters which I had sent back to her in order to allay her anxiety as to the possible consequences of her giddiness.

The sight of these letters caused me such a palpitation of the heart that I was compelled to sit down: it was a most evident sign of my defeat. Besides these two letters I found a third one signed "S." and addressed to M ** M **. I read the following lines:

"The mask who accompanied me back to my house would not, I believe, have uttered a single word if I had not told him that the charms of your witty mind were even more bewitching than those of your person; and his answer was, 'I have seen the one, and I believe in the other.' I added that I did not understand why you had not spoken to him, and he said, with a smile, 'I refused to be presented to her, and she punished me for it by not appearing to know that I was present.' These few words were all our dialogue. I intended to send you this note this morning, but found it impossible. Adieu."

After reading this note, which stated the exact truth, and which could be considered as proof, my heart began to beat less quickly. Delighted at seeing myself on the point of being convicted of injustice, I took courage, and I read the following letter:

"Owing to an excusable weakness, feeling curious to know what you would say about me to the countess after you had seen me, I took an opportunity of asking her to let me know all you said to her on the following day at latest, for I foresaw that you would pay me a visit in the afternoon. Her letter, which I enclose, and which I beg you to read, did not reach me till half an hour after you had left the convent.

"This was the first fatality.

"Not having received that letter when you called, I had not the courage to see you. This absurd weakness on my part was the second fatality, but the weakness you will, I hope, forgive. I gave orders to the lay sister to tell you that *I was ill for the whole day;* a very legitimate excuse, whether true or false, for it was an officious untruth, the corrective of which was to be found in the words 'for the whole day.' You had already left the convent, and I could not possibly send anyone to run after you, when the old fool informed me of her having told you that I was *engaged.*

"This was the third fatality.

"You cannot imagine what I had a mind to do and to say

[310]

to that foolish sister, but here one must say or do nothing; one must be patient and dissemble, thanking God when mistakes are the result of ignorance and not of wickedness — a very common thing in convents. I foresaw at once, at least partly, what would happen, and what has actually happened, for no reasonable being could, I believe, have foreseen it all. I guessed that, thinking yourself the victim of a joke, you would be incensed, and I felt miserable, for I did not see any way of letting you know the truth before the following Sunday. My heart longed ardently for that day. Could I possibly imagine that you would take a resolution not to come again to our church! I tried to be patient until that Sunday; but when I found myself disappointed in my hope, my misery became unbearable, and it will cause my death if you refuse to listen to my justification. Your letter has made me completely unhappy, and I shall not resist my despair if you persist in the cruel resolve expressed by your unfeeling letter. You have considered yourself trifled with; that is all you can say; but will this letter convince you of your error? And even believing yourself deceived in the most scandalous manner, you must admit that to write such an awful letter you must have supposed me an abominable wretch — a monster, such as a woman of noble birth and of refined education cannot possibly be. I enclose the two letters you sent back to me, with the idea of allaying my fears which you cruelly supposed very different to what they are in reality. I am a better physiognomist than you, and you must be quite certain that I have not acted thoughtlessly, for I have never thought you capable, I will not say of a crime, but even of an indelicate action. You must have read on my features the signs only of giddy impudence, and that is not my nature. You may be the cause of my death, you will certainly make me miserable for the remainder of my life, if you do not justify yourself; on my side I think the justification is complete.

"I hope that, even if you feel no interest in my life, you will think that you are bound in honour to come and speak to me. Come yourself to recall all you have written; it is your duty, and I deserve it. If you do not realise the fatal effect produced upon me by your letter, I must indeed pity you, in spite of my misery, for it proves that you have not the slightest knowledge of the human heart. But I feel certain that you will come back, provided the man to whom I trust this letter contrives to find you. Adieu! I expect life or death from you."

I did not require to read that letter twice; I was ashamed and in despair. M ** M ** was right. I called the Forlanese, inquired from him whether he had spoken to her in the morning, and whether she looked ill. He answered that he had found her looking more unhappy every day, and that her eyes were red from weeping.

"Go down again and wait," I said to him.

I began to write, and I had not concluded my long screed before the dawn of day; here are, word by word, the contents of the letter which I wrote to the noblest of women, whom in my unreasonable spite I had judged so wrongly.

"I plead guilty, madam; I cannot possibly justify myself, and I am perfectly convinced of your innocence. I should be disconsolate if I did not hope to obtain pardon, and you will not refuse to forgive me if you are kind enough to recollect the cause of my guilt. I saw you; I was dazzled, and I could not realise a happiness which seemed to me a dream; I thought myself the prey of one of those delightful illusions which vanish when we wake up. The doubt under which I was labouring could not be cleared up for twenty-four hours, and how could I express my feverish impatience as I was longing for that happy moment! It came at last! and my heart, throbbing with desire and hope, was flying towards you while I was in the parlour counting the minutes! Yet an hour passed almost rapidly, and not unnaturally, considering my impatience and the deep impression I felt at the idea of seeing you. But then, precisely at the very moment when I believed myself certain that I was going to gaze upon the beloved features which had been in one interview indelibly engraved upon my heart, I saw the most disagreeable face appear, and a creature announced that you were engaged for the whole day, and without giving me time to utter one word she disappeared! You may imagine my astonishment and . . . the rest. The lightning would not have produced upon me a more rapid, a more terrible effect! If you had sent me a line by that sister — a line from your hand — I would have gone away, if not pleased, at least submissive and resigned.

"But that was a fourth fatality which you have forgotten to add to your delightful and witty justification. Thinking myself scoffed at, my self-love rebelled, and indignation for the moment silenced love. Shame overwhelmed me! I thought that everybody could read on my face all the horror in my heart, and I saw in you, under the outward appearance of an angel, nothing but a fearful daughter of the Prince of Darkness. My mind was thoroughly upset, and at the end of eleven days I lost the small portion of good sense that was left in me — at least I must suppose so, as it is then that I wrote to you the letter of which you have so good a right to complain, and which at that time seemed to me a masterpiece of moderation.

"But I hope it is all over now, and this very day at eleven o'clock you will see me at your feet — tender, submissive, and repentant. You will forgive me, divine woman, or I will myself avenge you for the insult I have hurled at you. The only thing which I dare not ask from you as a great favour is to burn my first letter, and never to mention it again. I sent it only after I had written four, which I destroyed one after the other: you may therefore imagine the state of my heart.

"I have given orders to my messenger to go to your convent at once, so that my letter can be delivered to you as soon as you wake in the morning. He would never have discovered me, if my good angel had not made me go up to him at the door of the opera-house. But I shall not require his services any more: do not answer me, and receive all the devotion of a heart which adores you."

When my letter was finished, I called my Forlanese, gave him one sequin, and I made him promise me to go to Muran immediately, and to deliver my letter only to the nun herself. As soon as he had gone I threw myself on my bed, but anxiety and burning impatience would not allow me to sleep.

I need not tell the reader who knows the state of excitement under which I was labouring, that I was punctual in presenting myself at the convent. I was shown into the small parlour where I had seen her for the first time, and she almost immediately made her entrance. As soon as I saw her near the grating I fell on my knees, but she entreated me to rise at once as I might be seen. Her face was flushed with excitement, and her looks seemed to me heavenly. She sat down, and I took a seat opposite to her. We remained several minutes motionless, gazing at each other without speaking, but I broke the silence by asking her, in a voice full of love and anxiety, whether I could hope to obtain my pardon. She gave me her beautiful hand through the grating, and I covered it with tears and kisses.

"Our acquaintance," she said, "has begun with a violent storm; let us hope that we shall now enjoy it long in perfect and lasting calm. This is the first time that we speak to one another, but what has occurred must be enough to give us a thorough knowledge of each other. I trust that our intimacy will be as tender as sincere, and that we shall know how to have a mutual indulgence for our faults."

"Can such an angel as you have any?"

"Ah, my friend! who is without them?"

"When shall I have the happiness of convincing you of my devotion with complete freedom and in all the joy of my heart?"

"We will take supper together at my casino whenever you please, provided you give me notice two days beforehand; or I will go and sup with you in Venice, if it will not disturb your arrangements."

"It would only increase my happiness. I think it right to tell you that I am in very easy circumstances, and that, far from fearing expense, I delight in it: all I possess belongs to the woman I love."

"That confidence, my dear friend, is very agreeable to me, the more so that I have likewise to tell you that I am very rich, and that I could not refuse anything to my lover."

"But you must have a lover?"

"Yes; it is through him that I am rich, and he is entirely my master. I never conceal anything from him. The day after to-morrow, when I am alone with you, I will tell you more."

"But I hope that your lover . . ."

"Will not be there? Certainly not. Have you a mistress?"

"I had one, but, alas! she has been taken from me by violent means, and for the last six months I have led a life of complete celibacy."

"Do you love her still?"

"I cannot think of her without loving her. She has almost as great charms, as great beauty, as you have; but I foresee that you will make me forget her."

"If your happiness with her was complete, I pity you. She has been violently taken from you, and you shun society in order to feed your sorrow. I have guessed right, have I not? But if I happen to take possession of her place in your heart, no one, my sweet friend, shall turn me out of it."

"But what will your lover say?"

"He will be delighted to see me happy with such a lover as you. It is in his nature."

"What an admirable nature! Such heroism is quite beyond me!"

"What sort of a life do you lead in Venice?"

"I live at the theatres, in society, in the casinos, where I fight against fortune sometimes with good sometimes with bad success."

"Do you visit the foreign ambassadors?"

"No, because I am too much acquainted with the nobility; but I know them all."

"How can you know them if you do not see them?"

"I have known them abroad. In Parma the Duke de Montalegre, the Spanish ambassador; in Vienna I knew Count Rosemberg; in Paris, about two years ago, the French ambassador."

"It is near twelve o'clock, my dear friend; it is time for us to part. Come at the same hour the day after to-morrow, and I will give you all the instructions which you will require to enable you to come and sup with me."

"Alone?"

"Of course."

"May I venture to ask you for a pledge? The happiness which you promise me is so immense!"

"What pledge do you want?"

"To see you standing before that small window in the grating with permission for me to occupy the same place as Madame de S **."

She rose at once, and, with the most gracious smile, touched the spring; after a most expressive kiss, I took leave of her. She followed me with her eyes as far as the door, and her loving gaze would have rooted me to the spot if she had not left the room.

I spent the two days of expectation in a whirl of impatient joy, which prevented me from eating and sleeping; for it seemed to me that no other love had ever given me such happiness, or rather that I was going to be happy for the first time.

Irrespective of birth, beauty, and wit, which was the principal merit of my new conquest, prejudice was there to enhance a hundredfold my felicity, for she was a vestal; it was forbidden fruit, and who does not know that, from Eve down to our days, it was that fruit which has always appeared the most delicious! I was on the point of encroaching upon the rights of an all-powerful husband; in my eyes M ** M ** was above all the queens of the earth.

If my reason had not been the slave of passion, I should have known that my nun could not be a different creature from all the pretty women whom I had loved for the thirteen years that I had been labouring in the fields of love. But where is the man in love who can harbour such a thought? If it presents itself too often to his mind, he expels it disdainfully! M ** M ** could not by any means be otherwise than superior to all other women in the wide world.

Animal nature, which chemists call the animal kingdom, obtains through instinct the three various means necessary for the perpetuation of its species.

There are three real wants which nature has implanted in all human creatures. They must feed themselves, and to prevent that task from being insipid and tedious they have the agreeable sensation of appetite, which they feel pleasure in satisfying. They must propagate their respective species; an absolute necessity which proves the wisdom of the Creator, since without reproduction all would be annihilated by the constant law of degradation, decay, and death. And, whatever St. Augustine may say, human creatures would not perform the work of generation if they did not find pleasure in it, and if there was not in that great work an irresistible attraction for them. In the third place, all creatures have a determined and invincible propensity to destroy their enemies; and it is certainly a very wise ordination, for that feeling of self-preservation makes it a duty for them to do their best for the destruction of whatever can injure them.

Each species obeys these laws in its own way. The three sensations — hunger, desire, and hatred — are in animals the satisfaction of habitual instinct, and cannot be called pleasures, for they can be so only in proportion to the intelligence of the individual. Man alone is gifted with the perfect organs which render real pleasure peculiar to him; because, being endowed with the sublime faculty of reason, he foresees enjoyment, looks for it, composes, improves, and increases it by thought and recollection. I entreat you, dear reader, not to get weary of following me in my ramblings; for now that I am but the shadow of the once brilliant Casanova, I love to chatter; and if you were to give me the slip, you would be neither polite nor obliging.

Man comes down to the level of beasts whenever he gives himself up to the three natural propensities without calling reason and judgment to his assistance; but when the mind gives perfect equilibrium to those propensities, the sensations derived from them become true enjoyment, an unaccountable feeling which gives us what is called happiness, and which we experience without being able to describe it.

The voluptuous man who reasons, disdains greediness, rejects with contempt lust and lewdness, and spurns the brutal revenge which is caused by a first movement of anger: but he is dainty, and satisfies his appetite only in a manner in harmony with his nature and his tastes; he is amorous, but he enjoys himself with the object of his love only when he is certain that she will share his enjoyment, which can never be the case unless their love is mutual; if he is offended, he does not care for revenge until he has calmly considered the best means to enjoy it fully. If he is sometimes more cruel than necessary, he consoles himself with the idea that he has acted under the empire of reason; and his revenge is sometimes so noble that he finds it in forgiveness. Those three operations are the work of the soul which, to procure enjoyment for itself, becomes the agent of our passions. We sometimes suffer from hunger in order to enjoy better the food which will allay it; we delay the amorous enjoyment for the sake of making it more intense, and we put off the moment of our revenge in order to make it more certain. It is true, however, that one may die from indigestion, that we allow ourselves to be often deceived in love, and that the creature we want to annihilate often escapes our revenge; but perfection cannot be attained in anything, and those are risks which we run most willingly.

There is nothing, there can be nothing, dearer to a thinking being than life; yet the voluptuous men, those who try to enjoy it in the best manner, are the men who practise with the greatest perfection the difficult art of shortening life, of driving it fast.

They do not mean to make it shorter, for they would like to perpetuate it in the midst of pleasure, but they wish enjoyment to render its course insensible; and they are right, provided they do not fail in fulfilling their duties. Man must not, however, imagine that he has no other duties but those which gratify his senses; he would be greatly mistaken, and he might fall the victim of his own error. I think that my friend Horace made a mistake when he said to Florus:

Nec metuam quid de me judicet heres,
Quod non plura datis inveniet.

The happiest man is the one who knows how to obtain the greatest sum of happiness without ever failing in the discharge of his duties, and the most unhappy is the man who has adopted a profession in which he finds himself constantly under the sad necessity of foreseeing the future.

Perfectly certain that M ** M ** would keep her word, I went to the convent at ten o'clock in the morning, and she joined me in the parlour as soon as I was announced.

"Good heavens!" she exclaimed, "are you ill?"

"No, but I may well look so, for the expectation of happiness wears me out. I have lost sleep and appetite, and if my felicity were to be deferred my life would be the forfeit."

"There shall be no delay, dearest; but how impatient you are! Let us sit down. Here is the key of my casino. You will find some persons in it, because we must be served; but nobody will speak to you, and you need not speak to anyone. You must be masked, and you must not go there till two hours after sunset; mind, not before. Then go up the stairs opposite the street door, and at the top of those stairs you will see, by the light of a lamp, a green door, which you will open to enter the apartment, which you will find lighted. You will find me in the second room, and in case I should not be there you will wait for me a few minutes; you may rely upon my being punctual. You can take off your mask in that room, and make yourself comfortable; you will find some books and a good fire."

The description could not be clearer; I kissed the hand which was giving me the key of that mysterious temple, and I inquired from the charming woman whether I should see her in her conventual garb.

[318]

"I always leave the convent with it," she said, "but I have at the casino a complete wardrobe to transform myself into an elegant woman of the world, and even to disguise myself."

"I hope you will do me the favour to remain in the dress of a nun."

"Why so, I beg?"

"I love to see you in that dress."

"Ah! ah! I understand. You fancy that my head is shaved, and you are afraid. But comfort yourself, dear friend, my wig is so beautifully made that it defies detection; it is nature itself."

"Oh, dear! what are you saying? The very name of wig is awful. But no, you may be certain that I will find you lovely under all circumstances. I only entreat you not to put on that cruel wig in my presence. Do I offend you? Forgive me; I am very sorry to have mentioned that subject. Are you sure that no one can see you leave the convent?"

"You will be sure of it yourself when you have gone round the island and seen the small door on the shore. I have the key of a room opening on the shore, and I have every confidence in the sister who serves me."

"And the gondola?"

"My lover himself answers for the fidelity of the gondoliers."

"What a man that lover is! I fancy he must be an old man."

"You are mistaken; if he were old, I should be ashamed. He is not forty, and he has everything necessary to be loved — beauty, wit, sweet temper, and noble behaviour."

"And he forgives your amorous caprices?"

"What do you mean by caprices? A year ago he obtained possession of me, and before him I had never belonged to a man; you are the first who inspired me with a fancy. When I confessed it to him he was rather surprised, then he laughed, and read me a short lecture upon the risk I was running in trusting a man who might prove indiscreet. He wanted to know at least who you were before going any further, but it was too late. I answered for your discretion, and of course I made him laugh by my being so positively the guarantee of a man whom I did not know."

"When did you confide in him?"

"The day before yesterday, and without concealing anything from him. I have shown him my letters and yours; he thinks you are a Frenchman, although you represent yourself as a Venetian. He is very curious to know who you are, but you need not be afraid; I promise you faithfully never to take any steps to find it out myself."

"And I promise you likewise not to try to find out who is this wonderful man as wonderful as you are yourself. I am very miserable when I think of the sorrow I have caused you."

"Do not mention that subject any more; when I consider the matter, I see that only a conceited man would have acted differently."

Before leaving her, she granted me another token of her affection through the little window, and her gaze followed me as far as the door.

In the evening, at the time named by her, I repaired to the casino, and obeying all her instructions I reached a sitting-room in which I found my new conquest dressed in a most elegant costume. The room was lighted up by girandoles, which were reflected by the looking-glasses, and by four splendid candlesticks placed on a table covered with books. M ** M ** struck me as entirely different in her beauty to what she had seemed in the garb of a nun. She wore no cap, and her hair was fastened behind in a thick twist; but I passed rapidly over that part of her person, because I could not bear the idea of a wig, and I could not compliment her about it. I threw myself at her feet to show her my deep gratitude, and I kissed with rapture her beautiful hands; but M ** M ** thought fit to oppose some resistance. Oh, how sweet they are! those denials of a loving mistress, who delays the happy moment only for the sake of enjoying its delights better! As a lover respectful, tender, but bold, enterprising, certain of victory, I blended delicately the gentleness of my proceedings with the ardent fire which was consuming me; and stealing the most voluptuous kisses from the most beautiful mouth I felt as if my soul would burst from my body.

Wanting a little rest, and understanding each other as if by a natural instinct, she said to me:

"My friend, I have an appetite which promises to do honour to the supper; are you able to keep me good company?"

"Yes," I said, knowing well what I could do in that line, "yes, I can; and afterwards you shall judge whether I am able to sacrifice to Love as well as to Comus."

[320]

She rang the bell, and a woman, middle-aged but well dressed and respectable-looking, laid out a table for two persons; she then placed on another table close by all that was necessary to enable us to do without attendance, and she brought, one after the other, eight different dishes in Sèvres porcelain placed on silver heaters. It was a delicate and plentiful supper.

When I tasted the first dish I at once recognised the French style of cooking, and she did not deny it. We drank nothing but burgundy and champagne. She dressed the salad cleverly and quickly, and in everything she did I had to admire the graceful ease of her manners. It was evident that she owed her education to a lover who was a first-rate connoisseur. I was curious to know him, and as we were drinking some punch I told her that if she would gratify my curiosity in that respect I was ready to tell her my name.

"Let time, dearest," she answered, "satisfy our mutual curiosity."

M ** M ** had, amongst the charms and trinkets fastened to the chain of her watch, a small crystal bottle exactly similar to the one that I wore myself. I called her attention to that fact, and as mine was filled with cotton soaked in otto of roses I made her smell it.

"I have the same," she observed.

And she made me inhale its fragrance.

"It is a very scarce perfume," I said, "and very expensive."

"Yes; in fact it cannot be bought."

"Very true; the inventor of that essence wears a crown; it is the King of France; his majesty made a pound of it, which cost him thirty thousand crowns."

"Mine was a gift presented to my lover, and he gave it to me."

"Madame de Pompadour sent a small phial of it to M. de Mocenigo, the Venetian ambassador in Paris, through M. de B **, now French ambassador here."

"Do you know him?"

"I have had the honour to dine with him on the very day he came to take leave of the ambassador by whom he had been invited. M. de B ** is a man whom fortune has smiled upon, but he has captivated it by his merit; he is not less distinguished by his talents than by his birth; he is, I believe, Count de Lyon.

I recollect that he was nicknamed 'Belle Babet,' on account of his handsome face. There is a small collection of poetry written by him which does him great honour."

It was near midnight; we had made an excellent supper, and we were near a good fire. Besides, I was in love with a beautiful woman, and thinking that time was precious I became very pressing; but she resisted.

"Cruel darling, have you promised me happiness only to make me suffer the tortures of Tantalus? If you will not give way to love, at least obey the laws of nature: after such a delicious supper, go to bed."

"Are you sleepy?"

"Of course I am not; but it is late enough to go to bed. I will remain by your bedside, or even go away if you wish it."

"If you were to leave me, you would grieve me much."

"My grief would be as great as yours, believe me; but if I remain what shall we do!"

"We can lie down in our clothes on this sofa."

"With our clothes! Well, let it be so; I will let you sleep if you wish it; but you must forgive me if I do not sleep myself; for to sleep near you would be impossible."

"Wait a little."

She rose from her seat, turned the sofa crosswise, opened it, took out pillows, sheets, blankets, and in one minute we had a splendid bed, wide and convenient. She took a large handkerchief, which she wrapped round my head, and she gave me another, asking me to render her the same service. I began my task, dissembling my disgust for the wig, but a precious discovery caused me the most agreeable surprise; for, instead of the wig, my hands found the most magnificent hair I had ever seen. I uttered a scream of delight and admiration which made her laugh, and she told me that a nun was under no obligation other than to conceal her hair from the uninitiated. Thereupon she pushed me adroitly and made me fall on the sofa. She was very strong, and folding me in her arms she thought that I ought to forgive her for all the torture she was condemning me to. I had not obtained any essential favour. I contrived to undo five or six bows of ribbons, and my heart throbbed with pleasure. But her favours went no further; and my excitement increasing, I doubled my efforts; all in vain. At last, compelled to give way to fatigue, I fell asleep in her arms, holding her tightly against me. A noisy chime of bells woke us.

"What is the matter?" I exclaimed.

"Let us get up, dearest; it is time for me to return to the convent. Be satisfied for this time, dearest, and learn from me how to practise abstinence; we shall be happier another time. When I have gone, if you have nothing to hurry you, you can rest here."

She rang the bell, and the same woman who had appeared in the evening, and was most likely the secret minister and the confidante of her amorous mysteries, came in. After her hair had been dressed, she took off her gown, locked up her jewellery in her bureau, put on the stays of a nun, and assumed her monastic robes. The woman having gone out to call the gondoliers, M ** M ** kissed me warmly and tenderly, and said to me:

"I expect to see you the day after to-morrow, so as to hear from you which night I am to meet you in Venice; and then, my beloved lover, you shall be happy and I too. Fàrewell."

Pleased without being satisfied, I went to bed and slept soundly until noon.

I left the casino without seeing anyone, and being well masked I repaired to the house of Laura, who gave me a letter from my dear C ** C **. Here is a copy of it:

"I am going to give you, my best beloved, a specimen of my way of thinking; and I trust that, far from lowering me in your estimation, you will judge me, in spite of my youth, capable of keeping a secret and worthy of being your wife. Certain that your heart is mine, I do not blame you for having made a mystery of certain things, and not being jealous of what can divert your mind and help you to bear patiently our cruel separation, I can only delight in whatever procures you some pleasure. Listen now. Yesterday, as I was going along one of the halls, I dropped a tooth-pick which I held in my hand, and to get it again, I was compelled to displace a stool which happened to be in front of a crack in the partition. I have already become as curious as a nun — a fault very natural to idle people — I placed my eye against the small opening, and whom did I see? You in person, my darling, conversing in the most lively manner with my charming friend, Sister M ** M **. It would be difficult for you to imagine my surprise and joy. But those two feelings gave way soon to the fear of being seen and of exciting the curiosity of some inquisitive nun. I quickly replaced the stool, and I went away. Tell me all, dearest friend, you will make me happy. How could I cherish you with all my soul, and not be anxious to know the history of your adventure? Tell me if she knows you, and how you have made her acquaintance. She is my best friend, the one of whom I have spoken so often to you in my letters, without thinking it necessary to tell you her name. She is the friend who teaches me French, and has lent me books which gave me a great deal of information on a matter generally little known to women. If it had not been for her, the cause of the accident which has been so near costing me my life, would have been discovered. She gave me sheets and linen immediately; to her I owe my honour; but she has necessarily learned in that way that I have a lover, as I know that she has one; but neither of us has shown any anxiety to know the secrets of the other. Sister M ** M ** is a rare woman. I feel certain, dearest, that you love one another; it cannot be otherwise since you are acquainted; but as I am not jealous of that affection, I deserve that you should tell me all. I pity you both, however; for all you may do will, I fear, only irritate your passion. Everyone in the convent thinks that you are ill, and I am longing to see you. Come, at least once. Adieu!"

The letter of C ** C ** inspired me with the deepest esteem for her, but it caused me great anxiety, because, although I felt every confidence in my dear little wife, the small crack in the wall might expose M ** M ** and myself to the inquisitive looks of other persons. Besides, I found myself compelled to deceive, and honour forbade me to tell her the truth. I wrote to her immediately that her friendship for M ** M ** made it her duty to warn her friend at once that she had seen her in the parlour with a masked gentleman. I added that, having heard a great deal of M ** M **'s merit, and wishing to make her acquaintance, I had called on her under an assumed name; that I entreated her not to tell her friend who I was, but she might say that she had recognised in me the gentleman who attended their church. I assured her with barefaced impudence that there was no love between M ** M ** and me, but without concealing that I thought her a superior woman.

On St. Catherine's Day, the patroness of my dear C ** C **, I bethought myself of affording that lovely prisoner the pleasure of seeing me. As I was leaving the church after mass, and just as I was going to take a gondola, I observed that a man was following me. It looked suspicious, and I determined to ascertain whether I was right. The man took a gondola and followed mine. It might have been purely accidental; but, keeping on my guard for fear of surprise, I alighted in Venice at the Morosini Palace; the fellow alighted at the same place; his intentions were evident. I left the palace, and turning towards the Flanders Gate I stopped in a narrow street, took my knife in my hand, waited for the spy, seized him by the collar, and pushing him against the wall with the knife at his throat I commanded him to tell me what business he had with me. Trembling all over he would have confessed everything, but unluckily someone entered the street. The spy escaped and I was no wiser, but I had no doubt that for the future that fellow at least would keep at a respectful distance. It showed me how easy it would be for an obstinate spy to discover my identity, and I made up my mind never to go to Muran but with a mask, or at night.

The next day I had to see my beautiful nun in order to ascertain which day she would sup with me in Venice, and I went early to the convent. She did not keep me waiting, and her face was radiant with joy. She complimented me upon having resumed my attendance at their church; all the nuns had been delighted to see me again after an absence of three weeks.

"The abbess," she said, "told me how glad she was to see you, and that she was certain to find out who you are."

I then related to her the adventure of the spy, and we both thought that it was most likely the means taken by the sainted woman to gratify her curiosity about me.

"I have resolved not to attend your church any more."

"That will be a great deprivation to me, but in our common interest I can but approve your resolution."

She related the affair of the treacherous crack in the partition, and added:

"It is already repaired, and there is no longer any fear in that quarter. I heard of it from a young boarder whom I love dearly, and who is much attached to me. I am not curious to know her name, and she has never mentioned it to me."

"Now, darling angel, tell me whether my happiness will be postponed."

"Yes, but only for twenty-four hours; the new professed sister has invited me to supper in her room, and you must understand I cannot invent any plausible excuse for refusing her invitation."

"You would not, then, tell her in confidence the very legitimate obstacle which makes me wish that the new sisters never take supper?"

"Certainly not: we never trust anyone so far in a convent. Besides, dearest, such an invitation cannot be declined unless I wish to gain a most bitter enemy."

"Could you not say that you are ill?"

"Yes; but then the visits!"

"I understand; if you should refuse, the escape might be suspected."

"The escape! impossible; here no one admits the possibility of breaking out of the convent."

"Then you are the only one able to perform that miracle?"

"You may be sure of that; but, as is always the case, it is gold which performs that miracle."

"And many others, perhaps."

"Oh! the time has gone by for them! But tell me, my love, where will you wait for me to-morrow, two hours after the setting of the sun?"

"Could I not wait for you at your casino?"

"No, because my lover will take me himself to Venice."

"Your lover?"

"Yes, himself."

"It is not possible."

"Yet it is true."

"I can wait for you in St. John and St. Paul's Square behind the pedestal of the statue of Bartholomew of Bergamo."

"I have never seen either the square or the statue except in engravings; it is enough, however, and I will not fail. Nothing but very stormy weather could prevent me from coming to a rendezvous for which my heart is panting."

"And if the weather were bad?"

"Then, dearest, there would be nothing lost; and you would come here again in order to appoint another day."

I had no time to lose, for I had no casino. I took a second rower so as to reach St. Mark's Square more rapidly, and I immediately set to work looking for what I wanted. When a mortal is so lucky as to be in the good graces of the god Plutus, and is not crack-brained, he is pretty sure to succeed in everything; I had not to search very long before I found a casino suiting my purpose exactly. It was the finest in the neighbourhood of Venice, but, as a natural consequence, it was likewise the most expensive. It had belonged to the English ambassador, who had sold it cheap to his cook before leaving Venice. The owner let it to me until Easter for one hundred sequins, which I paid in advance on condition that he would himself cook the dinners and the suppers I might order.

I had five rooms furnished in the most elegant style, and everything seemed to be calculated for love, pleasure, and good cheer. The service of the dining-room was made through a sham window in the wall, provided with a dumb-waiter revolving upon itself, and fitting the window so exactly that masters and servants could not see each other. The drawing-room was decorated with magnificent looking-glasses, crystal chandeliers, girandoles in gilt, bronze, and with a splendid pier-glass placed on a chimney of white marble; the walls were covered with small squares of real china, representing little Cupids and naked amorous couples in all sorts of positions, well calculated to excite the imagination; elegant and very comfortable sofas were placed on every side. Next to it was an octagonal room, the walls, the ceiling, and the floor of which were entirely covered with splendid Venetian glass, arranged in such a manner as to reflect on all sides every position of the amorous couple enjoying the pleasures of love. Close by was a beautiful alcove with two secret outlets; on the right, an elegant dressing-room, on the left, a boudoir which seemed to have been arranged by the mother of Love, with a bath in Carrara marble. Everywhere the wainscots were embossed in ormolu or painted with flowers and arabesques.

After I had given my orders for all the chandeliers to be filled with wax-candles, and the finest linen to be provided wherever necessary, I ordered a most delicate and sumptuous supper for two, without regard to expense, and especially the most exquisite wines. I then took possession of the key of the principal entrance, and warned the master that I did not want to be seen by anyone when I came in or went out.

I observed with pleasure that the clock in the alcove had an alarum, for I was beginning, in spite of love, to be easily influenced by the power of sleep.

[327]

Everything being arranged according to my wishes, I went, as a careful and delicate lover, to purchase the finest slippers I could find, and a cap in Alençon point.

I trust my reader does not think me too particular; let him recollect that I was to receive the most accomplished of the sultanas of the master of the universe, and I told that fourth Grace that I had a casino. Was I to begin by giving her a bad idea of my truthfulness?

At the appointed time, that is two hours after sunset, I repaired to my palace; and it would be difficult to imagine the surprise of his honour the French cook, when he saw me arrive alone. Not finding all the chandeliers lighted up as I had ordered, I scolded him well, giving him notice that I did not like to repeat an order.

"I shall not fail, sir, another time, to execute your commands."

"Let the supper be served."

"Your honour ordered it for two."

"Yes, for two; and, this time, be present during my supper, so that I can tell you which dishes I find good or bad."

The supper came through the revolving dumb-waiter in very good order, two dishes at a time. I passed some remarks upon everything; but, to tell the truth, everything was excellent: game, fish, oysters, truffles, wine, dessert, and the whole served in very fine Dresden china and silver-gilt plate.

I told him that he had forgotten hard eggs, anchovies, and prepared vinegar to dress a salad. He lifted his eyes towards heaven, as if to plead guilty to a very heinous crime.

After a supper which lasted two hours, and during which I must certainly have won the admiration of my host, I asked him to bring me the bill. He presented it to me shortly afterwards, and I found it reasonable. I then dismissed him, and lay down in the splendid bed in the alcove; my excellent supper brought on very soon the most delicious sleep, which, without the burgundy and the champagne, might very likely not have visited me, if I had thought that the following night would see me in the same place, and in possession of a lovely divinity. It was broad daylight when I awoke, and after ordering the finest fruit and some ices for the evening I left the casino. In order to shorten a day which my impatient desires would have caused me to find very long, I went to the faro-table, and I saw with pleasure that

I was as great a favourite with fortune as with love. Everything proceeded according to my wishes, and I delighted in ascribing my happy success to the influence of my nun.

I was at the place of meeting one hour before the time appointed, and although the night was cold I did not feel it. Precisely as the hour struck I saw a two-oared gondola reach the shore and a mask come out of it, speak a few words to the gondolier, and take the direction of the statue. My heart was beating quickly, but seeing that it was a man I avoided him, and regretted not having brought my pistols. The mask, however, turning round the statue, came up to me with outstretched hands: I then recognised my angel, who was amused at my surprise and took my arm. Without speaking we went towards St. Mark's Square, and reached my casino, which was only one hundred yards from the St. Moses Theatre.

I found everything in good order; we went upstairs and I threw off my mask and my disguise; but M ** M ** took delight in walking about the rooms and in examining every nook of the charming place in which she was received. Highly gratified to see me admire the grace of her person, she wanted me likewise to admire in her attire the taste and generosity of her lover. She was surprised at the almost magic spell which, although she remained motionless, showed her lovely person in a thousand different manners. Her multiplied portraits, reproduced by the looking-glasses, and the numerous wax-candles disposed to that effect, offered to her sight a spectacle entirely new to her, and from which she could not withdraw her eyes. Sitting down on a stool I contemplated her elegant person with rapture. A coat of rosy velvet, embroidered with gold spangles, a vest to match, embroidered likewise in the richest fashion, breeches of black satin, diamond buckles, a solitaire of great value on her little finger, and on the other hand a ring: such was her toilet. Her black lace mask was remarkable for its fineness and the beauty of the design. To enable me to see her better she stood before me. I looked in her pockets, in which I found a gold snuff-box, a sweetmeat-box adorned with pearls, a gold case, a splendid opera-glass, handkerchiefs of the finest cambric, soaked rather than perfumed with the most precious essences. I examined attentively the richness and the workmanship of her two watches, of her chains, of her trinkets, brilliant with diamonds. The last article I found was a pistol; it was an English weapon of fine steel, and of the most beautiful finish.

"All I see, my divine angel, is not worthy of you; yet I cannot refrain from expressing my admiration for the wonderful, I might almost say adorable, being who wants to convince you that you are truly his mistress."

"This is what he said when I asked him to bring me to Venice, and to leave me. 'Amuse yourself,' he said, 'and I hope that the man whom you are going to make happy will convince you that he is worthy of it.'"

"He is indeed an extraordinary man, and I do not think there is another like him. Such a lover is a unique being; and I feel that I could not be like him, as deeply as I fear to be unworthy of a happiness which dazzles me."

"Allow me to leave you, and to take off these clothes alone."

"Do anything you please."

A quarter of an hour afterwards my mistress came back to me. Her hair was dressed like a man's; the front locks came down her cheeks, and the black hair, fastened with a knot of blue ribbon, reached the bend of her legs; her form was that of Antinous; her clothes alone, being cut in the French style, prevented the illusion from being complete. I was in a state of ecstatic delight, and I could not realise my happiness.

"No, adorable woman," I exclaimed, "you are not made for a mortal, and I do not believe that you will ever be mine. At the very moment of possessing you some miracle will wrest you from my arms. Your divine spouse, perhaps, jealous of a simple mortal, will annihilate all my hope. It is possible that in a few minutes I shall no longer exist."

"Are you mad, dearest? I am yours this very instant, if you wish it."

"Ah! if I wish it! Although fasting, come! Love and happiness will be my food!"

I was burning with ardent desires, and I would have satisfied them on the spot, if my adorable mistress had not calmed my impatience by these simple words:

"Wait until after supper."

I rang the bell; she shuddered.

"Do not be anxious, dearest."

And I showed her the secret of the sham window.

"You will be able to tell your lover that no one saw you."

"He will appreciate your delicate attention, and that will prove to him that you are not a novice in the art of love. But it is evident that I am not the only one who enjoys with you the delights of this charming residence."

"You are wrong, believe me: you are the first woman I have seen here. You are not, adorable creature, my first love, but you shall be the last."

"I shall be happy if you are faithful. My lover is constant, kind, gentle, and amiable; yet my heart has ever been fancy-free with him."

"Then his own heart must be the same; for if his love was of the same nature as mine you would never have made me happy."

"He loves me as I love you; do you believe in my love for you?"

"Yes, I want to believe in it; but you would not allow me to . . ."

"Do not say any more; for I feel that I could forgive you in anything, provided you told me all. The joy I experience at this moment is caused more by the hope I have of gratifying your desires than by the idea that I am going to pass a delightful night with you. It will be the first in my life."

"What! Have you never passed such a night with your lover?"

"Several; but friendship, compliance, and gratitude, perhaps, were then the only contributors to our pleasures; the most essential — love — was never present. In spite of that, my lover is like you; his wit is lively, very much the same as yours, and, as far as his features are concerned, he is very handsome; yet it is not you. I believe him more wealthy than you, although this casino almost convinces me that I am mistaken, but what does love care for riches? Do not imagine that I consider you endowed with less merit than he, because you confess yourself incapable of his heroism in allowing me to enjoy another love. Quite the contrary; I know that you would not love me as you do if you told me that you could be as indulgent as he is for one of my caprices."

"Will he be curious to hear the particulars of this night?"

"Most likely he will think that he will please me by asking what has taken place, and I will tell him everything, except such particulars as might humiliate him."

[331]

After the supper, which she found excellent, she made some punch, and she was a very good hand at it. But I felt my impatience growing stronger every moment, and I said:

"Recollect that we have only seven hours before us, and that we should be very foolish to waste them in this room."

"You reason better than Socrates," she answered, "and your eloquence has convinced me. Come!"

She led me to the elegant dressing-room, and I offered her the fine night-cap which I had brought for her, asking her at the same time to dress her hair like a woman. She took it with great pleasure, and begged me to go and undress myself in the drawing-room, promising to call me as soon as she was in bed.

I had not long to wait: when pleasure is waiting for us, we all go quickly to work. I fell into her arms, intoxicated with love and happiness, and during seven hours I gave her the most positive proofs of my ardour and of the feelings I entertained for her. At last the fatal alarum was heard: we had to stop our amorous transports; but before she left my arms she raised her eyes towards heaven as if to thank her Divine Master for having given her the courage to declare her passion to me.

Observing that I put the lace night-cap in her pocket she assured me that she would keep it all her life as a witness of the happiness which overwhelmed her. After drinking a cup of coffee we went out, and I left her at St. John and St. Paul's Square, promising to call on her the day after the morrow; I watched her until I saw her safe in her gondola, and I then went to bed. Ten hours of profound sleep restored me to my usual state of vigour.

CHAPTER IX

M ** M ** AND C ** C **: THE LAST FLING IN VENICE

ACCORDING to my promise, I went to see M ** M ** two days afterwards; but as soon as she came to the parlour she told me that her lover had said he was coming, and that she expected him every minute, and that she would be glad to see me the next day. I took leave of her; but near the bridge I saw a man, rather badly masked, coming out of a gondola. I looked at the gondolier, and I recognised him as being in the service of the

French ambassador. "It is he," I said to myself; and without appearing to observe him I watched him enter the convent. I had no longer any doubt as to his identity, and I returned to Venice delighted at having made the discovery, but I made up my mind not to say anything to my mistress.

I saw her on the following day, and we had a long conversation together, which I am now going to relate.

"My friend," she said to me, "came yesterday in order to bid farewell to me until the Christmas holidays. He is going to Padua, but everything has been arranged so that we can sup at his casino whenever we wish."

"Why not in Venice?"

"He has begged me not to go there during his absence. He is wise and prudent; I could not refuse his request."

"You are quite right. When shall we sup together?"

"Next Sunday, if you like."

"If I like is not the right expression, for I always like. On Sunday, then, I will go to the casino towards nightfall, and wait for you with a book. Have you told your friend that you were not very uncomfortable in my small palace?"

"He knows all about it; but, dearest, he is afraid of one thing — he fears a certain fatal plumpness . . . ."

"On my life, I never thought of that! But, my darling, do you not run the same risk with him?"

"No, it is impossible."

"I understand you. Then we must be very prudent for the future. I believe that, nine days before Christmas, the mask is no longer allowed, and then I shall have to go to your casino by water; otherwise, I might easily be recognised by the same spy who has already followed me once."

"Yes; the idea proves your prudence, and I can easily show you the place. I hope you will be able to come also during Lent, although we are told that at that time God wishes us to mortify our senses. Is it not strange that there is a time during which God wants us to amuse ourselves almost to frenzy, and another during which, in order to please Him, we must live in complete abstinence? What is there in common between a yearly observance and the Deity, and how can the action of the creature have any influence over the Creator, whom my reason cannot conceive otherwise than independent? It seems to me that if

God had created man with the power of offending Him, man would be right in doing everything that is forbidden to him, because the deficiencies of his organisation would be the work of the Creator Himself. How can we imagine God grieved during Lent?"

"My beloved one, you reason beautifully; but will you tell me where you have managed, in a convent, to pass the Rubicon?"

"Yes. My friend has given me some good books which I have read with deep attention, and the light of truth has dispelled the darkness which blinded my eyes. I can assure you that, when I look in my own heart, I find myself more fortunate in having met with a person who has brought light to my mind than miserable at having taken the veil; for the greatest happiness must certainly consist in living and in dying peacefully — a happiness which can hardly be obtained by listening to all the idle talk with which the priests puzzle our brains."

"I am of your opinion; but I admire you, for it ought to be the work of more than a few months to bring light to a mind prejudiced as yours was."

"There is no doubt that I should have seen light much sooner if I had not laboured under so many prejudices. There was in my mind a curtain dividing truth from error, and reason alone could draw it aside; but that poor reason — I had been taught to fear it, to repulse it, as if its bright flame would have devoured, instead of enlightening me. The moment it was proved to me that a reasonable being ought to be guided only by his own inductions I acknowledged the sway of reason, and the mist which hid truth from me was dispelled. The evidence of truth alone shone before my eyes, nonsensical trifles disappeared, and I have no fear of their resuming their influence over my mind, for every day it is getting stronger; and I may say that I only began to love God when my mind was disabused of priestly superstitions concerning Him."

"I congratulate you; you have been more fortunate than I, for you have made more progress in one year than I have made in ten."

"Then you did not begin by reading the writings of Lord Bolingbroke? Five or six months ago, I was reading *La Sagesse*, by Charron, and somehow or other my confessor heard of it;

when I went to him for confession, he took upon himself to tell me to give up reading that book. I answered that my conscience did not reproach me, and that I could not obey him. 'In that case,' replied he, 'I will not give you absolution.' 'That will not prevent me from taking the communion,' I said. This made him angry, and, in order to know what he ought to do, he applied to Bishop Diedo. His eminence came to see me, and told me that I ought to be guided by my confessor. I answered that we had mutual duties to perform, and that the mission of a priest in the confessional was to listen to me, to impose a reasonable penance, and to give me absolution; that he had not even the right of offering me any advice if I did not ask for it. I added that the confessor being bound to avoid scandal, if he dared to refuse me the absolution, which, of course, he could do, I would all the same go to the altar with the other nuns. The bishop, seeing that he was at his wit's end, told the priest to abandon me to my conscience. But that was not satisfactory to me, and my lover obtained a brief from the Pope authorising me to go to confession to any priest I like. All the sisters are jealous of the privilege; but I have availed myself of it only once, for the sake of establishing a precedent and of strengthening the right by the fact: for it is not worth the trouble. I always confess to the same priest, and he has no difficulty in giving me absolution, for I only tell him what I like!"

"And the rest you absolve yourself?"

"I confess to God, Who alone can know my thoughts and judge the degree of merit or of demerit to be attached to my actions."

Our conversation showed me that my lovely friend was what is called a free-thinker; but I was not astonished at it, because she felt a greater need of peace for her conscience than of gratification for her senses.

On the Sunday, after dinner, I took a two-oared gondola, and went round the island of Muran to reconnoitre the shore, and to discover the small door through which my mistress escaped from the convent: I lost my trouble and my time, for I did not become acquainted with the shore till the octave of Christmas, and with the small door six months afterwards. I shall mention the circumstance in its proper place.

As soon as it was time, I repaired to the temple; and while

I was waiting for the idol I amused myself in examining the books of a small library in the boudoir. They were not numerous, but they were well chosen and worthy of the place. I found there everything that has been written against religion, and all the works of the most voluptuous writers on pleasure; attractive books, the incendiary style of which compels the reader to seek the reality of the image they represent. Several folios, richly bound, contained nothing but erotic engravings. Their principal merit consisted much more in the beauty of the designs, in the finish of the work, than in the lubricity of the positions. I found amongst them the prints of the *Portier des Chatreux*, published in England; the engravings of Meursius, of Aloysia Sigea Toletana, and others, all very beautifully done. A great many small pictures covered the walls of the boudoir, and they were all masterpieces in the same style as the engravings.

I had spent an hour in examining all these works of art, the sight of which had excited me in the most irresistible manner, when I saw my beautiful mistress enter the room, dressed as a nun. Her appearance was not likely to act as a sedative, and therefore, without losing any time in compliments, I said to her:

"You arrive most opportunely. All these erotic pictures have fired my imagination, and it is in your garb of a saint that you must administer the remedy that my love requires."

"Let me put on another dress, darling; it will not take more than five minutes."

"Five minutes will complete my happiness, and then you can attend to your metamorphosis."

"But let me take off these woollen robes, which I dislike."

"No; I want you to receive the homage of my love in the same dress which you had on when you gave birth to it."

She uttered in the humblest manner a *fiat voluntas tua*, accompanied by the most voluptuous smile, and sank on the sofa: for one instant we forgot all the world besides. After that delightful ecstacy I assisted her to undress, and a simple gown of Indian muslin soon metamorphosed my lovely nun into a beautiful nymph.

After an excellent supper, we agreed not to meet again till the first day of the octave. She gave me the key of the gate on the shore, and told me that a blue ribbon attached to the window over the door would point it out by day, so as to prevent my making a mistake at night. I made her very happy by telling her that I would come and reside in her casino until the return of her friend. During the ten days that I remained there, I saw her four times, and I convinced her that I lived only for her.

During my stay in the casino I amused myself in reading and writing to C** C**, but my love for her had become a calm affection. The lines which interested me most in her letters were those in which she mentioned her friend. She often blamed me for not having cultivated the acquaintance of M** M**, and my answer was that I had not done so for fear of being known; I always insisted upon the necessity of discretion.

I do not believe in the possibility of equal love being bestowed upon two persons at the same time, nor do I believe it possible to keep love to a high degree of intensity if you give it either too much food or none at all. That which maintained my passion for M** M** in a state of great vigour was that I could never possess her without running the risk of losing her.

"It is impossible," I said to her once, "that some time or other one of the nuns should not want to speak to you when you are absent."

"No," she answered, "that cannot happen, because there is nothing more religiously respected in a convent than the right of a nun to deny herself, even to the abbess. A fire is the only circumstance I have to fear, because in that case there would be general uproar and confusion, and it would not appear natural that a nun should remain quietly locked up in her cell in the midst of such danger; my escape would then be discovered. I have contrived to gain over the lay sister and the gardener, as well as another nun, and that miracle was performed by my cunning assisted by my lover's gold. He answers for the fidelity of the cook and his wife who take care of the casino. He has likewise every confidence in the two gondoliers, although one of them is sure to be a spy of the State Inquisitors."

On Christmas Eve she announced the return of her lover, and she told him that on St. Stephen's Day she would go with him to the opera, and that they would afterwards spend the night together.

"I shall expect you, my beloved one," she added, "on the last day of the year, and here is a letter which I beg you not to read till you get home."

As I had to move in order to make room for her lover, I packed my things early in the morning, and, bidding farewell to a place in which during ten days I had enjoyed so many delights, I returned to the Bragadin Palace, where I read the following letter:

"You have somewhat offended me, my own darling, by telling me, respecting the mystery which I am bound to keep on the subject of my lover, that, satisfied to possess my heart, you left me mistress of my mind. That division of the heart and of the mind appears to me a pure sophism, and if it does not strike you as such you must admit that you do not love me wholly; for I cannot exist without mind, and you cannot cherish my heart if it does not agree with my mind. If your love cannot accept a different state of things it does not excel in delicacy. However, as some circumstance might occur in which you might accuse me of not having acted towards you with all the sincerity that true love inspires, and that it has a right to demand, I have made up my mind to confide to you a secret which concerns my friend, although I am aware that he relies entirely upon my discretion. I shall certainly be guilty of a breach of confidence, but you will not love me less for it, because, compelled to choose between you two, and to deceive either one or the other, love has conquered friendship; do not punish me for it, for it has not been done blindly, and you will, I trust, consider the reasons which have caused the scale to weigh down in your favour.

"When I found myself incapable of resisting my wish to know you and to become intimate with you, I could not gratify that wish without taking my friend into my confidence, and I had no doubt of his compliance. He conceived a very favourable opinion of your character from your first letter, not only because you had chosen the parlour of the convent for our first interview, but also because you appointed his casino at Muran instead of your own. But he likewise begged of me to allow him to be present at our first meeting-place, in a small closet — a true hiding-place, from which one can see and hear everything without being suspected by those in the drawing-room. You have not yet seen that mysterious closet, but I will show it to you on the last day of the year. Tell me, dearest, whether I could refuse that singular request to the man who was showing me such compliant kindness? I consented, and it was natural for me not to let you know it. You are therefore aware now that my friend was a witness of all we did and said during the first night that we spent together; but do not let that annoy you, for you pleased him in everything, in your behaviour towards me as well as in the witty sayings which you uttered to make me laugh. I was in great fear, when the conversation turned upon him, lest you would say something which might hurt his self-love; but, very fortunately, he heard only the most flattering compliments. Such is, dearest love, the sincere confession of my treason; but as a wise lover you will forgive me because it has not done you the slightest harm. My friend is extremely curious to ascertain who you are. But listen to me; that night you were natural and thoroughly amiable; would you have been the same if you had known that there was a witness? It is not likely; and if I had acquainted you with the truth, you might have refused your consent, and perhaps you would have been right.

"Now that we know each other, and that you entertain no doubt, I trust, of my devoted love, I wish to ease my conscience and to venture all. Learn then, dearest, that on the last day of the year, my friend will be at the casino, which he will leave only the next morning. You will not see him, but he will see us. As you are supposed not to know anything about it, you must feel that you will have to be natural in everything; otherwise, he might guess that I have betrayed the secret. It is especially in your conversation that you must be careful. My friend possesses every virtue except the theological one called faith, and on that subject you can say anything you like. You will be at liberty to talk literature, travels, politics, anything you please, and you need not refrain from anecdotes. In fact you are certain of his approbation.

"Now, dearest, I have only this to say: Do you feel disposed to allow yourself to be seen by another man while you are abandoning yourself to the sweet voluptuousness of your senses? That doubt causes all my anxiety, and I entreat from you an answer, yes or no. Do you understand how painful the doubt is for me? I expect not to close my eyes throughout the night, and I shall not rest until I have your decision. In case you should object to show your tenderness in the presence of a third person, I will take whatever determination love may suggest to me. But I hope you will consent, and even if you were not to perform the character of an ardent lover, it would not be of any consequence."

That letter certainly took me by surprise; but all things considered, thinking that my part was better than the one accepted by the lover, I laughed heartily at the proposal. I confess, however, that I should not have laughed if I had not known the nature of the individual who was to be the witness of my amorous exploits.

I spent the six following days with my three worthy friends, and at the *ridotto*, which at that time was opened on St. Stephen's Day. As I could not hold the cards there, the patricians alone having the privilege of holding the bank, I played morning and evening, and I constantly lost; for whoever punts must lose. But the loss of the four or five thousand sequins I possessed, far from cooling my love, seemed only to increase its ardour.

At the end of the year 1774 the Great Council promulgated a law forbidding all games of chance, the first effect of which was to close the *ridotto*. This law was a real phenomenon, and when the votes were taken out of the urn the senators looked at each other with stupefaction. They had made the law unwittingly, for three-fourths of the voters objected to it, and yet three-fourths of the votes were in favour of it. People said that it was a miracle of St. Mark's, who had answered the prayers of Monsignor Flangini, then censor-in-chief, now cardinal, and one of the three State Inquisitors.

On the day appointed I was punctual at the place of rendezvous, and I had not to wait for my mistress. She was in the dressing-room, where she had had time to attend to her toilet, and as soon as she heard me she came to me dressed with the greatest elegance.

"My friend is not yet at his post," she said to me; "but the moment he is there I will give you a wink."

"Where is the mysterious closet?"

"There it is. Look at the back of this sofa against the wall. All those flowers in relief have a hole in the centre which communicates with the closet behind that wall. There is a bed, a table, and everything necessary to a person who wants to spend the night in amusing himself by looking at what is going on in this room. I will show it to you whenever you like."

"Was it arranged by your lover's orders?"

"No; for he could not foresee that he would use it. He is at liberty to go away when he has had enough of it, or to sleep if he has a mind to; but if you play your part naturally he will not feel any weariness."

"I will be most natural, but I must be more polite."

"No, no politeness, I beg; for if you are polite, good-bye to nature. Where have you ever seen, I should like to know, two lovers, excited by all the fury of love, think of politeness?"

"You are right, darling; but I must be more delicate."

"Very well, delicacy can do no harm; but no more than usual. Your letter greatly pleased me; you have treated the subject like a man of experience."

I have already stated that my mistress was dressed most elegantly, but I ought to have added that it was the elegance of the Graces, and that it did not in any way prevent ease and simplicity. I only wondered at her having used some paint for the face, but it rather pleased me because she had applied it according to the fashion of the ladies of Versailles. The charm of that style consists in the negligence with which the paint is applied. The rouge must not appear natural; it is used to please the eyes, which see in it the marks of an intoxication heralding the most amorous fury. She told me that she had put some on her face to please her inquisitive friend, who was very fond of it.

"That taste," I said, "proves him to be a Frenchman."

As I was uttering these words, she made a sign to me; the friend was at his post, and now the play began.

"The more I look at you, beloved angel, the more I think you worthy of my adoration."

"But are you not certain that you do not worship a cruel divinity?"

"Yes, and therefore I do not offer my sacrifices to appease you, but to excite you. You shall feel all through the night the ardour of my devotion."

"You will not find me insensible to your offerings."

While we were bantering in this edifying fashion, the table had been laid, and we sat down to supper. She ate for two and I for four, our excellent appetite being excited by the delicate cheer. A sumptuous dessert was served in splendid silver-gilt plate, similar to the two candlesticks, which held four wax-candles each. Seeing that I admired them, she said:

"They are a present from my friend."

"It is a magnificent present; has he given you the snuffers likewise?"

"No."

"It is a proof that your friend is a great nobleman."

"How so?"

"Because great lords have no idea of snuffing the candle."

"Our candles have wicks which never require that operation."

"Good! Tell me who has taught you French."

"Old La Forest. I have been his pupil for six years. He has also taught me to write poetry; but you know a great many words which I never heard from him, such as *à gogo, frustratoire, rater, dorloter*. Who taught you these words?"

"The good company in Paris, and women particularly."

We made some punch, and amused ourselves in eating oysters after the voluptuous fashion of lovers; we sucked them in, one by one, after placing them on the other's tongue. Voluptuous reader, try it, and tell me whether it is not the nectar of the gods!

Dear reader, a picture must have shades, and there is nothing, no matter how beautiful in one point of view, that does not require to be sometimes veiled if you look at it from a different one. In order to paint the diversified scene which took place between me and my lovely mistress until the dawn of day, I should have to use all the colours of Aretino's palette. She resumed the costume of a nun, and entreating me to lie down and to write to her before returning to Venice, so as to let her know how I was, she left the casino.

I had no difficulty in obeying her, for I was truly in great need of rest; I slept until evening. As soon as I awoke, I wrote to her that my health was excellent, and that I felt quite inclined to begin our delightful contest all over again. I asked her to let me know how she was herself, and after I had dispatched my letter I returned to Venice.

*More and more engrossed by his infatuation for the voluptuous M ** M **, Casanova abandons the experiment of a colateral passion for C ** C **, who soon discovers the truth, but, far from showing any resentment, professes to be delighted that her "husband" has found a partner so worthy of him. Touched by such sublime generosity, he vows that his friendship for M ** M ** will in no* way interfere with the feeling which "bound him for ever" to his dear "wife." Meanwhile her rival, throwing precaution to the winds, accompanies him to the opera and the ridotto, where her winnings help to replenish his dwindling purse.

Once more it is carnival, when all Venice is seized with a Bacchanalian frenzy, as witness the following incident:

Laura having informed me that there was to be on a certain day a ball in the large parlour of the convent, I made up my mind to attend it in such a disguise that my two friends could not recognise me. I decided upon the costume of a Pierrot, because it conceals the form and the gait better than any other. I was certain that my two friends would be behind the grating, and that it would afford me the pleasant opportunity of seeing them together and of comparing them.

In Venice, during the carnival, that innocent pleasure is allowed in convents. The guests dance in the parlour, and the sisters remain behind the grating, enjoying the sight of the ball, which is over by sunset. Then all the guests retire, and the poor nuns are for a long time happy in the recollection of the pleasure enjoyed by their eyes. The ball was to take place in the afternoon of the day appointed for my meeting with M ** M ** in the evening at the casino of Muran, but that could not prevent me from going to the ball; besides, I wanted to see my dear C ** C **.

I have said before that the dress of a Pierrot is the costume which disguises the figure and the gait most completely; it has also the advantage, through a large cap, of concealing the hair, and the white gauze which covers the face does not allow the colour of the eyes or of the eyebrows to be seen; but in order to prevent the costume from hindering the movements of the mask, he must not wear anything underneath, and in winter a dress made of light calico is not particularly agreeable. I did not, however, pay any attention to that, and taking only a plate of soup I went to Muran in a gondola. I had no cloak, and in my pockets I had nothing but my handkerchief, my purse, and the key of the casino.

I went at once to the convent; the parlour was full; but thanks to my costume of Pierrot, which was seen in Venice but very seldom, everybody made room for me. I walked on, assuming the gait of a booby, the true characteristic of my costume, and I stopped near the dancers. After I had examined the Pantaloons, Punches, Harlequins, and Merry Andrews, I went near the grating, where I saw all the nuns and boarders, some seated, some standing, and without appearing to notice any of them in particular, I remarked my two friends together, and very intent upon the dancers. I then walked round the room, eyeing everybody from head to foot, and calling the general attention upon myself.

I chose for my partner in the minuet a pretty girl dressed as a Columbine, and I took her hand in so awkward a manner and with such an air of stupidity that everybody laughed and made room for us. My partner danced very well according to her costume, and I kept my character with such perfection that the laughter was general. After the minuet I danced twelve forlanas with the greatest vigour. Out of breath, I threw myself on a sofa, pretending to go to sleep, and the moment I began to snore everybody respected the slumbers of Pierrot. The quadrille lasted one hour, and I took no part in it; but immediately after it, a Harlequin approached me with the impertinence which belongs to his costume, and flogged me with his wand. It is Harlequin's weapon. In my quality of Pierrot I had no weapons; I seized him round the waist and carried him round the parlour, running all the time, while he kept on flogging me. I then put him down. Adroitly snatching his wand out of his hand, I lifted his Columbine on my shoulders, and pursued him, striking him with the wand, to the great delight and mirth of the company. The Columbine was screaming because she was afraid of my tumbling down. She had good reason to fear; for suddenly a foolish Merry Andrew came behind me, tripped me up, and down I tumbled. Everybody hooted Master Punch. I quickly picked myself up, and rather vexed I began a regular fight with the insolent fellow. He was of my size, but awkward, and he had nothing but strength; I threw him, and shaking him vigorously on all sides I contrived to deprive him of his hump and false stomach. The nuns, who had never seen such a merry sight, clapped their hands, everybody laughed loudly, and improving my opportunity I ran through the crowd and disappeared.

I was in a perspiration, and the weather was cold; I threw myself in a gondola, and in order not to get chilled I landed at the *ridotto.* I had two hours to spare before going to the casino of Muran, and I longed to enjoy the astonishment of my beautiful nun when she saw M. Pierrot standing before her. I spent those two hours in playing at all the banks, winning, losing, and performing all sorts of antics with complete freedom, being satisfied that no one could recognise me; enjoying the present, bidding defiance to the future, and laughing at all those reasonable beings who exercise their reason to avoid the misfortunes which they fear, destroying at the same time the pleasure that they might enjoy.

But two o'clock struck and gave me warning that Love and Comus were calling me to bestow new delights upon me. With my pockets full of gold and silver, I left the *ridotto,* hurried to Muran, entered the sanctuary, and saw my divinity leaning against the mantelpiece. She wore her convent dress; I come near her by stealth, in order to enjoy her surprise; I look at her, and I remain petrified, astounded.

The person I see is not M ** M **.

It is C ** C **, dressed as a nun, who, more astonished even than myself, does not utter one word or make a movement. I throw myself in an arm-chair in order to breathe and to recover from my surprise. The sight of C ** C ** had annihilated me, and my mind was as much stupefied as my body; I found myself in an inextricable maze.

It is M ** M **, I said to myself, who has played that trick upon me, but how has she contrived to know that I am the lover of C ** C **? Has C ** C ** betrayed my secret? But if she has betrayed it, how could M ** M ** deprive herself of the pleasure of seeing me, and consent to her place being taken by her friend and rival? That cannot be a mark of kind compliance, for a woman never carries it to such an extreme. I see in it only a mark of contempt — a gratuitous insult.

*It was a doleful night they passed together and a final proof that poor C ** C **'s reign was over. They spend the night in talking of M ** M **, C ** C ** trying to persuade him that her appearance there was intended as a gentle attention on the part of her friend after she had discovered that Casanova and C ** C ** had been lovers. He feels he has been slighted, tricked; and when they part, he sends back the key to the casino to M ** M ** in token of rupture. The quarrel, however, is made up. It turns out that M ** M ***

[345]

and her mysterious friend watched the nocturnal interview from a secret hiding-place and that she had realised her mistake. As for the friend, the amant en titre, *so often alluded to, his identity is at last revealed. He is none other than the French ambassador, the Abbé de Bernis, who, she declares, has become so interested in Casanova (according to the Memoirs he and M ** M ** were hidden for eight hours in the secret closet!) that he is burning to make his acquaintance. Casanova, rising to the occasion, professes himself delighted at the prospect of meeting his mistress's official lover, and a supper in the casino is arranged.*

I felt highly pleased with the supper-party I had arranged with M ** M **, and I ought to have been happy. Yet I was not so; but whence came the anxiety which was a torment to me? Whence? From my fatal habit of gambling. That passion was rooted in me; to live and to play were to me two identical things, and as I could not hold the bank I would go and punt at the *ridotto*, where I lost my money morning and night. That state of things made me miserable. Perhaps someone will say to me:

"Why did you play, when there was no need of it; when you were in want of nothing; when you had all the money you could wish to satisfy your fancies?"

That would be a troublesome question if I had not made it a law to tell the truth. Well, then, dear inquisitive reader, if I played with almost the certainty of losing, although no one, perhaps, was more sensible than I was to the losses made in gambling, it is because I had in me the evil spirit of avarice; it is because I loved prodigality, and because my heart bled when I found myself compelled to spend any money that I had not won at the gaming-table. It is an ugly vice, dear reader, I do not deny it. However, all I can say is that, during the four days previous to the supper, I lost all the gold won for me by M ** M **.

On the anxiously expected day I went to my casino, where at the appointed hour M ** M ** came with her friend, whom she introduced to me as soon as he had taken off his mask.

"I had an ardent wish, sir," said M. de Bernis to me, "to renew acquaintance with you, since I heard from madame that we had known each other in Paris."

With these words he looked at me attentively, as people will do when they are trying to recollect a person whom they have lost sight of. I then told him that we had never spoken to one another, and that he had not seen enough of me to recollect my features now.

"I had the honour," I added, "to dine with your excellency at M. de Mocenigo's house; but you talked all the time with Marshal Keith, the Prussian ambassador, and I was not fortunate enough to attract your attention. As you were on the point of leaving Paris to return to Venice, you went away almost immediately after dinner, and I have never had the honour of seeing you since that time."

"Now I recollect you," he answered, "and I remember asking whether you were not the secretary of the embassy. But from this day we shall not forget each other again; for the mysteries which unite us are of a nature likely to establish a lasting intimacy between us."

The amiable couple were not long before they felt thoroughly at ease, and we sat down to supper, of which, of course, I did the honours. The ambassador, a fine connoisseur in wines, found mine excellent, and was delighted to hear that I had them from Count Algarotti, who was reputed as having the best cellar in Venice.

My supper was delicate and abundant, and my manners towards my handsome guests were those of a private individual receiving his sovereign and his mistress. I saw that M ** M ** was charmed with the respect with which I treated her, and with my conversation, which evidently interested the ambassador highly. The serious character of a first meeting did not prevent the utterance of witty jests, for in that respect M. de Bernis was a true Frenchman. I have travelled much, I have deeply studied men, individually and in a body, but I have never met with true sociability except in Frenchmen; they alone know how to jest; and it is rare, delicate, refined jesting, which animates conversation and makes society charming.

During our delightful supper wit was never wanting, and the amiable M ** M ** led the conversation to the romantic combination which had given her occasion to know me. Naturally, she proceeded to speak of my passion for C ** C **, and she gave such an interesting description of that young girl that the ambassador listened with as much attention as if he had never seen the object of it. But that was his part, for he was not aware that I had been informed of his having witnessed from his hiding-place my silly interview with C ** C **. He told M ** M ** that he would have been delighted if she had brought her young friend to sup with us.

"That would be running too great a risk," answered the cunning nun, "but if you approve of it," she added, looking at me, "I can make you sup with her at my casino, for we sleep in the same room."

That offer surprised me much, but it was not the moment to show it, so I replied:

"It is impossible, madam, to add anything to the pleasure of your society; yet I confess I should be pleased if you could contrive to do us that great favour."

"Well, I will think of it."

"But," observed the ambassador, "if I am to be one of the party, I think it would be right to apprise the young lady of it."

"It is not necessary, for I will write to her to agree to whatever madam may propose to her. I will do so to-morrow."

I begged the ambassador to prepare himself with a good stock of indulgence for a girl of fifteen who had no experience of the world. In the course of the evening I related the history of O-Morphi, which greatly amused him. He entreated me to let him see her portrait. He informed me that she was still an inmate of the Parc-aux-cerfs, where she continued to be the delight of Louis XV., to whom she had given a child. My guests left me after midnight, highly pleased, and I remained alone.

The next morning, faithful to the promise I had made to my beautiful nun, I wrote to C ** C ** without informing her that there would be a fourth person at the projected supper, and having given my note to Laura I repaired to Muran, where I found the following letter from M ** M **:

"I could not sleep soundly, my love, if I did not ease my conscience of an unpleasant weight. Perhaps you did not approve of the *partie carrée* with our young friend, and you may not have objected out of mere politeness. Tell me the truth, dearest, for, should you not look forward to that meeting with pleasure, I can contrive to undo it without implicating you in any way; trust me for that. If, however, you have no objection to the party, it will take place as agreed. Believe me, I love your soul more than your heart — I mean than your person. Adieu."

Her fear was very natural, but out of shamefacedness I did not like to retract. M ** M ** knew me well, and as a skilful tactician she attacked my weak side.

Here is my answer:

"I expected your letter, my best beloved, and you cannot doubt it; because, as you know me thoroughly, you must be aware that I know you as well. Yes, I know your mind, and I know what idea you must entertain of mine, because I have exposed to you all my weakness and irritability by my sophisms. I do penance for it, dearest, when I think that having raised your suspicions your tenderness for me must have been weakened. Forget my visions, I beg, and be quite certain that for the future my soul will be in unison with yours. The supper must take place, it will be a pleasure for me; but let me confess that in accepting it I have shown myself more grateful than polite. C ** C ** is a novice, and I am not sorry to give her an opportunity of seeing the world. In what school could she learn better than yours? Therefore I recommend her to you, and you will please me much by continuing to show your care and friendship towards her, and by increasing, if possible, the sum of your goodness. I fear that you may entice her to take the veil, and if she did I would never console myself. Your friend has quite captivated me; he is a superior man, and truly charming."

Thus did I wittingly deprive myself of the power of drawing back; but I was able to realise the full force of the situation. I had no difficulty in guessing that the ambassador was in love with C ** C **, and that he had confessed as much to M ** M **, who, not being in a position to object to it, was compelled to show herself compliant, and to assist him in everything that could render his passion successful. She could certainly not do anything without my consent, and she had evidently considered the affair too delicate to venture upon proposing the party point-blank to me. They had, no doubt, put their heads together, so that by bringing the conversation on that subject I should find myself compelled, for the sake of politeness and perhaps of my inward feelings, to fall into the snare. The ambassador, whose profession it was to carry on intrigues skilfully, had succeeded well, and I had taken the bait as he wished. There was nothing left for me but to put a good face on the matter, not only so as not to show myself a very silly being, but also in order not to prove myself shamefully ungrateful towards a man who had granted me unheard-of privileges. Nevertheless, the consequence of it all was likely to be some coolness in my feelings towards both my mistresses. M ** M ** had become conscious of this after she had returned to the convent, and wishing to screen herself from all responsibility she had lost no time in writing to me that she would cause the projected supper to be abandoned, in case I should disapprove of it; but she knew very well that I would not accept her offer. Self-love is a stronger passion even than jealousy; it does not allow a man who has some pretension to wit to show himself jealous, particularly towards a person who is not tainted by that base passion, and has proved it.

The next day, having gone early to the casino, I found the ambassador already there, and he welcomed me in the most friendly manner. He told me that if he had known me in Paris he would have introduced me at the court, where I should certainly have made my fortune. Now, when I think of that, I say to myself, "That might have been the case, but of what good would it have been to me?" Perhaps I should have fallen a victim of the Revolution, like so many others. M. de Bernis himself would have been one of those victims if Fate had not allowed him to die in Rome in 1794. He died there unhappy, although wealthy, unless his feelings had undergone a complete change before his death, and I did not believe it.

I asked him whether he liked Venice, and he answered that he could not do otherwise than like that city, in which he enjoyed excellent health, and in which, with plenty of money, life could be enjoyed better than anywhere else.

"But I do not expect," he added, "to be allowed to keep this embassy very long. Be kind enough to let that remain between us; I do not wish to make M ** M ** unhappy."

We were conversing in all confidence when M ** M ** arrived with her young friend, who showed her surprise at seeing another man with me; but I encouraged her by the most tender welcome, and she recovered all her composure when she saw the delight of the stranger at being answered by her in good French. It gave us both an opportunity of paying the warmest compliments to the mistress who had taught her so well.

C ** C ** was truly charming; her looks, bright and modest at the same time, seemed to say to me, "You must belong to me." I wished to see her shine before our friends, and I contrived to conquer a cowardly feeling of jealousy which, in spite of myself, was beginning to get hold of me. I took care to make her talk on such subjects as I knew to be familiar to her. I developed her natural intelligence, and had the satisfaction of seeing her admired.

Applauded, flattered, animated by the satisfaction she could read in my eyes, C** C** appeared a prodigy to M. de Bernis; and, oh! what a contradiction of the human heart! I was pleased, yet I trembled lest he should fall in love with her! What an enigma! I was intent myself upon a work which would have caused me to murder any man who dared to undertake it.

During the supper, which was worthy of a king, the ambassador treated C** C** with the most delicate attentions. Wit, cheerfulness, decent manners, attended our delightful party, and did not expel the gaiety and the merry jests with which a Frenchman knows how to season every conversation.

An observing critic who, without being acquainted with us, wished to guess whether love was present at our happy party, might have suspected, perhaps, but he certainly could not have affirmed, that it was there. M** M** treated the ambassador as a friend. She showed no other feeling towards me than that of deep esteem, and she behaved to C** C** with the tender affection of a sister. M. de Bernis was kind, polite, and amiable with M** M**, but he never ceased to take the greatest interest in every word uttered by C** C**, who played her part to perfection, because she had only to follow her own nature, and, that nature being beautiful, C** C** could not fail to be most charming.

We had passed five delightful hours, and the ambassador seemed more pleased even than any of us. M** M** had the air of a person satisfied with her own work, and I was playing the part of an approving spectator. C** C** looked highly pleased at having secured the general approbation, and there was, perhaps, a slight feeling of vanity in her arising from the special attention which the ambassador had bestowed on her. She looked at me, smiling, and I could easily understand the language of her soul, by which she wished to tell me that she felt perfectly well the difference between the society in which she was then, and that in which her brother had given us such a disgusting specimen of his depravity.

After midnight it was time to think of our departure, and M. de Bernis undertook all the complimentary part. Thanking M ** M ** for the most agreeable supper he had ever made in his life, he contrived to make her offer a repetition of it for two days afterwards, and he asked me, for the sake of appearance, whether I should not find as much delight in that second meeting as himself. Could he have any doubt of my answering affirmatively? I believe not, for I had placed myself under the necessity of being compliant. All being agreed, we parted company.

The next day, when I thought of that exemplary supper, I had no difficulty in guessing what the ultimate result would be. The ambassador owed his great fortune entirely to the fair sex, because he possessed to the highest degree the art of *coddling* love; and as his nature was eminently voluptuous he found his advantage in it, because he knew how to call desires into existence, and this procured him enjoyments worthy of his delicate taste. I saw that he was deeply in love with C ** C **, and I was far from supposing him the man to be satisfied with looking at her lovely eyes. He certainly had some plan arranged, and M ** M **, in spite of all her honesty, was the prime manager of it: I knew that she would carry it on with such delicate skill that I should not see any evidence of it. Although I did not feel disposed to show more compliance than was strictly just, I foresaw that in the end I should be the dupe, and my poor C ** C ** the victim, of a cunningly-contrived trick. I could not make up my mind either to consent with a good grace, or to throw obstacles in the way; and, believing my dear little wife incapable of abandoning herself to anything likely to displease me, I allowed myself to be taken off my guard, and to rely upon the difficulty of seducing her. Stupid calculation! Self-love and shamefacedness prevented me from using my common sense. At all events, that intrigue kept me in a state of fever because I was afraid of its consequences, and yet curiosity mastered me to such an extent that I was longing for the result. I knew very well that a second edition of the supper did not imply that the same play would be performed a second time, and I foresaw that the changes would be strongly marked. But I thought myself bound in honour not to retract; I could not lead the intrigue, but I believed myself sufficiently skilful to baffle all their manœuvrings.

After all those considerations, however, considerations which enabled me to assume the countenance of false bravery, the inexperience of C ** C **, who, in spite of all the knowledge she had lately acquired, was only a novice, caused me great anxiety. It was easy to abuse her natural wish to be polite, but that fear gave way very soon before the confidence I had in M ** M **'s delicacy. I thought that, having seen how I had spent six hours with that young girl, knowing for a certainty that I intended to marry her, M ** M ** would never be guilty of such base treason. All these thoughts, worthy only of a weak and bashful jealousy, brought no conclusive decision; I had to follow the current and watch events.

At the appointed time I repaired to the casino, where I found my two lovely friends sitting by the fire.

"Good evening, my two divinities, where is our charming Frenchman?"

"He has not arrived yet," answered M ** M **, "but he will doubtless soon be here."

I took off my mask, and sitting between them, I gave them a thousand kisses, taking good care not to show any preference; and although I knew that they were aware of the unquestionable right I had upon both of them, I kept within the limits of the utmost decency. I congratulated them upon the mutual inclination they felt for each other, and I saw that they were pleased not to have to blush on that account.

More than one hour was spent in gallant and friendly conversation, without my giving any satisfaction to my burning desires. M ** M ** attracted me more than C ** C **, but I would not for the world have offended the charming girl. M ** M ** was beginning to show some anxiety about the absence of M. de Bernis, when the door-keeper brought her a note from him.

"A courier," he wrote, "who arrived two hours ago, prevents my being happy to-night, for I am compelled to pass it in answering the dispatches I have received. I trust that you will forgive and pity me. May I hope that you will kindly grant me on Friday the pleasure of which I am so unfortunately deprived to-day? Let me know your answer by to-morrow. I wish ardently, in that case, to find you with the same guests, to whom I beg you will present my affectionate compliments."

"Well," said M ** M **, "it is not his fault. We will sup without him. Will you come on Friday?"

"Yes, with the greatest pleasure. But what is the matter with you, dear C ** C **? You look sad."

"Sad, no; unless it should be for the sake of my friend, for I have never seen a more polite and more obliging gentleman."

"Very well, dear; I am glad he has rendered you so sensible."

"What do you mean? Could anyone be insensible to his merit?"

"Better still, but I agree with you. Only tell me if you love him?"

"Well, even if I loved him, do you think I would go and tell him? Besides, I am certain that he loves my friend."

The next day, however, when I came to think of that rather too lively night, during which, as is generally the case, Love had routed Reason, I felt some remorse. M ** M ** wanted to convince me of her love, and for that purpose she had combined all the virtues which I attached to my own affection — namely, honour, delicacy, and truth; but her temperament, of which her mind was the slave, carried her towards excess, and she prepared everything in order to give way to it, while she awaited the opportunity of making me her accomplice. She was coaxing love to make it compliant, and to succeed in mastering it, because her heart, enslaved by her senses, never reproached her. She likewise tried to deceive herself by endeavouring to forget that I might complain of having been surprised. She knew that to utter such a complaint I would have to acknowledge myself weaker or less courageous than she was, and she relied upon my being ashamed to make such a confession. I had no doubt whatever that the absence of the ambassador had been arranged and concerted beforehand. I could see still further: for it seemed evident to me that the two conspirators had foreseen that I would guess the artifice, and that, feeling stung to the quick, in spite of all my regrets, I would not show myself less generous than they had been themselves. The ambassador having first procured me a delightful night, how could I refuse to let him enjoy as pleasant a one? My friends had argued very well, for, in spite of all the objections of my mind, I saw that I could not on my side put any obstacle in their way. C ** C ** was no impediment to them; they were certain of conquering her the

moment she was not hindered by my presence. It rested entirely
with M ** M **, who had perfect control over her. Poor girl!
I saw her on the high road to debauchery, and it was my own
doing! I sighed when I thought of how little I had spared them
in our last orgy, and what would become of me if both of them
should happen to be, by my doing, in such a position as to be
compelled to run away from the convent? I could imagine both
of them thrown upon my hands, and the prospect was not particularly agreeable. It would be an *embarras de richesse*. In this
contest between reason and prejudice, between nature and sentiment, I could not make up my mind either to go to the supper or
to remain absent from it. "If I go," said I to myself, "the night
will pass with perfect decency, but I shall prove myself very
ridiculous, jealous, ungrateful, and even wanting in common
politeness: if I remain absent, C ** C ** is lost, at least in my
estimation; for I feel that my love will no longer exist, and then
good-bye to all idea of a marriage with her." In the perplexity
of mind in which I found myself, I felt a want of something more
certain than mere probabilities to base my decision upon. I put
on my mask, and repairing to the mansion of the French ambassador I addressed myself to the gate-keeper, saying that I had
a letter for Versailles, and that I would thank him to deliver it
to the courier when he went back to France with his excellency's
dispatches.

"But, sir," answered the man, "we have not had a special
courier for the last two months."

"What? Did not a special messenger arrive here last night?"

"Then he must have come in through the garret window or
down the chimney, for, on the word of an honest man, none
entered through the gate."

"But the ambassador worked all night?"

"That may be, sir, but not here, for his excellency dined with
the Spanish ambassador, and did not return till very late."

I had guessed rightly; I could no longer entertain any doubt.
It was all over; I could not draw back without shame. C **
C ** must resist, if the game was distasteful to her; no violence
would of course be offered to her. The die was cast!

Towards evening I went to the casino of Muran, and wrote
a short note to M ** M **, requesting her to excuse me if some
important business of M. de Bragadin's prevented me from

spending the night with her and with our two friends, to whom I sent my compliments as well as my apologies. After that I returned to Venice, but in rather an unpleasant mood; to divert myself I went to the gaming-table, and lost all night.

Two days afterwards, being certain that a letter from M ** M ** awaited me at Muran, I went over, and the door-keeper handed me a parcel in which I found a note from my nun and a letter from C ** C **, for everything was now in common between them.

Here is C ** C **'s letter:

"We were very sorry, dearest friend, when we heard that we should not have the happiness of seeing you. My dear M ** M **'s friend came shortly afterwards, and when he read your note he likewise expressed his deep regret. We expected to have a very dull supper, but the witty sayings of that gentleman enlivened us; and you cannot imagine of what follies we were guilty after partaking of some champagne punch. Our friend had become as gay as ourselves, and we spent the night in trios, not very fatiguing, but very pleasant. I can assure you that that man deserves to be loved; but he must acknowledge himself inferior to you in everything. Believe me, dearest, I shall ever love you, and you must for ever remain the master of my heart."

In spite of all my vexation, that letter made me laugh; but the note of M ** M ** was much more singular. Here are the contents of it:

"I am certain, my own beloved, that you told a story out of pure politeness; but you had guessed that I expected you to do so. You have made our friend a splendid present in exchange for the one he made you when he did not object to his M ** M ** bestowing her heart upon you. You possess that heart entirely, dearest, and you would possess it under all circumstances; but how sweet it is to flavour the pleasures of love with the charms of friendship! I was sorry not to see you, but I knew that if you had come we would not have had much enjoyment; for our friend, notwithstanding all his wit, is not exempt from some natural prejudices. As for C ** C **, her mind is now quite as free of them as our own; and I am glad she owes it to me. You must feel thankful to me for having completed her education, and for rendering her in every way worthy of you. I wish you had been hiding in the closet, where I am certain you would have spent some delightful hours. On Wednesday next I shall be yours, and all alone with you in your casino in Venice; let me know whether you will be at the usual hour near the statue of the hero Colleoni. In case you should be prevented, name any other day."

I had to answer those two letters in the same spirit in which they had been written, and in spite of all the bitter feelings which were then raging in my heart, my answers were to be as sweet as honey. I was in need of great courage, but I said to myself: *"George Dandin, tu l'as voulu!"* I could not refuse to pay the penalty of my own deeds, and I have never been able to ascertain whether the shame I felt was what is called shamefacedness. It is a problem which I leave to others.

In my letter to C ** C ** I had the courage, or the effrontery, to congratulate her, and to encourage her to imitate M ** M **, the best model, I said, I could propose to her.

I wrote to my nun that I would be punctual at the appointment near the statue; and amidst many false compliments, which ought to have betrayed the true state of my heart, ·I told her that I admired the perfect education she had given to C ** C **, but that I congratulated myself upon having escaped the torture I should have suffered in the mysterious observatory, for I felt that I could not have borne it.

On the Wednesday I was punctual at the rendezvous, and I had not to wait long for M ** M **, who came disguised in male attire.. "No theatre to-night," she said to me; "let us go to the *ridotto*, to lose or double our money." She had six hundred sequins; I had about one hundred. Fortune turned her back upon us, and we lost all. I expected that we would then leave that cut-throat place; but M ** M **, having left me for a minute, came back with three hundred sequins which had been given to her by her friend, whom she knew where to find. That money given by love or by friendship brought her luck for a short time, and she soon won back all we had lost; but in our greediness or impudence we continued to play, and finally we lost our last sequin. When we could play no longer, M ** M ** said to me:

"Now that we need not fear thieves, let us go to our supper."

That woman, religious and a free-thinker, a libertine and gambler, was wonderful in all she did. She had just lost five hundred pounds, and she was as completely at her ease as if she had won a very large sum. It is true that the money she had just lost had not cost her much.

As soon as we were alone, she found me sad and low-spirited, although I tried hard not to appear so; but, as for her, always the same, she was handsome, brilliant, cheerful, and amorous.

She thought she would bring back my spirits by giving me the fullest particulars of the night she had passed with C ** C ** and her friend, but she ought to have guessed that she was going the wrong way. That is a very common error; it comes from the mind, because people imagine that what they feel themselves others must feel likewise.

I was on thorns, and I tried everything to avoid that subject, and to lead the conversation into a different channel; for the amorous particulars, on which she was dwelling with apparent delight, vexed me greatly, and spite causing coldness, I was afraid of not playing my part very warmly.

Before leaving, M ** M ** asked me to go to her casino, to take some money and to play, taking her for my partner. I did so. I took all the gold I found, and playing the martingale, and doubling my stakes continuously, I won every day during the remainder of the carnival. I was fortunate enough never to lose the sixth card; and, if I had lost it, I should have been without money to play, for I had two thousand sequins on that card. I congratulated myself upon having increased the treasure of my dear mistress, who wrote to me that, for the sake of civility, we ought to have a supper *en partie carrée* on Shrove Monday. I consented.

That supper was the last I ever had in my life with C ** C **. She was in excellent spirits; but I had made up my mind, and as I paid all my attentions to M ** M **, C ** C ** imitated my example without difficulty, and she devoted herself wholly to her new lover. Foreseeing that we would, a little later, be all of us in each other's way, I begged M ** M ** to arrange everything so that we could be apart, and she contrived it marvellously well.

After supper, the ambassador proposed a game of faro, which our beauties did not know; he called for cards, and placed one hundred louis on the table before him; he dealt, and took care to make C ** C ** win the whole of that sum. It was the best way to make her accept it as pin-money. The young girl, dazzled by so much gold, and not knowing what to do with it, asked her friend to take care of it for her until such time as she should leave the convent to get married.

When the game was over, M** M** complained of a headache, and said that she would go to bed in the alcove: she asked me to come and lull her to sleep. We thus left the new lovers free to be as gay as they chose. Six hours afterwards, when the alarum warned us that it was time to part, we found them asleep in each other's embrace. I had myself passed an amorous and quiet night, pleased with M** M**, and without giving one thought to C** C**.

Though the infidelities of C** C** made me look at her with other eyes than before, and though I had now no intention of making her the companion of my life, I could not help feeling that it had rested with me to stop her on the brink of the stream, and I therefore considered it my duty always to be her friend.

If I had been more logical, the resolution I took with respect to her would doubtless have been of another kind. I should have said to myself: After seducing her, I myself have set the example of infidelity; I have bidden her to follow blindly the advice of her friend, although I knew that the advice and the example of M** M** would end in her ruin; I had insulted, in the most grievous manner, the delicacy of my mistress, and that before her very eyes; and after all this how could I ask a weak woman to do what a man, priding himself on his strength, would shrink from attempting? I should have stood self-condemned, and have felt that it was my duty to remain the same to her; but flattering myself that I was overcoming mere prejudices, I was in fact that most degraded of slaves, he who uses his strength to crush the weak.

The day after Shrove Tuesday, going to the casino of Muran, I found there a letter from M** M**, who gave me two pieces of bad news: that C** C** had lost her mother, and that the poor girl was in despair; and that the lay sister, whose rheum was cured, had returned to take her place. Thus C** C** was deprived of her friend at a time when she would have given her consolation, of which she stood in great need. C** C**, it seemed, had gone to share the rooms of her aunt, who, being very fond of her, had obtained permission from the superior.

This circumstance would prevent the ambassador taking any more suppers with her, and I should have been delighted if chance had put this obstacle in his path a few days sooner.

All these misfortunes seemed of small account compared with what I was afraid of, for C ** C ** might have to pay the price for her pleasures, and I so far regarded myself as the origin of her unhappiness as to feel bound never to abandon her, and this might have involved me in terrible complications.

M ** M ** asked me to sup with her and her lover on the following Monday. I went and found them both sad — he for the loss of his new mistress, and she because she had no longer a friend to make the seclusion of the convent pleasant.

About midnight M. de Bernis left us, saying in a melancholy manner that he feared he should be obliged to pass several months in Vienna on important diplomatic business. Before parting we agreed to sup together every Friday.

When we were alone M ** M ** told me that the ambassador would be obliged to me if in the future I would come to the casino two hours later. I understood that the good-natured and witty profligate had a very natural prejudice against indulging his amorous feelings except when he was certain of being alone.

On Good Friday, when I got to the casino, I found the lovers overwhelmed with grief. Supper was served, but the ambassador, downcast and absent, neither ate nor spoke, and M ** M ** was like a statue that moves at intervals by some mechanism. Good sense and ordinary politeness prevented me from asking any questions, but on M ** M ** leaving us together, M. de Bernis told me that she was distressed, and with reason, since he was obliged to set out for Vienna fifteen days after Easter. "I may tell you confidentially," he added, "that I believe I shall scarcely be able to return, but she must not be told, as she would be in despair." M ** M ** came back in a few minutes, but it was easy to see that she had been weeping.

After some commonplace conversation, M. de Bernis, seeing M ** M ** still low-spirited, said:

"Do not grieve thus, sweetheart, go I must; but my return is a matter of equal certainty when I have finished the important business which summons me to Vienna. You will still have the casino, but, dearest, both friendship and prudence make me advise you not to come here in my absence, for after I have left Venice I cannot depend upon the faith of the gondoliers in my service, and I suspect our friend here cannot flatter himself on his ability to get reliable ones. I may also tell you that I have strong reasons for suspecting that our intercourse is known to the State Inquisitors, who conceal their knowledge for political reasons; but I fancy the secret would soon come to light when I am no longer here, and when the nun who connives at your departure from the convent knows that it is no longer for me that you leave it. The only people whom I would trust are the housekeeper and his wife. I shall order them, before I go, to look upon our friend here as myself, and you can make arrangements with them. I trust all will go well till my return, if you will only behave discreetly. I will write to you under cover of the housekeeper, his wife will give you my letters as before, and in the same way you may reply. I must needs go, dearest one, but my heart is with you, and I leave you, till my return, in the hands of a friend, whom I rejoice to have known. He loves you, he has a heart and knowledge of the world, and he will not let you make any mistakes."

M ** M ** was so affected by what the ambassador had said that she entreated us to let her go, as she wished to be alone and to lie down. As she went we agreed to sup together on the following Thursday.

As soon as we were alone the ambassador impressed me with the absolute necessity of concealing from her that he was going to return no more. "I am going," said he, "to work in concert with the Austrian cabinet on a treaty which will be the talk of Europe. I entreat you to write to me unreservedly, and as a friend; and if you love our common mistress, have a care for her honour, and above all have the strength of mind to resist all projects which are certain to involve you in misfortune, and which will be equally fatal to both. You know what happened to Madame de Riva, a nun in the convent of S **. She had to disappear after it became known that she was with child, and M. de Frulai, my predecessor, went mad, and died shortly after. J. J. Rousseau told me that he died of poison, but he is a visionary who sees the black side of everything. For my part, I believe that he died of grief at not being able to do anything for the unfortunate woman, who afterwards procured a dispensation from her vows from the Pope, and having got married is now living at Padua without any position in society.

"Let the prudent and loyal friend master the lover: go and see M ** M ** sometimes in the parlour of the convent, but not here, or the boatmen will betray you. The knowledge which we both have that the girls are in a satisfactory condition is a great alleviation to my distress, but you must confess that you have been very imprudent. You have risked a terrible misfortune; consider the position you would have been in, for I am sure you would not have abandoned her. She had an idea that the danger might be overcome by means of drugs, but I convinced her that she was mistaken.

"In God's name, be discreet in the future, and write to me fully, for I shall always be interested in her fate, both from duty and sentiment."

We returned together to Venice, where we separated, and I passed the rest of the night in great distress. In the morning I wrote to the fair afflicted, and whilst endeavouring to console her to the best of my ability, I tried to impress on her the necessity for prudence and the avoidance of such escapades as might eventually ruin us.

Next day I received her reply, every word of which spelt despair. Nature had given her a disposition which had become so intensified by indulgence that the cloister was unbearable to her, and I foresaw the hard fights I should have to undergo.

We saw each other the Thursday after Easter, and I told her that I should not come to the casino before midnight. She had had four hours to pass with her lover in tears and regrets, amongst which she had often cursed her cruel fate and the foolish resolution which made her take the veil. We supped together, and although the meal was a rich and delicate one we did it little honour. When we had finished, the ambassador left, entreating me to remain, which I did, without thinking at all of the pleasures of a party of two, for Love lighteth not his torch at the hearts of two lovers who are full of grief and sorrow. M ** M ** had grown thin, and her condition excited my pity and shut out all other feelings. I held her a long time in my arms, covering her with tender and affectionate kisses, but I showed no intention of consoling her by amusements in which her spirit could not have taken part. She said, before we parted, that I had shown myself a true lover, and she asked me to consider myself from henceforth as her only friend and protector.

Next week, when we were together as usual, M. de Bernis called the housekeeper just before supper, and in his presence executed a deed in my behalf, which he made him sign. In this document he transferred to me all rights over the contents of the casino, and charged him to consider me in all things as his master.

We arranged to sup together two days after, to make our farewells, but on my arrival I found M ** M ** by herself, standing up, and pale as death, or rather as white as a statue of Carrara marble.

"He is gone," she said, "and he leaves me to your care. Fatal being, whom perchance I shall see no more, whom I thought I loved but as a friend, now you are lost to me I see my mistake. Before I knew him I was not happy, but neither was I unhappy as I now am."

*After the ambassador's departure Casanova and M ** M ** continued their meetings, employing various stratagems to escape detection; for, reading between the lines of the Memoirs, it would seem that M ** M **'s former freedom of movement was due to what we may term "diplomatic immunity" and that once her powerful friend had left Venice, it behoved her to be careful. Not daring any longer to trust hired boatmen to convey the lovers to Murano, Casanova himself steers the bark and on one occasion nearly perishes in a storm. In Venice, where he continues his old life, he makes friends with another ambassador, Mr. Murray, who represented Great Britain, not very worthily, if we are to believe the Memoirs. He is represented as a libertine of the first order, living openly with the beautiful and dissolute Ancilla, with whom he gives erotic exhibitions for his friends.*

As if the cup of his iniquities were not full enough, Casanova, by indulging his polemical vein at the expense of the Abbé Chiari, a local poet, falls foul of the latter's protector, the powerful Condulmer, who shortly afterwards is named State Inquisitor. "Having thus attained this diabolically eminent, or eminently diabolical position," observes Casanova, "he had not much difficulty in showing his colleagues the necessity of putting me under The Leads as a disturber of the peace of the Republic."

Already the shadow of this famous and dreaded prison is upon him. Before it swallows him up entirely, let us hear from him the epilogue to the Venetian Nights' Entertainment:

In the beginning of the winter the astounding news of the treaty between France and Austria was divulged — a treaty by which the political balance was entirely readjusted, and which was received with incredulity by the powers. The whole of Italy had reason to rejoice, for the treaty guarded that fair land from becoming the theatre of war on the slightest difference which might arise between the two powers. What astonished the most acute was that this wonderful treaty was conceived and carried out by a young ambassador who had hitherto been famed only as a wit. The first foundations had been laid in 1750 by Madame de Pompadour, Count Kaunitz (who was created a prince), and M. l'Abbé de Bernis, who was not known till the following year, when the king made him ambassador to Venice. The House of Bourbon and the House of Hapsburg had been foes for two hundred and forty years when this famous treaty was concluded; but it only lasted for forty years, and it is not likely that any treaty will last longer between two courts so essentially opposed to one another.

The Abbé de Bernis was created minister for foreign affairs some time after the ratification of the treaty; three years after he re-established the parliament, became a cardinal, was disgraced, and finally sent to Rome, where he died. *Mors ultima linea rerum est.*

Affairs fell out as I had foreseen, for nine months after he left Venice he conveyed to M ** M ** the news of his recall, though he did it in the most delicate manner. Nevertheless, M ** M ** felt the blow so severely that she would very possibly have succumbed, had I not been preparing her for it in every way I could think of. M. de Bernis sent me all instructions.

He directed that all the contents of the casino should be sold and the proceeds given to M ** M **, with the exception of the books and prints, which the housekeeper was ordered to bring to Paris. It was a nice breviary for a cardinal, but would to God they had nothing worse!

Whilst M ** M ** abandoned herself to grief I carried out the orders of M. de Bernis, and by the middle of January we had no longer a casino. She kept by her two thousand sequins and her pearls, intending to sell them later on to buy herself an annuity.

We were now only able to see each other at the grating; and

soon, worn with grief, she fell dangerously ill, and on the 2nd of February I recognised in her features the symptoms of approaching death. She sent me her jewel-case, with all her diamonds and nearly all her money, all the scandalous books she possessed, and all her letters, telling me that if she did not die I was to return her the whole, but that all belonged to me if, as she thought, she should succumb to the disease. She also told me that C** C** was aware of her state, and asked me to take pity on her, as my letters were her only comfort, and that she hoped to have strength to read them till her latest breath.

I burst into tears, for I loved her passionately, and I promised her to come and live in Muran until she recovered her health.

After languishing at death's door, sustained only by her lover's promises that if she recovered he would carry her off and live with her for the rest of their days, M** M** recovered. Casanova goes to congratulate her on her recovery. They meet in the convent parlour, only to realise that there are certain flames which, once extinguished, leave no embers. Still they continue on the best of terms, M** M** becoming a "sleeping partner" in his gambling enterprises, which finally would have ended in disaster, if the generous nun had not come to the rescue by selling the jewels which Bernis had given her. From her he learns the final vicissitudes of poor C** C**, but is powerless to help.

I found her very sad, for C** C**'s father was dead, and they had taken her out of the convent to marry her to a lawyer. Before leaving, C** C** had left a letter for me, in which she said that if I would promise to marry her at some time suitable to myself, she would wait for me, and refuse all other offers. I answered her straightforwardly that I had no property and no prospects, that I left her free, advising her not to refuse any offer which might be to her advantage.

In spite of this dismissal C** C** did not marry N** till after my flight from The Leads, when nobody expected to see me again in Venice. I did not see her for nineteen years, and then I was grieved to find her a widow, and poorly off. If I went to Venice now I should not marry her, for at my age marriage is an absurdity, but I would share with her my little all, and live with her as with a dear sister.

When I hear women talking about the bad faith and inconstancy of men, and maintaining that when men make promises of eternal constancy they are always deceivers, I confess that they are right, and join in their complaints. Still it cannot be helped, for the promises of lovers are dictated by the heart, and consequently the lamentations of women only make me want to laugh. Alas! we love without heeding reason, and cease to love in the same manner.

About this time I received a letter from the Abbé de Bernis, who wrote also to M ** M **. He told me that I ought to do my utmost to make our nun take a reasonable view of things, dwelling on the risks I should run in carrying her off and bringing her to Paris, where all his influence would be of no avail to obtain for us that safety so indispensable to happiness. I saw M ** M **; we showed each other our letters, she had some bitter tears, and her grief pierced me to the heart. I still had a great love for her in spite of my daily infidelities, and when I thought of those moments in which I had seen her given over to voluptuousness I could not help pitying her fate as I thought of the days of despair in store for her. But soon after this an event happened which gave rise to some wholesome reflections. One day, when I had come to see her, she said:

"They have just been burying a nun who died of consumption the day before yesterday in the odour of sanctity. She was called 'Maria Concetta.' She knew you, and told C ** C ** your name when you used to come to mass on feast days. C ** C ** begged her to be discreet, but the nun told her that you were a dangerous man, whose presence should be shunned by a young girl. C ** C ** told me all this after the mask of Pierrot."

"What was this saint's name when she was in the world?"

"Martha S **."

"I know her."

I then told M ** M ** the whole history of my loves with Nanette and Marton, ending with the letter she wrote me, in which she said that she owed me, indirectly, that eternal salvation to which she hoped to attain.

So, like the Don Juan *of Richard Strauss, Casanova ends his* Sinfonia Erotica *on a note of sadness and contrition — an effective ending, on the whole, which does credit to his sense of artistic fitness. He had the choice of several others, as has every author who invents a romance. For a romance it is from beginning to end, this luscious story of convent intrigue and "parties carrées" with a distinguished statesman.*

Having had the temerity of impressing a well-known historical character, such as the Abbé, later Cardinal, de Bernis, to serve as joint-hero of this erotic romance, Casanova should at least have taken the precaution of ordering his dates, if not his facts, to bear out his story. But it is in keeping with the character of the man that whenever ordinary reason counsels prudence, he must needs become more reckless than ever. Naturally critics of the Memoirs, such as Herr Gustav Gugitz, a leading authority in Casanoveriana, besides other historians, [1] have had no difficulty in demolishing this chronique scandaleuse.

*If it is true that the Abbé de Bernis was appointed ambassador to the Venetian Republic and was residing there in 1753, the year of the M** M**-C** C** episode, it is historically untrue that he led a life of debauchery in that city. Not only the cardinal's own Memoirs, but the accounts of contemporaries bear witness to the fact that, contrary to all expectation, given his reputation at Versailles and the precedent set up by his predecessors in Venice, the ambassador of Madame de Pompadour, this Bernis "chargé d'esprit et de cuisine," to quote one of the countless lampoons directed against her favourite, was one of the hardest-working, strictest-living diplomats that the* Serenissima *ever saw within her walls. The little abbé of Trianon, the gallant author of* petits vers, *whom Voltaire had ironically nicknamed Babet la Bouquetière, had at last got his chance of proving his mettle and he was making the most of it.*

The work which was then engrossing him and which was to be sprung on the world a few years hence [2] as one of the biggest diplo-

---

[1] *Frédéric Masson, the eminent historian, in his* Mémoires et lettres de Bernis, *indignantly refutes the Casanovian libel. Bernis, he says, "has a right to be believed when with one word he demolishes all that Casanova has written." The only exception to be made — and it is hardly a libel — is the authenticated excellence of the ambassadorial table. (For these and other references, see Charles Samaran's excellent work:* Jacques Casanova, Vénitien, *published by Calmann-Lévy, Paris.)*

[2] *This treaty, formally signed at Versailles on May 1, 1756, had been secretly negotiated at Sèvres during the previous summer, between Bernis and Starbemberg, the Austrian plenipotentiary. To this diplomatic success Bernis owed his appointment as prime minister the following year. Yet Casanova, who has been shuffling dates to suit the purposes of his story, does not hesitate to affirm that in 1754 — two years earlier! — Venice was startled to hear of the Franco-Austrian alliance, any more than to ask us to believe that the discreet Bernis, who was preparing his great coup, would have confided this important matter to him before leaving for Vienna — to say nothing of the fact that he did not leave Venice till the following year, when Casanova was already in prison!*

matic surprises in history was the treaty of alliance between France and Austria. But there is another and capital witness to the moral life led by Bernis in Venice — Giacomo Casanova himself, who in his Confutazione della Storia del governo veneto d'Amelot de la Houssaye, the work he composed to curry favour with the Venetian government so as to obtain his pardon after his escape from The Leads, explicitly praises the exemplary conduct of the French ambassador, whose acquaintance he seems to have made in Paris after his escape from prison. Herr Gugitz's theory that the original for the Abbé de Bernis of the Memoirs was a certain Louis Gabriel de Froulay, the abbé's predecessor at the French Embassy in Venice, whose intrigue with a nun and its tragic results are cited by the abbé as a warning, seems in every way acceptable.

As for M ** M ** and C ** C **, researches in the archives of San Giacomo di Galizzia, in Murano, which is evidently the convent alluded to in the Memoirs, have established the fact that a nun bearing the name of Maria Maddalena Pisani, and a pensioner of the name of Caterina Campana were members of the community at the time of the episode we are dealing with. In both cases the certified ages tally with those given by Casanova for his two heroines. In 1785 Maria Maddalena became abbess of the convent and died three years later. Caterina Campana left the convent after the death of her parents and became the wife of a lawyer. In the original manuscript of the Memoirs the name Maria Maddalena was at one time clearly legible under the erasure made by Casanova's hand. It may be also noted, by way of substantiating this identification, that Casanova mentions a present which he made C ** C ** on her name-day, the feast of St. Catherine.

The famous story of Casanova's Escape from The Leads, which now follows in the Memoirs, having already been published in a separate volume in Mr. Arthur Machen's translation,[1] is not included in the present volume.

For the information of readers unfamiliar with that story, the following summary will suffice:

On July 26th, 1755, Casanova was arrested in his house by Messer-Grande, the official representative of the Tribunal of Inquisitors, which for some time past had been keeping its eye on Senator

---

[1] Casanova's Escape from the Leads, by Arthur Machen (London, Casanova Society, 1925; New York, Alfred A. Knopf, 1925).

Bragadin's adopted son. The direct charges leading to his arrest and imprisonment were contained in a report submitted to the Tribunal by a certain Manuzzi (also spelt Manucci). According to this report, the text of which has been published, Casanova was a disturber of the peace, a dangerous character, who lived by exploiting his friends, defied the authorities, and, not content with ruining noble patricians, like Senator Bragadin and his friends, got their sons into mischief, as in the case of young Andrea Memmo, whose widowed mother had lodged a complaint. Casanova was also guilty of having forbidden books in his possession — works on magic, witchcraft, and necromancy. But one of the main charges — though Casanova says nothing about it — must certainly have been his affiliation with Freemasonry, into the "sublime trifles" of which he had been initiated in Lyons. Had the tribunal possessed positive proofs of his connection with the brotherhood, which was at that time beginning to make its influence felt in the politics of Europe, it is more than likely that Casanova would never have been seen alive after his arrest — a fate which befell several of his compatriots.

On the night of October 31st, 1756, Casanova, after a thwarted first attempt, escaped from prison in the company of a fellow-prisoner, Father Balbi, a Capuchin monk, under circumstances which — so some of his commentators think — call for further elucidation. By way of Bavaria, where he parted with Balbi, Casanova gained France and Paris.

CONTENTS

VOLUME II

CHAPTER X

Once more, then, I was in Paris, which I ought to regard as my fatherland, since I could return no more to that land which gave me birth: an unworthy country, yet, in spite of all, ever dear to me, possibly on account of early impressions and early prejudices, or possibly because the beauties of Venice are really unmatched in the world. But mighty Paris is a place of good luck or ill, as one takes it, and it was my part to catch the favouring gale.

Paris was not wholly new to me, as my readers know I had spent two years there, but I must confess that, having then no other aim than to pass the time pleasantly, I had merely devoted myself to pleasure and enjoyment. Fortune, to whom I had paid no court, had not opened to me her golden doors; but now I felt that I must treat her more reverently, and attach myself to the throng of her favoured sons whom she loads with her gifts. I understood now that the nearer one draws to the sun the more one feels the warmth of its rays. I saw that to attain my end I should have to employ all my mental and physical talents, that I must make friends of the great, and take the cue from all whom I found it to be my interest to please. To follow the plans suggested by these thoughts, I saw that I must avoid what is called bad company, that I must give up my old habits and pretensions, which would be sure to make me enemies, who would have no scruple in representing me as a trifler, and not fit to be trusted with affairs of any importance.

I think I thought wisely, and the reader, I hope, will be of the same opinion. "I will be reserved," said I, "in what I say and what I do, and thus I shall get a reputation for discretion which will bring its reward."

I was in no anxiety on the score of present needs, as I could reckon on a monthly allowance of a hundred crowns, which my adopted father, the good and generous M. de Bragadin, sent me, and I found this sum sufficient in the meanwhile, for with a little self-restraint one can live cheaply at Paris, and cut a good figure at the same time. I was obliged to wear a good suit of clothes, and to have a decent lodging; for in all large towns the most important thing is outward show, by which at the beginning one is always judged. My anxiety was only for the pressing needs of the moment — for to speak the truth I had neither clothes nor linen — in a word, nothing.

If my relations with the French ambassador are recalled, it will be found natural that my first idea was to address myself to him, as I knew him sufficiently well to reckon on his serving me.

Being perfectly certain that the porter would tell me that my lord was engaged, I took care to have a letter, and in the morning I went to the Palais Bourbon. The porter took my letter, and I gave him my address and returned home.

Wherever I went I had to tell the story of my escape from The Leads. This became a service almost as tiring as the flight itself had been, as it took me two hours to tell my tale, without the slightest bit of fancy-work; but I had to be polite to the curious inquirers, and to pretend that I believed them moved by the most affectionate interest in my welfare. In general, the best way to please is to take the benevolence of all with whom one has relation for granted.

I supped at Silvia's, and as the evening was quieter than the night before, I had time to congratulate myself on all the friendship they showed me. The girl was, as I have said, fifteen years old, and I was in every way charmed with her. I complimented the mother on the good results of her education, and I did not even think of guarding myself from falling a victim to her charms. I had taken so lately such well-founded and philosophical resolutions, and I was not yet sufficiently at my ease to value the pain of being tempted. I left at an early hour, impatient to see what kind of an answer the minister had sent me. I had not long to wait, and I received a short letter appointing a meeting for two o'clock in the afternoon. It may be guessed that I was punctual, and my reception by his excellency was most flattering. M. de Bernis expressed his pleasure at seeing me after my fortunate escape, and at being able to be of service to me. He told me that M ** M ** had informed him of my escape, and he had flattered himself that the first person I should go and see in Paris would be himself. He showed me the letters from M ** M ** relating to my arrest and escape, but all the details in the latter were purely imaginary and had no foundation in fact. M ** M ** was not to blame, as she could only write what she had heard, and it was not easy for anyone besides myself to know the real circumstances of my escape. The charming nun said that, no longer buoyed up by the hope of seeing either of the men who alone had made her in love with life, her existence had become a burden to her, and she was unfortunate in not being able to take any comfort in religion. "C ** C ** often comes to see me," she said, "but I grieve to say she is not happy with her husband."

I told M. de Bernis that the account of my flight from The Leads, as told by our friend, was wholly inaccurate, and I would therefore take the liberty of writing out the whole story with the minutest details. He challenged me to keep my word, assuring me that he would send a copy to M ** M **, and at the same time, with the utmost courtesy, he put a packet of a hundred louis in my hand, telling me that he would think what he could do for me, and would advise me as soon as he had any communication to make.

Thus furnished with ample funds, my first care was for my dress; and this done I went to work, and in a week sent my generous protector the result, giving him permission to have as many copies printed as he liked, and to make any use he pleased of it to interest in my behalf such persons as might be of service to me.

Three weeks after, the minister summoned me to say that he had spoken of me to M. Erizzo, the Venetian ambassador, who had nothing to say against me, but for fear of embroiling himself with the State Inquisitors declined to receive me. Not wanting anything from him, his refusal did me no harm. M. de Bernis then told me that he had given a copy of my history to Madame la Marquise de Pompadour, and he promised to take the first opportunity of presenting me to this all-powerful lady. "You can present yourself, my dear Casanova," added his excellence. "to the Duc de Choiseul, and M. de Boulogne, the comptroller. You will be well received, and with a little wit you ought to be able to make good use of the letters. He himself will give you the clue, and you will see that *he who listens obtains.* Try to invent some useful plan for the royal exchequer; don't let it be complicated or chimerical, and if you don't write it out at too great length I will give you my opinion on it."

I left the minister in a pleased and grateful mood, but extremely puzzled to find a way of increasing the royal revenue. I knew nothing of finance, and after racking my brains all that I could think of was new methods of taxation; but all my plans were either absurd or certain to be unpopular, and I rejected them all on consideration.

Casanova starts on his round of calls, beginning with the Duc de Choiseul, then prime minister, who receives him with the aloofness of the grand seigneur, but displays interest in the story of his flight. Choiseul sends him on to M. de Boulogne, the comptroller-general, where he meets the famous financier Paris-Duverney (the Memoirs persist in calling him "Paris du Vernai"), who had already done so much for French finance. Just then he was in need of twenty million francs for his military school, which he wanted to raise without taxation or treasury loan. Casanova at once announces he has a scheme which would give the king the interest of a hundred million without costing the Crown a penny. Although he maintains that at the moment he had not the slightest idea how this was to be accomplished — prompted, we may infer, by his "genius" — it is obvious that the scheme he had in mind was that of the banco lotto, *which was very popular at that time, not only in Italy, where it continues to this day, but in other continental countries. It was the day of lotteries. Two, of foreign origin, were already established in Paris.*

Although Casanova pretends the idea came to him as an inspiration, the fact is that he merely took over and espoused for his purposes a plan already worked out by the Calsabigi brothers, natives of Leghorn and experts in the lottery system. The older of the two brothers, Ranieri, might, and perhaps did, serve as a model for the new Casanovian avatar. Mathematician, financier, gambler, man of letters, [1] *indefatigable promoter of schemes, he appears, like Beaumarchais, a type of the complete adventurer of the eighteenth century — a type which, for all its depravity, compares not unfavourably with the modern profiteer and* arriviste.

The rôle played by Casanova in launching this scheme is made

[1] *Ranieri Calsabigi, besides translating into French for Madame de Pompadour the complete works of Metastasio, composed the libretti for the* Orpheus *and* Alcestes *of Gluck. In this connection it is interesting to recall that Casanova was also librettist in his leisure moments.*

plausible by the fact that Ranieri Calsabigi, the promoter and moving spirit of the whole affair, was confined to his bed by a chronic skin-disease and had to rely on his brother for all outside work. Under these conditions, rather than risk a dangerous rivalry with a man like Casanova, he may well have thought it to his interest to effect one of those combinazioni *dear to the heart of his countrymen, whereby the Venetian became partner in the scheme. At any rate, it is an established fact that Casanova was officially appointed one of the directors or receivers of the royal lottery. According to the* Memoirs *he was granted a salary of four thousand francs a year and allotted six receiving offices, five of which he promptly sold for two thousand francs each. With this sum as capital, he furnished his remaining office in the Rue St. Denis very elegantly and announced that every winning ticket bearing his signature would be paid within twenty-four hours at his office. As officially the lottery was not obliged to pay out before the end of a week after the drawing, Casanova's office was besieged by clients.*

The first drawing took place on April 18th, 1758, and proved a huge success, several of the big prizes falling on Paris. According to Casanova, the general receipts were two million francs, of which six hundred thousand went to the state and twenty thousand into his own pocket. There were four more drawings that year, and ten the following. One of the means for popularising the lottery is worthy of Casanova and may be of his invention. Each of the ninety numbers employed in the lotto *was given the name of a deserving young girl, with a bonus of two hundred francs for her if the number was among the five drawn.*

In a few months Casanova was at the top of the ladder, and Paris was at his feet:

In all the great houses I went to, and at the theatres, as soon as I was seen, everybody gave me money, asking me to lay it out as I liked and to send them the tickets, as, so far, the lottery was strange to most people. I thus got into the way of carrying about me tickets of all sorts, or rather of all prices, which I gave to people to choose from, going home in the evening with my pockets full of gold. This was an immense advantage to me, a kind of privilege which I enjoyed to the exclusion of the other receivers who were not in society, and did not drive a carriage like myself — no small point in one's favour, in a large town, where men are judged by the state they keep. I found I was thus able to go into any society, and to get credit anywhere.

I had hardly been a month in Paris when my brother Francis, with whom I had parted in 1752, arrived from Dresden with Madame Silvestre. He had been at Dresden for four years, taken up with the pursuit of his art, having copied all the battle-pieces in the Elector's Gallery. We were both of us glad to meet once more, but on my offering to see what my great friends could do for him with the Academicians, he replied with all an artist's pride that he was much obliged to me, but would rather not have any other patrons than his talents. "The French," said he, "have rejected me once, and I am far from bearing them ill-will on that account, for I would reject myself now if I were what I was then; but with their love of genius I reckon on a better reception this time."

His confidence pleased me, and I complimented him upon it, for I have always been of the opinion that true merit begins by doing justice to itself.

Francis painted a fine picture, which, on being exhibited at the Louvre, was received with applause. The Academy bought the picture for twelve thousand francs, my brother became famous, and in twenty-six years he made almost a million of money; but in spite of that, foolish expenditure, his luxurious style of living, and two bad marriages, were the ruin of him.

Although the great political revolution was still three decades off, Paris was already — had been for some time, in fact — in the throes of a social upheaval, which, though discernible for some time to the attentive observer, had only come to a head after the death of the Grand Monarch. All of a sudden the immutable strata of French society slid out of place, crumbled, collapsed, and inter-mingled, all except the hardest outer crust, on which the red heels strutted and pirouetted as if nothing were going on below the sur-face.

The first tangible result of this disruption and fermentation within was the formation of a Fourth Estate between the three officially recognised, a dangerous swampy region which had risen from the depth and was now working its way upwards. For the present it was wedged above the great middle stratum of French bourgeoisie, whose vigorous fibre had been sapped and drained too deeply by the blood-letting of the famous Revocation of 1685 and was taking on some sort of consistency, like the abscess hardening under the tooth. When finally, a hundred years later, it was officially recognised and

[6]

classified, it had already assumed such formidable dimensions that, socially speaking, it appeared a hemisphere and was so designated. Into this half-world, this demi-monde, in formation, Casanova plunges and splashes with delight. He is now in his proper element. Hobnobbing with every class of society, he is really at home, en famille, chez soi, with Silvia Baletti and her associates, the Italian Comedians. His gratitude and affection for Silvia, one of the greatest actresses of her day, who from the first had helped and be-mothered him, was so profound that he formally promised to marry her daughter, Manon Baletti. The story of Manon Baletti, the only official fiancée Casanova ever had, is not in the Memoirs, where her name is only mentioned on and off and the betrothal alluded to as a fait accompli, but it is in her letters.[1] The story is a pathetic one, for Manon's love, admiration, and confidence in her Giacomo are boundless. She is well educated, a good musician, a charming letter-writer, and, to judge by her portrait, unusually pretty. But the trouble is that she loves too well and makes no concealment of the fact. When finally, after a long period of waiting for her fiancé to redeem his word, seeing it is hopeless to wait any longer, she breaks off the engagement, Casanova is seized with rage and remorse.

His outburst at the time is very characteristic. It is true he has given Manon every provocation, never denying himself a fancy. At the moment he is philandering with Esther, or asserts he is, and is even contemplating marriage, he says. But the fact that his betrothed, the woman who is his by right of heritage and family agreement, his promessa, in fact, has given him the slip is a bitter blow. For in the recesses of that curious heart of his there lingers, almost unconsciously, the Latin sense of domesticity, the vision of the ultimate haven in which to cast anchor, the mirage of a hearth and family. Manon's "betrayal," as he calls it, is a rude awakening to the fact that socially he has become an outcast, even among his own kind. Hence his fury and resentment.

For the moment, however, he is still in the heyday of his social triumphs. Foremost among these must be counted his conquest of a

---

[1] *See Aldo Rava:* Lettere di donne a Giacomo Casanova *(Milan, 1912). A police note of 1753 suggests that during his first visit to Paris, Silvia was more than kind to her promising compatriot:* "Mademoiselle Silvia vit avec Casanova, italien, qu'on dit fils d'une comédienne. C'est elle qui l'entretient" *(quoted by Samaran).*

somewhat ancient, but socially and intellectually distinguished person, the Marquise d'Urfé, a great lady and former friend of the Regent. Having in her old age become immersed in occult sciences, her salon had become the rendezvous of all the famous quacks and charlatans, who in this "Age of Reason" flourished exceedingly. The most eminent of these, the celebrated Count of St. Germain, a forerunner of Cagliostro's, who was believed to have discovered the Elixir of Life, became from the outset Casanova's bête noire. The hatred with which this mysterious personage inspires him indicates something more than mere professional jealousy. It rather suggests that it was St. Germain, and not Casanova, who got the best of their encounters.

The introduction to Madame d'Urfé was the result of a boon-companionship between Casanova and her nephew, that amiable scapegrace the Comte de la Tour d'Auvergne, with whom he had fought a duel on one occasion and on whom he later accomplished a magic cure for sciatica. This is the story as he tells it:

Four or five days after, when I had almost forgotten the farce, I heard a carriage stopping at my door, and looking out of my window saw M. de la Tour d'Auvergne skipping nimbly out of the carriage.

"You were sure of success, then," said he, "as you did not come to see me the day after your astounding operation."

"Of course I was sure, but if I had not been too busy you would have seen me, for all that."

"May I take a bath?"

"No, don't bathe till you feel quite well."

"Very good. Everybody is in a state of astonishment at your feat, as I could not help telling the miracle to all my acquaintances. There are certainly some sceptics who laugh at me, but I let them talk."

"You should have kept your own counsel; you know what Paris is like. Everybody will be considering me as a master-quack."

"Not at all, not at all. I have come to ask a favour of you."

"What's that?"

"I have an aunt who enjoys a great reputation for her skill in the occult sciences, especially in alchemy. She is a woman of wit, very rich, and sole mistress of her fortune; in short, knowing her will do you no harm. She longs to see you, for she pretends to know you, and says that you are not what you seem. She has entreated me to take you to dine with her, and I hope you will accept the invitation. Her name is the Marchioness d'Urfé."

I did not know this lady, but the name of d'Urfé caught my attention directly, as I knew all about the famous Anne d'Urfé who flourished towards the end of the seventeenth century. The lady was the widow of her great-grandson, and on marrying into the family became a believer in the mystical doctrines of a science in which I was must interested, though I gave it little credit. I therefore replied that I should be glad to go, but on the condition that the party should not exceed the count, his aunt, and myself.

"She has twelve people every day to dinner, and you will find yourself in the company of the best society in Paris."

"My dear fellow, that's exactly what I don't want; for I hate to be thought a magician, which must have been the effect of the tales you have told."

"Oh, no! not at all; your character is well known, and you will find yourself in the society of people who have the greatest regard for you."

"Are you sure of that?"

"The Duchess de l'Oragnais told me that, four or five years ago, you were often to be seen at the Palais-Royal, and that you used to spend whole days with the Duchess d'Orleans; Madame de Bouflers, Madame de Blots, and Madame de Melfort have also talked to me about you. You are wrong not to keep up your old acquaintances. I know at least a hundred people of the first rank who are suffering from the same malady as that of which you cured me, and would give the half of their goods to be cured."

De la Tour d'Auvergne had reason on his side, but as I knew his wonderful cure had been due to a singular coincidence, I had no desire to expose myself to public ridicule. I therefore told him that I did not wish to become a public character, and that he must tell Madame d'Urfé that I would have the honour of calling on her in strict privacy only, and that she might tell me the day and hour on which I should kneel before her.

The same evening I had a letter from the count making an appointment at the Tuileries for the morrow; he was to meet me there, and take me to his aunt's to dinner. No one else was to be present.

[9]

The next day we met each other as had been arranged, and went to see Madame d'Urfé, who lived on the Quai des Theatins, on the same side as the Hôtel Bouillon.

Madame d'Urfé, a woman advanced in years, but still handsome, received me with all the courtly grace of the Court of the Regency. We spent an hour and a half in indifferent conversation, occupied in studying each other's character. Each was trying to get at the bottom of the other.

I had not much trouble in playing the part of the unenlightened, for such, in point of fact, was my state of mind, and Madame d'Urfé unconsciously betrayed the desire of showing her learning; this put me at my ease, for I felt sure I could make her pleased with me if I succeeded in making her pleased with herself.

At two o'clock the same dinner that was prepared every day for twelve was served for us three. Nothing worthy of note (so far as conversation went) was done at dinner, as we talked commonplace after the manner of people of fashion.

After the dessert Tour d'Auvergne left us to go and see the Prince de Turenne, who was in a high fever, and after he was gone Madame d'Urfé began to discuss alchemy and magic, and all the other branches of her beloved science, or rather infatuation. When we got on to the *magnum opus*, and I asked her if she knew the nature of the first matter, it was only her politeness which prevented her from laughing; but controlling herself, she replied graciously that she already possessed the philosopher's stone, and that she was acquainted with all the operations of the work. She then showed me a collection of books which had belonged to the great d'Urfé, and Renée of Savoy, his wife; but she had added to it manuscripts which had cost her more than a hundred thousand francs. Paracelsus was her favourite author, and according to her he was neither man, woman, nor hermaphrodite, and had the misfortune to poison himself with an overdose of his panacea, or universal medicine. She showed me a short manuscript in French, where the great work was clearly explained. She told me that she did not keep it under lock and key, because it was written in a cypher, the secret of which was known only to herself.

"You do not believe, then, in steganography."

"No, sir, and if you would like it, I will give you this which has been copied from the original."

"I accept it, madam, with all the more gratitude in that I know its worth."

From the library we went into the laboratory, at which I was truly astonished. She showed me matter that had been in the furnace for fifteen years, and was to be there for four or five years more. It was a powder of projection which was to transform instantaneously all metals into the finest gold. She showed me a pipe by which the coal descended to the furnace, keeping it always at the same heat. The lumps of coal were impelled by their own weight at proper intervals and in equal quantities, so that she was often three months without looking at the furnace, the temperature remaining the same the whole time. The cinders were removed by another pipe, most ingeniously contrived, which also answered the purpose of a ventilator.

The calcination of mercury was mere child's play to this wonderful woman. She showed me the calcined matter, and said that whenever I liked she would instruct me as to the process. I next saw the Tree of Diana of the famous Taliamed, whose pupil she was. His real name was Maillot, and according to Madame d'Urfé he had not, as was supposed, died at Marseilles, but was still alive; "and," added she, with a slight smile, "I often get letters from him. If the Regent of France," said she, "had listened to me he would be alive now. He was my first friend; he gave me the name of Egeria, and he married me to M. d'Urfé."

Casanova, who has primed himself with all the galimatias of the secret arts, is soon in high favour with the marquise, at whose table he is a constant guest.

The most enjoyable dinner I had was with Madame de Gergi, who came with the famous adventurer, known by the name of the Count de St. Germain. This individual, instead of eating, talked from the beginning of the meal to the end, and I followed his example in one respect as I did not eat, but listened to him with the greatest attention. It may safely be said that as a conversationalist he was unequalled.

St. Germain gave himself out for a marvel and always aimed at exciting amazement, which he often succeeded in doing. He was scholar, linguist, musician, and chemist, good-looking, and a perfect ladies' man. For a while he gave them paints and cosmetics; he flattered them, not that he would make them young again (which he modestly confessed was beyond him), but that their beauty would be preserved by means of a wash which, he said, cost him a lot of money, but which he gave away freely.

He had contrived to gain the favour of Madame de Pompadour, who had spoken about him to the king, for whom he had made a laboratory, in which the monarch — a martyr to boredom — tried to find a little pleasure — or distraction, at all events, by making dyes. The king had given him a suite of rooms at Chambord, and a hundred thousand francs for the construction of a laboratory, and according to St. Germain the dyes discovered by the king would have a materially beneficial influence on the quality of French fabrics.

This extraordinary man, intended by nature to be the king of impostors and quacks, would say in an easy, assured manner that he was three hundred years old, that he knew the secret of the Universal Medicine, that he possessed a mastery over nature, that he could melt diamonds, professing himself capable of forming, out of ten or twelve small diamonds, one large one of the finest water without any loss of weight. All this, he said, was a mere trifle to him. Notwithstanding his boastings, his barefaced lies, and his manifold eccentricities, I cannot say I thought him offensive. In spite of my knowledge of what he was and in spite of my own feelings, I thought him an astonishing man, as he was always astonishing me. I shall have something more to say of this character further on.

When Madame d'Urfé had introduced me to all her friends, I told her that I would dine with her whenever she wished, but that with the exception of her relations and St. Germain, whose wild talk amused me, I should prefer her to invite no company. St. Germain often dined with the best society in the capital, but he never ate anything, saying that he was kept alive by mysterious food known only to himself. One soon got used to his eccentricities, but not to his wonderful flow of words, which made him the soul of whatever company he was in.

By this time I had fathomed all the depths of Madame d'Urfé's character. She firmly believed me to be an adept of the first order, making use of another name for purposes of my own; and five or six weeks later she was confirmed in this wild idea on her asking me if I had deciphered the manuscript which pretended to explain the *magnum opus*.

"Yes," said I, "I have deciphered it, and consequently read it, and I now beg to return it you with my word of honour that I have not made a copy; in fact, I found nothing in it that I did not know before."

"Without the key, you mean, but of course you could never find out that."

"Shall I tell you the key?"

"Pray do so."

I gave her the word, which belonged to no language that I know of, and the marchioness was quite thunderstruck.

"This is too amazing," said she; "I thought myself the sole possessor of that mysterious word — for I had never written it down, laying it up in my memory — and I am sure I have never told anyone of it."

I might have informed her that the calculation which enabled me to decipher the manuscript furnished me also with the key, but the whim took me to tell her that a spirit had revealed it to me. This foolish tale completed my mastery over this truly learned and sensible woman on everything but her hobby. This false confidence gave me an immense ascendancy over Madame d'Urfé, and I often abused my power over her. Now that I am no longer the victim of those illusions which pursued me throughout my life, I blush at the remembrance of my conduct, and the penance I impose on myself is to tell the whole truth, and to extenuate nothing in these Memoirs.

The wildest notion in the good marchioness's brain was a firm belief in the possibility of communication between mortals and elementary spirits. She would have given all her goods to attain such communication, and she had several times been deceived by impostors who made her believe that she attained her aim.

"I did not think," said she, sadly, "that your spirit would have been able to force mine to reveal my secrets."

"There was no need to force your spirit, madam, as mine knows all things of his own power."

"Does he know the inmost secrets of my soul?"

"Certainly, and if I ask him he is forced to disclose all to me."

"Can you ask him when you like?"

"Oh, yes! provided I have paper and ink. I can even ask him questions through you by telling you his name."

"And will you tell it me?"

"I can do what I say; and, to convince you, his name is Paralis. Ask him a simple question in writing, as you would ask a common mortal. Ask him, for instance, how I deciphered your manuscript, and you shall see I will compel him to answer you."

Trembling with joy, Madame d'Urfé put her question, expressed it in numbers, then, following my method, in pyramid shape; and I made her extract the answer, which she wrote down in letters. At first she only obtained consonants, but by a second process which supplied the vowels she received a clear and sufficient answer. Her every feature expressed astonishment, for she had drawn from the pyramid the word which was the key to her manuscript. I left her, carrying with me her heart, her soul, her mind, and all the common sense which she had left.

De la Tour d'Auvergne having been obliged to rejoin his regiment, which was in garrison in Brittany, the marchioness and and I dined together almost every day and people looked upon me as her husband, and despite the improbability of the supposition, this was the only way in which they could account for the long hours we spent together. Madame d'Urfé thought that I was rich and looked upon my position at the lottery as a mere device for preserving my incognito.

I was the possessor in her estimation, not only of the philosopher's stone, but also of the power of speaking with the whole host of elementary spirits; from which premises she drew the very logical deduction that I could turn the world upside down if I liked, and be the blessing or the plague of France; and she thought my object in remaining incognito was to guard myself from arrest and imprisonment; which according to her would be the inevitable result of the minister's discovering my real character. These wild notions were the fruit of the nocturnal revelations of her genius, that is, of the dreams of her disordered spirit, which seemed to her realities. She did not seem to think that if I was endowed as she supposed, no one would have been able to arrest me, in the first place because I should have had foreknowledge of the attempt, and in the second place because my power would have been too strong for all bolts and bars. All this was clear enough, but strong passion and prejudice cannot reason.

One day, in the course of conversation, she said, with the utmost seriousness, that her genius had advised her that not even I had power to give her speech with the spirits, since she was a woman, and the genii only communicated with men, whose nature is more perfect. Nevertheless, by a process which was well known to me, I might make her soul pass into the body of a male child born of the mystic connection between a mortal and an immortal, or, in other words, between an ordinary man and a woman of a divine nature.

If I had thought it possible to lead back Madame d'Urfé to the right use of her senses I would have made the attempt, but I felt sure that her disease was without remedy, and the only course before me seemed to abet her in her ravings and to profit by them.

If I had spoken out like an honest man and told her that her theories were nonsensical, she would not have believed me; she would have thought me jealous of her knowledge, and I should have lost her favour without any gain to her or to myself. I thus let things take their course, and to speak the truth I was flattered to see myself treated as one of the most profound brothers of the Rosy Cross, as the most powerful of men by so distinguished a lady, who was in high repute for her learning, who entertained and was related to the first families of France, and had an income of eighty thousand francs, a splendid estate, and several magnificent houses in Paris. I was quite sure that she would refuse me nothing, and though I had no definite plan of profiting by her wealth I experienced a certain pleasure at the thought that I could do so if I would.

In spite of her immense fortune and her belief in her ability to make gold, Madame d'Urfé was miserly in her habits, for she never spent more than thirty thousand francs in a year, and she invested her savings in the exchange, and in this way had nearly doubled them. A brother used to buy her in government securities at their lowest rate and sell at their rise, and in this manner, being able to wait for their rise and fall, she had amassed a considerable sum.

She had told me more than once that she would give all she possessed to become a man, and that she knew I could do this for her if I would. One day, as she was speaking to me on this subject in a tone of persuasion almost irresistible, I told her that I must confess I had the power to do what she wanted, but that

I could not make up my mind to perform the operation upon her as I should have to kill her first. I thought this would effectually check her wish to go any further, but what was my surprise to hear her say:

"I know that, and what is more I know the death I shall have to die; but for all that I am ready."

"What, then, is that death, madam?"

"It is by the same poison which killed Paracelsus."

"Do you think that Paracelsus obtained the hypostasis?"

"No, but I know the reason of his not doing so."

"What is the reason?"

"It is that he was neither man nor woman, and a composite nature is incapable of the hypostasis, to obtain which one must be either the one or the other."

"Very true, but do you know how to make the poison, and that the thing is impossible without the aid of a salamander?"

"That may or may not be! I beseech you to inquire of the oracle whether there be anyone in Paris in possession of this potion."

It was easy to see that she thought herself in possession of it, so I had no hesitation in extracting her name from the oracular pyramid. I pretended to be astonished at the answer, but she said, boastfully:

"You see that all we want is a male child born of an immortal. This, I am advised, will be provided by you; and I do not think you will be found wanting out of a foolish pity for this poor old body of mine."

At these words I rose and went to the window, where I stayed for more than a quarter of an hour reflecting on her infatuation. When I returned to the table where she was seated she scanned my features attentively, and said, with much emotion, "Can it be done, my dear friend? I see that you have been weeping."

I did not try to undeceive her, and, taking my sword and hat, I took leave of her sadly. Her carriage, which was always at my disposal, was at the door, and I drove to the Boulevards, where I walked till the evening, wondering all the while at the extraordinary fantasies of the marchioness.

My brother had been made a member of the Academy, on the exhibition of a battle-piece which had taken all the critics by storm. The picture was purchased by the Academy for five hundred louis.

He had fallen in love with Caroline, and would have married her but for a piece of infidelity on her part, which so enraged him that in a week after he married an Italian dancer. M. de Sanci, the ecclesiastical commissioner, gave the wedding party. He was fond of the girl, and out of gratitude to my brother for marrying her he got him numerous orders among his friends, which paved the way to the large fortune and high repute which my brother afterwards attained.

M. Corneman, the banker, who was at my brother's wedding, spoke to me at considerable length on the great dearth of money, and asked me to discuss the matter with the comptroller-general.

He told me that one might dispose of government securities to an association of brokers at Amsterdam, and take in exchange the securities of any other country whose credit was higher than that of France, and that these securities could easily be realised. I begged him to say no more about it, and promised to see what I could do.

The plan pleased me, and I turned it over all night; and the next day I went to the Palais Bourbon to discuss the question with M. de Bernis. He thought the whole idea an excellent one, and advised me to go to Holland with a letter from M. de Choiseul for M. d'Afri, the ambassador at The Hague. He thought that the first person I should consult was M. de Boulogne, with whom he warned me to appear as if I was sure of my ground.

"As you do not require money in advance," said he, "you will be able to get as many letters of recommendation as you like."

The same day I went to the comptroller-general, who approved of my plan, and told me that M. le Duc de Choiseul would be at the Invalides the next day, and that I should speak to him at once, and take a letter he would write for me.

"For my part," said he, "I will credit our ambassador with twenty millions, and if, contrary to my hopes, you do not succeed, the paper can be sent back to France."

I answered that there would be no question of the paper being returned, if they would be content with a fair price.

"The margin will be a small one; however, you will hear

about that from the ambassador, who will have full instructions."

I felt so flattered by this mission that I passed the night in thinking it over. The next day I went to the Invalides, and M. de Choiseul, so famous for taking decisive action, had no sooner read M. de Boulogne's letter and spoken a few words to me on the subject, than he got me to write a letter for M. d'Afri, which he signed, sealed, returned to me, and wished me a prosperous journey.

I immediately got a passport from M. de Berkenrode, and the same day took leave of Madame Baletti and all my friends except Madame d'Urfé, with whom I was to spend the whole of the next day. I gave my clerk at the lottery office full authority to sign all tickets.

The accounts of Casanova's experiences in Holland, where he negotiates financial transactions for the French government, sells shares for the Marquise d'Urfé, wins the boundless gratitude and admiration of a wealthy Dutch merchant by a marvellous prediction regarding a ship reported to be lost at sea, turns the head of his charming daughter Esther by initiating her into his cabalistic tricks, participates in secret peace negotiations between the representatives of England and France, ousts St. Germain, who has come on a similar mission and who is finally obliged to fly to England, ending with Casanova's return to France, where, thanks to his Dutch transactions, government securities are now booming on the market and ministers eager to embrace him, belong too obviously to the ben trovato category of Casanovian exploits to merit serious attention.

*The facts of the case, as they transpire from diplomatic and police archives, are that Casanova did, in fact, visit Holland on two occasions, having found it expedient to leave Paris for a while. On the second occasion he brought a letter of recommendation from Choiseul to the French minister at The Hague, M. d'Afri, who, however, having taken Casanova's measure on the occasion of a former meeting, refused to have anything to do with him and so informed his superior in Paris. As for the generous merchant, M. d'O ** of the Memoirs, his identity has been established as a certain Hope,[1] a*

[1] *The omission of the aspirate in Mr. Hope's name would be natural enough in conversation, as they presumably spoke in French. But if Casanova had known the gentleman so intimately, it is hardly likely that he would have misspelt his name, which he must often have seen written.*

*well-known merchant of Amsterdam, who, unfortunately for Casa-
nova, had no daughter.*

*As for the fortune he claims to have made in Holland on his
second visit and which he squandered so liberally in Switzerland,
there has unfortunately come to light documentary proof that Casanova's fortunes on reaching the territory of the Confederation were so
low that he was obliged to pawn his wardrobe.*

*Amidst this amiable fantasy, where all is rose-coloured (in wilful
contrast perhaps to the darkness of his actual experiences), there
occurs a passage which brings us, and him, back to the material
plane of facts — sombre facts, which seem to fill him with foreboding.
Having gone to the theatre with his imaginary Esther, who had there
introduced him to a namesake of his, another Casanova, and his
daughter, he — Giacomo Casanova — is suddenly confronted with
a vision of his past in the person of that Thérèse Imer, who had
been the cause of his losing the favours of Senator Malipiero, and
who on a later occasion in Venice had accorded him hers for a brief
moment. This is how it happened:*

After a fine symphony, a concerto for the violin, another for
the hautbois, the Italian singer whose repute was so great and
who was styled Madame Trenti made her appearance. What
was my surprise when I recognised in her Thérèse Imer, wife of
the dancer Pompeati, whose name the reader may remember.
I had made her acquaintance eighteen years ago, when the old
senator Malipiero had struck me because we were playing together. I had seen her again at Venice in 1753, and then our
pastime had been of a more serious nature. She had gone to
Bayreuth, where she had been the margrave's mistress. I had
promised to go and see her, but C ** C ** and my fair nun M **
M ** had left me neither the time nor the wish to do so. Soon
after I was put under The Leads, and then I had other things to
think about. I was sufficiently self-controlled not to show my
astonishment, and listened to an aria which she was singing,
with her exquisite voice, beginning "*Eccoti giunta alfin, donna
infelice,*" words which seemed made for the case.

The applause seemed as if it would never come to an end.
Esther told me that it was not known who she was, but that she
was said to be a woman with a history, and to be very badly off.
"She goes from one town to another, singing at all the public
concerts, and all she receives is what those present choose to give
her on a plate which she takes round."

"Does she find that pay?"

"I should suspect not, as everyone has paid already at coming in. She cannot get more than thirty or forty florins. The day after to-morrow she will go to The Hague, then to Rotterdam, then back here again. She has been performing for six months, and she is always well received."

"Has she a lover?"

"She is said to have lovers in every town, but instead of enriching her they make her poorer. She always wears black, not only because she is a widow, but also on account of a great grief she is reported to have gone through. She will soon be coming round." I took out my purse, and counted out twelve ducats, which I wrapped in paper; my heart beating all the while in a ridiculous manner, for I had really nothing to be excited about.

When Thérèse was going along the seats in front of me, I glanced at her for an instant, and I saw that she looked surprised. I turned my head to speak to Esther, and when she was directly in front of me I put my little packet on the plate without looking at her, and she passed on. A little girl, four or five years old, followed her, and when she got to the end of the bench she came back to kiss my hand. I could not help recognising in her a facsimile of myself, but I concealed my emotion. The child stood still, and gazed at me fixedly, to my no small confusion. "Would you like some sweets, my dear?" said I, giving her my box, which I should have been glad to turn into gold. The little girl took it smilingly, made me a curtsy, and went on.

"Does it strike you, M. Casanova," said Esther, with a laugh, "that you and that little girl are as like each other as two peas?"

"Yes, indeed," added Mdlle. Casanova, "there is a striking likeness."

"These resemblances are often the work of chance."

"Just so," said Esther, with a wicked smile, "but you admit a likeness, don't you?"

"I confess I was struck with it, though of course I cannot judge so well as you."

After the concert M. d'O** arrived, and giving back his daughter to his care I betook myself to my lodging. I was just sitting down to a dish of oysters, before going to bed, when Thérèse made her appearance, holding her child by the hand. Although I had not expected her to visit me that evening, I was nevertheless not much surprised to see her. I, of course, rose to greet her, when all at once she fell fainting on the sofa, though whether the fainting fit was real or assumed I cannot say. Thinking that she might be really ill I played my part properly, and brought her to herself by sprinkling her with cold water and putting my vinaigrette to her nose. As soon as she came to herself she began to gaze at me without saying a word. At last, tired of her silence, I asked her if she would take any supper; and on her replying in the affirmative, I rang the bell and ordered a good supper for three, which kept us at the table till seven o'clock in the morning, talking over our various fortunes and misfortunes. She was already acquainted with most of my recent adventures, but I knew nothing at all about hers, and she entertained me with a recital of them for five or six hours.

Sophie, the little girl, slept in my bed till day, and her mother, keeping the best of her tale to the last, told me that she was my daughter, and showed me her baptismal certificate. The birth of the child fell in with the period at which I had been intimate with Thérèse, and her perfect likeness to myself left no room for doubt. I therefore raised no objections, but told the mother that I was persuaded of my paternity, and that, being in a position to give the child a good education, I was ready to be a father to her.

"She is too precious a treasure in my sight; if we were separated I should die."

"You are wrong; for if I took charge of the little girl I should see that she was well provided for."

"I have a son of twelve to whom I cannot give a proper education; take charge of him instead of Sophie."

"Where is he?"

"He is boarding, or rather in pawn, at Rotterdam."

"What do you mean by in pawn?"

"I mean that he will not be returned to me until I pay the person who has got him all my debts."

"How much do you owe?"

"Eighty florins. You have already given me sixty-two, give me four ducats more; you can then take my son, and I shall be the happiest of mothers. I will send my son to you at The Hague next week, as I think you will be there."

"Yes, my dear Thérèse; and instead of four ducats, here are twenty."

"We shall see each other again at The Hague."

She was grateful to excess, but I only felt pity for her and a sort of friendly interest, and kept quite cool, despite the ardour of her embraces. Seeing that her trouble was of no avail, she sighed, shed some tears, and, taking her daughter, she bid me adieu, promising once more to send me her son.

Thérèse was two years older than I. She was still pretty, and even handsome, but her charms no longer retained their first beauty, and my passion for her having been a merely physical one, it was no wonder that she had no longer any attraction for me. Her adventures during the six years in which I had lost her would certainly interest my readers, and form a pleasing episode in my book, and I would tell the tale if it were a true one; but not being a romance writer, I am anxious that this work shall contain the truth and nothing but the truth. Convicted by her amorous and jealous margrave of infidelity, she had been sent about her business. She was separated from her husband, Pompeati, had followed a new lover to Brussels, and there had caught the fancy of Prince Charles de Lorraine, who had obtained her the direction of all the theatres in the Austrian Low Countries. She had then undertaken this vast responsibility, entailing heavy expenditure, till at last, after selling all her diamonds and lace, she had fled to Holland to avoid arrest. Her husband killed himself at Vienna in a paroxysm caused by internal pain — he had cut open his stomach with a razor, and died tearing at his entrails.

Before leaving The Hague, he goes to call on Thérèse, who is now in that city:

It was not long before I saw that I should do well to get back to Amsterdam, but I did not care to break my word to Thérèse, whom I had promised to meet at The Hague. I received a letter from her while I was at the play, and the servant who brought it told me he was waiting to conduct me to her. I sent my own servant home, and set out on my quest.

My guide made me climb to the fourth floor of a somewhat wretched house, and there I found this strange woman in a small room attended by her son and daughter. The table stood in the midst of the room, and was covered with a black cloth, and the two candles standing upon it made it look like some sort of sepulchral altar. The Hague was a Court town. I was richly dressed;

my elaborate attire made the saddest possible contrast with the gloom of my surroundings. Thérèse, dressed in black and seated between her children at that black table, reminded me of Medea. To see these two fair young creatures vowed to a lot of misery and disgrace was a sad and touching sight. I took the boy between my arms, and pressing him to my breast called him my son. His mother told him to look upon me as his father from henceforth. The lad recognised me; he remembered, much to my delight, seeing me in the May of 1753, in Venice, at Madame Manzoni's. He was slight but strong; his limbs were well proportioned, and his features intellectual. He was thirteen years old.

His sister sat perfectly still, apparently waiting for her turn to come. I took her on my knee, and as I embraced her, Nature herself seemed to tell me that she was my daughter. She took my kisses in silence, but it was easy to see that she thought herself preferred to her brother, and was charmed with the idea. All her clothing was a slight frock, and I was able to feel every limb and to kiss her pretty little body all over, delighted that so sweet a being owed her existence to me.

"Mamma, dear," said she, "is not this fine gentleman the same we saw at Amsterdam, and who was taken for my papa because I am like him? But that cannot be, for my papa is dead."

"So he is, sweetheart; but I may be your dear friend, mayn't I? Would you like to have me for a friend?"

"Yes, yes!" she cried, and throwing her arms about my neck gave me a thousand kisses, which I returned with delight.

After we had talked and laughed together we sat down at table, and the heroine Thérèse gave me a delicate supper accompanied by exquisite wines. "I have never given the margrave better fare," said she, "at those nice little suppers we used to take together."

Wishing to probe the disposition of her son, whom I had engaged to take away with me, I addressed several remarks to him, and soon discovered that he was of a false and deceitful nature, always on his guard, taking care of what he said, and consequently speaking only from his head and not from his heart. Every word was delivered with a quiet politeness which, no doubt, was intended to please me.

I told him that this sort of thing was all very well on occasion; but that there were times when a man's happiness depended on his freedom from constraint; then and only then was his amiability, if he had any, displayed. His mother, thinking to praise him, told me that reserve was his chief characteristic, that she had trained him to keep his counsel at all times and places, and that she was thus used to his being reserved with her as with everyone else.

"All I can say is," said I, "your system is an abominable one. You may have strangled in their infancy all the finer qualities with which nature has endowed your son, and have fairly set him on the way to become a monster instead of an angel. I don't see how the most devoted father can possibly have any affection for a son who keeps all his emotions under lock and key."

This outburst, which proceeded from the tenderness I would fain have felt for the boy, seemed to strike his mother dumb.

"Tell me, my dear, if you feel yourself capable of showing me that confidence which a father has a right to expect of a good son, and if you can promise to be perfectly open and unreserved towards me?"

"I promise that I will die rather than tell you a falsehood."

"That's just like him," said the mother, "I have succeeded in inspiring him with the utmost horror of untruthfulness."

"That's all very well, my dear madam, but you might have pursued a still better course, and one which would have been still more conducive to his happiness."

"What is that?"

"I will tell you. It was not necessary to make him detest a lie; you should have rather endeavoured to make him a lover of the truth by displaying it to him in all its native beauty. This is the only way to make him lovable, and love is the sole bestower of happiness in this world."

"But isn't it the same thing not to lie and to tell the truth?" said the boy, with a smile which charmed his mother and displeased me.

"Certainly not; there is a great difference — for to avoid lying you have only to hold your tongue; and do you think that comes to the same thing as speaking the truth? You must open your mind to me, my son, and tell me all your thoughts, even if you blush in the recital. I will teach you how to blush, and soon you will have nothing to fear in laying open all your thoughts and deeds. When we know each other a little longer we shall see how we agree together. You must understand that I cannot look upon you as my son until I see cause to love you, and I cannot have you call me father till you treat me as the best friend you have. You may be quite sure that I shall find a way to discover your thoughts, however cleverly you try to hide them. If I find you deceitful and suspicious I shall certainly entertain no regard for you. As soon as I have finished my business at Amsterdam we will set out for Paris. I am leaving The Hague to-morrow, and on my return I hope to find you instructed by your mother in a system of morality more consonant with my views, and more likely to lead to your happiness."

On glancing at my little daughter, who had been listening to me with the greatest attention, I saw that her eyes were swimming with tears, which she could hardly retain.

"Why are you crying?" said the mother; "it is silly to cry." And with that the child ran to her mother and threw her arms round her neck.

"Would you like to come to Paris, too?" said I to her.

"Oh, yes! But mamma must come too, as she would die without me."

"What would you do if I told you to go?" said the mother.

"I would obey you, mamma, but how could I exist away from you?"

Thereupon my little daughter pretended to cry. I say pretended, as it was quite evident that the child did not mean what she said, and I am sure that her mother knew it as well as I.

It was really a melancholy thing to see the effects of a bad education on this young child, to whom nature had given intelligence and feeling. I took the mother on one side, and said that if she had intended to make actors of her children she had succeeded to admiration; but if she wished them to become useful members of society her system had failed lamentably, as they were in a fair way to become monsters of deceit. I continued making her the most pointed remonstrances until, in spite of her efforts to control herself, she burst into tears. However, she soon recovered her composure, and begged me to stay at The Hague a day longer, but I told her it was out of the question, and left the room. I came in again a few minutes after, and Sophie came up to me and said, in a loving little voice:

"If you are really my friend, you will give me some proof of your friendship."

"And what proof do you want, my dear?"

"I want you to come and sup with me to-morrow."

"I can't, Sophie dear, for I have just said no to your mother, and she would be offended if I granted you what I had refused her."

"Oh, no! she wouldn't; it was she who told me to ask you just now."

I naturally began to laugh, but on her mother calling the girl a little fool, and the brother adding that he had never committed such an indiscretion, the poor child began to tremble all over, and looked abashed. I reassured her as best I could, not caring whether what I said displeased her mother or not, and I endeavoured to instil into her principles of a very different nature to those in which she had been reared, while she listened with an eagerness which proved that her heart was still ready to learn the right way. Little by little her face cleared, and I saw that I had made an impression, and though I could not flatter myself that any good I might do her would be lasting in its effects as long as she remained under the bad influence of her mother, I promised to come and sup with her the next evening, "but on the condition," I said, "that you give me a plain meal, and one bottle of Chambertin only, for you are not too well off."

"I know that, but mamma says that you pay for everything."

This reply made me go off into a roar of laughter; and in spite of her vexation the mother was obliged to follow my example. The poor woman, hardened by the life she led, took the child's simplicity for stupidity, but I saw in her a rough diamond which only wanted polishing.

Thérèse told me that the wine did not cost her anything, as the son of the Rotterdam burgomaster furnished her with it, and that he would sup with us the next day if I would allow him to be present. I answered smilingly that I should be delighted to see him, and I went away after giving my daughter, of whom I felt fond, a tender embrace. I would have done anything to be entrusted with her, but I saw it would be no good trying to get possession of her, as the mother was evidently keeping her as a resource for her old age. This is a common way for adventuresses to look upon their daughters, and Thérèse was an adventuress in the widest acceptation of the term. I gave her twenty ducats to get clothes for my adopted son and Sophie, who, with spontaneous gratitude, and her eyes filled with tears, came and gave me a kiss. Joseph was going to kiss my hand, but I told him that it was degrading for one man to kiss another's hand, and that for the future he was to show his gratitude by embracing me as a son embraces his father.

Just as I was leaving, Thérèse took me to the closet where the two children were sleeping. I knew what she was thinking of; but all that was over long ago; I could think of no one but Esther.

The next day I found the burgomaster's son at my actress's house. He was a fine young fellow of twenty or twenty-one, but totally devoid of manner. He was Thérèse's lover, but he should have regulated his behaviour in my presence. Thérèse, seeing that he was posing as master of the field, and that his manners disgusted me, began to snub him, much to his displeasure, and after sneering at the poorness of the dishes, and praising the wine which he had supplied, he went out leaving us to finish our dessert by ourselves. I left myself at eleven, telling Thérèse that I should see her again before I went away. The Princesse de Galitzin, a Cantimir by birth, had asked me to dinner, and this made me lose another day.

Next day I heard from Madame d'Urfé, who enclosed a bill of exchange on Boaz for twelve thousand francs. She said that she had bought her shares for sixty thousand, that she did not wish to make anything of them, and that she hoped I would accept the overplus as my broker's fee. She worded her offer with too much courtesy for me to refuse it. The remainder of the letter was devoted to the wildest fancies. She said that her genius had revealed to her that I should bring back to Paris a boy born of the Mystical Marriage, and she hoped I would take pity on her. It was a strange coincidence, and seemed likely to attach the woman still more closely to her visionary theories. I laughed when I thought how she would be impressed by Thérèse's son, who was certainly not born of the Mystical Marriage.

[27]

In Amsterdam another phantom of his past — a very grim one this time — rises up before him. During that first period in Venice, the days of Marton and Nanette, while stopping in a country-house at Paséan, he played at love-making with a pretty child, the daughter of an honest couple living on the estate. Charmed and touched by her childish ways, he had, for once, refrained from taking advantage of her innocence — a fact he never ceased regretting, as he believed, perhaps sincerely, that he would have prevented the disaster which befell her after their parting had she really become his mistress. As it was, he felt himself to blame for having lighted a spark which, unquenched, flared up on the first occasion and caused the girl's ruin. It was a lesson to remember, not to kiss and run away, and henceforth he took care to extinguish himself any incipient conflagrations for which he was responsible. It was a case of noblesse oblige. This is the story he tells:

As I was going home I passed a tea-garden, and seeing a good many people going in and coming out I went in curious to know how these places were managed in Holland. Great heavens! I found myself the witness of an orgy, the scene a sort of cellar, a perfect cesspool of vice and debauchery. The discordant noise of the two or three instruments which formed the orchestra struck gloom to the soul and added to the horrors of the cavern. The air was dense with the fumes of bad tobacco, and vapours reeking of beer and garlic issued from every mouth. The company consisted of sailors, men of the lowest class, and a number of vile women. The sailors and the dregs of the people thought this den a garden of delight, and considered its pleasures compensation for the toils of the sea and the miseries of daily labour. There was not a single woman there whose aspect had anything redeeming about it. I was looking at the repulsive sight in silence, when a great hulking fellow, whose appearance suggested the blacksmith, and his voice the blackguard, came up to me and asked me in bad Italian if I would like to dance. I answered in the negative, but before leaving me he pointed out a Venetian woman who, he said, would oblige me if I gave her some drink.

Wishing to discover if she was anyone I knew I looked at her attentively, and seemed to recollect her features, although I could not decide who she could be. Feeling rather curious on the subject I sat down next to her, and asked if she came from Venice, and if she had left that country some time ago.

"Nearly eighteen years," she replied.

I ordered a bottle of wine, and asked if she would take any; she said yes, and added, if I liked, she would oblige me.

"I haven't time," I said; and I gave the poor wretch the change I received from the waiter. She was full of gratitude, and would have embraced me if I had allowed her.

"Do you like being at Amsterdam better than Venice?" I asked.

"Alas, no! for if I were in my own country I should not be following this dreadful trade."

"How old were you when you left Venice?"

"I was only fourteen and lived happily with my father and mother, who now may have died of grief."

"Who seduced you?"

"A rascally footman."

"In what part of Venice did you live?"

"I did not live in Venice, but at Friuli, not far off."

Friuli . . . eighteen years ago . . . a footman . . . I felt moved, and looking at the wretched woman more closely I soon recognized in her Lucie of Paséan. I cannot describe my sorrow, which I concealed as best I could, and tried hard to keep up my indifferent air. A life of debauchery rather than the flight of time had tarnished her beauty, and ruined the once exquisite outlines of her form. Lucie, that innocent and pretty maiden, grown ugly, vile, a common prostitute! It was a dreadful thought. She drank like a sailor, without looking at me, and without caring who I was. I took a few ducats from my purse, and slipped them into her hand, and without waiting for her to find out how much I had given her I left that horrible den.

I went to bed full of saddening thoughts. Not even under The Leads did I pass so wretched a day. I thought I must have risen under some unhappy star! I loathed myself. With regard to Lucie I felt the sting of remorse, but at the thought of M. d'O ** I hated myself. I considered that I should cause him a loss of three or four hundred thousand florins; and the thought was a bitter drop in the cup of my affection for Esther. I fancied she, as well as her father, would become my implacable foe; and love that is not returned is no love at all.

I spent a dreadful night. Lucie, Esther, her father, their hatred of me, and my hatred of myself, were the groundwork of my dreams. I saw Esther and her father, if not ruined, at all

[29]

events impoverished by my fault, and Lucie only thirty-two years old, and already deep in the abyss of vice, with an infinite prospect of misery and shame before her. The dawn was welcome indeed, for with its appearance a calm came to my spirit; it is the darkness which is terrible to a heart full of remorse.

As for the mythical Esther, it is time, he feels, to bid farewell to this airy vision, certain as he is of being able to invoke her again whenever it suits the purpose of his narrative:

The sad time of parting at last drew near, amid many regrets and tears from all of us. Esther gave me the two thousand pounds I had won so easily, and her father at my request gave me bills of exchange to the amount of a hundred thousand florins, with a note of two hundred thousand florins authorising me to draw upon him till the whole sum was exhausted. Just as I was going, Esther gave me fifty shirts and fifty handkerchiefs of the finest quality.

It was not my love for Manon Baletti, but a foolish vanity and a desire to cut a figure in the luxurious city of Paris, which made me leave Holland. But such was the disposition that Mother Nature had given me that fifteen months under The Leads had not been enough to cure this mental malady of mine. But when I reflect upon after events of my life I am not astonished that The Leads proved ineffectual, for the numberless vicissitudes which I have gone through since have not cured me — my disorder, indeed, being of the incurable kind. There is no such thing as destiny. We ourselves shape our lives, notwithstanding that saying of the Stoics, *Volentem ducit, nolentem trahit.*

After promising Esther to return before the end of the year, I set out with a clerk of the company who had brought the French securities, and I reached The Hague, where Boaz received me with a mingled air of wonder and admiration. He told me that I had worked a miracle; "but," he added, "to succeed thus you must have persuaded them that peace was on the point of being concluded."

"By no means," I answered; "so far from my persuading them, they are of the opposite opinion; but all the same I may tell you that peace is really imminent."

"If you like to give me that assurance in writing," said he, "I will make you a present of fifty thousand florins' worth of diamonds."

"Well," I answered, "the French ambassador is of the same opinion as myself; but I don't think the certainty is sufficiently great as yet for you to risk your diamonds upon it."

Next day I finished my business with the ambassador, and the clerk returned to Amsterdam.

I went to supper at Thérèse's, and found her children very well dressed. I told her to go on to Rotterdam the next day and wait for me there with her son, as I had no wish to give scandal at The Hague.

At Rotterdam Thérèse told me that she knew I had won half a million at Amsterdam, and that her fortune would be made if she could leave Holland for London. She had instructed Sophie to tell me that my good luck was the effect of the prayers she had addressed to Heaven on my behalf. I saw where the land lay, and I enjoyed a good laugh at the mother's craft, and the child's piety, and gave her a hundred ducats, telling her that she should have another hundred when she wrote to me from London. It was very evident that she thought the sum a very moderate one, but I would not give her any more. She waited for the moment when I was getting into my carriage to beg me to give her another hundred ducats, and I said, in a low tone, that she should have a thousand if she would give me her daughter. She thought it over for a minute, and then said that she could not part with her.

"I know very well why," I answered; and drawing a watch from my fob I gave it to Sophie, embraced her, and went on my way. I arrived at Paris on February 10th, and took sumptuous apartments near the Rue Montorgueil.

CHAPTER XI

The Fall and Rise of Giustina Wynne

HAVING left the lunar regions of Holland and Esther for the terra firma of Paris, where the presence of M. de Sartines, King Louis's very efficient lieutenant of police, and his carefully kept records seem to exercise a restraining influence on the memorialist's imagination, let us follow him once more. The romantic story he is going to tell us is as near the truth as anything to be found in the Memoirs:

During my journey from The Hague to Paris, short as it was, I had plenty of opportunities for seeing that the mental qualities of my adopted son were by no means equal to his physical ones.

As I have said, the chief point which his mother had impressed on him was reserve, which she had instilled into him out of regard for her own interests. My readers will understand what I mean, but the child, in following his mother's instructions, had gone beyond the bounds of moderation; he possessed reserve, it is true, but he was also full of dissimulation, suspicion, and hypocrisy — a fine trio of deceit in one who was still a boy. He not only concealed what he knew, but he pretended to know that which he did not. His idea of the one quality necessary to success in life was an impenetrable reserve, and to obtain this he had accustomed himself to silence the dictates of his heart, and to say no word that had not been carefully weighed. Giving other people wrong impressions passed with him for discretion, and his soul being incapable of a generous thought, he seemed likely to pass through life without knowing what friendship meant.

Knowing that Madame d'Urfé counted on the boy for the accomplishment of her absurd hypostasis, and that the more mystery I made of his birth the more extravagant would be her fancies about it, I told the lad that if I introduced him to a lady who questioned him by himself about his birth, he was to be perfectly open with her.

On my arrival at Paris my first visit was to my patron, whom I found in grand company, amongst whom I recognised the Venetian ambassador, who pretended not to know me.

"How long have you been in Paris?" said the minister, taking me by the hand.

"I have only just stepped out of my chaise."

"Then go to Versailles. You will find the Duc de Choiseul and the comptroller-general there. You have been wonderfully successful, go and get your meed of praise and come and see me afterwards. Tell the duke that Voltaire's appointment to be a gentleman-in-ordinary to the king is ready."

I was not going to start for Versailles at mid-day, but ministers in Paris are always talking in this style, as if Versailles were at the end of the street. Instead of going there, I went to see Madame d'Urfé.

She received me with the words that her genius had informed her that I should come to-day, and that she was delighted with the fulfilment of the prophecy.

"Corneman tells me that you have been doing wonders in Holland; but I see more in the matter than he does, as I am quite certain that you have taken over the twenty millions yourself. The funds have risen, and a hundred millions at least will be in circulation in the course of the next week. You must not be offended at my shabby present, for, of course, twelve thousand francs are nothing to you. You must look upon them as a little token of friendship.

"I am going to tell my servants to close all the doors, for I am too glad to see you not to want to have you all to myself."

A profound bow was the only reply I made to this flattering speech, and I saw her tremble with joy when I told her that I had brought a lad of twelve with me, whom I intended to place in the best school I could find that he might have a good education.

"I will send him myself to Viar, where my nephews are. What is his name? Where is he? I know well what this boy is, I long to see him. Why did you not alight from your journey at my house?"

Her questions and replies followed one another in rapid succession. I should have found it impossible to get in a word edgeways, even if I had wanted to, but I was very glad to let her expend her enthusiasm, and took good care not to interrupt her. On the first opportunity, I told her that I should have the pleasure of presenting the young gentleman to her the day after to-morrow, as on the morrow I had an engagement at Versailles.

"Does the dear lad speak French? While I am arranging for his going to school you must really let him come and live with me."

"We will discuss that question on the day after to-morrow, madam."

"Oh, how I wish the day after to-morrow was here!"

On leaving Madame d'Urfé I went to my lottery office and found everything in perfect order. I then went to the Italian play, and found Silvia and her daughter in the dressing-room.

"My dear friend," said she when she saw me, "I know that you have achieved a wonderful success in Holland, and I congratulate you."

I gave her an agreeable surprise by saying that I had been working for her daughter, and Marion herself blushed, and lowered her eyes in a very suggestive manner. "I will be with you at supper," I added, "and then we can talk at our ease." On leaving them I went to the amphitheatre, and what was my surprise to see in one of the first boxes Madame X ** C ** V **, with all her family. My readers will be glad to hear their history.

Madame X ** C ** V **, by birth a Greek, was the widow of an Englishman, by whom she had six children, four of whom were girls. On his death-bed he became a Catholic out of deference to the tears of his wife; but as his children could not inherit his forty thousand pounds invested in England without conforming to the Church of England, the family returned to London, where the widow complied with all the obligations of the law of England. What will people not do when their interests are at stake! though in a case like this there is no need to blame a person for yielding to prejudices which had the sanction of the law.

It was now the beginning of the year 1758, and five years before, when I was at Padua, I fell in love with the eldest daughter, but a few months after, when we were at Venice, Madame X ** C ** V ** thought good to exclude me from her family circle. The insult which the mother put upon me was softened by the daughter, who wrote me a charming letter, which I love to read even now. I may as well confess that my grief was the easier to bear as my time was taken up by my fair nun, M ** M **, and my dear C ** C **. Nevertheless, Mdlle. X ** C ** V **, though only fifteen, was of a perfect beauty, and was all the more charming in that to her physical advantages she joined those of a cultured mind.

Count Algarotti, the King of Prussia's chamberlain, gave her lessons, and several young nobles were among her suitors, her preference apparently being given to the heir of the family of Memmo de St. Marcuola. He died a year afterwards, while he was procurator.

My surprise at seeing this family at such a time and place may be imagined. Mdlle. X ** C ** V ** saw me directly, and pointed me out to her mother, who made a sign to me with her fan to come to their box.

[34]

She received me in the friendliest manner possible, telling me that we were not at Venice now, and that she hoped I would often come and see them at the Hôtel de Bretagne, in the Rue St. André des Arts. I told them that I did not wish to recall any events which might have happened at Venice, and her daughter having joined her entreaties to those of her mother, I promised to accept their invitation.

MdIle. X ** C ** V ** struck me as prettier than ever; and my love, after sleeping for five years, awoke to fresh strength and vigour. They told me that they were going to pass six months at Paris before returning to Venice. In return I informed them that I intended making Paris my home, that I had just left Holland, that I was going to Versailles the next day, so that I could not pay my respects to them till the day after. I also begged them to accept my services, in a manner which let them know I was a person of some importance.

MdIle. X ** C ** V ** said that she was aware that the results of my Dutch mission should render me dear to France, that she had always lived in hopes of seeing me once more, that my famous flight from The Leads had delighted them; "for," she added, "we have always been fond of you."

"I fancy your mother has kept her fondness for me very much to herself," I whispered to her.

"We won't say anything about that," said she in the same tone. "We learnt all the circumstances of your wonderful flight from a letter of sixteen pages you wrote to M. Memmo. We trembled with joy and shuddered with fear as we read it."

"How did you know I have been in Holland?"

"M. de la Popelinière told us about it yesterday."

M. de la Popelinière, the *fermier-général,* whom I had known seven years ago at Passi, came into the box just as his name was spoken. After complimenting me he said that if I could carry through the same operation for the India Company my fortune would be made.

"My advice to you is," he said, "to get yourself naturalised before it becomes generally known that you have made half a million of money."

"Half a million! I only wish I had!"

"You must have made that at the lowest calculation."

"On the contrary, I give you my assurance that if my claim

for brokerage is not allowed, the transaction will prove absolutely ruinous to me."

"Ah! no doubt you are right to take that tone. Meanwhile, everyone wants to make your acquaintance, for France is deeply indebted to you. You have caused the funds to recover in a very marked degree."

After the play was over I went to Silvia's, where I was received as if I had been the favourite child of the family; but on the other hand I gave them certain proofs that I wished to be regarded in that light. I was impressed with the idea that to their unshaken friendship I owed all my good luck, and I made the father, mother, the daughter, and the two sons, receive the presents I had got for them. The best was for the mother, who handed it on to her daughter. It was a pair of diamond earrings of great beauty, for which I had given fifteen thousand francs. Three days after, I sent her a box containing fine linen from Holland, and choice Mechlin and Alençon lace. Mario, who liked smoking, got a gold pipe; the father a choice gold and enamelled snuff-box, and I gave a repeater to the younger son, of whom I was very fond. I shall have occasion later on to speak of this lad, whose natural qualities were far superior to his position in life. But, you will ask, was I rich enough to make such presents? No, I was not, and I knew it perfectly well; but I gave these presents because I was afraid of not being able to do so if I waited.

I set out for Versailles at daybreak, and M. de Choiseul received me as before; his hair was being dressed, but for a moment he laid down his pen, which showed that I had become a person of greater importance in his eyes. After a slight but grateful compliment, he told me that if I thought myself capable of negotiating a loan of a hundred millions to bear interest at four per cent., he would do all in his power to help me. My answer was that I would think it over when I heard how much I was to have for what I had done already.

"But everybody says that you have made two hundred thousand florins by it."

"That would not be so bad; half a million of francs would be a fair foundation on which to build a fortune; but I can assure your excellence that there is not a word of truth in the report. I defy anyone to prove it; and till some substantial proof is offered, I think I can lay claim to brokerage."

"True, true. Go to the comptroller-general and state your views to him."

M. de Boulogne stopped the occupation on which he was engaged to give me a most friendly greeting, but when I said that he owed me a hundred thousand florins he smiled sardonically.

"I happen to know," he said, "that you have bills of exchange to the amount of a hundred thousand crowns payable to yourself."

"Certainly, but that money has no connection with my mission, as I can prove to you by referring to M. d'Afri. I have in my head an infallible project for increasing the revenue by twenty millions, in a manner which will cause no irritation."

"You don't say so! Communicate your plan, and I promise to get you a pension of a hundred thousand francs, and letters of nobility as well, if you like to become a Frenchman."

"I will think it over."

On leaving M. de Boulogne I went to the palace, where a ballet was going on before the Marquise de Pompadour.

She bowed to me as soon as she saw me, and on my approaching her she told me that I was an able financier, and that the "gentlemen below" could not appreciate my merits. She had not forgotten what I had said to her eight years before in the theatre at Fontainebleau. I replied that all good gifts were from above, whither, with her help, I hoped to attain.

On my return to Paris I went to the Hôtel Bourbon to inform my patron of the result of my journey. His advice to me was to continue to serve the government well, as its good fortune would come to be mine. On my telling him of my meeting with the X ** C ** V **'s, he said that M. de la Popelinière was going to marry the elder daughter.

I went to the Hôtel de Bretagne to pay my first call on Madame X ** C ** V **. The lady, though she was not over-fond of me, received me with great politeness. I possibly cut a better figure in her eyes when rich, and at Paris, than when we were in Venice. We all know that diamonds have the strange power of fascination, and that they form an excellent substitute for virtue!

Madame X ** C ** V ** had with her an old Greek named Zandiri, brother to M. de Bragadin's major-domo, who was just dead. I uttered some expressions of sympathy, and the boor did not take the trouble to answer me, but I was avenged for his foolish stiffness by the enthusiasm with which I was welcomed by everyone else. The eldest girl, her sisters, and the two sons almost overwhelmed me with friendliness. The eldest son was only fourteen and was a young fellow of charming manners, but evidently extremely independent, and sighed for the time when he would be able to devote himself to a career of profligacy, for which he was well fitted. Mdlle. X ** C ** V ** was both beautiful and charming in her manner, and had received an excellent education, of which, however, she made no parade. One could not stay in her presence without loving her, but she was no flirt, and I soon saw that she held out no vain hopes to those who had the misfortune not to please her. Without being rude she knew how to be cold, and it was all the worse for those whom her coldness did not show that their quest was useless.

The first hour I passed in her company chained me a captive to her triumphant car. I told her as much, and she replied that she was glad to have such a captive. She took the place in my heart where Esther had reigned a week before, but I freely confess that Esther yielded only because she was away. As to my attachment to Silvia's daughter, it was of such a nature as not to hinder me falling in love with any other woman who chanced to take my fancy. In the libertine's heart love cannot exist without substantial food, and women who have had some experience of the world are well aware of this fact. The youthful Baletti was a beginner, and so knew nothing of these things.

M. Farsetti, a Venetian of noble birth, a knight of Malta, a great student of the occult sciences, and a good Latin versifier, came in at one o'clock. Dinner was just ready and Madame X ** C ** V ** begged him to stay. She asked me also to dine with them, but wishing to dine with Madame d'Urfé I refused the invitation for the nonce.

M. Farsetti, who had known me very well in Venice, only noticed me by a side glance, and without showing any vexation I paid him back in the same coin. He smiled at Mdlle. X ** C ** V **'s praise of my courage. She noticed his expression, and as if to punish him for it went on to say that I had now the admiration of every Venetian, and that the French were anxious to have the honour of calling me a fellow-citizen. M. Farsetti asked me if my post at the lottery paid well. I replied, coolly, "Oh, yes, well enough for me to pay my clerks' salaries."

He understood the drift of my reply, and Mdlle. X ** C **
V ** smiled.

I found my supposed son with Madame d'Urfé, or rather in
that amiable visionary's arms. She hastened to apologise for
carrying him off, and I turned it off with a jest, having no other
course to take.

"I made him sleep with me," she said, "but I shall be obliged
to deprive myself of this privilege for the future, unless he
promises to be more discreet."

I thought the idea a grand one, and the little fellow, in spite
of his blushes, begged her to say how he had offended.

"We shall have the Comte de St. Germain," said Madame
d'Urfé, "to dinner. I know he amuses you, and I like you to
enjoy yourself at my house."

"For that, madam, your presence is all I need; nevertheless,
I thank you for considering me."

In due course St. Germain arrived, and in his usual manner
sat himself down, not to eat but to talk. With a face of imper-
turbable gravity he told the most incredible stories, which one
had to pretend to believe, as he was always either the hero of the
tale or an eye-witness of the event. All the same, I could not
help bursting into laughter when he told us of something that
happened as he was dining with the Fathers of the Council of Trent.

Madame d'Urfé wore on her neck a large magnet. She said
that it would one day happen that this magnet would attract the
lightning, and that she would consequently soar into the sun.
I longed to tell her that when she got there she could be no higher
up than on the earth, but I restrained myself; and the great
charlatan hastened to say that there could be no doubt about it,
and that he, and he only, could increase the force of the magnet
a thousand times. I said, dryly, that I would wager twenty
thousand crowns he would not so much as double its force, but
Madame d'Urfé would not let us bet, and after dinner she told
me in private that I should have lost, as St. Germain was a
magician. Of course I agreed with her.

A few days later, the magician set out for Chambord, where
the king had given him a suite of rooms and a hundred thousand
francs, that he might be at liberty to work on the dyes which
were to assure the superiority of French materials over those of
any other country. St. Germain had got over the king by ar-

ranging a laboratory where he occasionally tried to amuse himself, though he knew little about chemistry, but the king was a victim of an almost universal weariness. To enjoy a harem recruited from amongst the most ravishing beauties, and often from the ranks of neophytes, with whom pleasure had its difficulties, one would have needed to be a god, and Louis XV. was only a man after all.

It was the famous marquise who had introduced the adept to the king in the hope of his distracting the monarch's weariness, by giving him a taste for chemistry. Indeed, Madame de Pompadour was under the impression that St. Germain had given her the water of perpetual youth, and therefore felt obliged to make the chemist a good return. This wondrous water, taken according to the charlatan's directions, could not indeed make old age retire and give way to youth, but according to the marquise it would preserve one *in statu quo* for several centuries.

As a matter of fact, the water, or the giver of it, had worked wonders, if not on her body, at least on her mind; she assured the king that she was not getting older. The king was as much deluded by this grand impostor as she was, for one day he showed the Duc des Deux-Ponts a diamond of the first water, weighing twelve carats, which he fancied he had made himself. "I melted down," said Louis XV., "small diamonds weighing twenty-four carats, and obtained this one large one weighing twelve." Thus it came to pass that the infatuated monarch gave the impostor the suite formerly occupied by Marshal Saxe. The Duc des Deux-Ponts told me this story with his own lips, one evening, when I was supping with him and a Swede, the Comte de Levenhoop, at Metz.

Before I left Madame d'Urfé, I told her that the lad might be he who should make her to be born again, but that she would spoil all if she did not wait for him to attain the age of puberty. After what she had said about his misbehaviour, the reader will guess what made me say this. She sent him to board with Viar, gave him masters on everything, and disguised him under the name of the Comte d'Aranda, although he was born at Bayreuth, and though his mother never had anything to do with a Spaniard of that name. It was three or four months before I went to see him, as I was afraid of being insulted on account of the name which the visionary Madame d'Urfé had given him.

One day Tiretta came to see me in a fine coach. He told me that his elderly mistress wanted to become his wife, but that he would not hear of it, though she offered to endow him with all her worldly goods. I told him that if he gave in he might pay his debts, return to Trevisa, and live pleasantly there; but his destiny would not allow him to take my advice.

I had resolved on taking a country-house, and fixed on one called Little Poland, which pleased me better than all the others I had seen. It was well furnished, and was a hundred paces distant from the Madeleine Gate. It was situated on slightly elevated ground near the royal park, behind the Duc de Gram-mont's garden, and its owner had given it the name of Pleasant Warsaw. It had two gardens, one of which was on a level with the first floor, three reception rooms, large stables, coach-houses, baths, a good cellar, and a splendid kitchen. The master was called The Butter King, and always wrote himself down so; the name had been given to him by Louis XV. on the monarch's stopping at the house and liking the butter. The Butter King let me his house for a hundred louis per annum, and he gave me an excellent cook called The Pearl, a true blue-ribbon of the order of cooks, and to her he gave charge of all his furniture and the plate I should want for a dinner of six persons, engaging to get me as much plate as I wanted at the hire of a sou an ounce. He also promised to let me have what wine I wanted, and said all he had was of the best, and, moreover, cheaper than I could get it at Paris, as he had no gate-money to pay on it.

Matters having been arranged on these terms, in the course of a week I got a good coachman, two fine carriages, five horses, a groom, and two footmen. Madame d'Urfé, who was my first guest, was delighted with my new abode, and as she imagined that I had done it all for her, I left her in that flattering opinion. I never could believe in the morality of snatching from poor mortal man the delusions which make them happy. I also let her retain the notion that young d'Aranda, the count of her own making, was a scion of the nobility, that he was born for a mysterious operation unknown to the rest of mankind, that I was only his caretaker (here I spoke the truth), and that he must die and yet not cease to live. All these whimsical ideas were the products of her brain, which was only occupied with the impossible, and I thought the best thing I could do was to agree with everything.

If I had tried to undeceive her, she would have accused me of want of trust in her, for she was convinced that all her knowledge was revealed to her by her genius, who spoke to her only by night. After she had dined with me I took her back to her house, full of happiness.

Camille sent me a lottery ticket, which she had invested in at my office, and which proved to be a winning one, I think, for a thousand crowns or thereabouts. She asked me to come and sup with her, and bring the money with me. I accepted her invitation, and found her surrounded by all the girls she knew and their lovers. After supper I was asked to go to the opera with them, but we had scarcely got there when I lost my party in the crowd. I had no mask on, and I soon found myself attacked by a black domino, whom I knew to be a woman, and as she told me a hundred truths about myself in a falsetto voice, I was interested, and determined on finding out who she was. At last I succeeded in persuading her to come with me into a box, and as soon as we were in and I had taken off her mask I was astonished to find she was Mdlle. X ** C ** V **.

"I have come to the ball," said she, "with one of my sisters, my elder brother, and M. Farsetti. I left them to go into a box and change my domino."

"They must feel very uneasy."

"I dare say they do, but I am not going to take pity on them till the end of the ball."

Finding myself alone with her, and certain of having her in my company for the rest of the night, I began to talk of our old love-making; and I took care to say that I was more in love with her than ever. She listened to me kindly, did not oppose my embraces, and by the few obstacles she placed in my way I judged that the happy moment was not far off. Nevertheless I felt that I must practise restraint that evening, and she let me see that she was obliged to me.

"I heard at Versailles, my dear mademoiselle, that you are going to marry M. de la Popelinière."

"So they say. My mother wishes me to do so, and the old financier fancies he has got me in his talons already; but he makes a mistake, as I will never consent to such a thing."

"He is old, but he is very rich."

"He is very rich and very generous, for he promises me a

dowry of a million if I become a widow without children; and if I had a son he would leave me all his property."

"You wouldn't have much difficulty in complying with the second alternative."

"I shall never have anything to do with his money, for I should never make my life miserable by a marriage with a man whom I do not love, while I do love another."

"Another! Who is the fortunate mortal to whom you have given your heart's treasure?"

"I do not know if my loved one is fortunate. My lover is a Venetian, and my mother knows of it; but she says that I should not be happy, that he is not worthy of me."

"Your mother is a strange woman, always crossing your affections."

"I cannot be angry with her. She may possibly be wrong, but she certainly loves me. She would rather that I should marry M. Farsetti, who would be very glad to have me, but I detest him."

"Has he made a declaration in terms?"

"He has, and all the marks of contempt I have given him seem to have no effect."

"He clings hard to hope; but the truth is you have fascinated him."

"Possibly, but I do not think him susceptible of any tender or generous feeling. He is a visionary; surly, jealous, and envious in his disposition. When he heard me expressing myself about you in the manner you deserve, he had the impudence to say to my mother before my face that she ought not to receive you."

"He deserves that I should give him a lesson in manners, but there are other ways in which he may be punished. I shall be delighted to serve you in any way I can."

"Alas! if I could only count on your friendship I should be happy."

The sigh with which she uttered these words sent fire through my veins, and I told her that I was her devoted slave; that I had fifty thousand crowns which were at her service, and that I would risk my life to win her favours. She replied that she was truly grateful to me, and as she threw her arms about my neck our lips met, but I saw that she was weeping, so I took care that the fire which her kisses raised should be kept within bounds. She begged me to come and see her often, promising that as often as she could manage it we should be alone. I could ask no more, and after I had promised to come and dine with them on the morrow, we parted.

I passed an hour in walking behind her, enjoying my new position of intimate friend, and I then returned to my Little Poland. It was a short distance, for though I lived in the country I could get to any part of Paris in a quarter of an hour. I had a clever coachman, and capital horses not used to being spared. I got them from the royal stables, and as soon as I lost one I got·another from the same place, having to pay two hundred francs. This happened to me several times, for, to my mind, going fast is one of the greatest pleasures which Paris offers.

Having accepted an invitation to dinner at the X ** C ** V **'s, I did not give myself much time for sleep, and I went out on foot with a cloak on. The snow was falling in large flakes, and when I got to madame's I was as white as a sheet from head to foot. She gave me a hearty welcome, laughing, and saying that her daughter had been telling her how she had puzzled me, and that she was delighted to see me come to dinner without ceremony. "But," added she, "it's Friday to-day, and you will have to fast, though, after all, the fish is very good. Dinner is not ready yet. You had better go and see my daughter, who is still a-bed."

As may be imagined, this invitation had not to be repeated, for a pretty woman looks better in bed than anywhere else. I found Mdlle. X ** C ** V ** sitting up in bed writing, but she stopped as soon as she saw me.

"How is this, sweet lie-a-bed, not up yet?"

"Yes, I am staying in bed partly because I feel lazy, and partly because I am freer here."

"I was afraid you were not quite well."

"Nor am I. However, we will say no more about that now. I am just going to take some soup, as those who foolishly establish the institution of fasting were not polite enough to ask my opinion on the subject. It does not agree with my health, and I don't like it, so I am not going to get up even to sit at table, though I shall thus deprive myself of your society."

I naturally told her that in her absence dinner would have no savour; and I spoke the truth.

As the presence of her sister did not disturb us, she took out of her pocket-book an epistle in verse which I had addressed to her when her mother had forbidden me the house. "This fatal letter," said she, "which you called *The Phœnix*, has shaped my life and may prove the cause of my death."

I had called it *The Phœnix* because, after bewailing my unhappy lot, I proceeded to predict how she would afterwards give her heart to a mortal whose qualities would make him deserve the name of Phœnix. A hundred lines were taken up in the description of these imaginary mental and moral characteristics, and certainly the being who should have them all would be right worthy of worship, for he would be rather a god than a man.

"Alas!" said Mdlle. X ** C ** V **, "I fell in love with this imaginary being, and feeling certain that such an one must exist I set myself to look for him. After six months I thought I had found him. I gave him my heart, I received his, we loved each other fondly. But for the last four months we have been separated, and during the whole time I have only had one letter from him. Yet I must not blame him, for I know he cannot help it. Such is my sorry fate: I can neither hear from him nor write to him."

This story was a confirmation of a theory of mine — namely, that the most important events in our lives proceed often from the most trifling causes. My epistle was nothing better than a number of lines of poetry more or less well written, and the being I had delineated was certainly not to be found, as he surpassed by far all human perfections, but a woman's heart travels so quickly and so far! Mdlle. X ** C ** V ** took the thing literally, and fell in love with a chimera of goodness, and then was fain to turn this into a real lover, not thinking of the vast difference between the ideal and the real. For all that, when she thought that she had found the original of my fancy portrait, she had no difficulty in endowing him with all the good qualities I had pictured. Of course Mdlle. X ** C ** V ** would have fallen in love if I had never written her a letter in verse, but she would have done so in a different manner, and probably with different results.

As soon as dinner was served we were summoned to do justice

to the choice fish which M. de la Popelinière had provided. Madame X ** C ** V **, a narrow-minded Greek, was naturally bigoted and superstitious. In the mind of a silly woman the idea of an alliance between the most opposite of beings, God and the Devil, seems quite natural. A priest had told her that, since she had converted her husband, her salvation was secure, for the Scriptures solemnly promised a *soul for a soul* to everyone who would lead a heretic or a heathen within the fold of the Church. And as Madame X ** C ** V ** had converted her husband, she felt no anxiety about the life of the world to come, as she had done all that was necessary. However, she ate fish on the days appointed; the reason being that she preferred it to flesh.

Dinner over, I returned to the lady's bedside, and there stayed till nearly nine o'clock, keeping my passions well under control all the time. I was foppish enough to think that her feelings were as lively as mine, and I did not care to show myself less self-restrained than she, though I knew then, as I know now, that this was a false line of argument. It is the same with opportunity as with fortune; one must seize them when they come to us, or else they go by, often to return no more.

Not seeing Farsetti at the table, I suspected there had been a quarrel, and I asked my sweetheart about it; but she told me I was mistaken in supposing they had quarrelled with him, and that the reason of his absence was that he would never leave his house on a Friday. The deluded man had had his horoscope drawn, and learning by it that he would be assassinated on a Friday he resolved always to shut himself up on that day. He was laughed at, but persisted in the same course till he died four years ago at the age of seventy. He thought to prove by the success of his precautions that a man's destiny depends on his discretion, and on the precautions he takes to avoid the misfortunes of which he has had warning. This line of argument holds good in all cases except when the misfortunes are predicted in a horoscope; for either the ills predicted are avoidable, in which case the horoscope is a useless piece of folly, or else the horoscope is the interpreter of destiny, in which case all the precautions in the world are of no avail. The Chevalier Farsetti was therefore a fool to imagine he had proved anything at all. He would have proved a good deal for many people if he had gone out on a Friday and had chanced to have been assassinated. Picus de la

Mirandola, who believed in astrology, says, I have no doubt truly, "*Astra influunt, non cogunt.*" But would it have been a real proof of the truth of astrology if Farsetti had been assassinated on a Friday? In my opinion, certainly not.

The Comte d'Eigreville had introduced me to his sister, the Comtesse du Rumain, who had been wanting to make my acquaintance ever since she had heard of my oracle. It was not long before I made friends with her husband and her two daughters, the elder of whom, nicknamed "Cotenfau," married M. de Polignac later on. Madame du Rumain was handsome rather than pretty, but she won the love of all by her kindness, her frank courtesy, and her eagerness to be of service to her friends. She had a magnificent figure, and would have awed the whole bench of judges if she had pleaded before them.

At her house I got to know Mesdames de Valbelle and de Rancerolles, the Princess de Chimai, and many others who were then in the best society of Paris. Although Madame du Rumain was not a proficient in the occult sciences, she had nevertheless consulted my oracle more frequently than Madame d'Urfé. She was of the utmost service to me in connection with an unhappy circumstance of which I shall speak presently.

The day after my long conversation with Mdlle. X ** C ** V **, my servant told me that there was a young man waiting who wanted to give me a letter with his own hands. I had him in, and on my asking him from whom the letter came, he replied that I should find all particulars in the letter, and that he had orders to wait for an answer. The epistle ran as follows:

"I am writing this at two o'clock in the morning. I am weary and in need of rest, but a burden on my soul deprives me of sleep. The secret I am about to tell you will no longer be so grievous when I have confided in you; I shall feel eased by placing it in your breast. I am with child, and my situation drives me to despair. I was obliged to write to you because I felt I could not say it. Give me a word in reply."

My feelings on reading the above may be guessed. I was petrified with astonishment and could only write, "I will be with you at eleven o'clock."

No one should say that he has passed through great misfortunes unless they have proved too great for his mind to bear. The confidence of Mdlle. X ** C ** V ** showed me that she was

in need of support. I congratulated myself on having the preference, and I vowed to do my best for her did it cost me my life.
These were the thoughts of a lover, but for all that I could
not conceal from myself the imprudence of the step she had
taken. In such cases as these there is always the choice between
speaking or writing, and the only feeling which can give the
preference to writing is false shame, at bottom mere cowardice.
If I had not been in love with her, I should have found it easier
to have refused my aid in writing than if she had spoken to me,
but I loved her to distraction.

"Yes," said I to myself, "she can count on me. Her mishap
makes her all the dearer to me."

And below this there was another voice, a voice which whispered to me that if I succeeded in saving her my reward was
sure. I am well aware that more than one grave moralist will
fling stones at me for this avowal, but my answer is that such
men cannot be in love as I was.

I was punctual to my appointment, and found the fair unfortunate at the door of the hotel.

"You are going out, are you? Where are you going?"

"I am going to mass at the Church of the Augustinians."

"Is this a saint's day?"

"No; but my mother makes me go every day."

"I will come with you."

"Yes, do, give me your arm; we will go into the cloisters and
talk there."

Mdlle. X ** C ** V ** was accompanied by her maid, but she
knew better than to be in the way, so we left her in the cloisters.
As soon as we were alone she said to me:

"Have you read my letter?"

"Yes, of course; here it is, burn it yourself."

"No, keep it, and do so with your own hands."

"I see you trust in me, and I assure you I will not abuse your
trust."

"I am sure you will not. I am four months with child; I can
doubt it no longer, and the thought maddens me!"

"Comfort yourself, we will find some way to get over it."

"Yes; I leave all to you. You must procure an abortion."

"Never, dearest! that is a crime!"

"Alas! I know that well; but it is not a greater crime than

suicide, and there lies my choice: either to destroy the wretched witness of my shame, or to poison myself. For the latter alternative I have everything ready. You are my only friend, and it is for you to decide which it shall be. Speak to me! Are you angry that I have not gone to the Chevalier Farsetti before you?"

She saw my astonishment, and stopped short, and tried to wipe away the tears which escaped from her eyes. My heart bled for her.

"Laying the question of crime on one side," said I, "abortion is out of our power. If the means employed are not violent they are uncertain, and if they are violent they are dangerous to the mother. I will never risk becoming your executioner; but reckon on me, I will not forsake you. Your honour is as dear to me as your life. Be calm, and henceforth think that the peril is mine, not yours. Make up your mind that I shall find some way of escape, and that there will be no need to cut short that life, to preserve which I would gladly die. And allow me to say that when I read your note I felt glad, I could not help it, that at such an emergency you chose me before all others to be your helper. You will find that your trust was not given in vain, for no one loves you as well as I, and no one is so fain to help you. Later you shall begin to take the remedies I will get for you, but I warn you to be on your guard, for this is a serious matter — one of life and death. Possibly you have already told somebody about it — your maid or one of your sisters?"

"I have not told anybody but you, not even the author of my shame. I tremble when I think what my mother would do and say if she found out my situation. I am afraid she will draw her conclusions from my shape."

"So far there is nothing to be observed in that direction, the beauty of the outline still remains intact."

"But every day increases its size, and for that reason we must be quick in what we do. You must find a surgeon who does not know my name."

"I will not run the risk, it might lead to the discovery of the whole affair."

"What I should like you to do would be to take me to a midwife's. We can easily go without attracting any notice at the first ball at the opera."

"Yes, sweetheart, but that step is not necessary, and it might lead to our betrayal."

"No, no, in this great town there are midwives in every quarter, and we should never be known; we might keep our masks on all the time. Do me this kindness. A midwife's opinion is certainly worth having."

I could not refuse her request, but I made her agree to wait till the last ball, as the crowd was always greater, and we had a better chance of going out free from observation. I promised to be there in a black domino with a white mask in the Venetian fashion, and a rose painted beside the left eye. As soon as she saw me go out she was to follow me into a carriage. All this was carried out, but more if it anon.

I returned with her, and dined with them without taking any notice of Farsetti, who was also at the table, and had seen me come back from mass with her. We did not speak a word to one another; he did not like me and I despised him.

I must here relate a grievous mistake of which I was guilty, and which I have not yet forgiven myself.

I had promised to take Mdlle. X ** C ** V ** to a midwife, but I certainly ought to have taken her to a respectable woman's, for all we wanted to know was how a pregnant woman should regulate her diet and manner of living. But my evil genius took me by the Rue St. Louis, and there I saw the Montigni entering her house with a pretty girl whom I did not know, and so out of curiosity I went in after them. After amusing myself there, with Mdlle. X ** C ** V ** running in my head all the time, I asked the woman to give me the address of a midwife, as I wanted to consult one. She told me of a house in the Marais, where according to her dwelt the pearl of midwives, and began telling me some stories of her exploits, which all went to prove that the woman was an infamous character. I took her address, however, and as I should have to go there by night, I went the next day to see where the house was.

Mdlle. X ** C ** V ** was impatient to consult a midwife. On the night of the last ball she recognised me as we had agreed, and followed me out into the coach she saw me enter, and in less than a quarter of an hour we reached the house.

A woman of about fifty received us with great politeness, and asked what she could do.

Mdlle. X ** C ** V ** told her that she believed herself pregnant, and that she desired some means of concealing her misfortune. The wretch answered with a smile that she might as well tell her plainly that it would be easy to procure abortion. "I will do your business," said she, "for fifty louis, half to be paid in advance, and the rest when it's all over. I will trust in your honesty, and you will have to trust in mine. Give me the twenty-five louis down."

"If madame decides on taking your advice," said I, "I will bring you the money to-morrow."

I gave her two louis and left. Mdlle. X ** C ** V ** told me that she had no doubt of the infamy of this woman, as she was sure it was impossible to destroy the offspring without the risk of killing the mother also. "My only trust," said she, "is in you." I encouraged her in this idea, dissuading her from any criminal attempts, and assured her over and over again that she should not find her trust in me misplaced. All at once she complained of feeling cold, and asked if we had not time to warm ourselves in Little Poland, saying that she longed to see my pretty house. I was surprised and delighted with the idea. The night was too dark for her to see the exterior charms of my abode, she would have to satisfy herself with the inside, and leave the rest to her imagination. I thought my hour had come. I made the coach stop and we got down and walked some way, and then took another at the corner of the Rue de la Ferannerie. I promised the coachman six francs beyond his fare, and in a quarter of an hour he put us down at my door.

I rang with the touch of the master, the Pearl opened the door, and told me that there was nobody within, as I very well knew, but it was her habit to do so.

"Quick!" said I, "light us a fire, and bring some glasses and a bottle of champagne."

"Would you like an omelette?"

"Very well."

"Oh, I should like an omelette so much!" said Mdlle. X ** C ** V **. She was ravishing, and her laughing air seemed to promise me a moment of bliss. I sat down before the blazing fire and made her sit on my knee, covering her with kisses which she gave me back as lovingly. I had almost won what I wanted when she asked me in a sweet voice to stop. I obeyed, thinking

[51]

it would please her, feeling sure that she only delayed my victory to make it more complete, and that she would surrender after the champagne. I saw love, kindness, trust, and gratitude shining in her face, and I should have been sorry for her to think that I claimed her as a mere reward. No, I wanted her love, and nothing but her love.

We put on our masks and returned to the opera. On our way she dared to tell me that she should be obliged to decline my friendship if she had to pay for it so dearly.

"The emotions of love," I replied, "should yield to those of honour, and your honour as well as mine require us to continue friends. What I would have done for love I will now do for devoted friendship, and for the future I will die rather than make another attempt to gain those favours of which I thought you deemed me worthy."

We separated at the opera, and the vast crowd made me lose sight of her in an instant. Next day she told me that she had danced all night.

I returned to my house in a bad humour, trying in vain to justify a refusal which seemed humiliating and almost incredible. My good sense showed me, in spite of all sophisms, that I had been grievously insulted. I recollected the witty saying of Populia, who was never unfaithful to her husband except when she was with child —"*Non tollo vectorem*," said she, "*nisi navi plena.*"

I felt certain that I was not loved, and the thought grieved me; and I considered that it would be unworthy of me to love one whom I could no longer hope to possess. I resolved to avenge myself by leaving her to her fate, feeling that I could not allow myself to be duped as I had been.

The night brought wisdom with it, and when I awoke in the morning my mind was calm and I was still in love. I determined to act generously by the unfortunate girl. Without my aid she would be ruined; my course, then, would be to continue my services and to show myself indifferent to her favours. The part was no easy one, but I played it right well, and at last my reward came of itself.

What this "reward" was, it is easy to guess. It was obtained by means of a magic specific, recommended by Madame d'Urfé, who had been consulted in the matter. The story of the "aroph" (aroma

[52]

philosophorum) *of Paracelsus and the nightly* modus operandi *in a secret garret is neither convincing nor very entertaining, but it is in keeping with Casanova's erotic complex, which included a predilection for magical obscenities. Meanwhile the situation for the lady was getting serious and something had to be done to save her reputation. Fortunately Madame du Rumain, another* grande dame, *whose favour he had gained, came to the rescue:*

Three or four days afterwards I found her thoughtful but quiet. She told me that she had lost all hope of getting rid of her burden before the proper time. All the while, however, her mother persecuted her, and she would have to choose in a few days between making a declaration as to her state and signing the marriage contract. She would accept neither of these alternatives, and had decided on escaping from her home, and asked me to help her in doing so.

I had determined to help her, but I desired to save my reputation, for it might have been troublesome if it had been absolutely known that I had carried her off or furnished her with the means to escape. And as for any other alternative, neither of us had any idea of matrimony.

I left her and went to the Tuileries, where a sacred concert was being given. The piece was a motet composed by Moudonville, the words by the Abbé de Voisenon, whom I had furnished with the idea, *The Israelites on Mount Horeb.*

As I was getting out of my carriage, I saw Madame du Rumain descending alone from hers. I ran up to her, and received a hearty welcome. "I am delighted," said she, "to find you here, it is quite a piece of luck. I am going to hear this novel composition, and have two reserved seats. Will you do me the honour of accepting one?"

Although I had my ticket in my pocket I could not refuse so honourable an offer, so, giving her my arm, we walked up to two of the best places in the house.

At Paris no talking is allowed during the performance of sacred music, especially when the piece is heard for the first time; so Madame du Rumain could draw no conclusions from my silence throughout the performance, but she guessed that something was the matter from the troubled and absent expression of my face, which was by no means natural to me.

"M. Casanova," said she, "be good enough to give me your

company for an hour. I want to ask you two or three questions which can only be solved by your cabala. I hope you will oblige me, as I am very anxious to know the answers, but we must be quick as I have an engagement to sup in Paris."

It may be imagined that I did not wait to be asked twice, and as soon as we got to her house I went to work on the questions, and solved them all in less than half an hour.

When I had finished, "M. Casanova," said she, in the kindest manner possible, "what is the matter with you? You are not in your usual state of equanimity, and if I am not mistaken you are dreading some dire event. Or perhaps you are on the eve of taking some important resolution? I am not inquisitive, but if I can be of any service to you at Court, make use of me, and be sure that I will do my best. If necessary, I will go to Versailles to-morrow morning. I know all the ministers. Confide in me your troubles, if I cannot lighten them I can at least share them, and be sure I will keep your counsel."

Her words seemed to me a voice from heaven, a warning from my good genius to open my heart to this lady, who had almost read my thoughts, and had so plainly expressed her interest in my welfare. After gazing at her for some seconds without speaking, but with a manner that showed her how grateful I was: "Yes, madam," I said, "I am indeed critically situated, maybe on the verge of ruin, but your kindness has calmed my soul and made me once more acquainted with hope. You shall hear how I am placed. I am going to trust you with a secret of the most delicate description, but I can rely on your being as discreet as you are good. And if after hearing my story you deign to give me your advice, I promise to follow it and never to divulge its author."

After this beginning, which gained her close attention, I told her all the circumstances of the case, neither concealing the young lady's name nor any of the circumstances which made it my duty to watch over her welfare. All the same I said nothing about the aroph or the share I had taken in its exhibition.

After this weighty communication I stopped, and Madame du Rumain remained silent, as if lost in thought, for nearly a quarter of an hour. At last she rose, saying:

"I am expected at Madame de la Marque's, and I must go, as I am to meet the Bishop of Montrouge, to whom I want to speak, but I hope I shall eventually be able to help you. Come here the day after to-morrow, you will find me alone; above all, do nothing before you see me. Farewell."

I left her full of hope, and resolved to follow her advice and hers only in the troublesome affair in which I was involved.

The Bishop of Montrouge whom she was going to address on an important matter, the nature of which was well known to me, was the Abbé de Voisenon, who was thus named because he often went there. Montrouge is an estate near Paris, belonging to the Duc de la Valière.

I saw Mdlle. X ** C ** V ** the following day, and contented myself with telling her that in a couple of days I hoped to give her some good news. I was pleased with her manner, which was full of resignation, and trust in my endeavours.

The day after, I went to Madame du Rumain's punctually at eight. The porter told me that I should find the doctor with my lady, but I went upstairs all the same, and as soon as the doctor saw me he took his leave. His name was Herrenschwand, and all the ladies in Paris ran after him. Poor Poinsinet put him in a little one-act play called *Le Cercle*, which, though of very ordinary merit, was a great success.

"My dear sir," said Madame du Rumain, as soon as we were alone, "I have succeeded in my endeavours on your behalf, and it is now for you to keep secret my share in the matter. After I had pondered over the case of conscience you submitted to me, I went to the convent of C **, where the abbess is a friend of mine, and I entrusted her with the secret, relying on her discretion. We agreed that she should receive the young lady in her convent, and give her a good lay sister to nurse her through her confinement. Now you will not deny," said she, with a smile, "that the cloisters are of some use. Your young friend must go by herself to the convent with a letter for the abbess, which I will give her, and which she must deliver to the porter. She will then be admitted and lodged in a suitable chamber. She will receive no visitors nor any letters that have not passed through my hands. The abbess will bring her answers to me, and I will pass them on to you. You must see that her only correspondent must be yourself, and you must receive news of her welfare only through me. On your hand, in writing to her you must leave the address to be filled in by me. I had to tell the abbess the lady's name, but not yours, as she did not require it.

"Tell your young friend all about our plans, and when she is ready come and tell me, and I will give you the letter to the abbess. Tell her to bring nothing but what is strictly necessary, above all no diamonds or trinkets of any value. You may assure her that the abbess will be friendly, will come and see her every now and then, will give her proper books — in a word, that she will be well looked after. Warn her not to confide in the lay sister who will attend on her. I have no doubt she is an excellent woman, but she is a nun, and the secret might leak out. After she is safely delivered, she must go to confession and perform her Easter duties, and the abbess will give her a certificate of good behaviour; and she can then return to her mother, who will be too happy to see her to say anything more about the marriage, which, of course, she ought to give as her reason of her leaving home."

After many expressions of my gratitude to her, and of my admiration of her plan, I begged her to give me the letter on the spot, as there was no time to be lost. She was good enough to go at once to her desk, where she wrote as follows:

"My dear abbess, — The young lady who will give you this letter is the same of whom we have spoken. She wishes to spend three or four months under your protection, to recover her peace of mind, to perform her devotions, and to make sure that when she returns to her mother nothing more will be said about the marriage, which is partly the cause of her temporary separation from her family."

After reading it to me, she put it into my hands unsealed, that Mdlle. X ** C ** V ** might be able to read it. The abbess in question was a princess, and her convent was consequently a place above all suspicion. As Madame du Rumain gave me the letter, I felt such an impulse of gratitude that I fell on my knees before her. This generous woman was useful to me on another occasion, of which I shall speak later on.

After leaving Madame du Rumain I went straight to the Hôtel de Bretagne, where I saw Mdlle. X ** C ** V **, who had only time to tell me that she was engaged for the rest of the day, but that she would come to the garret at eleven o'clock that night, and that then we could talk matters over. I was overjoyed at this arrangement, as I foresaw that after this would come the awakening from a happy dream, and that I should be alone with her no more.

Before leaving the hotel I gave the word to Madelaine, who in turn got the scullion to have everything in readiness.

I kept the appointment, and had not long to wait for my mistress. After making her read the letter written by Madame du Rumain (whose name I withheld from her without her taking offence thereat) I put out the candle, and without troubling about the aroph, we set ourselves to the pleasant task of proving that we truly loved each other.

In the morning, before we separated, I gave her all the instructions I had received from Madame du Rumain; and we agreed that she should leave the house at eight o'clock with such things as she absolutely required, that she should take a coach to the Place Maubert, then send it away, and take another to the Place Antoine, and again, farther on, a third coach, in which she was to go to the convent named. I begged her not to forget to burn all the letters she had received from me, and to write to me from the convent as often as she could, to seal her letters, but to leave the address blank. She promised to carry out my instructions, and I then made her accept a packet of two hundred louis, of which she might chance to be in need. She wept, more for my situation than her own, but I consoled her by saying that I had plenty of money and powerful patrons.

"I will set out," said she, "the day after to-morrow, at the hour agreed on." And thereupon, I having promised to come to the house the day after her departure, as if I knew nothing about it, and to let her know what passed, we embraced each other tenderly, and I left her.

I was troubled in thinking about her fate. She had wit and courage, but when experience is wanting, wit often leads men to commit acts of great folly.

The day after the morrow I took a coach, and posted myself in a corner of the street by which she had to pass. I saw her come, get out of the coach, pay the coachman, go down a narrow street, and a few minutes after reappear again, veiled and hooded, carrying a small parcel in her hand. She then took another conveyance which went off in the direction we had agreed upon.

* * *

Mdlle. X ** C ** V ** had now been in the convent for a month, and her affair had ceased to be a common topic of conversation. I thought I should hear no more of it, but I was mistaken. I continued, however, to amuse myself, and my pleasure in spending freely quite prevented me from thinking about the future. The Abbé de Bernis, whom I went to see regularly once a week, told me one day that the comptroller-general often inquired how I was getting on. "You are wrong," said the abbé, "to neglect him." He advised me to say no more about my claims, but to communicate to him the means I had spoken of for increasing the revenues of the state. I laid too great store by the advice of the man who had made my fortune not to follow it. I went to the comptroller, and trusting in his probity, I explained my scheme to him. This was to pass a law by which every estate, except that left by father to son, should furnish the treasury with one year's income; every deed of gift formally drawn up being subject to the same provision. It seemed to me that the law could not give offence to anyone; the heir had only to imagine that he had inherited a year later than was actually the case. The minister was of the same opinion as myself, told me there would not be the slightest difficulty involved, and assured me that my fortune was made. In a week afterwards his place was taken by M. de Silhouette, and when I called on the new minister he told me coldly that when my scheme became law he would tell me. It became law two years afterwards, and when, as the originator of the scheme, I attempted to get my just reward, they laughed in my face.

Shortly after, the Pope died, and he was succeeded by the Venetian Rezzonico, who created my patron, the Abbé de Bernis, a cardinal. However, he had to go into exile by order of the king two days after his gracious majesty had presented him with the red cap: so good a thing it is to be the friend of kings!

The disgrace of my delightful abbé left me without a patron, but I had plenty of money, and so was enabled to bear this misfortune with resignation.

For having undone all the work of Cardinal Richelieu, for having changed the old enmity between France and Austria into friendship, for delivering Italy from the horrors of war which befell her whenever these countries had a bone to pick, although he was the first cardinal made by a pope who had had plenty of opportunities for discovering his character, merely because, on being asked, he had given it as his opinion that the Prince de

Soubise was not a fit person to command the French armies, this great ecclesiastic was driven into exile. The moment the Pompadour heard of this opinion of his, she decreed his banishment — a sentence which was unpopular with all classes of society; but they consoled themselves with epigrams, and the new cardinal was soon forgotten. Such is the character of the French people; it cares neither for its own misfortunes nor for those of others, if only it can extract laughter from them.

In my time epigrammatists and poetasters who assailed ministers or even the king's mistresses were sent to the Bastille, but the wits still persisted in being amusing, and there were some who considered a jest incomplete that was not followed by a prosecution. A man whose name I have forgotten — a great lover of notoriety — appropriated the following verses by the younger Crébillon, and went to the Bastille rather than disown them:

"All the world's turned upside down!
Jupiter has donned the gown — the King.
Venus mounts the council stair — the Pompadour.
Plutus trifles with the fair — M. de Boulogne.
Mercury in mail is dressed — Maréchal de Richelieu.
Mighty Mars has turned a priest — the Duc de Clermont,
     abbé of St. Germain-des-prés."

Crébillon, who was not the sort of man to conceal his writings, told the Duc de Choiseul that he had written some verses exactly like these, but that it was possible the prisoner had been inspired with precisely the same ideas. This jest was applauded, and the author of *The Sofa* was let alone.

Cardinal de Bernis passed ten years in exile, *procul negotiis*, but he was not happy, as he told me himself when I knew him in Rome fifteen years afterwards. It is said that it is better to be a minister than a king — an opinion which seems ridiculous when it is analysed. The question is, which is the better, independence or its contrary. The axiom may possibly be verified in a despotic government under an absurd, weak, or careless king who serves as a mere mask for his master the minister; but in all other cases it is an absurdity.

Cardinal de Bernis was never recalled; there is no instance of Louis XV. having ever recalled a minister whom he had disgraced; but on the death of Rezzonico he had to go to Rome to be present at the conclave, and there he remained as French ambassador.

About this time Madame d'Urfé conceived a wish to make the acquaintance of J. J. Rousseau, and we went to call upon him at Montmorenci, on the pretext of giving him music to copy — an occupation in which he was very skilled. He was paid twice the sum given to any other copyist, but he guaranteed that the work should be faultlessly done. At that period of his life copying music was the great writer's sole means of subsistence.

We found him to be a man of simple and modest demeanour, who talked well, but who was not otherwise distinguished either intellectually or physically. We did not think him what would be called a good-natured man, and as he was far from having the manners of good society Madame d'Urfé did not hesitate to pronounce him vulgar. We saw the woman with whom he lived, and of whom we had heard, but she scarcely looked at us. On our way home we amused ourselves by talking about Rousseau's eccentric habits.

I will here note down the visit of the Prince of Conti (father of the gentleman who is now known as the Conte de la Marche) to Rousseau.

The prince — a good-natured man — went by himself to Montmorenci, on purpose to spend a day in conversation with the philosopher, who was even then famous. He found him in the park, accosted him, and said that he had come to dine with him and to talk without restraint.

"Your highness will fare but badly," said Rousseau; "however, I will tell them to lay another knife and fork."

The philosopher gave his instructions, and came out and rejoined the prince, with whom he walked up and down for two or three hours. When it was dinner-time he took the prince into his dining-room, where the table was laid for three.

"Who is going to dine with us?" said the prince. "I thought we were to be alone."

"The third party," said Rousseau, "is my other self — a being who is neither my wife, nor my mistress, nor my servant-maid, nor my mother, nor my daughter, but yet personates all these characters at once."

"I dare say, my dear fellow, I dare say; but as I came to dine with you alone, I will not dine with your other self, but will leave you with all the rest of you to keep you company."

So saying the prince bade him farewell and went out. Rousseau did not try to keep him.

Some time after, my thoughts were occupied with a business speculation which all my calculations assured me would be extremely profitable. The plan was to produce on silks, by means of printing, the exquisite designs which are produced at Lyons by the tedious process of weaving, and thus to give customers excellent value at much lower prices. I had the requisite knowledge of chemistry, and enough capital to make the thing a success. I obtained the assistance of a man with the necessary technical skill and knowledge, intending to make him my manager.

I told my plan to the Prince de Conti, who encouraged me to persevere, promising me his patronage, and all the privileges I could wish for. That decided me to begin.

I rented a very large house near the Temple for a thousand crowns per annum. The house contained a spacious hall, in which I meant to put my workmen; another hall which was to be the shop; numerous rooms for my workpeople to live in; and a nice room for myself in case I cared to live on the premises.

I made the scheme into a company with thirty shares, of which I gave five to my designer, keeping the remaining twenty-five to distribute to those who were inclined to join the company. I gave one to a doctor who, on giving surety, became the store-keeper, and came to live in the house with his whole family; and I engaged four servants, a waiting-maid, and a porter. I had to give another share to an accountant, who furnished me with two clerks, who also took up their abode in the house. The carpenters, blacksmiths, and painters worked hard from morning to night, and in less than three weeks the place was ready. I told the manager to engage twenty girls to paint, who were to be paid every Saturday. I stocked the warehouse with three hundred pieces of sarcenet and camlet of different shades and colours to receive the designs, and I paid for everything in ready money.

I had made an approximate calculation with my manager that I should have to spend three hundred thousand francs, and that would not break me. If the worst happened I could fall back on my shares, which produced a good income, but I hoped

I should not be compelled to do this, as I wanted to have an income of two hundred thousand francs a year.

All the while I did not conceal from myself that the speculation might be my ruin, if custom did not come in, but on looking at my beautiful materials these fears were dispelled, especially as I heard everybody saying that I sold them much too cheap.

To set up the business I spent in the course of a month about sixty thousand francs, and my weekly expenses amounted to twelve hundred francs.

As for Madame d'Urfé she laughed every time she saw me, for she was quite certain that this business was only meant to put the curious off the scent and to preserve my incognito; so persuaded was she of my omnipotence.

The sight of twenty girls, all more or less pretty, the eldest of whom was not twenty-five, far from making me tremble as it ought, delighted me. I fancied myself in the midst of a seraglio, I amused myself by watching their meek and modest looks as they did their work under the direction of the foreman. The best paid did not get more than twenty-four sous a day, and all of them had excellent reputations, for they had been selected at her own request by the manager's wife, a devout woman of ripe age, whom I hoped to find obliging if the fancy seized me to test her choice. Manon Baletti did not share my satisfaction in them. She trembled to see me the owner of a harem, well knowing that sooner or later the barque of my virtue would run on the rocks. She scolded me well about these girls, though I assured her that none of them slept in the house.

This business increased my own ideas of my importance; partly from the thought that I was on the high road to fortune, and partly because I furnished so many people with the means of subsistence. Alas! I was too fortunate; and my evil genius soon crossed my career.

It was now three months since Mdlle. X ** C ** V ** had gone into the convent, and the time of her delivery drew near. We wrote to each other twice a week, and I considered the matter happily settled; M. de la Popelinière had married, and when Mdlle. X ** C ** V ** returned to her mother there would be nothing more to be said. But just at this period, when my happiness seemed assured, the hidden fire leapt forth and threatened to consume me; how, the reader will see.

One day after leaving Madame d'Urfé's I went to walk in the Tuileries. I had taken a couple of turns in the chief walk when I saw that an old woman, accompanied by a man dressed in black, was looking at me closely and communicating her observations to her companion. There was nothing very astonishing in this in a public place, and I continued my walk, and on turning again saw the same couple still watching me. In my turn I looked at them, and remembered seeing the man in a gaming-house, where he was known by the name of Castel-Bajac. On scrutinising the features of the hag, I at last succeeded in recollecting who she was; she was the woman to whom I had taken Mdlle. X ** C ** V **. I felt certain that she had recognised me, but not troubling myself about the matter I left the gardens to walk elsewhere. The day after next, just as I was going to get into my carriage, a man of evil aspect gave me a paper and asked me to read it. I opened it, but finding it covered with an illegible scrawl I gave it him back, telling him to read it himself. He did so, and I found myself summoned to appear before the commissary of police to answer to the plea which the midwife (whose name I forget) brought against me.

Although I could guess what the charge would be, and was certain that the midwife could furnish no proofs of her accusation, I went to an attorney I knew and told him to appear for me. I instructed him that I did not know any midwife in Paris whatsoever. The attorney waited on the commissary, and on the day after brought me a copy of the pleas.

The midwife said that I came to her one night, accompanied by a young lady about five months with child, and that, holding a pistol in one hand and a packet of fifty louis in the other, I made her promise to procure abortion. We both of us (so she said) had masks on, thus showing that we had been at the opera ball. Fear, she said, had prevented her from flatly refusing to grant my request; but she had enough presence of mind to say that she would have all in order by the next night; whereupon we left, promising to return. In the belief that we would not fail to keep the appointment, she went in to M. Castel-Bajac to ask him to hide in the next room that she might be protected from my fury, and that he might be a witness of what I said, but she had not seen me again. She added that she would have given information the day after the event if she had known who

I was, but since M. Castel-Bajac had told her my name on her recognising me in the Tuileries she had thought it her bounden duty to deliver me to the law that she might be compensated for the violence I had used to her. And this document was signed by the said Castel-Bajac as a witness.

"This is an evident case of libel," said my attorney, "at least, if she can't prove the truth of her allegations. My advice to you is to take the matter before the criminal lieutenant, who will be able to give you the satisfaction you require."

I authorised him to do what he thought advisable, and three or four days after, he told me that the lieutenant wished to speak to me in private, and would expect me the same day at three o'clock in the afternoon.

As will be expected, I was punctual to the appointment. I found the magistrate to be a polite and good-hearted gentleman. He was, in fact, the well-known M. de Sartine, who was the chief of police two years later. His office of criminal lieutenant was saleable, and M. de Sartine sold it when he was appointed head of the police.

As soon as I had made my bow, he asked me to sit down by him, and addressed me as follows:

"I have asked you to call upon me in the interests of both of us, as in your position our interests are inseparable. If you are innocent of the charge which has been brought against you, you are quite right to appeal to me; but before proceedings begin, you should tell me the whole truth. I am ready to forget my position as judge, and to give you my help, but you must see yourself that to prove the other side guilty of slander you must prove yourself innocent. What I want from you is an informal and strictly confidential declaration, for the case against you is a serious one, and of such a kind as to require all your efforts to wipe off this blot upon your honour. Your enemies will not respect your delicacy of feeling. They will press you so hard that you will either be obliged to submit to a shameful sentence, or to wound your feelings of honour in proving your innocence. You see I am confiding in you, for in certain cases honour seems so precious a thing to me that I am ready to defend it with all the power of the law. Pay me back, then, in the same coin, trust in me entirely, tell me the whole story without any reserves, and you may rely upon my good offices. All will be well

[64]

if you are innocent, for I shall not be the less a judge because I am your friend; but if you are guilty I am sorry for you, for I warn you that I shall be just."

After doing my best to express my gratitude to him, I said that my position did not oblige me to make any reservations on account of honour, and that I had, consequently, no informal statement to make him.

"The midwife," I added, "is absolutely unknown to me. She is most likely an abandoned woman, who with her worthy companion wants to cheat me of my money."

"I shall be delighted to think so," he answered, "but admitting the fact, see how chance favours her, and makes it a most difficult thing for you to prove your innocence.

"The young lady disappeared three months ago. She was known to be your intimate friend, you called upon her at all hours; you spent a considerable time with her the day before she disappeared, and no one knows what has become of her; but everyone's suspicions point at you, and paid spies are continually dogging your steps. The midwife sent me a requisition yesterday by her counsel, Vauversin. She says that the pregnant lady you brought to her house is the same whom Madame X ** C ** V ** is searching for. She also says that you both wore black dominoes, and the police have ascertained that you were both at the ball in black dominoes on the same night as that on which the midwife says you came to her house; you are also known to have left the ball-room together. All this, it is true, does not constitute full proof of your guilt, but it makes one tremble for your innocence."

"What cause have I to tremble?"

"What cause! Why, a false witness, easily enough hired for a little money, might swear with impunity that he saw you come from the opera together; and a coachman in the same way might swear he had taken you to the midwife's. In that case I should be compelled to order your arrest and examination, with a view to ascertain the name of the person whom you took with you. Do you realise that you are accused of procuring abortion; that three months have gone by without the lady's retreat having been discovered; that she is said to be dead? Do you realise, in short, what a very serious charge murder is?"

"Certainly; but if I die innocent, you will have condemned me wrongly, and will be more to be pitied than I."

[65]

"Yes, yes, but that wouldn't make your case any better. You may be sure, however, that I will not condemn an innocent man; but I am afraid that you will be a long time in prison before you succeed in proving your innocence. To be brief, you see that in twenty-four hours the case looks very bad, and in the course of a week it might look very much worse. My interest was aroused in your favour by the evident absurdity of the accusations, but it is the other circumstances about the case which make it a serious one for you. I can partly understand the circumstances, and the feelings of love and honour which bid you be silent. I have spoken to you, and I hope you will have no reserves with me. I will spare you all the unpleasant circumstances which threaten you, believing, as I do, that you are innocent. Tell me all, and be sure that the lady's honour will not suffer; but if, on the other hand, you are unfortunately guilty of the crimes laid to your charge, I advise you to be prudent, and to take steps which it is not my business to suggest. I warn you that in three or four days I shall cite you to the bar of the court, and that you will then find in me only the judge — just, certainly, but severe and impartial."

I was petrified, for these words showed me my danger in all its nakedness. I saw how I should esteem this worthy man's good offices, and said to him in quite another tone, that innocent as I was, I saw that my best course was to throw myself on his kindness respecting Mdlle. X ** C ** V **, who had committed no crime, but would lose her reputation by this unhappy business.

"I know where she is," I added, "and I may tell you that she would never have left her mother if she had not endeavoured to force her into a marriage she abhorred."

"Well, but the man is now married; let her return to her mother's house, and you will be safe, unless the midwife persists in maintaining that you incited her to procure abortion."

"There is no abortion in the matter; but other reasons prevent her returning to her family. I can tell you no more without obtaining the consent of another party. If I succeed in doing so I shall be able to throw the desired light on the question. Be kind enough to give me a second hearing on the day after to-morrow."

"I understand. I shall be delighted to hear what you have to say. I thank and congratulate you. Farewell!"

I was on the brink of the precipice, but I was determined to leave the kingdom rather than betray the honour of my poor dear sweetheart. If it had been possible, I would gladly have put an end to the case with money; but it was too late. I was sure that Farsetti had the chief hand in all this trouble, that he was continually on my track, and that he paid the spies mentioned by M. de Sartine. He it was who had set Vauversin, the barrister, after me, and I had no doubt that he would do all in his power to ruin me.

I felt that my only course was to tell the whole story to M. de Sartine, but to do that I required Madame du Rumain's permission.

The day after my interview with M. de Sartine I waited on Madame du Rumain at an early hour. Considering the urgency of the case I took the liberty of rousing her from her slumbers, and as soon as she was ready to receive me I told her all.

"There can be no hesitation in the matter," said this delightful woman. "We must make a confidant of M. de Sartine, and I will speak to him myself to-day without fail."

Forthwith she went to her desk and wrote to the criminal lieutenant asking him to see her at three o'clock in the afternoon. In less than an hour the servant returned with a note in which he said he would expect her. We agreed that I should come again in the evening, when she would tell me the result of her interview.

I went to the house at five o'clock, and had only a few minutes to wait.

"I have concealed nothing," said she; "he knows that she is on the eve of her confinement, and that you are not the father, which speaks highly for your generosity. I told him that as soon as the confinement was over, and the young lady had recovered her health, she would return to her mother, though she would make no confession, and that the child should be well looked after. You have now nothing to fear, and can calm yourself; but as the case must go on, you will be cited before the court the day after to-morrow. I advise you to see the clerk of the court on some pretext or other, and to make him accept a sum of money."

I was summoned to appear, and I appeared. I saw M. de Sartine, *sedentem pro tribunali*. At the end of the sitting he told

me that he was obliged to remand me, and that during my remand I must not leave Paris or get married, as all my civil
rights were in suspense pending the decision. I promised to follow his commands.

I acknowledged in my examination that I was at the ball in a
black domino on the night named in my accusation, but I denied
everything else. As for Mdlle. X ** C ** V **, I said that neither
I nor anyone of her family had any suspicion that she was with
child.

Recollecting that I was an alien, and that this circumstance
might make Vauversin call for my arrest, on the plea that I
might fly the kindgom, I thought the moment opportune for
making interest with the clerk of the court, and I accordingly
paid him a visit. After telling him of my fears, I slipped into his
hand a packet of three hundred louis, for which I did not ask for
a receipt, saying that they were to defray expenses if I were
mulcted in costs. He advised me to require the midwife to give
bail for her appearance, and I told my attorney to do so; but,
four days after, the following incident took place:

I was walking in the Temple Gardens, when I was accosted
by a Savoyard, who gave me a note in which I was informed
that somebody in an alley, fifty paces off, wanted to speak to
me. "Either a love affair or a challenge," I said to myself,
"let's see." I stopped my carriage, which was following me, and
went to the place.

I cannot say how surprised I was to see the wretched Castel-
Bajac standing before me. "I have only a word to say," said he,
when he saw me. "We will not be overheard here. The midwife is quite sure that you are the man who brought a pregnant
lady to her, but she is vexed that you are accused of making
away with her. Give her a hundred louis; she will then declare
to the court that she has been mistaken, and your trouble will
be ended. You need not pay the money till she has made her
declaration; we will take your word for it. Come with me and
talk it over with Vauversin. I am sure he will persuade you to
do as I suggest. I know where to find him, follow me at some
distance."

I had listened to him in silence, and I was delighted to see
that the rascals were betraying themselves. "Very good," said
I to the fellow, "you go on, and I will follow." I went after

him to the third floor of a house in the Rue aux Ours, where I found Vauversin the barrister. No sooner had I arrived than he went to business without any prefatory remarks.

"The midwife," he said, "will call on you with a witness apparently with the intention of maintaining to your face that you are her man; *but she won't be able to recognise you.* She will then proceed with the witness to the court, and will declare that she has made a mistake, and the criminal lieutenant will forthwith put an end to the proceedings. You will thus be certain of gaining your case against the lady's mother."

I thought the plan well conceived, and said that they would find me at the Temple any day up to noon.

"But the midwife wants a hundred louis badly."

"You mean that the worthy woman rates her perjury at that price. Well, never mind, I will pay the money, and you may trust to my word; but I can't do so before she has taken oath to her mistake before the court."

"Very good, but you must first give me twenty-five louis to reimburse me for my costs and fees."

"Certainly, if you will give me a formal receipt for the money."

He hesitated at first, but after talking it over the money proved too strong a bait, and he wrote out the receipt and I gave him twenty-five louis. He thanked me, and said that though Madame X ** C ** V ** was his client, he would let me know confidentially how best to put a stop to the proceedings. I thanked him with as much gratitude as if I had really intended to make use of his services, and I left to write and tell M. de Sartine what had taken place.

Three days afterwards I was told that a man and woman wanted to see me. I went down and asked the woman what she wanted.

"I want to speak to M. Casanova."

"I am he."

"Then I have made a mistake, for which I hope you will forgive me."

Her companion smiled, and they went off.

The same day Madame du Rumain had a letter from the abbess telling her that her young friend had given birth to a fine boy, who had been sent away to a place where he would be well looked after. She stated that the young lady could not leave the convent for the next six weeks, at the end of which time she could return to her mother with a certificate which would protect her from all annoyance.

Soon after the midwife was put in solitary confinement, Castel-Bajac was sent to the Bicêtre, and Vauversin's name was struck off the rolls. The suit instituted against me by Madame X ** C ** V ** went on till her daughter reappeared, but I knew that I had nothing to fear. The girl returned to her mother about the end of August armed with a certificate from the abbess, who said she had been under her protection for four months, during which time she had never left the convent or seen any persons from outside. This was perfectly true, but the abbess added that her only reason for her going back to her family was that she had nothing more to dread from the attentions of M. de la Popelinière, and in this the abbess lied.

Mdlle. X ** C ** V ** profited by the delight of her mother in seeing her again safe and sound, and made her wait on M. de Sartine with the abbess's certificate, stop all proceedings against me, and withdraw all the charges she had made. Her daughter told her that if I liked I might claim damages for libel, and that if she did not wish to injure her reputation she would say nothing more about what had happened.

The mother wrote me a letter of the most satisfactory character, which I had registered in court, thus putting an end to the prosecution. In my turn I wrote to congratulate her on the recovery of her daughter, but I never set foot in her house again, to avoid any disagreeable scenes with Farsetti.

Mdlle. X ** C ** V ** could not stay any longer in Paris, where her tale was known to everyone, and Farsetti took her to Brussels with her sister Madelaine. Some time after, her mother followed her, and they then went on to Venice, and there in three years' time she became a great lady. Fifteen years afterwards I saw her again, and she was a widow, happy enough apparently, and enjoying a great reputation on account of her rank, wit, and social qualities, but our connection was never renewed.

In four years the reader will hear more of Castel-Bajac. Towards the end of the same year (1759), before I went to Holland, I spent several hundred francs to obtain the release of the midwife.

I lived like a prince, and men might have thought me happy, but I was not. The enormous expenses I incurred, my love of spending money, and magnificent pleasures, warned me, in spite of myself, that there were rocks ahead. My business would have kept me going for a long time, if custom had not been paralysed by the war; but as it was, I, like everybody else, experienced the effect of bad times. My warehouse contained four hundred pieces of stuffs with designs on them, but as I could not hope to dispose of them before the peace, and as peace seemed a long way off, I was threatened with ruin.

With this fear I wrote to Esther to get her father to give me the remainder of my money, to send me a sharp clerk, and to join in my speculation. M. d'O ** said that if I would set up in Holland he would become responsible for everything and give me half profits, but I liked Paris too well to agree to so good an offer. I was sorry for it afterwards.

I spent a good deal of money at my private house, but the chief expense of my life, which was unknown to others but which was ruining me, was incurred in connection with the girls who worked in my establishment. With my complexion and my pronounced liking for variety, a score of girls, nearly all of them pretty and seductive, as most Paris girls are, was a reef on which my virtue made shipwreck every day. Curiosity had a good deal to do with it, and they profited by my impatience to take possession by selling their favours dearly. They all followed the example of the first favourite, and everyone claimed in turn an establishment, furniture, money, and jewels; and I knew too little of the value of money to care how much they asked. My fancy never lasted longer than a week, and often waned in three or four days, and the last comer always appeared the most worthy of my attentions.

As soon as I had made a new choice I saw no more of my old loves, but I continued to provide for them, and that with a good deal of money. Madame d'Urfé, who thought I was rich, gave me no trouble. I made her happy by using my oracle to second the magical ceremonies of which she grew fonder every day, although she never attained her aim. Manon Baletti, however, grieved me sorely by her jealousy and her well-founded reproaches. She could not understand — and I did not wonder at it — how I could put off marrying her if I really loved her. She accused me of deceiving her. Her mother died of consumption in our arms. Silvia had won my true friendship. I looked upon her as a most worthy woman, whose kindness of heart and purity of life deserved the esteem of all. I stayed in the family for three days after her death, sincerely sympathising with them in their affliction.

Thus ended, as far as Casanova was concerned, the romantic history of Mdlle. X ** C ** V **; for when they met a few months later in Holland, where she was travelling with her family and the inevitable Farsetti, it was as strangers, without speaking or greeting. Fifteen years later they met once more in Venice, but then a social gulf, which neither attempted to bridge, separated the Dowager-Countess Orsini-Rosenberg and the shabby adventurer.

Lady Mary Wortley Montagu, writing to her daughter from Venice on October 3rd, 1758, informs her that three beautiful ladies, four including the Signora Madre, have just left Venice for London and warns her to be careful about associating with them should they attempt to make her acquaintance on the pretext of having known her mother in Venice. In view of the Signora Madre's self-assurance, she thinks it is well to tell her daughter that she herself has only met these ladies in public resorts and at the house of the British resident (John Murray, Casanova's friend), who, as one of their professed admirers, had forced his wife to receive them. The father of the three beauties, she adds, was an Englishman called Wynne, who is believed to have been well off. According to the gossip of the town, this Wynne had come to Venice shortly after the death of his wife. In search of distraction he had been introduced by his gondolier to a very handsome Greek girl, who took his fancy and, after having presented him with three daughters, finally induced him to marry her. Shortly after the family had been increased by two sons, Wynne died, leaving each of his daughters fifteen hundred pounds. In order to receive this inheritance Mrs. Wynne had already been to England with her children and there proved the legality of her marriage. After her return to Venice all the young men were making love to her. It seems that the oldest daughter speaks English. In any case, it would be better to have as little to do with them as possible. On December 5th Lady Mary reports that the beautiful ladies are said to be still in Paris and have probably their reasons for stopping there.

THE FALL AND RISE OF GIUSTINA WYNNE

*Herr Gustav Gugitz, the leading German authority on Casanova, has traced the whole story of Mdlle. X ** C ** V **.[1] Her real name was Giustiniana-Franca-Antonia. She was born in Venice on January 21st, 1736, as the first-fruit of the secret loves of Sir Richard Wynne and Anna Gazini, his Greek mistress. From this it appears that Casanova is again juggling with dates when he asserts that Giustina was twelve years old in 1751, when they first met, and sixteen in 1759, at the time of her Parisian adventure; to say nothing of the fact that, even according to his own chronology, she must have been at least twenty, since twelve plus eight generally amount to that sum.*

Of her voyage to England and her stay in Paris in 1751, Giustina Wynne was later herself to give a description in her Pièces morales, *as well as of her return to Venice the following year and her life there for the next six years, the infatuation she inspired in the aged breast of Joseph Smith, the British consul (the air of the lagoons seems to have been fatal to the morals and decorum of Britain's representatives), and her own ardent passion for a young nobleman, introduced to her by the incautious Smith.*

Strange fatality! This young nobleman was none other than Andrea Memmo, the scapegrace patrician, the boon companion of Casanova in his early exploits in Venice and one of the direct causes of his imprisonment under The Leads; the same Memmo who throughout his life kept a tender affection for his old friend, with whom he continued to correspond until, a pillar of the state and laden with honours, he passed from this world, preceding his correspondent in Dux by only a few years.

If we are to believe the Pièces morales, *the course of true love was thwarted by Mrs. Wynne, who was dreaming of a finer* parti *for her lovely daughter than the dissolute young patrician, the associate of the undesirable Casanova, whom she had snubbed in Paris. So Giustina was kept a prisoner at home, where, "surrounded by five hundred volumes," she says, she made the best of her captivity by cultivating her mind. The results of this régime were so beneficial that she found, on regaining her liberty, the ardour of her passion had spent itself in the pursuit of knowledge. The prospect of re-visiting France and England and making a fine marriage contributed not a little to this change of sentiment, and it was with a light*

[1] Giacomo Casanova und sein Lebensroman, von Gustav Gugitz. Verlag Ed. Strache.

[73]

heart she bade farewell to that "tender friend," the still devoted Andrea, who accompanied the family as far as Milan.

Where and when the faux pas *was committed which was to involve her and Casanova in such trouble, it is difficult to say with absolute certainty. All that has been ascertained is that she was "in trouble" when she reached Paris. So it may well have been in Venice, and there can be little doubt that Memmo (the* Pièces morales *refer to the jilted lover as "M. M. . . .") was the other guilty party in this escapade. If we admit these probabilities as facts, it is equally credible that Memmo would have referred her to his friend Casanova in Paris as the "friend in need" and one especially qualified to help her out of her difficulties. It was doubtless owing to them and the resulting gossip in Paris that Giustina failed to find the* beau parti *of which she and her mother had been dreaming, either there or in England, where the family went on leaving France. But what she failed to find in these countries, she found waiting for her on her return to Venice next year in the person of the venerable Count Philipp, of the noble Austrian house of Orsini-Rosenberg, who represented his country as ambassador to the Venetian Republic. It was evidently decreed that Giustina was to finish as an old man's darling.*

For the four years that the marriage lasted, the count was doing his utmost to have his marriage sanctioned in Vienna, where his relatives, which included Prince Kaunitz, the brother of his first wife, looked askance on this mésalliance. *In vain he invoked the legitimate claims of the Wynne family to aristocratic rank, going even so far as to point out that the patrician Andrea Memmo had been a suitor for his wife's hand as proof that Giustina Wynne was considered a desirable match in Venice. His efforts and her own were unavailing to get the new countess "accepted" at court; and when he died, in Vienna, she retired to the family estate until she was finally able, after many efforts, to return to Venice. There she found the old welcome, and her house was soon the gathering-place of the most distinguished talents of the cosmopolitan* intelligenzia *residing in that city, among whom, we may suppose, was her former lover, Andrea Memmo, the ornament of the senate and the literary salons.*

Besides the Pièces morales, *already referred to, Giustina Wynne-Rosenberg published a series of works, all written in French and translated into several languages. On the appearance of the first of her books (1782), a description of the festivities given in Venice in honour of the visit of the future Czar Paul I., Casanova, then follow-*

ing the honourable profession of secret informer and moral censor for the Venetian government, took the opportunity of offering his respectful congratulations to the noble authoress, and at the same time sent her one of his own productions. These offerings were acknowledged in gracious though formal terms by the recipient.

For nine years Giustina continued to write and publish. The best of her works, entitled Les Morlaques, a study of racial customs, aroused the admiration of Goethe and Charles Nodier. It is interesting to see among the list of her published works a pamphlet dedicated to Andrea Memmo on the occasion of the marriage of his oldest daughter to Louis Mocenigo.

In 1791 Giustina died in Padua, mourned by the many friends and admirers which her talents, her charm, and her unfailing generosity to all who needed her help had earned for her. Two years later Andrea followed her, Casanova being the last of the three to lay down his pen for ever.

The avowal which Giustina noted in her Pièces morales might well serve as epitaph for their several tombs, in Padua, in Venice, and in Bohemia: "Ai-je donc fait bien moins de folies qu'un autre? — Tout au contraire: j'ai peut-être outre-passé la portion permise à chacun."

CHAPTER XII

"Moving On"

THE year 1760, Casanova being then thirty-five years of age, marks the beginning of those ceaseless wanderings across the map of Europe which were to continue for a quarter of a century. Though he will continue to speak of settling, of marrying, of turning monk, it is henceforth without conviction. Deep down in his heart he knows that he is no longer the master, but the sport of a capricious destiny — a destiny, it is true, which he has willed on himself by resolutely turning his back whenever Providence offered him the choice of safely navigating his barque along the charted ways which lead to safe harbours.

If we believe Casanova's own account, as set forth in his Memoirs, these migrations were prompted, for the most part, by the whims of his "genius," which would impel him to strike his tent and take to the road just when, as often as not, his pleasures and his interests *should have counselled him to stay. But although at first the mere lure of adventure, "the call of the road," doubtless did supply the main reason for seeking a change of scene, we shall find, or rather the various researches of commentators have found, that these peregrinations were due to less fantastic motives than those supplied by the Memoirs. During this second period of the Casanovian Odyssey it is more and more the warning hand of the law or the necessity of finding new hunting and poaching grounds, or both, which impels the nomad to "move on."*

These were doubtless the reasons for the journey to Germany and Switzerland, which follows the nebulous Dutch adventure. There had been the usual trouble with bills of exchange and promissory notes in Holland, on the one hand; on the other, there was a promising prospect of recouping himself for his losses at Cologne, which, after the unlucky affair at Minden, had become the headquarters of the French troops. This for Casanova and his like meant the blandishments of Paris and the resources of the Palais-Royal — in other words, Paradise Regained — within a day's journey from the Dutch frontier.

The adventures in Cologne and Bonn at the court of the Prince-Elector, with their carnival background, belong almost exclusively to the realm of Casanovian myths, as German commentators (notably Herr Gugitz) have had no difficulty in proving. That he visited those cities is doubtless true; for, as already mentioned, the table there was richly served for all who shared the appetites of our hero. It is also at least probable that he for a while was able to satisfy the most urgent of these. But what seems definitely disproved is that he was ever anything more than a looker-on at the spectacle. As for the pièce de résistance of the rich fare he asks us to enjoy with him in retrospect, the seduction of the burgomaster's wife and his clandestine meetings with her, this incredible story appears to have been imagined for the sorry purpose of wreaking a posthumous vengeance on a worthy magistrate whose duty compelled him to get rid of the undesirable characters that were disturbing the already troubled peace of Cologne.

Following the Roman principle of converting defeat into triumph, Casanova — then reduced to pawning his wardrobe — makes his allegedly splendid entry into Switzerland, squandering money, frequenting the best society and the worst, which welcomes him wherever he goes, finally settling for a while in Soleure, where his "adorable"

Madame Dubois keeps house for him — in fact, all the usual attractions of the Casanova tour are there, including Helvetian orgies and, needless to say, international swindling and gaming. But do what he will to spice his dishes, there is a table-d'hôte flavour about the Swiss bill of fare which hints at Ersatz. It is not until we come to the big morceau, *for which he has evidently been preparing, the "Visit to Voltaire," that we find again the old verve, the incisive and eager note which informs the best passages of the Memoirs.*

Although no record exists to prove that this visit ever took place as described by Casanova, the severest of his critics (for example, C. Samaran, A. Ravà, G. Gugitz) incline, in this case, to give him the benefit of the doubt. Despite obvious emendations and exaggerations, the interview at Les Délices, where Voltaire was then residing, is well in keeping with the character of both protagonists. Se non è vero . . . .

"M. de Voltaire," said I, "this is the happiest moment of my life. I have been your pupil for twenty years, and my heart is full of joy to see my master."

"Honour me with your attendance on my course for twenty years more, and promise me that you will bring me my fees at the end of that time."

"Certainly, if you promise to wait for me."

This Voltairean sally made all present laugh, as was to be expected, for those who laugh keep one party in countenance at the other's expense, and the side which has the laughter is sure to win; this is the rule of good society.

I was not taken by surprise, and waited to have my revenge.

Just then two Englishmen came in and were presented to him.

"These gentlemen are English," said Voltaire; "I wish I were."

I thought the compliment false and out of place; for the gentlemen were obliged to reply out of politeness that they wished they had been French, or if they did not care to tell a lie they would be too confused to tell the truth. I believe every man of honour should put his own nation first.

A moment after, Voltaire turned to me again and said that as I was a Venetian I must know Count Algarotti.

"I know him, but not because I am a Venetian, as seven-eighths of my dear countrymen are not even aware of his existence."

"I should have said, as a man of letters."

"I know him from having spent two months with him at Padua, seven years ago, and what particularly attracted my attention was the admiration he professed for M. de Voltaire."

"That is flattering for me, but he has no need of admiring anyone."

"If Algarotti had not begun by admiring others, he would never have made a name for himself. As an admirer of Newton he endeavoured to teach the ladies to discuss the theory of light."

"Has he succeeded?"

"Not as well as M. de Fontenelle in his *Plurality of Worlds*; however, one may say he has succeeded."

"True. If you see him at Bologna, tell him I am expecting to hear from him about Russia. He can address the letters to my banker, Bianchi, at Milan, and they will be sent on to me."

"I will not fail to do so if I see him."

"I have heard that the Italians do not care for his style."

"No; all that he writes is full of French idioms. His style is wretched."

"But do not these French turns increase the beauty of your language?"

"They make it insufferable, as French would be mixed with Italian or German even though it were written by M. de Voltaire."

"You are right; every language should preserve its purity. Livy has been criticised on this account; his Latin is said to be tainted with patavinity."

"When I began to learn Latin, the Abbé Lazzarini told me he preferred Livy to Sallust."

"The Abbé Lazzarini, author of the tragedy, *Ulisse il giovine*? You must have been very young; I wish I had known him. But I knew the Abbé Conti well; the same that was Newton's friend, and whose four tragedies contain the whole of Roman history."

"I also knew and admired him. I was young, but I congratulated myself on being admitted into the society of these great men. It seems as if it were yesterday, though it is many years ago; and now in your presence my inferiority does not humiliate me. I wish to be the younger son of all humanity."

"Better so than to be the chief and eldest. May I ask you to what branch of literature you have devoted yourself?"

"To none; but that, perhaps, will come afterwards. In the meanwhile I read as much as I can, and try to study character on my travels."

"That is the way to become learned, but the book of humanity is too vast. Reading a history is the easier way."

"Yes, if history did not lie. One is not sure of the truth of the facts. It is tiring, while the study of the world is amusing. Horace, whom I know by heart, is my guide-book."

"Algarotti, too, is very fond of Horace. Of course you are fond of poetry?"

"It is my passion."

"Have you made many sonnets?"

"Ten or twelve I like, and two or three thousand which in all probability I have not read twice."

"The Italians are mad after sonnets."

"Yes; if one can call it a madness to desire to put thought into measured harmony. The sonnet is difficult because the thought has to be fitted exactly into the fourteen lines."

"It is Procrustes' bed, and that's the reason you have so few good ones. As for us, we have not one; but that is the fault of our language."

"And of the French genius, which considers that a thought when extended loses all its force."

"And you do not think so?"

"Pardon me, it depends on the kind of thought. A witty saying, for example, will not make a sonnet; in French or Italian it belongs to the domain of epigram."

"What Italian poet do you like best?"

"Ariosto; but I cannot say I love him better than the others, for he is my only love."

"You know the others, though?"

"I think I have read them all, but all their lights pale before Ariosto's. Fifteen years ago I read all you have written against him, and I said that you would retract when you had read his works."

"I am obliged to you for thinking that I had not read them. As a matter of fact I had done so, but I was young. I knew Italian very imperfectly, and being prejudiced by the learned Italians who adore Tasso I was unfortunate enough to publish a criticism on Ariosto which I thought my own, while it was only the echo of those who had prejudiced me. I adore your Ariosto."

"Ah! M. de Voltaire, I breathe again. But be good enough to have the work in which you turned this great man into ridicule excommunicated."

"What use would that be? All my books are excommunicated; but I will give you a good proof of my retractation."

I was astonished! The great man began to recite the two fine passages from the thirty-fourth and thirty-fifth cantos, in which the divine poet speaks of the conversation of Astolpho with St. John, and he did it without missing a single line or committing the slightest fault against the laws of prosody. He then pointed out the beauties of the passages with his natural insight and with a great man's genius. I could not have had anything better from the lips of the most skilled commentators in Italy. I listened to him with the greatest attention, hardly daring to breathe, and waiting for him to make a mistake, but I had my trouble for nothing. I turned to the company crying that I was more than astonished, and that all Italy should know what I had seen. "And I, sir," said the great man, "will let all Europe know of the amends I owe to the greatest genius our continent has produced."

Greedy of the praise which he deserved so well, Voltaire gave me the next day his translation, which Ariosto begins thus:

Quindi avvien che tra principi e signori.

The lines were as follows:

Les Papes, les Césars, apaisant leur querelle,
Jurent sur l'Evangile une paix éternelle;
Vous les voyez l'un de l'autre ennemis;
C'était pour se tromper qu'ils s'étaient réunis:
Nul serment n'est gardé, nul accord n'est sincère;
Quand la bouche a parlé, le cœur dit le contraire.
Du ciel qu'ils attestaient, ils bravaient le courroux:
L'intérêt est le Dieu qui les gouverne tous.

At the end of the recitation, which gained the applause of all who heard it, although not one of them knew Italian, Madame Denis, his niece, asked me if I thought the passage her uncle had just recited one of the finest the poet had written.

"Yes, but not the finest."

"It ought to be; for without it Signor Lodovico would not have gained his apotheosis."

"He has been canonised, then? I was not aware of that."

At these words the laugh, headed by Voltaire, went for Madame Denis. Everybody laughed except myself, and I continued to look perfectly serious.

Voltaire was vexed at not seeing me laugh like the rest, and asked me the reason.

"Are you thinking," said he, "of some more than human passage?"

"Yes," I answered.

"What passage is that?"

"The last thirty-six stanzas of the twenty-third canto, where the poet describes in detail how Roland became mad. Since the world has existed no one has discovered the springs of madness, unless Ariosto himself, who became mad in his old age. These stanzas are terrible, and I am sure they must have made you tremble."

"Yes, I remember they render love dreadful. I long to read them again."

"Perhaps the gentleman will be good enough to recite them," said Madame Denis, with a side glance at her uncle.

"Willingly," said I, "if you will have the goodness to listen to me."

"You have learnt them by heart, then, have you?" said Voltaire.

"Yes, it was a pleasure and no trouble. Since I was sixteen, I have read over Ariosto two or three times every year; it is my passion, and the lines have naturally become linked in my memory without my having given myself any pains to learn them. I know it all, except his long genealogies and his historical tirades, which fatigue the mind and do not touch the heart. It is only Horace that I know throughout, in spite of the often prosaic style of his epistles, which are certainly far from equalling Boileau's."

"Boileau is often too lengthy; I admire Horace, but as for Ariosto, with his forty long cantos, there is too much of him."

"It is fifty-one cantos, M. de Voltaire."

The great man was silent, but Madame Denis was equal to the occasion.

[81]

"Come, come," said she, "let us hear the thirty-six stanzas which earned the author the title of divine, and which are to make us tremble."

I then began, in an assured voice, but not in that monotonous tone adopted by the Italians, with which the French so justly reproach us. The French would be the best reciters if they were not constrained by the rhyme, for they say what they feel better than any other people. They have neither the passionate monotonous tone of my fellow-countrymen, nor the sentimentality of the Germans, nor the fatiguing mannerisms of the English; to every period they give its proper expression, but the recurrence of the same sounds partly spoils their recitation. I recited the fine verses of Ariosto, as if it had been rhythmic prose, animating it by the sound of my voice and the movements of my eyes, and by modulating my intonation according to the sentiments with which I wished to inspire my audience. They saw how hardly I could restrain my tears, and every eye was wet; but when I came to the stanza:

> *Poi ch'allargare il freno al dolor puote,*
> *Chè resta solo, e senza altrui rispetto,*
> *Giù dagli occhi rigando per le gote*
> *Sparge un fiume di lacrime sul petto,*

my tears coursed down my cheeks to such an extent that everyone began to sob. M. de Voltaire and Madame Denis threw their arms round my neck, but their embraces could not stop me, for Roland, to become mad, had to notice that he was in the same bed in which Angelica had lately been found in the arms of the too fortunate Medor, and I had to reach the next stanza. For my voice of sorrow and wailing I substituted the expression of that terror which arose naturally from the contemplation of his fury, which was in its effects like a tempest, a volcano, or an earthquake.

When I had finished I received with a sad air the congratulations of the audience. Voltaire cried:

"I always said so; the secret of drawing tears is to weep one's self, but they must be real tears, and to shed them the heart must be stirred to its depths. I am obliged to you, sir," he added, embracing me, "and I promise to recite the same stanzas myself to-morrow, and to weep like you."

He kept his word.

"It is astonishing," said Madame Denis, "that intolerant Rome should not have condemned the song of Roland."

"Far from it," said Voltaire, "Leo X. excommunicated whoever should dare to condemn it. The two great families of Este and Medici interested themselves in the poet's favour. Without that protection it is probable that the one line on the donation of Rome by Constantine to Silvester, where the poet speaks *puzza forte,* would have sufficed to put the whole poem under an interdict."

"I believe," said I, "that the line which has excited the most talk is that in which Ariosto throws doubt on the general resurrection. Ariosto," I added, "in speaking of the hermit who would have hindered Rhodomonte from getting possession of Isabella, widow of Zerbin, paints the African, who wearied of the hermit's sermons, seizes him and throws him so far that he dashes him against a rock, against which he remains in a dead swoon, so that *che al novissimo di forse fia desto.*"

This *forse,* which may possibly have only been placed there as a flower of rhetoric or as a word to complete the verse, raised a great uproar, which would doubtless have greatly amused the poet if he had had time!

"It is a pity," said Madame Denis, "that Ariosto was not more careful in these hyperbolical expressions."

"Be quiet, niece, they are full of wit. They are all golden grains, which are dispersed throughout the work in the best taste."

The conversation was then directed towards various topics, and at last we got to the Ecossaise we had played at Soleure.

They knew all about it.

M. de Voltaire said that if I liked to play it at his house he would write to M. de Chavigni to send the Lindane, and that he himself would play Montrose. I excused myself by saying that Madame ** was at Bâle and that I should be obliged to go on my journey the next day. At this he exclaimed loudly, aroused the whole company against me, and said at last that he should consider my visit as an insult unless I spared him a week at least of my society.

"Sir," said I, "I have only come to Geneva to have the honour of seeing you, and now that I have obtained that favour I have nothing more to do."

"Have you come to speak to me, or for me to speak to you?"

"In a measure, of course, to speak to you, but much more for you to speak to me."

"Then stay here three days at least; come to dinner every day, and we will have some conversation."

The invitation was so flattering and pressing that I could not refuse it with a good grace. I therefore accepted, and I then left to go and write.

I had not been back for a quarter of an hour when a syndic of the town, an amiable man, whom I had seen at M. de Voltaire's, and whose name I shall not mention, came and asked me to give him supper. "I was present," said he, "at your argument with the great man, and though I did not open my mouth I should much like to have an hour's talk with you." By way of reply, I embraced him, begging him to excuse my dressing-gown, and telling him that I should be glad if he would spend the whole night with me.

The worthy man spent two hours with me, without saying a word on the subject of literature, but to please me he had no need to talk of books, for he was a disciple of Epicurus and Socrates, and the evening was spent in telling little stories, in bursts of laughter, and in accounts of the various kinds of pleasure obtainable at Geneva.

Next morning, young Fox came to see me with the two Englishmen I had seen at M. de Voltaire's. They proposed a game of quinze, which I accepted, and after losing fifty louis I left off, and we walked about the town till dinner-time.

We found the Duc de Villars at Délices; he had come there to consult Dr. Tronchin, who had kept him alive for the last ten years.

I was silent during the repast, but at dessert, M. de Voltaire, knowing that I had reasons for not liking the Venetian government, introduced the subject; but I disappointed him, as I maintained that in no country could a man enjoy more perfect liberty than in Venice.

"Yes," said he, "provided he resigns himself to play the part of a dumb man."

And seeing that I did not care for the subject, he took me by the arm to his garden, of which, he said, he was the creator. The principal walk led to a pretty running stream.

"'Tis the Rhone," said he, "which I send into France."

"It does not cost you much in carriage, at all events," said I.

He smiled pleasantly and showed me the principal street of Geneva, and Mont Blanc, which is the highest point of the Alps.

Bringing back the conversation to Italian literature, he began to talk nonsense with much wit and learning, but always concluding with a false judgment. I let him talk on. He spoke of Homer, Dante, and Petrarch, and everybody knows what he thought of these great geniuses, but he did himself wrong in writing what he thought. I contented myself with saying that if these great men did not merit the esteem of those who studied them, it would at all events be a long time before they had to come down from the high place in which the praise of centuries had placed them.

The Duc de Villars and the famous Tronchin came and joined us. The doctor, a tall fine man, polite, eloquent without being a conversationalist, a learned physician, a man of wit, a favourite pupil of Boerhaave, without scientific jargon, or charlatanism, or self-sufficiency, enchanted me. His system of medicine was based on regimen, and to make rules he had to be a man of profound science. I have been assured, but can scarcely believe it, that he cured a consumptive patient of a secret disease by means of the milk of an ass, which he had submitted to thirty strong frictions of mercury by four sturdy porters.

As to Villars he also attracted my attention, but in quite a different way to Tronchin. On examining his face and manner I thought I saw before me a woman of seventy dressed as a man, thin and emaciated, but still proud of her looks, and with claims to past beauty. His cheeks and lips were painted, his eyebrows blackened, and his teeth were false; he wore a huge wig, which exhaled amber, and at his buttonhole was an enormous bunch of flowers which touched his chin. He affected a gracious manner, and he spoke so softly that it was often impossible to hear what he said. He was excessively polite and affable, and his manners were those of the Regency. His whole appearance was supremely ridiculous. I was told that in his youth he was a lover of the fair sex, but now that he was no longer good for anything he had modestly made himself into a woman, and had four pretty pets in his employ, who took turns in the disgusting duty of warming his old carcase at night.

[85]

Villars was governor of Provence, and had his back eaten up with cancer. In the course of nature he should have been buried ten years ago, but Tronchin kept him alive with his regimen and by feeding the wounds on slices of veal. Without this the cancer would have killed him. His life might well be called an artificial one.

I accompanied M. de Voltaire to his bedroom, where he changed his wig and put on another cap, for he always wore one on account of the rheumatism to which he was subject. I saw on the table the *Summa* of St. Thomas, and among other Italian poets the *Secchia Rapita* of Tassoni.

"This," said Voltaire, "is the only tragi-comic poem which Italy has. Tassoni was a monk, a wit, and a genius as well as a poet."

"I will grant his poetical ability but not his learning, for he ridiculed the system of Copernicus, and said that if his theories were followed astronomers would not be able to calculate lunations or eclipses."

"Where does he make that ridiculous remark?"

"In his academical discourses."

"I have not read them, but I will get them."

He took a pen and noted the name down, and said:

"But Tassoni has criticised Petrarch very ingeniously."

"Yes, but he has dishonoured taste and literature, like Muratori."

"Here he is. You must allow that his learning is immense."

"*Est ubi peccat.*"

Voltaire opened a door, and I saw a hundred great files full of papers.

"That's my correspondence," said he. "You see before you nearly fifty thousand letters, to which I have replied."

"Have you a copy of your answers?"

"Of a good many of them. That's the business of a servant of mine, who has nothing else to do."

"I know plenty of booksellers who would give a good deal to get hold of your answers."

"Yes; but look out for the booksellers when you publish anything, if you have not yet begun; they are greater robbers than Barabbas."

"I shall not have anything to do with these gentlemen till I am an old man."

"Then they will be the scourge of your old age."

Thereupon I quoted a Macaronic verse by Merlin Coccæus.

"Where's that from?"

"It's a line from a celebrated poem in twenty-four cantos."

"Celebrated?"

"Yes; and, what is more, worthy of being celebrated; but to appreciate it one must understand the Mantuan dialect."

"I could make it out, if you could get me a copy."

"I shall have the honour of presenting you with one to-morrow."

"You will oblige me extremely."

We had to leave his room and spend two hours in the company, talking over all sorts of things. Voltaire displayed all the resources of his brilliant and fertile wit, and charmed everyone in spite of his sarcastic observations, which did not even spare those present, but he had an inimitable manner of lancing a sarcasm without wounding a person's feelings. When the great man accompanied his witticisms with a graceful smile he could always get a laugh.

He kept up a notable establishment and an excellent table, a rare circumstance with his poetic brothers, who are rarely favourites of Plutus as he was. He was then sixty years old, and had a hundred and twenty thousand francs a year. It has been said maliciously that this great man enriched himself by cheating his publishers; whereas the fact was that he fared no better than any other author, and instead of duping them was often their dupe. The Cramers must be excepted, whose fortune he made. Voltaire had other ways of making money than by his pen; and as he was greedy of fame, he often gave his works away on the sole condition that they were to be printed and published. During the short time I was with him, I was a witness of such a generous action; he made a present to his bookseller of the *Princess of Babylon*, a charming story which he had written in three days.

After a good night's sleep I awoke in an active mood, and began to write a letter to Voltaire in blank verse, which cost me four times the pains that rhymed verses would have done. I sent it to him with the poem of Théophile Falengue, but I made a mistake in doing so, as I might have known he would not care for it; one cannot appreciate what one does not understand. I then went to Mr. Fox, where I found the two Englishmen, who offered me my revenge. I lost a hundred louis, and was glad to see them set out for Lausanne.

At noon I went to M. de Voltaire's. He was not to be seen, but Madame Denis consoled me for his absence. She had wit, learning without pretension, taste, and a great hatred for the King of Prussia, whom she called a villain. She asked about my beautiful housekeeper, and congratulated me on having married her to a respectable man. Although I feel now that she was quite right, I was far from thinking so then; the impression was too fresh on my mind. Madame Denis begged me to tell her how I had escaped from The Leads, but as the story was rather a long one I promised to satisfy her another time.

M. de Voltaire did not dine with us; he appeared, however, at five o'clock, holding a letter in his hand.

"Do you know," said he, "the Marquis Albergati Capacelli, senator of Bologna, and Count Paradisi?"

"I do not know Paradisi, but I know Albergati by sight and by reputation; he is not a senator, but one of the Forty, who at Bologna are Fifty."

"Dear me! That seems rather a riddle!"

"Do you know him?"

"No, but he has sent me Goldoni's *Theatre*, the translation of my *Tancred*, and some Bologna sausages, and he says he will come and see me."

"He will not come; he is not such a fool."

"How a fool? Would there be anything foolish in coming to see me?"

"Certainly not, as far as you are concerned; but very much so for his own sake."

"Would you mind telling me why?"

"He knows what he would lose; for he enjoys the idea you seem to have of him, and if he came you would see his nothingness, and good-bye to the illusion. He is a worthy man with six thousand sequins a year, and a craze for the theatre. He is a good actor enough, and has written several comedies in prose, but they are fit neither for the study nor the stage."

"You certainly give him a coat which does not make him look any bigger."

"I assure you it is not quite small enough."

"But tell me how he can belong to the Forty and the Fifty?"

"Just as at Bâle noon is at eleven."

"I understand; just as your Council of Ten is composed of seventeen members."

"Exactly; but the cursed Forty of Bologna are men of another kind."

"Why cursed?"

"Because they are not subject to the fisc, and are thus enabled to commit whatever crimes they like with perfect impunity; all they have got to do is to live outside the state borders on their revenues."

"That is a blessing, and not a curse; but let me return to our subject. I suppose the Marquis Albergati is a man of letters?"

"He writes well enough, but he is fond of the sound of his own voice, his style is prolix, and I don't think he has much brains."

"He is an actor, I think you said?"

"Yes, and a very good one; above all, when he plays the lover's part in one of his own plays."

"Is he a handsome man?"

"Yes, on the stage, but not elsewhere; his face lacks expression."

"But his plays give satisfaction?"

"Not to persons who understand play writing; they would be hissed if they were intelligible."

"And what do you think of Goldoni?"

"I have the highest opinion of him. Goldoni is the Italian Molière."

"Why does he call himself poet to the Duke of Parma?"

"No doubt to prove that a wit as well as a fool has his weak points; in all probability the duke knows nothing about it. He also calls himself a barrister, though he is such only in his own imagination. Goldoni is a good play writer, and nothing more. Everybody in Venice knows me for his friend, and I can therefore speak of him with authority. He does not shine in society, and in spite of the fine satire of his works he is a man of an extremely gentle disposition."

"So I have been told. He is poor, and wants to leave Venice. The managers of the theatres where they play his pieces will not like that."

"People talked about getting him a pension, but the project has been relegated to the Greek Kalends, as they said that if he had a pension he would write no more."

"Cumæ refused to give a pension to Homer, for fear that all the blind men would ask for a pension."

We spent a pleasant day, and he thanked me heartily for the copy of the *Macaronicon*, which he promised to read. He introduced me to a Jesuit he had in his household, who was called Adam, and he added, after telling me his name, "not the first Adam." I was told afterwards that Voltaire used to play backgammon with him, and when he lost he would throw the dice and the box at his head. If Jesuits were treated like that all the world over, perhaps we should have none but inoffensive Jesuits at last, but that happy time is still far off.

After having enjoyed a calm and refreshing sleep for ten hours, I felt myself able to enjoy the delightful society of M. de Voltaire. I went to his house, but I was disappointed in my hopes, as it pleased the great man to be in a fault-finding and sarcastic mood the whole day. He knew I had to leave on the morrow.

He began by thanking me at table for my present of Merlin Coccæus.

"You certainly gave it me with good intentions," said he, "but I owe you no thanks for praising it so highly, as you made me lose four hours in reading nonsense."

I felt my hair stand on end, but I mastered my emotions, and told him quietly enough that one day, perhaps, he would find himself obliged to praise the poem more highly than I had done. I quoted several instances of the insufficiency of a first perusal.

"That's true," said he; "but as for your Merlin, I will read him no more. I have put him beside Chapelain's *Pucelle*."

"Which pleases all the critics, in spite of its bad versification, for it is a good poem, and Chapelain was a real poet though he wrote bad verses. I cannot overlook his genius."

My freedom must have shocked him, and I might have guessed it when he told me he had put the *Macaronicon* beside the *Pucelle*. I knew that there was a poem of the same title in circulation which passed for Voltaire's; but I also knew that he disavowed it, and I thought that would make him conceal the vexation my explanation must have caused him. It was not so, however; he contradicted me sharply, and I closed with him.

"Chapelain," said I, "has the merit of having rendered his subject-matter pleasant, without pandering to the tastes of his readers by saying things shocking to modesty and piety. So thinks my master Crébillon."

"Crébillon! You cite a weighty authority. But how is my friend Crébillon your master, may I ask?"

"He taught me to speak French in less than two years, and as a mark of my gratitude I translated his *Radamiste* into Italian Alexandrines. I am the first Italian who has dared to use this metre in our language."

"The first? I beg your pardon, as that honour belongs to my friend Pierre Jacques Martelli."

"I am sorry to be obliged to tell you that you are making a mistake."

"Why, I have his works, printed at Bologna, in my room!"

"I don't deny that, I am only talking about the metre used by Martelli. What you are thinking of must be verses of fourteen syllables, without alternative masculine and feminine rhymes. However, I confess that he thinks he has imitated the French Alexandrines, and his preface made me explode with laughter. Did you read it?"

"Read it? I always read prefaces, and Martelli proves there that his verses have the same effect in Italian as our Alexandrine verses have in French."

"Exactly, that's what's so amusing. The worthy man is quite mistaken, and I only ask you to listen to what I have to say on the subject. Your masculine verse has only twelve poetic syllables, and the feminine thirteen. All Martelli's lines have fourteen syllables, except those that finish with a long vowel, which at the end of a line always counts as two syllables. You will observe that the first hemistich in Martelli always consists of seven syllables, while in French it only has six. Your friend Pierre Jacques was either stone deaf or very hard of hearing."

"Then you have followed our theory of versification rigorously."

"Just so, in spite of the difficulty, as nearly all our words end with a short syllable."

"What reception has been accorded to your innovation?"

"It has not been found pleasing, because nobody knows how to recite my verses; but I hope to triumph when I deliver them myself before our literary clubs."

[91]

"Do you remember any of your version of the *Radamiste?*"

"I remember it all."

"You have a wonderful memory; I should be glad to hear it."

I began to recite the same scene that I had recited to Crébillon ten years before, and I thought M. de Voltaire listened with pleasure.

"It doesn't strike one as at all harsh," said he.

This was the highest praise he would give me. In his turn the great man recited a passage from *Tancred*, which had not as yet been published, and which was afterwards considered, and rightly, as a masterpiece.

We should have got on very well if we had kept to that, but on my quoting a line of Horace to praise one of his pieces, he said that Horace was a great master who had given precepts which would never be out of date. Thereupon I answered that he himself had violated one of them, but that he had violated it grandly.

"Which is that?"

"You do not write, *Contentus paucis lectoribus.*"

"If Horace had had to combat the hydra-headed monster of superstition, he would have written as I have written — for all the world."

"It seems to me that you might spare yourself the trouble of combating what you will never destroy."

"That which I cannot finish others will, and I shall always have the glory of being the first in the field."

"Very good; but supposing you succeed in destroying superstition, what are you going to put in its place?"

"I like that. If I deliver the race of man from a wild beast which is devouring it, am I to be asked what I intend to put in its place?"

"It does not devour it; on the contrary, it is necessary to its existence."

"Necessary to its existence! That is a horrible blasphemy, the falsity of which will be seen in the future. I love the human race; I would fain see men like myself, free and happy, and superstition and freedom cannot go together. Where do you find an enslaved and yet a happy people?"

"You wish, then, to see the people sovereign?"

"God forbid! There must be a sovereign to govern the masses."

"In that case you must have superstition, for without it the masses will never obey a mere man decked with the name of monarch."

"I will have no monarch; the word expresses despotism, which I hate as I do slavery."

"What do you mean, then? If you wish to put the government in the hands of one man, such a man, I maintain, will be a monarch."

"I would have a sovereign ruler of a free people, of which he is the chief by an agreement which binds them both, which would prevent him from becoming a tyrant."

"Addison will tell you that such a sovereign is a sheer impossibility. I agree with Hobbes, of two evils choose the least. A nation without superstition would be a nation of philosophers, and philosophers would never obey. The people will only be happy when they are crushed and downtrodden, and bound in chains."

"This is horrible; and you are of the people yourself. If you have read my works you must have seen how I show that superstition is the enemy of kings."

"Read your works? I have read and re-read them, especially in places where I have differed from you. Your ruling passion is the love of humanity. *Est ubi peccas.* This blinds you. Love humanity, but love it as it is. It is not fit to receive the blessings you would lavish on it, and which would only make it more wretched and perverse. Leave men their devouring monster, it is dear to them. I have never laughed so heartily as at Don Quixote assailed by the galley-slaves whom his generosity had set free."

"I am sorry that you have such a bad opinion of your fellow-creatures. And, by the way, tell me whether there is freedom in Venice."

"As much as can be expected under an aristocracy. Our liberty is not so great as that which the English enjoy, but we are content."

"Even under The Leads?"

"My imprisonment was certainly despotic; but as I had knowingly abused my liberty I am satisfied that the government was within its rights in shutting me up without the usual formalities."

"All the same, you made your escape."

"I used my rights as they had used theirs."

"Very good! But as far as I can see, no one in Venice is really free."

"That may be; but you must agree that the essence of freedom consists in thinking you have it."

"I shall not agree to that so easily. You and I see liberty from very different points of view. The aristocrats, the members of the government even, are not free at Venice; for example, they cannot travel without permission."

"True, but that is a restriction of their own making to preserve their power. Would you say that a Bernese is not free, because he is subject to the sumptuary laws, which he himself had made?"

"Well, well, I wish the people made the laws everywhere."

After this lively answer, he abruptly asked me what part I came from.

"From Roche," said I. "I should have been very sorry to leave Switzerland without seeing the famous Haller. In my travels I render homage to my learned contemporaries, and you come the last and best."

"You must have liked Haller."

"I spent three of the happiest days of my life with him."

"I congratulate you. He is a great man and worthy of all honour."

"I think as you do, and I am glad to hear you doing him justice; I am sorry he was not so just towards you."

"Well, you see we may be both of us mistaken."

At this reply, the quickness of which constituted its chief merit, everybody present began to laugh and applaud.

No more was said of literature, and I became a silent actor till M. de Voltaire retired, when I approached Madame Denis, and asked her if she had any commands for me at Rome. I went home well pleased at having compelled the giant of intellect to listen to reason, as I then thought foolishly enough; but there was a rankling feeling left in my heart against him which made me, ten years later, criticise all he had written.

I am sorry now for having done so, though on reading my censures over again I find that in many places I was right. I should have done better, however, to have kept silence, to have respected his genius, and to have suspected my own opinions. I should have considered that if it had not been for those quips and cranks which made me hate him on the third day, I should have thought him wholly sublime. This thought alone should have silenced me, but an angry man always thinks himself right. Posterity on reading my attack will rank me among the Zoyluses, and the humble apology I now make to the great man's shades may not be read.

If we meet in the halls of Pluto, the more peccant parts of our mortal nature purged away, all will be made up; he will receive my heartfelt apologies, and he will be my friend, I his sincere admirer.

I spent part of the night and the whole of the following day in writing down my conversations with Voltaire, and they amounted nearly to a volume, of which I have only given a mere abridgment. I set out the next day, after dining with the syndic, who accompanied me as far as Anneci, where I spent the night. Next day I dined at Aix, with the intention of lying at Chambéri, but my destiny ordered otherwise.

CHAPTER XIII

SENTIMENTAL JOURNEYINGS

*F*ROM *Switzerland Casanova makes his way southward, stopping in Aix (the modern Aix-les-Bains), then, as now, a watering- and gambling-place, where he falls in with his "second M** M **," a nun in distress, who bears so strange a resemblance to his Venetian nun that he recapitulates his amours for the sake of "auld lang syne." Leaving in a hurry, ostensibly to escape the snares of a dangerous couple of adventurers, he makes for Grenoble. There he casts a horoscope for Mdlle. Ramon, which foretells that she will shortly become the king's mistress, a prophecy the young lady and her family promptly set to work to realise by removing to Paris, where, needless to say, her destiny was accomplished as announced. In a pious mood he makes the pilgrimage to the Fountain of Vaucluse, evokes the shades of Laura and Petrach, embracing and "watering with his tears" the ground on which they trod, to the astonishment of a stolid British couple, the Chevalier*

Stuard (sic.) *and his frigid companion, whom he apostrophises in true Rousseauesque fashion in an impassioned improvisation on the divine passion of love.*

Via Marseilles, Nice, and Genoa, meeting with the usual adventures, Casanova gains Florence, where, to his joy and amazement, he finds Teresa Lanti, whom he had met and loved so well in Rimini seventeen years ago, when, as Bellino, she was masquerading as a male soprano. Teresa, now a famous singer, after accumulating riches, though happily married, is still faithful to his memory. Her masquerading days are not over, however, for the handsome young brother who accompanies her is, in fact, none other than the fruit of her youthful passion for Casanova. Nothing moves the latter's entrails so deeply as the sight of his progeny, wherever and whenever he encounters it during his travels. The quartet, husband, wife-mistress, brother-son, father-lover, spend blissful hours together. They might have been prolonged, had not poor Casanova, once more the victim of designing villains whom he had trusted, received the order to leave Tuscany.

It was during this visit to Tuscany that Casanova formed two acquaintances destined to be the cause of future trouble to him: Giacomo Passano, alias Ascanio Pogamas, and the dancer Corticelli — arcades ambo. When shortly he will be looking for accomplices to carry out the reincarnation hoax on the Marquise d'Urfé, the memory of their roguish faces will recur to him.

From Florence to Rome was a matter of thirty-six hours — just as long as it takes a Casanova to go from one Thérèse to another, and no longer, as we shall see.

It was midnight when I passed under the Porta del Popolo, for one may enter the Eternal City at any time. I was then taken to the custom-house, which is always open, and my mails were examined. The only thing they are strict about at Rome is books, as if they feared the light. I had about thirty volumes, all more or less against the Papacy, religion, or the virtues inculcated thereby. I had resolved to surrender them without any dispute, as I felt tired and wanted to go to bed, but the clerk told me politely to count them and leave them in his charge for the night, and he would bring them to my hotel in the morning. I did so, and he kept his word. He was well enough pleased when he touched the two sequins with which I rewarded him.

I put up at the Ville de Paris, in the Piazza di Spagna. It

is the best inn in the town. All the world, I found, was drowned in sleep, but when they let me in they asked me to wait on the ground-floor while a fire was lighted in my room. All the seats were covered with dresses, petticoats, and chemises, and I heard a small feminine voice begging me to sit on her bed. I approached and saw a laughing mouth, and two black eyes shining like carbuncles.

"What splendid eyes!" said I, "let me kiss them."

By way of reply she hid her head under the coverlet.

"Who are you, my angel?"

"I am Thérèse, the innkeeper's daughter, and this is my sister." There was another girl beside her, whom I had not seen, as her head was under the bolster.

"How old are you?"

"Nearly seventeen."

"I hope I shall see you in my room to-morrow morning."

"Have you any ladies with you?"

"No."

"That's a pity, as we never go to the gentlemen's rooms."

"Lower the coverlet a little; I can't hear what you say."

"It's too cold."

"Dear Thérèse, your eyes make me feel as if I were in flames."

She put her head back at this, and I grew daring. I caressed her in a somewhat lively manner, and when she let me see her face I thought I saw delight rather than anger in her eyes and on her cheeks, and I felt hopeful with regard to her. I was just going to begin again, when a handsome chambermaid came to tell me that my room was ready and my fire lighted.

"Farewell till to-morrow," said I to Thérèse, but she only answered by turning on her side to go to sleep.

I went to bed after ordering dinner for one o'clock, and I slept till noon, dreaming of Thérèse. When I woke up, Costa told me that he had found out where my brother lived, and had left a note at the house. This was my brother Jean, then about thirty, and a pupil of the famous Raphael Mengs. This painter was then deprived of his pension on account of a war which obliged the King of Poland to live at Warsaw, as the Prussians occupied the whole electorate of Saxe. I had not seen my brother for ten years, and I kept our meeting as a holiday. I was sitting down to table when he came, and we embraced each other with transport. We spent an hour in telling, he his small adventures, and I my grand ones, and he told me that I should not stay at the hotel, which was too dear, but come and live at the Chevalier Mengs's house, which contained an empty room, where I could stay at a much cheaper rate.

"As to your table, there is a restaurant in the house where one can get a capital meal."

"Your advice is excellent," said I, "but I have not the courage to follow it, as I am in love with my landlord's daughter"; and I told him what had happened the night before.

"That's a mere nothing," said he, laughing; "you can cultivate her acquaintance without staying in the house."

I let myself be persuaded, and I promised to come to him the following day; and then we proceeded to take a walk about Rome.

I had many interesting memories of my last visit, and I wanted to renew my acquaintance with those who had interested me at that happy age when such impressions are so durable because they touch the heart rather than the mind; but I had to make up my mind to a good many disappointments, considering the space of time that had elapsed since I had been in Rome.

I went to the Minerva to find Donna Cecilia; she was no more in this world. I found out where her daughter Angelica lived, and I went to see her, but she gave me a poor reception, and said that she really scarcely remembered me.

"I can say the same," I replied, "for you are not the Angelica I used to know. Good-bye, madam!"

The lapse of time had not improved her personal appearance. I found out also where the printer's son, who had married Barbaruccia, lived, but I put off the pleasure of seeing him till another time, and also my visit to the Reverend Father Georgi, who was a man of great repute in Rome. Gaspar Vivaldi had gone into the country.

My brother took me to Madame Cherubini. I found her mansion to be a splendid one, and the lady welcomed me in the Roman manner. I thought her pleasant and her daughters still more so, but I thought the crowd of lovers too large and too miscellaneous. There was too much luxury and ceremony, and the girls, one of whom was as fair as Love himself, were too polite to everybody. An interesting question was put to me, to which I answered in such a manner as to elicit another question but to no purpose. I saw that the rank of my brother, who had introduced me, prevented my being thought a person of any consequence, and on hearing an abbé say, "He's Casanova's brother," I turned to him and said:

"That's not correct; you should say Casanova's my brother."

"That comes to the same thing."

"Not at all, my dear abbé."

I said these words in a tone which commanded attention, and another abbé said:

"The gentleman is quite right; it does *not* come to the same thing."

The first abbé made no reply to this. The one who had taken my part, and was my friend from that moment, was the famous Winckelmann, who was unhappily assassinated at Trieste twelve years afterwards.

While I was talking to him, Cardinal Alexander Albani arrived. Winckelmann presented me to his eminence, who was nearly blind. He talked to me a great deal, without saying anything worth listening to. As soon as he heard that I was the Casanova who had escaped from The Leads, he said in a somewhat rude tone that he wondered I had the hardihood to come to Rome, where on the slightest hint from the State Inquisitors at Venice an *ordine santissimo* would re-consign me to my prison. I was annoyed by this unseemly remark, and replied in a dignified voice:

"It is not my hardihood in coming to Rome that your eminence should wonder at, but a man of any sense would wonder at the Inquisitors if they had the hardihood to issue an *ordine santissimo* against me; for they would be perplexed to allege any crime in me as a pretext for thus infamously depriving me of my liberty."

This reply silenced his eminence. He was ashamed at having taken me for a fool, and to see that I thought him one. Shortly after, I left and never set foot in that house again.

The Abbé Winckelmann went out with my brother and myself, and as he came with me to my hotel he did me the honour of staying to supper. Winckelmann was the second volume of the celebrated Abbé de Voisenon. He called for me next day, and we went to Villa Albani to see the Chevalier Mengs, who was then living there and painting a ceiling.

My landlord Roland (who knew my brother) paid me a visit at supper. Roland came from Avignon and was fond of good living. I told him I was sorry to be leaving him to stay with my brother, because I had fallen in love with his daughter Thérèse, although I had only spoken to her for a few minutes, and had only seen her head.

"You saw her in bed, I will bet."

"Exactly, and I should very much like to see the rest of her. Would you be so kind as to ask her to step up for a few minutes?"

"With all my heart."

She came upstairs, seeming only too glad to obey her father's summons. She had a lithe, graceful figure, her eyes were of surpassing brilliancy, her features exquisite, her mouth charming; but taken altogether I did not like her so well as before. In return, my poor brother became enamoured of her to such an extent that he ended by becoming her slave. He married her next year, and two years afterwards he took her to Dresden. I saw her five years later with a pretty baby; but after ten years of married life she died of consumption.

I found Mengs at the Villa Albani; he was an indefatigable worker, and extremely original in his conceptions. He welcomed me, and said he was glad to be able to lodge me at his house in Rome, and that he hoped to return home himself in a few days, with his whole family. I was astonished with the Villa Albani. It had been built by Cardinal Alexander, and had been wholly constructed from antique materials to satisfy the cardinal's love for classic art; not only the statues and the vases, but the columns, the pedestals — in fact, everything was Greek. He was a Greek himself, and had a perfect knowledge of antique work, and had contrived to spend comparatively little money compared with the masterpiece he had produced. If a sovereign monarch had had a villa like the cardinal's built, it would have cost him fifty million francs, but the cardinal made a much cheaper bargain.

As he could not get any ancient ceilings, he was obliged to have them painted, and Mengs was undoubtedly the greatest and the most laborious painter of his age. It is a great pity that death carried him off in the midst of his career, as otherwise he would have enriched the stores of art with numerous masterpieces. My brother never did anything to justify his title of pupil of this great artist. When I come to my visit to Spain in 1767, I shall have some more to say about Mengs.

As soon as I was settled with my brother I hired a carriage, a coachman, and a footman, whom I put into fancy livery, and I called on Monsignor Cornaro, auditor of the rota, with the intention of making my way into good society, but fearing lest he as a Venetian might get compromised, he introduced me to Cardinal Passionei, who spoke of me to the sovereign pontiff.

Before I pass on to anything else, I will inform my readers of what took place on the occasion of my second visit to this odd cardinal, a great enemy of the Jesuits, a wit, and a man of letters.

Cardinal Passionei received me in a large hall where he was writing. He begged me to wait till he had finished, but he could not ask me to take a seat as he occupied the only chair that his vast room contained.

When he had put down his pen, he rose, came to me, and after informing me that he would tell the Holy Father of my visit, he added:

"My brother Cornaro might have made a better choice, as he knows the Pope does not like me."

"He thought it better to choose the man who is esteemed than the man who is merely liked."

"I don't know whether the Pope esteems me, but I am sure he knows I don't esteem him. I both liked and esteemed him before he was pope, and I concurred in his election, but since he has worn the tiara it's a different matter; he has shown himself too much of a *coglione*."

"The conclave ought to have chosen your eminence."

"No, no; I'm a root-and-branch reformer, and my hand would not have been stayed for fear of the vengeance of the guilty, and God alone knows what would have come of that. The only cardinal fit to be pope was Tamburini; but it can't be helped now. I hear people coming; good-bye, come again to-morrow."

What a delightful thing to have heard a cardinal call the Pope a fool, and name Tamburini as a fit person. I did not lose a moment in noting this pleasant circumstance down: it was too precious a morsel to let slip. But who was Tamburini? I had never heard of him. I asked Winckelmann, who dined with me.

[101]

"He's a man deserving of respect for his virtues, his character, his firmness, and his far-seeing intelligence. He has never disguised his opinions of the Jesuits, whom he styles the fathers of deceits, intrigues, and lies; and that's what made Passionei mention him. I think, with him, that Tamburini would be a great and good pope."

I will here note down what I heard at Rome nine years later from the mouth of a tool of the Jesuits. The Cardinal Tamburini was at the last gasp, and the conversation turned upon him, when somebody else said:

"This Benedictine cardinal is an impious fellow after all; he is on his death-bed, and he has asked for the viaticum, without wishing to purify his soul by confession."

I did not make any remark, but feeling as if I should like to know the truth of the matter I asked somebody about it next day, my informant being a person who must have known the truth, and could not have had any motive for disguising the real facts of the case. He told me that the cardinal had said mass three days before, and that if he had not asked for a confessor it was doubtless because he had nothing to confess. Unfortunate are they that love the truth, and do not seek it out at its source. I hope the reader will pardon this digression, which is not without interest.

Next day I went to see Cardinal Passionei, who told me I was quite right to come early, as he wanted to learn all about my escape from The Leads, of which he had heard some wonderful tales told.

"I shall be delighted to satisfy your eminence, but the story is a long one."

"All the better; they say you tell it well."

"But, my lord, am I to sit down on the floor?"

"No, no; your dress is too good for that."

He rang his bell, and having told one of his gentlemen to send up a seat, a servant brought in a stool. A seat without a back and without arms! It made me quite angry. I cut my story short, told it badly, and had finished in a quarter of an hour.

"I write better than you speak," said he.

"My lord, I never speak well except when I am at my ease."

"But you are not afraid of me?"

"No, my lord, a true man and a philosopher can never make me afraid; but this stool of yours . . ."

"You like to be at your ease, above all things.

"Take this, it is the funeral oration of Prince Eugène; I make you a present of it. I hope you will approve of my Latinity. You can kiss the Pope's feet to-morrow at ten o'clock."

When I got home, as I reflected on the character of this strange cardinal — a wit, haughty, vain, and boastful — I resolved to make him a fine present. It was the *Pandectarum liber unicus* which M. de F ** had given me at Berne, and which I did not know what to do with. It was a folio well printed on fine paper, choicely bound, and in perfect preservation. As chief librarian the present should be a valuable one to him, all the more as he had a large private library, of which my friend the Abbé Winckelmann was librarian. I therefore wrote a short Latin letter, which I enclosed in another to Winckelmann, whom I begged to present my offering to his eminence. I thought it was as valuable as his funeral oration at any rate, and I hoped that he would give me a more comfortable chair for the future.

Next morning, at the time appointed, I went to Monte Cavallo, which ought to be called Monte Cavalli, as it gets its name from two fine statues of horses standing on a pedestal in the midst of the square, where the Holy Father's palace is situated.

I had no real need of being presented to the Pope by anyone, as any Christian is at liberty to go in when he sees the door open. Besides I had known His Holiness when he was Bishop of Padua; but I had preferred to claim the honour of being introduced by a cardinal.

After saluting the Head of the Faithful, and kissing the holy cross embroidered on his holy slipper, the Pope put his right hand on my left shoulder, and said he remembered that I always forsook the assembly at Padua, when he intoned the Rosary.

"Holy Father, I have much worse sins than that on my conscience, so I come prostrate at your feet to receive your absolution."

He then gave me his benediction, and asked me very graciously what he could do for me.

"I beg Your Holiness to plead for me, that I may be able to return to Venice."

"We will speak of it to the ambassador, and then we will speak again to you on the matter. Do you often go and see Cardinal Passionei?"

"I have been three times. He gave me his funeral oration on Prince Eugène, and in return I sent him the *Pandects*."

"Has he accepted them?"

"I think so, Holy Father."

"If he has, he will send Winckelmann to pay you for them."

"That would be treating me like a bookseller; I will not receive any payment."

"Then he will return the volume of the *Pandects;* we are sure of it, he always does so."

"If his eminence returns me the *Pandects*, I will return him his funeral oration."

At this the Pope laughed till his sides shook.

"We shall be pleased to hear the end of the story without anyone being informed of our innocent curiosity."

With these words, a long benediction delivered with much unction informed me that my audience was at an end.

As I was leaving His Holiness's palace, I was accosted by an old abbé, who asked me respectfully if I were not the M. Casanova who had escaped from The Leads.

"Yes," said I, "I am the man."

"Heaven be praised, worthy sir, that I see you again in such good estate!"

"But whom have I the honour of addressing?"

"Don't you recollect me? I am Momolo, formerly gondolier at Venice."

"Have you entered holy orders, then?"

"Not at all, but here everyone wears the cassock. I am the first *scopatore* (sweeper) of His Holiness the Pope."

"I congratulate you on your appointment, but you mustn't mind me laughing."

"Laugh as much as you like. My wife and daughters laugh when I put on the cassock and bands, and I laugh myself, but here the dress gains one respect. Come and see us."

"Where do you live?"

"Behind the Trinity of Monti; here's my address."

"I will come to-night."

I went home delighted with this meeting, and determined to enjoy the evening with my Venetian boatman. I got my brother to come with me, and I told him how the Pope had received me.

The Abbé Winckelmann came in the afternoon and informed

me that I was fortunate enough to be high in favour with his cardinal, and that the book I had sent him was very valuable; it was a rare work, and in much better condition than the Vatican copy.

"I am commissioned to pay you for it."

"I have told his eminence that it was a present."

"He never accepts books as presents, and he wants yours for his own library; and as he is librarian of the Vatican Library he is afraid lest people might say unpleasant things."

"That's all very well, but I am not a bookseller; and as this book only cost me the trouble of accepting it, I am determined only to sell it at the same price. Pray ask the cardinal to honour me by accepting it."

"He is sure to send it back to you."

"He can if he likes, but I will send back his funeral oration, as I am not going to be under an obligation to anyone who refuses to take a present from me."

Next morning the eccentric cardinal returned me my *Pandects*, and I immediately returned his funeral oration, with a letter in which I pronounced it a masterpiece of composition, though I had barely glanced over it in reality. My brother told me I was wrong, but I did not trouble what he said, not caring to guide myself by his rulings.

In the evening my brother and I went to the *scopatore santissimo*, who was expecting me, and had announced me to his family as a prodigy of a man. I introduced my brother, and proceeded to a close scrutiny of the family. I saw an elderly woman, four girls, of whom the eldest was twenty-four, two small boys, and above all universal ugliness. It was not inviting for a man of voluptuous tastes, but I was there, and the best thing was to put a good face on it; so I stayed and enjoyed myself. Besides the general ugliness, the household presented the picture of misery, for the *scopatore santissimo* and his numerous family were obliged to live on two hundred Roman crowns a year, and as there are no perquisites attached to the office of apostolic sweeper, he was compelled to furnish all needs out of this slender sum. In spite of that Momolo was a most generous man. As soon as he saw me seated he told me he should have liked to give me a good supper, but there was only pork chops and a polenta.

"They are very nice," said I; "but will you allow me to send for half a dozen flasks of Orvieto from my lodging?"

"You are master here."

I wrote a note to Costa, telling him to bring the six flasks directly, with a cooked ham. He came in half an hour, and the four girls cried when they saw him, "What a fine fellow!" I saw Costa was delighted with this reception, and said to Momolo:

"If you like him as well as your girls I will let him stay."

Costa was charmed with such honour being shown him, and after thanking me went into the kitchen to help the mother with the polenta.

The large table was covered with a clean cloth, and soon after they brought in two huge dishes of polenta and an enormous pan full of chops. We were just going to begin when a knocking on the street door was heard.

"'Tis Signora Maria and her mother," said one of the boys.

At this announcement I saw the four girls pulling a wry face. 'Who asked them?" said one. "What do they want?" said another. "What troublesome people they are!" said a third. "They might have stayed at home," said the fourth. But the good, kindly father said, "My children, they are hungry, and they shall share what Providence has given us."

I was deeply touched with the worthy man's kindness. I saw that true Christian charity is more often to be found in the breasts of the poor than the rich, who are so well provided for that they cannot feel for the wants of others.

While I was making these wholesome reflections the two hungry ones came in. One was a young woman of a modest and pleasant aspect, and the other her mother, who seemed very humble and as if ashamed of their poverty. The daughter saluted the company with that natural grace which is a gift of nature, apologising in some confusion for her presence, and saying that she would not have taken the liberty to come if she had known there was company. The worthy Momolo was the only one who answered her, and he said, kindly, that she had done quite right to come, and put her a chair between my brother and myself. I looked at her and thought her a perfect beauty.

Then the eating began and there was no more talking. The polenta was excellent, the chops delicious, and the ham perfect, and in less than an hour the board was as bare as if there had been nothing on it; but the Orvieto kept the company in good spirits. They began to talk of the lottery which was to be drawn the day after next, and all the girls mentioned the numbers on which they had risked a few bajocchi.

"If I could be sure of one number," said I, "I would stake something on it."

Mariuccia told me that if I wanted a number she could give me one. I laughed at this offer, but in the gravest way she named me the number 27.

"Is the lottery still open?" I asked the Abbé Momolo.

"Till midnight," he replied, "and if you like I will go and get the number for you."

"Here are fifty crowns," said I, "put twenty-five crowns on 27 — this for these five young ladies; and the other twenty-five on 27 coming out the fifth number, and this I will keep for myself."

He went out directly and returned with the two tickets.

My pretty neighbour thanked me and said she was sure of winning, but that she did not think I should succeed as it was not probable that 27 would come out fifth.

"I am sure of it," I answered, "for you are the fifth young lady I saw in this house." This made everybody laugh. Momolo's wife told me I would have done much better if I had given the money to the poor, but her husband told her to be quiet, as she did not know my intent. My brother laughed, and told me I had done a foolish thing. "I do, sometimes," said I, "but we shall see how it turns out, and when one plays one is obliged either to win or lose."

I managed to squeeze my fair neighbour's hand, and she returned the pressure with all her strength. From that time I knew my fate with Mariuccia was sealed. I left them at midnight, begging the worthy Momolo to ask me again in two days' time, that we might rejoice together over our gains. On our way home my brother said I had either become as rich as Crœsus or had gone mad. I told him that both suppositions were incorrect, that Mariuccia was as handsome as an angel, and he agreed.

Next day Mengs returned to Rome, and I supped with him and his family. He had an exceedingly ugly sister, who, for all that, was a good and talented woman. She had fallen deeply in love with my brother, and it was easy to see that the flame was not yet extinguished, but whenever she spoke to him, which she did whenever she could get an opportunity, he looked another way.

She was an exquisite painter of miniatures, and a capital hand at catching a likeness. To the best of my belief she is still living at Rome with Maroni her husband. She often used to speak of my brother to me, and one day she said that he must be the most thankless of men or he would not despise her so. I was not curious enough to inquire what claim she had to his gratitude.

Mengs's wife was a good and pretty woman, attentive to her household duties and very submissive to her husband, though she could not have loved him, for he was anything but amiable. He was obstinate and fierce in his manner, and when he dined at home he made a point of not leaving the table before he was drunk; out of his own house he was temperate to the extent of not drinking anything but water. His wife carried her obedience so far as to serve as his model for all the nude figures he painted. I spoke to her one day about this unpleasant obligation, and she said that her confessor had charged her to fulfil it, "for," said he, "if your husband has another woman for model he will be sure to enjoy her before painting her, and that sin would be laid to your charge."

After supper, Winckelmann, who was as far gone as all the other male guests, played with Mengs's children. There was nothing of the pedant about this philosopher; he loved children and young people, and his cheerful disposition made him delight in all kinds of enjoyment.

Next day, as I was going to pay my court to the Pope, I saw Momolo in the first ante-chamber, and I took care to remind him of the polenta for the evening.

As soon as the Pope saw me, he said:

"The Venetian ambassador has informed us that if you wish to return to your native land, you must go and present yourself before the secretary of the Tribunal."

"Most Holy Father, I am quite ready to take this step, if Your Holiness will grant me a letter of commendation written with your own hand. Without this powerful protection I should never dream of exposing myself to the risk of being again shut up in a place from which I escaped by a miracle and the help of the Almighty."

"You are gaily dressed; you do not look as if you were going to church."

"True, most Holy Father, but neither am I going to a ball."

"We have heard all about the presents being sent back. Confess that you did so to gratify your pride."

"Yes, but also to lower a pride greater than mine."

The Pope smiled at this reply, and I knelt down and begged him to permit me to present the volume of *Pandects* to the Vatican Library. By way of reply he gave me his blessing, which signifies, in papal language, "Rise; your request is granted."

"We will send you," said he, "a mark of our *singular affection* for you without your having to pay any fees."

A second blessing bid me begone. I have often felt what a good thing it would be if this kind of dismissal could be employed in general society to send away importunate petitioners, to whom one does not dare say, "Go away!"

I was extremely curious to know what the Pope had meant by "a mark of our singular affection." I was afraid that it would be a blessed rosary, with which I should not have known what to do.

When I got home I sent the book by Costa to the Vatican, and then I went to dine with Mengs. While we were eating the soup the winning numbers from the lottery were brought in. My brother glanced at them and looked at me with astonishment. I was not thinking of the subject at that moment, and his gaze surprised me.

"Twenty-seven," he cried, "came out fifth."

"All the better," said I, "we shall have some amusement out of it."

I told the story to Mengs, who said:

"It's a lucky folly for you this time; but it always is a folly."

He was quite right, and I told him that I agreed with him; but I added that to make a worthy use of the fifteen hundred Roman crowns which fortune had given me I should go and spend fifteen days at Naples.

"I will come too," said the Abbé Alfani. "I will pass for your secretary."

"With all my heart," I answered, "I shall keep you to your word."

I asked Winckelmann to come and eat polenta with the *scopatore santissimo,* and told my brother to show him the way; and I then called on the Marquis Belloni, my banker, to look into my accounts, and to get a letter of credit on the firm at Naples who were his agents. I still had two hundred thousand francs. I had jewellery worth thirty thousand francs, and fifty thousand florins at Amsterdam.

I got to Momolo's in the dusk of the evening, and I found Winckelmann and my brother already there; but instead of mirth reigning round the board I saw sad faces on all sides.

"What's the matter with the girls?" I asked Momolo.

"They are vexed that you did not stake for them in the same way as you did for yourself."

"People are never satisfied. If I had staked for them as I did for myself, and the number had come out first instead of fifth, they would have got nothing, and they would have been vexed then. Two days ago they had nothing, and now that they have twenty-seven crowns apiece they ought to be contented."

"That's just what I tell them, but all women are the same."

"And men, too, dear countryman, unless they are philosophers. Gold does not spell happiness, and mirth can only be found in hearts devoid of care. Let us say no more about it, but be happy."

Costa placed a basket containing ten packets of sweets upon the table.

"I will distribute them," said I, "when everybody is here."

On this, Momolo's second daughter told me that Mariuccia and her mother were not coming, but that they would send them the sweets.

"Why are they not coming?"

"They had a quarrel yesterday," said the father, "and Mariuccia, who was in the right, went away saying that she would never come here again."

"You ungrateful girls!" said I to my host's daughters, "don't you know that it is to her that you owe your winnings, for she gave me the number twenty-seven, which I should never have thought of. Quick! think of some way to make her come, or I will go away and take all the sweets with me."

"You are quite right," said Momolo.

The mortified girls looked at one another and begged their father to fetch her.

"No," said he, "that won't do; you made her say that she would never come here again, and you must make up the quarrel."

They held a short consultation, and then, asking Costa to go with them, they went to fetch her.

In half an hour they returned in triumph, and Costa was quite proud of the part he had taken in the reconciliation. I then distributed the sweets, taking care to give the two best packets to the fair Mary.

A noble polenta was placed upon the board, flanked by two large dishes of pork chops. But Momolo, who knew my tastes, and whom I had made rich in the person of his daughters, added to the feast some delicate dishes and some excellent wine. Mariuccia was simply dressed, but her elegance and beauty and the modesty of her demeanour completely seduced me.

We could only express our mutual flames by squeezing each other's hands; and she did this so feelingly that I could not doubt her love. As we were going out I took care to go downstairs beside her and asked if I could not meet her by herself, to which she replied by making an appointment with me for the next day at eight o'clock at the Trinity of Monti.

Mariuccia was tall and shapely, a perfect picture, as fair as a white rose, and calculated to inspire voluptuous desires. She had beautiful light brown hair, dark blue eyes, and exquisitely arched eyelids. Her mouth, the vermilion of her lips, and her ivory teeth were all perfect. Her well-shaped forehead gave her an air approaching the majestic. Kindness and gaiety sparkled in her eyes; while her plump white hands, her rounded fingertips, her pink nails, her breast, which the corset seemed scarcely able to restrain, her dainty feet, and her prominent hips, made her worthy of the chisel of Praxiteles. She was just on her eighteenth year, and so far had escaped the connoisseurs. By a lucky chance I came across her in a poor and wretched street, and I was fortunate enough to ensure her happiness.

It may easily be believed that I did not fail to keep the appointment, and when she was sure I had seen her she went out of the church. I followed her at a considerable distance: she entered a ruined building, and I after her. She climbed a flight of steps which seemed to be built in air, and when she had reached the top she turned.

"No one will come and look for me here," said she, "so we can talk freely together."

I sat beside her on a stone, and I then declared my passionate love for her.

"Tell me," I added, "what I can do to make you happy; for I wish to possess you, but first to show my deserts."

"Make me happy, and I will yield to your desires, for I love you."

"Tell me what I can do."

"You can draw me out of the poverty and misery which overwhelm me. I live with my mother, who is a good woman, but devout to the point of superstition; she will damn my soul in her efforts to save it. She finds fault with my keeping myself clean, because I have to touch myself when I wash, and that might give rise to evil desires. If you had given me the money you made me win in the lottery as a simple alms she would have made me refuse it, because you might have had intentions. She allows me to go by myself to mass because our confessor told her she might do so; but I dare not stay away a minute beyond the time, except on feast days, when I am allowed to pray in the church for two or three hours. We can only meet here, but if you wish to soften my lot in life you can do as follows:

"A fine young man, who is a hairdresser, and bears an excellent character, saw me at Momolo's a fortnight ago, and met me at the church door next day and gave me a letter. He declared himself my lover, and said that if I could bring him a dowry of four hundred crowns, he could open a shop, furnish it, and marry me.

"'I am poor,' I answered, 'and I have only a hundred crowns in charity tickets, which my confessor keeps for me.' Now I have two hundred crowns, for if I marry, my mother will willingly give me her share of the money you made us gain. You can therefore make me happy by getting me tickets to the amount of two hundred crowns more. Take the tickets to my confessor, who is a very good man and fond of me; he will not say anything to my mother about it."

"I needn't go about seeking for charity tickets, my angel. I will take two hundred piastres to your confessor to-morrow, and you must manage the rest yourself. Tell me his name, and to-morrow I will tell you what I have done, but not here, as the wind and the cold would be the death of me. You can leave me to find out a room where we shall be at our ease, and without any danger of people suspecting that we have spent an hour together. I will meet you at the church to-morrow at the same hour, and when you see me follow me."

Mariuccia told me her confessor's name, and allowed me all the caresses possible in our uncomfortable position. The kisses she gave me in return for mine left no doubt in my mind as to her love for me. As nine o'clock struck I left her, perishing with cold, but burning with desire; my only thought being where to find a room in which I might possess myself of the treasure the next day.

On leaving the ruined palace, instead of returning to the Piazza di Spagna I turned to the left and passed along a narrow and dirty street only inhabited by people of the lowest sort. As I slowly walked along, a woman came out of her house and asked me politely if I were looking for anybody.

"I am looking for a room to let."

"There are none here, sir, but you will find a hundred in the square."

"I know it, but I want the room to be here, not for the sake of the expense, but that I may be sure of being able to spend an hour or so of a morning with a person in whom I am interested. I am ready to pay anything."

"I understand what you mean, and you should have a room in my house if I had one to spare, but a neighbour of mine has one on the ground-floor, and if you will wait a moment I will go and speak to her."

"You will oblige me very much."

"Kindly step in here."

I entered a poor room, where all seemed wretchedness, and I saw two children doing their lessons. Soon after, the good woman came back and asked me to follow her. I took several pieces of money from my pocket, and put them down on the only table which this poor place contained. I must have seemed very generous, for the poor mother came and kissed my hand with the utmost gratitude. So pleasant is it to do good, that now when I have nothing left the remembrance of the happiness I have given to others at small cost is almost the only pleasure I enjoy.

I went to a neighbouring house where a woman received me in an empty room, which she told me she would let cheaply if I would pay three months in advance, and bring in my own furniture.

"What do you ask for the three months' rent?"

"Three Roman crowns."

"If you will see to the furnishing of the room this very day I will give you twelve crowns."

"Twelve crowns! What furniture do you want?"

"A good clean bed, a small table covered with a clean cloth, four good chairs, and a large brazier with plenty of fire in it, for I am nearly perishing of cold here. I shall only come occasionally in the morning, and I shall leave by noon at the latest."

"Come at three o'clock, then, to-day, and you will find everything to your satisfaction."

From there I went to the confessor. He was a French monk, about sixty, a fine and benevolent-looking man, who won one's respect and confidence.

"Reverend father," I began, "I saw at the house of Abbé Momolo, *scopatore santissimo*, a young girl named Mary, whose confessor you are. I fell in love with her, and offered her money to try and seduce her. She replied that instead of trying to lead her into sin I would do better to get her some charity tickets that she might be able to marry a young man who loved her, and would make her happy. I was touched by what she said, but my passion still remained. I spoke to her again, and said that I would give her two hundred crowns for nothing, and that her mother should keep them.

"'That would be my ruin,' said she; 'my mother would think the money was the price of sin, and would not accept it. If you are really going to be so generous, take the money to my confessor, and ask him to do what he can for my marriage.'

"Here, then, reverend father, is the sum of money for the good girl; be kind enough to take charge of it, and I will trouble her no more. I am going to Naples the day after to-morrow, and I hope when I come back she will be married."

The good confessor took the hundred sequins and gave me a receipt, telling me that in interesting myself on behalf of Mariuccia I was making happy a most pure and innocent dove, whom he had confessed since she was five years old, and that he had often told her that she might communicate without making her confession because he knew she was incapable of mortal sin.

"Her mother," he added, "is a sainted woman, and as soon as I have inquired into the character of the future husband I will soon bring the marriage about. No one shall ever know from whom this generous gift comes."

After putting this matter in order I dined with the Chevalier Mengs, and I willingly consented to go with the whole family to the Aliberti Theatre that evening. I did not forget, however, to go and inspect the room I had taken. I found all my orders executed, and I gave twelve crowns to the landlady and took the key, telling her to light the fire at seven every morning.

So impatient did I feel for the next day to come that I thought the opera detestable, and the night for me was a sleepless one.

Next morning I went to the church before the time, and when Mariuccia came, feeling sure that she had seen me, I went out. She followed me at a distance, and when I got to the door of the lodging I turned for her to be sure that it was I, and then went in and found the room well warmed. Soon after, Mariuccia came in, looking timid, confused, and as if she were doubtful of the path she was treading. I clasped her in my arms, and re-assured her by my tender embraces; and her courage rose when I showed her the confessor's receipt, and told her that the worthy man had promised to care for her marriage. She kissed my hand in a transport of delight, assuring me that she would never forget my kindness. Then, as I urged her to make me a happy man, she said:

"We have three hours before us, as I told my mother I was going to give thanks to God for having made me a winner in the lottery."

I had to go to Naples, but I assured her that the desire of embracing her once more before her marriage would hasten my return to Rome. I promised to take another hundred crowns to her confessor, advising her to spend the money she had won in the lottery on her trousseau.

"I shall be at Momolo's to-night, dearest, and you must come, too; but we must appear indifferent to each other, though our hearts be full of joy, lest those malicious girls suspect our mutual understanding."

"It is all the more necessary to be cautious," she replied, "as I have noticed that they suspect that we love each other."

Before we parted she thanked me for what I had done for her, and begged me to believe that, her poverty notwithstanding, she had given herself for love alone.

I was the last to leave the house, and I told my landlady that I should be away for ten or twelve days. I then went to the confessor to give him the hundred crowns I had promised my mistress. When the good old Frenchman heard that I had made this fresh sacrifice that Mariuccia might be able to spend her lottery winnings on her clothes, he told me that he would call on the mother that very day and urge her to consent to her daughter's marriage, and also learn where the young man lived. On my return from Naples I heard that he had faithfully carried out his promise.

I was sitting at table with Mengs when a chamberlain of the Holy Father called. When he came in he asked M. Mengs if I lived there, and on that gentleman pointing me out, he gave me, from his holy master, the cross of the Order of the Golden Spur with the diploma, and a patent under the pontifical seal, which, in my quality as doctor of laws, made me a prothonotary-apostolic *extra urbem*.

I felt that I had been highly honoured, and told the bearer that I would go and thank my new sovereign and ask his blessing the next day. The Chevalier Mengs embraced me as a brother, but I had the advantage over him in not being obliged to pay anything, whereas the great artist had to disburse twenty-five Roman crowns to have his diploma made out. There is a saying at Rome, *Sine effusione sanguinis non fit remissio*, which may be interpreted, *Nothing without money*; and as a matter of fact, one can do anything with money in the Holy City.

Feeling highly flattered at the favour the Holy Father had shown me, I put on the cross, which depended from a broad red ribbon — red being the colour worn by the Knights of St. John of the Lateran, the companions of the palace, *comites palatini*, or count-palatins. About the same time poor Cahusac, author of the opera of *Zoroaster*, went mad for joy on the receipt of the same order. I was not so bad as that, but I confess, to my shame, that I was so proud of the decoration that I asked Winckelmann whether I should be allowed to have the cross set with diamonds and rubies. He said I could if I liked, and if I wanted such a cross he could get me one cheap. I was delighted, and bought it to make a show at Naples, but I had not the face to wear it in Rome. When I went to thank the Pope I wore the cross in my buttonhole out of modesty. Five years afterwards, when I was at Warsaw, Czartoryski, a Russian prince-palatine, made me leave it off by saying:

"What are you doing with that wretched bauble? It's a drug in the market, and no one but an impostor would wear it now."

The popes knew this quite well, but they continued to give the cross to ambassadors while they also gave it to their *valets de chambre*. One has to wink at a good many things in Rome.

In the evening Momolo gave me a supper by way of celebrating my new dignity. I recouped him for the expense by holding a bank at faro, at which I was dexterous enough to lose forty crowns to the family, without having the slightest partiality to Mariuccia, who won like the rest. She found the opportunity to tell me that her confessor had called on her, that she had told him where her future husband lived, and that the worthy monk had obtained her mother's consent to the hundred crowns being spent on her trousseau.

I noticed that Momolo's second daughter had taken a fancy to Costa, and I told Momolo that I was going to Naples, but that I would leave my man in Rome, and that if I found a marriage had been arranged on my return I would gladly pay the expenses of the wedding.

Costa liked the girl, but he did not marry her then for fear of my claiming the first-fruits. He was a fool of a peculiar kind, though fools of all sorts are common enough. He married her a year later after robbing me, but I shall speak of that again.

Next day, after I had breakfasted and duly embraced my brother, I set out in a nice carriage with the Abbé Alfani, Le Duc preceding me on horseback, and I reached Naples at a time when everybody was in a state of excitement because an eruption of Vesuvius seemed imminent. At the last stage the innkeeper made me read the will of his father, who had died during the eruption of 1754. He said that in the year 1761 God would overwhelm the sinful town of Naples, and the worthy host consequently advised me to return to Rome. Alfani took the thing seriously, and said that we should do well to be warned by so evident an indication of the will of God. The event was predicted, therefore it had to happen. Thus a good many people reason, but as I was not of the number I proceeded on my way.

In Naples, where, as he often assures us, Fortune was ever kind to him, his paternal entrails receive another shock. This time it is the beautiful Leonilda, the honorary mistress of the Duke of Montalone, who, with the duke's approval, he nearly marries. But when he goes to call on the young lady's mother — oh, horror! oh, joy! — whom does he see? Lucrezia Castelli, the Neapolitan lawyer's handsome wife, and now his no less handsome widow, with whom in Rome, in Tivoli, in Frascati, he had tasted such unforgettable joys. Once more it is "just seventeen years ago," and once more he is more than willing to marry the mother and live happily with her for the rest of his days, if she will consent to take their daughter with them, for he cannot bear the thought of separating from his "Giacomina." But Lucrezia's first duty is towards her daughter, who being in the excellent hands of the elderly and impotent duke, must remain where she is. So the matter is dropped and Casanova, after settling a share of his winnings as dowry on his daughter, bids farewell to mother, daughter, and their generous protector.

Stopping in Rome, where the carnival has just begun, Casanova is the guest of honour at the marriage of Mariuccia (after, we need hardly say, the usual tenderly protracted farewell). Then, retracing his itinerary, with the obbligato *accompaniment of amorous exploits, he regains Paris, where his infatuated marquise is impatiently awaiting the promised accomplishment of her rejuvenation. There let us rejoin him.*

CHAPTER XIV

From Paris to Augsburg

A T TEN o'clock in the morning, cheered by the pleasant feeling of being once more in that Paris which is so imperfect, but which is the only true town in the world, I called on my dear Madame d'Urfé, who received me with open arms. She told me that the young Count d'Aranda was quite well, and if I liked she would ask him to dinner the next day. I told her I should be delighted to see him, and then I informed her that the operation by which she was to become a man could not be performed till Querilinto, one of the three chiefs of the Fraternity of the Rosy Cross, was liberated from the dungeons of the Inquisition, at Lisbon.

"This is the reason," I added, "that I am going to Augsburg in the course of next month, where I shall confer with the Earl of Stormont as to the liberation of the adept, under the pretext of a mission from the Portuguese government. For these purposes I shall require a good letter of credit, and some watches and snuff-boxes to make presents with, as we have to win over certain of the profane."

"I will gladly see to all that, but you need not hurry yourself, as the Congress will not meet till September."

"Believe me, it will never meet at all, but the ambassadors of the belligerent powers will be there all the same. If, contrary to my expectation, the Congress is held, I shall be obliged to go to Lisbon. In any case, I promise to see you again in the ensuing winter. The fortnight that I have to spend here will enable me to defeat a plot of St. Germain's."

"St. Germain — he would never dare to return to Paris."

"I am certain that he is here in disguise. The state messenger who ordered him to leave London has convinced him the English minister was not duped by the demand for his person to be given up, made by the Comte d'Afri in the name of the king to the States-General."

All this was mere guesswork, and it will be seen that I guessed rightly.

Madame d'Urfé then congratulated me on the charming girl whom I had sent from Grenoble to Paris. Valenglard had told her the whole story.

"The king adores her," said she, "and before long she will make him a father. I have been to see her at Passi with the Duchesse de l'Oraguais."

"She will give birth to a son who will make France happy, and in thirty years' time you will see wondrous things, of which, unfortunately, I can tell you nothing until your transformation. Did you mention my name to her?"

"No, I did not; but I am sure you will be able to see her, if only at Madame Varnier's."

She was not mistaken; but shortly afterwards an event happened which made the madness of this excellent woman much worse. Towards four o'clock, as we were talking over my travels and our designs, she took a fancy to walk in the Bois du Boulogne. She begged me to accompany her, and I acceded to her request. We walked into the deepest recesses of the wood and sat down under a tree.

"It is eighteen years," said she, "since I fell asleep on the same spot that we now occupy. During my sleep the divine Horosmadis came down from the sun and stayed with me till I awoke. As I opened my eyes I saw him leave me and ascend to heaven. He left me with child, and I bore a girl which he took away from me ten years ago, no doubt to punish me for having so far forgotten myself as to love a mortal after him. My lovely Iriasis was like him."

"You are quite sure that M. d'Urfé was not the child's father?"

".M. d'Urfé did not know me after he saw me lying beside the divine Anael."

"That's the genius of Venus."

"He too left me on account of my sinning with an Arab."

"The Arab was sent to you by an enemy of Anael's, the genius of Mercury."

"It must have been so; it was a great misfortune."

"On the contrary, it rendered you more fit for transformation."

We were walking towards the carriage when all at once we saw St. Germain, but as soon as he noticed us he turned back and we lost sight of him.

"Did you see him?" said I. "He is working against us, but our genie makes him tremble."

"I am quite thunderstruck. I will go and impart this piece of news to the Duc de Choiseul to-morrow morning. I am curious to hear what he will say when I tell him."

As we were going back to Paris I left Madame d'Urfé, and walked to the Porte St. Denis to see my brother. He and his wife received me with cries of joy. I thought the wife very pretty but very wretched, for Providence had not allowed my brother to prove his manhood, and she was unhappily in love with him. I say unhappily, because her love kept her faithful to ·him, and if she had not been in love she might easily have found a cure for her misfortune, as her husband allowed her perfect liberty. She grieved bitterly, for she did not know that my brother was impotent, and fancied that the reason of his abstention was that he did not return her love; and the mistake was an excusable one, for he was like a Hercules, and indeed he was one, except where it was most to be desired. Her grief threw her into a consumption of which she died five or six years later. She did not mean her death to be a punishment to her husband, but we shall see that it was so.

The next day I called on Madame Varnier to give her Madame Morin's letter. I was cordially welcomed, and Madame Varnier was kind enough to say that she had rather see me than anybody else in the world; her niece had told her such strange things about me that she had got quite curious. This, as is well known, is a prevailing complaint with women.

"You shall see my niece," she said, "and she will tell you all about herself."

She wrote her a note, and put Madame Morin's letter under the same envelope.

"If you want to know what my niece's answer is," said Madame Varnier, "you must dine with me."

I accepted the invitation, and she immediately told her servant that she was not at home to anyone.

The small messenger who had taken the note to Passi returned at four o'clock with the following epistle:

"The moment in which I see the Chevalier de Seingalt once more will be one of the happiest of my life. Ask him to be at your house at ten o'clock the day after to-morrow, and if he can't come then, please let me know."

After reading the note and promising to keep the appointment, I left Madame Varnier and called on Madame de Rumain, who told me I must spend a whole day with her as she had several questions to put to my oracle.

Next day Madame d'Urfé told me the reply she had from the Duc de Choiseul, when she told him that she had seen the Comte de St. Germain in the Bois du Boulogne.

"I should not be surprised," said the minister, "considering that he spent the night in my closet."

The duke was a man of wit and a man of the world. He only kept secrets when they were really important ones; very different from those make-believe diplomatists, who think they give themselves importance by making a mystery of trifles of no consequence. It is true that the Duc de Choiseul very seldom thought anything of great importance; and, in point of fact, if there were less intrigue and more truth about diplomacy (as there ought to be), concealment would be rather ridiculous than necessary.

The duke had pretended to disgrace St. Germain in France that he might use him as a spy in London; but Lord Halifax was by no means taken in by this stratagem. However, all governments have the politeness to afford one another these services, so that none of them can reproach the others.

The small Comte d'Aranda after caressing me affectionately begged me to come and breakfast with him at his boarding-house, telling me that Mdlle. Viar would be glad to see me.

The next day I took care not to fail in my appointment with the fair lady. I was at Madame Varnier's a quarter of an hour before the arrival of the dazzling brunette, and I waited for her with a beating at the heart which showed me that the small favours she had given me had not quenched the flame of love. When she made her appearance the stoutness of her figure carried respect with it, so that I did not feel as if I could come forward and greet her tenderly; but she was far from thinking that more respect was due to her than when she was at Grenoble, poor but also pure. She kissed me affectionately and told me as much.

"They think I am happy," said she, "and envy my lot; but can one be happy after the loss of one's self-respect? For the last six months I have only smiled, not laughed; while at Grenoble I laughed heartily from true gladness. I have diamonds, lace, a beautiful house, a superb carriage, a lovely garden, waiting-maids, and a maid of honour who perhaps despises me; and although the highest Court ladies treat me like a princess, I do not pass a single day without experiencing some mortification."

"Mortification?"

"Yes; people come and bring pleas before me, and I am obliged to send them away as I dare not ask the king anything."

"Why not?"

"Because I cannot look on him as my lover only; he is always my sovereign, too. Ah! happiness is to be sought for in simple homes, not in pompous palaces."

[122]

"Happiness is gained by complying with the duties of whatever condition of life one is in, and you must constrain yourself to rise to that exalted station in which destiny has placed you."

"I cannot do it; I love the king and I am always afraid of vexing him. I am always thinking that he does too much for me, and thus I dare not ask for anything for others."

"But I am sure the king would be only too glad to show his love for you by benefiting the persons in whom you take an interest."

"I know he would, and that thought makes me happy, but I cannot overcome my feeling of repugnance to asking favours. I have a hundred louis a month for pin-money, and I distribute it in alms and presents, but with due economy, so that I am not penniless at the end of the month. I have a foolish notion that the chief reason the king loves me is that I do not importune him."

"And do you love him?"

"How can I help it? He is good-hearted, kindly, handsome, and polite to excess; in short, he possesses all the qualities to captivate a woman's heart.

"He is always asking me if I am pleased with my furniture, my clothes, my servants, and my garden, and if I desire anything altered. I thank him with a kiss, and tell him that I am pleased with everything."

"Does he ever speak of the scion you are going to present to him?"

"He often says that I ought to be careful of myself in my situation. I am hoping that he will recognise my son as a prince of the blood; he ought in justice to do so, as the queen is dead."

"To be sure he will."

"I should be very happy if I had a son. I wish I felt sure that I would have one. But I say nothing about this to anyone. If I dared speak to the king about the horoscope, I am certain he would want to know you; but I am afraid of evil tongues."

"So am I. Continue in your discreet course and nothing will come to disturb your happiness, which may become greater, and which I am pleased to have procured for you."

We did not part without tears. She was the first to go, after kissing me and calling me her best friend. I stayed a short time with Madame Varnier to compose my feelings, and I told her that I should have married her instead of drawing her horoscope.

"She would no doubt have been happier. You did not foresee, perhaps, her timidity and her lack of ambition."

"I can assure you that I did not reckon upon her courage or ambition. I laid aside my own happiness to think only of hers. But what is done cannot be recalled, and I shall be consoled if I see her perfectly happy at last. I hope, indeed, she will be so, above all if she is delivered of a son."

I dined with Madame d'Urfé, and we decided to send back Aranda to his boarding-school that we might be more free to pursue our cabalistic operations; and afterwards I went to the opera, where my brother had made an appointment with me. He took me to sup at Madame Vanloo's, and she received me in the friendliest manner possible.

"You will have the pleasure of meeting Madame Blondel and her husband," said she.

The reader will recollect that Madame Blondel was Manon Baletti, whom I was to have married.

"Does she know I am coming?" I inquired.

"No, I promise myself the pleasure of seeing her surprise."

"I am much obliged to you for not wishing to enjoy my surprise as well. We shall see each other again, but not to-day, so I must bid you farewell; for as I am a man of honour I hope never to be under the same roof as Madame Blondel again."

With this I left the room, leaving everybody in astonishment, and not knowing where to go I took a coach and went to sup with my sister-in-law, who was extremely glad to see me. But all through supper-time this charming woman did nothing but complain of her husband, saying that he had no business to marry her, knowing that he could not show himself a man.

"Why did you not make the trial before you married?"

"Was it for me to propose such a thing? How should I suppose that such a fine man was impotent? But I will tell you how it all happened. As you know, I was a dancer at the Comédie Italienne, and I was the mistress of M. de Sauci, the ecclesiastical commissioner. He brought your brother to my house, I liked him, and before long I saw that he loved me. My lover advised me that it was an opportunity for getting married and making my fortune. With this idea I conceived the plan of not granting him any favours. He used to come and see me in the morning, and often found me in bed; we talked together, and his passions seemed to be aroused, but it all ended in kissing. On my part, I was waiting for a formal declaration and a proposal of marriage. At that period, M. de Sauci settled an annuity of a thousand crowns on me on the condition that I left the stage.

"In the spring M. de Sauci invited your brother to spend a month in his country-house. I was of the party, but for propriety's sake it was agreed that I should pass as your brother's wife. Casanova enjoyed the idea, looking upon it as a jest, and not thinking of the consequences. I was therefore introduced as his wife to my lover's family, as also to his relations, who were judges, officers, and men about town, and to their wives, who were all women of fashion. Your brother was in high glee that to play our parts properly we were obliged to sleep together. For my part, I was far from disliking the idea, or at all events I looked upon it as a short cut to the marriage I desired.

"But how can I tell you? Though tender and affectionate in everything, your brother slept with me for a month without our attaining what seemed the natural result under the circumstances."

"You might have concluded, then, that he was impotent; for unless he were made of stone, or had taken a vow of chastity, his conduct was inexplicable."

"The fact is, that I had no means of knowing whether he was capable or incapable of giving me substantial proof of his love."

"Why did you not ascertain his condition for yourself?"

"A feeling of foolish pride prevented me from putting him to the test. I did not suspect the truth, but imagined reasons flattering to myself. I thought that he loved me so truly that he would not do anything before I was his wife. That idea prevented me humiliating myself by making him give me some positive proof of his powers."

"That supposition would have been tenable, though highly improbable, if you had been an innocent young maid, but he knew perfectly well that your novitiate was long over."

"Very true; but what can you expect of a woman impelled by love and vanity?"

"Your reasoning is excellent, but it comes rather late."

"Well, at last we went back to Paris, your brother to his house, and I to mine, while he continued his courtship, and I could not understand what he meant by such strange behaviour. M. de Sauci, who knew that nothing serious had taken place between us, tried in vain to solve the enigma. 'No doubt he is afraid of getting you with child,' he said, 'and of thus being obliged to marry you.' I began to be of the same opinion, but I thought it a strange line for a man in love to take.

"M. de Nesle, an officer in the French Guards, who had a pretty wife I had met in the country, went to your brother's to call on me. Not finding me there he asked why we did not live together. Your brother replied openly that our marriage had been a mere jest. M. de Nesle then came to me to inquire if this were the truth, and when he heard that it was he asked me how I would like him to make Casanova marry me. I answered that I should be delighted, and that was enough for him. He went again to your brother, and told him that his wife would never have associated with me on equal terms if I had not been introduced to her as a married woman; that the deceit was an insult to all the company at the country-house, which must be wiped out by his marrying me within the week or by fighting a duel. M. de Nesle added that if he fell he would be avenged by all the gentlemen who had been offended in the same way. Casanova replied, laughing, that so far from fighting to escape marrying me, he was ready to break a lance to get me. 'I love her,' he said, 'and if she loves me I am quite ready to give her my hand. Be kind enough,' he added, 'to prepare the way for me, and I will marry her whenever you like.'

"M. de Nesle embraced him, and promised to see to everything; he brought me the joyful news, and in a week all was over. M. de Nesle gave us a splendid supper on our wedding-day, and since then I have had the title of his wife. It is an empty title, however, for, despite the ceremony and the fatal yes, I am no wife, for your brother is completely impotent. I am an unhappy wretch, and it is all his fault, for he ought to have known his own condition. He has deceived me horribly."

"But he was obliged to act as he did; he is more to be pitied than to be blamed. I also pity you, but I think you are in the wrong, for after his sleeping with you for a month without giving any proof of his manhood you might have guessed the truth. Even if you had been a perfect novice, M. de Sauci ought to have known what was the matter."

"All that seems very reasonable, but nevertheless neither of us thought of it; your brother looks such a Hercules."

"There are two remedies open to you; you can either have your marriage annulled, or you can take a lover; and I am sure that my brother is too reasonable a man to offer any opposition to the latter course."

"I am perfectly free, but I can neither avail myself of a divorce nor of a lover; for the wretch treats me so kindly that I love him more and more, which doubtless makes my misfortune harder to bear."

The poor woman was so unhappy that I should have been delighted to console her, but it was out of the question. However, the mere telling of her story had afforded her some solace, and after kissing her in such a way as to convince her that I was not like my brother, I wished her good-night.

The next day I called on Madame Vanloo, who informed me that Madame Blondel had charged her to thank me for having gone away, while her husband wished me to know that he was sorry not to have seen me to express his gratitude.

"He seems to have found his wife a maid, but that's no fault of mine; and Manon Baletti is the only person he ought to be grateful to. They tell me that he has a pretty baby, and that he lives at the Louvre, while she has another house in the Rue Neuve-des-Petits-Champs."

"Yes, but he has supper with her every evening."

"It's an odd way of living."

"I assure you it answers capitally. Blondel regards his wife as his mistress. He says that that keeps the flame of love alight, and that as he never had a mistress worthy of being a wife, he is delighted to have a wife worthy of being a mistress."

The next day I devoted entirely to Madame de Rumain, and we were occupied with knotty questions till the evening. I left her well pleased. The marriage of her daughter, Mdlle. Cotenfau, with M. de Polignac, which took place five or six years later, was the result of our cabalistic calculations.

The fair stocking-seller of the Rue des Prouvères, whom I had loved so well, was no longer in Paris. She had gone off with a M. de Langlade, and her husband was inconsolable. Camille was ill. Coralline had become the titulary mistress of the Comte de la Marche, son of the Prince of Conti, and the issue of this union was a son, whom I knew twenty years later. He called himself the Chevalier de Montréal and wore the cross of the Knights of Malta. Several other girls I had known were widowed and in the country, or had become inaccessible in other ways.

Such was the Paris of my day. The actors on its stage changed as rapidly as the fashions.

I devoted a whole day to my old friend Baletti, who had left the theatre and married a pretty ballet-girl on the death of his father; he was making experiments with a view to finding the philosopher's stone.

I was agreeably surprised at meeting the poet Poinsinet at the Comédie Française. He embraced me again and again, and told me that M. du Tillot had overwhelmed him with kindness at Parma.

"He could not get me anything to do," said Poinsinet, "because a French poet is rather at a discount in Italy."

"Have you heard anything of Lord Lismore?"

"Yes, he wrote to his mother from Leghorn, telling her that he was going to the Indies, and that if you had not been good enough to give him a thousand louis he would have been a prisoner at Rome."

"His fate interests me extremely, and I should be glad to call on his lady-mother with you."

"I will tell her that you are in Paris, and I am sure that she will invite you to supper, for she has the greatest desire to talk to you."

"How are you getting on here? Are you still content to serve Apollo?"

"He is not the god of wealth by any means. I have no money and no room, and I shall be glad of a supper, if you will ask me. I will read you my play, the *Cercle*, which has been accepted. I am sure it will be successful."

The *Cercle* was a short prose play, in which the poet satirised the jargon of Dr. Herrenschwand, brother of the doctor I had consulted at Soleure. The play proved to be a great success.

I took Poinsinet home to supper, and the poor nursling of

the muses ate for four. In the morning he came to tell me that the Countess of Lismore expected me to supper.

I found the lady, still pretty, in company with her aged lover, M. de St. Albin, Archbishop of Cambrai, who spent all the revenues of his see on her. This worthy prelate was one of the illegitimate children of the Duc d'Orléans, the famous Regent, by an actress. He supped with us, but he only opened his mouth to eat, and his mistress only spoke of her son, whose talents she lauded to the skies, though he was in reality a mere scamp; but I felt in duty bound to echo what she said. It would have been cruel to contradict her. I promised to let her know if I saw anything more of him.

Poinsinet, who was hearthless and homeless, as they say, spent the night in my room, and in the morning I gave him two cups of chocolate and some money wherewith to get a lodging. I never saw him again, and a few years after he was drowned, not in the fountain Hippocrene, but in the Guadalquivir. He told me that he had spent a week with M. de Voltaire, and that he had hastened his return to Paris to obtain the release of the Abbé Morellet from the Bastille.

I had nothing more to do at Paris, and I was only waiting for some clothes to be made and for a cross of the order with which the Holy Father had decorated me, to be set with diamonds and rubies.

I had waited for five or six days when an unfortunate incident obliged me to take a hasty departure. I am loth to write what follows, for it was all my own fault that I was nearly losing my life and my honour. I pity those simpletons who blame fortune and not themselves for their misfortunes.

I was walking in the Tuileries at ten o'clock in the morning, when I was unlucky enough to meet the Dangenancour and another girl. This Dangenancour was a dancer at the opera-house, whom I had desired to meet previously to my last departure from Paris. I congratulated myself on the lucky chance which threw her in my way, and accosted her, and had not much trouble in inducing her to dine with me at Choisi.

We walked towards the Pont-Royal, where we took a coach. After dinner had been ordered we were taking a turn in the garden, when I saw a carriage stop and two adventurers whom I knew getting out of it, with two girls, friends of the ones I

had with me. The wretched landlady, who was standing at the
door, said that if we liked to sit down together she could give us
an excellent dinner, and I said nothing, or rather I assented to
the yes of my two nymphs. The dinner was excellent, and after
the bill was paid, and we were on the point of returning to Paris,
I noticed that a ring, which I had taken off to show to one of
the adventurers, named Santis, was still missing. It was an
exceedingly pretty minature, and the diamond setting had cost
me twenty-five louis. I politely begged Santis to return me the
ring, and he replied with the utmost coolness that he had done so
already.

"If you had returned it," said I, "it would be on my finger,
and you see that it is not."

He persisted in his assertion; the girls said nothing, but
Santis's friend, a Portuguese, named Xavier, dared to tell me
that he had seen the ring returned.

"You're a liar," I exclaimed; and without more ado I took
hold of Santis by the collar, and swore I would not let him go
till he returned me my ring. The Portuguese rose to come to
his friend's rescue, while I stepped back and drew my sword,
repeating my determination not to let them go. The landlady
came on the scene and began to shriek, and Santis asked me to
give him a few words apart. I thought in all good faith that he
was ashamed to restore the ring before company, but that he
would give it me as soon as we were alone. I sheathed my
sword, and told him to come with me. Xavier got into the
carriage with the four girls, and they all went back to Paris.

Santis followed me to the back of the inn, and then assuming
a pleasant smile he told me that he had put the ring into his
friend's pocket for a joke, but that I should have it back at
Paris.

"That's an idle tale," I exclaimed, "your friend said that he
saw you return it, and now he has escaped me. Do you think
that I am green enough to be taken in by this sort of thing?
You're a couple of robbers."

So saying, I stretched out my hand for his watch-chain,
but he stepped back and drew his sword. I drew mine, and we
had scarcely crossed swords when he thrust, and I parrying
rushed in and ran him through and through. He fell to the
ground calling, "Help!" I sheathed my sword, and, without

troubling myself about him, got into my coach and drove back to Paris.

I got down in the Place Maubert, and walked by a circuitous way to my hotel. I was sure that no one could have come after me there, as my landlord did not even know my name.

I spent the rest of the day in packing up my trunks, and after telling Costa to place them on my carriage I went to Madame d'Urfé. After I had told her of what had happened, I begged her, as soon as that which she had for me was ready, to send it to me at Augsburg by Costa. I should have told her to entrust it to one of her own servants, but my good genius had left me that day. Besides, I did not look upon Costa as a thief.

When I got back to the hotel I gave the rascal his instructions, telling him to be quick and to keep his own counsel, and I then gave him money for the journey.

I left Paris in my carriage, drawn by four hired horses, which took me as far as the second post, and I did not stop till I got to Strasburg, where I found Desarmoises and my Spaniard.

There was nothing to keep me in Strasburg, so I wanted to cross the Rhine immediately; but Desarmoises persuaded me to come with him to see an extremely pretty woman who had only delayed her departure for Augsburg in the hope that we might journey there together.

"You know the lady," said the false marquis, "but she made me give my word of honour that I would not tell you. She has only her maid with her, and I am sure you will be pleased to see her."

My curiosity made me give in. I followed Desarmoises, and came into a room where I saw a nice-looking woman whom I did not recognise at first. I collected my thoughts, and the lady turned out to be a dancer whom I had admired on the Dresden boards eight years before. She was then mistress to Count Brühl, but I had not even attempted to win her favour. She had an excellent carriage, and as she was ready to go to Augsburg I immediately concluded that we could make the journey together very pleasantly.

After the usual compliments had passed, we decided on leaving for Augsburg the following morning. The lady was going to Munich, but as I had no business there we agreed that she should go by herself.

"I am quite sure," she said, afterwards, "that you will come too, for the ambassadors do not assemble at Augsburg till next September."

We supped together, and next morning we started on our way; she in her carriage with her maid, and I in mine with Desarmoises, preceded by Le Duc on horseback. At Rastadt, however, we made a change, the Renaud (as she was called) thinking that she would give less opportunity for curious surmises by riding with me, while Desarmoises went with the servant. We soon became intimate. She told me about herself, or pretended to, and I told her all that I did not want to conceal. I informed her that I was an agent of the Court of Lisbon, and she believed me, while, for my part, I believed that she was only going to Munich and Augsburg to sell her diamonds.

We began to talk about Desarmoises, and she said that it was well enough for me to associate with him, but I should not countenance his styling himself marquis.

"But," said I, "he is the son of the Marquis Desarmoises, of Nancy."

"No, he isn't; he is only a retired messenger, with a small pension from the department of foreign affairs. I know the Marquis Desarmoises; he lives at Nancy, and is not so old as our friend."

"Then one can't see how he can be Desarmoises's father."

"The landlord of the inn at Strasburg knew him when he was a messenger."

"How did you make his acquaintance?"

"We met at the table d'hôte. After dinner he came up to my room, and told me he was waiting for a gentleman who was going to Augsburg, and that we might make the journey together. He told me the name, and after questioning him I concluded that the gentleman was yourself, so here we are, and I am very glad of it. But listen to me; I advise you to drop all false styles and titles. Why do you call yourself Seingalt?"

"Because it's my name, but that doesn't prevent my old friends calling me Casanova, for I am both. You understand?"

"Oh, yes! I understand. Your mother is at Prague, and as she doesn't get her pension on account of the war, I am afraid she must be rather in difficulties."

"I know it, but I do not forget my filial duties. I have sent her some money."

"That's right. Where are you going to stay at Augsburg?"

"I shall take a house, and if you like you shall be the mistress and do the honours."

"That would be delightful! We will give little suppers, and play cards all night."

"Your programme is an excellent one."

"I will see that you get a good cook; all the Bavarian cooks are good. We shall cut a fine figure, and people will say we love each other madly."

"You must know, dearest, that I do not understand jokes at the expense of fidelity."

"You may trust me for that. You know how I lived at Dresden."

"I will trust you, but not blindly, I promise you. And now let us address each other in the same way; you must call me *tu*. You must remember we are lovers."

"Kiss me!"

The fair Renaud did not like travelling by night; she preferred to eat a good supper, to drink heavily, and to go to bed just as her head began to whirl. The heat of the wine made her into a Bacchante, hard to appease; but when I could do no more I told her to leave me alone, and she had to obey.

When we reached Augsburg we alighted at the Three Moors, but the landlord told us that though he could give us a good dinner he could not put us up, as the whole of the hotel had been engaged by the French ambassador. I called on M. Corti, the banker to whom I was accredited, and he soon got me a furnished house with a garden, which I took for six months. The Renaud liked it immensely.

No one had yet arrived at Augsburg. The Renaud contrived to make me feel that I should be lonely at Augsburg without her, and succeeded in persuading me to come with her to Munich. We put up at the Stag, and made ourselves very comfortable, while Desarmoises went to stay somewhere else. As my business and that of my new mate had nothing in common, I gave her a servant and a carriage to herself, and made myself the same allowance.

The Abbé Gama had given me a letter from the Commenda-tore Almada for Lord Stormont, the English ambassador at the Court of Bavaria. This nobleman being then at Munich I hastened to deliver the letter. He received me very well, and promised to do all he could as soon as he had time, as Lord Halifax had told him all about it. On leaving his Britannic lordship's I called on M. de Folard, the French ambassador, and gave him a letter from M. de Choiseul. M. de Folard gave me a hearty welcome, and asked me to dine with him the next day, and the day after introduced me to the Elector.

During the four fatal weeks I spent at Munich, the ambassador's house was the only one I frequented. I call these weeks fatal, and with reason, for in them I lost all my money, I pledged jewels (which I never recovered) to the amount of forty thousand francs, and finally I lost my health. My assassins were the Renaud and Desarmoises, who owed me so much and paid me so badly.

The third day after my arrival I had to call on the Dowager Electress of Saxony. It was my brother-in-law, who was in her train, that made me go, by telling me that it must be done, as she knew me and had been inquiring for me. I had no reason to repent of my politeness in going, as the Electress gave me a good reception, and made me talk to any extent. She was extremely curious, like most people who have no employment, and have not sufficient intelligence to amuse themselves.

I have done a good many foolish things in the course of my existence. I confess it as frankly as Rousseau, and my Memoirs are not so egotistic as those of that unfortunate genius; but I never committed such an act of folly as I did when I went to Munich, where I had nothing to do. But it was a crisis in my life. My evil genius had made me commit one folly after another since I left Turin. The evening at Lord Lismore's, my connection with Desarmoises, my party at Choisi, my trust in Costa, my union with the Renaud, and, worse than all, my folly in letting myself play at faro at a place where the knavery of the gamesters is renowned all over Europe, followed one another in fatal succession. Among the players was the famous, or rather infamous, Afflisio, the friend of the Duc de Deux-Ponts, whom the duke called his aide-de-camp, and who was known for the keenest rogue in the world.

I played every day, and as I often lost money on my word of honour, the necessity of paying the next day often caused me the utmost anxiety. When I had exhausted my credit with the bankers, I had recourse to the Jews who require pledges, and in this Desarmoises and the Renaud were my agents, the latter of whom ended by making herself mistress of all my property. This was not the worst thing she did to me; for she gave me a disease which devoured her interior parts and left no marks outwardly, and was thus all the more dangerous, as the freshness of her complexion seemed to indicate the most perfect health. In short, this serpent, who must have come from hell to destroy me, had acquired such a mastery over me that she persuaded me that she would be dishonoured if I called in a doctor during our stay at Munich, as everybody knew that we were living together as man and wife.

I cannot imagine what had become of my wits to let myself be so beguiled, while every day I renewed the poison that she had poured into my veins.

My stay at Munich was a kind of curse; throughout that dreadful month I seemed to have a foretaste of the pains of the damned. The Renaud loved gaming, and Desarmoises was her partner. I took care not to play with them, for the false marquis was an unmitigated cheat and often tricked with less skill than impudence. He asked disreputable people to my house and treated them at my expense; every evening scenes of a disgraceful character took place.

The Dowager Electress mortified me extremely by the way she addressed me on my last two visits to her.

"Everybody knows what kind of a life you lead here, and the way the Renaud behaves, possibly without your knowing it. I advise you to have done with her, as your character is suffering."

She did not know what a thraldom I was under. I had left Paris for a month, and I had neither heard of Madame d'Urfé nor of Costa. I could not guess the reason, but I began to suspect my Italian's fidelity. I also feared lest my good Madame d'Urfé might be dead or have come to her senses, which would have come to the same thing so far as I was concerned; and I could not possibly return to Paris to obtain the information which was so necessary both for calming my mind and refilling my purse.

I was in a terrible state, and my sharpest pang was that I began to experience a certain abatement of my vigour, the natural result of advancing years. I had no longer that daring born of youth and the knowledge of one's strength, and I was not yet old enough to have learnt how to husband my forces. Nevertheless, I made an effort and took a sudden leave of my mistress, telling her I would await her at Augsburg. She did not try to detain me, but promised to rejoin me as soon as possible; she was engaged in selling her jewellery. I set out preceded by Le Duc, feeling very glad that Desarmoises had chosen to stay with the wretched woman to whom he had introduced me. When I reached my pretty house at Augsburg I took to my bed, determined not to rise till I was cured or dead. M. Carli, my banker, recommended to me a doctor named Cephalides, a pupil of the famous Fayet, who had cured me of a similar complaint several years before. This Cephalides was considered the best doctor in Augsburg. He examined me and declared he could cure me by sudorifics without having recourse to the knife. He began his treatment by putting me on a severe regimen, ordering baths, and applying mercury locally. I endured this treatment for six weeks, at the end of which time I found myself worse than at the beginning. I had become terribly thin, and I had two enormous inguinal tumours. I had to make up my mind to have them lanced, but though the operation nearly killed me it did not make me any better. He was so clumsy as to cut the artery, causing great loss of blood which was arrested with difficulty, and would have proved fatal if it had not been for the care of M. Algardi, a Bolognese doctor in the service of the Prince-Bishop of Augsburg.

I had had enough of Cephalides, and Dr. Algardi prepared in my presence eighty-six pills containing eighteen grains of manna. I took one of these pills every morning, drinking a large glass of curds after it, and in the evening I had another pill with barley water, and this was the only sustenance I had. This heroic treatment gave me back my health in two months and a half, in which I suffered a great deal of pain; but I did not begin to put on flesh and get back my strength till the end of the year.

It was during this time that I heard about Costa's flight with my diamonds, watches, snuff-box, linen, rich suits, and a hundred louis which Madame d'Urfé had given him for the journey. The worthy lady sent me a bill of exchange for fifty thousand francs, which she had happily not entrusted to the robber, and the money rescued me very opportunely from the state to which my imprudence had reduced me.

At this period I made another discovery of an extremely vexatious character; namely, that Le Duc had robbed me. I would have forgiven him if he had not forced me to a public exposure, which I could only have avoided with the loss of my honour. However, I kept him in my service till my return to Paris at the commencement of the following year.

Towards the end of September, when everybody knew that the Congress would not take place, the Renaud passed through Augsburg with Desarmoises on her way to Paris; but she dared not come and see me for fear I should make her return my goods, of which she had taken possession without telling me. Four or five years later she married a man named Böhmer, the same that gave the Cardinal de Rohan the famous necklace, which he supposed was destined for the unfortunate Marie Antoinette. The Renaud was at Paris when I returned, but I made no endeavour to see her, as I wished, if possible, to forget the past. I had every reason to do so, for amongst all the misfortunes I had gone through during that wretched year the person I found most at fault was myself. Nevertheless, I would have given myself the pleasure of cutting off Desarmoises's ears; but the old rascal, who, no doubt, foresaw what kind of treatment I was likely to mete to him, made his escape. Shortly after, he died miserably of consumption in Normandy.

My health had scarcely returned, when I forgot all my woes and began once more to amuse myself. My excellent cook, Anna Midel, who had been idle so long, had to work hard to satisfy my ravenous appetite. My landlord and pretty Gertrude, his daughter, looked at me with astonishment as I ate, fearing some disastrous results. Dr. Algardi, who had saved my life, prophesied a dyspepsia which would bring me to the tomb, but my need of food was stronger than his arguments, to which I paid no kind of attention; and I was right, for I required an immense quantity of nourishment to recover my former state, and I soon felt in a condition to renew my sacrifices to the deity for whom I had suffered so much.

I fell in love with the cook and Gertrude, who were both young and pretty. I imparted my love to both of them at once, for I had foreseen that if I attacked them separately I should conquer neither. Besides, I felt that I had not much time to lose, as I had promised to sup with Madame d'Urfé on the first night of the year 1761 in a suite of rooms she had furnished for me in the Rue du Bacq. She had adorned the rooms with superb tapestry made for Réné of Savoy, on which were depicted all the operations of the Great Work. She wrote to me that she had heard that Santis had recovered from the wound I had given him, and had been committed to the Bicêtre for fraud.

Gertrude and Anna Midel occupied my leisure moments agreeably enough during the rest of my stay at Augsburg, but they did not make me neglect society. I spent my evenings in a very agreeable manner with Count Max de Lamberg, who occupied the position of field-marshal to the prince-bishop. His wife had all the attractions which collect good company together. At this house I made the acquaintance of the Baron von Selentin, a captain in the Prussian service, who was recruiting for the King of Prussia at Augsburg. I was particularly drawn to the Count Lamberg by his taste for literature. He was an extremely learned man, and has published some excellent works. I kept up a correspondence with him till his death, by his own fault, in 1792, four years from the time of my writing. I say by his fault, but I should have said by the fault of his doctors, who treated him mercurially for a disease which was not venereal; and this treatment not only killed him but took away his good name.

His widow is still alive, and lives in Bavaria, loved by her friends and her daughters, who all made excellent marriages.

At this time a miserable company of Italian actors made their appearance in Augsburg, and I got them permission to play in a small and wretched theatre. As this was the occasion of an incident which diverted me, the hero, I shall impart it to my readers in the hope of its amusing them also.

CHAPTER XV

"Chevalier de Seingalt"

A WOMAN, ugly enough, but lively like all Italians, called on me, and asked me to intercede with the police to obtain permission for her company to act in Augsburg. In spite of her ugliness she was a poor fellow-countrywoman, and without asking her name, or ascertaining whether the company was good or bad, I promised to do my best, and had no difficulty in obtaining the favour.

I went to the first performance, and saw to my surprise that the chief actor was a Venetian, and a fellow-student of mine, twenty years before, at St. Cyprian's College. His name was Bassi, and like myself he had given up the priesthood. Fortune had made an actor of him, and he looked wretched enough, while I, the adventurer, had a prosperous air.

I felt curious to hear his adventures, and I was also actuated by that feeling of kindliness which draws one towards the companions of one's youthful and especially one's school days, so I went to the back as soon as the curtain fell. He recognised me directly, gave a joyful cry, and after he had embraced me he introduced me to his wife, the woman who had called on me, and to his daughter, a girl of thirteen or fourteen, whose dancing had delighted me. He did not stop here, but turning to his mates, of whom he was chief, introduced me to them as his best friend. These worthy people, seeing me dressed like a lord, with a cross on my breast, took me for a cosmopolitan charlatan who was expected at Augsburg, and Bassi, strange to say, did not undeceive them. When the company had taken off its stage rags and put on its everyday rags, Bassi's ugly wife took me by the arm and said I must come and sup with her. I let myself be led, and we soon got to just the kind of room I had imagined. It was a huge room on the ground-floor, which served for kitchen, dining-room, and bedroom all at once. In the middle stood a long table, part of which was covered with a cloth which looked as if it had been in use for a month, and at the other end of the room somebody was washing certain earthenware dishes in a dirty pan. This den was lighted by one candle stuck in the neck of a broken bottle, and as there were no snuffers Bassi's wife snuffed it cleverly with her finger and thumb, wiping her hand on the table-cloth after throwing the burnt wick on the floor. An actor with long moustaches, who played the villain in the various pieces, served an enormous dish of hashed-up meat, swimming in a sea of dirty water dignified with the name of sauce; and the hungry family proceeded to tear pieces of bread off the loaf with their fingers or teeth, and then to dip them in the dish; but as all did the same no one had a right to be disgusted. A large pot of ale passed from hand to hand, and with all this misery mirth displayed itself on every countenance, and I had to ask myself what is happiness. For a second course there was a dish of fried pork, which was devoured with great relish. Bassi was kind enough not to press me to take part in this banquet, and I felt obliged to him.

The meal over, he proceeded to impart to me his adventures, which were ordinary enough, and like those which many a poor devil has to undergo; and while he talked his pretty daughter sat on my knee. Bassi brought his story to an end by saying that he was going to Venice for the carnival, and was sure of making a lot of money. I wished him all the luck he could desire, and on his asking me what profession I followed, the fancy took me to reply that I was a doctor.

"That's a better trade than mine," said he, "and I am happy to be able to give you a valuable present."

"What is that?" I asked.

"The receipt for the Venetian Specific, which you can sell at two florins a pound, while it will only cost you four gros."

"I shall be delighted; but tell me, how is the treasury?"

"Well, I can't complain for a first night. I have paid all expenses, and have given my actors a florin apiece. But I am sure I don't know how I am to play to-morrow, as the company has rebelled; they say they won't act unless I give each of them a florin in advance."

"They don't ask very much, however."

"I know that, but I have no money, and nothing to pledge; but they will be sorry for it afterwards, as I am sure I shall make at least fifty florins to-morrow."

"How many are there in the company?"

"Fourteen, including my family. Could you lend me ten florins? I would pay you back to-morrow night."

"Certainly, but I should like to have you all to supper at the nearest inn to the theatre. Here are the ten florins."

The poor devil overflowed with gratitude, and said he would order supper at a florin a head, according to my instructions. I thought the sight of fourteen famished actors sitting down to a good supper would be rather amusing.

The company gave a play the next evening, but as only thirty or at most forty people were present, poor Bassi did not know where to turn to pay for the lighting and the orchestra. He was in despair; and instead of returning my ten florins he begged me to lend him another ten, still in the hope of a good house next time. I consoled him by saying we would talk it over after supper, and that I would go to the inn to wait for my guests.

I made the supper last three hours by dint of passing the bottle freely. My reason was that I had taken a great interest in a young girl from Strasburg, who played singing chamber-maids. Her features were exquisite and her voice charming, while she made me split my sides with laughing at her Italian pronounced with an Alsatian accent, and at her gestures, which were of the most comic description.

I was determined to possess her in the course of the next twenty-four hours, and before the party broke up I spoke as follows:

"Ladies and gentlemen, I will engage you myself for a week at fifty florins a day on the condition that you acknowledge me as your manager for the time being, and pay all the expenses of the theatre. You must charge the prices I name for seats, five members of the company to be chosen by me must sup with me every evening. If the receipts amount to more than fifty florins, we will share the overplus between us."

My proposal was welcomed with shouts of joy, and I called for pen, ink, and paper, and drew up the agreement.

"For to-morrow," I said to Bassi, "the prices for admission shall remain the same, but the day after we will see what can be done. You and your family will sup with me to-morrow, as also the young Alsatian, whom I could never separate from her dear Harlequin."

He issued bills of an enticing description for the following evening; but, in spite of all, the pit only contained a score of common people, and nearly all the boxes were empty.

Bassi had done his best, and when we met at supper he came up to me looking extremely confused, and gave me ten or twelve florins.

"Courage!" said I; and I proceeded to share them among the guests present.

We had a good supper, and I kept them at table till midnight, giving them plenty of choice wine and playing a thousand pranks with Bassi's daughter and the young Alsatian, who sat one on each side of me. I did not heed the jealous Harlequin, who seemed not to relish my familiarities with his sweetheart. The latter lent herself to my endearments with a bad enough grace, as she hoped Harlequin would marry her, and consequently did not want to vex him. When supper was over, we rose, and I took her between my arms, laughing, and caressing her in a manner which seemed too suggestive to the lover, who tried to pull me away. I thought this rather too much in my turn, and seizing him by his shoulders I dismissed him with a hearty kick, which he received with great humility. However, the situation assumed a melancholy aspect, for the poor girl began to weep bitterly. Bassi and his wife, two hardened sinners, laughed at her tears, and Bassi's daughter said that her lover had offered me great provocation; but the young Alsatian continued weeping, and told me that she would never sup with me again if I did not make her lover return.

"I will see to all that," said I; and four sequins soon made her all smiles again. She even tried to show me that she was not really cruel, and that she would be still less so if I could manage the jealous Harlequin. I promised everything, and she did her best to convince me that she would be quite complaisant on the first opportunity. I ordered Bassi to give notice that the pit would be two florins and the boxes a ducat, but that the gallery would be opened freely to the first comers.

"We shall have nobody there," said he, looking alarmed.

"Maybe, but that remains to be seen. You must request twelve soldiers to keep order, and I will pay for them."

"We shall want some soldiers to look after the mob which will besiege the gallery, but as for the rest of the house . . ."

"Again I tell you, we shall see. Carry out my instructions, and whether they prove successful or no, we will have a merry supper as usual."

The next day I called upon the Harlequin in his little den of a room, and with two louis, and a promise to respect his mistress, I made him as soft as a glove.

Bassi's bills made everybody laugh. People said he must be mad; but when it was ascertained that it was the lessee's speculation, and that I was the lessee, the accusation of madness was turned on me, but what did I care? At night the gallery was full an hour before the rise of the curtain; but the pit was empty, and there was nobody in the boxes with the exception of Count Lamberg, a Genoese abbé named Bolo, and a young man who appeared to me a woman in disguise.

The actors surpassed themselves, and the thunders of applause from the gallery enlivened the performance.

When we got to the inn, Bassi gave me the three ducats for the three boxes, but of course I returned them to him; it was quite a little fortune for the poor actors. I sat down at table between Bassi's wife and daughter, leaving the Alsatian to her lover. I told the manager to persevere in the same course, and to let those laugh who would, and I made him promise to play all his best pieces.

When the orgy was over I emptied my purse on the table, and enjoyed the eagerness with which they shared a score of sequins.

This indulgence at a time when I had not yet recovered my full strength made me enjoy a long sleep. Just as I awoke I was handed a summons to appear before the burgomaster. I made haste with my toilet, for I felt curious to know the reason of this citation, and I was aware I had nothing to fear. When I appeared, the magistrate addressed me in German, to which I turned a deaf ear, for I only knew enough of that language to ask for necessaries. When he was informed of my ignorance of German he addressed me in Latin, not of the Ciceronian kind by any means, but in that peculiar dialect which obtains at most of the German universities.

"Why do you bear a false name?" he asked.

"My name is not false. You can ask Carli, the banker, who has paid me fifty thousand florins."

"I know that; but your name is Casanova, so why do you call yourself Seingalt?"

"I take this name, or rather I have taken it, because it belongs to me, and in such a manner that if anyone else dared to take it I should contest it as my property by every legitimate resource."

"Ah! and how does this name belong to you?"

"Because I invented it; but that does not prevent my being Casanova as well."

"Sir, you must choose between Casanova and Seingalt; a man cannot have two names."

"The Spaniards and Portuguese often have half a dozen names."

"But you are not a Spaniard or a Portuguese; you are an Italian: and, after all, how can one invent a name?"

"It's the simplest thing in the world."

"Kindly explain."

"The alphabet belongs equally to the whole human race; no one can deny that. I have taken eight letters and combined them in such a way as to produce the word 'Seingalt.' It pleased me, and I have adopted it as my surname, being firmly persuaded that as no one had borne it before, no one could deprive me of it, or carry it without my consent."

"This is a very odd idea. Your arguments are rather specious than well grounded, for your name ought to be none other than your father's name."

"I suspect that there you are mistaken; the name you yourself bear because your father bore it before you, has not existed from all eternity; it must have been invented by an ancestor of yours who did not get it from his father, or else your name would have been Adam. Does your worship agree to that?"

"I am obliged to; but all this is strange, very strange."

"You are again mistaken. It's quite an old custom, and I engage to give you by to-morrow a long list of names invented by worthy people still living, who are allowed to enjoy their names in peace and quietness without being cited to the town hall to explain how they got them."

"But you will confess that there are laws against false names?"

"Yes, but I repeat this name is my true name. Your name, which I honour, though I do not know it, cannot be more true than mine, for it is possible that you are not the son of the gentleman you consider your father."

He smiled and escorted me out, telling me that he would make inquiries about me of M. Carli.

I took the part of going to M. Carli's myself. The story made him laugh. He told me that the burgomaster was a Catholic, a worthy man, well to do, but rather thick-headed; in short, a fine subject for a joke.

The following morning M. Carli asked me to breakfast, and afterwards to dine with the burgomaster.

"I saw him yesterday," said he, "and we had a long talk, in the course of which I succeeded in convincing him on the question of names, and he is now quite of your opinion."

I accepted the invitation with pleasure, as I was sure of seeing some good company. I was not undeceived; there were some charming women and several agreeable men. Amongst others, I noticed the woman in man's dress I had seen at the theatre. I watched her at dinner, and I was the more convinced that she was a woman. Nevertheless, everybody addressed her as a man, and she played the part to admiration. I, however, being in search of amusement, and not caring to seem as if I were taken in, began to talk to her in a strain of gallantry as one talks to a woman, and I contrived to let her know that if I were not sure of her sex I had very strong suspicions. She pretended not to understand me, and everyone laughed at my feigned expression of offence.

After dinner, while we were taking coffee, the pretended gentleman showed a canon who was present a portrait on one of her rings. It represented a young lady who was in the company, and was an excellent likeness — an easy enough matter, as she was very ugly. My conviction was not disturbed, but when I saw the impostor kissing the young lady's hand with mingled affection and respect, I ceased jesting on the question of her sex. M. Carli took me aside for a moment, and told me that in spite of his effeminate appearance this individual was a man, and was shortly going to marry the young lady whose hand he had just kissed.

"It may be so," said I, "but I can't believe it all the same."

However, the pair were married during the carnival, and the husband obtained a rich dowry with his wife. The poor girl died of grief in the course of a year, but did not say a word till she was on her death-bed. Her foolish parents, ashamed of having been deceived so grossly, dared not say anything, and got the female swindler out of the way; she had taken good care, however, to lay a firm hold on the dowry. The story became known, and gave the good folk of Augsburg much amusement, while I became renowned for my sagacity in piercing the disguise.

I continued to enjoy the society of my two servants and of the fair Alsatian, who cost me a hundred louis. At the end of a week my agreement with Bassi came to an end, leaving him with some money in his pocket. He continued to give performances, returning to the usual prices and suppressing the free gallery. He did very fair business.

I left Augsburg towards the middle of December.

I was vexed on account of Gertrude, who believed herself with child, but could not make up her mind to accompany me to France. Her father would have been pleased for me to take her; he had no hopes of getting her a husband, and would have been glad enough to get rid of her by my making her my mistress.

We shall hear more of her in the course of five or six years, as also of my excellent cook, Anna Midel, to whom I gave a present of four hundred florins. She married shortly afterwards, and when I visited the town again I found her unhappy.

I could not make up my mind to forgive Le Duc, who rode on the coachman's box, and when we were in Paris, half-way along the Rue St. Antoine, I made him take his trunk and get down; and I left him there without a character, in spite of his entreaties. I never heard of him again, but I still miss him, for, in spite of his great failings, he was an excellent servant. Perhaps I should have called to mind the important services he had rendered me at Stuttgart, Soleure, Naples, Florence, and Turin; but I could not pass over his impudence in compromising me before the Augsburg magistrate. If I had not succeeded in bringing a certain theft home to him, it would have been laid to my door, and I should have been dishonoured.

I had done a good deal in saving him from justice, and, besides, I had rewarded him liberally for all the special services he had done me.

From Augsburg I went to Bâle by way of Constance, where I stayed at the dearest inn in Switzerland. The landlord, Imhoff, was the prince of cheats, but his daughters were amusing, and after a three days' stay I continued my journey. I got to Paris on the last day of the year 1761, and I left the coach at the house in the Rue du Bacq, where my good angel Madame d'Urfé had arranged me a suite of rooms with the utmost elegance.

I spent three weeks in these rooms without going anywhere, in order to convince the worthy lady that I had only returned to Paris to keep my word to her, and make her be born again a man.

We spent the three weeks in making preparations for this divine operation, and our preparations consisted of devotions to each of the seven planets on the days consecrated to each of the intelligences. After this I had to seek, in a place which the spirits would point out to me, for a maiden, the daughter of an adept, whom I was to impregnate with a male child in a manner only known to the Fraternity of the Rosy Cross. Madame d'Urfé was to receive the child into her arms the moment it was born, and to keep it beside her in bed for seven days. At the end of the seven days she would die with her lips on the lips of the child, who would thus receive her reasonable soul, whereas before it had only possessed a vegetal soul.

This being done, it was to be my part to care for the child with the magisterium which was known to me, and as soon as it had attained to its third year Madame d'Urfé would begin to recover her self-consciousness, and then I was to begin to initiate her in the perfect knowledge of the Great Work.

The operation must take place under the full moon during the months of April, May, or June. Above all, Madame d'Urfé was to make a will in favour of the child, whose guardian I was to be till its thirteenth year.

This sublime madwoman had no doubts whatever as to the truth of all this, and burned with impatience to see the virgin who was destined to be the vessel of election. She begged me to hasten my departure.

I had hoped, in obtaining my answers from the oracle, that she would be deterred by the prospect of death, and I reckoned on the natural love of life making her defer the operation for an indefinite period. But such was not the case, and I found myself obliged to keep my word, in appearance at all events, and to go on my quest for the mysterious virgin.

What I wanted was some young hussy whom I could teach the part, and I thought of the Corticelli. She had been at

Prague for the last nine months, and when we were at Bologna I had promised to come and see her before the end of the year. But as I was leaving Germany — by no means a land of pleasant memories to me — I did not think it was worth while going out of my way for such a trifle in the depth of winter. I resolved to send her enough money for the journey, and to let her meet me in some French town.

M. de Fouquet, a friend of Madame d'Urfé's, was Governor of Metz, and I felt sure that, with a letter of introduction from Madame d'Urfé, this nobleman would give me a distingushed reception. Besides, his nephew, the Comte de Lastic, whom I knew well, was there with his regiment. For these reasons I chose Metz as a meeting-place with the virgin Corticelli, to whom this new part would certainly be a surprise. Madame d'Urfé gave me the necessary instructions, and I left Paris on January 25th, 1762, loaded with presents. I had a letter of credit to a large amount, but I did not make use of it as my purse was abundantly replenished.

I took no servant, for after Costa's robbing me and Le Duc's cheating me I felt as if I could not trust in anyone. I got to Metz in two days, and put up at the Roi Dagobert, an excellent inn, where I found the Comte de Louvenhaupt, a Swede, whom I had met at the house of the Princess of Anhalt-Zerbst, mother of the Empress of Russia. He asked me to sup with him and the Duc de Deux-Ponts, who was travelling incognito to Paris to visit Louis XV., whose constant friend he was.

The day after my arrival I took my letters to the governor, who told me I must dine with him every day. M. de Lastic had left Metz, much to my regret, as he would have contributed in no small degree to the pleasure of my stay. The same day I wrote to the Corticelli, sending her fifty louis, and telling her to come with her mother as soon as possible, and to get someone who knew the way to accompany her. She could not leave Prague before the beginning of Lent, and to make sure of her coming I promised that I would make her fortune.

In four or five days I knew my way about the town, but I did not frequent polite assemblies, preferring to go to the theatre, where a comic opera singer had captivated me. Her name was Raton, and she was only fifteen, after the fashion of actresses who always subtract at least two or three years from their age.

However, this failing is common to women, and is a pardonable one, since to be youthful is the greatest of all advantages to them. Raton was not so much handsome as attractive.

I kept Raton at a louis a day till the arrival of the Corticelli, and she had to be faithful to me, as I never let her go out of my sight. I liked the girl so well and found her so pleasant that I was sorry that the Corticelli was coming; however, I was told of her arrival one night just as I was leaving my box at the theatre. My footman told me in a loud voice that my lady wife, my daughter, and a gentleman had just arrived from Frankfort, and were awaiting me at the inn.

"Idiot," I exclaimed, "I have no wife and no daughter."

However, all Metz heard that my family had arrived.

The Corticelli threw her arms round my neck, laughing as usual, and her mother presented me to the worthy man who had accompanied them from Prague to Metz. He was an Italian named Monti, who had lived for a long time at Prague, where he taught his native language. I saw that M. Monti and the old woman were suitably accommodated, and I then led the young fool into my room. I found her changed for the better; she had grown, her shape was improved, and her pleasant manners made her a very charming girl.

CHAPTER XVI

HOCUS–POCUS

"WHY did you allow your mother to call herself my wife, little simpleton? Do you think that's a compliment to my judgment? She might have given herself out for your governess, as she wishes to pass you off as my daughter."

"My mother is an obstinate old woman who had rather be whipped at the cart-tail than call herself my governess. She has very narrow ideas, and always thinks that governess and procuress mean the same thing."

"She's an old fool, but we will make her hear reason either with her will or in spite of it. But you look well dresssed, have you made your fortune?"

"At Prague I captivated the affections of Count N**, and he proved a generous lover. But let your first action be to send back M. Monti. The worthy man has his family at Prague to look after; he can't afford to stay here long."

"True, I will see about it directly."

The coach started for Frankfort the same evening, and summoning Monti I thanked him for his kindness and paid him generously, so he went off well pleased.

I had nothing further to do at Metz, so I took leave of my new friends, and in two days' time I was at Nancy, where I wrote to Madame d'Urfé that I was on my way back with a virgin, the last of the family of Lascaris, who had once reigned at Constantinople. I begged her to receive her from my hands, at a country-house which belonged to her, where we should be occupied for some days in cabalistic ceremonies.

She answered that she would await us at Pont-Carré, an old castle four leagues distant from Paris, and that she would welcome the young princess with all possible kindness.

"I owe her all the more friendship," added the sublime madwoman, "as the family of Lascaris is connected with the family of d'Urfé, and as I am to be born again in the seed of the happy virgin."

I felt that my task would be not exactly to throw cold water on her enthusiasm, but to hold it in check and to moderate its manifestations. I therefore explained to her by return of post that she must be content to treat the virgin as a countess, not a princess, and I ended by informing her that we should arrive, accompanied by the countess's governess, on the Monday of Holy Week.

I spent twelve days at Nancy, instructing the young madcap in the part she had to play, and endeavouring to persuade her mother that she must be content herself with being the Countess Lascaris's humble servant. It was a task of immense difficulty; it was not enough to show her that our success depended on her submitting; I had to threaten to send her back to Bologna by herself. I had good reason to repent of my perseverance. That woman's obstinacy was an inspiration of my good angel's, bidding me avoid the greatest mistake I ever made.

On the day appointed we reached Pont-Carré. Madame d'Urfé, whom I had advised of the exact hour of our arrival, had the drawbridge of the castle lowered, and stood in the archway in the midst of her people, like a general surrendering with all the honours of war. The dear lady, whose madness was but an excess of wit, gave the false princess so distinguished a reception that she would have shown her amazement if I had not warned her of what she might expect. Thrice did she clasp her to her breast with a tenderness that was quite maternal, calling her her beloved niece, and explaining the entire pedigrees of the families of Lascaris and d'Urfé to make the countess understand how she came to be her niece. I was agreeably surprised to see the polite and dignified air with which the Italian wench listened to all this; she did not even smile, though the scene must have struck her as extremely laughable.

As soon as we got into the castle Madame d'Urfé proceeded to cense the new-comer, who received the attention with all the dignity of an opera queen, and then threw herself into the arms of the priestess, who received her with enthusiastic affection.

At dinner the countess was agreeable and talkative, which won her Madame d'Urfé's entire favour; her broken French being easily accounted for. Laura, the countess's mother, only knew her native Italian, and so kept silence. She was given a comfortable room, where her meals were brought to her, and which she only left to hear mass.

The castle was a fortified building, and had sustained several sieges in the civil wars. As its name, Pont-Carré, indicated, it was square, and was flanked by four crenelated towers and surrounded by a broad moat. The rooms were vast, and richly furnished in an old-fashioned way. The air was full of venomous gnats who devoured us and covered our faces with painful bites; but I had agreed to spend a week there, and I should have been hard put to it to find a pretext for shortening the time. Madame d'Urfé had a bed next her own for her niece, but I was not afraid of her attempting to satisfy herself as to the countess's virginity, as the oracle had expressly forbidden it under pain of failure. The operation was fixed for the fourteenth day of the April moon.

On that day we had a temperate supper, after which I went to bed. A quarter of an hour afterwards Madame d'Urfé came, leading the virgin Lascaris. She undressed her, scented her, cast a lovely veil over her body, and when the countess was laid beside me she remained, wishing to be present at an operation which was to result in her being born again in the course of nine months.

The act was consummated in form, and then Madame d'Urfé left us alone for the rest of the night, which was well employed. Afterwards, the countess slept with her aunt till the last day of the moon, when I asked the oracle if the Countess Lascaris had conceived. That well might be, for I had spared nothing to that intent; but I thought it more prudent to make the oracle reply that the operation had failed because the small Count d'Aranda had watched us behind a screen. Madame d'Urfé was in despair, but I consoled her by a second reply, in which the oracle declared that though the operation could only be performed in France in April, it could take place out of that realm in May; but the inquisitive young count, whose influence had proved so fatal, must be sent for at least a year to some place a hundred leagues from Paris. The oracle also indicated the manner in which he was to travel; he was to have a tutor, a servant, and all in order.

The oracle had spoken, and no more was wanted. Madame d'Urfé thought of an abbé she liked for his tutor, and the count was sent to Lyons, with strong letters of commendation to M. de Rochebaron, a relation of his patroness. The young man was delighted to travel, and never had any suspicion of the way in which I had slandered him. It was not a mere fancy which suggested this course of action. I had discovered that the Corticelli was making up to him, and that her mother favoured the intrigue. I had surprised her twice in the young man's room, and though he only cared for the girl as a youth cares for all girls, the Signora Laura did not at all approve of my opposing her daughter's designs.

Our next task was to fix on some foreign town where we could again attempt the mysterious operation. We settled on Aix-la-Chapelle, and in five or six days all was ready for the journey.

The Corticelli, angry with me for having thwarted her in her projects, reproached me bitterly, and from that time began to be my enemy; she even allowed herself to threaten me if I did not get back the pretty boy, as she called him.

"You have no business to be jealous," said she, "and I am the mistress of my own actions."

"Quite right, my dear," I answered; "but it is my business to see that you do not behave like a prostitute in your present position."

The mother was in a furious rage, and said that she and her daughter would return to Bologna, and to quiet them I promised to take them there myself as soon as we had been to Aix-la-Chapelle.

Nevertheless, I did not feel at ease, and to prevent any plots taking place I hastened our departure.

We started in May, in a travelling carriage containing Madame d'Urfé, myself, the false Lascaris, and her maid and favourite named Brougnole. We were followed by a coach with two seats; in it were the Signora Laura and another servant. Two men-servants in full livery sat on the outside of our travelling carriage. We stopped a day at Brussels, and another at Liège. At Aix there were many distinguished visitors, and at the first ball we attended Madame d'Urfé presented the Lascaris to two Princesses of Mecklenburg as her niece. The false countess received their embraces with much ease and modesty, and attracted the particular attention of the Margrave of Bayreuth and the Duchess of Württemberg, his daughter, who took possession of her, and did not leave her till the end of the ball. I was on thorns the whole time, in terror lest the heroine might make some dreadful slip. She danced so gracefully that everybody gazed at her, and I was the person who was complimented on her performance. I suffered a martyrdom, for these compliments seemed to be given with malicious intent. I suspected that the ballet-girl had been discovered beneath the countess, and I felt myself dishonoured. I succeeded in speaking privately to the young wanton for a moment, and begged her to dance like a young lady, and not like a chorus girl; but she was proud of her success, and dared to tell me that a young lady might know how to dance as well as a professional dancer, and that she was not going to dance badly to please me. I was so enraged with her impudence that I would have cast her off that instant if it had been possible; but as it was not, I determined that her punishment should lose none of its sharpness by waiting; and whether it be a vice or a virtue, the desire of revenge is never extinguished in my heart till it is satisfied.

The day after the ball Madame d'Urfé presented her with a

casket containing a beautiful watch set with brilliants, a pair of diamond ear-rings, and a ring containing a ruby of fifteen carats. The whole was worth sixty thousand francs. I took possession of it to prevent her going off without my leave.

In the meantime I amused myself with play and making bad acquaintances. The worst of all was a French officer, named d'Aché, who had a pretty wife and a daughter prettier still. Before long the daughter had taken possession of the heart which the Corticelli had lost, but as soon as Madame d'Aché saw that I preferred her daughter to herself she refused to receive me at her house.

I had lent d'Aché ten louis, and I consequently felt myself entitled to complain of his wife's conduct; but he answered rudely that as I only went to the house after his daughter, his wife was quite right; that he intended his daughter to make a good match, and that if my intentions were honourable I had only to speak to the mother. His manner was still more offensive than his words, and I felt enraged, but knowing the brutal drunken characteristics of the man, and that he was always ready to draw cold steel for a yes or a no, I was silent and resolved to forget the girl, not caring to become involved with a man like her father.

I had almost cured myself of my fancy when, a few days after our conversation, I happened to go into a billiard-room where d'Aché was playing with a Swiss named Schmit, an officer in the Swedish army. As soon as d'Aché saw me he asked whether I would lay the ten louis he owed me against him.

"Yes," said I, "that will make double or quits."

Towards the end of the match d'Aché made an unfair stroke, which was so evident that the marker told him of it; but as this stroke made him the winner, d'Aché seized the stakes and put them in his pocket without heeding the marker or the other player, who, seeing himself cheated before his very eyes, gave the rascal a blow across the face with his cue. D'Aché parried the blow with his hand, and drawing his sword rushed at Schmit, who had no arms. The marker, a sturdy young fellow, caught hold of d'Aché round the body, and thus prevented murder. The Swiss went out, saying:

"We shall see each other again."

The rascally Frenchman cooled down, and said to me:

"Now, you see, we are quits."

"Very much quits."

"That's all very well; but, by God! you might have prevented the insult which has dishonoured me."

"I might have done so, but I did not care to interfere. You are strong enough to look after yourself. Schmit had not his sword but I believe him to be a brave man; and he will give you satisfaction if you will return him his money, for there can be no doubt that you lost the match."

An officer, named de Pyène, took me up and said that he himself would give me the twenty louis which d'Aché had taken, but that the Swiss must give satisfaction. I had no hesitation in promising that he would do so, and said I would bring a reply to the challenge the next morning.

I had no fears myself. The man of honour ought always to be ready to use the sword to defend himself from insult, or to give satisfaction for an insult he has offered. I know that the law of duelling is a prejudice which may be called, and perhaps rightly, barbarous, but it is a prejudice which no man of honour can contend against, and I believed Schmit to be a thorough gentleman.

I called on him at daybreak, and found him still in bed. As soon as he saw me, he said:

"I am sure you have come to ask me to fight with d'Aché. I am quite ready to burn powder with him, but he must first pay me the twenty louis he robbed me of."

"You shall have them to-morrow, and I will attend you. D'Aché will be seconded by M. de Pyène."

"Very good. I shall expect you at daybreak."

Two hours after, I saw de Pyène, and we fixed the meeting for the next day, at six o'clock in the morning. The arms were to be pistols. We chose a garden, half a league from the town, as the scene of the combat.

At daybreak I found the Swiss waiting for me at the door of his lodgings, carolling the *ranz-des-vaches*, so dear to his fellow-countrymen. I thought that a good omen.

"Here you are," said he; "let us be off, then."

On the way, he observed, "I have only fought with men of honour up to now, and I don't much care for killing a rascal; it's hangman's work."

"I know," I replied, "that it's very hard to have to risk one's life against a fellow like that."

"There's no risk," said Schmit, with a laugh. "I am certain that I shall kill him."

"How can you be certain?"

"I shall make him tremble."

He was right. This secret is infallible when it is applied to a coward. We found d'Aché and de Pyène on the field, and five or six others who must have been present from motives of curiosity.

D'Aché took twenty louis from his pocket and gave them to his enemy, saying:

"I may be mistaken, but I hope to make you pay dearly for your brutality." Then turning to me, he said:

"I owe you twenty louis also"; but I made no reply.

Schmit put the money in his purse with the calmest air imaginable, and making no reply to the other's boast placed himself between two trees, distant about four paces from one another, and drawing two pistols from his pocket said to d'Aché:

"Place yourself at a distance of ten paces, and fire first. I shall walk to and fro between these two trees, and you may walk as far if you like to do so when my turn comes to fire."

Nothing could be clearer or more calmly delivered than this explanation.

"But we must decide," said I, "who is to have the first shot."

"There is no need," said Schmit, "I never fire first; besides, the gentleman has a right to the first shot."

De Pyène placed his friend at the proper distance and then stepped aside, and d'Aché fired on his antagonist, who was walking slowly to and fro without looking at him. Schmit turned round in the coolest manner possible, and said:

"You have missed me, sir; I knew you would. Try again."

I thought he was mad, and that some arrangement would be come to; but nothing of the kind. D'Aché fired a second time, and again missed; and Schmit, without a word, but as calm as death, fired his first pistol in the air, and then covering d'Aché with his second pistol hit him in the forehead and stretched him dead on the ground. He put back his pistols into his pocket and went off directly by himself, as if he were merely continuing his walk. In two minutes I followed his example, after ascertaining that the unfortunate d'Aché no longer breathed.

I was in a state of amazement. Such a duel was more like a combat of romance than a real fact. I could not understand it; I had watched the Swiss, and had not noticed the slightest change pass over his face.

I breakfasted with Madame d'Urfé, whom I found inconsolable. It was the full moon, and at three minutes past four exactly I ought to perform the mysterious creation of the child in which she was to be born again. But the Lascaris, on whom the work was to be wrought, was twisting and turning in her bed, contorting herself in such a way that it would be impossible for me to accomplish the prolific work.

My grief, when I heard what had happened, was hypocritical; in the first place because I no longer felt any desire for the girl, and in the second because I thought I saw a way in which I could make use of the incident to take vengeance on her.

I lavished consolations on Madame d'Urfé; and on consulting the oracle I found that the Lascaris had been defiled by an evil genius, and that I must search for another virgin whose purity must be under the protection of more powerful spirits. I saw that my madwoman was perfectly happy with this, and I left her to visit the Corticelli, whom I found in bed with her mother beside her.

"You have convulsions, have you, dearest?" said I.

"No, I haven't. I am quite well, but all the same I shall have them till you give me back my jewel-casket."

"You are getting wicked, my poor child; this comes of following your mother's advice. As for the casket, if you are going to behave like this probably you will never have it."

"I will reveal all."

"You will not be believed; and I shall send you back to Bologna without letting you take any of the presents which Madame d'Urfé has given you."

"You ought to have given me back the casket when I declared myself with child."

Signora Laura told me that this was only too true, though I was not the father.

"Who is, then?" I asked.

"Count N**, whose mistress she was at Prague."

It did not seem probable, as she had no symptoms of pregnancy; still it might be so. I was obliged to plot myself to bring the plots of these two rascally women to nought, and without saying anything to them I shut myself up with Madame d'Urfé to inquire of the oracle concerning the operation which was to make her happy.

After several answers, more obscure than any returned from the oracular tripod at Delphi, the interpretation of which I left to the infatuated Madame d'Urfé, she discovered herself — and I took care not to contradict her — that the Countess Lascaris had gone mad. I encouraged her fears, and succeeded in making her obtain from a cabalistic pyramid the statement that the reason the princess had not conceived was that she had been defiled by an evil genius — an enemy of the Fraternity of the Rosy Cross. This put Madame d'Urfé fairly on the way, and she added on her own account that the girl must be with child by a gnome.

She then erected another pyramid to obtain guidance on our quest, and I so directed things that the answer came that she must write to the moon.

This mad reply, which should have brought her to her senses, only made her more crazy than ever. She was quite ecstatic, and I am sure that if I had endeavoured to show her the nothingness of all this I should have had nothing for my trouble. Her conclusion would probably have been that I was possessed by an evil spirit, and was no longer a true Rosy Cross. But I had no idea of undertaking a cure which would have done me harm and her no good. Her chimerical notions made her happy, and the cold naked truth would doubtless have made her unhappy.

She received the order to write to the moon with the greater delight as she knew what ceremonies were to be observed in addressing that planet; but she could not dispense with the assistance of an adept, and I knew she would reckon on me. I told her I should always be ready to serve her, but that, as she knew herself, we should have to wait for the first phase of the new moon. I was very glad to gain time, for I had lost heavily at play, and I could not leave Aix-la-Chapelle before a bill, which I had drawn on M. d'O** of Amsterdam, was cashed. In the meantime we agreed that as the Countess Lascaris had become mad, we must not pay any attention to what she might say, as the words would not be hers but would proceed from the evil spirit who possessed her.

[158]

Nevertheless, we determined that as her state was a pitiable one, and should be as much alleviated as possible, she should continue to dine with us, but that in the evening she was to go to her governess and sleep with her.

After having thus disposed Madame d'Urfé to disbelieve whatever the Corticelli cared to tell her, and to concentrate all her energies on the task of writing to Selenis, the intelligence of the moon, I set myself seriously to work to regain the money I had lost at play; and here my cabala was no good to me. I pledged the Corticelli's casket for a thousand louis, and proceeded to play in an English club where I had a much better chance of winning than with Germans or Frenchmen.

Three or four days after d'Aché's death, his widow wrote me a note begging me to call on her. I found her in company with de Pyène. She told me in a lugubrious voice that her husband had left many debts unsettled, and that his creditors had seized everything she possessed; and that she was thus unable to pay the expenses of a journey, though she wanted to take her daughter with her to Colmar, and there to rejoin her family.

"You caused my husband's death," she added, "and I ask you to give me a thousand crowns; if you refuse me I shall commence a lawsuit against you, for as the Swiss officer has left, you are the only person I can prosecute."

"I am surprised at your taking such a tone towards me," I replied, coldly, "and were it not for the respect I feel for your misfortune, I should answer as bitterly as you deserve. In the first place I have not a thousand crowns to throw away, and if I had I would not sacrifice my money to threats. I am curious to know what kind of a case you could get up against me in the courts of law. As for Schmit, he fought like a brave gentleman, and I don't think you could get much out of him if he were still here. Good day, madam."

I had scarcely got fifty paces from the house when I was joined by de Pyène, who said that rather than Madame d'Aché should have to complain of me he would cut my throat on the spot. We neither of us had swords.

"Your intention is not a very flattering one," said I, "and there is something rather brutal about it. I had rather not have any affair of the kind with a man whom I don't know and to whom I owe nothing."

[159]

"You are a coward."

"I would be, you mean, if I were to imitate you. It is a matter of perfect indifference to me what opinion you may have on the subject."

"You will be sorry for this."

"Maybe, but I warn you that I never go out unattended by a pair of pistols, which I keep in good order and know how to use." So saying I showed him the pistols, and took one in my right hand.

At this the bully uttered an oath and we separated.

At a short distance from the place where this scene had occurred I met a Neapolitan named Maliterni, a lieutenant-colonel and *aide* to the Prince de Condé, commander-in-chief of the French army. This Maliterni was a boon companion, always ready to oblige, and always short of money. We were friends, and I told him what had happened.

"I should be sorry," said I, "to have anything to do with a fellow like de Pyène, and if you can rid me of him I promise you a hundred crowns."

"I dare say that can be managed," he replied, "and I will tell you what I can do to-morrow."

In point of fact, he brought me news the next day that my cut-throat had received orders from his superior officer to leave Aix-la-Chapelle at daybreak and at the same time he gave me a passport from the Prince de Condé.

I confess that this was very pleasant tidings. I have never feared to cross my sword with any man, though I never sought the barbarous pleasure of spilling men's blood; but on this occasion I felt an extreme dislike to a duel with a fellow who was probably of the same caste as his friend d'Aché.

I therefore gave Maliterni my heartiest thanks, as well as the hundred crowns I had promised him, which I considered so well employed that I did not regret their loss.

Maliterni, who was a jester of the first water, and a creature of the Marshal d'Estrées, was lacking neither in wit nor knowledge; but he was deficient in a sense of order and refinement. He was a pleasant companion, for his gaiety was inexhaustible and he had a large knowledge of the world. He attained the rank of field-marshal in 1768, and went to Naples to marry a rich heiress, whom he left a widow a year after.

The day after de Pyène's departure I received a note from Mdlle. d'Aché, begging me, for the sake of her sick mother, to come and see her. I answered that I would be at such a place at such a time, and that she could say what she liked to me.

I found her at the place and time I appointed, with her mother, whose illness, it appeared, did not prevent her from going out. She called me her persecutor, and said that since the departure of her best friend, de Pyène, she did not know where to turn; that she had pledged all her belongings, and that I, who was rich, ought to aid her, if I were not the vilest of men.

"I feel for your condition," I replied, "as I feel your abuse of me; and I cannot help saying that you have shown yourself the vilest of women in inciting de Pyène, who may be an honest man for all I know, to assassinate me. In fine, rich or not, and though I owe you nothing, I will give you enough money to take your property out of pawn, and I may possibly take you to Colmar myself, but you must first consent to my giving your charming daughter a proof of my affection."

"And you dare to make this horrible proposal to me?"

"Horrible or not, I do make it."

"I will never consent."

"Good day, madam."

I called the waiter to pay him for the refreshments I had ordered, and I gave the girl six double louis, but her proud mother forbade her to accept the money from me. I was not surprised, in spite of her distress; for the mother was in reality still more charming than the daughter, and she knew it. I ought to have given her the preference, and thus have ended the dispute, but who can account for his whims? I felt that she must hate me, for she did not care for her daughter, and it must have humiliated her bitterly to be obliged to regard her as a victorious rival.

I left them still holding the six double louis, which pride or scorn had refused, and I went to the faro-table and decided in sacrificing them to fortune; but that capricious deity, as proud as the haughty widow, refused them, and though I left them on the board for five deals I almost broke the bank. An Englishman, named Martin, offered to go shares with me, and I accepted, as I knew he was a good player; and in the course of eight or ten days we did such good business that I was not only able to take the casket out of pledge and to cover all losses, but made a considerable profit in addition.

About this period, the Corticelli, in her rage against me, had told Madame d'Urfé the whole history of her life, of our acquaintance, and of her pregnancy. But the more truthfully she told her story so much the more did the good lady believe her to be mad, and we often laughed together at the extraordinary fancies of the traitress. Madame d'Urfé put all her trust in the instructions which Selenis would give in reply to her letter.

Nevertheless, as the girl's conduct displeased me, I made her eat her meals with her mother, while I kept Madame d'Urfé company. I assured her that we should easily find another vessel of election, the madness of the Countess Lascaris having made her absolutely incapable of participating in our mysterious rites.

Before long, d'Aché's widow found herself obliged to give me her Mimi; but I won her by kindness, and in such a way that the mother could pretend with decency to know nothing about it. I redeemed all the goods she had pawned, and although the daughter had not yet yielded entirely to my ardour, I formed the plan of taking them to Colmar with Madame d'Urfé. To make up the good lady's mind, I resolved to let that be one of the instructions from the moon, and this she would not only obey blindly but would have no suspicions as to my motive.

I managed the correspondence between Selenis and Madame d'Urfé in the following manner:

On the day appointed, we supped together in a garden beyond the town walls, and in a room on the ground-floor of the house I had made all the necessary preparations, the letter which was to fall from the moon, in reply to Madame d'Urfé's epistle, being in my pocket. At a little distance from the chamber of ceremonies I had placed a large bath filled with lukewarm water and perfumes pleasing to the deity of the night, into which we were to plunge at the hour of the moon, which fell at one o'clock.

When we had burnt incense, we sprinkled the essences appropriate to the cult of Selenis; holding the letter concealed in my left hand, with the right I graciously led Madame d'Urfé to the brink of the bath. Here stood an alabaster cup containing spirits of wine which I kindled, repeating magical words which I did not understand, but which she said after me, giving me the letter addressed to Selenis. I burnt the letter in the flame of the spirits, beneath the light of the moon, and the credulous lady told me she saw the characters she had traced ascending in the rays of the planet.

We then got into the bath, and the letter, which was written in silver characters on green paper, appeared on the surface of the water in the course of ten minutes. As soon as Madame d'Urfé saw it, she picked it up reverently and got out of the bath with me.

We dried and scented ourselves. I told Madame d'Urfé that she might read the epistle, which she had placed on a scented silk cushion. She obeyed, and I saw sadness visibly expressed on her features when she saw that her hypostasis was deferred till the arrival of Querilinthus, whom she would see with me at Marseilles in the spring of next year. The genius also said that the Countess Lascaris could now only do her harm, and that she should consult me as to the best means of getting rid of her. The letter ended by ordering her not to leave at Aix a lady who had lost her husband, and had a daughter who was destined to be of great service to the fraternity of the R.C. She was to take them to Alsace, and not to leave them till they were there, and safe from that danger which threatened them if they were left to themselves.

Madame d'Urfé, who with all her folly was an exceedingly benevolent woman, commended the widow to my care enthusiastically, and seemed impatient to hear her whole history. I told her all the circumstances which I thought would strengthen her in her resolution to befriend them, and promised to introduce the ladies to her at the first opportunity.

We returned to Aix, and spent the night in discussing the phantoms which coursed through her brain. All was going on well, and my only care was for the journey to Aix, and how to obtain the complete enjoyment of Mimi after having so well deserved her favours.

I had a run of luck at play the next day, and in the evening I gave Madame d'Aché an agreeable surprise by telling her that I should accompany her and her Mimi to Colmar. I told her that I should begin by introducing her to the lady whom I had the honour to accompany, and I begged her to be ready by the next day as the marchioness was impatient to see her. I could see that she could scarcely believe her ears, for she thought Madame d'Urfé was in love with me, and she could not understand her desire to make the acquaintance of two ladies who might be dangerous rivals.

I conducted them to Madame d'Urfé at the appointed hour, and they were received with a warmth which surprised them exceedingly, for they could not be expected to know that their recommendation came from the moon. We made a party of four, and while the two ladies talked together in the fashion of ladies who have seen the world, I paid Mimi particular attention, which her mother understood very well, but which Madame d'Urfé attributed to the young lady's connection with the Rosy Cross.

In the evening we all went to a ball, and there the Corticelli, who was always trying to annoy me, danced as no young lady would dance. She executed rapid steps, pirouetted, cut capers, and showed her legs; in short, she behaved like a ballet-girl. I was on thorns. An officer, who either ignored, or pretended to ignore, my supposed relation to her, asked me if she was a professional dancer. I heard another man behind me say that he thought he remembered seeing her on the boards at Prague. I resolved on hastening my departure, as I foresaw that if I stayed much longer at Aix the wretched girl would end by costing me my life.

As I have said, Madame d'Aché had a good society manner, and this put her in Madame d'Urfé's good graces, who saw in her politeness a new proof of the favour of Selenis. Madame d'Aché felt, I suppose, that she owed me some return after all I had done for her, and left the ball early, so that when I took Mimi home I found myself alone with her, and at perfect liberty to do what I liked.

In three days' time I provided the mother and daughter with their outfit, and we left Aix gladly in an elegant and convenient travelling carriage which I had provided. Half an hour before we left I made an acquaintance which afterwards proved fatal to me. A Flemish officer, unknown to me, accosted me, and painted his destitute condition in such sad colours that I felt obliged to give him twelve louis. Ten minutes after, he gave me a paper in which he acknowledged the debt, and named the time in which he could pay it. From the paper I ascertained that his name was Malingan. In ten months the reader will hear the results.

Just as we were starting I showed the Corticelli a carriage with four places, in which she, her mother, and the two maids, were to travel. At this she trembled, her pride was wounded, and for a moment I thought she was going out of her mind; she rained sobs, abuse, and curses on me. I stood the storm unmoved, however, and Madame d'Urfé only laughed at her niece's paroxysms, and seemed delighted to find herself sitting opposite to me with the servant of Selenis beside her, while Mimi was highly pleased to be so close to me.

We got to Liège at nightfall on the next day, and I contrived to make Madame d'Urfé stay there the day following, wishing to get horses to take us through the Ardennes, and thus to have the charming Mimi longer in my possession.

I rose early and went out to see the town. By the great bridge, a woman, so wrapped up in a black mantilla that only the tip of her nose was visible, accosted me, and asked me to follow her into a house with an open door which she showed me.

"As I have not the pleasure of knowing you," I replied, "prudence will not allow me to do so."

"You do know me, though," she replied, and taking me to the corner of a neighbouring street she showed me her face. What was my surprise to see the fair Stuart of Avignon, the statue of the Fountain of Vaucluse. I was very glad to meet her.

In my curiosity I followed her into the house, to a room on the first floor, where she welcomed me most tenderly. It was all no good, for I felt angry with her, and despised her advances, no doubt, because I had Mimi, and wished to keep all my love for her. However, I took three louis out of my purse and gave them to her, asking her to tell me her history.

"Stuart," she said, "was only my keeper; my real name is Ransom, and I am the mistress of a rich landed proprietor. I got back to Liège after many sufferings."

"I am delighted to hear that you are more prosperous now, but it must be confessed that your behaviour at Avignon was both preposterous and absurd. But the subject is not worth discussing. Good day, madam."

I then returned to my hotel to write an account of what I had seen to the Marquis Grimaldi.

The next day we left Liège, and were two days passing through the Ardennes. This is one of the strangest tracts in Europe: a vast forest, the traditions of which furnished Ariosto with some splendid passages.

There is no town in the forest, and though one is obliged to cross it to pass from one country to another, hardly any of the necessaries of life are to be found in it.

The inquirer will seek in vain for vices or virtues, or manners of any, kind. The inhabitants are devoid of correct ideas, but have wild notions of their own on the power of men they style scholars. It is enough to be a doctor to enjoy the reputation of an astrologer and a wizard. Nevertheless the Ardennes have a large population, as I was assured that there were twelve hundred churches in the forest. The people are good-hearted and even pleasant, especially the young girls; but as a general rule the fair sex is by no means fair in those quarters. In this vast district watered by the Meuse is the town of Bouillon — a regular hole, but in my time it was the freest place in Europe. The Duke of Bouillon was so jealous of his rights that he preferred the exercise of his prerogatives to all the honours he might have enjoyed at the Court of France. We stayed a day at Metz, but did not call on anyone; and in three days we reached Colmar, where we left Madame d'Aché, whose good graces I had completely won. Her family, in extremely comfortable circumstances, received the mother and daughter with great affection. Mimi wept bitterly when I left her, but I consoled her by saying that I would come back before long. Madame d'Urfé seemed not to mind leaving them, and I consoled myself easily enough. While congratulating myself on having made mother and daughter happy, I adored the secret paths and ways of Divine Providence.

On the following day we went to Sulzbach, where the Baron of Schaumburg, who knew Madame d'Urfé, gave us a warm welcome. I should have been sadly bored in this dull place if it had not been for gaming. Madame d'Urfé, finding herself in need of company, encouraged the Corticelli to hope to regain my good graces, and, consequently, her own. The wretched girl, seeing how easily I had defeated her projects, and to what a pass of humiliation I had brought her, had changed her part, and was now submissive enough. She flattered herself that she would regain the favour she had completely lost, and she thought the day was won when she saw that Madame d'Aché and her daughter stayed at Colmar. But what she had more at heart than either my friendship or Madame d'Urfé's was the jewel-casket; but she dared not ask for it, and her hopes of seeing it again were growing dim. By her pleasantries at table which made Madame d'Urfé laugh she succeeded in giving me a few amorous twinges; but still I did not allow my feelings to relax my severity, and she continued to sleep with her mother.

A week after our arrival at Sulzbach I left Madame d'Urfé with the Baron of Schaumburg, and I went to Colmar in the hope of good fortune. But I was disappointed, as the mother and daughter had both made arrangements for getting married.

A rich merchant, who had been in love with the mother eighteen years before, seeing her a widow and still pretty, felt his early flames revive, and offered his hand and was accepted. A young advocate found Mimi to his taste, and asked her in marriage. The mother and daughter, fearing the results of my affection, and finding it would be a good match, lost no time in giving their consent. I was entertained in the family, and supped in the midst of a numerous and choice assemblage; but seeing that I should only annoy the ladies and tire myself in waiting for some chance favour if I stayed, I bade them adieu and returned to Sulzbach the next morning. I found there a charming girl from Strasburg, named Salzmann, three or four gamesters who had come to drink the waters, and several ladies, to whom I shall introduce the reader in the ensuing chapter.

CHAPTER XVII

LONDON

*I*N THE *month of June, 1763 — the fatal year which, according to the Memoirs, marks the definite decline of his unstable fortunes — Casanova arrives for the first time in England. The ostensible object of this journey was to bring that precocious young scamp Giuseppe Pompeati, who under the assumed name of Count d'Aranda had been educated in Paris at the expense of the Marquise d'Urfé, back to his mother, Thérèse Imer. This extraordinary woman, whose adventurous career, starting in Venice simultaneously with Casanova's, forms a strange parallel to his own, was now settled in London, where, as Madame Cornelis — her final and most* *successful avatar — she had become a well-known figure of the cos-mopolitan half-world. As former mistress of the Margrave of Bay-reuth and of Prince Charles of Lorraine she had acquired sufficient knowledge of the great world to play the fine lady in the ever-widen-ing sphere of her election. Her speciality was to organise subscrip-tion balls and entertainments on a lavish scale, managing at the same time to give them an air of exclusiveness which was calculated to appeal to insular snobbery. Mutual interests of a more practical and far-reaching order than Giacomo's alleged fatherhood of Thérèse's daughter, Sophie, and probably a sort of reciprocal esteem and pro-fessional solidarity, seem to have been the basis of the long, though often strained, relationship between the two Venetian adventurers.*

In Paris he had left the aged marquise, continuing to "revel in the joys of her regeneration" after a second and even more elaborate hoax had been staged at Marseilles, the most tangible results of which were the "planetary offerings," in the shape of precious metals and stones, that Casanova appropriated for his own uses. He was there-fore well equipped for making his bow before the elegant clientèle of his good friend "Madame Cornelis." Let us listen to him for a while:

When I got to Calais I consigned my post-chaise to the care of the landlord of the inn, and hired a packet. There was only one available for a private party, there being another for public use at six francs apiece. I paid six guineas in advance, taking care to get a proper receipt, for I knew that at Calais a man finds himself in an awkward position if he is unable to support his claim by documents.

Before the tide was out Clairmont got all my belongings on board, and I ordered my supper. The landlord told me that louis were not current in England, and offered to give me guineas in exchange for mine; but I was surprised when I found he gave me the same number of guineas as I had given him of louis. I wanted him to take the difference — four per cent. — but he refused, saying that he did not allow anything when the English gave him guineas for louis. I do not know whether he found his system a profitable one on the whole, but it was certainly so for me.

The young Count d'Aranda, to whom I had restored his humble name of Trenti, was quite resigned, but proud of having given me a specimen of his knowingness by riding post. We were just going to sit down at table, well pleased with one another, when I heard a loud conversation in English going on near my door, and mine host came in to tell me what it was about.

"It's the courier of the Duke of Bedford, the English ambassador," said he; "he announces the approach of his master, and is disputing with the captain of the packet. He says he hired the boat by letter, and that the captain had no right to let it to you. The master maintains that he has received no such letter, and no one can prove that he is telling a lie."

I congratulated myself on having taken the packet and paid the earnest-money, and went to bed. At daybreak the landlord said that the ambassador had arrived at midnight, and that his man wanted to see me.

He came in and told me that the nobleman, his master, was in a great hurry to get to London, and that I should oblige him very much by yielding the boat to him.

I did not answer a word, but wrote a note which ran as follows:

"My lord duke may dispose of the whole of the packet, with the exception of the space necessary for my own accommodation, that of two other persons, and my luggage. I am delighted to have the opportunity of obliging the English ambassador."

The valet took the note, and returned to thank me on behalf of his master, who stipulated, however, that he should be allowed to pay for the packet.

"Tell him that it is out of the question, as the boat is paid for already."

"He will give you the six guineas."

"Tell your master that I cannot allow him to pay. I do not buy to sell again."

The duke called on me in the course of half an hour, and said that we were both of us in the right.

"However," he added, "there is a middle course, let us adopt it, and I shall be just as much indebted to you."

"What is that, my lord?"

"We will each pay half."

"My desire to oblige you, my lord, will not allow me to refuse, but it is I who will be indebted to you for the honour your lordship does me. We will start as soon as you like, and I can make my arrangements accordingly."

He shook my hand and left the room, and when he had gone

I found three guineas on the table. He had placed them there without my noticing them. An hour afterwards I returned his call, and then told the master to take the duke and his carriages on board.

We took two hours and a half in crossing the Channel; the wind was strong, but we made a good passage.

The stranger who sets his foot on English soil has need of a good deal of patience. The custom-house officials made a minute, vexatious, and even an impertinent perquisition; but as the duke and ambassador had to submit, I thought it best to follow his example; besides, resistance would be useless. The Englishman, who prides himself on his strict adherence to the law of the land, is curt and rude in his manner, and the English officials cannot be compared to the French, who know how to combine politeness with the exercise of their rights.

England is different in every respect from the rest of Europe; even the country has a different aspect, and the water of the Thames has a taste peculiar to itself. Everything has its own characteristics, and the fish, cattle, horses, men, and women are of a type not found in any other land. Their manner of living is wholly different from that of other countries, especially their cookery. The most striking feature in their character is their national pride; they exalt themselves above all other nations.

My attention was attracted by the universal cleanliness, the beauty of the country, the goodness of the roads, the reasonable charges for posting, the quickness of the horses, although they never go beyond a trot; and lastly, the construction of the towns on the Dover road; Canterbury and Rochester for instance, though large and populous, are like long passages; they are all length and no breadth.

We got to London in the evening and stopped at the house of Madame Cornelis, as Thérèse called herself. She was originally married to an actor named Imer, then to the dancer Pompeati, who committed suicide at Venice by ripping up his stomach with a razor.

In Holland she had been known as Madame Trenti, but at London she had taken the name of her lover Cornelius Rigerboos, whom she had contrived to ruin.

She lived in Soho Square, almost facing the house of the Venetian ambassador. When I arrived I followed the instructions I had received in her last letter. I left her son in the carriage, and sent up my name, expecting she would fly to meet me; but the porter told me to wait, and in a few minutes a servant in grand livery brought me a note in which Madame Cornelis asked me to get down at the house to which her servant would conduct me. I thought this rather strange behaviour, but still she might have her reasons for acting in this manner, so I did not let my indignation appear. When we got to the house, a fat woman named Rancour, and two servants, welcomed us, or rather welcomed my young friend; for the lady embraced him, told him how glad she was to see him, and did not appear to be aware of my existence.

Our trunks were taken in, and Madame Rancour, having ascertained which belonged to Cornelis, had them placed in a fine suite of three rooms, and said, pointing out to him the apartment and the two servants:

"This apartment and the two servants are for you, and I, too, am your most humble servant."

Clairmont told me that he had put my things in a room which communicated with Cornelis's. I went to inspect it, and saw directly that I was being treated as if I were a person of no consequence. The storm of anger was gathering, but, wonderful to relate, I subdued myself, and did not say a word.

"Where is your room?" I said to Clairmont.

"Near the roof, and I am to share it with one of those two louts you saw."

The worthy Clairmont, who knew my disposition, was surprised at the calm with which I said:

"Take your trunk there."

"Shall I open yours?"

"No. We will see what can be done to-morrow."

I still kept on my mask, and returned to the room of the young gentleman, who seemed to be considered as my master. I found him listening with a foolish stare to Madame Rancour, who was telling him of the splendid position his mother occupied, her great enterprise, her immense credit, the splendid house she had built, her thirty-three servants, her two secretaries, her six horses, her country-house, etc., etc.

"How is my sister Sophie?" said the young gentleman.

"Her name is Sophie, is it? She is only known as Miss Cornelis. She is a beauty, a perfect prodigy, she plays at sight on several instruments, dances like Terpsichore, speaks English, French, and Italian equally well — in a word, she is really wonderful. She has a governess and a maid. Unfortunately, she is rather short for her age; she is eight."

She was ten, but as Madame Rancour was not speaking to me I refrained from interrupting her.

My lord Cornelis, who felt very tired, asked at what hour they were to sup.

"At ten o'clock and not before," said the duenna, "for Madame Cornelis is always engaged till then. She is always with her lawyer, on account of an important lawsuit she has against Sir Frederick Fermer."

I could see that I should learn nothing worth learning by listening to the woman's gossip, so I took my hat and cane and went for a walk in the immense city, taking care not to lose my way.

It was seven o'clock when I went out, and a quarter of an hour after, seeing a number of people in a coffee-house, I entered it. It was the most notorious place in London, the resort of all the rascally Italians in town. I had heard of it at Lyons, and had taken a firm resolve never to set my foot in it, but almighty chance made me go there unknown to myself. But it was my only visit.

I sat down by myself and called for a glass of lemonade, and before long a man came and sat by me to profit by the light. He had a printed paper in his hand, and I could see that the words were Italian. He had a pencil with which he scratched out some words and letters, writing the corrections in the margin. Idle curiosity made me follow him in his work, and I noticed him correcting the word "*ancora*," putting in an *h* in the margin. I was irritated by this barbarous spelling, and told him that for four centuries "*ancora*" had been spelt without an *h*.

"Quite so," said he, "but I am quoting from Boccaccio, and one should be exact in quotations."

"I apologise, sir; I see you are a man of letters."

"Well, in a small way. My name is Martinelli."

"Then you are in a great way indeed. I know you by repute, and if I am not mistaken you are a relation of Calsabigi, who has spoken of you to me. I have read some of your satires."

"May I ask to whom I have the honour of speaking?"

"My name is Seingalt. Have you finished your edition of the *Decameron?*"

"I am still at work on it, and trying to increase the number of my subscribers."

"If you will be so kind I should be glad to be of the number."

"You do me honour."

He gave me a ticket, and seeing that it was only for a guinea I took four, and telling him I hoped to see him again at the same coffee-house, the name of which I asked him, he told it me, evidently astonished at my ignorance; but his surprise vanished when I informed him that I had only been in London for an hour, and that it was my first visit to the great city.

"You will experience some trouble in finding your way back," said he, "allow me to accompany you."

When we had got out he gave me to understand that chance had led me to the Orange Coffee House, the most disreputable house in London.

"But you go there."

"Yes, but I can say with Juvenal:

'*Cantabit vacuus coram latrone viator.*'

The rogues can't hurt me; I know them and they know me; we never trouble each other."

"You have been a long time in London, I suppose."

"Five years."

"I presume you know a good many people."

"Yes, but I seldom wait on anyone but Lord Spencer. I am occupied with literary work and live all by myself. I don't make much, but enough to live on. I live in furnished apartments, and have twelve shirts and the clothes you see on my back, and that is enough for my happiness.

'*Nec ultra deos lacesso.*' "

I was pleased with this honest man, who spoke Italian with the most exquisite correctness.

On the way back I asked him what I had better do to get a comfortable lodging. When he heard the style in which I wished to live and the time I proposed to spend in London, he advised me to take a house completely furnished.

"You will be given an inventory of the goods," said he, "and as soon as you get a surety your house will be your castle."

"I like the idea," I answered, "but how shall I find such a house?"

"That is easily done."

He went into a shop, begged the mistress to lend him the *Advertiser*, noted down several advertisements, and said:

"That's all we have to do."

The nearest house was in Pall Mall and we went to see it. An old woman opened the door to us, and showed us the ground-floor and the three floors above. Each floor contained two rooms, and a closet. Everything shone with cleanliness; linen, furniture, carpets, mirrors, and china, and even the bells and the bolts on the doors. The necessary linen was kept in a large press, and in another was the silver plate and several sets of china. The arrangements in the kitchen were excellent, and, in a word, nothing was lacking in the way of comfort. The rent was twenty guineas a week, and, not stopping to bargain, which is never of any use in London, I told Martinelli that I would take it on the spot.

Martinelli translated what I said to the old woman, who told me that if I liked to keep her on as housekeeper I need not have a surety, and that it would only be necessary for me to pay for each week in advance. I answered that I would do so, but that she must get me a servant who could speak French or Italian as well as English. She promised to get one in a day's time, and I paid her four weeks' rent on the spot, for which she gave me a receipt under the name of the Chevalier de Seingalt. This was the name by which I was known during the whole of my stay in London.

Thus in less than two hours I was comfortably settled in a town which is sometimes described as a chaos, especially for a stranger. But in London everything is easy to him who has money and is not afraid of spending it. I was delighted to be able to escape so soon from a house where I was welcomed so ill, though I had a right to the best reception; but I was still more pleased at the chance which had made me acquainted with Martinelli, whom I had known by repute for six years.

When I got back Madame Cornelis had not yet arrived, though ten o'clock had struck. Young Cornelis was asleep on the sofa. I was enraged at the way the woman treated me, but I resolved to put a good face on it.

Before long three loud knocks announced the arrival of Madame Cornelis in a sedan-chair, and I heard her ascending the stairs. She came in and seemed glad to see me, but did not come and give me those caresses which I had a right to expect. She ran to her son and took him on her knee, but the sleepy boy did not respond to her kisses with any great warmth.

"He is very tired, like myself," said I, "and considering that we are travellers in need of rest you have kept us waiting a long time."

I do not know whether she would have answered at all, or, if so, what her answer would have been, for just at that moment a servant came in and said that supper was ready. She rose and did me the honour to take my arm, and we went into another room which I had not seen. The table was laid for four, and I was curious enough to inquire who was the fourth person.

"It was to have been my daughter, but I left her behind, as when I told her that you and her brother had arrived she asked me if you were well."

"And you have punished her for doing so?"

"Certainly, for in my opinion she ought to have asked for her brother first and then for you. Don't you think I was right?"

"Poor Sophie! I am sorry for her. Gratitude has evidently more influence over her than blood relationship."

"It is not a question of sentiment, but of teaching young persons to think with propriety."

"Propriety is often far from proper."

The woman told her son that she was working hard to leave him a fortune when she died, and that she had been obliged to summon him to England as he was old enough to help her in her business.

"And how am I to help you, my dear mother?"

"I give twelve balls and twelve suppers to the nobility, and the same number to the middle classes in the year. I have often as many as six hundred guests at two guineas a head. The expenses are enormous, and alone as I am I must be robbed, for I can't be in two places at once. Now that you are here you can keep everything under lock and key, keep the books, pay and receive accounts, and see that everyone is properly attended to at the assemblies; in fine, you will perform the duties of the master."

"And do you think that I can do all that?"

"You will easily learn it."

"I think it will be very difficult."

"One of my secretaries will come and live with you, and instruct you in everything. During the first year you will only have to acquire the English language, and to be present at my assemblies, that I may introduce you to the most distinguished people in London. You will get quite English before long."

"I would rather remain French."

"That's mere prejudice, my dear, you will like the sound of Mister Cornelis by-and-bye."

"Cornelis?"

"Yes; that is your name."

"It's a very funny one."

"I will write it down, so that you may not forget it."

Thinking that her dear son was joking, Madame Cornelis looked at me in some astonishment, and told him to go to bed, which he did instantly. When we were alone she said he struck her as badly educated, and too small for his age.

"I am very much afraid," said she, "that we shall have to begin his education all over again. What has he learnt in the last six years?"

"He might have learnt a great deal, for he went to the best boarding-school in Paris; but he only learnt what he liked, and what he liked was not much. He can play the flute, ride, fence, dance a minuet, change his shirt every day, answer politely, make a graceful bow, talk elegant trifles, and dress well. As he never had any application, he doesn't know anything about literature; he can scarcely write, his spelling is abominable, his arithmetic limited, and I doubt whether he knows in what continent England is situated."

"He has used the six years well, certainly."

"Say, rather, he has wasted them; but he will waste many more."

"My daughter will laugh at him; but then it is I who have had the care of her education. He will be ashamed when he finds her so well instructed, though she is only eight."

"He will never see her at eight, if I know anything of reckoning; she is fully ten."

"I think I ought to know the age of my own daughter. She

knows geography, history, languages, and music; she argues correctly, and behaves in a manner which is surprising in so young a child. All the ladies are in love with her. I keep her at a school of design all day; she shows a great taste for drawing. She dines with me on Sundays, and if you would care to come to dinner next Sunday you will confess that I have not exaggerated her capacities."

It was Monday. I said nothing, but I thought it strange that she did not seem to consider that I was impatient to see my daughter. She should have asked me to meet her at supper the following evening.

"You are just in time," said she, "to witness the last assembly of the year; for in a few weeks all the nobility will leave town in order to pass the summer in the country. I can't give you a ticket, as they are only issued to the nobility, but you can come as my friend and keep close to me. You will see everything. If I am asked who you are, I will say that you have superintended the education of my son in Paris, and have brought him back to me."

"You do me too much honour."

We continued talking till two o'clock in the morning, and she told me all about the suit she had with Sir Frederick Fermer. He maintained that the house she had built at a cost of ten thousand guineas belonged to him as he had furnished the money. In equity he was right, but according to English law wrong, for it was she who had paid the workmen, the contractors, and the architect; it was she that had given and received receipts, and signed all documents. The house, therefore, belonged to her, and Fermer admitted as much; but he claimed the sum he had furnished, and here was the kernel of the whole case, for she had defied him to produce a single acknowledgment of money received.

"I confess," said this honest woman, "that you have often given me a thousand pounds at a time, but that was a friendly gift, and nothing to be wondered at in a rich Englishman, considering that we were lovers and lived together."

She won her suit four times over in two years, but Fermer took advantage of the intricacies of English law to appeal again and again, and now he had gone to the House of Lords, the appeal to which might last fifteen years.

"This suit," said the honest lady, "dishonours Fermer."

"I should think it did, but you surely don't think it honours you."

"Certainly I do."

"I don't quite understand how you make that out."

"I will explain it all to you."

"We will talk it over again."

In the three hours for which we talked together this woman did not once ask me how I was, whether I was comfortable, how long I intended to stay in London, or whether I had made much money. In short she made no inquiries whatever about me, only saying with a smile, but not heedlessly:

"I never have a penny to spare."

Her receipts amounted to more than twenty-four thousand pounds per annum, but her expenses were enormous and she had debts.

I avenged myself on her indifference by not saying a word about myself. I was dressed simply but neatly, and had not any jewellery or diamonds about my person.

I went to bed annoyed with her, but glad to have discovered the badness of her heart. In spite of my longing to see my daughter I determined not to take any steps to meet her till the ensuing Sunday, when I was invited to dinner.

Early next morning I told Clairmont to put all my goods and chattels in a carriage, and when all was ready I went to take leave of young Cornelis, telling him I was going to live in Pall Mall, and leaving him my address.

"You are not going to stay with me, then?" said he.

"No, your mother doesn't know how to welcome or to treat me."

"I think you are right. I shall go back to Paris."

"Don't do anything so silly. Remember that here you are at home, and that in Paris you might not find a roof to shelter you. Farewell; I shall see you on Sunday."

I was soon settled in my new house, and I went out to call on M. Zuccato, the Venetian ambassador. I gave him M. Morosini's letter, and he said, coldly, that he was glad to make my acquaintance. When I asked him to present me at Court, the insolent fool only replied with a smile, which might fairly be described as contemptuous. It was the aristocratic pride coming out, so I returned his smile with a cold bow, and never set foot in his house again.

On leaving Zuccato I called on Lord Egremont, and finding him ill left my letter with the porter. He died a few days after, so M. Morosini's letters were both useless through no fault of his. We shall learn presently what was the result of the little note.

I then went to the Comte de Guerchi, the French ambassador, with a letter from the Marquis Chauvelin, and I received a warm welcome. This nobleman asked me to dine with him the following day, and told me that if I liked he would present me at Court after chapel on Sunday. It was at that ambassador's table that I made the acquaintance of the Chevalier d'Eon, the secretary of the embassy, who afterwards became famous. This Chevalier d'Eon was a handsome woman who had been an advocate and a captain of dragoons before entering the diplomatic service; she served Louis XV. as a valiant soldier and a diplomatist of consummate skill. In spite of her manly ways I soon recognised her as a woman; her voice was not that of a *castrato*, and her shape was too rounded to be a man's. I say nothing of the absence of hair on her face, as that might be an accident.

In the first days of my stay in London I made the acquaintance of my bankers, who held at least three hundred thousand francs of my money. They all honoured my drafts and offered their services to me, but I did not make use of their good offices.

I visited the theatres of Covent Garden and Drury Lane, but I could not extract much enjoyment out of the performances as I did not know a word of English. I dined at all the taverns, high and low, to get some insight into the peculiar manners of the English. In the morning I went on 'Change, where I made some friends. It was there that a merchant to whom I spoke got me a Negro servant who spoke English, French, and Italian with equal facility; and the same individual procured me a cook who spoke French. I also visited the bagnios where a rich man can sup, bathe, and sleep with a fashionable courtesan, of which species there are many in London. It makes a magnificent debauch and only costs six guineas. The expense may be reduced to a hundred francs, but economy in pleasure is not to my taste.

On Sunday I made an elegant toilet and went to Court about eleven, and met the Comte de Guerchi as we had arranged. He introduced me to George III., who spoke to me, but in such a low voice that I could not understand him and had to reply by a bow. The queen made up for the king, however, and I was delighted to observe that the proud ambassador from my beloved Venice was also present. When M. de Guerchi introduced me under the name of the Chevalier de Seingalt, Zuccato looked astonished, for M. Morosini had called me Casanova in his letter. The queen asked me from what part of France I came, and understanding from my answer that I was from Venice, she looked at the Venetian ambassador, who bowed as if to say that he had no objection to make. Her majesty then asked me if I knew the ambassadors extraordinary, who had been sent to congratulate the king, and I replied that I had the pleasure of knowing them intimately, and that I had spent three days in their society at Lyons, where M. Morosini gave me letters for my Lord d'Egremont and M. Zuccato.

"M. Querini amused me extremely," said the queen; "he called me a little devil."

"He meant to say that your highness is as witty as an angel."

I longed for the queen to ask me why I had not been presented by M. Zuccato, for I had a reply on the tip of my tongue that would have deprived the ambassador of his sleep for a week, while I should have slept soundly, for vengeance is a divine pleasure, especially when it is taken on the proud and foolish; but the whole conversation was a compound of nothings, as is usual in courts.

After my interview was over I got into my sedan-chair and went to Soho Square. A man in court dress cannot walk the streets of London without being pelted with mud by the mob, while the gentlemen look on and laugh. All customs must be respected; they are all at once worthy and absurd.

When I got to the house of Madame Cornelis, I and my Negro, Jarbe, were shown upstairs, and conducted through a suite of gorgeous apartments to a room where the lady of the house was sitting with two English ladies and two English gentlemen. She received me with familiar politeness, made me sit down in an arm-chair beside her, and then continued the conversation in English without introducing me. When her steward told her that dinner was ready, she gave orders for the children to be brought down.

I had long desired this meeting, and when I saw Sophie I ran to meet her; but she, who had profited by her mother's instructions, drew back with profound courtesy and a compliment learnt by heart. I did not say anything for fear it should embarrass her, but I felt grieved to the heart.

Madame Cornelis then brought forward her son, telling the company that I had brought him to England after superintending his education for six years. She spoke in French, so I was glad to see that her friends understood that language.

We sat down to table; Madame Cornelis between her two children, and I between the two Englishwomen, one of whom delighted me by her pleasant wit. I attached myself to her as soon as I noticed that the mistress of the house only spoke to me by chance and that Sophie did not look at me. She was so like me that no mistake was possible. I could see that she had been carefully tutored by her mother to behave in this manner, and I felt this treatment to be both absurd and impertinent. I did not want to let anyone see that I was angry, so I began to discourse in a pleasant strain on the peculiarities of English manners, taking care, however, not to say anything which might wound the insular pride of the English guests. My idea was to make them laugh and to make myself agreeable, and I succeeded, but not a word did I speak to Madame Cornelis; I did not so much as look at her.

The lady next to me, after admiring the beauty of my lace, asked me what was the news at Court.

"It was all news to me," said I, "for I went there to-day for the first time."

"Have you seen the king?" said Sir Joseph Cornelis.

"My dear, you should not ask such questions," said his mother.

"Why not?"

"Because the gentleman may not wish to answer them."

"On the contrary, madam, I like being questioned. I have been teaching your son for the last six years to be always asking something, for that is the way to acquire knowledge. He who asks nothing knows nothing."

I had touched her to the quick, and she fell into a sulky silence.

"You have not told me yet," said the lad, "whether you saw the king."

"Yes, my man, I saw the king and the queen, and both their majesties did me the honour to speak to me."

"Who introduced you?"

"The French ambassador."

"I think you will agree with me," said the mother, "that last question was a little too much."

"Certainly it would be if it were addressed to a stranger, but not to me who am his friend. You will notice that the reply he extracted from me did me honour. If I had not wished it to be known that I had been at Court, I should not have come here in this dress."

"Very good; but as you like to be questioned, may I ask you why you were not presented by your own ambassador?"

"Because the Venetian ambassador would not present me, knowing that his government have a bone to pick with me."

By this time we had come to the dessert, and poor Sophie had not uttered a syllable.

"Say something to M. de Seingalt," said her mother.

"I don't know what to say," she answered. "Tell M. de Seingalt to ask me some questions, and I will answer to the best of my ability."

"Well, Sophie, tell me in what studies you are engaged at the present time."

"I am learning drawing; if you like I will show you some of my work."

"I will look at it with pleasure; but tell me how you think you have offended me; you have a guilty air."

"I, sir? I do not think I have done anything amiss."

"Nor do I, my dear; but as you do not look at me when you speak I thought you must be ashamed of something. Are you ashamed of your fine eyes? You blush. What have you done?"

"You are embarrassing her," said the mother. "Tell him, my dear, that you have done nothing, but that a feeling of modesty and respect prevents you from gazing at the persons you address."

"Yes," said I; "but if modesty bids young ladies lower their eyes, politeness should make them raise them now and again."

No one replied to this objection, which was a sharp cut for the absurd woman; but after an interval of silence we rose from the table, and Sophie went to fetch her drawings.

"I won't look at anything, Sophie, unless you will look at me."

"Come," said her mother, "look at the gentleman."

She obeyed as quickly as lightning, and I saw the prettiest eyes imaginable.

"Now," said I, "I know you again, and perhaps you may remember having seen me."

"Yes, although it is six years ago since we met, I recognised you directly."

"And yet you did not look me in the face! If you knew how impolite it was to lower your eyes when you are addressing anyone, you would not do it. Who can have given you such a bad lesson?"

The child glanced towards her mother, who was standing by a window, and I saw who was her preceptress.

I felt that I had taken sufficient vengeance, and began to examine her drawings, to praise them in detail, and to congratulate her on her talents. I told her that she ought to be thankful to have a mother who had given her so good an education. This indirect compliment pleased Madame Cornelis, and Sophie, now free from all restraint, gazed at me with an expression of childlike affection which ravished me. Her features bore the imprint of a noble soul within, and I pitied her for having to grow up under the authority of a foolish mother. Sophie went to the piano, played with feeling, and then sang some Italian airs, to the accompaniment of the guitar, too well for her age. She was too precocious, and wanted much more discretion in her education than Madame Cornelis was able to give her.

When her singing had been applauded by the company, her mother told her to dance a minuet with her brother, who had learnt in Paris, but danced badly for want of a good carriage. His sister told him so with a kiss, and then asked me to dance with her, which I did very readily. Her mother, who thought she had danced exquisitely, as was indeed the case, told her that she must give me a kiss. She came up to me, and drawing her on my knee I covered her face with kisses, which she returned with the greatest affection. Her mother laughed with all her heart, and then Sophie, beginning to be doubtful again, went up to her and asked if she were angry. Her mother comforted her with a kiss.

After we had taken coffee, which was served in the French

fashion, Madame Cornelis showed me a magnificent hall which she had built, in which she could give supper to four hundred persons seated at one table. She told me, and I could easily believe her, that there was not such another in all London.

The last assembly was given before the prorogation of Parliament; it was to take place in four or five days. She had a score of pretty girls in her service, and a dozen footmen all in full livery.

"They all rob me," said she, "but I have to put up with it. What I want is a sharp man to help me and watch over my interests; if I had such an one I should make an immense fortune in a comparatively short time; for when it is a question of pleasure, the English do not care what they spend."

I told her I hoped she would find such a man and make the fortune, and then I left her, admiring her enterprise.

When I left Soho Square I went to St. James's Park to see Lady Harrington, for whom I bore a letter, as I have mentioned. This lady lived in the precincts of the Court, and received company every Sunday. It was allowable to play in her house, as the park is under the jurisdiction of the Crown. In any other place there is no playing cards or singing on Sundays. The town abounds in spies, and if they have reason to suppose that there is any gaming or music going on, they watch for their opportunity, slip into the house, and arrest all the bad Christians, who are diverting themselves in a manner which is thought innocent enough in any other country. But to make up for this severity the Englishman may go in perfect liberty to the tavern or the brothel, and sanctify the Sabbath as he pleases.

I called on Lady Harrington, and, having sent up my letter, she summoned me into her presence. I found her in the midst of about thirty persons, but the hostess was easily distinguished by the air of welcome she had for me.

After I had made my bow she told me she had seen me at Court in the morning, and that without knowing who I was she had been desirous of making my acquaintance. Our conversation lasted three-quarters of an hour, and was composed of those frivolous observations and idle questions which are commonly addressed to a traveller.

The lady was forty, but she was still handsome. She was well known for her gallantries and her influence at Court. She introduced me to her husband and her four daughters, charming girls of a marriageable age. She asked me why I had come to London when everybody was on the point of going out of town. I told her that as I always obeyed the impulse of the moment, I should find it difficult to answer her question; besides, I intended staying for a year, so that the pleasure would be deferred but not lost.

My reply seemed to please her by its character of English independence, and she offered with exquisite grace to do all in her power for me.

"In the meanwhile," said she, "we will begin by letting you see all the nobility at Madame Cornelis's on Thursday next. I can give you a ticket to admit to ball and supper. It is two guineas."

I gave her the money, and she took the ticket again, writing on it, "Paid. — Harrington."

"Is this formality necessary, my lady?"

"Yes; or else they would ask you for the money at the doors."

I did not think it necessary to say anything about my connection with the lady of Soho Square.

While Lady Harrington was making up a rubber at whist, she asked me if I had any other letters for ladies.

"Yes," said I, "I have one which I intend to present to-morrow. It is a singular letter, being merely a portrait."

"Have you got it about you?"

"Yes, my lady."

"May I see it?"

"Certainly. Here it is."

"It is the Duchess of Northumberland. We will go and give it her."

"With pleasure."

"Just wait till they have marked the game."

Lord Percy had given me this portrait as a letter of introduction to his mother.

"My dear duchess," said Lady Harrington, "here is a letter of introduction which this gentleman begs to present to you."

"I know, it is M. de Seingalt. My son has written to me about him. I am delighted to see you, Chevalier, and I hope you will come and see me. I receive thrice a week."

"Will your ladyship allow me to present my valuable letter in person?"

"Certainly. You are right."

I played a rubber of whist for very small stakes, and lost fifteen guineas, which I paid on the spot. Directly afterwards, Lady Harrington took me apart, and gave me a lesson which I deem worthy of record.

"You paid in gold," said she; "I suppose you had no bank-notes about you?"

"Yes, my lady, I have notes for fifty and a hundred pounds."

"Then you must change one of them or wait till another time to pay, for in England to pay in gold is a solecism only pardonable in a stranger. Perhaps you noticed that the lady smiled?"

"Yes; who is she?"

"Lady Coventry, sister of the Duchess of Hamilton."

"Ought I to apologise?"

"Not at all, the offence is not one of those which require an apology. She must have been more surprised than offended, for she made fifteen shillings by your paying her in gold."

I was vexed by this small mischance, for Lady Coventry was an exquisitely beautiful brunette. I comforted myself, however, without much trouble.

The same day I made the acquaintance of Lord Hervey, the nobleman who conquered Havana, a pleasant and intelligent person. He had married Miss Chudleigh, but the marriage was annulled. This celebrated Miss Chudleigh was maid of honour to the Princess Dowager of Wales, and afterwards became Duchess of Kingston. As her history is well known I shall say something more of her in due course. I went home well enough pleased with my day's work.

The next day I began dining at home, and found my cook very satisfactory; for, besides the usual English dishes, he was ac-quainted with the French system of cooking, and did fricandeaus, cutlets, ragouts, and, above all, the excellent French soup, which is one of the principal glories of France.

My table and my house were not enough for my happiness. I was alone, and the reader will understand by this that Nature had not meant me for a hermit. I had neither a mistress nor a friend, and at London one may invite a man to dinner at a tavern where he pays for himself, but not to one's own table. One day I was invited by a younger son of the Duke of Bedford to eat oysters and drink a bottle of champagne. I accepted the invitation, and he ordered the oysters and the champagne, but we drank two bottles, and he made me pay half the price of the second bottle. Such are manners on the other side of the Channel. People laughed in my face when I said that I did not care to dine at a tavern as I could not get any soup.

"Are you ill?" they said. "Soup is only fit for invalids."

The Englishman is entirely carnivorous. He eats very little bread, and calls himself economical because he spares himself the expense of soup and dessert, which circumstance made me remark that an English dinner is like eternity; it has no beginning and no end. Soup is considered very extravagant, as the very servants refuse to eat the meat from which it has been made. They say it is only fit to give to dogs. The salt beef which they use is certainly excellent. I cannot say the same for their beer, which was so bitter that I could not drink it. However, I could not be expected to like beer after the excellent French wines with which the wine merchant supplied me, certainly at a very heavy cost.

I had been a week in my new home without seeing Martinelli. He came on a Monday morning, and I asked him to dine with me. He told me that he had to go to the Museum, and my curiosity to see the famous collection which is such an honour to England made me accompany him. It was there that I made the acquaintance of Dr. Mati, of whom I shall speak in due course.

At dinner Martinelli made himself extremely pleasant. He had a profound knowledge of the English manners and customs which it behoved me to know if I wished to get on. I happened to speak of the impoliteness of which I had been guilty in paying a gaming debt in gold instead of paper, and on this text he preached me a sermon on the national prosperity, demonstrating that the preference given to paper shows the confidence which is felt in the Bank, which may or may not be misplaced, but which is certainly a source of wealth. This confidence might be destroyed by a too large issue of paper money, and if that ever took place by reason of a protracted or unfortunate war, bankruptcy would be inevitable, and no one could calculate the final results.

After a long discussion on politics, national manners, literature,

in which subjects Martinelli shone, we went to Drury Lane
Theatre, where I had a specimen of the rough insular manners.
By some accident or other the company could not give the piece
that had been announced, and the audience were in a tumult.
Garrick, the celebrated actor, who was buried twenty years later
in Westminister Abbey, came forward and tried in vain to restore order. He was obliged to retire behind the curtain. Then
the king, the queen, and all the fashionables left the theatre, and
in less than an hour the house was gutted, till nothing but the
bare walls were left.

After this destruction, which went on without any authority
interposing, the mad populace rushed to the taverns to consume
gin and beer. In a fortnight the theatre was refitted and the
piece announced again, and when Garrick appeared before the
curtain to implore the indulgence of the house, a voice from
the pit shouted, "On your knees." A thousand voices took up the
cry "On your knees," and the English Roscius was obliged to
kneel down and beg forgiveness. Then came a thunder of applause, and everything was over. Such are the English, and,
above all, the Londoners. They hoot the king and the royal
family when they appear in public, and the consequence is, that
they are never seen, save on great occasions, when order is kept
by hundreds of constables.

One day, as I was walking by myself, I saw Sir Augustus
Hervey, whose acquaintance I had made, speaking to a gentleman, whom he left to come to me. I asked him whom he had
been speaking to.

"That's the brother of Earl Ferrers," said he, "who was
hanged a couple of months ago for murdering one of his people."

"And you speak to his brother?"

"Why shouldn't I?"

"Is he not dishonoured by the execution of his relative?"

"Dishonoured! Certainly not; even his brother was not dishonoured. He broke the law, but he paid for it with his life,
and owed society nothing more. He's a man of honour, who
played high and lost; that's all. I don't know that there is any
penalty in the statute book which dishonours the culprit; that
would be tyrannical, and we would not bear it. I may break
any law I like, so long as I am willing to pay the penalty. It is
only a dishonour when the criminal tries to escape punishment
by base or cowardly actions."

"How do you mean?"

"To ask for the royal mercy, to beg forgiveness of the people, and the like."

"How about escaping from justice?"

"That is no dishonour, for to fly is an act of courage; it continues the defiance of the law, and if the law cannot exact obedience, so much the worse for it. It is an honour for you to have escaped from the tyranny of your magistrates; your flight from The Leads was a virtuous action. In such cases man fights with death and flees from it. *Vir fugiens denuo pugnabit.*"

"What do you think of highway robbers, then?"

"I detest them as wretches dangerous to society, but I pity them when I reflect that they are always riding towards the gallows. You go out in a coach to pay a visit to a friend three or four miles out of London. A determined and agile-looking fellow springs upon you with his pistol in his hand, and says, 'Your money or your life.' What would you do in such a case?"

"If I had a pistol handy I would blow out his brains, and if not I would give him my purse and call him a scoundrelly assassin."

"You would be wrong in both cases. If you killed him, you would be hanged, for you have no right to take the law into your own hands; and if you called him an assassin, he would tell you that he was no assassin as he attacked you openly and gave you a free choice. Nay, he is generous, for he might kill you and take your money as well. You might, indeed, tell him he has an evil trade, and he would tell you that you were right, and that he would try to avoid the gallows as long as possible. He would then thank you and advise you never to drive out of London without being accompanied by a mounted servant, as then no robber would dare to attack you. We English always carry two purses on our journeys; a small one for the robbers and a large one for ourselves."

What answer could I make to such arguments, based as they were upon the national manners? England is a rich sea, but strewn with reefs, and those who voyage there would do well to take precautions. Sir Augustus Hervey's discourse gave me great pleasure.

Going from one topic to another, as is always the way with a desultory conversation, Sir Augustus deplored the fate of an unhappy Englishman who had absconded to France with seventy thousand pounds, and had been brought back to London, and was to be hanged.

"How could that be?" I asked.

"The Crown asked the Duc de Nivernois to extradite him, and Louis XV. granted the request to make England assent to some articles of the peace. It was an act unworthy of a king, for it violates the right of nations. It is true that the man is a wretch, but that has nothing to do with the principle of the thing."

"Of course they have got back the seventy thousand pounds?"

"Not a shilling of it."

"How was that?"

"Because no money was found on him. He has most likely left his little fortune to his wife, who can marry again as she is still young and pretty."

"I wonder the police have not been after her."

"Such a thing is never thought of. What could they do? It's not likely that she would confess that her husband left her the stolen money. The law says robbers shall be hanged, but it says nothing about what they have stolen, as they are supposed to have made away with it. Then if we had to take into account the thieves who had kept their theft and thieves who had spent it, we should have to make two sets of laws, and make all manner of allowances; the end of it would be inextricable confusion. It seems to us Englishmen that it would not be just to ordain two punishments for theft. The robber becomes the owner of what he has stolen; true, he got it by violence, but it is none the less his, for he can do what he likes with it. That being the case, everyone should be careful to keep what he has, since he knows that once stolen he will never see it again. I have taken Havana from Spain: this was robbery on a large scale."

He talked at once like a philosopher and a faithful subject of his king.

Engaged in this discussion we walked towards the Duchess of Northumberland's, where I made the acquaintance of Lady Rochefort, whose husband had just been appointed Spanish ambassador. This lady's gallantries were innumerable, and furnished a fresh topic of conversation every day.

The day before the assembly at Soho Square Martinelli dined

with me, and told me that Madame Cornelis was heavily in debt, and dared not go out except on Sundays, when debtors are privileged.

"The enormous and unnecessary expense which she puts herself to," said he, "will soon bring her to ruin. She owes four times the amount of her assets, even counting in the house, which is a doubtful item, as it is the subject of litigation."

This news only distressed me for her children's sake, for I thought that she herself well deserved such a fate.

I went in due time to the assembly, and the secretary at the door wrote down my name as I handed in my ticket. When Madame Cornelis saw me she said she was delighted I had come in by ticket, and that she had had some doubts as to whether I would come.

"You might have spared yourself the trouble of doubting," said I, "for after hearing that I had been to Court you might have guessed that a matter of two guineas would not have kept me away. I am sorry for our old friendship's sake that I did not pay the money to you; you might have known that I would not condescend to be present in the modest manner you indicated."

This address, delivered with an ironical accent, embarrassed Madame Cornelis, but Lady Harrington, a great supporter of hers, came to her rescue.

"I have a number of guineas to hand over to you, my dear Cornelis, and amongst others two from M. de Seingalt, who, I fancy, is an old friend of yours. Nevertheless, I did not dare to tell him so," she added, with a sly glance in my direction.

"Why not, my lady? I have known Madame Cornelis for many years."

"I should think you have," she answered, laughing, "and I congratulate you both. I suppose you know the delightful Miss Sophie too, Chevalier?"

"Certainly, my lady, whoso knows the mother knows the daughter."

"Quite so, quite so."

Sophie was standing by, and after kissing her fondly Lady Harrington said:

"If you love yourself, you ought to love her, for she is the image of you."

"Yes, it is a freak of nature."

"I think there is something more than a freak in this instance."

With these words the lady took Sophie's hand, and leaning on my arm she led us through the crowd, and I had to bear in silence the remarks of everyone.

"There is Madame Cornelis's husband."

"That must be M. Cornelis."

"Oh! there can be no doubt about it."

"No, no," said Lady Harrington, "you are all quite wrong."

I got tired of these remarks, which were all founded on the remarkable likeness between myself and Sophie. I wanted Lady Harrington to let the child go, but she was too much amused to do so.

"Stay by me," she said, "if you want to know the names of the guests." She sat down, making me sit on one side and Sophie on the other.

Madame Cornelis then made her appearance, and everyone asked her the same questions, and made the same remarks about me. She said bravely that I was her best and her oldest friend, and that the likeness between me and her daughter might possibly be capable of explanation. Everyone laughed and said it was very natural that it should be so. To change the subject, Madame Cornelis remarked that Sophie had learnt the minuet and danced it admirably.

"Then fetch a violin player," said Lady Harrington, "that we may have the pleasure of witnessing the young artist's performance."

The ball had not yet begun, and as soon as the violinist appeared, I stepped forward and danced with Sophie, to the delight of the select circle of spectators.

The ball lasted all night without ceasing, as the company ate by relays, and at all times and hours; the waste and prodigality were worthy of a prince's palace. I made the acquaintance of all the nobility and the royal family, for they were all there, with the exception of the king and queen, and the Prince of Wales. Madame Cornelis must have received more than twelve hundred guineas, but the outlay was enormous, without any control or safeguard against thefts which must have been perpetrated on all sides. She tried to introduce her son to everybody, but the poor lad looked like a victim, and did nothing but make profound bows. I pitied him from my heart.

As soon as I got home I went to bed and spent the whole of the next day there. The day after I went to the Staven Tavern, as I had been told that the prettiest girls in London resorted to it. Lord Pembroke gave me this piece of information; he went there very frequently himself. When I got to the tavern I asked for a private room, and the landlord, perceiving that I did not know English, accosted me in French, and came to keep me company. I was astonished at his grave and reverend manner of speaking, and did not like to tell him that I wanted to dine with a pretty Englishwoman. At last, however, I summoned up courage to say, with a great deal of circumlocution, that I did not know whether Lord Pembroke had deceived me in informing me that I should find the prettiest girls in London at his house.

"No, sir," said he, "my lord has not deceived you, and you can have as many as you like."

"That's what I came for."

He called out some name, and, a tidy-looking lad making his appearance, he told him to get me a wench just as though he were ordering a bottle of champagne. The lad went out, and presently a girl of herculean proportions entered.

"Sir," said I, "I don't like the looks of this girl."

"Give her a shilling and send her away. We don't trouble ourselves about ceremonies in London."

This put me at my ease, so I paid my shilling and called for a prettier wench. The second was worse than the first, and I sent her away, and ten others after her, while I could see that my fastidiousness amused the landlord immensely.

"I'll see no more girls," said I at last, "let me have a good dinner. I think the procurer must have been making game of me for the sake of the shillings."

"It's very likely; indeed it often happens so when a gentleman does not give the name and address of the wench he wants."

In the evening as I was walking in St. James's Park, I remembered it was a Ranelagh evening, and wishing to see the place I took a coach and drove there, intending to amuse myself till midnight, and to find a beauty to my taste.

I was pleased with the rotunda. I had some tea, I danced some minuets, but I made no acquaintances; and although I saw several pretty women, I did not dare to attack any of them. I got tired, and as it was near midnight I went out thinking to find my coach, for which I had not paid, still there, but it was gone, and I did not know what to do. An extremely pretty woman who was waiting for her carriage in the doorway, noticed my distress, and said that if I lived anywhere near Whitehall, she could take me home. I thanked her gratefully, and told her where I lived. Her carriage came up, her man opened the door, and she stepped in on my arm, telling me to sit beside her, and to stop the carriage when it got to my house.

As soon as we were in the carriage, I burst out into expressions of gratitude; and after telling her my name I expressed my regret at not having seen her at Soho Square.

"I was not in London," she replied, "I returned from Bath to-day."

I apostrophised my happiness in having met her. I covered her hands with kisses, and dared to kiss her on the cheek; and finding that she smiled graciously, I fastened my lips on hers, and before long had given her an unequivocal mark of the ardour with which she inspired me.

She took my attentions so easily that I flattered myself I had not displeased her, and I begged her to tell me where I could call on her and pay my court while I remained in London, but she replied:

"We shall see each other again; we must be careful."

I swore secrecy, and urged her no more. Directly after the carriage stopped, I kissed her hand and was set down at my door, well pleased with the ride home.

For a fortnight I saw nothing of her, but I met her again in a house where Lady Harrington had told me to present myself, giving her name. It was Lady Betty German's, and I found her out, but was asked to sit down and wait as she would be in soon. I was pleasantly surprised to find my fair friend of Ranelagh in the room, reading a newspaper. I conceived the idea of asking her to introduce me to Lady Betty, so I went up to her and proffered my request, but she replied politely that she could not do so not having the honour to know my name.

"I have told you my name, madam. Do you not remember me?"

"I remember you perfectly, but a piece of folly is not a title of acquaintance."

I was dumbfounded at the extraordinary reply, while the

lady calmly returned to her newspaper, and did not speak another word till the arrival of Lady Betty.

The fair philosopher talked for two hours without giving the least sign of knowing who I was, although she answered me with great politeness whenever I ventured to address her. She turned out to be a lady of high birth and of great reputation.

Happening to call on Martinelli, I asked him who was the pretty girl who was kissing her hands to me from the house opposite. I was pleasantly surprised to hear that she was a dancer named Binetti. Four years ago she had done me a great service at Stuttgart, but I did not know she was in London. I took leave of Martinelli to go and see her, and did so all the more eagerly when I heard that she had parted from her husband, though they were obliged to dance together at the Haymarket.

She received me with open arms, telling me that she had recognised me directly.

"I am surprised, my dear elder," said she, "to see you in London."

She called me "elder" because I was the oldest of her friends.

"Nor did I know that you were here. I came to town after the close of the opera. How is it that you are not living with your husband?"

"Because he games, loses, and despoils me of all I possess. Besides, a woman of my condition, if she be married, cannot hope that a rich lover will come and see her, while if she be alone she can receive visits without any constraint."

"I shouldn't have thought they would be afraid of Binetti; he used to be far from jealous."

"Nor is he jealous now; but you must know that there is an English law which allows the husband to arrest his wife and her lover if he find them *in flagrante delicto*. He only wants two witnesses, and it is enough that they are sitting together on a bed. The lover is forced to pay to the husband the half of all he possesses. Several rich Englishmen have been caught in this way, and now they are very shy of visiting married women, especially Italians."

"So you have much to be thankful for. You enjoy perfect liberty, can receive any visitors you like, and are in a fair way to make a fortune."

"Alas! my dear friend, you do not know all. When he has information from his spies that I have had a visitor, he comes to me in a sedan-chair at night, and threatens to turn me out into the street if I do not give him all the money I have. He is a terrible rascal!"

I left the poor woman, after giving her my address, and telling her to come and dine with me whenever she liked. She had given me a lesson on the subject of visiting ladies. England has very good laws, but most of them are capable of abuse. The oath which jurymen have to take to execute them to the letter has caused several to be interpreted in a manner absolutely contrary to the intention of the legislators, thus placing the judges in a difficult predicament. Thus new laws have constantly to be made, and new glosses to explain the old ones.

My Lord Pembroke, seeing me at my window, came in, and after examining my house, including the kitchen, where the cook was at work, told me that there was not a nobleman in town who had such a well-furnished and comfortable house. He made a calculation, and told me that if I wanted to entertain my friends I should require three hundred pounds a month. "You can't live here," said he, "without a pretty girl, and those who know that you keep bachelor's hall are of opinion that you are very wise, and will save a great deal of useless expense."

"Do you keep a girl, my lord?"

"No, for I am unfortunate enough to be disgusted with a woman after I have had her for a day."

"Then you require a fresh one every day?"

"Yes, and without being as comfortable as you I spend four times as much. You must know that I live in London like a stranger. I never dine at my own house. I wonder at your dining alone."

"I can't speak English. I like soup and good wine, and that is enough to keep me from your taverns."

"I expect so, with your French tastes."

"You will confess that they are not bad tastes."

"You are right, for, good Englishman as I am, I get on very well in Paris."

He burst out laughing when I told him how I had dispatched a score of wenches at the Staven Tavern, and that my disappointment was due to him.

"I did not tell you what names to send for, and I was wrong."

"Yes, you ought to have told me."

"But even if I did they wouldn't have come, for they are not at the orders of the procuress. If you will promise to pay them as I do, I will give you some tickets which will make them come."

"Can I have them here?"

"Just as you like."

"That will be most convenient for me. Write out the tickets and let them know French if you can."

"That's the difficulty; the prettiest only speak English."

"Never mind, we shall understand each other well enough for the purpose I dare say."

He wrote several tickets for four and six guineas each; but one was marked twelve guineas.

"She is doubly pretty, is she?" said I.

"Not exactly, but she has cuckolded a duke of Great Britain who keeps her, and only uses her once or twice a month."

"Would you do me the honour of testing the skill of my cook?"

"Certainly, but I can't make an appointment."

"And supposing I am out."

"I'll go to the tavern."

Having nothing better to do I sent Jarbe to one of the four-guinea wenches, telling him to advise her that she would dine with me. She came. She did not attract me sufficiently to make me attempt more than some slight toying. She went away well pleased with her four guineas, which she had done nothing to earn. Another wench, also at four guineas, supped with me the following evening. She had been very pretty, and, indeed, was so still, but she was too melancholy and quiet for my taste, and I could not make up my mind to tell her to undress.

The third day, not feeling inclined to try another ticket, I went to Covent Garden, and on meeting an attractive young person I accosted her in French, and asked her if she would sup with me.

"How much will you give me at dessert?"

"Three guineas."

"Come along."

After the play I ordered a good supper for two, and she

displayed an appetite after mine own heart. When we had supped I asked for her name and address, and I was astonished to find that she was one of the girls whom Lord Pembroke had assessed at six guineas. I concluded that it was best to do one's own business, or, at any rate, not to employ noblemen as agents. As to the other tickets, they procured me but little pleasure. The twelve-guinea one, which I had reserved for the last, as a choice morsel, pleased me the least of all, and I did not care to cuckold the noble duke who kept her.

Lord Pembroke was young, handsome, rich, and full of wit. I went to see him one day, and found him just getting out of bed. He said he would walk with me and told his valet to shave him.

"But," said I, "there's not a trace of beard on your face."

"There never is," said he, "I get myself shaved three times a day."

"Three times."

"Yes, when I change my shirt I wash my hands; when I wash my hands I have to wash my face, and the proper way to wash a man's face is with a razor."

"When do you make these three ablutions?"

"When I get up, when I dress for dinner, and when I go to bed, for I should not like the woman who is sleeping with me to feel my beard."

We had a short walk together, and then I left him as I had some writing to do. As we parted, he asked me if I dined at home. I replied in the affirmative, and foreseeing that he intended dining with me I warned my cook to serve us well, though I did not let him know that I expected a nobleman to dinner. Vanity has more than one string to its bow.

I had scarcely got home when Madame Binetti came in, and said that if she were not in the way, she would be glad to dine with me. I gave her a warm welcome, and she said I was really doing her a great service, as her husband would suffer the torments of hell in trying to find out with whom she had dined.

This woman still pleased; and though she was thirty-five, nobody would have taken her for more than twenty-five. Her appearance was in every way pleasing. Her lips were of the hue of the rose, disclosing two exquisite rows of teeth. A fine complexion, splendid eyes, and a forehead where Innocence might have been well enthroned, all this made an exquisite picture. If you add to this, that her breast was of the rarest proportions, you will understand that more fastidious tastes than mine would have been satisfied with her.

She had not been in my house for half an hour when Lord Pembroke came in. They both uttered an exclamation, and the nobleman told me that he had been in love with her for the last six months; that he had written ardent letters to her of which she had taken no notice.

"I never would have anything to do with him," said she, "because he is the greatest profligate in all England; and it's a pity," she added, "because he is a kind-hearted nobleman."

This explanation was followed by a score of kisses, and I saw that they were agreed.

We had a choice dinner in the French style, and Lord Pembroke swore he had not eaten so good a dinner for the last year.

"I am sorry for you," he said, "when I think of you being alone every day."

Madame Binetti was as much a *gourmet* as the Englishman, and when we rose from table we felt inclined to pass from the worship of Comus to that of Venus; but the lady was too experienced to give the Englishman anything more than a few trifling kisses.

I busied myself in turning over the leaves of some books I had brought the day before, and left them together to their heart's content; but to prevent them asking me to give them another dinner I said that I hoped chance would bring about such another meeting on another occasion.

At six o'clock, after my guests had left me, I dressed and went to Vauxhall, where I met a French officer named Malingan, to whom I had given some money at Aix-la-Chapelle. He said he would like to speak to me, so I gave him my name and address. I also met a well-known character, the Chevalier Goudar, who talked to me about gaming and women. Malingan introduced me to an individual who he said might be very useful to me in London. He was a man of forty, and styled himself son of the late Theodore, the pretender to the throne of Corsica, who had died miserably in London fourteen years before, after having been imprisoned for debt for seven years. I should have done better if I had never gone to Vauxhall that evening.

The entrance-fee at Vauxhall was half the sum charged at Ranelagh, but in spite of that the amusements were of the most varied kinds. There was good fare, music, walks in solitary alleys, thousands of lamps, and a crowd of London beauties, both high and low.

In the midst of all these pleasures I was dull, because I had no girl to share my abode or my good table, and make it dear to me. I had been in London for six weeks; and in no other place had I been alone for so long.

My house seemed intended for keeping a mistress with all decency, and as I had the virtue of constancy a mistress was all I wanted to make me happy. But how was I to find a woman who should be the equal of those women I had loved before? I had already seen half a hundred of girls whom the town pronounced to be pretty, and who did not strike me as even passable. I thought the matter over continually, and at last an odd idea struck me.

I called the old housekeeper, and told her by the servant, who acted as my interpreter, that I wanted to let the second or third floor for the sake of company; and although I was at perfect liberty to do what I liked with the house, I would give her half a guinea a week extra. Forthwith I ordered her to affix the following bill to the window: —

Second or third floor to be let, furnished, to a young lady speaking English and French, who receives no visitors, either by day or night.

The old Englishwoman, who had seen something of the world, began to laugh so violently when the document was translated to her that I thought she would have choked.

"What are you laughing at, my worthy woman? "

"Because this notice is a laughing matter."

"I suppose you think I shall have no applications? "

"Not at all, the doorstep will be crowded from morn to night, but I shall leave it all to Fanny. Only tell me how much to ask."

"I will arrange about the rent in my interview with the young lady. I don't think I shall have so many inquiries, for the young lady is to speak French and English, and also to be respectable. She must not receive any visits, not even from her father and mother, if she has them."

"But there will be a mob in front of the house reading the notice."

"All the better. Nothing is the worse for being a little odd."

It happened just as the old woman had foretold; as soon as the notice was up, everybody stopped to read it, made various comments, and passed on. On the second day after it was up, my Negro told me that my notice was printed in full in the *St. James's Chronicle*, with some amusing remarks. I had the paper brought up to me, and Fanny translated it. It ran as follows:

"The landlord of the second and third floors probably occupies the first floor himself. He must be a man of the world and of good taste, for he wants a young and pretty lodger; and as he forbids her to receive visits, he will have to keep her company himself."

He added:

"The landlord should take care lest he become his own dupe, for it is very likely that the pretty lodger would only take the room to sleep in, and possibly only to sleep in now and then; and if she chose she would have a perfect right to refuse to receive the proprietor's visits."

These sensible remarks delighted me, for after reading them I felt forewarned.

Such matters as these give their chief interest to the English newspapers. They are allowed to gossip about everything, and the writers have the knack of making the merest trifles seem amusing. Happy is the nation where anything may be written and anything said!

Lord Pembroke was the first to come and congratulate me on my idea, and he was succeeded by Martinelli; but he expressed some fears as to the possible consequences, "for," said he, "there are plenty of women in London who would come and lodge with you to be your ruin."

"In that case," I answered, "it would be a case of Greek meeting Greek; however, we shall see. If I am taken in, people will have the fullest right to laugh at me, for I have been warned."

I will not trouble my readers with an account of the hundred women who came in the first ten days, whom I refused on one pretext or another, though some of them were not wanting in grace and beauty. But one day, when I was at dinner, I received a visit from a girl of from twenty to twenty-four years, simply but elegantly dressed; her features were sweet and gracious, though somewhat grave, her complexion pale, and her hair black. She gave me a bow which I had to rise to return, and as I remained standing she politely begged me not to put myself out, but to continue my dinner. I begged her to be seated and to take dessert, but she refused with an air of modesty which delighted me.

This fair lady said, not in French, but in Italian worthy of a Siennese, its purity was so perfect, that she hoped I would let her have a room on the third floor, and that she would gladly submit to all my conditions.

"You may only make use of one room if you like, but all the floor will belong to you."

"Although the notice says the rooms will be let cheaply, I shall not be able to afford more than one room. Two shillings a week is all I can spend."

"That's exactly what I want for the whole suite of rooms; so you can use them all. My maid will wait on you, get you whatever food you may require, and wash your linen as well. You can also employ her to do your commissions, so that you need not go out for trifles."

"Then I will dismiss my maid," she said; "she robs me of little, it is true, but still too much for my small means. I will tell your maid what food to buy for me every day, and she shall have six sols a week for her pains."

"That will be ample. I should advise you to apply to my cook's wife, who will get your dinner and supper for you as cheaply as you could buy it."

"I hardly think so, for I am ashamed to tell you how little I spend."

⊦ "Even if you only spend two sols a day, she will give you two sols' worth. All the same I advise you to be content with what you get from the kitchen, without troubling about the price, for I usually have provision made for four, though I dine alone, and the rest is the cook's perquisite. I merely advise you to the best of my ability, and I hope you will not be offended at my interest in your welfare."

"Really, sir, you are too generous."

"Wait a moment, and you will see how everything will be settled comfortably."

I told Clairmont to order up the maid and the cook's wife, and I said to the latter:

"For how much could you provide dinner and supper for this young lady, who is not rich, and only wants to eat to live?"

"I can do it very cheaply; for you usually eat alone, and have enough for four."

"Very good; then I hope you will treat her very well for the sum she gives you."

"I can only afford five sols a day."

"That will do nicely."

I gave orders that the bill should be taken down directly, and that the young lady's room should be made comfortable. When the maid and the cook's wife had left the room, the young lady told me that she should only go out on Sundays to hear mass at the Bavarian ambassador's chapel, and once a month to a person who gave her three guineas to support her.

"You can go out when you like," said I, "and without rendering an account to anybody of your movements."

She begged me not to introduce anyone to her, and to tell the porter to deny her to anyone who might come to the door to make inquiries. I promised that her wishes should be respected, and she went away saying that she was going for her trunk.

I immediately ordered my household to treat her with the utmost respect. The old housekeeper told me that she had paid the first week in advance, taking a receipt, and had gone, as she had come, in a sedan-chair. Then the worthy old woman made free to tell me to be on my guard.

"Against what? If I fall in love with her, so much the better; that is just what I want. What name did she give you?"

"Mistress Pauline. She was quite pale when she came and she went away covered with blushes."

CHAPTER XVIII

The Charpillon

*T*HE *romantic story of Pauline, who turns out to be a Portuguese lady of very high degree and whom a mysterious fate tears from his arms at the height of their felicity, under circumstances similar to those which brought about the parting with Henriette, belongs too obviously to the category of the interpolated romance, which had become a popular device of the novelist of those days, to have any biographical value. Artistically its purpose here would seem to be once more that of contrasting the romantic love-idyll with the crude verities of a Casanovian existence. At the same time it is the swan-song of the romantic lover whose rôle in the Memoirs is now over.[1] For Nemesis in the person of Mdlle. Charpillon is already drawing near.*

[1]*As if to forestall the reader's making the remark for himself, Casanova points out the analogy between the two episodes:*

The analogy between my parting with Pauline and my parting with Henriette fifteen years before, was exceedingly striking; the two women were of very similar character, and both were equally beautiful, though their beauty was of a different kind. Thus I fell madly in love with the second as with the first, both being equally intelligent. The fact that one had more talent and less prejudices than the other must have been an effect of their different educations. Pauline had the fine pride of her nation, her mind was of a serious cast, and her religion was more of an affair of the heart than the understanding. She was also a far more ardent mistress than Henriette. I was successful with both of them because I was rich, if I had been a poor man I should never have known either of them. I have half forgotten them, as everything is forgotten in time, but when I recall them to my memory I find that Henriette made the profounder impression on me, no doubt because I was twenty-five when I knew her, while I was thirty-seven in London.

The older I get, the more I feel the destructive effects of old age; and I regret bitterly that I could not discover the secret of remaining young and happy for ever. Vain regrets! We must finish as we began, helpless and devoid of sense.

Simultaneously with parting from Pauline and romance in general, the Memoirs give the coup de grâce, *to that other romantic, but not fictitious, person: the Marquise d'Urfé:*

The 1st of August was a fatal day for both of us. Pauline received a letter from Lisbon, which summoned her home without delay, and I had a letter from Paris announcing the death of Madame d'Urfé. Madame du Rumain told me that on the evidence of her maid the doctors had pronounced her

A Flemish officer, the man whom I had helped at Aix-la-Chapelle, had called on me several times, and had even dined three or four times with me. I reproached myself for not having been polite enough to return his call, and when we met in the street, and he reproached me for not having been to see him, I was obliged to blush. He had his wife and daughter with him, and some feeling of shame and a good deal of curiosity made me call on him.

When he saw me he threw his arms about my neck, calling me his preserver. I was obliged to receive all the compliments which knaves make to honest men when they hope to take them in. A few moments after, an old woman and a girl came in, and I was introduced as the Chevalier de Seingalt, of whom he had spoken so often. The girl, affecting surprise, said she had known a M. Casanova, who was very like me. I answered that Casanova was my name as well as Seingalt, but that I had not the happiness of recollecting her.

"My name was Anspergher when I saw you," she replied, "but now it is Charpillon; and considering that we only met once, and that I was only thirteen at the time, I do not wonder at your not recollecting me. I have been in London with my mother and aunts for the last four years."

"But where had I the pleasure of speaking to you?"

"At Paris."

"In what part of Paris?"

---

death to be due to an overdose of the liquid she called "The Panacea." She added that a will had been found which savoured of a lunatic asylum, for she had left all her wealth to the son or daughter that should be born of her, declaring that she was with child. I was to be the governor of the infant; this vexed me exceedingly, as I knew I should be the laughing-stock of Paris for a week at least. Her daughter, the Comtesse de Chatelet, had taken possession of all her real estate and of her pocket-book, which contained, to my surprise, four hundred thousand francs. It was a great shock for me, but the contents of the two letters Pauline had received was a greater blow.

What Casanova's reasons were for killing off his generous patron twelve years before her real death, which took place in 1775, we may not know, though we may surmise. It is probable that after the last hoax the lady's family brought her round to her senses. In this connection it is interesting to consult the curious series of letters written by Casanova's accomplice, the so-called Count Passano, alias Pogamas, denouncing the former to the Marquise. These letters, discovered in a provincial library near the ancestral home of the d'Urfé family, have been published by M. Samaran in his admirable work, already mentioned.

[205]

"In the Bazaar. You were with a charming lady, and you gave me these buckles" (she showed me them on her shoes), "and you also did me the honour to kiss me."

I recollected the circumstance, and the reader will remember that I was with Madame Baret, the fair stocking-seller.

"Now I remember you," said I; "but I do not recognise your aunt."

"This is the sister of the one you saw, but if you will take tea with us you will see her."

"Where do you live?"

"In Denmark Street, Soho."

The name Charpillon reminded me that I was the bearer of a letter for her, and drawing it from my pocket-book I gave it her, saying that the document ought to cement our acquaintance.

"What!" she exclaimed, "a letter from the dear ambassador Morosini. How delighted I am to have it! And you have actually been all these months in London without giving it me?"

"I confess I am to blame, but, as you see, the note has no address on it. I am grateful for the chance which has enabled me to discharge my commission to-day."

"Come and dine with us to-morrow."

"I cannot do so, as I am expecting Lord Pembroke to dinner."

"Will you be alone?"

"I expect so."

"I am glad to hear it; you will see my aunt and myself appearing on the scene."

"Here is my address; and I shall be delighted if you will come and see me."

She took the address, and I was surprised to see her smile as she read it.

"Then you are the Italian," she said, "who put up that notice that amused all the town?"

"I am."

"They say the joke cost you dear."

"Quite the reverse; it resulted in the greatest happiness."

"But now that the beloved object has left you, I suppose you are unhappy?"

"I am; but there are sorrows so sweet that they are almost joys."

"Nobody knows who she was, but I suppose you do?"

"Yes."

"Do you make a mystery of it?"

"Surely, and I would rather die than reveal it."

"Ask my aunt if I may take some rooms in your house; but I am afraid my mother would not let me."

"Why, do you want to lodge cheaply?"

"I don't want to lodge cheaply, but I should like to punish the audacious author of that notice."

"How would you punish me?"

"By making you fall in love with me, and then tormenting you. It would have amused me immensely."

"Then you think that you can inspire me with love, and at the same time form the dreadful plan of tyrannising over the victim of your charms. Such a project is monstrous, and, unhappily for us poor men, you do not look a monster. Nevertheless, I am obliged to you for your frankness, and I shall be on my guard."

"Then you must take care never to see me, or else all your efforts will be in vain."

As the Charpillon had laughed merrily through the whole of this dialogue, I took it all as a jest, but I could not help admiring her manner, which seemed made for the subjugation of men. But though I knew it not, the day I made that woman's acquaintance was a luckless one for me, as my readers will see.

It was towards the end of the month of September, 1763, when I met the Charpillon, and from that day I began to die. If the lines of ascent and declination are equal, now, on this first day of November, 1797, I have about four more years of life to reckon on, which will pass by swiftly, according to the axiom *Motus in fine velocior*.

The Charpillon, who was well known in London, and I believe is still alive, was one of those beauties in whom it is difficult to find any positive fault. Her hair was chestnut coloured, and astonishingly long and thick, her blue eyes were at once languorous and brilliant, her skin, faintly tinged with a rosy hue, was of a dazzling whiteness; she was tall for her age, and seemed likely to become as tall as Pauline. Her breast was perhaps a little small, but perfectly shaped, her hands were white and plump, her feet small, and her gait had something noble and gracious. Her features were of that exquisite sensibility which gives so much charm to the fair sex, but nature had given her a beautiful body and a deformed soul. This siren had formed a design to wreck my happiness even before she knew me, and as if to add to her triumph she told me as much.

I left Malingan's house not like a man who, fond of the fair sex, is glad to have made the acquaintance of a beautiful woman, but in a state of stupefaction that the image of Pauline, which was always before me, was not strong enough to overcome the influence of a creature like the Charpillon, whom in my heart I could not help despising.

I calmed myself by saying that this strong impression was due to novelty, and by hoping that I should soon be disenchanted.

"She will have no charm," said I, "when I have once possessed her, and that will not be long in coming."

Perhaps the reader will think that I was too presumptuous, but why should I suppose that there would be any difficulty? She had asked me to dinner herself, she had surrendered herself entirely to Morosini, who was not the man to sigh for long at any woman's feet, and must have paid her, for he was not young enough nor handsome enough to inspire her with a fancy for him. Without counting my physical attractions, I had plenty of money, and I was not afraid of spending it; and so I thought I could count on an easy victory.

Pembroke had become an intimate friend of mine since my proceedings with regard to Schwerin. He admired my conduct in not making any claim on the general for half my loss. He had said we would make a pleasant day of it together, and when he saw that my table was laid for four he asked who the other guests were to be. He was extremely surprised when he heard that they were the Charpillon and her aunt, and that the girl had invited herself when she heard he was to dine with me.

"I once took a violent fancy for the little hussy," said he. "It was one evening when I was at Vauxhall, and I offered her twenty guineas if she would come and take a little walk with me in a dark alley. She said she would come if I gave her the money in advance, which I was fool enough to do. She went with me, but as soon as we were alone she ran away, and I could not catch her again, though I looked for her all the evening."

"You ought to have boxed her ears before everybody."

"I should have got into trouble, and people would have laughed at me besides. I preferred to despise her and the money too. Are you in love with her?"

"No; but I am curious, as you were."

"Take care! she will do all in her power to entrap you."

She came in and went up to my lord with the most perfect coolness, and began to chatter away to him without taking any notice of me. She laughed, joked, and reproached him for not having pursued her at Vauxhall. Her stratagem, she said, was only meant to excite him the more.

"Another time," she added, "I shall not escape you."

"Perhaps not, my dear, for another time I shall take care not to pay in advance."

"Oh, fie! you degrade yourself by talking about paying."

"I suppose I honour you."

"We never talk of such things."

Lord Pembroke laughed at her impertinences, while she made a vigorous assault on him, for his coolness and indifference piqued her.

She left soon after dinner, making me promise to dine with her the day after next.

I passed the next day with the amiable nobleman who initiated me into the mysteries of the English bagnio, an entertainment which I shall not describe, for it is well known to all who care to spend six guineas.

On the day appointed, my evil destiny made me go to the Charpillon's; the girl introduced me to her mother, whom I at once recollected, although she had aged and altered since I had seen her.

In the year 1759 a Genevan named Bolomé had persuaded me to sell her jewels to the extent of six thousand francs, and she had paid me in bills drawn by her and her two sisters on this Bolomé, but they were then known as Anspergher. The Genevan became bankrupt before the bills were due, and the three sisters disappeared. As may be imagined, I was surprised to find them in England, and especially to be introduced to them by the Charpillon, who, knowing nothing of the affair of the jewels, had not told them that Seingalt was the same as Casanova, whom they had cheated of six thousand francs.

"I am delighted to see you again," were the first words I addressed to her.

"I recollect you, sir; that rascal Bolomé . . ."

"We will discuss that subject another time. I see you are ill."

"I have been at death's door, but I am better now. My daughter did not tell me your proper name."

"Yes, she did. My name is Seingalt as well as Casanova. I was known by the latter name at Paris when I made your daughter's acquaintance, though I did not know then that she was your daughter."

Just then the grandmother, whose name was also Anspergher, came in with the two aunts, and a quarter of an hour later three men arrived, one of whom was the Chevalier Goudar, whom I had met at Paris. I did not know the others who were introduced to me under the names of Rostaing and Caumon. They were three friends of the household, whose business it was to bring in dupes.

Such was the infamous company in which I found myself, and though I took its measure directly, yet I did not make my escape, nor did I resolve never to go to the house again. I was fascinated; I thought I would be on my guard and be safe, and as I only wanted the daughter I looked on all else as of little moment.

At table I led the conversation, and thought that my prey would soon be within my grasp. The only thing which annoyed me was that the Charpillon, after apologising for having made me sit down to such a poor dinner, invited herself and all the company to sup with me on any day I liked to mention. I could make no opposition, so I begged her to name the day herself, and she did so, after a consultation with her worthy friends.

After coffee had been served we played four rubbers of whist, at which I lost, and at midnight I went away ill pleased with myself, but with no purpose of amendment, for this sorceress had got me in her toils.

All the same, I had the strength of mind to refrain from seeing her for two days, and on the third, which was the day appointed for the cursed supper, she and her aunt paid me a call at nine o'clock in the morning.

"I have come to breakfast with you, and to discuss a certain question," said she, in the most engaging manner.

"Will you tell me your business now, or after breakfast?"

"After breakfast; for we must be alone."

We had our breakfast, and then the aunt went into another room, and the Charpillon, after describing the monetary situation of the family, told me that it would be much relieved if her aunt could obtain a hundred guineas.

"What would she do with the money?"

"She would make the Balm of Life, of which she possesses the secret, and no doubt she would make her fortune, too."

She then began to dilate on the marvellous properties of the balm, on its probable success in a town like London, and on the benefits which would accrue to myself, for of course I should share in the profits. She added that her mother and aunt would give me a written promise to repay the money in the course of six years.

"I will give you a decided answer after supper."

I then began to caress her, but it was all in vain. She made her escape and ran to her aunt, while I followed her, feeling obliged to laugh as she did. She gave me her hand, and said:

"Farewell, till this evening."

When they were gone, I reflected over what had passed and thought this first scene of no bad augury. I saw that I should get nothing out of her without spending a hundred guineas, and I determined not to attempt to bargain, but I would let her understand that she must make up her mind not to play prude. The game was in my hands, and all I had to do was to take care not to be duped.

In the evening the company arrived, and the girl asked me to hold a bank till supper was ready ; but I declined, with a burst of laughter that seemed to puzzle her.

"At least, let us have a game of whist," said she.

"It seems to me," I answered, "that you don't feel very anxious to hear my reply."

"You have made up your mind, I suppose?"

"I have, follow me."

She followed me into an adjoining room, and after she had seated herself on a sofa, I told her that the hundred guineas were at her disposal.

"Then please to give the money to my aunt, otherwise these gentlemen might think I got it from you by some improper means."

"I will do so."

I tried to get possession of her, but in vain; and I ceased my endeavours when she said:

"You will get nothing from me either by money or violence; but you can hope for all when I find you really nice and quiet."

I re-entered the drawing-room, and feeling my blood boiling I began to play to quiet myself. She was as gay as ever, but her gaiety tired me. At supper I had her on my right hand, but the hundred impertinences which, under other circumstances, would have amused me, only wearied me, after the two rebuffs I had received from her.

After supper, just as they were going, she took me aside, and told me that if I wanted to hand over the hundred guineas she would tell her aunt to go with me into the next room.

"As documents have to be executed," I replied, "it will take some time; we will talk of it again."

"Won't you fix the time?"

I drew out my purse full of gold, and showed it her, saying:

"The time depends entirely on you."

When my hateful guests were gone, I began to reflect, and came to the conclusion that this young adventuress had determined to plunder me without giving me anything in return. I determined to have nothing more to do with her, but I could not get her beauty out of my mind.

I felt I wanted some distraction, something that would give me new aims and make me forget her. With this idea I went to see my daughter, taking with me an immense bag of sweets.

As soon as I was in the midst of the little flock, the delight became general, Sophie distributing the sweetmeats to her friends, who received them gratefully.

I spent a happy day, and for a week or two I paid several visits to Harwich. The mistress treated me with the utmost politeness and my daughter with boundless affection, always calling me "dear papa."

In less than three weeks I congratulated myself on having forgotten the Charpillon, and on having replaced her by innocent amours, though one of my daughter's schoolmates pleased me rather too much for my peace of mind.

Such was my condition when one morning the favourite aunt of the Charpillon paid me a call, and said that they were all mystified at not having seen me since the supper I had given them, especially herself, as her niece had given her to understand that I would furnish her with the means of making the Balm of Life.

"Certainly; I would have given you the hundred guineas if your niece had treated me as a friend, but she has refused me favours a vestal might have granted, and you must be aware that she is by no means a vestal."

"Don't mind my laughing. My niece is an innocent, giddy girl; she loves you, but she is afraid you have only a passing whim for her. She is in bed now with a bad cold, and if you will come and see her I am sure you will be satisfied."

These artful remarks, which had no doubt been prepared in advance, ought to have aroused all my scorn, but instead of that they awakened the most violent desires. I laughed in chorus with the old woman, and asked what would be the best time to call.

"Come now, and give one knock."

"Very good, then you may expect me shortly."

I congratulated myself on being on the verge of success, for after the explanation I had had with the aunt, and having, as I thought, a friend in her, I did not doubt that I should succeed.

I put on my great coat, and in less than a quarter of an hour I knocked at their door. The aunt opened to me, and said:

"Come back in a quarter of an hour; she has been ordered a bath, and is just going to take it."

"This is another imposture. You're as bad a liar as she is."

"You are cruel and unjust, and if you will promise to be discreet, I will take you up to the third floor, where she is bathing."

"Very good; take me." She went upstairs, I following on tiptoe, and pushed me into a room, and shut the door upon me. The Charpillon was in a huge bath, with her head towards the door, and the infernal coquette, pretending to think it was her aunt, did not move, and said:

"Give me the towels, aunt."

When she caught sight of me, or rather pretended to do so, she gave a shriek, huddled her limbs together, and said, with affected anger:

"Begone!"

"You needn't exert your voice, for I am not going to be duped."

"Begone!"

"Not so, give me a little time to collect myself."

"I tell you, go!"

"Calm yourself, and don't be afraid of my showing you any violence; that would suit your game too well."

"My aunt shall pay dearly for this."

"She will find me her friend. I won't touch you."

"Leave the room."

"I have told you I am not going, and that you need not fear."

She then, pretending kindliness, said:

"Please leave me; I will not fail to show my gratitude."

Seeing that she got nothing, and that I refrained from touching her, she turned her back to me to give me to understand that it was no pleasure to her to look at me.

The aunt came in and I went out without a word, well pleased to find myself despising a character wherein profit and loss usurped the place of feeling.

The aunt came to me as I was going out of the house, and after inquiring if I were satisfied begged me to come into the parlour.

"Yes," said I, "I am perfectly satisfied — to know you and your niece. Here is the reward."

With these words I drew a bank-note for a hundred pounds from my pocket-book, and was foolish enough to give it her, telling her that she could make her balm, and need not trouble to give me any document, as I knew it would be of no value. I had not the strength to go away without giving her anything, and the procuress was sharp enough to know it.

When I got home I reflected on what had happened, and pronounced myself the conqueror with great triumph. I felt well at ease, and felt sure that I should never set foot in that house again. There were seven of them altogether, including servants, and the need of subsisting made them do anything for a living; and when they found themselves obliged to make use of men, they summoned the three rascals I have named, who were equally dependent on them.

Five or six days afterwards, I met the little hussy at Vauxhall in company with Goudar. I avoided her at first, but she came up to me reproaching me for my rudeness. I replied coolly enough, but affecting not to notice my manner, she asked me to come into an arbour with her and take a cup of tea.

"No, thank you," I replied, "I prefer supper."

"Then I will take some too, and you will give it me, won't you, just to show that you bear no malice?"

I ordered supper for four and we sat down together as if we had been intimate friends.

Her charming conversation combined with her beauty gradually drew me under her charm, and as the drink began to exercise its influence over me, I proposed a turn in one of the dark walks, expressing a hope that I should fare better than Lord Pembroke. She said gently, and with an appearance of sincerity that deceived me, that she wanted to be mine, but by day and on the condition that I would come and see her every day.

"I will do so, but first give me one little proof of your love."

"Most certainly not."

I got up to pay the bill, and then I left without a word, refusing to take her home. I went home by myself and went to bed.

The first thought when I awoke was that I was glad she had not taken me at my word; I felt very strongly that it was to my interest to break off all connection between that creature and myself. I felt the strength of her influence over me, and that my only way was to keep away from her, or to renounce all pretension to the possession of her charms.

The latter plan seemed to me impossible, so I determined to adhere to the first; but the wretched woman had resolved to defeat all my plans. The manner in which she succeeded must have been the result of a council of the whole society.

A few days after the Vauxhall supper Goudar called on me, and began by congratulating me on my resolution not to visit the Anspberghers any more, "for," said he, "the girl would have made you more and more in love with her, and in the end she would have reduced you to beggary."

"You must think me a great fool. If I had found her kind I should have been grateful, but without squandering all my money; and if she had been cruel, instead of ridiculous, I might have given her what I have already given her every day, without reducing myself to beggary."

"I congratulate you; it shows that you are well off. But have you made up your mind not to see her again?"

"Certainly."

"Then you are not in love with her?"

"I have been in love, but I am so no longer; and in a few days she will have passed completely out of my memory. I had almost forgotten her when I met her with you at Vauxhall."

"You are not cured. The way to be cured of an amour does not lie in flight, when the two parties live in the same town. Meetings will happen, and all the trouble has to be taken over again."

"Then do you know a better way?"

"Certainly; you should satiate yourself. It is quite possible that the creature is not in love with you, but you are rich and she has nothing. You might have had her for so much, and you could have left her when you found her to be unworthy of your constancy. You must know what kind of woman she is."

"I should have tried this method gladly, but I found her out."

"You could have got the best of her, though, if you had gone to work in the proper way. You should never have paid in advance. I know everything."

"What do you mean?"

"I know she has cost you a hundred guineas, and that you have not won so much as a kiss from her. She boasts that she took you in, though you pride yourself on your craft."

"It was an act of charity towards her aunt."

"Yes, to make her Balm of Life; but you know if it had not been for the niece the aunt would never have had the money."

"Perhaps not, but how come you who are of their party to be talking to me in this fashion?"

"I swear to you I only speak out of friendship for you, and I will tell you how I came to make the acquaintance of the girl, her mother, her grandmother, and her two aunts, and then you will no longer consider me as of their party.

"Sixteen months ago I saw M. Morosini walking about Vauxhall by himself. He had just come to England to congratulate the king on his accession to the throne, on behalf of the Republic of Venice. I saw how enchanted he was with the London beauties, and I went up to him and told him that all these beauties were at his service. This made him laugh, and on my repeating that it was not a jest he pointed out one of the girls, and asked if she would be at his service. I did not know her, so I asked him to wait awhile, and I would bring him the information he required. There was no time to be lost, and I could see that the girl was not a vestal virgin, so I went up to her and told her that the Venetian ambassador was amorous of her, and that I would take her to him if she would receive his visits. The aunt said that a nobleman of such an exalted rank could only bring honour to her niece. I took their address, and on my way back to the ambassador I met a friend of mine who is learned in such commodities, and after I had showed him the address he told me it was the Charpillon."

"And it was she?"

"It was. My friend told me she was a young Swiss girl who was not yet in the general market, but who would soon be there, as she was not rich, and had a numerous train to support.

"I rejoined the Venetian, and told him that his business was done, and asked him at what time I should introduce him the next day, warning him that as she had a mother and aunts she would not be alone.

"'I am glad to hear it,' said he, 'and also that she is not a common woman.' He gave me an appointment for the next day, and we parted.

"I told the ladies at what hour I should have the pleasure of introducing the great man to them, and after warning them that they must appear not to know him I went home.

"The following day I called on M. de Morosini, and took him to Denmark Street incognito. We spent an hour in conversation, and then went away without anything being settled. On the way back the ambassador told me that he should like to have the girl on conditions which he would give me in writing at his residence.

"These conditions were that she should live in a furnished house free of rent, without any companion, and without receiving any visitors. His excellency would give her fifty guineas a month and pay for supper whenever he came. He told me to get the house if his conditions were received. The mother was to sign the agreement.

"The ambassador was in a hurry, and in three days the agreement was signed; but I obtained a document from the mother promising to let me have the girl for one night as soon as the Venetian had gone; it was known he was only stopping in London for a year."

Goudar extracted the document in question from his pocket, and gave it me. I read it and re-read it with as much surprise as pleasure, and he then proceeded with his story.

"When the ambassador had gone, the Charpillon, finding herself at liberty once more, had Lord Baltimore, Lord Grosvenor, and M. de Saa, the Portuguese ambassador, in turn, but no titular lover. I insisted on having my night with her according to agreement, but both mother and daughter laughed at me when I spoke of it. I cannot arrest her, because she is a minor, but I will have the mother imprisoned on the first opportunity, and you will see how the town will laugh. Now you know why I go to their house; and I assure you you are wrong if you think I have any part in their councils. Nevertheless, I know they are discussing how they may catch you, and they will do so if you do not take care."

"Tell the mother that I have another hundred guineas at her service if she will let me have her daughter for a single night."

"Do you mean that?"

"Assuredly, but I am not going to pay in advance."

"That's the only way not to be duped. I shall be glad to execute your commission."

I kept the rogue to dinner, thinking he might be useful to me. He knew everything and everybody, and told me a number of amusing anecdotes. Although a good-for-nothing fellow, he had his merits.

He had written several works, which, though badly constructed, showed he was a man of some wit. He was then writing his "Chinese Spy," and every day he wrote five or six news-letters from the various coffee-houses he frequented. I wrote one or two letters for him, with which he was much pleased.

The next morning, what was my surprise to see the Charpillon, who said with an air that I should have taken for modesty in any other woman:

"I don't want you to give me any breakfast, I want an explanation, and to introduce Miss Lorenzi to you."

I bowed to her and to her companion, and then said:

"What explanation do you require?"

At this, Miss Lorenzi, whom I had never seen before, thought proper to leave us, and I told my man that I was not at home to anybody. I ordered breakfast to be served to the companion of the nymph, that she might not find the waiting tedious.

"Sir," said the Charpillon, "is it a fact that you charged the Chevalier Goudar to tell my mother that you would give a hundred guineas to spend the night with me?"

"No, not to spend a night with you, but after I had passed it. Isn't the price enough?"

"No jesting, sir, if you please. There is no question of bargaining; all I want to know is whether you think you have a right to insult me, and that I am going to bear it?"

"If you think yourself insulted, I may, perhaps, confess I was wrong; but I confess I did not think I should have to listen to any reproaches from you. Goudar is one of your intimate friends, and this is not the first proposal he has taken to you. I could not address you directly, as I know your arts only too well."

"I shall not pay any attention to your abuse of myself; I will only remind you of what I said — 'that neither money nor violence were of any use,' and that your only way was to make me in love with you by gentle means. Show me where I have broken my word! It is you that have foresworn yourself in coming into my bath-room, and in sending such a brutal message to my mother. No one but a rascal like Goudar would have dared to take such a message."

"Goudar a rascal, is he? Well, he is your best friend. You know he is in love with you, and that he only got you for the ambassador in the hope of enjoying you himself. The document in his possession proves that you behaved badly towards him. You are in his debt, discharge it, and then call him a rascal if you have the conscience to do so. You need not trouble to weep, for I know the source of those tears; it is defiled."

"You know nothing of it. I love you, and it is hard to have you treat me so."

"You love me? You have not taken the best way to prove it."

"As good a way as yours. You have behaved to me as if I were the vilest of prostitutes, and yesterday you seemed to think I was a brute beast, the slave of my mother. You should have written to me in person, and without the intervention of so vile an agent; I should have replied in the same way, and you need not have been afraid that you would be deceived."

"Supposing I had written, what would your answer have been?"

"I should have put all money matters out of question. I should have promised to content you on the condition that you would come and court me for a fortnight without demanding the slightest favour. We should have lived a pleasant life; we should have gone to the theatre and to the parks. I should have become madly in love with you. Then I should have given myself up to you for love, and nothing but love. I am ashamed to say that hitherto I have only given myself out of mere complaisance. Unhappy woman that I am! but I think nature meant me to love, and I thought when I saw you that my happy star had sent you to England that I might know the bliss of true affection. Instead of this you have only made me unhappy. You are the first man that has seen me weep; you have troubled my peace at home, for my mother shall never have the sum you promised her were it for nothing but a kiss."

"I am sorry to have injured you, though I did not intend to do so; but I really don't know what I can do."

"Come and see us, and keep your money, which I despise. If you love me, come and conquer me like a reasonable and not a brutal lover; and I will help you, for now you cannot doubt that I love you."

All this seemed so natural to me that I never dreamed it contained a trap. I was caught, and I promised to do what she wished, but only for a fortnight. She confirmed her promise, and her countenance became once more serene and calm. The Charpillon was a born actress.

She got up to go, and on my begging a kiss as a pledge of our reconciliation she replied, with a smile, the charm of which she well knew, that it would not do to begin by breaking the term of our agreement, and she left me more in love than ever, and full of repentance for my conduct.

The siren keeps her promise in the letter, but not in the spirit, with the result that the baffled and furious lover gives her a thrashing, which she richly deserved. Her vengeance is to feign remorse and effect a reconciliation, on the understanding that she will henceforth live with Casanova, as she had already done with his countryman Morosini. Needless to say, since the gods have struck him with madness in order to destroy him, he falls into the trap and engages a house in Chelsea — "our country-house," as he calls it. The girl moves in her belongings, and all seems for the best, but again the reward is withheld from him under one pretext or another. Seeing him submissive and patient, she begins to taunt him (one cannot help admiring her temerity!), till, losing all control, he knocks her down. A tragedy might have followed had not the landlord interfered.

The man fortunately spoke Italian, and told me that she wanted to go away, and advised me to let her do so, or she might make it awkward for me, and he himself would be obliged to witness against me.

"Tell her to begone as fast as she likes," said I, "and to keep out of my sight for ever."

She finished dressing, staunched the blood, and went off in a sedan-chair, while I remained petrified, feeling that I did not deserve to live, and finding her conduct utterly outrageous and incomprehensible.

After an hour's consideration I decided on sending her back her trunk, and then I went home and to bed, telling my servants I was not at home to anyone.

I spent twenty-four hours in pondering over my wrongs, and at last my reason told me that the fault was mine; I despised myself. I was on the brink of suicide, but happily I escaped that fate.

I was just going out when Goudar came up and made me go in with him, as he said he wanted to speak to me. After telling me that the Charpillon had come home with a swollen cheek which prevented her showing herself, he advised me to abandon all claims on her or her mother, or the latter would bring a false accusation against me which might cost me my life. Those who know England, and especially London, will not need to be informed as to the nature of this accusation, which is so easily brought in England; it will suffice to say that through it Sodom was overwhelmed.

"The mother has engaged me to mediate," said Goudar, "and if you leave her alone, she will do you no harm."

I spent the day with him, foolishly complaining, and telling him that he could assure the mother that I would take no proceedings against her, but that I should like to know if she had the courage to receive this assurance from my own lips.

"I will carry your message," said he, "but I pity you; for you are going into their nets again, and will end in utter ruin."

I fancied they would be ashamed to see me; but I was very

much mistaken, for Goudar came back laughing, and said the mother expressed a hope that I should always be the friend of the family. I ought to have refused to have anything more to do with them, but I had not the strength to play the man. I called at Denmark Street the same evening, and spent an hour without uttering a syllable. The Charpillon sat opposite to me, with eyes lowered to a piece of embroidery, while from time to time she pretended to wipe away a tear as she let me see the ravages I had worked on her cheek.

I saw her every day and always in silence till the fatal mark had disappeared, but during these mad visits the poison of desire was so instilled into my veins that if she had known my state of mind she might have despoiled me of all I possessed for a single favour.

When she was once more as beautiful as ever I felt as if I must die if I did not hold her in my arms again, and I bought a magnificent pier-glass and a splendid breakfast service in Dresden china, and sent them to her with an amorous epistle which must have made her think me either the most extravagant or the most cowardly of men. She wrote in answer that she would expect me to sup with her in her room, that she might give me the tenderest proofs of her gratitude.

This letter sent me completely mad with joy, and in a paroxysm of delight I resolved to surrender to her keeping the two bills of exchange which Bolomé had given me, and which gave me power to send her mother and aunts to prison.

Full of the happiness that awaited me, and enchanted with my own idiotic heroism, I went to her in the evening. She received me in the parlour with her mother, and I was delighted to see the pier-glass over the mantel, and the china displayed on a little table. After a hundred words of love and tenderness she asked me to come up to her room, and her mother wished us good night. I was overwhelmed with joy. After a delicate little supper I took out the bills of exchange, and after telling her their history gave them up to her, to show that I had no intention of avenging myself on her mother and aunts. I made her promise that she would never part with them, and she said she would never do so, and with many expressions of gratitude and wonder at my generosity she locked them up with great care.

Then I thought it was time to give her some marks of my passion, and I found her kind; but she began to weep bitterly.

For a quarter of an hour I remained silent and motionless, as if petrified. At last I rose with apparent coolness, and took my cloak and sword.

"What!" said she, "are you not going to spend the night with me?"

"No."

"But we shall see each other to-morrow?"

"I hope so. Good-night."

I left that infernal abode, and went home to bed.

At eight o'clock the next morning Jarbe told me that the Charpillon wanted to see me, and that she had sent away her chairman.

"Tell her that I can't see her."

But I had hardly spoken when she came in, and Jarbe went out. I addressed her with the utmost calmness, and begged her to give me back the two bills of exchange I had placed in her hands the night before.

"I haven't got them about me; but why do you want me to return them to you?"

At this question I could contain myself no longer, and launched a storm of abuse at her. It was an explosion which relieved nature, and ended with an involuntary shower of tears. My infamous seductress stood as calmly as Innocence itself; and when I was so choked with sobs that I could not utter a word, she said she had only been cruel because her mother had made her swear an oath never to give herself to anyone in her own house, and that she had only come now to convince me of her love, to give herself up to me without reserve, and never to leave me any more if I wished it.

The reader who imagines that at these words rage gave place to love, and that I hastened to obtain the prize, does not know the nature of the passion so well as the vile woman whose plaything I was. From hot love to hot anger is a short journey, but the return is slow and difficult. If there be only anger in a man's breast it may be subdued by tenderness, by submission, and affection; but when to anger is added a feeling of indignation at having been shamefully deceived, it is impossible to pass suddenly to thoughts of love and voluptuous enjoyment. With me mere anger has never been of long duration, but when I am indignant the only cure is forgetfulness.

The Charpillon knew perfectly well that I would not take her at her word, and this kind of science was inborn in her. The instinct of women teaches them greater secrets than all the philosophy and the research of men.

In the evening this monster left me, feigning to be disappointed and disconsolate, and saying:

"I hope you will come and see me again when you are once more yourself."

She had spent eight hours with me, during which time she had only spoken to deny my suppositions, which were perfectly true, but which she could not afford to let pass. I had not taken anything all day, in order that I might not be obliged to offer her anything or to eat with her.

After she had left me I took some soup and then enjoyed a quiet sleep, for which I felt all the better. When I came to consider what had passed the day before I concluded that the Charpillon was repentant, but I seemed no longer to care anything about her.

Here I may as well confess, in all humility, what a change love worked on me in London, though I had attained the age of thirty-eight. Here closed the first act of my life; the second closed when I left Venice in 1783, and probably the third will close here, as I amuse myself by writing these Memoirs. Thus, the three-act comedy will finish, and if it be hissed, as may possibly be the case, I shall not hear the sounds of disapproval. But as yet the reader has not seen the last and I think the most interesting scene of the first act.

I went for a walk in the Green Park and met Goudar. I was glad to see him, as the rogue was useful to me.

"I have just been at the Charpillons'," he began; "they were all in high spirits. I tried in vain to turn the conversation on you, but not a word would they utter."

"I despise them entirely," I rejoined, "I don't want to have anything more to do with them."

He told me I was quite right, and advised me to persevere in my plan. I made him dine with me, and then we went to see the well-known procuress, Mrs. Wells, and saw the celebrated courtesan, Kitty Fisher, who was waiting for the Duke of ** to take her to a ball. She was magnificently dressed, and it is no exaggeration to say that she had on diamonds worth five hundred thousand francs. Goudar told me that if I liked I might have her then and there for ten guineas. I did not care to do so, however, for, though charming, she could only speak English, and I liked to have all my senses, including that of hearing, gratified. When she had gone, Mrs. Wells told us that Kitty had eaten a bank-note for a thousand guineas, on a slice of bread and butter, that very day. The note was a present from Sir ** Akins, brother of the fair Mrs. Pitt. I do not know whether the bank thanked Kitty for the present she had made it.

I spent an hour with a girl named Kennedy, a fair Irishwoman, who could speak a sort of French, and behaved most extravagantly under the influence of champagne; but the image of the Charpillon was still before me, though I knew it not, and I could not enjoy anything. I went home feeling sad and ill pleased with myself. Common sense told me to drive all thoughts of that wretched woman out of my head, but something I called honour bade me not leave her the triumph of having won the two bills of exchange from me for nothing, and made me determine to get them back by fair means or foul.

M. Malingan, at whose house I had made the acquaintance of this creature, came and asked me to dinner. He had asked me to dine with him several times before, and I had always refused, and now I would not accept until I had heard what guests he had invited. The names were all strange to me, so I agreed to come.

When I arrived I found two young ladies from Liège, in one of whom I got interested directly. She introduced me to her husband, and to another young man who seemed to be the cavalier of the other lady, her cousin.

The company pleased me, and I was in hopes that I should spend a happy day, but my evil genius brought the Charpillon to mar the feast. She came into the room in high glee, and said to Malingan:

"I should not have come to beg you to give me a dinner if I had known that you would have so many guests, and if I am at all in the way I will go."

Everybody welcomed her, myself excepted, for I was on the rack. To make matters worse, she was placed at my left hand. If she had come in before we sat down to dinner I should have made some excuse and gone away, but as we had begun the soup a sudden flight would have covered me with ridicule. I adopted the plan of not looking at her, reserving all my politeness for the lady on my right. When the meal was over Malingan took me apart, and swore to me that he had not invited the Charpillon, but I was not convinced, though I pretended to be for politeness' sake.

The two ladies from Liège and their cavaliers were embarking for Ostend in a few days, and in speaking of their departure the one to whom I had taken a fancy said that she was sorry to be leaving England without having seen Richmond. I begged her to give me the pleasure of showing it her, and without waiting for an answer I asked her husband and all the company to be present, excepting the Charpillon, whom I pretended not to see.

The invitation was accepted.

"Two carriages," I said, "holding four each, shall be ready at eight o'clock, and we shall be exactly eight."

"No, nine, for I am coming," said the Charpillon, giving me an impudent stare, "and I hope you will not drive me away."

"No, that would be impolite, I will ride in front on horseback."

"Oh, not at all! Emilie shall sit on my lap."

Emilie was Malingan's daughter, and as everybody seemed to think the arrangement an extremely pleasant one I had not the courage to resist. A few moments after, I was obliged to leave the room for a few moments, and when I came back I met her on the landing. She told me I had insulted her grievously, and that unless I made amends I should feel her vengeance.

"You can begin your vengeance," I said, "by returning my bills of exchange."

"You shall have them to-morrow, but you had better try and make me forget the insult you have put on me."

I left the company in the evening, having arranged that we should all breakfast together the next day.

At eight o'clock the two carriages were ready, and Malingan, his wife, his daughter, and the two gentlemen got into the first vehicle, and I had to get into the second with the ladies from Liège and the Charpillon, who seemed to have become very intimate with them. This made me ill-tempered, and I sulked the whole way. We were an hour and a quarter on the journey, and when we arrived I ordered a good dinner, and then we proceeded to view the gardens; the day was a beautiful one, though it was autumn.

Whilst we were talking the Charpillon came up to me and said she wanted to return the bills in the same place in which I had given her them. As we were at some distance from the others I pelted her with abuse, telling her of her perfidy and of her corruption at an age when she should have retained some vestiges of innocence, calling her by the name she deserved, as I reminded her how often she had already prostituted herself; in short I threatened her with my vengeance if she pushed me to extremities. But she was as cold as ice, and opposed a calm front to the storm of invective I rained in her ears. However, as the other guests were at no great distance, she begged me to speak more softly, but they heard me and I was very glad of it.

At last we sat down to dinner, and the wretched woman contrived to get a place beside me, and behaved all the while as if I were her lover, or at any rate as if she loved me. She did not seem to care what people thought of my coldness, while I was in a rage, for the company must either have thought me a fool or else that she was making game of me.

After dinner we returned to the garden, and the Charpillon, determined to gain the victory, clung to my arm and after several turns led me towards the maze where she wished to try her power. She made me sit down on the grass beside her, and attacked me with passionate words and tender caresses, and by displaying the most interesting of her charms she succeeded in seducing me, but still I do not know whether I was impelled by love or vengeance, and I am inclined to think that my feelings were a compound of both passions.

"What! you would deceive me again?"

"No, no, but we have done enough now. I promise to spend the night in your arms in your own house."

For a moment I lost my senses. I only saw the deceitful wretch who had profited by my foolish credulity so many times, and I resolved to enjoy or take vengeance. I held her down with my left arm, and drawing a small knife from my pocket I opened it with my teeth and pricked her neck, threatening to kill her if she resisted me.

"Do as you like," she said with perfect calm, "I only ask

you to leave me my life, but after you have satisfied yourself I will not leave the spot; I will not enter your carriage unless you carry me by force, and everybody shall know the reason."

This threat had no effect, for I had already got back my senses, and I pitied myself for being degraded by a creature for whom I had the greatest contempt, in spite of the almost magical influence she had over me, and the furious desires she knew how to kindle in my breast. I rose without a word, and taking my hat and cane I hastened to leave a place where unbridled passion had brought me to the brink of ruin.

My readers will scarcely believe me (but it is nevertheless the exact truth) when I say that the impudent creature hastened to rejoin me, and took my arm again as if nothing had happened. A girl of her age could not have played the part so well unless she had been already tried in a hundred battles. When we rejoined the company I was asked if I were ill, while nobody noticed the slightest alteration in her.

When we got back to London I excused myself under the plea of a bad headache, and returned home.

The adventure had made a terrible impression on me, and I saw that if I did not avoid all intercourse with this girl I should be brought to ruin. There was something about her I could not resist. I therefore resolved to see her no more, but feeling ashamed of my weakness in giving her the bills of exchange I wrote her mother a note requesting her to make her daughter return them, or else I should be compelled to take harsh measures.

In the afternoon I received the following reply: —

"Sir, — I am exceedingly surprised at your addressing yourself to me about the bills you handed to my daughter. She tells me she will give you them back in person when you show more discretion, and have learnt to respect her."

This impudent letter so enraged me that I forgot my vow of the morning. I put two pistols in my pocket and proceeded to the wretched woman's abode to compel her to return me my bills if she did not wish to be soundly caned.

I only took the pistols to overawe the two male rascals who supped with them every evening. I was furious when I arrived, but when I passed by the door I saw a handsome young hairdresser, who did the Charpillon's hair every Saturday evening, going into the house.

I did not want a stranger to be present at the scene I meant to make, so I waited at the corner of the street for the hairdresser to go. After I had waited half an hour Rostaing and Cauman, the two supports of the house, came out and went away, much to my delight. I waited on; eleven struck, and the handsome barber had not yet gone. A little before midnight a servant came out with a lamp, I suppose to look for something that had fallen out of the window. I approached noiselessly, stepped in and opened the parlour door, which was close to the street, and saw . . . the Charpillon and the barber stretched on the sofa.

When the slut saw me she gave a shriek. Her gallant I caned soundly until he escaped in the confusion consequent on the servants, mother, and aunts all rushing into the room. While this was going on the Charpillon, half-naked, remained crouched behind the sofa, trembling lest the blows should begin to descend on her. Then the three hags set upon me like furies; but their abuse only irritated me, and I broke the pier-glass, the china, and the furniture, and as they still howled and shrieked I roared out that if they did not cease I would break their heads. At this they began to calm.

I threw myself upon the fatal sofa, and bade the mother return me the bills of exchange; but just then the watchman came in.

There is only one watchman to a district, which he perambulates all night with a lantern in one hand and a staff in the other. On these men the peace of the great city depends. I put three or four crowns into his hand and said "Go away," and so saying shut the door upon him. Then I sat down once more and asked again for the bills of exchange.

"I have not got them; my daughter keeps them."

"Call her."

The two maids said that whilst I was breaking the china she had escaped by the street door, and that they did not know what had become of her. Then the mother and aunts began to shriek, weep, and exclaim:

"My poor daughter alone in the streets of London at midnight! My dear niece, alas! alas! she is lost. Cursed be the hour when you came to England to make us all unhappy!"

My rage had evaporated, and I trembled at the thought of this young frightened girl running about the streets at such an hour.

"Go and look for her at the neighbours' houses," I said to the servants, "no doubt you will find her. When you tell me she is safe, you shall have a guinea apiece."

When the three Gorgons saw I was interested, their tears, complaints, and invectives began again with renewed vigour, while I kept silence as much as to say that they were in the right. I awaited the return of the servants with impatience, and at last at one o'clock they came back with looks of despair.

"We have looked for her everywhere," said they, "but we can't find her."

I gave them the two guineas as if they had succeeded, whilst I sat motionless reflecting on the terrible consequences of my anger. How foolish is man when he is in love!

I was idiot enough to express my repentance to the three old cheats. I begged them to seek for her everywhere when dawn appeared, and to let me know of her return that I might fall at her feet to beg pardon, and never see her face again. I also promised to pay for all the damage I had done, and to give them a full receipt for the bills of exchange. After these acts, done to the everlasting shame of my good sense, after this apology made to procuresses who laughed at me and my honour, I went home, promising two guineas to the servant who should bring me tidings that her young mistress had come home.

On leaving the house I found the watchman at the door; he had been waiting to see me home. It was two o'clock. I threw myself on my bed, and the six hours of sleep I obtained, though troubled by fearful dreams, probably saved me from madness.

At eight o'clock I heard a knock at the door, and on opening the window found it was one of the servants from the house of my foes. I cried out to let her in, and I breathed again on hearing that Miss Charpillon had just arrived in a sedan-chair in a pitiable condition, and that she had been put to bed.

"I made haste to come and tell you," said the cunning maid, "not for the sake of your two guineas, but because I saw you were so unhappy."

This duped me directly. I gave her the two guineas, and made her sit down on my bed, begging her to tell me all about her mistress's return. I did not dream that she had been schooled by my enemies; but during the whole of this period I was deprived of the right use of my reason.

The slut began by saying that her young mistress loved me, and had only deceived me in accordance with her mother's orders.

"I know that," I said, "but where did she pass the night?"

"At a shop which she found open, and where she was known from having bought various articles there. She is in bed with a fever, and I am afraid it may have serious consequences."

"Tell her that I am coming to pass the day beside her bed, and bring me her reply."

"I will send the other girl if you like."

"No, she only speaks English."

She went away, and as she had not returned by three o'clock I decided on calling to hear how she was. I knocked at the door, and one of the aunts appeared and begged me not to enter as the two friends of the house were there in a fury against me, and her niece lay in a delirium, crying out "There's Seingalt, there's Seingalt! He's going to kill me. Help! help!" "For God's sake, sir, go away!"

I went home desperate, without the slightest suspicion that it was all a lie. I spent the whole day without eating anything; I could not swallow a mouthful. All night I kept awake, and though I took several glasses of strong waters I could obtain no rest.

At nine o'clock the next morning I knocked at the Charpillon's door, and the old aunt came and held it half open as before. She forbade me to enter, saying that her niece was still delirious, continually calling on me in her transports, and that the doctor had declared that if the disease continued its course she had not twenty-four hours to live.

I gave her a bank-note for ten guineas and went away, like the fool I was. On my way back I met Goudar, who was quite frightened at my aspect. I begged him to go and see how the Charpillon really was, and then to come and pass the rest of the day with me. An hour after, he came back and said he had found them all in tears and that the girl was *in extremis*.

"Did you see her?"

"No, they said she could see no one."

"Do you think it is all true?"

"I don't know what to think. The girl told me it was all your fault."

I then told him the whole story. He could only pity me, but when he heard that I had neither eaten nor slept for the last forty-eight hours he said very wisely that if I did not take care I should lose my reason or my life. I knew it, but I could find no remedy. He spent the day with me and did me good. As I could not eat I drank a good deal, and not being able to sleep I spent the night in striding up and down my room like a man beside himself.

On the third day, having heard nothing positive about the Charpillon, I went out at seven o'clock in the morning to call on her. After I had waited a quarter of an hour in the street, the door was partly opened, and I saw her mother all in tears, but she would not let me come in. She said her daughter was in the last agony. At the same instant a pale and thin old man came out telling the mother that we must resign ourselves to the will of God. I asked the infamous creature if it were the doctor.

"The doctor is no good now," said the old hypocrite, weeping anew, "he is a minister of the Gospel, and there is another of them upstairs. My poor daughter! In another hour she will be no more."

I felt as if an icy hand had closed upon my heart. I burst into tears and left the woman, saying:

"It is true that my hand dealt the blow, but her death lies at your door."

As I walked away my knees seemed to bend under me, and I entered my house determined to commit suicide.

With this fearful idea, I gave orders that I was not at home to anyone. As soon as I got to my room I put my watches, rings, snuff-boxes, purse, and pocket-book in my casket, and shut it up in my escritoire. I then wrote a letter to the Venetian ambassador, informing him that all my property was to go to M. de Bragadin after my death. I sealed the letter and put it with the casket, and took the key with me, and also silver to the amount of a few guineas. I took my pistols and went out with the firm intention of drowning myself in the Thames, near the Tower of London.

Pondering over my plan with the utmost coolness, I went and bought some balls of lead as large as my pockets would hold, and as heavy as I could bear, to carry to the Tower, where I intended to go on foot. On my way I was strengthened in my purpose by the reflection that if I continued to live I should be tormented for the remainder of my days by the pale shade of the Charpillon reproaching me as her murderer. I even congratulated myself on being able to carry out my purpose without any effort, and I also felt a secret pride in my courage.

I walked slowly on account of the enormous weight I bore, which would assure me a speedy passage to the bottom of the river.

By Westminster Bridge my good fortune made me meet Sir Edgar **, a rich young Englishman, who lived a careless and joyous life. I had made his acquaintance at Lord Pembroke's, and he had dined with me several times. We suited one another, his conversation was agreeable, and we had passed many pleasant hours together. I tried to avoid him, but he saw me, and came up and took me by the arm in a friendly manner.

"Where are you going? Come with me, unless you are going to deliver some captive. Come along, we shall have a pleasant party."

"I can't come, my dear fellow, let me go."

"What's the matter? I hardly recognised you, you looked so solemn."

"Nothing is the matter."

"Nothing? You should look at your face in the glass. Now I feel quite sure that you are going to commit a foolish action."

"Not at all."

"It's no good denying it."

"I tell you there's nothing the matter with me. Good-bye, I shall see you again."

"It's no good, I won't leave you. Come along, we will walk together."

His eyes happening to fall on my breeches pocket he noticed my pistol, and putting his hand on the other pocket he felt the other pistol, and said:

"You are going to fight a duel; I should like to see it. I won't interfere with the affair, but neither will I leave you."

I tried to put on a smile, and assured him that he was mistaken, and that I was only going for a walk to pass the time.

"Very good," said Edgar, "then I hope my society is as pleasant to you as yours is to me; I won't leave you. After we have taken a walk we will go and dine at the Canon. I will get two girls to come and join us, and we shall have a gay little party of four."

"My dear friend, you must excuse me; I am in a melancholy mood, and I want to be alone to get over it."

"You can be alone to-morrow, if you like, but I am sure you will be all right in the next three hours, and if not, why I will share your madness. Where did you think of dining?"

"Nowhere; I have no appetite. I have been fasting for the last three days, and I can only drink."

"Ah! I begin to see daylight. Something has crossed you, and you are going to let it kill you as it killed one of my brothers. I must see what can be done."

Edgar argued, insisted, and joked till at last I said to myself, "A day longer will not matter, I can do the deed when he leaves me, and I shall only have to bear with life a few hours longer."

When Edgar heard that I had no particular object in crossing the bridge he said that we had better turn back, and I let myself be persuaded; but in half an hour I begged him to take me somewhere where I could wait for him, as I could not bear the weight of the lead any longer. I gave him my word of honour that I would meet him at the Canon.

As soon as I was alone I emptied my pockets, and put the leaden balls into a cupboard. Then I lay down and began to consider whether the good-natured young man would prevent me committing suicide, as he had already made me postpone it.

I reasoned, not as one that hopes, but rather as one that foresaw that Edgar would hinder me from shortening my days. Thus I waited in the tavern for the young Englishman, doubtful whether he was doing me a service or an injury.

Although Edgar was a profligate, he was a sensible man, and my story made him furious. He threw his arms around my neck, and told me he should always think the day on which he rescued me from death for so unworthy an object the happiest in his life. He could scarcely credit the infamy of the Charpillon and her mother. He told me I could have the mother arrested, though I had not got the bills of exchange, as her mother's letter acknowledging her daughter's possession of the bills was sufficient evidence.

Without informing him of my intention, I resolved that moment to have her arrested. Before we parted we swore eternal friendship, but the reader will see before long what a penance the kind Englishman had to do for befriending me.

The next day I went to the attorney I had employed against Count Schwerin. After hearing my story he said that I had an undoubted claim, and that I could arrest the mother and the two aunts.

Without losing time I went before a magistrate, who took my sworn information and granted me a warrant. The same official who had arrested Schwerin took charge of the affair; but as he did not know the women by sight it was necessary that someone who did should go with him, for though he was certain of surprising them there might be several other women present, and he might not arrest the right ones.

As Goudar would not have undertaken the delicate task of pointing them out, I resolved on accompanying him myself.

I made an appointment with him at an hour when I knew they would be all in the parlour. He was to enter directly the door was opened, and I would come in at the same instant and point out the women he had to arrest. In England all judicial proceedings are conducted with the utmost punctuality, and everything went off as I had arranged. The bailiff and his subaltern stepped into the parlor and I followed in their footsteps. I pointed out the mother and the two sisters and then made haste to escape, for the sight of the Charpillon, dressed in black, standing by the hearth, made me shudder. I felt cured, certainly; but the wounds she had given me were not yet healed, and I cannot say what might have happened if the Circe had had the presence of mind to throw her arms about my neck and beg for mercy.

As soon as I had seen these women in the hands of justice I fled, tasting the sweets of vengeance, which are very great, but yet a sign of unhappiness. The rage in which I had arrested the three procuresses, and my terror in seeing the woman who had well-nigh killed me, showed that I was not really cured. To be so I must fly from them and forget them altogether.

The next morning Goudar came and congratulated me on the bold step I had taken, which proved, he said, that I was either cured or more in love than ever. "I have just come from Denmark Street," he added, "and I only saw the grandmother, who was weeping bitterly, and an attorney, whom no doubt she was consulting."

"Then you have heard what has happened?"

"Yes, I came up a minute after you had gone and I stayed till the three old sluts made up their minds to go with the constable. They resisted and said he ought to leave them till the next day, when they would be able to find someone to bail them. The two bravos drew their swords to resist the law, but the other constable disarmed them one after the other, and the three women were led off. The Charpillon wanted to accompany them, but it was judged best that she should remain at liberty, in order to try and set them free."

Goudar concluded by saying that he should go and see them in prison, and if I felt disposed to come to an arrangement he would mediate between us. I told him that the only arrangement I would accept was the payment of the six thousand francs, and that they might think themselves very lucky that I did not insist on having my interest, and thus repaying myself in part for the sums they had cheated out of me.

A fortnight elapsed without my hearing any more of the matter. The Charpillon dined with them every day, and, in fact, kept them. It must have cost her a good deal, for they had two rooms, and their landlord would not allow them to have their meals prepared outside the prison. Goudar told me that the Charpillon said she would never beg me to listen to her mother, though she knew she had only to call on me to obtain anything she wanted. She thought me the most abominable of men. If I feel obliged to maintain that she was equally abominable, I must confess that on this occasion she showed more strength of mind than I; but whereas I had acted out of passion, her misdeeds were calculated, and tended solely to her own interests.

For the whole of this fortnight I had sought for Edgar in vain, but one morning he came to see me, looking in high spirits.

"Where have you been hiding all this time?" said I, "I have been looking for you everywhere."

"Love has been keeping me a prisoner," said he, "I have got some money for you."

"For me? From what quarter?"

"On behalf of the Anspergers. Give me a receipt and the necessary declaration, for I am going to restore them myself to the poor Charpillon, who has been weeping for the last fortnight."

"I dare say she has, I have seen her weep myself; but I like the way in which she has chosen the being who delivered me from her chains as a protector. Does she know that I owe my life to you?"

"She only knew that I was with you at Ranelagh when you saw her dancing instead of dying, but I have told her the whole story since."

"No doubt she wants you to plead with me in her favour."

"By no means. She has just been telling me that you are a monster of ingratitude, for she loved you and gave you several proofs of her affection, but now she hates you."

"Thank Heaven for that! The wretched woman! It's curious she should have selected you as her lover by way of taking vengeance on me, but take care! she will punish you."

"It may be so, but at all events it's a pleasant kind of punishment."

"I hope you may be happy, but look to yourself; she is a mistress in all sorts of deceit."

Edgar counted me out two hundred and fifty guineas, for which I gave him a receipt and the declaration he required, and with these documents he went off in high spirits.

After this I might surely flatter myself that all was at an end between us, but I was mistaken.

Just about this time the Crown Prince of Brunswick, now the reigning duke, married the King of England's sister. The Common Council presented him with the freedom of the City, and the Goldsmiths' Company admitted him into their society, and gave him a splendid golden box containing the documents which made him a London citizen. The prince was the first gentleman in Europe, and yet he did not disdain to add this new honour to a family illustrious for fourteen hundred years.

On this occasion Lady Harrington was the means of getting Madame Cornelis two hundred guineas. She lent her room in Soho Square to a confectioner who gave a ball and supper to a thousand persons at three guineas each. I paid my three guineas, and had the honour of standing up all the evening with six hundred others, for the table only seated four hundred, and there were several ladies who were unable to procure seats.

That evening I saw Lady Grafton seated beside the Duke of Cumberland. She wore her hair without any powder, and all the

other ladies were exclaiming about it, and saying how very unbe-
coming it was. They could not anathematize the innovator too
much, but in less than six months Lady Grafton's style of doing
the hair became common, crossed the Channel, and spread all
over Europe, though it has been given another name. It is still
in fashion, and is the only method that can boast the age of
thirty years, though it was so unmercifully ridiculed at first.

The supper for which the giver of the feast had received three
thousand guineas, or sixty-five thousand francs, contained a
most varied assortment of delicacies, but as I had not been
dancing, and did not feel taken with any of the ladies present, I
left at one in the morning. It was Sunday, a day on which all
persons, save criminals, are exempt from arrest; but, nevertheless, the following adventure befell me:—

I was dressed magnificently, and was driving home in my
carriage, with my Negro and another servant seated behind me;
and just as we entered Pall Mall I heard a voice crying, "Good-
night, Seingalt." I put my head out of the window to reply, and
in an instant the carriage was surrounded by men armed with
pistols, and one of them said:

"In the king's name!"

My servant asked what they wanted, and they answered:

"To take him to Newgate, for Sunday makes no difference
to criminals."

"And what crime have I committed?"

"You will hear that in prison."

"My master has a right to know his crime before he goes to
prison," said the Negro.

"Yes, but the magistrate's abed."

The Negro stuck to his position, however, and the people who
had come up declared with one consent that he was in the right.

The head-constable gave in, and said he would take me to
a house in the City.

"Then drive to the City," said I, "and have done with it."

We stopped before the house, and I was placed in a large
room on the ground-floor, furnished solely with benches and long
tables. My servant sent back the carriage, and came to keep me
company. The six constables said they could not leave me, and
told me I should send out for some meat and drink for them.
I told my Negro to give them what they wanted, and to be as
amicable with them as was possible.

As I had not committed any crime, I was quite at ease; I knew that my arrest must be the effect of a slander, and as I was aware that London justice was speedy and equitable, I thought I should soon be free. But I blamed myself for having transgressed the excellent maxim, never to answer anyone in the night time; for if I had not done so I should have been in my house, and not in prison. The mistake, however, had been committed, and there was nothing to be done but to wait patiently. I amused myself by reflecting on my rapid passage from a numerous and exalted assemblage to the vile place I now occupied, though I was still dressed like a prince.

At last the day dawned, and the keeper of the tavern came to see who the prisoner was. I could not help laughing at him when he saw me, for he immediately began to abuse the constables for not awaking him when I came; he had lost the guinea I should have paid for a private room. At last news was brought that the magistrate was sitting, and that I must be brought up.

A coach was summoned, and I got into it, for if I had dared to walk along the streets in my magnificent attire the mob would have pelted me.

I went into the hall of justice, and all eyes were at once attracted towards me; my silks and satins appeared to them the height of impertinence.

At the end of the room I saw a gentleman sitting in an armchair, and concluded him to be my judge. I was right, and the judge was blind. He wore a broad band round his head, passing over his eyes. A man beside me, guessing I was a foreigner, said in French:

"Be of good courage, Mr. Fielding is a just and equitable magistrate."

I thanked the kindly unknown, and was delighted to see before me this famous and estimable writer, whose works are an honour to the English nation.

When my turn came the clerk of the court told Mr. Fielding my name; at least, so I presume.

"Signor Casanova," said he, in excellent Italian, "be kind enough to step forward. I wish to speak to you."

I was delighted to hear the accents of my native tongue, and making my way through the press I came up to the bar of the court, and said:

"*Eccomi, Signore.*"

He continued to speak Italian, and said:

"Signor de Casanova, of Venice, you are condemned to perpetual confinement in the prisons of His Majesty the King of Great Britain."

"I should like to know, sir, for what crime I am condemned. Would you be kind enough to inform me as to its nature?"

"Your demand is a reasonable one, for with us no one is condemned without knowing the cause of his condemnation. You must know, then, that the accusation (which is supported by two witnesses) charges you with intending to do grievous bodily harm to the person of a pretty girl; and as this pretty girl aforesaid goes in dread of you, the law decrees that you must be kept in prison for the rest of your days."

"Sir, this accusation is a groundless calumny; to that I will take oath! It is very possible indeed that the girl may fear my vengeance when she comes to consider her own conduct, but I can assure you that I have had no such designs hitherto, and I don't think I ever shall."

"She has two witnesses."

"Then they are false ones. But may I ask your worship the name of my accuser?"

"Miss Charpillon."

"I thought as much; but I have never given her aught but proofs of my affection."

"Then you have no wish to do her any bodily harm?"

"Certainly not."

"Then I congratulate you. You can dine at home; but you must find two sureties. I must have an assurance from the mouths of two householders that you will never commit such a crime."

"Whom shall I find to do so?"

"Two well-known Englishmen, whose friendship you have gained, and who know that you are incapable of such an action. Send for them, and if they arrive before I go to dinner I will set you at liberty."

The constable took me back to prison, where I had passed the night, and I gave my servants the addresses of all the householders I recollected, bidding them explain my situation, and to be as quick as possible. They ought to have come before noon, but London is such a large place! They did not arrive, and the magistrate went to dinner. I comforted myself by the thought that he would sit in the afternoon, but I had to put up with a disagreeable experience.

The chief constable, accompanied by an interpreter, came to say that I must go to Newgate. This is a prison where the most wretched and abject criminals are kept.

I signified to him that I was awaiting bail, and that he could take me to Newgate in the evening if it did not come, but he only turned a deaf ear to my petition. The interpreter told me in a whisper that the fellow was certainly paid by the other side to put me to trouble, but that if I liked to bribe him I could stay where I was.

"How much will he want?" I asked.

The interpreter took the constable aside, and then told me that I could stay where I was for ten guineas.

"Then say that I should like to see Newgate."

A coach was summoned, and I was taken away.

When I got to this abode of misery and despair, a hell, such as Dante might have conceived, a crowd of wretches, some of whom were to be hanged in the course of the week, greeted me by deriding my elegant attire. I did not answer them, and they began to get angry and to abuse me. The gaoler quieted them by saying that I was a foreigner and did not understand English, and then took me to a cell, informing me how much it would cost me, and of the prison rules, as if he felt certain that I should make a long stay. But in the course of half an hour, the constable who had tried to get ten guineas out of me told me that bail had arrived and that my carriage was at the door.

I thanked God from the bottom of my heart, and soon found myself in the presence of the blind magistrate. My bail consisted of Pegu, my tailor, and Maisonneuve, my wine merchant, who said they were happy to be able to render me this slight service. In another part of the court I noticed the infamous Charpillon, Rostaing, Goudar, and an attorney. They made no impression on me, and I contented myself with giving them a look of profound contempt.

My two sureties were informed of the amount in which they were to bail me, and signed with a light heart and then the magistrate said, politely:

"Signor Casanova, please to sign your name for double the amount, and you will then be a free man again."

I went towards the clerk's table, and on asking the sum I was to answer for was informed that it was forty guineas, each of my sureties signing for twenty. I signed my name, telling Goudar that if the magistrate could have seen the Charpillon he would have valued her beauty at ten thousand guineas. I asked the names of the two witnesses, and was told that they were Rostaing and Bottarelli. I looked contemptuously at Rostaing, who was as pale as death, and averting my face from the Charpillon out of pity I said:

"The witnesses are worthy of the charge."

I saluted the judge with respect, although he could not see me, and asked the clerk if I had anything to pay. He replied in the negative, and a dispute ensued between him and the attorney of my fair enemy, who was disgusted on hearing that she could not leave the court without paying the costs of my arrest.

Just as I was going, five or six well-known Englishmen appeared to bail me out, and were mortified to hear that they had come too late. They begged me to forgive the laws of the land, which are only too often converted into a means for the annoyance of foreigners.

At last, after one of the most tedious days I have ever spent, I returned home and went to bed, laughing at the experience I had undergone.

Thus ended the first act of the comedy; the second began the next morning. I was just getting up, when I heard a noise at the street door, and on putting my head out of the window I saw Pocchini, the scoundrel who had robbed me at Stuttgart, trying to get into my house. I cried out wrathfully that I would having nothing to do with him, and slammed down my window.

A little later Goudar put in an appearance. He had got a copy of the St. James's Chronicle, containing a brief report of my arrest, and of my being set at liberty under a bail of eighty guineas. My name and the lady's were disguised, but Rostaing and Bottarelli were set down plainly, and the editor praised their conduct. I felt as if I should like to know Bottarelli, and begged Goudar to take me to him and Martinelli, happening to call just then, said he would come with us.

We entered a wretched room on the third floor of a wretched house, and there we beheld a picture of the greatest misery. A woman and five children clothed in rags formed the foreground, and in the background was Bottarelli, in an old dressing-gown, writing at a table worthy of Philemon and Baucis. He rose as we came in, and the sight of him moved me to compassion. I said:

"Do you know me, sir?"

"No, sir, I do not."

"I am Casanova, against whom you bore false witness; whom you tried to cast into Newgate."

"I am very sorry, but look around you and say what choice have I? I have no bread to give my children. I will do as much in your favour another time for nothing."

"Are you not afraid of the gallows?"

"No, for perjury is not punished with death; besides it is very difficult to prove."

"I have heard you are a poet."

"Yes. I have lengthened the *Didone* and abridged the *Demetrio*."

"You are a great poet, indeed!"

I felt more contempt than hatred for the rascal, and gave his wife a guinea, for which she presented me with a wretched pamphlet by her husband: *The Secrets of the Freemasons Displayed.*" Bottarelli had been a monk in his native city, Pisa, and had fled to England with his wife, who had been a nun.

About this time M. de Saa surprised me by giving me a letter from my fair Portuguese, which confirmed the sad fate of poor Clairmont. Pauline said she was married to Count Al**. I was astonished to hear M. de Saa observe that he had known all about Pauline from the moment she arrived in London. That is the hobby of all diplomatists; they like people to believe that they are omniscient. However, M. de Saa was a man of worth and talent, and one could excuse this weakness as an incident inseparable from his profession; while most diplomatists only make themselves ridiculous by their assumption of universal knowledge.

M. de Saa had been almost as badly treated by the Charpillon as myself, and we might have condoled with one another, but the subject was not mentioned.

A few days afterwards, as I was walking idly about, I passed a place called the Parrot Market. As I was amusing myself by looking at these curious birds, I saw a fine young one in a cage, and asked what language it spoke. They told me that it was quite young and did not speak at all yet, so I bought it for ten guineas. I thought I would teach the bird a pretty speech, so I had the cage hung by my bed, and repeated dozens of times every day the following sentence: "*The Charpillon is a bigger wh**e than her mother.*"

The only end I had in view was my private amusement, and in a fortnight the bird had learnt the phrase with the utmost exactness; and every time it uttered the words it accompanied them with a shriek of laughter which I had not taught it, but which made me laugh myself.

One day Goudar heard the bird, and told me that if I sent it to the Exchange I should certainly get fifty guineas for it. I welcomed the idea, and resolved to make the parrot the instrument of my vengeance against the woman who had treated me so badly. I secured myself from fear of the law, which is severe in such cases, by entrusting the bird to my Negro, to whom such merchandise was very suitable.

For the first two or three days my parrot did not attract much attention, its observations being in French; but as soon as those who knew the subject of them heard it, its audience increased and bids were made. Fifty guineas seemed rather too much, and my Negro wanted me to lower the price, but I would not agree, having fallen in love with this odd revenge.

In the course of a week Goudar came to inform me of the effect the parrot's criticism had produced in the Charpillon family. As the vendor was my Negro, there could be no doubt as to whom it belonged, and who had been its master of languages. Goudar said that the Charpillon thought my revenge very ingenious, but that the mother and aunts were furious. They had consulted several counsel, who agreed in saying that a parrot could not be indicted for libel, but that they could make me pay dearly for my jest if they could prove that I had been the bird's instructor. Goudar warned me to be careful of owning to the fact, as two witnesses would suffice to undo me.

The facility with which false witnesses may be procured in London is something dreadful. I have myself seen the word "evidence" written in large characters in a window; this is as much as to say that false witnesses may be procured within.

The *St. James's Chronicle* contained an article on my parrot, in which the writer remarked that the ladies whom the bird insulted must be very poor and friendless, or they would have bought it at once, and have thus prevented the thing from becoming the talk of the town. He added:

"The teacher of the parrot has no doubt made the bird an instrument of his vengeance, and has displayed his wit in doing so; he ought to be an Englishman."

I met my good friend Edgar, and asked him why he had not bought the little slanderer.

"Because it delights all who know anything about the object of the slander," said he.

At last Jarbe found a purchaser for fifty guineas, and I heard afterwards that Lord Grosvenor had bought it to please the Charpillon, with whom he occasionally diverted himself.

Thus my relations with that girl came to an end. I have seen her since with the greatest indifference, and without any renewal of the old pain.

The story of Marie-Anne-Geneviève Charpillon, or Charpillion, and of her worthy family is to be found not only in the Memoirs of their victim, but in the police records of the time. With the aid of the latter, M. Charles Samaran has reconstructed the family history. This edifying document proves that, whatever Casanova may have added to embellish his tale, it was scarcely in his or anyone's power to blacken the reputation of his heroine and her familiars. The grandmother's name was Catherine Brunner; she was a native of Berne, which in the eighteenth century enjoyed an unenviable fame for its underworld and "low life" resorts. Working in association with her three sisters and the daughter she had by a compatriot named Augspurgher (the form Ansperger, given in the Memoirs, seems to be a mis-spelling), she drove a prosperous if disreputable trade, principally in Paris and London. But it was only in the third generation, in the captivating person of Marie-Anne Charpillon, that their ignominious talents were to come to full fruition. When Casanova made her acquaintance, she was only seventeen years old. It was not their first meeting. Four years earlier, when shopping in Paris with the mistress of the hour, Madame Baret, he had been so struck by the looks of the child, which she then was, that he had presented her with a pair of ear-rings for which she had been clamouring. Ten years after the Casanova affair Marie-Anne Charpillon became the mistress of the famous John Wilkes, another acquaintance of our hero. [1]

The episode of the Hanoverian sisters, which rounds off the London experiences (this form of the "sister complex" is a recurring and favourite theme in the Memoirs), is evidently an attempt to rehabilitate the discomfited hero and to reassure the reader that as a champion in the lists of Venus he has yet many a lance to break before being carried off the field. In relegating it to the Casanovian ben trovati and dismissing it as such, we feel we are not depriving our readers of any essential enjoyment.

Arriving at leisure and departing in haste seems henceforth to be the traveller's motto. London proved no exception, as we shall see:

In the month I had spent with the Hanoverians I had dissipated the whole of the sum resulting from the sale of the precious stones, and I found that I was in debt to the amount of four hundred guineas. I resolved to go to Lisbon by sea, and sold my diamond cross, six or seven gold snuff-boxes (after removing the portraits), all my watches except one, and two great trunks full of clothes. I then discharged my debts and found I was eighty guineas to the good, this being what remained of the fine fortune I had squandered away like a fool or a philosopher, or, perhaps, a little like both. I left my fine house where I had lived so pleasantly, and took a little room at a guinea a week. I still kept my Negro, as I had every reason to believe him to be a faithful servant.

After taking these measures I wrote to M. de Bragadin, begging him to send me two hundred sequins.

Thus having made up my mind to leave London without owing a penny to anyone, and under obligations to no man's purse, I waited for the bill of exchange from Venice. When it came I resolved to bid farewell to all my friends and to try my fortune in Lisbon, but such was not the fate which the fickle goddess had assigned to me.

A fortnight after the departure of the Hanoverians (it was

---

[1] *According to M. Edouard Maynial (Casanova et son temps), it was the Charpillon episode in Casanova's Memoirs which inspired Pierre Louÿs with the first idea for his well-known novel La Femme et le pantin.*

the end of February in the year 1764), my evil genius made me go to the Canon Tavern, where I usually dined in a room by myself. The table was laid and I was just going to sit down, when Baron Stenau came in and begged me to have my dinner brought into the next room, where he and his mistress were dining.

"I thank you, " said I, "for the solitary man grows weary of his company."

I saw the English woman I had met at Sartori's, the same to whom the baron had been so generous. She spoke Italian, and was attractive in many ways, so I was well pleased to find myself opposite to her, and we had a pleasant dinner.

After a fortnight's abstinence it was not surprising that she inspired me with desires, but I concealed them nevertheless, for her lover seemed to respect her. I only allowed myself to tell the baron that I thought him the happiest of men.

Towards the close of the dinner the girl noticed three dice on the mantel and took them up, saying:

"Let us have a wager of a guinea, and spend it on oysters and champagne."

We could not refuse, and the baron having lost called the waiter and gave him his orders.

While we were eating the oysters she suggested that we should throw again to see which should pay for the dinner.

We did so and she lost.

I did not like my luck, and wishing to lose a couple of guineas I offered to throw against the baron. He accepted, and to my annoyance I won. He asked for his revenge and lost again.

"I don't want to win your money," said I, "and I will give you your revenge up to a hundred guineas."

He seemed grateful and we went on playing, and in less than half an hour he owed me a hundred guineas.

"Let us go on," said he.

"My dear baron, the luck's against you; you might lose a large sum of money. I really think we have had enough."

Without heeding my politeness, he swore against fortune and against the favour I seemed to be showing him. Finally he got up, and taking his hat and cane, went out, saying:

"I will pay you when I come back."

As soon as he had gone the girl said:

"I am sure you have been regarding me as your partner at play."

"If you have guessed that, you will also have guessed that I think you charming."

"Yes, I think I have."

"Are you angry with me?"

"Not in the least."

"You shall have the fifty guineas as soon as he has paid me."

"Very good, but the baron must know nothing about it."

"Of course not."

The bargain was scarcely struck before I began to show her how much I loved her. I had every reason to congratulate myself on her complaisance, and I thought this meeting a welcome gleam of light when all looked dark around me. We had to make haste, however, as the door was only shut with a catch. I had barely time to ascertain her address and the hour at which she could see me, and whether I should have to be careful with her lover. She replied that the baron's fidelity was not of a character to make him very exacting. I put the address in my pocket, and promised to pass a night with her.

The baron came in again, and said:

"I have been to a merchant to discount this bill of exchange, and though it is drawn on one of the best houses in Cadiz, and made out by a good house in London, he would not have anything to do with it."

I took the bill and saw some millions mentioned on it, which astonished me.

The baron said with a laugh that the currency was Portuguese milreis, and that they amounted to five hundred pounds sterling.

"If the signatures are known," said I, "I don't understand why the man won't discount it. Why don't you take it to your banker?"

"I haven't got one. I came to England with a thousand gold pieces in my pocket, and I have spent them all. As I have not got any letters of credit I cannot pay you unless the bill is discounted. If you have got any friends on the Exchange, however, you could get it done."

"If the names prove good ones I will let you have the money to-morrow morning."

"Then I will make it payable to your order."

[248]

He put his name to it, and I promised to send him either the money or the bill before noon on the day following. He gave me his address and begged me to come and dine with him, and so we parted.

The next day I went to Bosanquet, who told me that Mr. Leigh was looking out for bills of exchange on Cadiz, and I accordingly waited on him. He exclaimed that such paper was worth more than gold to him, and gave me five hundred and twenty guineas, of course after I had endorsed it.

I called on the baron and gave him the money I had just received, and he thanked me and gave me back the hundred guineas. Afterwards we had dinner, and fell to talking of his mistress.

"Are you in love with her?" said I.

"No; I have plenty of others, and if you like her you can have her for ten guineas."

I liked this way of putting it, though I had not the slightest idea of cheating the girl out of the sum I had promised her. On leaving the baron I went to see her, and as soon as she heard that the baron had paid me she ordered a delicious supper, and made me spend a night that obliterated all my sorrows from my memory. In the morning, when I handed over the fifty guineas, she said that as a reward for the way in which I kept my promise I could sup with her whenever I liked to spend six guineas. I promised to come and see her often.

The next morning I received a letter through the post, written in bad Italian, and signed, "*Your obedient godson, Daturi.*" This godson of mine was in prison for debt, and begged me to give him a few shillings to buy some food.

I had nothing particular to do, the appellation of *godson* made me curious, and so I went to the prison to see Daturi, of whose identity I had not the slightest idea. He was a fine young man of twenty; he did not know me, nor I him. I gave him his letter, and begging me to forgive him he drew a paper from his pocket and showed me his certificate of baptism, on which I saw my own name inscribed beside his name and those of his father and mother, the parish of Venice, where he was born, and the church in which he was baptized; but still I racked my memory in vain; I could not recollect him.

"If you will listen to me," he said, "I can set you right; my mother has told me the story a hundred times."

"Go on," said I, "I will listen"; and as he told his story I remembered who he was.

This young man whom I had held at the font as the son of the actor Daturi was possibly my own son. He had come to London with a troupe of jugglers to play the illustrious part of clown, or *pagliazzo*, but having quarrelled with the company he had lost his place and had got into debt to the extent of ten pounds sterling, and for this debt he had been imprisoned. Without saying anything to him about my relations with his mother, I set him free on the spot, telling him to come to me every morning, as I would give him two shillings a day for his support.

A week after I had done this good work I felt that I had caught the fearful disease from which the god Mercury had already delivered me three times, though with great danger and peril of my life. I had spent three nights with the fatal English woman, and the misfortune was doubly inconvenient under the circumstances. I was on the eve of a long sea voyage, and though Venus may have risen from the waves of the sea, sea air is by no means favourable to those on whom she has cast her malign aspect. I knew what to do, and resolved to have my case taken in hand without delay.

I left my house, not with the intention of reproaching the English woman after the manner of fools, but rather of going to a good surgeon, with whom I could make an agreement to stay in his house till my cure was completed.

I had my trunks packed just as if I was going to leave London, excepting my linen, which I sent to my washerwoman, who lived at a distance of six miles from town, and drove a great trade.

The very day I meant to change my lodging a letter was handed to me. It was from Mr. Leigh, and ran as follows:

"The bill of exchange I discounted for you is a forgery, so please send me at your earliest convenience the five hundred and twenty guineas; and if the man who has cheated you will not reimburse the money, have him arrested. For Heaven's sake do not force me to have you arrested to-morrow, and whatever you do make haste, for this may prove a hanging matter."

Fortunately I was by myself when I received the letter. I fell upon my bed, and in a moment I was covered with a cold sweat, while I trembled like a leaf. I saw the gallows before me, for nobody would lend me the money, and they would not wait for my remittance from Venice to reach me.

To my shuddering fit succeeded a burning fever. I loaded my pistols, and went out with the determination of blowing out Baron Stenau's brains, or putting him under arrest if he did not give me the money. I reached his house, and was informed that he had sailed for Lisbon four days ago.

This Baron Stenau was a Livonian, and four months after these events he was hanged at Lisbon. I only anticipate this little event in his life because I might possibly forget it when I come to my sojourn at Riga.

As soon as I heard he was gone I saw there was no remedy and that I must save myself. I had only ten or twelve guineas left, and this sum was insufficient. I went to Trèves, a Venetian Jew to whom I had a letter from Count Algarotti, the Venetian banker. I did not think of going to Bosanquet, or Sanhel, or Salvador, who might possibly have got wind of my trouble, while Trèves had no dealings with these great bankers, and discounted a bill for a hundred sequins readily enough.

With the money in my pocket I made my way to my lodging, while deadly fear dogged every step. Leigh had given me twenty-four hours' breathing time, and I did not think him capable of breaking his word, still it would not do to trust to it. I did not want to lose my linen nor three fine suits of clothes which my tailor was keeping for me, and yet I had need of the greatest promptitude.

I called in Jarbe and asked him whether he would prefer to take twenty guineas and his dismissal, or to continue in my service. I explained that he would have to wait in London for a week, and join me at the place from which I wrote to him.

"Sir," said he, "I should like to remain in your service, and I will rejoin you wherever you please. When are you leaving?"

"In an hour's time; but say not a word, or it will cost me my life."

"Why can't you take me with you?"

"Because I want you to bring my linen which is at the wash, and my clothes which the tailor is making. I will give you sufficient money for the journey."

"I don't want anything. You shall pay me what I have spent when I rejoin you. Wait a moment."

He went out and came back again directly, and holding out sixty guineas, said:

"Take this, sir, I entreat you, my credit is good for as much more in case of need."

"I thank you, my good fellow, but I will not take your money, but be sure I will not forget your fidelity."

My tailor lived close by and I called on him, and seeing that my clothes were not yet made up I told him that I should like to sell them, and also the gold lace that was to be used in the trimming. He instantly gave me thirty guineas, which meant a gain to him of twenty-five per cent. I paid the week's rent of my lodging, and after bidding farewell to my Negro I set out with Daturi. We slept at Rochester, as my strength would carry me no farther. I was in convulsions, and had a sort of delirium. Daturi was the means of saving my life.

I had ordered post-horses to continue our journey, and Daturi of his own authority sent them back and went for a doctor, who pronounced me to be in danger of an apoplectic fit and ordered a copious blood-letting, which restored my calm. Six hours later he pronounced me fit to travel. I got to Dover early in the morning, and had only half an hour to stop, as the captain of the packet said that the tide would not allow of any delay. The worthy sailor little knew how well his views suited mine. I used this half hour in writing to Jarbe, telling him to rejoin me at Calais, and Mrs. Mercier, my landlady, to whom I had addressed the letter, wrote to tell me that she had given it him with her own hands. However, Jarbe did not come. We shall hear more of this Negro in the course of two years.

The fever and the virus that was in my blood put me in danger of my life, and on the third day I was *in extremis*. A fourth blood-letting exhausted my strength, and left me in a state of coma which lasted for twenty-four hours. This was succeeded by a crisis which restored me to life again, but it was only by dint of the most careful treatment that I found myself able to continue my journey a fortnight after my arrival in France.

Weak in health, grieved at having been the innocent cause of the worthy Mr. Leigh's losing a large sum of money, humiliated by my flight from London, indignant with Jarbe, and angry at being obliged to abandon my Portuguese project, I got into a post-chaise with Daturi, not knowing where to turn or where to go, or whether I had many more weeks to live.

I had written to Venice asking M. de Bragadin to send the sum I have mentioned to Brussels instead of London.

When I got to Dunkirk, the day after I left Paris, the first person I saw was the merchant S **, the husband of that Thérèse whom my readers may remember, the niece of Tiretta's mistress, with whom I had been in love seven years ago. The worthy man recognised me, and seeing his astonishment at the change in my appearance I told him I was recovering from a long illness, and then asked after his wife.

"She is wonderfully well," he answered, "and I hope we shall have the pleasure of seeing you to dinner to-morrow."

I said I wanted to be off at daybreak, but he would not hear of it, and protested he would be quite hurt if I went away without seeing his wife and his three children. At last I appeased him by saying that we would sup together.

My readers will remember that I had been on the point of marrying Thérèse, and this circumstance made me ashamed of presenting myself to her in such a sorry plight.

In a quarter of an hour the husband arrived with his wife and three children, the eldest of whom looked about six. After the usual greetings and tiresome inquiries after my health, Thérèse sent back the two younger children, rightly thinking that the eldest would be the only one in whom I should take any interest. He was a charming boy; and as he was exactly like his mother, the worthy merchant had no doubts as to the parentage of the child.

I laughed to myself at finding my offspring thus scattered all over Europe. At supper Thérèse gave me news of Tiretta. He had entered the Dutch East India Company's service, but having been concerned in a revolt at Batavia, he had only escaped the gallows by flight. I had my own thoughts as to the similarity between his destiny and mine, but I did not reveal them. After all it is an easy enough matter for an adventurous man who does not look where he is going, to get hanged for a mere trifle.

The next day, when I got to Tournay, I saw some grooms walking fine horses up and down, and I asked to whom they belonged.

"To the Comte de St. Germain, the adept, who has been here a month, and never goes out. Everybody who passes through the place wants to see him; but he is invisible."

This was enough to give me the same desire, so I wrote him a letter, expressing my wish to speak to him, and asking him to name an hour. His reply, which I have preserved, ran as follows:

"The gravity of my occupation compels me to exclude everyone, but you are an exception. Come whenever you like, you will be shown in. You need not mention my name nor your own. I do not ask you to share my repast, for my food is not suitable to others — to you least of all, if your appetite is what it used to be."

At nine o'clock I paid my call, and found he had grown a beard two inches long. He had a score of retorts before him, full of liquids in various stages of digestion. He told me he was experimenting with colours for his own amusement, and that he had established a hat factory for Count Cobenzl, the Austrian ambassador at Brussels. He·added that the count had only given him a hundred and fifty thousand florins, which were insufficient. Then we spoke of Madame d'Urfé.

"She poisoned herself," said he, "by taking too strong a dose of the Universal Medicine, and her will shows that she thought herself to be with child. If she had come to me, I could have really made her so, though it is a difficult process, and science has not advanced far enough for us to be able to guarantee the sex of the child."

When he heard the nature of my disease, he wanted me to stay three days at Tournay for him to give me fifteen pills, which would effectually cure me, and restore me to perfect health. Then he showed me his *magistrum*, which he called *atboeter*. It was a white liquid contained in a well-stoppered phial. He told me that this liquid was the universal spirit of nature, and that if the wax on the stopper was pricked ever so lightly, the whole of the contents would disappear. I begged him to make the experiment. He gave me the phial and a pin, and I pricked the wax, and lo! the phial was empty.

"It is very fine," said I, "but what good is all this?"

"I cannot tell you; that is my secret."

He wanted to astonish me before I went, and asked me if I had any money about me. I took out several pieces and put them on the table. He got up, and without saying what he was going to do he took a burning coal and put it on a metal plate, and placed a twelve-sols piece with a small black grain on the coal. He then blew it, and in two minutes it seemed on fire.

"Wait a moment," said the alchemist, "let it get cool"; and it cooled almost directly.

"Take it; it is yours," said he.

I took up the piece of money and found it had become gold. I felt perfectly certain that he had smuggled my silver piece away, and had substituted a gold piece coated with silver for it. I did not care to tell him as much, but to let him see that I was not taken in, I said:

"It is really very wonderful, but another time you should warn me what you are going to do, so that the operation might be attentively watched, and the piece of money noted before being placed on the burning coal."

"Those that are capable of entertaining doubts of my art," said the rogue, "are not worthy to speak to me."

This was his usual style of arrogance, to which I was accustomed. This was the last time I saw this celebrated and learned impostor; he died at Schlesing six or seven years after. The piece of money he gave me was pure gold, and two months after, Field-marshal Keith took such a fancy to it that I gave it him.

I left Tournay the next morning, and stopped at Brussels to await the answer of the letter which I had written to M. de Bragadin. Five days after, I got the letter with a bill of exchange for two hundred ducats.

CHAPTER XIX

TALKS WITH THE GREAT: FREDERICUS REX AND CATHERINE OF RUSSIA

*H*AVING *for the nonce somewhat worn out his welcome in the western countries of Europe, Casanova turns his face eastwards in search of "fresh woods and pastures new." After a short stay at Brunswick, where the good-natured heir to the throne, a London acquaintance, overlooking a little amorous poaching in the royal preserves, intervenes in trouble arising over a bill of exchange — solved, as usual, to the complete satisfaction of the chevalier's honour — Casanova arrives in Berlin.*

According to the Memoirs, this visit to the Prussian capital was due to nothing more than a traveller's whim; but the fact that the younger of the Calsabigi brothers was renewing there with considerable success his Paris lottery enterprise was doubtless an added consideration. Unfortunately King Frederick was just then on the point of withdrawing his patronage from the lottery, which was to cease functioning as a state institution and therefore needed reorganising on a private basis. Consulted by his old associate, Casanova drew up a plan for attracting shareholders, which, however, Calsabigi rejected. This scheme having failed, Casanova bethought himself of applying direct to the king and offering him the services of his manifold capacities. He set about it as follows:

The fifth day after my arrival at Berlin I presented myself to the lord-marshal, who since the death of his brother had been styled Lord Keith. I had seen him in London after his return from Scotland, where he had been reinstated in the family estates, which had been confiscated for Jacobitism. Frederick the Great was supposed to have brought this about. Lord Keith lived at Berlin, resting on his laurels, and enjoying the blessings of peace.

With his old simplicity of manner he told me he was glad to see me again, and asked if I proposed making any stay at Berlin. I replied that I would willingly do so if the king would give me a suitable office. I asked him if he would speak a word in my favour; but he replied that the king liked to judge men's characters for himself, and would often discover merit where no one had suspected its presence, and *vice versa.*

He advised me to intimate to the king in writing that I desired to have the honour of an interview. "When you speak to him," the good old man added, "you may say that you know me, and the king will doubtless address me on the subject, and you may be sure what I say shall not be to your disadvantage."

"But, my lord, how can I write to a monarch of whom I know nothing, and who knows nothing of me? I should not have thought of such a step."

"I dare say, but don't you wish to speak to him?"

"Certainly."

"That is enough. Your letter will make him aware of your desire and nothing more."

"But will he reply?"

"Undoubtedly; he replies to everybody. He will tell you when and where he will see you. His majesty is now at Sans-Souci. I am curious to know the nature of your interview with the monarch, who, as you can see, is not afraid of being imposed on."

When I got home I wrote a plain but respectful letter to the king, asking where and at what time I could introduce myself to him.

In two days I received a letter signed *"Frederick,"* in which the receipt of my letter was acknowledged, and I was told that I should find his majesty in the garden of Sans-Souci at four o'clock.

As may be imagined I was punctual to my appointment. I was at Sans-Souci at three, clad in a simple black dress. When I got into the courtyard there was not so much as a sentinel to stop me, so I went on, mounted a stair, and opened a door in front of me. I found myself in a picture-gallery, and the curator came up to me and offered to show me over it.

"I have not come to admire these masterpieces," I replied, "but to see the king, who informed me in writing that I should find him in the garden."

"He is now at a concert playing the flute; he does so every day after dinner. Did he name any time?"

"Yes, four o'clock, but he will have forgotten that."

"The king never forgets anything; he will keep the appointment, and you will do well to go into the garden and await him."

I had been in the garden for some minutes when I saw him appear, followed by his reader and a pretty damsel. As soon as he saw me he accosted me, taking off his old hat, and pronouncing my name. Then he asked in a terrible voice what I wanted of him. This greeting surprised me, and my voice stuck in my throat.

"Well, speak out. Are you not the person who wrote to me?"

"Yes, sire, but I have forgotten everything now. I thought that I should not be awed by the majesty of a king, but I was mistaken. My lord-marshal should have warned me."

"Then he knows you? Let us walk. What is it that you want? What do you think of my garden?"

His inquiries after my needs and of his garden were simultaneous. To any other person I should have answered that I did not know anything about gardening, but this would have been equivalent to refusing to answer the question; and no monarch, even if he be a philosopher, could endure that. I therefore replied that I thought the garden superb.

"But," he said, "the gardens of Versailles are much finer."

"Yes, sire, but that is chiefly on account of the fountains."

"True, but it is not my fault; there is no water here. I have spent more than three hundred thousand crowns to get water, but unsuccessfully."

"Three hundred thousand crowns, sire! If your majesty had spent them all at once, the fountains should be here."

"Oh, oh! I see you are acquainted with hydraulics."

I could not say that he was mistaken, for fear of offending him, so I simply bent my head, which might mean either yes or no. Thank God the king did not trouble to test my knowledge of the science of hydraulics, with which I was totally unacquainted.

He kept on the move all the time, and as he turned his head from one side to the other hurriedly asked me what forces Venice could put into the field in war time.

"Twenty men-of-war, sire, and a number of galleys."

"What are the land forces?"

"Seventy thousand men, sire; all of whom are subjects of the Republic, and assessing each village at one man."

"That is not true; no doubt you wish to amuse me by telling me these fables. Give me your opinion on taxation."

This was the first conversation I had ever had with a monarch. I made a rapid review of the situation, and found myself much in the same position as an actor of the improvised comedy of the Italians, who is greeted by the hisses of the gods if he stops short a moment. I therefore replied with all the airs of a doctor of finance that I could say something about the theory of taxation.

"That's what I want," he replied, "for the practice is no business of yours."

"There are three kinds of taxes, considered as to their effects. The first is ruinous, the second a necessary evil, and the third invariably beneficial."

"Good! Go on."

"The ruinous impost is the royal tax, the necessary is the military, and the beneficial is the popular."

As I had not given the subject any thought I was in a disagreeable position, for I was obliged to go on speaking, and yet not to talk nonsense.

"The royal tax, sire, is that which deplenishes the purses of the subject to fill the coffers of the king."

"And that kind of tax is always ruinous, you think."

"Always, sire; it prevents the circulation of money — the soul of commerce and the mainstay of the state."

"But if the tax be levied to keep up the strength of the army, you say it is a necessary evil."

"Yes, it is necessary and yet evil, for war is an evil."

"Quite so; and now about the popular tax."

"This is always a benefit, for the monarch takes with one hand and gives with the other; he improves towns and roads, founds schools, protects the sciences, cherishes the arts; in fine, he directs this tax towards improving the condition and increasing the happiness of his people."

"There is a good deal of truth in that. I suppose you know Calsabigi?"

"I ought to, your majesty, as he and I established the Genoa Lottery at Paris seven years ago."

"In what class would you put this taxation, for you will agree that it is taxation of a kind?"

"Certainly, sire, and not the least important. It is beneficial when the monarch spends his profits for the good of the people."

"But the monarch may lose?"

"Once in fifty."

"Is that conclusion the result of a mathematical calculation?"

"Yes, sire."

"Such calculations often prove deceptive."

"Not so, may it please your majesty, when God remains neutral."

"What has God got to do with it?"

"Well, sire, we will call it destiny or chance."

"Good! I may possibly be of your opinion as to the calculation, but I don't like your Genoese Lottery. It seems to me an elaborate swindle, and I would have nothing more to do with it, even if it were positively certain that I should never lose."

"Your majesty is right, for the confidence which makes the people risk their money in a lottery is perfectly fallacious."

This was the end of our strange dialogue, and stopping before a building he looked me over, and then, after a short silence, observed:

"Do you know that you are a fine man?"

"Is it possible that, after the scientific conversation we have had, your majesty should select the least of the qualities which adorn your lifeguardsmen for remark?"

The king smiled kindly, and said:

"As you know Marshal Keith, I will speak to him of you."

With that he took off his hat, and bade me farewell. I retired with a profound bow.

Three or four days after, the marshal gave me the agreeable news that I had found favour in the king's eyes, and that his majesty thought of employing me.

I was curious to learn the nature of this employment, and being in no kind of hurry I resolved to await events in Berlin. The time passed pleasantly enough, for I was either with Calsabigi, Baron Treidel, or my landlady, and when these resources failed me, I used to walk in the park, musing over the events of my life.

Calsabigi had no difficulty in obtaining permission to continue the lottery on his own account, and he boldly announced that henceforward he would conduct the lottery on his own risk. His audacity was crowned with success, and he obtained a profit of a hundred thousand crowns. With this he paid most of his debts, and gave his mistress ten thousand crowns, she returning the document entitling her to that amount. After this lucky drawing it was easy to find guarantors, and the lottery went on successfully for two or three years.

Nevertheless Calsabigi ended by becoming bankrupt and died poor enough in Italy. He might be compared to the Danaides; the more he got the more he spent. His mistress eventually made a respectable marriage and returned to Paris, where she lived in comfort.

At the period of which I am speaking, the Duchess of Brunswick, the king's sister, came to pay him a visit. She was accompanied by her daughter who married the Crown Prince of Prussia in the following year. I saw the king in a suit of lustring trimmed with gold lace, and black silk stockings on his legs. He looked truly comic, and more like a theatrical heavy father than a great king. He came into the hall with his sister on his arm and attracted universal attention, for only very old men could remember seeing him without his uniform and top-boots.

One evening at the theatre he recognises in Madame Denis, the prima ballerina, one of his earliest loves, dating from the days when he was still a pupil at Dr. Gozzi's and she the little daughter of Pantaloon. Together they evoke their childish idyll, which they decide to continue on a more substantial basis. Having thus satis-factorily settled the essential business of finding a mistress, he proceeds to take in the principal sights of the town:

Some days after, Madame Denis took me to Potsdam to show me all the sights of the town. Our intimacy offended no one, for she was generally believed to be my niece, and the general who kept her either believed the report, or like a man of sense pretended to believe it.

Amongst other notable things I saw at Potsdam was the sight of the king commanding the first battalion of his grenadiers, all picked men, the flower of the Prussian army.

The room which we occupied at the inn faced a walk by which the king passed when he came from the castle. The shutters were all closed, and our landlady told us that on one occasion when a pretty dancer called La Reggiana was sleeping in the same room, the king had seen her *in puris naturalibus.* This was too much for his modesty, and he had ordered the shutters to be closed, and closed they had remained, though this event was four years old. The king had some cause to fear, for he had been severely treated by La Barbarina. In the king's bedroom we saw her portrait, that of La Cochois, sister to the actress who became Marchioness d'Argens, and that of Maria Theresa, with whom Frederick had been in love, or rather he had been in love with the idea of becoming emperor. After we had admired the beauty and elegance of the castle, we could not help admiring the way in which the master of the castle was lodged. He had a mean room, and slept on a little bed with a screen around it. There was no dressing-gown and no slippers. The valet showed us an old cap which the king put on when he had a cold; it looked as if it must be very uncomfortable. His majesty's bureau was a table covered with pens, paper, half-burnt manuscripts, and an ink-pot; beside it was a sofa. The valet told us that these manuscripts contained the history of the last Prussian war, and the king had been so annoyed by their accidentally getting burnt that he had resolved to have no more to do with the work. He probably changed his mind, for the book, which is little esteemed, was published shortly after his death.

Five or six weeks after my curious conversation with the monarch, Marshal Keith told me that his majesty had been pleased to create me a tutor to the new corps of Pomeranian cadets which he was just establishing. There were to be fifteen cadets and five tutors, so that each should have the care of three pupils. The salary was six hundred crowns and board found. The duty of the tutors was to follow or accompany the cadets wherever they went, Court included. I had to be quick in making up my mind, for the four others were already installed, and his majesty did not like to be kept waiting. I asked Lord Keith where the college was, and I promised to give him a reply by the next day.

I had to summon all my powers of self-restraint to my assistance when I heard this extravagant proposal as coming from a man who was so discreet in most things, but my astonishment was increased when I saw the abode of these fifteen young noblemen of rich Pomerania. It consisted of three or four great rooms almost devoid of furniture, several whitewashed bedrooms, containing a wretched bed, a deal table, and two deal chairs. The young cadets, boys of twelve or thirteen, all looked dirty and untidy, and were boxed up in a wretched uniform which matched admirably their rude and rustic faces. They were in company with their four governors, whom I took for their servants, and who looked at me in a stupefied manner, not daring to think that I was to be their future colleague.

Just as I was going to bid an eternal farewell to this abode of misery, one of the governors put his head out of the window and exclaimed:

"The king is riding up."

I could not avoid meeting him, and besides, I was glad enough to see him again, especially in such a place.

His majesty came up with his friend Icilius, examined everything, and saw me, but did not honour me with a word. I was elegantly dressed, and wore my cross set with brilliants. But I had to bite my lips so as not to burst out laughing when Frederick the Great got in a towering rage at a chamber utensil which stood beside one of the beds, and which did not appear to be in a very cleanly condition.

"Whose bed is this?" cried the monarch.

"Mine, sire," answered a trembling cadet.

"Good! but it is not you I am angry with; where is your governor?"

The fortunate governor presented himself, and the monarch, after honouring him with the title of *blockhead*, proceeded to scold him roundly. However, he ended by saying that there was a servant, and that the governor ought to see that he did his work properly.

This disgusting scene was enough for me, and I hastened to call on Marshal Keith to announce my determination. The old soldier laughed at the description I gave him of the academy, and said I was quite right to despise such an office, but that I ought, nevertheless, to go and thank the king before I left Berlin. I said I did not feel inclined for another interview with such a man, and he agreed to present my thanks and excuses in my stead.

I made up my mind to go to Russia, and began my preparations in good earnest. Baron Treidel supported my resolve by offering to give me a letter of introduction to his sister, the Duchess of Courland. I wrote to M. de Bragadin to give me a letter for a banker at St. Petersburg, and to remit me through him every month a sum which would keep me in comfort.

Baron Bodisson, a Venetian who wanted to sell the king a picture by Andrea del Sarto, asked me to come with him to Potsdam and the desire of seeing the monarch once again made me accept the invitation. When I reached Potsdam I went to see the parade at which Frederick was nearly always to be found. When he saw me he came up and asked me in a familiar manner when I was going to start for St. Petersburg.

"In five or six days, if your majesty has no objection."

"I wish you a pleasant journey; but what do you hope to do in that land?"

"What I hoped to do in this land — namely, to please the sovereign."

"Have you got an introduction to the empress?"

"No, but I have an introduction to a banker."

"Ah! that's much better. If you pass through Prussia on

your return I shall be delighted to hear of your adventures in Russia."

"Farewell, sire."

Such was the second interview I had with this great king, whom I never saw again.

Arriving at Mitau, the capital of the dukedom of Courland, with six horses to his carriage and three ducats in his pocket, he ingratiates himself with the old duke by pretending to be an authority on mining, accompanies the latter on a tour of inspection of the mineral mines, which need developing, and, thanks to his manservant Lambert, who has had some training as an engineer, acquits himself so well of his task as expert adviser that he is handsomely rewarded for his services by the duke, who also gives him a letter to his son, Charles-Ernest de Biron, general of a Russian infantry regiment, then in garrison at Riga. This introduction was worth more to Casanova than the ducal thalers, for in Charles-Ernest, Prince of Courland, he met a man after his own heart.[1] Already the young general had formed a gambling association with a trio of more or less illustrious and quite unscrupulous adventurers, one of

---

[1] *Ernest-Charles de Biron, younger son of the reigning Duke of Courland, ex-regent of Russia, is the type of the high-born swindler so often to be met with in Casanova's day. The friendship between the prince and the adventurer, which started at Riga, was maintained for many years. When, three years after the Riga meeting, the prince was arrested in Paris for swindling and forgery and transferred to the Bastille, a number of letters from Casanova were seized among his papers. Of these unfortunately only summaries were preserved among the police archives, with the exception of one curious letter, which, though unsigned, was attributed to the same source by the official hand which had to classify the prince's papers. This letter, which under the seal of the greatest secrecy sets forth in detail a process for making gold, bears the following marginal note: "Casanova est un illustre fripon, exilé du royaume le 6 novembre 1767. La pièce mentionnée ci-contre et plusieurs lettres dont il sera parlé plus bas constatent une partie des faits qui le concernent. Il ne serait pas indifférent de voir le dossier de ce particulier." Unfortunately nothing else seems to have been discovered by the officials, judging from a note added to the one mentioned. The letter with its notes was discovered after the capture of the Bastille and published shortly afterwards — the word 'fripon' in the note having been tactfully altered to 'aventurier' — in the Mémoires historiques et authentiques sur la Bastille, by Carra. The book, which had a great success, inspired the Journal de Paris with an article on the Prince of Courland and his relations with Casanova, echoes of which reached Bohemia and the circle at Dux. Far from denying the authorship of the letter, Count Waldstein's librarian with characteristic effrontery declares: "Pour moi, je m'en fais un honneur immortel," and himself reproduces the text of the letter. (See: Mémoires, Garnier edition, Vol. VII.)*

them being Campioni, the Italian dancer, an old acquaintance of our hero's. It was natural, under these circumstances, that Riga offered especial attractions and opportunities, which Casanova was not the man to forgo. A two-months' sojourn was not too much to exhaust these, but two of the bank-holders of the aforesaid association — which, needless to say, Casanova had joined — having had to decamp, the latter also decided to continue his travels eastward.

At Riga Casanova has his first glimpse of the great Catherine:

Catherine II., wishing to show herself to her new subjects, over whom she was in reality supreme, though she had put the ghost of a king in the person of Stanislas Poniatowski, her former favourite, on the throne of Poland, came to Riga, and it was then I saw this great sovereign for the first time. I was a witness of the kindness and affability with which she treated the Livonian nobility, and of the way in which she kissed the young ladies, who had come to kiss her hand, upon the mouth. She was surrounded by the Orloffs and by other nobles who had assisted in placing her on the throne. For the comfort and pleasure of her loyal subjects the empress graciously expressed her intention of holding a bank at faro of ten thousand roubles.

Instantly the table and the cards were brought forward, and the piles of gold placed in order. She took the cards, pretended to shuffle them, and gave them to the first comer to cut. She had the pleasure of seeing her bank broken at the first deal, and indeed this result was to be expected, as anybody not an absolute idiot could see how the cards were going. The next day the empress set out for Mitau, where triumphal arches were erected in her honour. They were made of wood, as stone is scarce in Poland, and indeed there would not have been time to build stone arches.

The day after her arrival great alarm prevailed, for news came that a revolution was ready to burst out at St. Petersburg, and some even said that it had begun. The rebels wished to have forth from his prison the hapless Ivan Ivanovitz, who had been proclaimed emperor in his cradle, and dethroned by Elizabeth Petrovna. Two officers to whom the guardianship of the prince had been confided had killed the poor innocent monarch when they saw that they would be overpowered.

The assassination of the innocent prince created such a sensation that the wary Panin, fearing for the results, sent courier after courier to the empress urging her to return to St. Petersburg and show herself to the people. Catherine was thus obliged to leave Mitau twenty-four hours after she had entered it, and after hastening back to the capital she arrived only to find that the excitement had entirely subsided. For politic reasons the assassins of the wretched Ivan were rewarded, and the bold man who had endeavoured to rise by her fall was beheaded.

He is to see more of the empress very shortly, for he is soon on his way to St. Petersburg:

I left Riga with the thermometer indicating fifteen degrees of frost, but though I travelled day and night, not leaving the carriage for the sixty hours for which my journey lasted, I did not feel the cold in the least. I had taken care to pay all the stages in advance and Marshal Braun, Governor of Livonia, had given me the proper passport. On the box seat was a French servant who had begged me to allow him to wait on me for the journey in return for a seat beside the coachman. He kept his word and served me well, and though he was but ill clad he bore the horrible cold for two days and three nights without appearing to feel it. It is only a Frenchman who can bear such trials; a Russian in similar attire would have been frozen to death in twenty-four hours, despite plentiful doses of corn brandy.

I lost sight of this individual when I arrived at St. Petersburg, but I met him again three months after, richly dressed, and occupying a seat beside mine at the table of M. de Czernitscheff. He was the *uchitel* of the young count, who sat beside him. But I shall have occasion to speak more at length of the office of *uchitel*, or tutor, in Russia.

As for Lambert, who was beside me in the carriage, he did nothing but eat, drink, and sleep the whole way; seldom speaking, for he stammered, and could only talk about mathematical problems, on which I was not always in the humour to converse. He was never amusing, never had any sensible observation to make on the varied scenes through which we passed; in short, he was a fool, and wearisome to all save himself.

I was only stopped once, and that was at Nawa, where the authorities demanded a passport, which I did not possess. I told the governor that as I was a Venetian, and only travelled for pleasure, I did not conceive a passport would be necessary, my Republic not being at war with any other power, and Russia having no embassy at Venice.

"Nevertheless," I added, "if your excellency wills it I will turn back; but I shall complain to Marshal Braun, who gave me the passport for posting, knowing that I had not the political passport."

After rubbing his forehead for a minute, the governor gave me a pass, which I still possess, and which brought me into St. Petersburg, without my having to allow the custom-house officers to inspect my trunks.

Between Koporie and St. Petersburg there is only a wretched hut for the accommodation of travellers. The country is a wilderness, and the inhabitants do not even speak Russian. The district is called Ingria, and I believe the jargon spoken has no affinity with any other language. The principal occupation of the peasants is robbery, and the traveller does well not to leave any of his effects alone for a moment.

I got to St. Petersburg just as the first rays of the sun began to gild the horizon. It was in the winter solstice, and the sun rose at the extremity of an immense plain at twenty-four minutes past nine, so I am able to state that the longest night in Russia consists of eighteen hours and three-quarters.

I got down in a fine street called the Millione. I found a couple of empty rooms, which the people of the house furnished with two beds, four chairs, and two small tables, and rented to me very cheaply. Seeing the enormous stoves, I concluded they must consume a vast amount of wood, but I was mistaken. Russia is the land of stoves as Venice is that of cisterns. I have inspected the interior of these stoves in summer-time as minutely as if I wished to find out the secret of making them; they are twelve feet high by six broad, and are capable of warming a vast room. They are only refuelled once in twenty-four hours, for as soon as the wood is reduced to the state of charcoal a valve is shut in the upper part of the stove.

It is only in the houses of noblemen that the stoves are refuelled twice a day, because servants are strictly forbidden to close the valve, and for a very good reason.

If a gentleman chance to come home and order his servants to warm his room before he goes to bed, and if the servant is careless enough to close the valve before the wood is reduced to charcoal, then the master sleeps his last sleep, being suffocated in three or four hours. When the door is opened in the morning he is found dead, and the poor devil of a servant is immediately hanged, whatever he may say. This sounds severe, and even cruel; but it is a necessary regulation, or else a servant would be able to get rid of his master on the smallest provocation.

After I had made an agreement for my board and lodging, both of which were very cheap (now St. Petersburg is as dear as London), I bought some pieces of furniture which were necessaries for me, but which were not as yet much in use in Russia, such as a commode, a bureau, etc.

German is the language principally spoken in St. Petersburg, and I did not speak German much better then than I do now, so I had a good deal of difficulty in making myself understood, and usually excited my auditors to laughter.

After dinner my landlord told me that the Court was giving a masked ball to five thousand persons to last sixty hours. He gave me a ticket, and told me I only needed to show it at the entrance of the imperial palace.

I decided to use the ticket, for I felt that I should like to be present at so numerous an assembly, and as I had my domino still by me a mask was all I wanted. I went to the palace in a sedan-chair, and found an immense crowd assembled, and dancing going on in several halls, in each of which an orchestra was stationed. There were long counters loaded with eatables and drinkables at which those who were hungry or thirsty ate or drank as much as they liked. Gaiety and freedom reigned everywhere, and the light of a thousand wax-candles illuminated the hall. Everything was wonderful, and all the more so from its contrast with the cold and darkness that were without. All at once I heard a masquer beside me say to another:

"There's the czarina."

We soon saw Gregory Orloff, for his orders were to follow the empress at a distance.

I followed the masquer, and I was soon persuaded that it was really the empress, for everybody was repeating it, though no one openly recognised her. Those who really did not know her jostled her in the crowd, and I imagined that she would be delighted at being treated thus, as it was a proof of the success of her disguise. Several times I saw her speaking in Russian to one masquer and another. No doubt she exposed her vanity to some rude shocks, but she had also the inestimable advantage of hearing truths which her courtiers would certainly not tell her. The masquer who was pronounced to be Orloff followed her everywhere, and did not let her out of his sight for a moment. He could not be mistaken, as he was an exceptionally tall man and had a peculiar carriage of the head.

Among the masquers Casanova discovers to his delight one of the most cherished of his Parisian amours, Madame Baret, the mercer's wife, now fairly launched in the gallant world as Madame de l'Anglade, mistress of the Polish ambassador and by profession an actress, though, as she herself admits, she can neither act nor sing. As her protector has just left her, she counts on Casanova to get her out of the country.

Despite the Orloff decree against gaming, Casanova finds no difficulty in indulging in his favourite and essential pastime. His remarks on the conditions under which it was carried on have the value of expert opinion:

I played for small stakes and won a few roubles. I made friends with Baron Lefort at supper, and he afterwards told me of the vicissitudes he had experienced.

As I was praising the noble calmness with which a certain prince had lost a thousand roubles to him, he laughed and said that the fine gamester I had mentioned played upon credit but never paid.

"How about his honour?"

"It is not affected by the non-payment of gaming debts. It is an understood thing in Russia that one who plays on credit and loses may pay or not pay as he wishes, and the winner only makes himself ridiculous by reminding the loser of his debt."

"Then the holder of the bank has the right to refuse to accept bets which are not backed by ready money."

"Certainly; and nobody has a right to be offended with him for doing so. Gaming is in a very bad state in Russia. I know young men of the highest rank whose chief boast is that they know how to conquer fortune; that is, to cheat. One of the Matuschkins goes so far as to challenge all foreign cheats to master him. He has just received permission to travel for three years, and it is an open secret that he wishes to travel that he may exercise his skill. He intends returning to Russia laden with the spoils of the dupes he has made."

St. Petersburg was swarming with adventurers of every nation-

ality, for with the recent accession to the throne of the "Semiramis of the North," the new capital of Russia was becoming a veritable land of Cockaigne for the demi-monde *of Europe. What a happy change for our hero after the austerity and pettiness of most of the German capitals, and how Voltaire's "Our light comes from the north!" must have found an echo in his heart! He is soon in the thick of things, making new acquaintances and renewing with the old ones he meets at every turn the oft-tried* combinazioni *in which he excels. He is quick also to adopt local customs, as witness the following:*

As I was walking away from Catherinhoff with Zinowieff I noticed a young country-woman whose beauty astonished me. I pointed her out to the young officer, and we made for her; but she fled away with great activity to a little cottage, where we followed her. We went in and saw the father, mother, and some children, and in a corner the timid form of the fair maiden.

Zinowieff (who, by the way, was for twenty years Russian ambassador at Madrid) had a long conversation in Russian with the father. I did not understand what was said, but I guessed it referred to the girl because, when her father called her, she advanced submissively, and stood modestly before us.

The conversation over, Zinowieff went out, and I followed him after giving the master of the house a rouble. Zinowieff told me what had passed, saying that he had asked the father if he would let him have the daughter as a maid-servant, and the father had replied that it should be so with all his heart, but that he must have a hundred roubles for her, as she was still a virgin. "So you see," added Zinowieff, "the matter is quite simple."

"How simple?"

"Why, yes; only a hundred roubles."

"And supposing me to be inclined to give that sum?"

"Then she would be your servant, and you could do anything you liked with her, except kill her."

"And supposing she is not willing?"

"That never happens, but if it did you could have her beaten."

"Well, if she is satisfied and I enjoy her, can I still continue to keep her?"

"You will be her master, I tell you, and can have her arrested if she attempts to escape, unless she can return the hundred roubles you gave for her."

"What must I give her per month?"

"Nothing, except enough to eat and drink. You must also let her go to the baths on Saturday and to the church on Sunday."

"Can I make her come with me when I leave St. Petersburg?"

"No, unless you obtain permission and find a surety, for though the girl would be your slave she would still be a slave to the empress."

"Very good; then will you arrange this matter for me? I will give the hundred roubles, and I promise you I will not treat her as a slave. But I hope you will care for my interests, as I do not wish to be duped."

"I promise you you shall not be duped; I will see to everything. Would you like her now?"

"No, to-morrow."

Balsamo Cagliostro, evidently scenting an affinity, gives Casanova proofs of his powers of counterfeiting with brush and pen, which border on the marvellous. "You ought to make this talent serve you in good stead," Casanova remarks approvingly, adding the warning, "but be careful, or it may cost you your life." [1] *Ten years later they met again. The promised record of this meeting between the two great adventurers — Cagliostro then in all his glory, Casanova at his lowest depth — is unfortunately not included in the Memoirs. If a link between the two great mystifiers of the eighteenth century, the Count of St. Germain and the Count of Cagliostro (by some held to be one and the same person) can be established, it is possible that the Chevalier de Seingalt helped to forge it.*

We returned to St. Petersburg in a phaeton, and the next day at nine o'clock I called on Zinowieff, who said he was delighted to do me this small service. On the way he said that if I liked he could get me a perfect seraglio of pretty girls in a few days.

"No," said I, "one is enough." And I gave him the hundred roubles.

We arrived at the cottage, where we found the father, mother, and daughter. Zinowieff explained his business crudely enough,

---

[1] *In the last volume of the Memoirs, Casanova, then over seventy years of age, refers to this meeting. "Twenty years ago," he observes, "I told Cagliostro (who called himself Count Pellegrini in those days) not to set foot in Rome, and if he had followed this counsel he would not have died miserably in a Roman prison."*

after the custom of the country, and the father thanked St. Nicholas for the good luck he had sent him. He spoke to his daughter, who looked at me and softly, uttered the necessary *yes*.

Zinowieff then gave the hundred roubles to the father, who handed them to his daughter, and she only took them to return them to her mother. My servant and coachman were then called in to witness an arrangement of which they knew nothing.

I called her Zaira, and she got into the carriage and returned with me to St. Petersburg in her coarse clothes, without a chemise of any kind. After I had dropped Zinowieff at his lodging I went home, and for four days I was engaged in collecting and arranging my slave's toilet, not resting till I had dressed her modestly in the French style. In less than three months she had learnt enough Italian to tell me what she wanted and to understand me. She soon loved me, and afterwards she got jealous. But we shall hear more of her.

This is what we hear (Casanova, it should be remarked, has been out all night celebrating in Franco-Russian fashion):

I got home, and, fortunately for myself, escaped the bottle which Zaira flung at my head, and which would infallibly have killed me if it had hit me. She threw herself on to the ground, and began to strike it with her forehead. I thought she had gone mad, and wondered whether I had better call for assistance; but she became quiet enough to call me assassin and traitor, with all the other abusive epithets that she could remember. To convict me of my crime she showed me twenty-five cards, placed in order, and on them she displayed the various enormities of which I had been guilty.

I let her go on till her rage was somewhat exhausted, and then, having thrown her divining apparatus into the fire, I looked at her in pity and anger, and said that we must part the next day, as she had narrowly escaped killing me. I confessed that I had been with Bomback, and that there had been a girl in the house; but I denied all the other sins of which she accused me. I then went to sleep without taking the slightest notice of her, in spite of all she said and did to prove her repentance.

I woke after a few hours to find her sleeping soundly, and I began to consider how I could best rid myself of the girl, who would probably kill me if we continued living together. Whilst I was absorbed in these thoughts she awoke, and falling at my feet wept and professed her utter repentance, and promised never to touch another card as long as I kept her.

At last I could resist her entreaties no longer, so I took her in my arms and forgave her; and we did not part till she had received undeniable proofs of the return of my affection. I intended to start for Moscow in three days, and she was delighted when she heard she was to go.

Three circumstances had won me this young girl's furious affection. In the first place I often took her to see her family, with whom I always left a rouble; in the second I made her eat with me; and in the third I had beaten her three of four times when she had tried to prevent me going out.

In Russia beating is a matter of necessity, for words have no force whatever. A servant, mistress, or courtesan understands nothing but the lash. Words are altogether thrown away, but a few good strokes are entirely efficacious. The servant, whose soul is still more enslaved than his body, reasons somewhat as follows, after he has had a beating:

"My master has not sent me away, but beaten me; therefore he loves me, and I ought to be attached to him."

It is the same with the Russian soldier, and in fact with everybody. Honour stands for nothing, but with the knout and brandy one can get anything from them except heroical enthusiasm.

Papanelopulo laughed at me when I said that as I liked my Cossack I should endeavour to correct him with words only, when he took too much brandy.

"If you do not beat him," he said, "he will end by beating you"; and he spoke the truth.

One day, when he was so drunk as to be unable to attend on me, I began to scold him, and threatened him with the stick if he did not mend his ways. As soon as he saw my cane lifted, he ran at me and got hold of it; and if I had not knocked him down immediately, he would doubtless have beaten me. I dismissed him on the spot. There is not a better servant in the world than a Russian. He works without ceasing, sleeps in front of the door of his master's bedroom to be always ready to fulfil his orders, never answering his reproaches, incapable of theft. But after drinking a little too much brandy he becomes a perfect monster; and drunkenness is the vice of the whole nation.

A coachman knows no other way of resisting the bitter cold to which he is exposed, than by drinking rye brandy. It sometimes happens that he drinks till he falls asleep, and then there is no awaking for him in this world. Unless one is very careful, it is easy to lose an ear, the nose, a cheek, or a lip by frost bites. One day as I was walking out on a bitterly cold day, a Russian noticed that one of my ears was frozen. He ran up to me and rubbed the affected part with a handful of snow till the circulation was restored. I asked him how he had noticed my state, and he said he had remarked the livid whiteness of my ear, and this, he said, was always a sign that the frost had taken it. What surprised me most of all is that sometimes the part grows again after it has dropped off. Prince Charles of Courland assured me that he had lost his nose in Siberia, and that it had grown again the next summer. I have been assured of the truth of this by several Russians.

It had been announced that a magnificent tournament, to which all the nobility of Russia were invited, was to inaugurate the huge new amphitheatre built by the Italian architect Rinaldini at St. Petersburg. But owing to the persistent bad weather, the fête had to be postponed and with it the arrival of that "dear Prince of Courland" with whom Casanova doubtless intended improving that very shining hour. To console himself for this disappointment Casanova takes his Zaira for a trip to Moscow:

Having made all arrangements for my journey to Moscow, I got into my sleeping carriage with Zaira, having a servant behind who could speak both Russian and German. For twenty-four roubles the *chevochic* (hirer out of horses) engaged to carry me to Moscow in six days and seven nights with six horses. This struck me as being extremely cheap. The distance is seventy-two Russian stages, almost equivalent to five hundred Italian miles, or a hundred and sixty French leagues.

We set out just as a cannon shot from the citadel announced the close of day. It was towards the end of May, in which month there is literally no night at St. Petersburg. Without the report of the cannon no one would be able to tell when the day ended and the night began. One can read a letter at midnight, and the moonlight makes no appreciable difference. This continual day lasts for eight weeks, and during that time no one lights a candle. At Moscow it is different; a candle is always necessary at midnight if one wishes to read.

We reached Novgorod in forty-eight hours, and here the *chevochic* allowed us a rest of five hours. I saw a circumstance there which surprised me very much, though one has no business to be surprised at anything if one travels much, and especially in a land of half savages. I asked the *chevochic* to drink, but he appeared to be in great melancholy. I inquired what was the matter and he told Zaira that one of his horses had refused to eat, and that it was clear that if he could not eat he could not work. We followed him into the stable, and found the horse looking oppressed by care, its head lowered and motionless; it had evidently got no appetite. His master began a pathetic oration, looking tenderly at the animal, as if to arouse it to a sense of duty, and then taking its head, and kissing it lovingly, he put it into the manger, but to no purpose. Then the man began to weep bitterly, but in such a way that I had the greatest difficulty to prevent myself laughing, for I could see that he wept in the hope that his tears might soften the brute's heart. When he had wept some time he again put the horse's head into the manger, but again to no purpose. At this he got furious and swore to be avenged. He led the horse out of the stable, tied it to a post, and beat it with a thick stick for a quarter of an hour so violently that my heart bled for the poor animal. At last the *chevochic* was tired out, and taking the horse back to the stable he fastened up his head once more, and to my astonishment it began to devour its provender with the greatest appetite. At this the master jumped for joy, laughed, sang, and committed a thousand extravagancies, as if to show the horse how happy it had made him. I was beside myself with astonishment, and concluded that such treatment would have succeeded nowhere but in Russia, where the stick seems to be the panacea or universal medicine.

They tell me, however, that the stick is gradually going out of fashion. Peter the Great used to beat his generals black and blue, and in his days a lieutenant had to receive with all submission the cuffs of his captain, who bent before the blows of his major, who did the same to his colonel, who received chastisement from his general. So I was informed by old General Woyakoff, who was a pupil of Peter the Great, and had often been beaten by the great emperor, the founder of St. Petersburg.

It seems to me that I have scarcely said anything about

this great and famous capital, which in my opinion is built on somewhat precarious foundations. No one but Peter could have thus given the lie to nature by building his immense palaces of marble and granite on mud and shifting sand. They tell me that the town is now in its manhood, to the honour of the great Catherine; but in the year 1765 it was still in its minority, and seemed to me only to have been built with the childish aim of seeing it fall into ruins. Streets were built with certainty of having to repair them in six months' time. The whole place proclaimed itself to be the whim of a despot. If it is to be durable constant care will be required, for nature never gives up its rights and reasserts them when the constraint of man is withdrawn. My theory is that sooner or later the soil must give way and drag the vast city with it.

We reached Moscow in the time the *chevochic* had promised. As the same horses were used for the whole journey, it would have been impossible to travel more quickly. A Russian told me that the Empress Elizabeth had done the journey in fifty-two hours.

"You mean that she issued a ukase to the effect that she had done it," said a Russian of the old school; "and if she had liked she could have travelled more quickly still; it was only a question of the wording of the ukase."

Even when I was in Russia it was not allowable to doubt the infallibility of a ukase, and to do so was equivalent to high treason. One day I was crossing a canal at St. Petersburg by a small wooden bridge; Melissino, Papanelopulo, and some other Russians were with me. I began to abuse the wooden bridge, which I characterised as both mean and dangerous. One of my companions said that on such a day it would be replaced by a fine stone bridge, as the empress had to pass there on some state occasion. The day named was three weeks off, and I said plainly that it was impossible. One of the Russians looked askance at me, and said there was no doubt about it, as a ukase had been published ordering that the bridge should be built. I was going to answer him but Papanelopulo gave my hand a squeeze, and whispered "*Taci!*" (hush).

The bridge was not built, but I was not justified, for the empress published another ukase in which she declared it to be her gracious pleasure that the bridge should not be built till the following year. If anyone would see what a pure despotism is like, let him go to Russia.

The Russian sovereigns use the language of despotism on all occasions. One day I saw the empress, dressed in man's clothes, going out for a ride. Her master of the horse, Prince Repnin, held the bridle of the horse, which suddenly gave him a kick which broke his ankle-bone. The empress instantly ordained that the horse should be taken away, and that no one should mount it again under pain of death. All official positions in Russia have military rank assigned to them, and this sufficiently indicates the nature of the government. The coachman-in-chief of her imperial highness holds the rank of colonel, as also does her chief cook. The *castrato* Luini was a lieutenant-colonel and the painter Toretti only a captain, because he had only eight hundred roubles a year, while the coachman had three thousand. The sentinels at the doors of the palace have their muskets crossed, and ask those who wish to pass through what is their rank. When I was asked this question, I stopped short; but the quick-witted officer asked me how much I had a year, and on my replying, at a hazard, three thousand roubles, he gave me the rank of general and I was allowed to pass. I saw the czarina for a moment; she stopped at the door and took off her gloves to give her hands to be kissed by the officer and the two sentinels. But such means as this she had won the affection of the corps, commanded by Gregorius Gregorovitch Orloff, on which her safety depended in case of revolution.

I made the following notes when I saw the empress hearing mass in her chapel: The protopapa, or bishop, received her at the door to give her the holy water, and she kissed his episcopal ring, while the prelate, whose beard was a couple of feet in length, lowered his head to kiss the hands of his temporal sovereign and spiritual head, for in Russia the he or she on the throne is the spiritual as well as temporal head of the Church.

She did not evidence the least devotion during mass; hypocrisy did not seem to be one of her vices. Now she smiled at one of her suite, now at another, and occasionally she addressed the favourite, not because she had anything to say to him, but to make him an object of envy to the others.

One evening, as she was leaving the theatre where Metastasio's *Olympiade* had been performed, I heard her say:

"The music of that opera has given the greatest pleasure to everyone, so of course I am delighted with it; but it wearies me, nevertheless. Music is a fine thing, but I cannot understand how anyone who is seriously occupied can love it passionately. I will have Buranello here, and I wonder whether he will interest me in music, but I am afraid nature did not constitute me to feel all its charms."

She always argued in that way. In due time I will set down her words to me when I returned from Moscow. When I arrived at that city I got down at a good inn, where they gave me two rooms and a coach-house for my carriage. After dinner I hired a small carriage and a guide who could speak French. My carriage was drawn by four horses, for Moscow is a vast city composed of four distinct towns, and many of the streets are rough and ill paved. I had five or six letters of introduction, and I determined to take them all. I took Zaira with me, as she was as curious to see everything as a girl of fourteen naturally is. I do not remember what feast the Greek Church was keeping on that day, but I shall never forget the terrific bell-ringing with which my ears were assailed, for there are churches everywhere. The country people were engaged in sowing their grain, to reap it in September. They laughed at our southern custom of sowing eight months earlier, as unnecessary and even prejudicial to the crops, but I do not know where the right lies. Perhaps we may both be right, for there is no master to compare with experience.

I took the introductions I had received from Narischkin, Prince Repnin, the worthy Papanelopulo, and Melissino's brother. The next morning the whole of the persons at whose houses I had left letters called on me. They all asked Zaira and myself to dinner, and I accepted the invitation of the first comer, M. Dimidoff, who promised to dine with the rest on the following days. Zaira, who had been tutored by me to some extent, was delighted to show me that she was worthy of the position she occupied. She was exquisitely dressed and won golden opinions everywhere, for our hosts did not care to inquire whether she were my daughter, my mistress, or my servant, for in this matter, as in many others, the Russians are excessively indulgent. Those who have not seen Moscow have not seen Russia, for the people of St. Petersburg are not really Russians at all. Their court manners are very different from their manners *au naturel,* and it may be said with truth that the Russian is as a stranger in St. Petersburg. The citizens of Moscow, and especially the rich ones, speak with pity of those who, for one reason or another, had expatriated themselves; and with them to expatriate one's self is to leave Moscow, which they consider as their native land. They look on St. Petersburg with an envious eye, and call it the ruin of Russia. I do not know whether this is a just view to take of the case, I merely repeat what I have heard.

In the course of a week I saw all the sights of Moscow — the manufactures, the churches, the remains of the old days, the museums, the libraries (of no interest to my mind), not forgetting the famous bell. I noticed that their bells are not allowed to swing like ours, but are motionless, being rung by a rope attached to the clapper.

I thought the Moscow women more handsome than those of St. Petersburg, and I attribute this to the great superiority of the air. They are gentle and accessible by nature; and to obtain the favour of a kiss on the lips, one need only make a show of kissing their hands.

There was good fare in plenty, but no delicacy in its composition or arrangement. Their table is always open to friends and acquaintances, and a friend may bring in five or six persons to dinner, and even at the end of the meals you will never hear a Russian say, "We have had dinner; you have come too late." Their souls are not black enough for them to pronounce such words as these. Notice is given to the cook, and the dinner begins over again. They have a delicious drink, the name of which I do not remember; but it is much superior to the sherbet of Constantinople. The numerous servants are not given water, but a light, nourishing, and agreeable fluid, which may be purchased very cheaply. They all hold St. Nicholas in the greatest reverence, only praying to God through the mediation of this saint, whose picture is always suspended in the principal room of the house. A person coming in makes first a bow to the image and then a bow to the master, and if perchance the image is absent, the Russian, after gazing all round, stands confused and motionless, not knowing what to do. As a general rule the Muscovites are the most superstitious Christians in the world. Their liturgy is in Greek, of which the people understand nothing, and the clergy, themselves extremely ignorant, gladly leave them completely in the dark on all matters connected with religion. I could never make them understand that the only reason for the Roman Christians making the sign of the Cross from left to right, is that we say *spiritus sancti*, while they say *agion pneuma*.

"If you said *pneuma agion*," I used to say, "then you would cross yourselves like us, and if we said *sancti spiritus* we should cross ourselves like you."

"The adjective," replied my interlocutor, "should always precede the substantive, for we should never utter the name of God without first giving Him some honourable epithet."

Such are nearly all the differences which divide the two Churches, without reckoning the numerous idle tales which they have as well as ourselves, and which are by no means the least cherished articles of their faith.

We returned to St. Petersburg by the way we had come, but Zaira would have liked me never to leave Moscow. She had become so much in love with me by force of constant association that I could not think without a pang of the moment of separation. The day after our arrival in the capital I took her to her home, where she showed her father all the little presents I had given her, and told him of the honour she had received as my daughter, which made the good man laugh heartily.

The first piece of news I heard was that a ukase had been issued, ordering the erection of a temple dedicated to God in the Moscöi opposite the house where I resided. The empress had entrusted Rinaldi, the architect, with the erection. He asked her what emblem he should put above the portal, and she replied:

"No emblem at all, only the name of God in large letters."

"I will put a triangle."

"No triangle at all; but only the name of God in whatever language you like, and nothing more."

The second piece of news was that Bomback had fled and had been captured at Mitau, where he believed himself in safety. M. de Simolia had arrested him. It was a grave case, for he had deserted; however, he was given his life, and sent into barracks at Kamstchatka. Crèvecœur and his mistress had departed, carrying some money with them, and a Florentine adventurer named Biliotti had fled with eighteen thousand roubles belonging

to Papanelopulo, but a certain Bori, the worthy Greek's facto-
tum, had caught him at Mitau and brought him back to St.
Petersburg, where he was now in prison. Prince Charles of
Courland arrived about this time, and I hastened to call upon
him as soon as he advised me of his coming. He was lodging in
a house belonging to Count Dimidoff, who owned large iron
mines, and had made the whole house of iron, from attic to base-
ment. The prince had brought his mistress with him, but she
was still in an ill-humour, and he was beginning to get heartily
sick of her. The man was to be pitied, for he could not get rid
of her without finding her a husband, and this husband became
more difficult to find every day. When the prince saw how
happy I was with my Zaira, he could not help thinking how
easily happiness may be won; but the fatal desire for luxury and
empty show spoils all, and renders the very sweets of life as
bitter as gall.

I was indeed considered happy, and I liked to appear so, but
in my heart I was wretched. Ever since my imprisonment under
The Leads, I had been subject to hæmorrhoids, which came
on three or four times a year. At St. Petersburg I had a serious
attack, and the daily pain and anxiety embittered my existence.
A vegetarian doctor called Senapios, for whom I had sent, gave
me the sad news that I had a blind or incomplete fistula in the
rectum, and according to him nothing but the cruel bistoury
would give me any relief, and indeed he said I had no time to
lose. I had to agree, in spite of my dislike to the operation; but
fortunately the clever surgeon whom the doctor summoned pronounced that if I would have patience nature itself would give
me relief. I had much to endure, especially from the severe
dieting to which I was subjected, but which doubtless did me
good.

Colonel Melissino asked me to be present at a review which
was to take place at three versts from St. Petersburg, and was
to be succeeded by a dinner to twenty-four guests, given by
General Orloff. I went with the prince, and saw a cannon fired
twenty times in a minute, testing the performance with my
watch.

My neighbour at dinner was the French ambassador. Wishing
to drink deeply, after the Russian fashion, and thinking the
Hungarian wine as innocent as champagne, he drank so bravely

that at the end of dinner he had lost the use of his legs. Count Orloff made him drink still more, and then he fell asleep and was laid on a bed.

The gaiety of the meal gave me some idea of Russian wit. I did not understand the language, so M. Zinowieff translated the curious sallies to me while the applause they had raised was still resounding.

Melissino rose to his feet, holding a large goblet full of Hungarian wine in his hand. There was a general silence to listen to him. He drank the health of General Orloff in these words:

"May you die when you become rich."

The applause was general, for the allusion was to the unbounded generosity of Orloff. The general's reply struck me as better still, but it was equally rugged in character. He, too, took a full cup, and turning to Melissino, said:

"May you never die till I slay you!"

The applause was furious, for he was their host and their general.

The Russian wit is of the energetic kind, devoid of grace; all they care about is directness and vigour.

Voltaire had just sent the empress his *Philosophy of History*, which he had written for her and dedicated to her. A month after, an edition of three thousand copies came by sea, and was sold out in a week, for all the Russians who knew a little French were eager to possess a copy of the work. The leaders of the Voltaireans were two noblemen, named, respectively, Stroganoff and Schuvaloff. I had seen verses written by the former of these as good as Voltaire's own verses, and twenty years later I saw an ode by the latter of which Voltaire would not have been ashamed, but the subject was ill chosen; for it treated of the death of the great philosopher who had so studiously avoided using his pen on melancholy themes. In those days all Russians with any pretensions to literature read nothing but Voltaire, and when they had read all his writings they thought themselves as wise as their master. To me they seemed pigmies mimicking a giant. I told them that they ought to read all the books from which Voltaire had drawn his immense learning, and then, perhaps, they might become as wise as he. I remember the saying of a wise man at Rome: "Beware of the man of one book." I wonder whether the Russians are more profound now; but that is

a question I cannot answer. At Dresden I knew Prince Bilosel-
ski, who was on his way back to Russia after having been ambassador at Turin. He was the author of an admirable work
on metaphysics, and the analysis of the soul and reason.

Count Panin was the tutor of Paul Petrovitch, heir-presump-
tive to the throne. The young prince had a severe master, and
dared not even applaud an air at the opera unless he first received
permission to do so from his mentor.

When a courier brought the news of the sudden death of
Francis I., Emperor of Germany and of the Holy Roman Empire, the czarina being at Czarsko-Zelo, the count minister-tutor
was in the palace with his pupil, then eleven years old. The
courier came at noon, and gave the dispatch into the hands of
the minister, who was standing in the midst of a crowd of
courtiers of whom I was one. The prince imperial was at his
right hand. The minister read the dispatch in a low voice, and
then said:

"This is news indeed. The Emperor of the Romans has died
suddenly."

He then turned to Paul, and said to him:

"Full court mourning, which your highness will observe for
three months longer than the empress."

"Why so?" said Paul.

"Because, as Duke of Holstein, your highness has a right to
attend the diet of the empire, a privilege," he added, turning to
us, "which Peter the Great desired in vain."

I noted the attention with which the Grand Duke Paul listened
to his mentor, and the care with which he concealed his joy at
the news. I was immensely pleased with this way of giving instruction. I said as much to Prince Lobkowitz, who was standing by me, and he refined on my praises. This prince was
popular with everyone. He was even preferred to his predecessor, Prince Esterhazy; and this was saying a great deal, for
Esterhazy was adored in Russia. The gay and affable manner of
Prince Lobkowitz made him the life and soul of all the parties
at which he was present. He was a constant courtier of the
Countess Braun, the reigning beauty, and everyone believed his
love had been crowned with success, though no one could assert
as much positively.

There was a great review held at a distance of twelve or fourteen versts from St. Petersburg, at which the empress and all her train of courtiers were present. The houses of the two or three adjoining villages were so few and small that it would be impossible for all the company to find a lodging. Nevertheless I wished to be present, chiefly to please Zaira, who wanted to be seen with me on such an occasion. The review was to last three days; there were to be fireworks, and a mine was to be exploded besides the evolutions of the troops. I went in my travelling carriage, which would serve me for a lodging if I could get nothing better.

We arrived at the appointed place at eight o'clock in the morning; the evolutions lasted till noon. When they were over we went towards a tavern and had our meal served to us in the carriage, as all the rooms in the inn were full.

After dinner my coachman tried in vain to find me a lodging, so I disposed myself to sleep all night in the carriage; and so I did for the whole time of the review, and fared better than those who had spent so much money to be ill lodged. Melissino told me that the empress thought my idea a very sensible one. As I was the only person who had a sleeping carriage, which was quite a portable house in itself, I had numerous visitors, and Zaira was radiant to be able to do the honours.

I had a good deal of conversation during the review with Count Tott, brother of the nobleman who was employed at Constantinople, and known as Baron Tott. We had known each other at Paris, and afterwards at The Hague, where I had the pleasure of being of service to him. He had come to St. Petersburg with Madame de Soltikoff, whom he had met at Paris, and whose lover he was. He lived with her, went to Court, and was well received by everyone.

Two or three years after, the empress ordered him to leave St. Petersburg on account of the troubles in Poland. It was said that he kept up a correspondence with his brother, who was endeavouring to intercept the fleet under the command of Alexis Orloff. I never heard what became of him after he left Russia, where he obliged me with the loan of five hundred roubles, which I have not yet been able to return to him.

M. Maruzzi, by calling a Venetian merchant, and by birth a Greek, having left trade to live like a gentleman, came to St. Petersburg when I was there, and was presented at Court. He was a fine-looking man, and was admitted to all the great houses. The empress treated him with distinction because she had thoughts of making him her agent at Venice. He paid his court to the Countess Braun, but he had rivals there who were not afraid of him. He was rich enough, but did not know how to spend his money; and avarice is a sin which meets with no pity from the Russian ladies.

I went to Czarsko-Zelo, Peterhoff, and Cronstadt, for if you want to say you have been in a country you should see as much as possible of it. I wrote notes and memorandums on several questions with the hope of them procuring me a place in the civil service, and all my productions were laid before the empress but with no effect. In Russia they do not think much of foreigners unless they have specially summoned them; those who come of their own account rarely make much, and I suspect the Russians are right.

I thought of leaving Russia at the beginning of the autumn, but I was told by MM. Panin and Alsuwieff that I ought not to go without having spoken to the empress.

"I should be sorry to do so," I replied, "but as I can't find anyone to present me to her, I must be resigned."

At last Panin told me to walk in a garden frequented by her majesty at an early hour, and he said that meeting me, as it were by chance, she would probably speak to me. I told him I should like him to be with her, and he accordingly named a day.

I repaired to the garden, and as I walked about I marvelled at the statuary it contained, all the statues being made of the worst stone, and executed in the worst possible taste. The names cut beneath them gave the whole the air of a practical joke. A weeping statue was Democritus; another, with grinning mouth, was labelled Heraclitus; an old man with a long beard was Sappho; and an old woman, Avicenna; and so on.

As I was smiling at this extraordinary collection, I saw the czarina, preceded by Count Gregorius Orloff, and followed by two ladies, approaching. Count Panin was on her left hand. I stood by the hedge to let her pass, but as soon as she came up to me she asked, smilingly, if I had been interested in the statues. I replied, following her steps, that I presumed they had been placed there to impose on fools, or to excite the laughter of those acquainted with history.

[285]

"From what I can make out," she replied, "the secret of the matter is that my worthy aunt was imposed on, and indeed she did not trouble herself much about such trifles. But I hope you have seen other things in Russia less ridiculous than these statues?"

I entertained the sovereign for more than an hour with my remarks on the things of note I had seen in St. Petersburg. The conversation happened to turn on the King of Prussia, and I sang his praises; but I censured his terrible habit of always interrupting the person whom he was addressing. Catherine smiled and asked me to tell her about the conversation I had had with this monarch, and I did so to the best of my ability. She was then kind enough to say that she had never seen me at the *Courtag*, which was a vocal and instrumental concert given at the palace, and open to all. I told her that I had only attended once, as I was so unfortunate as not to have a taste for music. At this she turned to Panin, and said smilingly that she knew someone else who had the same misfortune. If the reader remembers what I heard her say about music as she was leaving the opera, he will pronounce my speech to have been a very courtier-like one, and I confess it was; but who can resist making such speeches to a monarch, and above all, a monarch in petticoats?

The czarina turned from me to speak to M. Bezkoi, who had just come up, and as M. Panin left the garden I did so too, delighted with the honour I had had.

The empress, who was a woman of moderate height and yet of a majestic appearance, thoroughly understood the art of making herself loved. She was not beautiful, but yet she was sure of pleasing by her geniality and her wit, and also by that exquisite tact which made one forget the awfulness of the sovereign in the gentleness of the woman.

A few days after, Count Panin told me that the empress had twice asked after me, and that this was a sure sign I had pleased her. He advised me to look out for another opportunity of meeting her, and said that for the future she would always tell me to approach whenever she saw me, and that if I wanted some employment she might possibly do something for me.

Though I did not know what employ I could ask for in that disagreeable country, I was glad to hear that I could have easy access to the Court. With that idea I walked in the garden every day, and here follows my second conversation with the empress: —

She saw me at a distance and sent an officer to fetch me into her presence. As everybody was talking of the tournament, which had to be postponed on account of the bad weather, she asked me if this kind of entertainment could be given at Venice. I told her some amusing stories on the subject of shows and spectacles, and in this relation I remarked that the Venetian climate was more pleasant than the Russian, for at Venice fine days were the rule, while at St. Petersburg they were the exception, though the year is younger there than anywhere else.

"Yes," she said, "in your country it is eleven days older."

"Would it not be worthy of your majesty to put Russia on an equality with the rest of the world in this respect, by adopting the Gregorian calendar? All the Protestants have done so, and England, who adopted it fourteen years ago, has already gained several millions. All Europe is astonished that the old style should be suffered to exist in a country where the sovereign is the head of the Church, and whose capital contains an academy of science. It is thought that Peter the Great, who made the year begin in January, would have also abolished the old style if he had not been afraid of offending England, which then kept trade and commerce alive throughout your vast empire."

"You know," she replied, with a sly smile, "that Peter the Great was not exactly a learned man."

"He was more than a man of learning, the immortal Peter was a genius of the first order. Instinct supplied the place of science with him; his judgment was always in the right. His vast genius, his firm resolve, prevented him from making mistakes, and helped him to destroy all those abuses which threatened to oppose his great designs."

Her majesty seemed to have heard me with great interest, and was about to reply when she noticed two ladies whom she summoned to her presence. To me she said:

"I shall be delighted to reply to you at another time"; and then turned towards the ladies.

The time came in eight or ten days, when I was beginning to think she had had enough of me, for she had seen me without summoning me to speak to her.

She began by saying that what I desired should be done was

already done. "All the letters sent to foreign countries and all the important state records are marked with both dates."

"But I must point out to your majesty that by the end of the century the difference will be of twelve days, not eleven."

"Not at all; we have seen to that. The last year of this century will not be accounted as a leap year. It is fortunate that the difference is one of eleven days, for as that is the number which is added every year to the epact our epacts are almost the same. As to the celebration of Easter, that is a different question. Your equinox is on March the 21st, ours on the 10th, and the astronomers say we are both wrong; sometimes it is we who are wrong and sometimes you, as the equinox varies. You know you are not even in agreement with the Jews, whose calculation is said to be perfectly accurate: and, in fine, this difference in the time of celebrating Easter does not disturb in any way public order or the progress of the government."

"Your majesty's words fill me with admiration, but the Festival of Christmas . . ."

"I suppose you are going to say that we do not celebrate Christmas in the winter solstice as should properly be done. We know it, but it seems to one a matter of no account. I would rather bear with this small mistake than grievously afflict vast numbers of my subjects by depriving them of their birthdays. If I did so, there would be no open complaints uttered, as that is not the fashion in Russia; but they would say in secret that I was an Atheist, and that I disputed the infallibility of the Council of Nice. You may think such complaints matter for laughter, but I do not, for I have much more agreeable motives for amusement."

The czarina was delighted to mark my surprise. I did not doubt for a moment that she had made a special study of the whole subject. M. Alsuwieff told me, a few days after, that she had very possibly read a little pamphlet on the subject, the statements of which exactly coincided with her own. He took care to add, however, that it was very possible her highness was profoundly learned on the matter, but this was merely a courtier's phrase.

What she said was spoken modestly and energetically, and her good humour and pleasant smile remained unmoved throughout. She exercised a constant self-control over herself, and herein appeared the greatness of her character, for nothing is more difficult. Her demeanour, so different from that of the Prussian king, showed her to be the greater sovereign of the two; her frank geniality always gave her the advantage, while the short, curt manners of the king often exposed him to being made a dupe. In an examination of the life of Frederick the Great, one cannot help paying a deserved tribute to his courage, but at the same time one feels that if it had not been for repeated turns of good fortune he must have succumbed, whereas Catherine was little indebted to the favours of the blind deity. She succeeded in enterprises which, before her time, would have been pronounced impossibilities, and it seemed her aim to make men look upon her achievements as of small account.

CHAPTER XX

STORY OF THE FAMOUS DUEL

*A*MONG *the various accomplishments on which Casanova prided himself that of successful duellist is not the least — a very necessary accomplishment in those days for all who wished to make a career, whether in the half-world or the great world. Doubtless the chevalier possessed all the essential physical and moral qualities to make him a good combatant, but the ease with which he disposes of all his adversaries was doubtless due in a large measure to a certain* estocade *which he had learnt in his youth (where and how he does not say) and which he declares never failed him. As his duels were generally fought without witnesses and, according to his own accounts, invariably terminated, after a few passes, with the triumphal thrust which put his opponent* hors de combat, *we are left to infer that the blow in question may not have been among those regarded as strictly regular by sticklers for the classic* duello — *but we know already Casanova's opinion of sticklers in general.*

Under these circumstances it is not surprising that Casanova refused to fight with any weapon but the sword. The pistols he carried — and on occasion knew how to use — were meant to defend his life, not that curious thing he called his "honour." But it so happened that in the most famous of all his encounters it was with the pistol and not the sword that he had to defend both life and honour. This

[289]

was the famous duel with Count Branicki, near Warsaw, whither he had gone on leaving Russia. The story of this duel ranks in Casanovian annals with The Escape from The Leads, *and, like the latter, was one of the especially prepared* morceaux *which Casanova was wont to recite when called upon to entertain the company. It has two notable advantages over the* Escape: *that of brevity and certified truth, Count Branicki himself having in later years assured the Prince de Ligne (uncle of Count Waldstein and a friend and admirer of the latter's librarian at Dux) that the latter's strange story could be believed. We give it in full:*

Madame Binetti, whom I had last seen in London, arrived at Warsaw with her husband and Pic the dancer. She had a letter of introduction to the king's brother, who was a general in the Austrian service, and then resided at Warsaw. I heard that the day they came, when I was at supper at the palatin's. The king was present, and said he should like to keep them in Warsaw for a week and see them dance, if a thousand ducats would satisfy them.

I went to see Madame Binetti and to give her the good news the next morning. She was very much surprised to meet me in Warsaw, and still more so at the news I gave her. She called Pic, who seemed undecided, but as we were talking it over, Prince Poniatowski came in to acquaint them with his majesty's wishes, and the offer was accepted. In three days Pic arranged a ballet; the costumes, the scenery, the music, the dancers — all were ready, and Tomatis put it on handsomely to please his generous master. The couple gave such satisfaction that they were engaged for a year. The Catai was furious, as Madame Binetti threw her completely into the shade, and, worse still, drew away her lovers. Tomatis, who was under the Catai's influence, made things so unpleasant for Madame Binetti that the two dancers became deadly enemies.

In ten or twelve days Madame Binetti was settled in a well-furnished house; her plate was simple but good, her cellar full of excellent wine, her cook an artist, and her adorers numerous, amongst them being Moszciuski and Branicki, the king's friends.

The pit was divided into two parties, for the Catai was resolved to make a stand against the new-comer, though her talents were not to be compared to Madame Binetti's. She danced in the first ballet, and her rival in the second. Those who applauded the first greeted the second in dead silence, and *vice versa*. I had great obligations towards Madame Binetti, but my duty also drew me towards the Catai, who numbered in her party all the Czartoryskis and their following, Prince Lubomirski, and other powerful nobles. It was plain that I could not desert to Madame Binetti without earning the contempt of the other party.

Madame Binetti reproached me bitterly, and I laid the case plainly before her. She agreed that I could not do otherwise, but begged me to stay away from the theatre in future, telling me that she had got a rod in pickle for Tomatis which would make him repent of his impertinence. She called me her oldest friend; and indeed I was very fond of her, and cared nothing for the Catai despite her prettiness.

Xavier Branicki, the royal postoli, Knight of the White Eagle, colonel of Uhlans, the king's friend, was the chief adorer of Madame Binetti. The lady probably confided her displeasure to him, and begged him to take vengeance on the manager, who had committed so many offences against her. Count Branicki in his turn probably promised to avenge her quarrel, and, if no opportunity of doing so arose, to create an opportunity. At least, this is the way in which affairs of this kind are usually managed, and I can find no better explanation for what happened. Nevertheless, the way in which the Pole took vengeance was very original and extraordinary.

On the 20th of February Branicki went to the opera, and, contrary to his custom, went to the Catai's dressing-room, and began to pay his court to the actress, Tomatis being present. Both he and the actress concluded that Branicki had had a quarrel with her rival, and though she did not much care to place him in the number of her adorers, she yet gave him a good reception, for she knew it would be dangerous to despise his suit openly.

When the Catai had completed her toilet, the gallant postoli offered her his arm to take her to her carriage, which was at the door. Tomatis followed, and I too was there, awaiting my carriage. Madame Catai came down, the carriage-door was opened, she stepped in, and Branicki got in after her, telling the astonished Tomatis to follow them in the other carriage. Tomatis replied that he meant to ride in his own carriage, and begged the colonel to get out. Branicki paid no attention, and told the coachman to drive on. Tomatis forbade him to stir, and the man, of course, obeyed the master. The gallant postoli was therefore obliged to get down, but he bade his hussar give Tomatis a box on the ear, and this order was so promptly and vigorously obeyed that the unfortunate man was on the ground before he had time to recollect that he had a sword. He got up eventually and drove off, but he would eat no supper, no doubt because he had a blow to digest. I was to have supped with him, but after this scene I had really not the face to go. I went home in a melancholy and reflective mood, wondering whether the whole had been concerted; but I concluded that this was impossible, as neither Branicki nor Binetti could have foreseen the impoliteness and cowardice of Tomatis.

The reader will see how tragically the matter ended.

On reflection I concluded that Branicki had not done an ungentlemanly thing in getting into Tomatis's carriage; he had merely behaved with impetuosity, as if he were the Catai's lover. It also appeared to me that, considering the affront he had received from the jealous Italian, the box on the ear was a very moderate form of vengeance. A blow is bad, of course, but not so bad as death; and Branicki might very well have run his sword through the manager's body. Certainly, if Branicki had killed him he would have been stigmatised as an assassin, for though Tomatis had a sword the Polish officer's servants would never have allowed him to draw it, nevertheless I could not help thinking that Tomatis should have tried to take the servant's life, even at the risk of his own. He wanted no more courage for that than in ordering the king's favourite to come out of the carriage. He might have foreseen that the Polish noble would be stung to the quick, and would surely attempt to take speedy vengeance.

The next day the encounter was the subject of all conversations. Tomatis remained indoors for a week, calling for vengeance in vain. The king told him he could do nothing for him, as Branicki maintained he had only given insult for insult. I saw Tomatis, who told me in confidence that he could easily take vengeance, but that it would cost him too dear. He had spent forty thousand ducats on the two ballets, and if he had avenged himself he would have lost it nearly all, as he would be obliged to leave the kingdom. The only consolation he had was that his great friends were kinder to him than ever, and the king himself honoured him with peculiar attention. Madame Binetti was triumphant. When I saw her she condoled with me ironically on the mishap that had befallen my friend. She wearied me; but I could not guess that Branicki had only acted at her instigation, and still less that she had a grudge against me. Indeed, if I had known it, I should only have laughed at her, for I had nothing to dread from her bravo's dagger. I had never seen him nor spoken to him; he could have no opportunity for attacking me. He was never with the king in the morning and never went to the palatin's to supper, being an unpopular character with the Polish nobility. This Branicki was said to have been originally a Cossack, Branecki by name. He became the king's favourite and assumed the name of Branicki, pretending to be of the same family as the illustrious marshal of that name, who was still alive; but he, far from recognising the pretender, ordered his shield to be broken and buried with him as the last of his race. However that may be, Branicki was the tool of the Russian party, the determined enemy of those who withstood Catherine's design of Russianising the ancient Polish constitution. The king liked him out of habit, and because he had peculiar obligations to him.

The life I lived was really exemplary. I indulged neither in love affairs nor gaming. I worked for the king, hoping to become his secretary. I paid my court to the princess-palatine, who liked my company, and I played tressette with the palatin himself.

On the 4th of March, St. Casimir's Eve, there was a banquet to which I had the honour to be invited. Casimir was the name of the king's eldest brother, who held the office of grand chamberlain. After dinner the king asked me if I intended going to the theatre where a Polish play was to be given for the first time. Everybody was interested in this novelty, but it was a matter of indifference to me as I did not understand the language, and I told the king as much.

"Never mind," said he, "come in my box."

This was too flattering an invitation to be refused, so I obeyed the royal command and stood behind the king's chair. After the second act a ballet was given, and the dancing of Madame

Caracci, a Piedmontese, so pleased his majesty that he went to the unusual pains of clapping her.

I only knew the dancer by sight, for I had never spoken to her. She had some talents. Her principal admirer was Count Poninski, who was always reproaching me when I dined with him for visiting the other dancers to the exclusion of Madame Caracci. I thought of his reproach at the time, and determined to pay her a visit after the ballet to congratulate her on her performance and the king's applause. On my way I passed by Madame Binetti's dressing-room, and seeing the door open I stayed a moment. Count Branicki came up, and I left with a bow and passed on to Madame Caracci's dressing-room. She was astonished to see me, and began with kindly reproaches for my neglect; to which I replied with compliments, and then giving her a kiss I promised to come and see her.

Just as I embraced her, who should enter but Branicki, whom I had left a moment before with Madame Binetti. He had clearly followed me in the hopes of picking a quarrel. He was accompanied by Bininski, his lieutenant-colonel. As soon as he appeared, politeness made me stand up and turn to go, but he stopped me.

"It seems to me I have come at a bad time; it looks as if you loved this lady."

"Certainly, my lord; does not your excellency consider her as worthy of love?"

"Quite so; but as it happens I love her too, and I am not the man to bear any rivals."

"As I know that, I shall love her no more."

"Then you give her up?"

"With all my heart; for everyone must yield to such a noble as you are."

"Very good; but I call a man that yields a coward."

"Isn't that rather a strong expression?"

As I uttered these words I looked proudly at him and touched the hilt of my sword. Three or four officers were present and witnessed what passed.

I had hardly gone four paces from the dressing-room when I heard myself called "Venetian coward." In spite of my rage I restrained myself, and turned back saying, coolly and firmly, that perhaps a Venetian coward might kill a brave Pole outside

the theatre; and without awaiting a reply I left the building by
the chief staircase.

I waited vainly outside the theatre for a quarter of an hour
with my sword in my hand, for I was not afraid of losing forty
thousand ducats like Tomatis. At last, half perishing with cold,
I called my carriage and drove to the palatin's, where the king
was to sup.

The cold and loneliness began to cool my brain, and I congratulated myself on my self-restraint in not drawing my sword
in the actress's dressing-room; and I felt glad that Branicki had
not followed me down the stairs, for his friend Bininski had a
sabre, and I should probably have been assassinated.

Although the Poles are polite enough, there is still a good deal
of the old leaven in them. They are still Dacians and Sarma-
tians at dinner, in war, and in friendship, as they call it, but
which is often a burden hardly to be borne. They can never
understand that a man may be sufficient company for himself,
and that it is not right to descend on him in a troop and ask him
to give them dinner.

I made up my mind that Madame Binetti had excited Branicki
to follow me, and possibly to treat me as he had treated Tomatis.
I had not received a blow certainly, but I had been called a coward. I had no choice but to demand satisfaction, but I also determined to be studiously moderate throughout. In this frame
of mind I got down at the palatin's, resolved to tell the whole
story to the king, leaving his majesty the task of compelling his
favourite to give me satisfaction.

As soon as the palatin saw me, he reproached me in a friendly
manner for keeping him waiting, and we sat down to tressette.
I was his partner, and committed several blunders. When it
came to losing a second game he said:

"Where is your head to-night?"

"My lord, it is four leagues away."

"A respectable man ought to have his head in the game, and
not at a distance of four leagues."

With these words the prince threw down his cards and began
to walk up and down the room. I was rather startled, but I got
up and stood by the fire, waiting for the king. But after I had
waited thus for half an hour a chamberlain came from the palace,
and announced that his majesty could not do himself the honour
of supping with my lord that night.

This was a blow for me, but I concealed my disappointment. Supper was served, and I sat down as usual at the left hand of the palatin, who was annoyed with me, and showed it. We were eighteen at table, and for once I had no appetite. About the middle of the supper Prince Gaspard Lubomirski came in, and chanced to sit down opposite me. As soon as he saw me he condoled with me in a loud voice for what had happened.

"I am sorry for you," said he, "but Branicki was drunk, and you really shouldn't count what he said as an insult."

"What has happened?" became at once the general question. I held my tongue, and when they asked Lubomirski he replied that as I kept silence it was his duty to do the same.

Thereupon the palatin, speaking in his friendliest manner, said to me:

"What has taken place between you and Branicki?"

"I will tell you the whole story, my lord, in private after supper."

The conversation became indifferent, and after the meal was over, the palatin took up his stand by the small door by which he was accustomed to leave the room, and there I told him the whole story. He sighed, condoled with me, and added:

"You had good reason for being absent-minded at cards."

"May I presume to ask your excellency's advice?"

"I never give advice in these affairs, in which you must do everything or nothing."

The palatin shook me by the hand, and I went home and slept for six hours. As soon as I awoke I sat up in bed, and my first thought was *everything or nothing*. I soon rejected the latter alternative, and I saw that I must demand a duel to the death. If Branicki refused to fight I should be compelled to kill him, even if I were to lose my head for it.

Such was my determination; to write to him proposing a duel at four leagues from Warsaw, this being the limit of the starostia, in which duelling was forbidden on pain of death. I wrote as follows, for I have kept the rough draft of the letter to this day:

"Warsaw,

"March 5th, 1766. 5 A.M.

"My Lord, — Yesterday evening your excellency insulted me with a light heart, without my having given you any cause or reason for doing so. This seems to indicate that you hate me, and would gladly efface me from the land of the living. I both can and will oblige you in this matter. Be kind enough, therefore, to drive me in your carriage to a place where my death will not subject your lordship to the vengeance of the law, in case you obtain the victory, and where I shall enjoy the same advantage if God give me grace to kill your lordship. I should not make this proposal unless I believed your lordship to be of a noble disposition.

"I have the honour to be, etc."

I sent this letter an hour before daybreak to Branicki's lodging in the palace. My messenger had orders to give the letter into the count's own hands, to wait for him to rise, and also for an answer.

In half an hour I received the following answer:

"Sir, — I accept your proposal, and shall be glad if you will have the kindness to inform me when I shall have the honour of seeing you.

"I remain, sir, etc."

I answered this immediately, informing him I would call on him the next day, at six o'clock in the morning.

Shortly after, I received a second letter, in which he said that I might choose the arms and place, but that our differences must be settled in the course of the day.

I sent him the measure of my sword, which was thirty-two inches long, telling him he might choose any place beyond the ban. In reply, I had the following:

"Sir, — You will greatly oblige me by coming now. I have sent my carriage.

"I have the honour to be, etc."

I replied that I had business all the day, and that as I had made up my mind not to call upon him, except for the purpose of fighting, I begged him not to be offended if I took the liberty of sending back his carriage.

An hour later Branicki called in person, leaving his suite at the door. He came into the room, requested some gentlemen who were talking with me to leave us alone, locked the door after them, and then sat down on my bed. I did not understand what all this meant, so I took up my pistols.

"Don't be afraid," said he, "I am not come to assassinate you, but merely to say that I accept your proposal, on condition only that the duel shall take place to-day. If not, never."

[297]

"It is out of the question. I have letters to write, and some business to do for the king."

"That will do afterwards. In all probability you will not fall, and if you do I am sure the king will forgive you. Besides, a dead man need fear no reproaches."

"I want to make my will."

"Come, come, you needn't be afraid of dying; it will be time enough for you to make your will in fifty years."

"But why should your excellency not wait till to-morrow?"

"I don't want to be caught."

"You will have nothing of the kind to fear from me."

"I dare say, but unless we make haste the king will have us both arrested."

"How can he, unless you have told him about our quarrel?"

"Ah, you don't understand! Well, I am quite willing to give you satisfaction, but it must be to-day or never."

"Very good. This duel is too dear to my heart for me to leave you any pretext for avoiding it. Call for me after dinner, for I shall want all my strength."

"Certainly. For my part I like a good supper after, better than a good dinner before."

"Everyone to his taste."

"True. By the way, why did you send me the length of your sword. I intend to fight with pistols, for I never use swords with unknown persons."

"What do you mean? I beg of you to refrain from insulting me in my own house. I do not intend to fight with pistols, and you cannot compel me to do so, for I have your letter giving me the choice of weapons."

"Strictly speaking, no doubt you are in the right; but I am sure you are too polite not to give way, when I assure you that you will lay me under a great obligation by doing so. Very often the first shot is a miss, and if that is the case with both of us, I promise to fight with swords as long as you like. Will you oblige me in the matter?"

"Yes, for I like your way of asking, though, in my opinion, a pistol duel is a barbarous affair. I accept, but on the following conditions: You must bring two pistols, charge them in my presence, and give me the choice. If the first shot is a miss, we will fight with swords till the first blood or to the death, whichever you prefer. Call for me at three o'clock, and choose some place where we shall be secure from the law."

"Very good. You are a good fellow, allow me to embrace you. Give me your word of honour not to say a word about it to anyone, for if you did we should be arrested immediately."

"You need not be afraid of my talking; the project is too dear to me."

"Good. Farewell till three o'clock."

As soon as the brave braggart had left me, I placed the papers I was doing for the king apart, and went to Campioni, in whom I had great confidence.

"Take this packet to the king," I said, "if I happen to be killed. You may guess, perhaps, what is going to happen, but do not say a word to anyone, as it would mean loss of honour to me."

"I understand. You may reckon on my discretion, and I hope the affair may be ended honourably and prosperously for you. But take a piece of friendly advice — don't spare your opponent, were it the king himself, for it might cost you your life. I know that by experience."

"I will not forget. Farewell."

We kissed each other, and I ordered an excellent dinner, for I had no mind to be sent to Pluto fasting. Campioni came in to dinner at one o'clock, and at dessert I had a visit from two young counts, with their tutor, Bertrand, a kindly Swiss. They were witnesses to my cheerfulness and the excellent appetite with which I ate. At half-past two I dismissed my company, and stood at the window to be ready to go down directly Branicki's carriage appeared. He drove up in a travelling carriage and six; two grooms, leading saddle horses, went in front, followed by his two aide-de-camps and two hussars. Behind his carriage stood four servants. I hastened to descend, and found my enemy was accompanied by a lieutenant-general and an armed footman. The door was opened, the general gave me his place, and I ordered my servants not to follow me but await my orders at the house.

"You might want them," said Branicki; "they had better come along."

"If I had as many as you, I would certainly agree to your proposition; but as it is I shall do still better without any at all.

If need be, your excellency will see that I am tended by your own servants."

He gave me his hand, and assured me they should wait on me before himself.

I sat down, and we went off.

It would have been absurd if I had asked where we were going, so I held my tongue, for at such moments a man should take heed to his words. Branicki was silent, and I thought the best thing I could do would be to engage him in a trivial conversation.

"Does your excellency intend spending the spring at Warsaw?"

"I had thought of doing so, but you may possibly send me to pass the spring somewhere else."

"Oh, I hope not!"

"Have you seen any military service?"

"Yes; but may I ask why your excellency asks me the question, for . . ."

"I had no particular reason; it was only for the sake of saying something."

We had driven about half an hour when the carriage stopped at the door of a large garden. We got down and, following the postoli, reached a green arbour which, by the way, was not at all green on that 5th of March. In it was a stone table on which the footman placed two pistols, a foot and a half long, with a powder flask and scales. He weighed the powder, loaded them equally, and laid them down crosswise on the table.

This done, Branicki said boldly:

"Choose your weapon, sir."

At this the general called out:

"Is this a duel, sir?"

"Yes."

"You cannot fight here; you are within the ban."

"No matter."

"It does matter; and I, at all events, refuse to be a witness. I am on guard at the castle, and you have taken me by surprise."

"Be quiet; I will answer for everything. I owe this gentleman satisfaction, and I mean to give it him here."

"M. Casanova," said the general, "you cannot fight here."

"Then why have I been brought here? I shall defend myself wherever I am attacked."

"Lay the whole matter before the king, and you shall have my voice in your favour."

"I am quite willing to do so, general, if his excellency will say that he regrets what passed between us last night."

Branicki looked fiercely at me, and said wrathfully that he had come to fight and not to parley.

"General," said I, "you can bear witness that I have done all in my power to avoid this duel."

The general went away with his head between his hands, and throwing off my cloak I took the first pistol that came to my hand. Branicki took the other, and said that he would guarantee upon his honour that my weapon was a good one.

"I am going to try its goodness on your head," I answered.

He turned pale at this, threw his sword to one of his servants, and bared his throat, and I was obliged, to my sorrow, to follow his example, for my sword was the only weapon I had, with the exception of the pistol. I bared my chest also, and stepped back five or six paces, and he did the same.

As soon as we had taken up our positions I took off my hat with my left hand, and begged him to fire first.

Instead of doing so immediately he lost two or three seconds in sighting, aiming, and covering his head by raising the weapon before it. I was not in a position to let him kill me at his ease, so I suddenly aimed and fired on him just as he fired on me. That I did so is evident, as all the witnesses were unanimous in saying that they heard only one report. I felt I was wounded in my left hand, and so I put it into my pocket, and I ran towards my enemy who had fallen. All of a sudden, as I knelt beside him, three bare swords were flourished over my head, and three noble assassins prepared to cut me down beside their master. Fortunately, Branicki had not lost consciousness or the power of speaking, and he cried out in a voice of thunder:

"Scoundrels! have some respect for a man of honour."

This seemed to petrify them. I put my right hand under the postoli's armpit, while the general helped him on the other side, and thus we took him to the inn, which happened to be near at hand.

Branicki stooped as he walked, and gazed at me curiously,

apparently wondering where all the blood on my clothes came from.

When we got to the inn, Branicki laid himself down in an arm-chair. We unbuttoned his clothes and lifted up his shirt, and he could see himself that he was dangerously wounded. My ball had entered his body by the seventh rib on the right hand, and had gone out by the second false rib on the left. The two wounds were ten inches apart, and the case was of an alarming nature, as the intestine must have been pierced. Branicki spoke to me in a weak voice: —

"You have killed me, so make haste away, as you are in danger of the gibbet. The duel was fought in the ban, and I am a high court officer, and a Knight of the White Eagle. So lose no time, and if you have not enough money take my purse."

I picked up the purse which had fallen out, and put it back in his pocket, thanking him, and saying it would be useless to me, for if I were guilty I was content to lose my head. "I hope," I added, "that your wound will not be mortal, and I am deeply grieved at your obliging me to fight."

With these words I kissed him on his brow and left the inn, seeing neither horses nor carriage, nor servant. They had all gone off for a doctor, surgeon, priest, and the friends and relatives of the wounded man.

I was alone and without any weapon, in the midst of a snow-covered country, my hand was wounded, and I had not the slightest idea which was the way to Warsaw.

I took the road which seemed most likely, and after I had gone some distance I met a peasant with an empty sleigh.

"*Warszawa?* " I cried, showing him a ducat.

He understood me, and lifted a coarse mat, with which he covered me when I got into the sleigh, and then set off at a gallop.

All at once Bininski, Branicki's bosom-friend, came galloping furiously along the road with his bare sword in his hand. He was evidently running after me. Happily he did not glance at the wretched sleigh in which I was, or else he would undoubtedly have murdered me. I got at last to Warsaw, and went to the house of Prince Adam Czartoryski to beg him to shelter me, but there was nobody there. Without delay I determined to seek refuge in the convent of the Recollets, which was handy.

I rang at the door of the monastery, and the porter seeing me covered with blood hastened to shut the door, guessing the object of my visit. But I did not give him the time to do so, but honouring him with a hearty kick forced my way in. His cries attracted a troop of frightened monks. I demanded sanctuary, and threatened them with vengeance if they refused to grant it. One of their number spoke to me, and I was taken to a little den which looked more like a dungeon than anything else. I offered no resistance, feeling sure that they would change their tune before very long. I asked them to send for my servants, and when they came I sent for a doctor and Campioni. Before the surgeon could come the Palatin of Polduchia was announced. I never had the honour of speaking to him, but after hearing the history of my duel he was so kind as to give me all the particulars of a duel he had fought in his youthful days. Soon after came the Palatin of Kalisch, Prince Jablenowski, Prince Sanguska, and the Palatin of Wilna, who all joined in a chorus of abuse of the monks who had lodged me so scurvily. The poor religious excused themselves by saying that I had ill-treated their porter, which made my noble friends laugh; but I did not laugh, for my wound was very painful. However, I was immediately moved into two of their best guest-rooms.

The ball had pierced my hand by the metacarpus under the index finger, and had broken the first phalanges. Its force had been arrested by a metal button on my waistcoat, and it had only inflicted a slight wound on my stomach close to the navel. However, there it was and it had to be extracted, for it pained me extremely. An empiric named Gendron, the first surgeon my servants had found, made an opening on the opposite side of my hand which doubled the wound. While he was performing this painful operation I told the story of the duel to the company, concealing the anguish I was enduring. What a power vanity exercises on the moral and physical forces! If I had been alone I should probably have fainted.

As soon as the empiric Gendron was gone, the palatin's surgeon came in and took charge of the case, calling Gendron a low fellow. At the same time Prince Lubomirski, the husband of the palatin's daughter, arrived, and gave us all a surprise by recounting the strange occurrences which had happened after the duel. Bininski came to where Branicki was lying, and seeing his wound rode off furiously on horseback, swearing to strike me dead wherever he found me. He fancied I would be with Tomatis, and went to his house. He found Tomatis with his mistress, Prince Lubomirski, and Count Moszczinski but no Casanova was visible. He asked where I was, and on Tomatis replying that he did not know he discharged a pistol at his head. At this dastardly action Count Moszczinski seized him and tried to throw him out of the window, but the madman got loose with three cuts of his sabre, one of which slashed the count on the face and knocked out three of his teeth.

"After this exploit," Prince Lubomirski continued, "he seized me by the throat and held a pistol to my head, threatening to blow out my brains if I did not take him in safety to the court where his horse was, so that he might get away from the house without any attack being made on him by Tomatis's servants; and I did so immediately. Moszczinski is in the doctor's hands, and will be laid up for some time.

"As soon as it was reported that Branicki was killed, his Uhlans began to ride about the town swearing to avenge their colonel, and to slaughter you. It is very fortunate that you took refuge here.

"The chief marshal has had the monastery surrounded by two hundred dragoons, ostensibly to prevent your escape, but in reality to defend you from Branicki's soldiers.

"The doctors say that the postoli is in great danger if the ball has wounded the intestines, but if not they answer for his recovery. His fate will be known to-morrow. He now lies at the lord chamberlain's, not daring to have himself carried to his apartments at the palace. The king has been to see him, and the general who was present told his majesty that the only thing that saved your life was your threat to aim at Branicki's head. This frightened him, and to keep your ball from his head he stood in such an awkward position that he missed your vital parts. Otherwise he would undoubtedly have shot you through the heart, for he can split a bullet into two halves by firing against the blade of a knife. It was also a lucky thing for you that you escaped Bininski, who never thought of looking for you in the wretched sleigh."

"My lord, the most fortunate thing for me is that I did not kill my man outright. Otherwise I should have been cut to pieces just as I went to his help by three of his servants, who stood over me with drawn swords. However, the postoli ordered them to leave me alone.

"I am sorry for what has happened to your highness and Count Moszczinski; and if Tomatis was not killed by the madman it is only because the pistol was only charged with powder."

"That's what I think, for no one heard the bullet; but it was a mere chance."

"Quite so."

Just then an officer of the palatin's came to me with a note from his master, which ran as follows:

"Read what the king says to me, and sleep well."

The king's note was thus conceived:

"Branicki, my dear uncle, is dangerously wounded. My surgeons are doing all they can for him, but I have not forgotten Casanova. You may assure him that he is pardoned, even if Branicki should die."

I kissed the letter gratefully, and showed it to my visitors, who lauded this generous man, truly worthy of being a king.

After this pleasant news I felt in need of rest, and my lords left me. As soon as they were gone, Campioni, who had come in before and had stood in the background, came up to me and gave me back the packet of papers, and with tears of joy congratulated me on the happy issue of the duel.

Next day I had shoals of visitors, and many of the chiefs of the party opposed to Branicki sent me purses full of gold. The persons who brought the money on behalf of such a lord or lady, said that being a foreigner I might be in need of money, and that was their excuse for the liberty they had taken. I thanked and refused them all, and sent back at least four thousand ducats, and was very proud of having done so. Campioni thought it was absurd, and he was right, for I repented afterwards of what I had done. The only present I accepted was a dinner for four persons, which Prince Adam Czartoryski sent me in every day, though the doctor would not let me enjoy it, he being a great believer in diet.

The wound in my stomach was progressing favourably, but on the fourth day the surgeons said my hand was becoming gangrened, and they agreed that the only remedy was amputation. I saw this announced in the *Court Gazette* the next morning, but as I had other views on the matter I laughed heartily at the paragraph. The sheet was printed at night, after the king had placed his initials to the copy. In the morning several persons came to condole with me, but I received their sympathy with great irreverence. I merely laughed at Count Clary, who said I would surely submit to the operation; and just as he uttered the words the three surgeons came in together.

"Well, gentlemen," said I, "you have mustered in great strength; why is this?"

My ordinary surgeon replied that he wished to have the opinion of the other two before proceeding to amputation, and they would require to look at the wound.

The dressing was lifted and gangrene was declared to be undoubtedly present, and execution was ordered that evening. The butchers gave me the news with radiant faces, and assured me I need not be afraid as the operation would certainly prove efficacious.

"Gentlemen," I replied, "you seem to have a great many solid scientific reasons for cutting off my hand; but one thing you have not got, and that is my consent. My hand is my own, and I am going to keep it."

"Sir, it is certainly gangrened; by to-morrow the arm will begin to mortify, and then you will have to lose your arm."

"Very good; if that prove so you shall cut off my arm, but I happen to know something of gangrene, and there is none about me."

"You cannot know as much about it as we do."

"Possibly; but as far as I can make out, you know nothing at all."

"That's rather a strong expression."

"I don't care whether it be strong or weak; you can go now."

In a couple of hours everyone whom the surgeons had told of my obstinacy came pestering me. Even the prince-palatin wrote to me that the king was extremely surprised at my lack of courage. This stung me to the quick, and I wrote the king a long letter, half in earnest, half in jest, in which I laughed at the ignorance of the surgeons, and at the simplicity of those who took whatever they said for gospel truth. I added that as an arm without a hand would be quite as useless as no arm at all, I meant to wait till it was necessary to cut off the arm.

My letter was read at Court, and people wondered how a man with gangrene could write a long letter of four pages. Lubomirski told me kindly that I was mistaken in laughing at my friends, for the three best surgeons in Warsaw could not be mistaken in such a simple case.

"My lord, they are not deceived themselves, but they want to deceive me."

"Why should they?"

"To make themselves agreeable to Branicki, who is in a dangerous state, and might possibly get better if he heard that my hand had been taken off."

"Really, that seems an incredible idea to me!"

"What will your highness say on the day when I am proved to be right?"

"I shall say you are deserving of the highest praise, but the day must first come."

"We shall see this evening, and I give you my word that if any gangrene has attacked the arm, I will have it cut off to-morrow morning."

Four surgeons came to see me. My arm was pronounced to be highly œdematous, and of a livid colour up to the elbow; but when the lint was taken off the wound I could see for myself that it was progressing admirably. However, I concealed my delight. Prince Augustus Sulkowski and the Abbé Gouvel were present; the latter being attached to the palatin's court. The judgment of the surgeons was that the arm was gangrened, and must be amputated by the next morning at latest.

I was tired of arguing with these rascals, so I told them to bring their instruments, and that I would submit to the operation. At this they went away in high glee, to tell the news at the Court, to Branicki, to the palatin, and so forth. I merely gave my servants orders to send them away when they came.

I can dwell no more on this matter, though it is interesting enough to me. However, the reader will no doubt be obliged to me by my simply saying that a French surgeon in Prince Sulkowski's household took charge of the case in defiance of professional etiquette, and cured me perfectly, so I have my hand and my arm to this day.

On Easter Day I went to mass with my arm in a sling. My cure had only lasted three weeks, but I was not able to put the hand to any active employment for eighteen months afterwards. Everyone was obliged to congratulate me on having held out against the amputation, and the general consent declared the surgeons grossly ignorant, while I was satisfied with thinking them very great knaves.

I must here set down an incident which happened three days after the duel.

I was told that a Jesuit father from the bishop of the diocese wanted to speak to me in private, and I had him shown in, and asked him what he wanted.

"I have come from my lord bishop," said he, "to absolve you from the ecclesiastical censure which you have incurred by duelling."

"I am always delighted to receive absolution, father, but only after I have confessed my guilt. In the present case I have nothing to confess; I was attacked, and I defended myself. Pray thank my lord for his kindness. If you like to absolve me without confession, I shall be much obliged."

"If you do not confess, I cannot give you absolution, but you can do this: ask me to absolve you, supposing you have fought a duel."

"Certainly; I shall be glad if you will absolve me, supposing I have fought a duel."

The delightful Jesuit gave me absolution in similar terms. He was like his brethren — never at a loss when a loophole of any kind is required.

Three days before I left the monastery, that is on Holy Thursday, the marshal withdrew my guard. After I had been to mass on Easter Day, I went to Court, and as I kissed the king's hand, he asked me (as had been arranged) why I wore my arm in a sling. I said I had been suffering from a chill, and he replied, with a meaning smile:

"Take care not to catch another."

After my visit to the king, I called on Branicki, who had made daily inquiries after my health, and had sent me back my sword. He was condemned to stay in bed for six weeks longer, at least, for the wad of my pistol had got into the wound, and in extracting it the opening had to be enlarged, which retarded his recovery. The king had just appointed him chief huntsman, not so exalted an office as chamberlain, but a more lucrative one. It was said he had got the place because he was such a good shot; but if that were the reason I had a better claim to it, for I had proved the better shot — for one day at all events.

I entered an enormous ante-room in which stood officers, footmen, pages, and lackeys, all gazing at me with the greatest astonishment. I asked if my lord was to be seen, and begged the door-keeper to send in my name. He did not answer, but sighed, and went into his master's room. Directly after, he came out and begged me, with a profound bow, to step in.

Branicki, who was dressed in a magnificent gown and supported by pillows and cushions, greeted me by taking off his night-cap. He was as pale as death.

"I have come here, my lord," I began, "to offer you my service and to assure you how I regret that I did not pass over a few trifling words of yours."

"You have no reason to reproach yourself, M. Casanova."

"Your excellency is very kind. I am also come to say that by fighting with me you have done me an honour which completely swallows up all offence, and I trust that you will give me your protection for the future."

"I confess I insulted you, but you will allow that I have paid for it. As to my friends, I openly say that they are my enemies unless they treat you with respect. Bininski has been cashiered, and his nobility taken from him; he is well served. As to my protection you have no need of it, the king esteems you highly, like myself, and all men of honour. Sit down; we will be friends. A cup of chocolate for this gentleman. You seem to have got over your wound completely."

"Quite so, my lord, except as to the use of my fingers, and that will take some time."

"You were quite right to withstand those rascally surgeons, and you had good reason for your opinion that the fools thought to please me by rendering you one-handed. They judged my heart by their own. I congratulate you on the preservation of your hand, but I have not been able to make out how my ball could have wounded you in the hand after striking your stomach."

Just then the chocolate was brought, and the chamberlain came in and looked at me with a smile. In five minutes the room was full of lords and ladies who had heard I was with

Branicki, and wanted to know how we were getting on. I could see that they did not expect to find us on such good terms, and were agreeably surprised. Branicki asked the question which had been interrupted by the chocolate and the visitors over again.

"Your excellency will allow me to assume the position I was in as I received your fire."

"Pray do so."

I rose and placed myself in the position, and he said he understood how it was.

A lady said:

"You should have put your hand behind your body."

"Excuse me, madam, but I thought it better to put my body behind my hand."

This sally made Branicki laugh, but his sister said to me:

"You wanted to kill my brother, for you aimed at his head."

"God forbid, madam! my interest lay in keeping him alive to defend me from his friends."

"But you said you were going to fire at his head."

"That's a mere figure of speech, just as one says, 'I'll blow your brains out.' The skilled duellist, however, always aims at the middle of the body; the head does not offer a large enough surface."

"Yes," said Branicki, "your tactics were superior to mine, and I am obliged to you for the lesson you gave me."

"Your excellency gave me a lesson in heroism of far greater value."

"You must have had a great deal of practice with the pistol," continued his sister.

"Not at all, madam, I regard the weapon with detestation. This unlucky shot was my first; but I have always known a straight line, and my hand has always been steady."

"That's all one wants," said Branicki. "I have those advantages myself, and I am only too well pleased that I did not aim so well as usual."

"Your ball broke my first phalanges. Here it is, you see, flattened by my bone. Allow me to return it to you."

"I am sorry to say I can't return yours, which I suppose remains on the field of battle."

"You seem to be getting better, thank God!"

"The wound is healing painfully. If I had imitated you I

should no longer be in the land of the living; I am told you made an excellent dinner?"

"Yes, my lord, I was afraid I might never have another chance of dining again."

"If I had dined, your ball would have pierced the intestine; but being empty it yielded to the bullet, and let it pass by harmlessly."

I heard afterwards that on the day of the duel Branicki had gone to confession and mass, and had communicated. The priest could not refuse him absolution, if he said that honour obliged him to fight; for this was in accordance with the ancient laws of chivalry. As for me I only addressed these words to God:

"Lord, if my enemy kill me, I shall be damned; deign, therefore, to preserve me from death. Amen."

After a long and pleasant conversation I took leave of the hero to visit the high constable, Count Bielinski, brother of Countess Salmor. He was a very old man, but the sovereign administrator of justice in Poland. I had never spoken to him, but he had defended me from Branicki's Uhlans, and had made out my pardon, so I felt bound to go and thank him.

I sent in my name, and the worthy old man greeted me with: "What can I do for you?"

"I have come to kiss the hand of the kindly man that signed my pardon, and to promise your excellency to be more discreet in future."

"I advise you to be more discreet indeed. As for your pardon, thank the king; for if he had not requested me especially to grant it you, I should have had you beheaded."

"In spite of the extenuating circumstances, my lord?"

"What circumstances? Did you or did you not fight a duel?"

"That is not a proper way of putting it; I was obliged to defend myself. You might have charged me with fighting a duel if Branicki had taken me outside the ban, as I requested, but as it was he took me where he willed and made me fight. Under these circumstances I am sure your excellency would have spared my head."

"I really can't say. The king requested that you should be pardoned, and that shows he believes you to be deserving of pardon; I congratulate you on his good will. I shall be pleased if you will dine with me to-morrow."

"My lord, I am delighted to accept your invitation."

The illustrious old constable was a man of great intelligence. He had been a bosom-friend of the celebrated Poniatowski, the king's father. We had a good deal of conversation together at dinner the next day.

"What a comfort it would have been to your excellency's friend," said I, "if he could have lived to see his son crowned King of Poland."

"He would never have consented."

The vehemence with which he pronounced these words gave me a deep insight into his feelings. He was of the Saxon party. The same day, that is on Easter Day, I dined at the palatin's.

"Political reasons," said he, "prevented me from visiting you at the monastery; but you must not think I had forgotten you, for you were constantly in my thoughts. I am going to lodge you here, for my wife is very fond of your society; but the rooms will not be ready for another six weeks."

"I shall take the opportunity, my lord, of paying a visit to the Palatin of Kiowia, who has honoured me with an invitation to come and see him."

"Who gave you the invitation?"

"Count Brühl, who is at Dresden; his wife is daughter of the palatin."

"This journey is an excellent idea, for this duel of yours has made you innumerable enemies, and I only hope you will have to fight no more duels. I give you fair warning; be on your guard, and never go on foot, especially at night."

I spent a fortnight in going out to dinner and supper every day. I had become the fashion, and wherever I went I had to tell the duel story over again. I was rather tired of it myself, but the wish to please and my own self-love were too strong to be resisted. The king was nearly always present, but feigned not to hear me. However, he once asked me if I had been insulted by a patrician in Venice, whether I should have called him out immediately.

"No, sire, for his patrician pride would have prevented his complying, and I should have had my pains for my trouble."

"Then what would you have done?"

"Sire, I should have contained myself, though if a noble Venetian were to insult me in a foreign country he would have to give me satisfaction."

I called on Prince Moszczinski, and Madame Binetti happened to be there; the moment she saw me she made her escape. "What has she against me?" I asked the count.

"She is afraid of you, because she was the cause of the duel, and now Branicki, who was her lover, will have nothing more to say to her. She hoped he would serve you as he served Tomatis, and instead of that you almost killed her bravo. She lays the fault on him for having accepted your challenge, but he has resolved to have done with her."

This Count Moszczinski was both good-hearted and quick-witted, and so generous that he ruined himself by making presents. His wounds were beginning to heal, but though I was the indirect cause of his mishap, far from bearing malice against me he had become my friend.

The person whom I should have expected to be most grateful to me for the duel was Tomatis, but on the contrary he hated the sight of me and hardly concealed his feelings. I was the living reproach of his cowardice; my wounded hand seemed to show him that he had loved his money more than his honour. I am sure he would have preferred Branicki to have killed me, for then he would have become an object of general execration, and Tomatis would have been received with less contempt in the great houses he still frequented.

I resolved to pay a visit to the discontented party who only recognised the new king on compulsion, and some of whom had not recognised him at all; so I set out with my true friend Campioni and one servant.

Prince Charles of Courland had started for Venice, where I had given him letters for my illustrious friends who would make his visit a pleasant one. The English ambassador, who had given me an introduction to Prince Adam, had just arrived at Warsaw. I dined with him at the prince's house, and the king signified his wish to be of the party. I heard a good deal of conversation about Madame de Geoffrin, an old sweetheart of the king's whom he had just summoned to Warsaw. The Polish monarch, of whom I cannot speak in too favourable terms, was yet weak enough to listen to the slanderous reports against me, and refused to make my fortune. I had the pleasure of convincing him that he was mistaken, but I will speak of this later on.

I arrived at Leopol the sixth day after I had left Warsaw,

having stopped a couple of days at Prince Zamoiski's; he had forty thousand ducats a year, but also — epilepsy.

"I would give all my goods," said he, "to be cured."

I pitied his young wife. She was very fond of him, and yet had to deny him, for his disease always came on him in moments of amorous excitement. She had the bitter task of constantly refusing him, and even of running away if he pressed her hard. This great nobleman, who died soon after, lodged me in a splendid room utterly devoid of furniture. This is a Polish custom; one is supposed to bring one's furniture with one.

At Leopol I put up at an hotel, but I soon had to move from thence to take up my abode with the famous Kaminska, the deadly foe of Branicki, the king, and all that party. She was very rich, but she has since been ruined by conspiracies. She entertained me sumptuously for a week, but the visit was agreeable to neither side, as she could only speak Polish and German. From Leopol I proceeded to a small town, the name of which I forget (the Polish names are very crabbed), to take an introduction from Prince Lubomirski to Joseph Rzewuski, a little old man who wore a long beard as a sign of mourning for the innovations that were being introduced into his country. He was rich, learned, superstitiously religious, and exceedingly polite. I stayed with him for three days. He was the commander of a stronghold containing a garrison of five hundred men.

On the first day, as I was in his room with some other officers, about eleven o'clock in the morning, another officer came in, whispered to Rzewuski, and then came up to me and whispered in my ear, "Venice and St. Mark."

"St. Mark," I answered aloud, "is the patron saint and protector of Venice"; and everybody began to laugh.

It dawned upon me that "*Venice and St. Mark*" was the watchword, and I began to apologise profusely, and the word was changed.

The old commander spoke to me with great politeness. He never went to Court, but he had resolved on going to the Diet to oppose the Russian party with all his might. The poor man, a Pole of the true old leaven, was one of the four whom Repnin arrested and sent to Siberia.

After taking leave of this brave patriot, I went to Christianpol, where lived the famous palatin Potocki, who had been one of the lovers of the empress Anna Ivanovna. He had founded the town in which he lived and called it after his own name. This nobleman, still a fine man, kept a splendid court. He honoured Count Brühl by keeping me at his house for a fortnight, and sending me out every day with his doctor, the famous Styrneus, the sworn foe of Van Swieten, a still more famous physician. Although Styrneus was undoubtedly a learned man, I thought him somewhat extravagant and empirical. His system was that of Asclepiades, considered as exploded since the time of the great Boerhaave; nevertheless, he effected wonderful cures.

In the evenings I was always with the palatin and his court. Play was not heavy, and I always won, which was fortunate and indeed necessary for me. After an extremely agreeable visit to the palatin I returned to Leopol, where I amused myself for a week with a pretty girl who afterwards so captivated Count Potocki, starost of Sniatin, that he married her. This is purity of blood with a vengeance in your noble families!

Leaving Leopol I went to Palavia, a splendid palace on the Vistula, eighteen leagues distant from Warsaw. It belonged to the prince-palatin, who had built it himself.

Howsoever magnificent an abode may be, a lonely man will weary of it unless he has the solace of books or of some great idea. I had neither, and boredom soon made itself felt.

As a rule, the Polish women are ugly; a beauty is a miracle, and a pretty woman a rare exception. At the end of a week of feasting and weariness, I returned to Warsaw.

In this manner I saw Podolia and Volkynia, which were rebaptized a few years later by the names of Galicia and Lodomeria, for they are now part of the Austrian Empire. It is said, however, that they are more prosperous than they ever were before.

At Warsaw I found Madame Geoffrin the object of universal admiration; and everybody was remarking with what simplicity she was dressed. As for myself, I was received not coldly, but positively rudely. People said to my face:

"We did not expect to see you here again. Why did you come back?"

"To pay my debts."

This behaviour astonished and disgusted me. The prince-palatin even seemed quite changed towards me. I was still invited to dinner, but no one spoke to me. However, Prince Adam's sister asked me very kindly to come and sup with her, and I accepted the invitation with delight. I found myself seated opposite the king, who did not speak one word to me the whole time. He had never behaved to me thus before.

The next day I dined with the Countess Oginski, and in the course of dinner the countess asked where the king had supped the night before; nobody seemed to know, and I did not answer. Just as we were rising, General Roniker came in, and the question was repeated.

"At Princess Strasnikowa's," said the general, "and M. Casanova was there."

"Then why did you not answer my question?" said the countess to me.

"Because I am very sorry to have been there. His majesty neither spoke to me nor looked at me. I see I am in disgrace, but for the life of me I know not why."

On leaving the house I went to call on Prince Augustus Sulkowski, who welcomed me as of old, but told me that I had made a mistake in returning to Warsaw, as public opinion was against me.

"What have I done?"

"Nothing; but the Poles are always inconsistent and changeable. *Sarmatarum virtus veluti extra ipsos.* This inconstancy will cost us dear sooner or later. Your fortune was made, but you missed the turn of the tide, and I advise you to go."

"I will certainly do so, but it seems to me rather hard."

When I got home my servant gave me a letter which some unknown person had left at my door. I opened it and found it to be anonymous, but I could see it came from a well-wisher. The writer said that the slanderers had got the ears of the king, and that I was no longer a *persona grata* at Court, as he had been assured that the Parisians had burnt me in effigy for my absconding with the lottery money, and that I had been a strolling player in Italy and little better than a vagabond.

Such calumnies are easy to utter but hard to refute in a foreign country. At all Courts hatred, born of envy, is ever at work. I might have despised the slanders and left the country, but I had contracted debts and had not sufficient money to pay them and my expenses to Portugal, where I thought I might do something.

I no longer saw any company, with the exception of Campioni, who seemed more distressed than myself. I wrote to Venice and everywhere else, where there was a chance of my getting funds; but one day the general who had been present at the duel called on me, and told me (though he seemed ashamed of his task) that the king requested me to leave the ban in the course of a a week.

Such a piece of insolence made my blood boil, and I informed the general that he might tell the king that I did not feel inclined to obey such an unjust order, and that if I left I would let all the world know that I had been compelled to do so by brute force.

"I cannot take such a message as that," said the general, kindly. "I shall simply tell the king that I have executed his orders, and no more; but of course you must follow your own judgment."

In the excess of my indignation I wrote to the king that I could not obey his orders and keep my honour. I said in my letter:

"My creditors, sire, will forgive me for leaving Poland without paying my debts, when they learn that I have only done so because your majesty gave me no choice."

I was thinking how I could ensure this letter reaching the king, when who should arrive but Count Moszczinski. I told him what had happened, and asked if he could suggest any means of delivering the letter.

"Give it to me," said he; "I will place it in the king's hands."

As soon as he had gone I went out to take the air, and called on Prince Sulkowski, who was not at all astonished at my news. As if to sweeten the bitter pill I had to swallow, he told me how the Empress of Austria had ordered him to leave Vienna in twenty-four hours, merely because he had complimented the Archduchess Christina on behalf of Prince Louis of Württemberg.

The next day Count Moszczinski brought me a present of a thousand ducats from the king, who said that my leaving Warsaw would probably be the means of preserving my life, as in that city I was exposed to danger which I could not expect to escape eventually.

This referred to five or six challenges I had received, and to which I had not even taken the trouble to reply. My enemies might possibly assassinate me, and the king did not care to be constantly anxious on my account. Count Moszczinski added that the order to leave carried no dishonour with it, considering by whom it had been delivered, and the delay it gave me to make my preparations.

The consequence of all this was that I not only gave my word to go, but that I begged the count to thank his majesty for his kindness, and the interest he had been pleased to take in me.

When I gave in, the generous Moszczinski embraced me, begged me to write to him, and accept a present of a travelling carriage as a token of his friendship. He informed me that Madame Binetti's husband had gone off with his wife's maid, taking with him her diamonds, jewels, linen, and even her silver plate, leaving her to the tender mercies of the dancer, Pic. Her admirers had clubbed together to make up to her for what her husband had stolen. I also heard that the king's sister had arrived at Warsaw from Bialistock, and it was hoped that her husband would follow her. This husband was the real Count Branicki, and the Branicki, or rather Branecki, or Bragnecki, who had fought with me, was no relation to him whatever.

The following day I paid my debts, which amounted to about two hundred ducats, and I made preparations for starting for Breslau, the day after, with Count Clary, each of us having his own carriage. Clary was one of those men to whom lying has become a sort of second nature; whenever such an one opens his mouth, you may safely say to him, "You have lied, or you are going to lie." If they could feel their own degradation, they would be much to be pitied, for by their own fault at last no one will believe them even when by chance they speak the truth. This Count Clary, who was not one of the Clarys of Teplitz, could neither go to his own country nor to Vienna, because he had deserted the army on the eve of a battle. He was lame, but he walked so adroitly that his defect did not appear. If this had been the only truth he concealed, it would have been well, for it was a piece of deception that hurt no one. He died miserably in Venice.

We reached Breslau in perfect safety, and without experiencing any adventures. Campioni, who had accompanied me as far as Württemberg, returned, but rejoined me at Vienna in the course of seven months. Count Clary had left Breslau, and I thought I would make the acquaintance of the Abbé Bastiani, a celebrated Venetian whose fortune had been made by the King of Prussia. He was canon of the cathedral, and received me cordially; in fact, each mutually desired the other's acquaintance. He was a fine well-made man, fair-complexioned, and at least six feet high. He was also witty, learned, eloquent, and gifted with a persuasive voice; his cook was an artist, his library full of choice volumes, and his cellar a very good one. He was well lodged on the ground-floor, and on the first floor he accommodated a lady, of whose children he was very fond, possibly because he was their father. The canon showed me all the letters he had received from the King of Prussia before he had been made canon. He was the son of a tailor at Venice, and became a friar, but having committed some peccadillo which got him into trouble, he was fortunate enough to be able to make his escape. He fled to The Hague, and there met Tron, the Venetian ambassador, who lent him a hundred ducats with which he made his way to Berlin and favour with the king. Such are the ways by which men arrive at fortune! *Sequere deum!*

On the event of my departure from Breslau I went to pay a call on a baroness for whom I had a letter of introduction from her son, who was an officer of the Polish Court. I sent up my name and was asked to wait a few moments as the baroness was dressing. I sat down beside a pretty girl, who was neatly dressed in a mantle with a hood. I asked her if she were waiting for the baroness like myself.

"Yes, sir," she replied, "I have come to offer myself as governess for her three daughters."

"What! Governess at your age?"

"Alas! sir, age has nothing to do with necessity. I have neither father nor mother. My brother is a poor lieutenant who cannot help me; what can I do? I can only get a livelihood by turning my good education to account."

"What will your salary be?"

"Fifty wretched crowns, enough to buy my dresses."

"It's very little."

"It is as much as people give."

"Where are you living now?"

"With a poor aunt, where I can scarce earn enough bread to keep me alive by sewing from morning till night."

"If you liked to become my governess instead of becoming a children's governess, I would give you fifty crowns, not per year, but per month."

"Your governess? Governess to your family, you mean, I suppose?"

"I have no family; I am a bachelor, and I spend my time in travelling. I leave at five o'clock to-morrow morning for Dresden, and if you like to come with me there is a place for you in my carriage. I am staying at such an inn. Come there with your trunk, and we will start together."

"You are joking; besides, I don't know you."

"I am not jesting; and we should get to know each other perfectly well in twenty-four hours; that is ample time."

My serious air convinced the girl that I was not laughing at her; but she was still very much astonished, while I was very much astonished to find I had gone so far when I had only intended to joke. In trying to win over the girl I had won over myself. It seemed to me a rare adventure, and I was delighted to see that she was giving it her serious attention by the side glances she kept casting in my direction to see if I was laughing at her. I began to think that fate had brought us together that I might become the architect of her fortune. I had no doubt whatever as to her goodness or her feelings for me, for she completely infatuated my judgment. To put the finishing stroke on the affair I drew out two ducats and gave them her as an earnest of her first month's wages. She took them timidly, but seemed convinced that I was not imposing on her.

By this time the baroness was ready, and she welcomed me very kindly; but I said I could not accept her invitation to dine with her the following day, as I was leaving at daybreak. I replied to all the questions that a fond mother makes concerning her son, and then took leave of the worthy lady. As I went out I noticed that the would-be governess had disappeared. The rest of the day I spent with the canon, making good cheer, playing ombre, drinking hard, and talking about girls or literature. The next day my carriage came to the door at the time I had arranged, and I went off without thinking of the girl I had met at the baroness's. But we had not gone two hundred paces when the postillion stopped, a bundle of linen whirled through the window into the carriage, and the governess got in. I gave her a hearty welcome by embracing her, and made her sit down beside me, and so we drove off.

CHAPTER XXI

CASTLES IN SPAIN

*H*AVING *refurbished his somewhat tarnished laurels with the Polish exploit — which, as he tells us, everyone was asking him to recount — Casanova, after a short visit to Dresden, where his mother, his sister, and his brother Giovanni, director of the state gallery, gave him the prodigal's welcome, resumes his wanderings. His stays in the various capitals become ever shorter. The old hectoring ways with police officers and magistrates, the letters from and to illustrious personages, all the old expedients for ingratiating himself and cutting a dash, are losing their efficacy. The order to "move on" is repeated with almost monotonous regularity. Casanova at forty is a marked man.*

While taking the waters at Spa, in Belgium, he runs across his ex-colleague and fellow-reprobate, the notorious Croce, now parading as a marquis with his pseudo-marquise, a young Belgian girl, with whom he had eloped. The story of the hapless Charlotte Lamothe, whom Croce, though knowing himself to be the father of the child she was about to bear, abandoned to his friend's care when disaster overtook him, is one of those "glimpses of reality" which, whenever they occur in the Memoirs, show that their author could respond to calls of genuine distress and at moments, at least, put into practice the chivalry on which he prided himself. This is the brief story of Charlotte[1] as we find it in the Memoirs:

To prepare her for the fatal news I asked her if she would approve of her lover exposing himself to assassination for the sake of bidding adieu to her rather than making his escape.

"I should blame him for doing so," she replied. "He ought to escape by all means, if only to save his life for my sake. Has

---

[1] *M. Charles Samaran publishes in his book on Casanova an extract from the register of the Foundling Hospital in Paris which bears out the truth of Casanova's statements regarding the birth and parentage of Charlotte's child.*

my husband done so? Speak openly to me. My spirit is strong enough to resist even so fatal a blow, for I know I have a friend in you. Speak."

"Well, I will tell you all. But first of all remember this: you must look upon me as a tender father who will never let you want, so long as life remains to him."

"In that case I cannot be called unfortunate, for I have a true friend. Say on."

I told all that Croce had told me, not omitting his last words: "*I commend Charlotte to your care; I would that she had never known me.*"

For a few minutes she remained motionless, as one turned into stone. By her attitude, by her laboured and unequal breath, I could divine somewhat of the battle between love, and anger, and sorrow, and pity, that was raging in the noble breast. I was cut to the heart. At last she wiped away the big tears that began to trickle down her cheeks, and turning to me sighed and said:

"Dear friend, since I can count on you, I am far indeed from utter misery."

"I swear to you, Charlotte, that I will never leave you till I place you again in your husband's hands, provided I do not die before."

"That is enough. I swear eternal gratitude and to be as submissive to you as a good daughter ought to be."

The religion and philosophy with which her heart and mine were fortified, though she made no parade of either, began to calm her spirit, and she proceeded to make some reflections on Croce's unhappy lot, but all in pity not in anger, excusing his inveterate passion for play. She had often heard from Croce's lips the story of the Marseilles girl whom he had left penniless in an inn at Milan, commending her to my care. She thought it something wonderful that I should again be intervening as the tutelary genius; but her situation was much the worse, for she was with child.

"There's another difference," I added, "for I made the fortune of the first by finding her an honest husband, whereas I should never have the courage to adopt the same method with the second."

"While Croce lives I am no man's wife but his, nevertheless I am glad to find myself free."

When we were back in the house, I advised her to send away the servant and to pay his journey to Besançon, where she had taken him. Thus all unpleasantness would be avoided. I made her sell all that remained of her poor lover's wardrobe, as also his carriage, for mine was a better one. She showed me all she had left, which only amounted to some sets of linen and three or four dresses.

We remained at Spa without going out of doors. She could see that my love was a tenderer passion than the love of a father, and she told me so, and that she was obliged to me for the respect with which I treated her. We sat together for hours, she folded in my arms, whilst I gently kissed her beautiful eyes, and asked no more. I was happy in her gratitude and in my powers of self-restraint. When temptation was too strong I left the beautiful girl till I was myself again, and such conquests made me proud. In the affection between us there was somewhat of the purity of a man's first love.

I wanted a small travelling cap, and the servant of the house went to my former lodging to order one. Mercy brought several for me to choose from. She blushed when she saw me, but I said nothing to her. When she had gone I told Charlotte the whole story, and she laughed with all her heart when I reminded her of the bruise on my face when we first met, and informed her that Mercy had given it me. She praised my firmness in rejecting her repentance, and agreed with me in thinking that the whole plan had been concerted between her and her aunt.

We left Spa without any servant, and when we reached Liège we took the way of the Ardennes, as she was afraid of being recognised if we passed through Brussels. At Luxemburg we engaged a servant, who attended on us till we reached Paris. All the way Charlotte was tender and affectionate, but her condition prescribed limits to her love, and I could only look forward to the time after her delivery. We got down at Paris at the Hôtel Montmorenci, in the street of the same name.

Paris struck me quite as a new place. Madame d'Urfé was dead, my friends had changed their houses and their fortunes; the poor had become rich and the rich poor, new streets and buildings were rising on all sides; I hardly knew my way about the town. Everything was dearer; poverty was rampant, and luxury at its highest pitch. Perhaps Paris is the only city where so great a change could take place in the course of five or six years.

The first call I made was on Madame du Rumain, who was delighted to see me. I repaid her the money she had so kindly lent me in the time of my distress. She was well in health, but harassed by so many anxieties and private troubles that she said Providence must have sent me to her to relieve her of all her griefs by my cabala. I told her that I would wait on her at any hour or hours; and this, indeed, was the least I could do for the woman who had been so kind to me.

My brother had gone to live in the Faubourg St. Antoine. Both he and his wife (who remained constant to him, despite his physical disability) were overjoyed to see me, and entreated me to come and stop with them. I told them I should be glad to do so, as soon as the lady who had travelled with me had got over her confinement. I did not think proper to tell them her story, and they had the delicacy to refrain from questioning me on the subject. The same day I called on Princess Lubomirska and Tomatis, begging them not to take it amiss if my visits were few and far between, as the lady they had seen at Spa was approaching her confinement, and demanded all my care.

After the discharge of these duties I remained constantly by Charlotte's side. On October 8th I thought it would be well to take her to Madame Lamarre, a midwife, who lived in the Faubourg St. Denis, and Charlotte was of the same opinion. We went together, she saw the room, the bed, and heard how she would be tended and looked after, for all of which I would pay. At nightfall we drove to the place, with a trunk containing all her effects.

As we were leaving the Rue Montmorenci our carriage was obliged to stop to allow the funeral of some rich man to go by. Charlotte covered her face with her handkerchief, and whispered in my ear:

"Dearest, I know it is a foolish superstition, but to a woman in my condition such a meeting is of evil omen."

"What, Charlotte! I thought you were too wise to have such silly fears. A woman in childbed is not a sick woman, and no woman ever died of giving birth to a child except some other disease intervened."

"Yes, my dear philosopher, it is like a duel; there are two

men in perfect health, when all of a sudden there comes a sword-thrust, and one of them is dead."

"That's a witty idea. But bid all gloomy thoughts go by, and after your child is born, and we have placed it in good hands, you shall come with me to Madrid, and there I hope to see you happy and contented."

All the way I did my best to cheer her, for I knew only too well the fatal effects of melancholy on a pregnant woman, especially in such a delicate girl as Charlotte.

When I saw her completely settled I returned to the hotel, and the next day I took up my quarters with my brother. However, as long as my Charlotte lived, I only slept at his house, for from nine in the morning till after midnight I was with my dear.

On October 13th Charlotte was attacked with a fever which never left her. On the 17th she was happily delivered of a boy, who was immediately taken to the church and baptized at the express wishes of the mother. Charlotte wrote down what its name was to be — Jacques (after me), Charles (after her), son of Antonio della Croce and of Charlotte de ** (she gave her real name). When it was brought from the church she told Madame Lamarre to carry it to the Foundling Hospital, with the certificate of baptism in its linen. I vainly endeavoured to persuade her to leave the care of the child to me. She said that if it lived the father could easily reclaim it. On the same day, October 18th, the midwife gave me the following certificate, which I still possess.

It was worded as follows: —

"We, J. B. Dorival, Councillor to the King, Commissary of the Chatelet, formerly Superintendent of Police in the City of Paris, do certify that there has been taken to the Hospital for Children a male infant, appearing to be one day old, brought from the Faubourg St. Denis by the midwife Lamarre, and bearing a certificate of baptism to the effect that its name is Jacques Charles, son of Antonio della Croce and of Charlotte de **. Wherefore, we have delivered the above certificate at our office in the City of Paris, this 18th day of October, in the year of our Lord, 1767, at seven o'clock in the afternoon.

"Dorival."

If any of my readers have any curiosity to know the real name of the mother, I have given them the means of satisfying it.

[325]

After this I did not leave the bed of the invalid for a single instant. In spite of all the doctor's care the fever increased, and at five o'clock in the morning of October 26th, she succumbed to it. An hour before she sighed her last, she bade me the last farewell in the presence of the venerable ecclesiastic who had confessed her at midnight. The tears which gather fast as I write these words are probably the last honours I shall pay to this poor victim of a man who is still alive, and whose destiny seemed to be to make women unhappy.

I sat weeping by the bed of her I loved so dearly, and in vain Madame Lamarre tried to induce me to come and sit with her. I loved the poor corpse better than all the world outside.

At noon my brother and his wife came to see me; they had not seen me for a week, and were getting anxious. They saw the body lovely in death; they understood my tears, and mingled theirs with mine. At last I asked them to leave me, and I remained all night by Charlotte's bed, resolved not to leave it till her body had been consigned to the grave.

The day before this morning of unhappy memory my brother had given me several letters, but I had not opened any of them. On my return from the funeral I proceeded to do so, and the first one was from M. Dandolo, announcing the death of M. de Bragadin; but I could not weep. For twenty-two years M. de Bragadin had been as a father to me, living poorly, and even going into debt that I might have enough. He could not leave me anything, as his property was entailed, while his furniture and his library would become the prey of his creditors. His two friends, who were my friends also, were poor, and could give me nothing but their love. The dreadful news was accompanied by a bill of exchange for a thousand crowns, which he had sent me twenty-four hours before his death, foreseeing that it would be the last gift he would ever make me.

I was overwhelmed, and thought that Fortune had done her worst to me.

I spent three days in my brother's house without going out. On the fourth I began to pay an assiduous court to Princess Lubomirska, who had written the king, her brother, a letter that must have mortified him, as she proved beyond a doubt that the tales he had listened to against me were mere calumny. But your kings do not allow so small a thing to vex or mortify them.

Besides, Stanislas Augustus had just received a dreadful insult from Russia. Repnin's violence in kidnapping the three senators who had spoken their minds at the Diet was a blow which must have pierced the hapless king to the heart.

The princess had left Warsaw more from hatred than love; though such was not the general opinion. As I had decided to visit the Court of Madrid before going to Portugal, the princess gave me a letter of introduction to the powerful Count of Aranda; and the Marquis Caracedillo, who was still at Paris, gave me three letters, one for Prince de la Catolica, the Neapolitan ambassador at Madrid, one for the Duke of Lossada, the king's favourite and lord high steward, and a third for the Marquis Mora Pignatelli.

On November 4th I went to a concert with a ticket that the princess had given me. When the concert was half-way through I heard my name pronounced, accompanied by scornful laughter. I turned round and saw the gentleman who was speaking contemptuously of me. It was a tall young man sitting between two men advanced in years. I stared him in the face, but he turned his head away and continued his impertinencies, saying, amongst other things, that I had robbed him of a million francs at least by my swindling his late aunt, the Marchioness d'Urfé.

"You are an impudent liar," I said to him, "and if we were out of this room I would give you a kick to teach you to speak respectfully."

With these words I made my way out of the hall, and on turning my head round I saw that the two elderly men were keeping the young blockhead back. I got into my carriage and waited some time, and as he did not come I drove to the theatre and chanced to find myself in the same box as Madame Valville. She informed me that she had left the boards, and was kept by the Marquis de Brunel.

"I congratulate you, and wish you good luck."

"I hope you will come to supper at my house."

"I should be only too happy, but unfortunately I have an engagement; but I will come and see you if you will give me your address."

So saying, I slipped into her hand a rouleau, it being the fifty louis I owed her.

"What is this?"

"The money you lent me so kindly at Königsberg."

"This is neither the time nor the place to return it. I will only take it at my own house, so please do not insist."

I put the money back into my pocket, she gave me her address, and I left her. I felt too sad to visit her alone.

Two days later, as I was at table with my brother, my sister-in-law, and some young Russians whom he was teaching to paint, I was told that a Chevalier St. Louis wanted to speak to me in the ante-chamber. I went out, and he handed me a paper without making any preface. I opened the document, and found it was signed "Louis." The great king ordered me to leave Paris in twenty-four hours and his realm of France within three weeks, and the reason assigned was: "*It is our good pleasure.*"

Having, as he naïvely puts it, "informed all my friends of the great honour his majesty had done me" and declined Madame du Rumain's offer to appeal on his behalf to the king, Casanova bids farewell to France: "Fair and beloved France, that went so well in those days, despite lettres de cachet, *despite* corvées, *despite the people's misery and the king's 'good pleasure,' dear France, where art thou now? Thy sovereign is the people now, the most brutal and tyrannical sovereign in the world . . . ."*

Little has so far been ascertained regarding Casanova's Spanish sojourn, which lasted about a year (from the end of 1767 to the end of 1768). He seems to have spent some time in Madrid and Barcelona and to have been afforded the opportunity of comparing the prisons of Castille with those of Catalonia, from the inside as well as the outside, an opportunity he made the most of by composing his Confutazione della Storia del governo veneto, *an attack on a work by Amelot de la Houssaye which represented the Venetian government in an unfavourable light, hoping by this means to ingratiate himself with the authorities of this city and win his pardon.*

In Madrid he found Raphael Mengs, whom he had known in Rome when his brother was studying under the painter. Mengs, who was then in high favour, appears to have befriended the adventurer at first, and then, finding him incorrigible, to have given him up as a bad job. In Madrid he also met the son of his arch-enemy Manuzzi (also spelt Manucci), the spy who had got him put under The Leads. As the young man happened to be the very intimate friend of the Venetian ambassador, Mocenigo, Casanova was as willing to let bygones be bygones as Manuzzi junior to

*make amends for his father's misdeeds, especially as he himself was
posing as a count. But Casanova was always his own worst
enemy. Having had every proof of young Manuzzi's desire to befriend him, he foolishly behind his back made fun of his assumed
title (the Chevalier de Seingalt had a passion for exposing titular
frauds!) thereby earning the lasting wrath of the upstart and losing
all chance of the ambassador's using his influence on his behalf.*

Regarding his lettre de cachet, *Casanova maintains that, far
from being anything to his discredit, the fact that he was allowed to
leave the kingdom at his leisure (i.e., on November 20th, a fortnight
later) and that the order was presented to him by a Chevalier de
St. Louis, proves that he was accorded honourable treatment, and
not, as his enemies later pretended, shamefully expelled from France.*

The love-*motif of this Spanish* fantasia *— a somewhat conventional "local colour" motif of the* Gil Blas *period (the days of*
Carmen *were yet to come!) — is furnished by the intrigue with
Doña Ignazia, the daughter of the hidalgo-cobbler. It is introduced
as follows:*

By way of amusing myself I began to go to the theatre, and
to the masked balls which the Count of Aranda had established.
They were held in a room built for the purpose, and named *Los
Scannos del Peral.* A Spanish play is full of absurdities, but I
rather relished the representations. The *Autos Sacramentales*
were still represented; they were afterwards prohibited. I could
not help remarking the strange way in which the boxes were constructed by order of the wretched police. Instead of being
boarded in front they are perfectly open, being kept up by small
pillars. A devotee once said to me at the theatre that this was
a very wise regulation, and he was surprised that it was not
carried into force in Italy.

"Why so?"

"Because lovers, who feel sure that no one in the pit can
see them, may commit improprieties."

I only answered with a shrug of the shoulders.

In a large box opposite to the stage sat *los padres* of the Holy
Inquisition to watch over the morals of actors and audience. I
was gazing on them when of a sudden the sentinel at the door of
the pit called out "*Dios!*" and at this cry all the actors and all
the audience, men and women, fell down on their knees, and remained kneeling till the sound of a bell in the street ceased to be

heard. This bell betokened that a priest was passing by carrying the viaticum to some sick man. I felt very much inclined to laugh, but I had seen enough of Spanish manners to refrain. All the religion of the Spaniards is in outward show and ceremony. A profligate woman before yielding to the desires of her lover covers the picture of Christ, or the Virgin, with a veil. If the lover laughed at this absurdity he would run a risk of being denounced as an Atheist, and most probably by the wretched woman who had sold him her charms.

In Madrid, and possibly all over Spain, a gentleman who takes a lady to a private room in an inn must expect to have a servant in the room the whole of the time, that he may be able to swear that the couple took no indecent liberties with each other. In spite of all, profligacy is rampant at Madrid, and also the most dreadful hypocrisy, which is more offensive to true piety than open sin. Men and women seemed to have come to an agreement to set the whole system of surveillance utterly at nought. However, commerce with women is not without its dangers; whether it be endemic or a result of dirty habits, one has often good reasons to repent the favours one has obtained.

The masked ball quite captivated me. The first time I went to see what it was like and it only cost me a doubloon (about eleven francs), but ever after it cost me four doubloons, for the following reason: An elderly gentleman, who sat next me at supper, guessed I was a foreigner by my difficulty in making myself understood by the waiter, and asked me where I had left my lady friend.

"I have not got one; I came by myself to enjoy this delightful and excellently-managed entertainment."

"Yes, but you ought to come with a companion; then you could dance. At present you cannot do so, as every lady has her partner, who will not allow her to dance with anyone else."

"Then I must be content not to dance, for, being a stranger, I do not know any lady whom I can ask to come with me."

"As a stranger you would have much less difficulty in securing a partner than a citizen of Madrid. Under the new fashion, introduced by the Count of Aranda, the masked ball has become the rage of all the women in the capital. You see there are about two hundred of them on the floor to-night; well, I should think there are at least four thousand girls in Madrid who are sighing for someone to take them to the ball, for, as you may know, no woman is allowed to come by herself. You would only have to go to any respectable people, give your name and address, and ask to have the pleasure of taking their daughter to the ball. You would have to send her a domino, mask, and gloves; and you would take her and bring her back in your carriage."

"And if the father and mother refused?"

"Then you would make your bow and go, leaving them to repent of their folly, for the girl would sigh, and weep, and moan, bewail parental tyranny, call Heaven to witness the innocency of going to a ball, and finally go into convulsions."

This oration, which was uttered in the most persuasive style, made me quite gay, for I scented an intrigue from afar. I thanked the masquer (who spoke Italian very well) and promised to follow his advice and to let him know the results.

"I shall be delighted to hear of your success, and you will find me in the box, where I shall be glad if you will follow me now to be introduced to the lady who is my constant companion."

I was astonished at so much politeness, and told him my name and followed him. He took me into a box where there were two ladies and an elderly man. They were talking about the ball, so I put in a remark or two on the same topic, which seemed to meet with approval. One of the two ladies, who retained some traces of her former beauty, asked me, in excellent French, what circles I moved in.

"I have only been a short time in Madrid, and not having been presented at Court I really know no one."

"Really! I quite pity you. Come and see me, you will be welcome. My name is Pichona, and anybody will tell you where I live."

"I shall be delighted to pay my respects to you, madam."

What I liked best about the spectacle was a wonderful and fantastic dance which was struck up at midnight. It was the famous *fandango*, of which I had often heard, but of which I had absolutely no idea. I had seen it danced on the stage in France and Italy, but the actors were careful not to use those voluptuous gestures which make it the most seductive in the world. It cannot be described. Each couple only dances three steps, but the gestures and the attitudes are the most lascivious imaginable.

Everything is represented, from the sigh of desire to the final ecstacy; it is a very history of love. I could not conceive a woman refusing her partner anything after this dance, for it seemed made to stir up the senses. I was so excited at this Bacchanalian spectacle that I burst out into cries of delight. The masquer who had taken me to his box told me that I should see the *fandango* danced by the Gitanas with good partners."

"But," I remarked, "does not the Inquisition object to this dance?"

Madame Pichona told me that it was absolutely forbidden, and would not be danced unless the Count of Aranda had given permission.

I heard afterwards that, on the count forbidding the *fandango*, the ball-room was deserted with bitter complaints, and on the prohibition being withdrawn everyone was loud in his praise.

The next day I told my infamous page to get me a Spaniard who would teach me the *fandango*. He brought me an actor, who also gave me Spanish lessons, for he pronounced the language admirably. In the course of three days the young actor taught me all the steps so well that, by the confession of the Spaniards themselves, I danced it to perfection.

For the next ball I determined to carry the masquer's advice into effect, but I did not want to take a courtesan or a married woman with me, and I could not reasonably expect that any young lady of family would accompany me.

It was St. Anthony's Day, and passing the Church of the Soledad, I went in, with the double motive of hearing mass and of procuring a partner for the next day's ball.

I noticed a fine-looking girl coming out of the confessional, with contrite face and lowered eyes, and I noted where she went. She knelt down in the middle of the church, and I was so attracted by her appearance that I registered a mental vow to the effect that she should be my first partner. She did not look a person of condition, nor, so far as I could see, was she rich, and nothing about her indicated the courtesan, though women of that class go to confession in Madrid like everybody else. When mass was ended, the priest distributed the Eucharist, and I saw her rise and approach humbly to the holy table, and there receive the communion. She then returned to the church to finish her devotions, and I was patient enough to wait till they were over.

At last she left, in company with another girl, and I followed her at a distance. At the end of a street her companion left her to go into her house, and she, retracing her steps, turned into another street and entered a small house, one story high. I noted the house and the street (Calle del Desinjaño) and then walked up and down for half an hour, that I might not be suspected of following her. At last I took courage and walked in, and, on my ringing a bell, I heard a voice:

"Who is there?"

"Honest folk," I answered, according to the custom of the country; and the door was opened. I found myself in the presence of a man, a woman, the young devotee I had followed, and another girl, somewhat ugly.

My Spanish was bad, but still it was good enough to express my meaning, being a stranger, and having no partner to take to the ball, I had come to ask him to give me his daughter for my partner, supposing he had a daughter. I assured him that I was a man of honour, and that the girl should be returned to him after the ball in the same condition as when she started.

"Señor," said he, "there is my daughter, but I don't know you and don't know whether she wants to go."

"I should like to go, if my parents will allow me."

"Then you know this gentleman?"

"I have never seen him, and I suppose he has never seen me."

"You speak the truth, señora."

The father asked me my name and address, and promised I should have a decisive answer by dinner-time, if I dined at home. I begged him to excuse the liberty I had taken, and to let me know his answer without fail, so that I might have time to get another partner if it were unfavourable to me.

Just as I was beginning to dine my man appeared. I asked him to sit down, and he informed me that his daughter would accept my offer, but that her mother would accompany her and sleep in the carriage. I said that she might do so if she liked, but I should be sorry for her on account of the cold.

"She shall have a good cloak," said he; and he proceeded to inform me that he was a cordwainer.

"Then I hope you will take my measure for a pair of shoes."

"I daren't do that; I'm an hidalgo, and if I were to take anyone's measure I should have to touch his foot, and that would be a degradation. I am a cobbler, and that is not inconsistent with my nobility."

"Then, will you mend these boots?"

"I will make them like new; but I see they want a lot of work; it will cost you a pezzo duro, about five francs."

I told him that I thought his terms very reasonable, and he went out with a profound bow, refusing absolutely to dine with me.

Here was a cobbler who despised bootmakers because they had to touch the foot, and they, no doubt, despised him because he touched old leather. Unhappy pride! how many forms it assumes, and who is without his own peculiar form of it?

The next day I sent to the gentleman-cobbler's a tradesman with dominoes, masks, and gloves; but I took care not to go myself nor to send my page, for whom I had an aversion which almost amounted to a presentiment. I hired a carriage to seat four, and at nightfall I drove to the house of my pious partner, who was quite ready for me. The happy flush on her face was a sufficient index to me of the feelings of her heart. We got into the carriage with the mother, who was wrapped up in a vast cloak, and at the door of the dancing-room we descended, leaving the mother in the carriage. As soon as we were alone my fair partner told me that her name was Donna Ignazia.

We entered the ball-room and walked round several times. Donna Ignazia was in such a state of ecstacy that I felt her trembling, and augured well for my amorous projects. Though liberty, nay, licence, seemed to reign supreme, there was a guard of soldiers ready to arrest the first person who created any disturbance. We danced several minuets and square dances, and at ten o'clock we went to the supper-room, our conversation being very limited all the while, she not speaking for fear of encouraging me too much, and I on account of my poor knowledge of the Spanish language. I left her alone for a moment after supper, and went to the box, where I expected to find Madame Pichona, but it was occupied by masquers, who were unknown to me, so I rejoined my partner, and we went on dancing the minuets and quadrilles till the *fandango* was announced. I took my place with my partner, who danced it admirably, and seemed astonished to find herself so well supported by a foreigner. This dance had excited both of us, so, after taking her to the buffet and giving her the best wines and liqueurs procurable, I asked her if she were content with me. I added that I was deeply in love with her, that unless she found some means of making me happy I should undoubtedly die of love. I assured her that I was ready to face all hazards.

"By making you happy," she replied, "I shall make myself happy, too. I will write to you to-morrow, and you will find the letter sewn into the hood of my domino."

"You will find me ready to do anything, fair Ignazia, if you will give me hope."

At last the ball was over, and we went out and got into the carriage. The mother woke up, and the coachman drove off, and I, taking the girl's hands, would have kissed them. However, she seemed to suspect that I had other intentions, and held my hands clasped so tightly that I believe I should have found it a hard task to pull them away. In this position Donna Ignazia proceeded to tell her mother all about the ball, and the delight it had given her. She did not let go my hands till we got to the corner of their street, when the mother called out to the coachman to stop, not wishing to give her neighbours occasion for slander by stopping in front of their own house.

During the course of his amours with Donna Ignazia, Casanova was imprisoned for a short time at the fortress of El Buen Retiro, owing, he says, to the malevolence of his Spanish servant, who had denounced him to the alcalde for harbouring weapons. Afterwards Casanova seems to have enjoyed a short hour of popularity. Whatever may be the truth of his alleged intimacy with the great, his portraits of some of the leading personalities of the day, and his keen sense for picturesque details, make interesting reading:

I had not long returned to my lodging when Mengs called for me in his carriage. The ambassador gave me a most gracious reception, and overwhelmed Mengs with compliments for having endeavoured to shelter me. At dinner I told the story of my sufferings at Buen Retiro, and the conversation I had just had with the Count of Aranda, who had returned me my letters. The company expressed a desire to see them, and everyone gave an opinion on the matter.

The guests were Abbé Bigliardi, the French consul, Don Rodrigues de Campomanes, and the famous Don Pablo d'Olavides. Everyone spoke his mind, and the ambassador condemned the letters as too *ferocious*. On the other hand, Campomanes approved them, saying that they were not abusive, and were wonderfully adapted to my purpose — namely, to force the reader to do me prompt justice, were the reader to be the king himself. Olavides and Bigliardi echoed this sentiment. Mengs sided with the ambassador, and begged me to come and live with him, so as not to be liable to any more inconveniences from spying servants. I did not accept this invitation till I had been pressed for some time, and I noted the remark of the ambassador, who said I owed Mengs this reparation for the indirect affront he had received.

I was delighted to make the acquaintance of Campomanes and Olavides, men of intellect and of a stamp very rare in Spain. They were not exactly men of learning, but they were above religious prejudices, and were not only fearless in throwing public scorn upon them but even laboured openly for their destruction. It was Campomanes who had furnished Aranda with all the damaging matter against the Jesuits. By a curious coincidence, Campomanes, the Count of Aranda, and the General of the Jesuits, were all squint-eyed. I asked Campomanes why he hated the Jesuits so bitterly, and he replied that he looked upon them in the same light as the other religious orders, whom he considered a parasitical and noxious race, and would gladly banish them all, not only from the peninsula but from the face of the earth.

He was the author of all the pamphlets that had been written on the subject of mortmain; and as he was an intimate friend of the ambassador's, M. Mocenigo had furnished him with an account of the proceedings of the Venetian Republic against the monks. He might have dispensed with this source of information if he had read the writings of Father Paul Sarpi on the same subject. Quicksighted, firm, with the courage of his opinions, Campomanes was the fiscal of the Supreme Council of Castille, of which Aranda was president. Everyone knew him to be a thoroughly honest man, who acted solely for the good of the state. Thus statesmen and officials had warm feelings of respect for him, while the monks and bigots hated the sound of his name, and the Inquisition had sworn to be his ruin. It was said openly that he would either become a bishop or perish in the cells of the holy brotherhood. The prophecy was only partly fulfilled. Four years after my visit to Spain he was incarcerated in the dungeons of the Inquisition, but he obtained his release after three years' confinement by doing public penance. The leprosy which eats out the heart of Spain is not yet cured. Olavides was still more harshly treated, and even Aranda would have fallen a victim if he had not the good sense to ask the king to send him to France as his ambassador. The king was very glad to do so, as otherwise he would have been forced to deliver him up to the infuriated monks.

Charles III. (who died a madman) was a remarkable character. He was as obstinate as a mule, as weak as a woman, as gross as a Dutchman, and a thorough-paced bigot. It was no wonder that he became the tool of his confessor.

At the time of which I am speaking the cabinet of Madrid was occupied in a curious scheme. A thousand Catholic families had been enticed from Switzerland to form a colony in the beautiful but deserted region called the Sierra Morena, well known all over Europe by its mention in *Don Quixote*. Nature seemed there to have lavished all her gifts; the climate was perfect, the soil fertile, and streams of all kinds watered the land, but in spite of all it was almost depopulated.

Desiring to change this state of things, his Catholic majesty had decided to make a present of all the agricultural products for a certain number of years to industrious colonists. He had consequently invited the Swiss Catholics, and had paid their expenses for the journey. The Swiss arrived, and the Spanish government did its best to provide them with lodging and spiritual and temporal superintendence. Olavides was the soul of this scheme. He conferred with the ministers to provide the population with magistrates, priests, a governor, craftsmen of all kinds to build churches and houses, and especially a bull-ring, a necessity for the Spaniards, but a perfectly useless provision as far as the simple Swiss were concerned.

In the documents which Don Pablo Olavides had composed on the subject he demonstrated the inexpediency of establishing any religious orders in the new colony, but if he could have proved his opinion to be correct with foot and rule he would none the less have drawn on his head the implacable hatred of the monks, and of the bishop in whose diocese the new colony was situated. The secular clergy supported Olavides, but the

[337]

monks cried out against his impiety, and as the Inquisition was eminently monkish in its sympathies persecution had already begun, and this was one of the subjects of conversation at the dinner at which I was present.

I listened to the arguments, sensible and otherwise, which were advanced, and I finally gave my opinion, as modestly as I could, that in a few years the colony would vanish like smoke; and this for several reasons.

"The Swiss," I said, "are very peculiar people; if you transplant them to a foreign shore, they languish and die; they become a prey to home-sickness. When this once begins in a Switzer, the only thing is to take him home to the mountain, the lake, or the valley, where he was born, or else he will infallibly die."

"It would be wise, I think," I continued, "to endeavour to combine a Spanish colony with the Swiss colony, so as to effect a mingling of races. At first, at all events, their rulers, both spiritual and temporal, should be Swiss, and, above all, you would have to ensure them complete immunity from the Inquisition. The Swiss who has been bred in the country, has peculiar customs and manners of love-making, of which the Spanish Church might not exactly approve; but the least attempt to restrain their liberty in this respect would immediately bring about a general home-sickness."

At first Olavides thought I was joking, but he soon found out that my remarks had some sense in them. He begged me to write out my opinions on the subject, and to give him the benefit of my knowledge. I promised to do so, and Mengs fixed a day for him to come and dine with me at his house.

The next day I moved my household goods to Mengs's house, and began my philosophical and physiological treatise on the colony.

I called on Don Emmanuel de Roda, who was a man of letters, a *rara avis* in Spain. He liked Latin poetry, had read some Italian, but very naturally gave the palm to the Spanish poets. He welcomed me warmly, begged me to come and see him again, and told me how sorry he had been at my unjust imprisonment.

The Duke of Lossada congratulated me on the way in which the Venetian ambassador spoke of me everywhere, and encouraged me in my idea of getting some place under Government, promising to give me his support in the matter.

The Prince de la Cattolica invited me to dinner with the Venetian ambassador; and in the course of three weeks I had made a great number of valuable acquaintances. I thought seriously of seeking employment in Spain, as not having heard from Lisbon I dared not go there on the chance of finding something to do. I had not received any letters from Pauline of late, and had no idea as to what had become of her.

I passed a good many of my evenings with a Spanish lady, named Sabatini, who gave *tertullas* or assemblies, frequented chiefly by fifth-rate literary men. I also visited the Duke of Medina-Sidonia, a well-read and intelligent man, to whom I had been presented by Don Domingo Varnier, one of the gentlemen of the king's chamber, whom I had met at Mengs's house. I paid a good many visits to Donna Ignazia, but as I was never left alone with her these visits became tiresome. When I suggested a party of pleasure with her and her cousins, she replied that she would like it as much as I, but as it was Lent and near Holy Week, in which God died for our salvation, it was more fit to think of penance than pleasure. After Easter, she said, we might consider the matter. Ignazia was a perfect example of the young Spanish devotee.

A fortnight after, the king and Court left Madrid for Aranjuez. M. de Mocenigo asked me to come and stay with him, as he would be able to present me at Court. As may be imagined, I should have been only too glad to accept, but on the eve of my departure, as I was driving with Mengs, I was suddenly seized with a fever, and was convulsed so violently that my head was dashed against the carriage window, which it shivered to fragments. Mengs ordered the coachman to drive home, and I was put to bed. In four hours I was seized with a sweating fit, which lasted ten or twelve hours. The bed and two mattresses were soaked through with my perspiration, which dripped on to the floor beneath. The fever abated in forty-eight hours, but left me in such a state of weakness that I was kept to my bed for a whole week, and could not go to Aranjuez till Holy Saturday. The ambassador welcomed me warmly, but on the night I arrived a small lump which I had felt in the course of the day grew as large as an egg, and I was unable to go to mass on Easter

Day. In five days the excrescence became as large as an average melon, much to the amazement of Manucci and the ambassador, and even of the king's surgeon, a Frenchman, who declared he had never seen the like before. I was not alarmed personally, for, as I suffered no pain and the lump was quite soft, I guessed it was only a collection of lymph, the remainder of the evil humours which I had sweated away in a fever. I told the surgeon the history of the fever and begged him to lance the abscess, which he did, and for four days the opening discharged an almost incredible amount of matter. On the fifth day the wound was almost healed, but the exhaustion had left me so weak that I could not leave my bed.

Such was my situation when I received a letter from Mengs. It is before me at the present moment, and I give below a true copy.

"Yesterday the rector of the parish in which I reside affixed to the church door a list of those of his parishioners who are Atheists and have neglected their Easter duties. Amongst them your name figures in full, and the aforesaid rector has reproached me bitterly for harbouring a heretic. I did not know what answer to make, for I feel sure that you could have stopped in Madrid a day longer to discharge the duties of a Christian, even if it were only out of regard for me. The duty I owe to the king, my master, the care I am bound to take of my reputation, and my fears of being molested, all make me repuest you to look upon my house as yours no longer. When you return to Madrid you may go where you will, and my servants shall transport your effects to your new abode.

"I am, etc.,

"Antonio Raphael Mengs."

I was so annoyed by this rude, brutal, and ungrateful letter, that if I had not been seven leagues from Madrid, and in a state of the utmost weakness, Mengs should have suffered for his insolence. I told the messenger who had brought it to begone, but he replied that he had orders to await my reply. I crushed the letter in my hand and flung it at his face, saying:

"Go and tell your unworthy master what I did with his letter, and tell him that is the only answer that such a letter deserves."

The innocent messenger went his way in great amazement.

My anger gave me strength, and having dressed myself and

[340]

summoned a sedan-chair I went to church, and was confessed by a Grey Friar, and at six o'clock the next morning I received the Sacrament.

My confessor was kind enough to give me a certificate to the effect that I had been obliged to keep my bed since my arrival *al sitio*, and that in spite of my extreme weakness I had gone to church, and had confessed and communicated like a good Christian. He also told me the name of the priest who had affixed the paper containing my name to the door of the church.

When I returned to the ambassador's house I wrote to this priest, telling him that the certificate enclosed would inform him as to my reasons for not communicating. I expressed a hope that, being satisfied of my orthodoxy, he would not delay in removing my name from his church doors, and I concluded by begging him to hand the enclosed letter to the Chevalier Mengs.

To the painter I wrote that I felt that I had deserved the shameful insult he had given me by my great mistake in acceding to his request to honour him by staying in his house. However, as a good Christian who had just received the Holy Communion, I told him that his brutal behaviour was forgiven; but I bade him to take to heart the line, well known to all honest people, and doubtless unknown to him:

Turpius ejicitur quam non admittitur hospes.

After sending the letter I told the ambassador what had happened, to which he replied:

"I am not at all surprised at what you tell me. Mengs is only liked for his talents in painting; in everything else he is well known to be little better than a fool."

As a matter of fact he had only asked me to stay with him to gratify his own vanity. He knew that all the town was talking of my imprisonment and of the satisfaction the Count of Aranda had accorded me, and he wanted people to think that his influence had obtained the favour that had been shown me. Indeed, he had said in a moment of exaltation that I should have compelled the Alcalde Messa to escort me not to my own house but to his, as it was in his that I had been arrested.

Mengs was an exceedingly ambitious and a very jealous man; he hated all his brother painters. His colour and design were excellent, but his invention was very weak, and invention is as necessary to a great painter as a great poet.

[341]

When Mengs was beaten in an argument, instead of acknowledging his defeat, he invariably became brutal and insulting. He died at the age of fifty, and is regarded by posterity as a Stoic philosopher, a scholar, and a compendium of all the virtues; and this opinion must be ascribed to a fine biography of him in royal quarto, choicely printed, and dedicated to the King of Spain. This panegyric is a mere tissue of lies. Mengs was a great painter, and nothing else; and if he had only produced the splendid picture which hangs over the high altar of the chapel royal at Dresden he would deserve eternal fame, though indeed he is indebted to the great Raphael for the idea of the painting.

We shall hear more of Mengs when I describe my meeting with him at Rome, two or three years later.

I was still weak and confined to my room when Manucci came to me, and proposed that I should go with him to Toledo.

"The ambassador," he said, "is going to give a grand official dinner to the ambassadors of the other powers, and as I have not been presented at Court I am excluded from being present. However, if I travel, my absence will not give rise to any remarks. We shall be back in five or six days."

I was delighted to have the chance of seeing Toledo, and of making the journey in a comfortable carriage, so I accepted. We started the next morning, and reached Toledo in the evening of the same day. For Spain we were lodged comfortably enough, and the next day we went out under the charge of a cicerone, who took us to the Alcazar, the Louvre of Toledo, formerly the palace of the moorish kings. Afterwards we inspected the cathedral, which is well worthy of a visit, on account of the riches it contains. I saw the great tabernacle used on Corpus Christi. It is made of silver, and is so heavy that it requires thirty strong men to lift it. The Archbishop of Toledo has three hundred thousand duros a year, and his clergy have four hundred thousand, amounting to two million francs in French money. One of the canons, as he was showing me the urns containing the relics, told me that one of them contained the thirty pieces of silver for which Judas betrayed our Lord. I begged him to let me see them, to which he replied severely that the king himself would not have dared to express such indecent curiosity.

I hastened to apologise, begging him not to take offence at a stranger's heedless questions; and this seemed to calm his anger.

The Spanish priests are a band of knaves, but one has to treat them with more respect than one would pay to honest men elsewhere. The following day we were shown the museum of natural history. It was rather a dull exhibition; but, at all events, one could laugh at it without exciting the wrath of the monks and the terrors of the Inquisition. We were shown, amongst other wonders, a stuffed dragon, and the man who exhibited it said:

"This proves, gentlemen, that the dragon is not a fabulous animal"; but I thought there was more of art than nature about the beast. He then showed us a basilisk, but instead of slaying us with a glance, it only made us laugh. The greatest wonder of all, however, was nothing else than a Freemason's apron, which, as the curator very sagely declared, proved the existence of such an order, whatever some might say.

The journey restored me to health, and when I returned to Aranjuez, I proceeded to pay my court to all the ministers. The ambassador presented me to Marquis Grimaldi, with whom I had some conversations on the subject of the Swiss colony, which was going on badly. I reiterated my opinion that the colony should be composed of Spaniards.

"Yes," said he, "but Spain is thinly populated everywhere, and your plan would amount to impoverishing one district to make another rich."

"Not at all, for if you took ten persons who are dying of poverty in the Asturias, and placed them in the Sierra Morena, they would not die till they had begotten fifty children. This fifty would beget two hundred and so on."

My scheme was laid before a commission and the marquis promised that I should be made governor of the colony if the plan was accepted.

An Italian Opéra Comique was then amusing the Court, with the exception of the king, who had no taste for music. His majesty bore a considerable resemblance to a sheep in the face, and it seemed as if the likeness went deeper, for sheep have not the slightest idea of sound. His favourite pursuit was sport, and the reason will be given later on.

An Italian musician at the Court desired to compose some music for a new opera, and as there was no time to send to Italy I offered to compose the libretto. My offer was accepted, and by the next day the first act was ready. The music was composed in four days, and the Venetian ambassador invited all the ministers to the rehearsal in the grand hall of his palace. The music was pronounced exquisite; the two other acts were written, and in a fortnight the opera was put upon the stage. The musician was rewarded handsomely, but I was considered too grand to work for money and my reward was paid me in the court money of compliments. However, I was glad to see that the ambassador was proud of me and that the ministers' esteem for me seemed increased.

I often saw the king's gentleman of the chamber, Don Domingo Varnier, another gentleman in the service of the Princess of the Asturias, and one of the princess's bed-chamber women. This most popular princess succeeded in suppressing a good deal of the old etiquette, and the tone of her Court lost the air of solemnity common in Spanish society. It was a strange thing to see the King of Spain always dining at eleven o'clock, like the Parisian cordwainers in the seventeenth century. His meal always consisted of the same dishes, he always went out hunting at the same hour, coming back in the evening thoroughly fatigued.

The king was ugly, but everything is relative, he was handsome compared with his brother, who was terrifically ugly.

This brother never went anywhere without a picture of the Virgin, which Mengs had painted for him. It was two feet high by three and a half broad. The figure was depicted as seated on the grass with legs crossed after the Eastern fashion, and uncovered up to the knees. It was, in reality, a voluptuous painting; and the prince mistook for devotion that which was really a sinful passion, for it was impossible to look upon the figure without desiring to have the original within one's arms. However, the prince did not see this, and was delighted to find himself in love with the mother of the Saviour. In this he was a true Spaniard; they only love pictures of this kind, and interpret the passions they excite in the most favourable sense.

At Madrid I had seen a picture of the Madonna with the Child at her breast. It was the altar-piece of a chapel in the Calle St. Jeronimo. The place was filled all day by the devout, who came to adore the Mother of God, whose figure was only interesting by reason of her magnificent breast. The alms given at this chapel were so numerous, that in the hundred and fifty years since the picture had been placed there, the clergy had been able to purchase numerous lamps and candlesticks of silver, and vessels of silver gilt, and even of gold. The doorway was always blocked by carriages, and a sentinel was placed there to keep order amongst the coachmen; no nobleman would pass by without going in to pray to the Virgin, and to contemplate those *beata ubera, quæ lactaverunt æterni patris filium.* But there came a change.

When I returned to Madrid I wanted to pay a visit to the Abbé Pico, and told my coachman to take another way so as to avoid the crush in front of the chapel.

"It is not so frequented now, señor," said he, "I can easily get by it."

He went on his way, and I found the entrance to the chapel deserted. As I was getting out of the carriage I asked my coachman what was the reason for the change, and he replied:

"Oh, señor! men are getting more wicked every day."

This reason did not satisfy me, and when I had taken my chocolate with the abbé, an intelligent and venerable old man, I asked him why the chapel in question had lost its reputation.

He burst out laughing, and replied:

"Excuse me, I really cannot tell you. Go and see for yourself; your curiosity will soon be satisfied."

As soon as I left him I went to the chapel, and the state of the picture told me all. The breast of the Virgin had disappeared under a handkerchief which some profane brush had dared to paint over it. The beautiful picture was spoilt; the magic and fascination had disappeared. Even the teat had been painted out; the Child held on to nothing, and the head of the Virgin no longer appeared natural. This disaster had taken place at the end of the Carnival of 1768. The old chaplain died, and the Vandal who succeeded him pronounced the painting to be a scandalous one, and robbed it of all its charm.

He may have been in the right as a fool, but as a Christian and a Spaniard he was certainly in the wrong, and he was probably soon convinced of the mistake he had made by the diminution in the offerings of the faithful.

My interest in the study of human nature made me call on this priest, whom I expected to find a stupid old man.

I went one morning, but instead of being old, the priest was an active, clever-looking man of thirty, who immediately offered me chocolate with the best grace imaginable. I refused, as was my duty as a stranger, and indeed the Spaniards offer visitors chocolate so frequently at all hours that if one accepted it all one would be choked.

I lost no time in exordiums, but came to the point at once, by saying that as a lover of paintings I had been grieved at finding the magnificent Madonna spoilt.

"Very likely," he replied, "but it was exactly the physical beauty of the picture that rendered it in my eyes unfit to represent one whose aspect should purify and purge the senses, instead of exciting them. Let all the pictures in the world be destroyed, if they be found to have caused the commission of one mortal sin."

"Who allowed you to commit this mutilation? The Venetian State Inquisitors, even M. Barberigo, though he is a devout man, would have put you under The Leads for such a deed. The love of Paradise should not be allowed to interfere with the fine arts, and I am sure that St. Luke himself (who was a painter as you know) would condemn you if he could come to life again."

"Sir, I needed no one's leave or licence. I have to say mass at that altar every day, and I am not ashamed to tell you that I was unable to consecrate. You are a man and a Christian, you can excuse my weakness. That voluptuous picture drew away my thoughts from holy things."

"Who obliged you to look at it?"

"I did not look at it; the Devil, the enemy of God, made me see it in spite of myself."

"Then you should have mutilated yourself like Origen. Your generative organs, believe me, are not so valuable as the picture you have ruined."

"Sir, you insult me."

"Not at all, I have no intention of doing so."

That young priest showed me the door with such brusqueness that I felt sure he would inform against me to the Inquisition. I knew he would have no difficulty in finding out my name, so I resolved to be beforehand with him.

Both my fear and my resolve were inspired by an incident which I shall mention as an episode.

A few days before, I had met a Frenchman named Ségur, who had just come out of the prisons of the Inquisition. He had been shut up for three years for committing the following crime:

In the hall of his house there was a fountain, composed of a marble basin and the statue of a naked child, who discharged the water in the same way as the well-known statue of Brussels, that is to say, by his virile member. The child might be a Cupid or an Infant Jesus, as you pleased, but the sculptor had adorned the head with a kind of aureole; and so the fanatics declared that it was a mocking of God.

Poor Ségur was accused of impiety, and the Inquisition dealt with him accordingly.

I felt that my fault might be adjudged as great as Ségur's, and not caring to run the risk of a like punishment I called on the bishop, who held the office of Grand Inquisitor, and told him word for word the conversation I had had with the iconoclast chaplain. I ended by craving pardon, if I had offended the chaplain, as I was a good Christian, and orthodox on all points.

I had never expected to find the Grand Inquisitor of Madrid a kindly and intelligent, though ill-favoured prelate; but so it was, and he did nothing but laugh from the beginning to the end of my story, for he would not let me call it a confession.

"The chaplain," he said, "is himself blameworthy and unfit for his position, in that he has adjudged others to be as weak as himself; in fact, he has committed a wrong against religion. Nevertheless, my dear son, it was not wise of you to go and irritate him."

As I had told him my name he showed me, smilingly, an accusation against me, drawn up by someone who had witnessed the fact. The good bishop gently chid me for having called the friar-confessor of the Duke of Medina an ignoramus. He had refused to admit that a priest might say mass a second time on a high festival, after breaking his fast, on the command of his sovereign prince, who, by the hypothesis, had not heard mass before.

"You were quite right in your contention," said the Inquisitor, "but yet every truth is not good to utter, and it was wrong to call the man an ignoramus in his presence. For the future you would do well to avoid all idle discussion on religious matters, both on dogma and discipline. And I must also tell you, in order that you may not leave Spain with any harsh ideas on the Inquisition, that the priest who affixed your name to the church

door amongst the excommunicated has been severely repri-
manded. He ought to have given you a fatherly admonition,
and, above all, inquired as to your health, as we know that you
were seriously ill at the time."

Thereupon I knelt down and kissed his hand, and went my
way, well pleased with my call.

To go back to Aranjuez. As soon as I heard that the ambassador could not put me up at Madrid, I wrote to the worthy
cobbler, Don Diego, that I wanted a well-furnished room, a
closet, a good bed, and an honest servant. I informed him how
much I was willing to spend a month, and said I would leave
Aranjuez as soon as I heard that everything was ready.

I was a good deal occupied with the question of colonising the
Sierra Morena; I wrote principally on the subject of the civil
government, a most important item in a scheme for a new colony.
My articles pleased the Marquis Grimaldi and flattered Mocenigo; for the latter hoped that I should become governor of the
colony, and that his embassy would thereby shine with a bor-
rowed light.

My labours did not prevent my amusing myself, and I frequented the society of those about the Court who could tell me
most of the king and royal family. Don Varnier, a man of much
frankness and intelligence, was my principal source of information.

I asked him one day whether the king was fond of Gregorio
Squillace only because he had once been his wife's lover.

"That's an idle calumny," he replied. "If the epithet of
'chaste' can be applied to any monarch, Charles III. certainly
deserves it better than any other. He has never touched any
woman in his life except his wife, not only out of respect for the
sanctity of marriage, but also as a good Christian. He has
avoided this sin that his soul may remain pure, and so as not
to have the shame of confessing it to his chaplain. He enjoys
an iron constitution, sickness is unknown to him, and he is a
thorough Spaniard in temperament. Ever since his marriage he
has paid his duty to his wife every day, except when the state of
her health compelled her to call for a truce. In such seasons this
chaste husband brought down his fleshly desires by the fatigue of
hunting and by abstinence. You can imagine his distress at being left a widower, for he would rather die than take a mistress.

His only resource was in hunting, and in so planning out his day that he should have no time left wherein to think of women. It was a difficult matter, for he cares neither for reading nor writing, music wearies him, and conversation of a lively turn inspires him with disgust.

"He has adopted the following plan, in which he will persevere till his dying day: He dresses at seven, then goes into his closet and has his hair dressed. At eight o'clock he says his prayers, then hears mass, and when this is over he takes chocolate and an enormous pinch of snuff, over which his big nose ruminates for some minutes; this is his only pinch in the whole day. At nine o'clock he sees his ministers, and works with them till eleven. Then comes dinner, which he always takes alone, then a short visit to the Princess of the Asturias, and at twelve sharp he gets into his carriage and drives to the hunting-grounds. At seven o'clock he takes a morsel wherever he happens to be, and at eight o'clock he comes home, so tired that he often goes to sleep before he can get his clothes off. Thus he keeps down the desires of the flesh."

"Poor voluntary martyr!"

"He thought of marrying a second time, but when Adelaide of France saw his portrait she was quite frightened and refused him. He was very mortified, and renounced all thoughts of marriage; and woe to the courtier who should advise him to get a mistress!"

In further speaking of his character Don Domingo told me that the ministers had good cause for making him inaccessible, as whenever anyone did succeed in getting at him and asked a favour he made a point of granting it, as it was at such times that he felt himself really a king.

"Then he is not a hard man, as some say?"

"Not at all. Kings seldom have the reputation they deserve. The most accessible monarchs are the least generous; they are overwhelmed with importunate requests, and their first instinct is always to refuse."

"But as Charles III. is so inaccessible he can have no opportunity of either granting or refusing."

"People catch him when he is hunting; he is usually in a good humour then. His chief defect is his obstinacy; when he has once made up his mind there is no changing it.

"He has the greatest liking for his brother, and can scarce refuse him anything, though he must be master in all things. It is thought he will give him leave to marry for the sake of his salvation; the king has the greatest horror of illegitimate children, and his brother has three already."

There were an immense number of persons at Aranjuez, who persecuted the ministers in the hope of getting employment.

"They will go back as they come," said Don Domingo, "and that is empty-handed."

"Then they ask impossibilities?"

"They don't ask anything. 'What do you want?' says a minister.

"'What your excellency will let me have.'

"'What can you do?'

"'I am ready to do whatever your excellency pleases to think best for me.'

"'Please leave me. I have no time to waste.'"

That is always the way. Charles III. died a madman; the Queen of Portugal is mad; the King of England has been mad, and, as some say, is not really cured. There is nothing astonishing in it; a king who tries to do his duty is almost forced into madness by his enormous task.

I took leave of M. Mocenigo three days before he left Aranjuez, and I embraced Manucci affectionately. He had been most kind to me throughout my stay.

After the break with Manucci, Casanova, who, for once, takes the blame on himself, finding himself persona non grata *in Madrid, moves on to Valentia, where he picks up with the infamous Nina, a Venetian courtesan kept by the viceroy of Barcelona. Though warned to be careful, he follows the lady to Barcelona, where to his surprise and disgust he encounters once more his evil genius Passano-Pogamas, the Genoese adventurer who had helped him to dupe the Marquise d'Urfé. Passano, who is also prowling round the golden cage under the guise of a painter, is unmasked by his old confederate (who remembers his treachery on the former occasion) and goes off swearing vengeance. Follows a midnight attack on "Don Jaime" Casanova, who dispatches one of his assailants, is arrested, and passes six weeks in the citadel, where he composes from memory his famous refutation of Houssaye's* History of the Venetian Government.

EPILOGUE

Although assured on his release that his arrest was due to a mis-apprehension regarding his passports, "Don Jaime" is none the less requested to leave the country.

When, in January, 1769, he crossed the frontier, he knew that the last of his castles in Spain had vanished for ever.

EPILOGUE

With the vanishing of the mirage vanishes also the Wanderlust. *Henceforth Casanova has but one object in view: make his peace with the* Serenissima — *return to Venice. As a first step in this direction, and as a proof of his good citizenship, he has already composed his* Refutation. *The next thing is to get it published, if possible in Switzerland, which is conveniently near to Venetian territory.*

On his way to Switzerland, Casanova passes through Aix-in-Provence, which at carnival time was the meeting-place of the Provençal nobility. There, besides winning a little money at the tables, he might perhaps get a glimpse of his long-lost Henriette among the merry-makers. It was worth trying.

It was in the old Provençal capital that a curious meeting took place. Hearing one day of the arrival of a male and female pilgrim, said to be high-born Italians, Casanova goes to satisfy his curiosity:

We found the lady sitting in an arm-chair, looking very tired. She was young, beautiful, and melancholy-looking, and in her hands she held a brass crucifix some six inches long. She laid it down when we came in, and got up and received us most graciously. Her companion, who was arranging cockle-shells on his black mantle, did not stir; he seemed to say, by glancing at his wife, that we must confine our attentions to her. He seemed a man of twenty-four or twenty-five years of age. He was short and badly hung, and his face bore all the indications of daring, impudence, sarcasm, and imposture. His wife, on the other hand, was all meekness and simplicity, and had that modesty which adds so much to the charm of feminine beauty. They only spoke just enough French to make themselves understood on their journey, and when they heard me addressing them in Italian they seemed much relieved.

The lady told me she was a Roman, but I could have guessed as much from her accent. I judged the man to be a Neapolitan or Sicilian. Their passport, dated Rome, called him Balsamo, while she bore the names of Serafina Feliciani, which she still retains. Ten years later we shall hear more of this couple under the name of Cagliostro.

During this visit to Aix the mysterious Henriette for the last time crosses the stage, without revealing her presence. Having caught a chill, Casanova falls dangerously ill and for days lies at death's door. Day and night he is tended by a strange woman, who disappears as soon as he is out of danger. The innkeeper is unable or unwilling to tell him where she came from or who sent her. Haunted by the memory of Henriette, which his illness has served to intensify, he determines to make a last effort to see her. So, on leaving Aix, he tells his coachman to drive to the manor where, six years ago, he had been her unsuspecting guest. To his surprise, he is met at the door by the charitable woman who had nursed him during his illness and who informs him that it was her mistress, Henriette, who had sent her when she had heard of his plight. As for the latter, she was still at Aix, where she had been all the time of his stay there. Doubtless he must have seen her without knowing it. She at least had recognised him. Respecting her incognito, Casanova, after writing her a long letter, which he leaves with the servant, goes on his way. At Marseilles, his first stop, he receives the following letter from Henriette:

"My Dear Old Friend, — Nothing could be more romantic than our meeting at my country-house six years ago, and now again, after a parting of so many years. Naturally we have both grown older, and though I love you still, I am glad you did not recognise me. Not that I have become ugly, but I am stout, and this gives me another look. I am a widow, and well enough off to tell you that if you lack money you will find some ready for you in Henriette's purse. Do not come back to Aix to see me, as your return might give rise to gossip; but if you chance to come here again after some time, we may meet, though not as old acquaintances. I am happy to think that I have perhaps prolonged your days by giving you a nurse for whose trustworthiness I would answer. If you would like to correspond with me I should be happy to do my part. I am very curious to know what happened to you after your flight from The Leads, and after the proofs you have given me of your discretion I think I shall be able to tell you how we came to meet at Cesena, and how I returned to my country. The first part is a secret for everyone; only M. d'Antoine is acquainted with a portion of the story. I am grateful for the reticence you have observed, though Marcoline must have delivered the message I gave her. Tell me what has become of that beautiful girl. Farewell!"

I replied, accepting her offer to correspond, and I told her the whole story of my adventures. From her I received forty letters, in which the history of her life is given. If she die before me, I shall add these letters to my Memoirs, but at present she is alive and happy, though advanced in years.

After a visit to Turin, where he gathers subscriptions for his forthcoming publication, Casanova, well satisfied with the result, proceeds to Lugano and gets to work:

I spent the whole of the next month in my room, working assiduously, and only going out to mass on feast days, to dine with M. de R **, and to walk with his wife and her child.

At the end of a month my first volume was printed and stitched, and the manuscript of the second volume was ready for the press. Towards the end of October the printer sent in the entire work in three volumes, and in less than a year the edition was sold out.

My object was not so much to make money as to appease the wrath of the Venetian Inquisitors; I had gone all over Europe, and experienced a violent desire to see my native land once more.

Amelot de la Houssaye had written his book from the point of view of an enemy of Venice. His history was rather a satire, containing learned and slanderous observations mingled together. It had been published for seventy years, but hitherto no one had taken the trouble to refute it. If a Venetian had attempted to do so he would not have obtained permission from his government to print it in the States of Venice, for the state policy is to allow no one to discuss the actions of the authorities, whether in praise or blame; consequently no writer had attempted to refute the French history, as it was well known that the refutation would be visited with punishment and not with reward.

My position was an exceptional one. I had been persecuted by the Venetian government, so no one could accuse me of being partial; and by my exposing the calumnies of Amelot before all Europe I hoped to gain a reward, which after all would only be an act of justice.

I had been an exile for fourteen years, and I thought the Inquisitors would be glad to repair their injustice on the pretext of rewarding my patriotism.

My readers will see that my hopes were fulfilled, but I had to wait for five more years instead of receiving permission to return at once.

M. de Bragadin was dead, and Dandolo and Barbaro were the only friends I had left at Venice, and with their aid I contrived to subscribe fifty copies of my book in my native town.

For five years Casanova continued to wander up and down Italy, waiting for the longed-for amnesty, the permission to return to Venice. In Parma, Bologna, Tuscany, Rome, Naples, he passes, lingers, returns, scenting the wind, catching the echoes, gauging his opportunities of making advances towards the desired goal. At Rome, where he spends several months, he finds in Cardinal de Bernis, the French ambassador, a generous and discreet protector, is received in his circle, and pays his way by amusing the distinguished company with the tale of his exploits. His bête noire *for the time being is Voltaire, whom he attacks with tongue and pen on every occasion, with more wit and reason than most of his compatriots. Polemist, apologist, historian, translator, sonneteer, he can even rise to the heights of a religious ode, "On the Redemption," which he delivers before a learned assembly (including, among other princes of the Church, his friend de Bernis), "pouring out a torrent of tears," with the result that "all the Academicians wept."*

In spite of these and other ephemeral successes of the familiar kind — the latter taking place more and more en famille *under the auspices of his complacent ex-mistresses — he feels that it is time to relinquish the rôle of brilliant* jeune premier *and to strive for more substantial honours. Italy, he felt, needed a worthy translation of Homer's* Iliad, *and who was better qualified to give it her than Casanova, who, ever since he left England, had been studying it in the original with increasing delight?*

Florence, of all cities, offering the best facilities for this task, to Florence he goes, resolved to make a final bid for fame and, if not fortune, at least an honourable independence. It was high time; for, as he observes: "All the friends whose purses had been open for me were dead. M. Barbaro, who died this year of consumption, left me in his will only six miserable sequins a month for the rest of my life, and M. Dandolo, who was the only friend that remained to me, could only give me another six sequins."

But it was evidently fated that Casanova and Florence were never to agree for long. Despite his efforts to lead a studious life and avoid the old pitfalls, he was suspected before very long of being connected with a dangerous set of swindlers who had fleeced a young English nobleman, and ordered to leave the Grand Duke's states.

Most of the following year, 1772, is spent at Bologna, where he is heartily welcomed by a former boon companion of his Paris days, Cardinal Brancaforte. "We had met," says Casanova, "at the Lodge of Freemasons, for the members of the Sacred College were by no means afraid of their own anathemas. We had also some very pleasant little suppers with pretty sinners . . . ." For Bologna he has many a good word to say: "the freest town in Italy," where living is cheap and the cult of letters almost universal — not a pretence, as in Florence. Despite the Inquisition, the press is almost free and printing cheap.

While he is busy in Bologna with his literary projects, his friends in Venice are busy trying to obtain his pardon. Finally they advise him to take up his residence as near as possible to the Venetian border, so that the State Inquisitors might satisfy themselves of his good conduct.

Such a hint is as good as a command, and, leaving pleasant Bologna, he makes for Trieste. As he draws nearer to the cradle of his youth, he indulges in some bitter heart-searchings. So at Ancona:

It was in Ancona that I had begun to enjoy life; and when I thought it over, it was quite a shock to find that this was thirty years ago, for thirty years is a long period in a man's life. And yet I felt quite young, in spite of the tenth lustrum so near at hand for me.

What a difference I found between my youth and my middle age! I could scarcely recognise myself. I was then happy, but now unhappy; then all the world was before me, and the future seemed a gorgeous dream, and now I was obliged to confess that my life had been all in vain. I might live twenty years more, but I felt that the happy time was passed away, and the future seemed all dreary.

I reckoned up my forty-seven years, and saw fortune fly away. This in itself was enough to sadden me, for without the favours of the fickle goddess life was not worth living, for me at all events.

My object, then, was to return to my country; it was as if I struggled to undo all that I had done. All I could hope for was to soften the hardships of the slow but certain passage to the grave.

These are the thoughts of declining years and not of youth. The young man looks only to the present, believes that the sky will always smile upon him, and laughs at philosophy as it vainly preaches of old age, misery, repentance, and, worst of all, abhorred death.

Such were my thoughts twenty-six years ago; what must they be now, when I am all alone, poor, despised, and impotent. They would kill me if I did not resolutely subdue them, for whether for good or ill my heart is still young. Of what use are desires when one can no longer satisfy them? I write to kill ennui, and I take pleasure in writing. Whether I write sense or nonsense, what matters? I am amused, and that is enough.

At Trieste he manages to gain the good graces of the Austrian governor and the Venetian consul, who put him in the way of rendering service to the Venetian government — opportunities he avails himself of to such good effect that he receives a monetary recompense as acknowledgment and encouragement for his work. Here and at Gorizia he composes the first volumes of his history of the Polish troubles (Istoria delle turbolenze della Polonia), *which were then culminating, as he had foreseen, in the partition of that unhappy country.*

At last, on September 10th, 1774, the Venetian consul, Marco Monti, brought Casanova the good news that the newly-elected Council of Ten and the three new Inquisitors had granted his pardon and that he was free to return to Venice. A few days later, in a letter to his friend Count Lamberg, he gives vent to his joy: "I am mad with joy . . . . Never has the dread Tribunal of the State Inquisitors granted a citizen a more ample pardon than the one accorded to me!"

In Venice the return of Casanova was the topic of the day and when he appears at last on the Piazza, the Merceria, the Rialto, as erect, as disdainful, as hawk-eyed as ever, who should say that the world he set out to conquer was not at his feet? Is he not still the friend of the Memmos, the Mocenigos, the Morosinis, the Dandolos, the Grimanis, even, it is hinted, the very private guest of the all-powerful Three, whom he regales with his countless stories, not omitting, needless to say, that already legendary exploit, the escape from The Leads?

EPILOGUE

The story of Casanova's last Venetian sojourn, lasting over eight years, is not told in the Memoirs, which break off abruptly, while he is still in Trieste, with the characteristic: "Three years later I saw her again at Padua" (he is speaking of the actress Irene). "Her daughter had become a charming girl, and our acquaintance was renewed in the tenderest manner." In the absence of the concluding volumes — whether lost, destroyed, or never written has so far not been definitely ascertained — the chronicle of those years and the ones which followed up to the death of the adventurer has been established, as best it could be, from the notes and correspondence discovered at Dux and elsewhere.

On the one hand, we have the record of Casanova's literary activities, which, during this Venetian period, seem to have been as intense as they were varied, including his translation of the Iliad, *a volume of Venetian anecdotes,* Aneddoti Viniziani, *an account of his famous duel in Poland, entitled* Il Duello, ovvero Saggia della vita di G. C. *veneziano, a theatrical periodical,* Messager de Thalie, *correspondence with the famous scholar Simon Stratico, the ambassador Sebastiano Foscarini, etc. On the other, alas! we have the record, only recently come to light, of less avowable though quite official activities, in the shape of secret reports to the inquisitorial tribunal regarding the corruption of public morality in every form, whether literary, social, or religious. These activities extend over the last two years of his stay in Venice.*

Whether Casanova in the rôle of government spy — "member of the Secret Service" would be the euphemistic modern designation — is more deserving of pity or contempt, depends on the moral evaluation we feel inclined to apply to all or any of his actions. The exhilarating national pastime of trying to adjust the moral balance will scarcely conduce to the pleasure of reading certain documents.

"In 1782," recounts M. Charles Samaran, "there appeared in the book-shops of Venice a small anonymous work entitled Nè amori nè donne, ovvero la stalla d'Augia ripulita. *Unnoticed at first, there was soon a run on the book when it became known that it was a sort of mythological* roman à clef, *full of scandalous disclosures." It was, in fact, a merciless satire on old Grimani, one of Casanova's benefactors. That there had recently been a falling-out between the two was common knowledge. There could be no doubt as to the authorship — the allusions were too transparent — nor probably was it intended that there should be. Had Casanova once*

more yielded to the temptation of biting off his nose to spite his face, or was it his way of extricating himself from a position which had become intolerable, and, at the same time, avenging himself for a forced humiliation? Given the man, either theory is at least admissible.

Casanova's own comment on this incident is as follows: "Either I am not made for Venice, I said to myself, or Venice is not made for me, or both. In this uncertainty, a very disagreeable incident came to my rescue by obliging me to take a decision. I determined to leave my country, much as one gives up a house which pleases one, but where one is obliged to put up with a bad neighbour, who causes trouble and who yet cannot be ejected."

In January, 1783, at fifty-eight years of age, Casanova is once more a wanderer on the face of the earth. After spending some months in Vienna, the return of spring brings a fit of home-sickness. He had sworn, very likely, never to set foot again on the shores of his ungrateful city, for when, in June, he arrives once more in Venice, it is only to be rowed through the canals as far as his house, to gaze at old familiar things — then, without alighting from the gondola, to depart for ever.

Through the Tyrol, Austria, Holland, Belgium, he takes his way as far as Paris, where he arrives in September. If on his last visit he found Paris changed and unfriendly, he finds it now a desert. In the streets, the cafés, not a face to greet him. In vain he scans the theatre-bills — that social register which so far has never failed him — for a familiar name: Coraline and Camille Veronese, those twin stars, whom he and all Paris had worshipped, had set for ever — Silvia Baletti, hardly a memory — her daughter Manon, once his promessa, already in her grave — her brother, disappeared. That air of Paris, once so light, so sparkling, was now poisoned with politics. The very police seemed to ignore him!

His brother, the painter François, whose lodging at the Louvre he shared, having agreed with him that Paris was played out as far as the Casanovas were concerned, the two set out for Germany. At Dresden they hold a family council. Berlin, St. Petersburg, Vienna, seem for the moment to offer the best fields for exploiting their several talents. Vienna, which is first tried, proves a lucky choice for François, who quickly obtains the favours of Prince Kaunitz and of the Viennese public, to whom he remained faithful till his death, in 1802.

EPILOGUE

As for Giacomo, he, too, finally found employment in Vienna, as secretary to the Venetian ambassador Foscarini. For a year all went well and it looked as if the wanderer had at last settled down, when the sudden death of his employer left him once more stranded. In vain he looks for employment, thinks in despair of turning monk —it was not for the first time — then sets out for Berlin in the hope of finding employment at the Academy. Stopping on the way at Teplitz, in Bohemia, he is invited to dine with a young Bohemian nobleman, a descendant of the great Wallenstein — Count Waldstein-Wartenberg, whose acquaintance he had already made at Paris. Aware that the young count took an interest in the occult sciences, Casanova adroitly brought round the conversation to a subject on which he could talk so well, with the result that Waldstein insisted on his paying him a visit at his ancestral castle at Dux, not far from Teplitz. The visit lasted, with short interruptions, for fourteen years.

But though the "Herr Bibliothekar" of Dux castle had inscribed the Inveni portum over his door, there was as yet no question of Spes et Fortuna valete! On the contrary, over his quiet anchorage those twin stars, Hope and Fortune, that he had followed all his life twinkled more brightly than ever. If his "genius," whose mysterious behests had kept him wandering for half a century through the length and breadth of Europe, had decreed that he should moor his barque in this Bohemian backwater, it was for a reason easy to divine — the accomplishment of his destiny, his supreme avatar: Casanova the World-Prophet.

Here the great work he had been meditating for years, his message to mankind, the fruit of all his labours, was to be brought to light for the delectation of generations to come, the confusion of his enemies, and the vindication — not without considerable material profits to himself — of his own sublime talents. The title of this monument of human science, philosophy, and political wisdom was Icosameron ou Histoire d'Edouard et d'Elisabeth qui passèrent quatre vingts ans chez les Mégamicres habitans aborigènes du Protocosme dans l'intérieur de notre globe, traduite de l'anglois. It slumbers in six dust-covered volumes in the nirvana of unread masterpieces.

To console himself for the failure of his magnum opus — printed partly or entirely at his own expense at Prague — and also as a distraction from his other serious labours, which cover almost every branch of human learning — Casanova began to classify and elaborate the biographical notes he had amassed through his long lifetime.

As he worked, chuckling to himself at the unbridled licence, the taunting cynicism, the impudent triumphs of his heroes and heroines, real and imagined, the conviction grew on him that the work could never be published.

Writing in 1792 to his friend Opiz, one of his faithful Bohemian admirers, he laughingly admits as much: "Je vous dirai donc à la hâte que je me porte assez bien, que je travaille onze heures par jour à mes mémoires dont je suis au dixième tome. Je ne me repose un peu que lorsque je me vois dans la douce obligation de répondre à mes amis, qui m'honorent d'un commerce épistolaire suivi. —Pour ce qui regarde mes mémoires, plus l'ouvrage avance, plus je me vois convaincu qu'il est fait pour être brûlé. Par là vous voyés que tant que j'en serai le maître, il ne verra certainement pas le jour. Il est d'une nature qu'il fait passer la nuit au lecteur, mais le *Cinisme*, que j'y ai mis, est outré et il passe les bornes que la convenance a mis à la discretion. Mais vous ne sauriés croire combien cela m'amuse. Je me suis aperçu *sans rougir* que je m'aime plus que personne, mais notés, que je rougis de ce que je ne rougis pas, et cette érubescence secondaire me justifie vis-à-vis de moi-même, car des autres je ne me soucie pas . . . ."

But Opiz, Count Maximilian Lamberg, and Count Waldstein's uncle, the Prince de Ligne, as representative and enlightened a tribunal of contemporary taste as any writer could wish, were of a different opinion. Already the successful publication of Histoire de ma Fuite (*the* Escape from The Leads), *which had preceded that of the unlucky* Icosameron, *had whetted the appetite of these and many other connoisseurs for a full account of Casanova's adventures, which for years had been one of the major themes of European gossip.*

It is to the encouragement and solicitude of these faithful friends that we owe the composition and, probably, the conservation of those famous Memoirs, which, for all their aberrations, constitute one of the most curious and fascinating documents bearing on the life of pre-revolutionary Europe.

Under what conditions this work and the many others composed by the indefatigable librarian at Dux were carried out can be seen from the following sketch given by Mr. Arthur Machen in the Appendix to his English version of the Memoirs:

"*As the Prince de Ligne (from whose Memoirs we learn these particulars) remarks, Casanova's life had been a stormy and adven-*

turous one, and it might have been expected that he would have found his patron's library a pleasant refuge after so many toils and travels. But the man carried rough weather and storm in his own heart, and found daily opportunities of mortification and resentment. The coffee was ill made, the macaroni not cooked in the true Italian style, the dogs bayed during the night, he had been made to dine at a small table, the parish priest had tried to convert him, the soup had been served too hot on purpose to annoy him, he had not been introduced to a distinguished guest, the count had lent a book without telling him, a groom had not taken off his hat; such were his complaints. The fact is Casanova felt his dependent position and his utter poverty, and was all the more determined to stand to his dignity as a man who had talked with all the crowned heads of Europe, and had fought a duel with the Polish general. And he had another reason for finding life bitter — he had lived beyond his time. Louis XV. was dead, and Louis XVI. had been guillotined; the Revolution had come; and Casanova, his dress, and his manners, appeared as odd and antique as some 'blood' of the Regency would appear to us of these days. Sixty years before, Marcel, the famous dancing-master, had taught young Casanova how to enter a room with a lowly and ceremonious bow; and still, though the eighteenth century is drawing to a close, old Casanova enters the rooms of Dux with the same stately bow, and now everyone laughs. Old Casanova treads the grave measures of the minuet; they applauded his dancing once, but now everyone laughs. Young Casanova was always dressed in the height of the fashion; but the age of powder, wigs, velvets, and silks has departed, and old Casanova's attempts at elegance ('Strass' diamonds have replaced the genuine stones with him) are likewise greeted with laughter. No wonder the old adventurer denounces the whole house as Jacobins and canaille; the world, he feels, is permanently out of joint for him; everything is cross, and everyone is in a conspiracy to drive the iron into his soul.

"At last these persecutions, real or imaginary, drive him away from Dux; he considers his genius bids him go, and, as before, he obeys. Casanova has but little pleasure or profit out of this his last journey; he has to dance attendance in ante-chambers; no one will give him any office, whether as tutor, librarian, or chamberlain. In one quarter only is he well received — namely, by the famous Duke of Weimar; but in a few days he becomes madly jealous of the duke's more famous protégés, Goethe and Wieland, and goes off

declaiming against them and German literature generally — with which literature he was wholly unacquainted. From Weimar to Berlin; where there are Jews to whom he has introductions. Casanova thinks them ignorant, superstitious, and knavish; but they lend him money, and he gives bills on Count Wallenstein, which are paid. In six weeks the wanderer returns to Dux, and is welcomed with open arms; his journeys are over at last.

"But not his troubles. A week after his return there are straw-berries at dessert; everyone is served before himself, and when the plate comes round to him it is empty. Worse still; his portrait is missing from his room, and is discovered salement placardé à la porte des lieux d'aisance!

"Five more years of life remained to him. They were passed in such petty mortifications as we have narrated, in grieving over his affreuse vieillesse, *and in laments over the conquest of his native land Venice, once so splendid and powerful. His appetite began to fail, and with it failed his last source of pleasure. So death came to him somewhat as a release. He received the sacraments with devotion, exclaimed:*

"'Grand Dieu, et vous tous témoins de ma mort, j'ai vécu en philosophe, et je meurs en Chrétien,' *and so died.*

"The Prince de Ligne draws the following portrait under the name of Adventuros:

"'He would be a handsome man if he were not ugly; he is tall and strongly built, but his dark complexion and his glittering eyes give him a fierce expression. He is easier to annoy than amuse; he laughs little but makes others laugh by the peculiar turn he gives to his conversation. He knows everything except those matters on the knowledge of which he chiefly prides himself — namely, dancing, the French language, good taste, and knowledge of the world. Everything about him is comic, except his comedies; and all his writings are philosophical, saving those which treat of philosophy. He is a perfect well of knowledge, but he quotes Homer and Horace ad nauseam.'"*

Other Da Capo titles of interest

AMERICANS IN PARIS. By George Wickes. New foreword by Virgil Thomson. 302 pages, 16 pages of photos (0-306-80127-2) $6.95

CONSUELO: A Romance of Venice. By George Sand. 799 pages (0-306-80102-7) $8.95

LAND OF THE FREE. By Archibald MacLeisch. Introduction by A. D. Coleman. A dramatic mating of poetry and photographs. 93 pages, 88 photos (0-306-80080-2) $7.95

MAUPRAT. By George Sand. New introduction by Diane Johnson. 324 pages (0-306-80077-2) $6.95

OSCAR WILDE. By H. Montgomery Hyde. 410 pages, 53 photos (0-306-80147-7) $8.95

THE TRUE LIFE OF SWEENEY TODD: A Novel in Collage. By Cozette de Charmoy. 94 pages, illustrated (0-306-80060-8) $5.95

TRAVEL IN VOGUE. 255 pages, 128 illustrations (0-306-80185-X) $10.95

Available at your bookstore

or Order Directly from DA CAPO PRESS
233 Spring Street, New York, New York 10013